Market-Led Strategic Change

A Guide to Transforming the Process of Going to Market

Third edition

Nigel F. Piercy

Professor of Strategic Marketing
Cranfield School of Management

Published in association with
The Chartered Institute of Marketing

ELSEVIER
BUTTERWORTH
HEINEMANN

AMSTERDAM BOSTON HEIDELBERG LONDON NEW YORK OXFORD
PARIS SAN DIEGO SAN FRANCISCO SINGAPORE SYDNEY TOKYO

Dedication
This book is dedicated to the memory of my mother,
Helena G. Piercy (1911–2001)

Elsevier Butterworth-Heinemann
Lineacre House, Jordan Hill, Oxford OX2 8DP
200 Wheeler Road, Burlington, MA 01803

First published by HarperCollins Publishers Ltd 1991
First published as a paperback edition by Butterworth-Heinemann 1992
Second edition 1997
Reprinted 1998
Reissued with new cover 2000
Third edition 2002
Reprinted 2003, 2005

British Library Cataloguing in Publication Data
A catalogue record for this book is available from the British Library

Library of Congress Cataloguing in Publication Data
A catalogue record for this book is available from the Library of Congress

ISBN 0 7506 5225 X

For information on all Butterworth-Heinemann publications visit
our website at www.bh.com

Working together to grow
libraries in developing countries

www.elsevier.com | www.bookaid.org | www.sabre.org

ELSEVIER   BOOK AID International   Sabre Foundation

Composition by Genesis Typesetting, Laser Quay, Rochester, Kent
Printed and bound in Great Britain by Biddles Ltd, King's Lynn, Norfolk

Contents

Preface to the third edition

So, now it is time for the new, revitalized and improved product – *Market-Led Strategic Change III* – to be unleashed on an unsuspecting world! Well, some things have changed and some have not. This is still a book aimed squarely at people of practice – whether managers, students or analysts, not theoreticians. I have no patience with academic views, which seem to be based on the premise that 'the trouble with good practice, is that you have to ask if it works in theory'!

This is a book with attitude. Undoubtedly, some will not like that attitude. Sorry – it's the only one I've got.

Changes in the third edition

The focus of the book is not 'marketing' in the conventional sense, but an emphasis on the 'process of going to market', to underline the point that customers and how we perform in the market is an issue for *everyone* in the organization, not the concern of the marketing department (if there still is one). I am convinced that this simple fact is one of the most powerful ideas that we must embrace and practise.

The book is aimed at managers and management students, and the goal is to provide them with tools and ideas for achieving superior performance in the marketplace. Within that focus, there have been a number of changes to the structure of the book. In Part I, I have added a chapter that expands on the central issue of customer value as the focus of strategy, reflecting the evolution of strategic thinking from emphasis on brands and relationships to value. This describes a new world for business where transparency and value in customer terms come to the fore. This will be uncomfortable for many executives, but it is the future for all of us.

I have also developed a new Part II for the third edition, reflecting three of the most central issues which have surfaced in my work with executives and MBA students, and which provide a platform for examining the strategic pathway in Part III. These three issues are: (inevitably) the *Internet* as a tool in the process of going to market, the competitive impact of e-business models and the status of the dot.coms; the need for *totally integrated marketing* (which includes many of the issues that we previously considered as 'Marketing Organization'); and the issue of *strategy and creativity*, as part of the process of reinvention and renewal of companies to survive in the new 'speed-of-light' environment.

The strategic pathway model has been amended slightly to include customer focus and market sensing as part of the pathway, because people have told me that makes the intention clearer, but otherwise the model remains largely as in the last edition – a mechanism for surfacing the most critical issues of market strategy facing an organization, by examining market choices, value propositions, and the key relationships on which they depend.

In response to reader feedback, I have reduced the number of cases from twelve to six. There are two reasons for this: to make the third edition of the book more accessible than the second edition, and because additional case material is available in my book *Tales From the Marketplace: Stories of Revolution, Reinvention and Renewal* (Oxford: Butterworth-Heinemann, 1999), both in book format and as downloads from the publisher's web pages (www.businesscases.org). Part I has two new cases alongside the Avis story of achieving customer focus – Huntingdon Life Sciences and Barclays Bank. Part II also has two completely new cases – Priceline.com and Dyson Appliances. The Trolley-wars case has been made longer and more detailed than the version in the last edition, because these stories provide an excellent way of putting together all the issues in the book, and because it has proved to be interesting material for readers and students.

Incidentally, I have taken the forms for the worksheets and diagnostics out of this edition of the book, mainly because publishing blank forms did not seem a good way to use the limited space available, when there is so much else to do. However, the worksheets and diagnostics from the last editions, as well as some new ones, are included in the *Tutor's Manual for Market-Led Strategic Change*, published by Butterworth-Heinemann alongside the new book. This means that readers who want to use the book for specific in-company development work or as part of course delivery can get access to supporting tools in the *Tutor's Manual*, while the reader of the book does not have to fight his/her way through a bunch of forms.

Lastly, there has been an effort to update the examples and literature references, and to remove some of the worst examples of poor humour (admittedly, in most cases only to replace them with new examples of poor humour). On a point of style – some readers have suggested that there were too many examples and illustrations in the last edition, which made it difficult to follow the argument in places. In response, I have reduced the number of minor examples, and placed many of the larger illustrations in boxes as exhibits, called Reality Checks, to improve the flow of the text.

Acknowledgements

Many colleagues, industrial contacts, research collaborators, students and others have continued to play a part in reshaping the *Market-Led Strategic Change* book, and no attempt can be made to list them all here. I would, however, like to express my continuing gratitude to my friend William Giles. William taught me much about market planning, and we collaborated in a variety of consultancy and writing projects. Sadly, William died in 1993. He is greatly and frequently missed for numerous reasons, both personal and professional.

I would also like to express my appreciation to Professor David W. Cravens of Texas Christian University, from whom I have learned a great deal in the last several years in our research and writing collaborations. I have also had the privilege of working with James Mac Hulbert and Noel Capon of Columbia Business School and have learned a great deal from that partnership, which has impacted on the revision of this book, as well as the book we have produced together.

I would like to thank my colleagues Dr Carolyn Strong and Dr Nikala Lane, and Niall Piercy, for their proof-reading efforts, which inevitably identified disagreements and disputes to be resolved within the text, as well as the typing errors they were actually asked to find.

Lastly, on a personal note, I would like to thank my wife, Nikala, and my son, Niall, for their support and encouragement in my work, particularly at a time when many who had pretended to be friends turned out not to be.

Naturally, the shortcomings and limitations of this book, and any errors contained, remain the responsibility of the author (until such time as he can find someone else to blame, as he usually does, or so say Nikala and Niall, but what do they know?*).

Nigel F. Piercy

---

* *Nikala*: Is there any chance at all of some *new* jokes for the fourth edition, please?

About the author

Professor Nigel F. Piercy B.A., M.A., Ph.D., FCIM is Professor of Strategic Marketing and Director of the Strategic Sales Research Consortium at Cranfield School of Management. In addition to UK business school experience, he has been a visiting professor at: Texas Christian University; the University of California, Berkeley; Columbia Graduate School of Business, New York; and the Fuqua School of Business, Duke University, North Carolina. He has presented seminars and workshops at business schools throughout the world. He has managerial experience in retailing, and was in business planning with Amersham International plc (now Nycomed Amersham plc).

He has extensive experience as a consultant and management workshop speaker with many organizations in different parts of the world – he has worked with managers and management students in the UK, the USA, Europe, Sweden, Greece, the Far East, South Africa and Zimbabwe. He focuses on issues of market strategy development, planning and implementation, and recent client companies include Amey plc, British Telecom, Allied Dunbar, Ford Cellular, AT&T, Honeywell, AIB Group, ICL and *Yellow Pages*, as well as other smaller organizations. He also presents and chairs management development programmes for: the Chartered Institute of Marketing; the Institute of Management; the Institute of Directors; the Swedish Insitute of Management; the Tavistock Institute; and Henley Management College.

Professor Piercy has written ten books and around 200 articles and papers appearing in the management literature throughout the world. Recent books include: *Marketing Strategy & Competitive Positioning* (with Graham Hooley and John Saunders) (Hemel Hempstead: Prentice-Hall, 1998) and *Tales*

From the Marketplace: Stories of Revolution, Reinvention and Renewal (Oxford: Butterworth-Heinemann, 1999). Among other awards and prizes, he was the UK Marketing Author of the Year for three years. He has published academic papers in the *Journal of Marketing*, the *Journal of the Academy of Marketing Science*, the *Journal of World Business* and the *Journal of Business Research*, and has written on management and marketing issues in *The Sunday Times* and *The Independent* newspapers.

What readers said about *Market-Led Strategic Change*

'Much is known about good marketing practice, but little is known about how to transform a company into a first-rate marketing company. Nigel Piercy has provided the best guide I've seen to creating a market-led company – replete with worksheets, diagnostics, and many convincing illustrative cases . . . a very useful and readable book that will make a contribution to many companies that manage to read it and act on it.'

Professor Philip Kotler

S. C. Johnson & Son Distinguished Professor of International Marketing, Northwestern University, Evanston, IL, USA

'Professor Piercy lives up to his promise to provide management with a number of tools and techniques to help implement marketing effectively in their own companies so that customer considerations and satisfaction are put at the top of the management agenda. A very practical manual, full of good useful advice . . . I enjoyed reading it.'

Professor John O'Shaugnessy

(formerly) Professor of Business, Columbia University, New York, USA

'It is not just the chapter titles which are provocative. The more closely one reads the contents of the individual chapters, it becomes apparent that they constitute a healthy mix of foundation material (informative), well-reasoned questioning of certain heretofore unchallenged assumptions and practices (provocative), and clear directions to managers as to how the content of the

individual chapters can be put to use in organizations (instruc-
tive) . . . I was looking for new insights, needless to say I was not
disappointed . . . an outstanding contribution.'

Professor P. Rajan Varadarajan

*Foley's Professor of Marketing, Texas A & M University, College
Station, Texas, USA*

'This is a marvelous, thought-provoking book on how to cultivate
and implement a customer-focused strategy within a company. In
a time when many marketing texts seem depressingly similar, this
book is different and that is very much to the good . . . No reader
will walk away from this book without substantial new ideas on
making customer-focused marketing work. On that basis, I think
it is a book that should be on the shelf of every person seriously
concerned with market strategy.'

Professor Bruce H. Clark

Northeastern University

'Every once in a while one reads a book and thinks "This makes
so much sense, why didn't someone write it before?" Anyone
seriously interested in the management of marketing is likely to
have this reaction to Nigel Piercy's *Market-Led Strategic Change* . . .
Refreshing in its candor, stimulating in its arguments, practical in
its applicability, Professor Piercy is to be congratulated. Buy it!'

Professor James M. Hulbert

*Kopf Professor of International Marketing, Graduate School of
Business, Columbia University, New York*

'This book is aimed at the reflective practitioner who wants to get
things done. It is a management perspective on marketing, where
marketing is not just the Marketing and Sales Department but a
way of life that permeates every corner of the company. *Market-
Led Strategic Change* demonstrates the author's ability to combine
systematic analysis with practical advice for action. The book is
rich in practical examples from the author's own experience and
research.'

Professor Evert Gummesson

Professor of Marketing, University of Stockholm, Sweden

'By now everyone knows (or should know) what marketing *is* and
what benefits will accrue to the marketing oriented organization.
The problem is not *WHAT* but *HOW*. Virtually all the recent work

on competitiveness and competitive success . . . confirms that "it ain't what you do, it's the way that you do it". In his new pragmatic and practitioner-oriented book Nigel Piercy provides usable insights and advice on *how* to establish, develop, deliver and sustain long-term customer satisfaction which can be the only guaranteed road to survival and success. I will use the book myself both as an educator and a senior manager/company director.'

Professor Michael J. Baker

Emeritus Professor of Marketing, University of Strathclyde, Scotland, UK

'Once in a while comes a book that is clearly a classic. Nigel Piercy writes for managers responsible for designing and implementing profit-effective strategies – that is, *all* managers. The key is a practical obsession with serving customers, with the creation of long-term customer satisfaction. The ideal of customer-oriented management has long been preached by theoreticians. But in this remarkable book it is now made realistic and actionable. No marketing manager can afford to be without this book. Nor can any non-marketing manager.'

Professor Gordon R. Foxall

Professor of Consumer Policy, University of Keele, UK

'I have always enjoyed reading what Nigel Piercy has to say about marketing, because he always has something interesting and useful to say. This book is no exception. It is creative, original, punchy, practical, challenging, thought-provoking, actionable, and a very enjoyable read to boot. I shall definitely be recommending it to as many people as possible. It will make an enormous contribution to marketing practice.'

Professor Malcolm McDonald

Professor of Marketing, Cranfield School of Management, UK

'British business has been in search of the customer-driven organization for three decades. This book is an important step forward in the pursuit of this elusive goal . . . There are no quick-fixes in the world of market-led change. This practical book helps lay out a way forward for the manager caught up in the politics of delivering success to his organization.'

David M. Battye

Associate Director, Harbridge House Consulting Group, London, UK

'There are too many books on marketing theory and too few on how to change the culture of a company to make it market responsive. Nigel Piercy's book is pragmatic and has the whiff of battle and the real world about it.'

Sir John Harvey-Jones

(formerly) Chairman, ICI plc, UK

'Essentially management is about change and, for a commercial undertaking, very much about the change necessary to secure and grow markets. Professor Piercy's book *Market-Led Strategic Change* both teaches and reminds us what it takes to develop and deliver that business essential, the marketing plan ... I very much enjoyed reading the book and I am happy to admit that I learned from it.'

Sir Graham Day

(formerly) Chairman, British Aerospace, UK

PART I

The Customer Value Imperative

CHAPTER 1

New marketing:

The renaissance of the marketplace

The main goal of this book is very simple. I want to infect you with the incredible excitement that surrounds taking products and services to market in new and better ways, and to build a passion and enthusiasm for creating customer value better than others do. The goal is relevance and new marketing to meet the demands of new customers, not just repackaging the old stuff that you can find in traditional textbooks. I also take exception to writers, trainers and teachers who seem determined to make business boring. The process of taking business ideas into reality is not boring, it is incredible fun. I think we have a problem with what seems to be the 'MBA mantra' to be boring and tedious as a substitute for being innovative and creative. It is almost as if every business school in the world has an unwritten set of MBA Commandments, to which you have to agree if you want to be a 'proper' manager. In fact, it must look something like this:

'The goal is relevance and new marketing to meet the demands of new customers'

THE MBA CODE OF PRACTICE

Thou shall never smile again.

Thou shall dedicate thy career to being a boring, humourless jerk, for is this not how thy professors are moulded?

Thou shall spread the message that plans and systems matter more than doing things.

3

> Thou shall live by the dictum that those things which cannot be measured precisely and validly to six decimal points, simply do not exist (little things like customer satisfaction and customer value shall not trouble thee . . .)
>
> Thou shall dedicate thyself to driving the creative and unconventional people out of thy organization, for do not they deserve to be in an agency somewhere, where they can do no harm?
>
> Thou shall worship at the alter of bureaucracy, for is not the neatness of the organization chart a measure of thy true worth?
>
> Thy mission is to attend meetings for the rest of thy life, for is not the number of such meetings a measure of thy productivity?

Oh all right, I am exaggerating a bit, but not that much.

In the context of going back to having fun, this is a book about the process of going to market, not marketing – the difference is explained shortly. It also sets out to be controversial not conventional. Partly, this is because the book is grounded in working with managers in companies and revelling in the creativity and innovation taking place in the marketplace, not in traditional marketing theory – it is sad that these should be such different things, but they are. On these questions there is really quite a lot left to be said, and even more to be *done*.

'this is a book about the process of going to market, not marketing'

There is a small problem with the conventional marketing view of how companies take their products and services to a customer, which is getting more deadly by the day – it assumes and relies on the existence of a world which is alien and unrecognizable to executives who actually have to *manage* such things for real. It rests on implicit assumptions such as the formalization and integration of 'marketing' in an organization, not to mention explicit assumptions that market strategies are specifically formulated and directly lead to related marketing programmes. It assumes that the whole market problem is solved by marketing research to fully understand customers and markets. All these assumptions come from the page of the idealistic, ivory-tower, prescriptive textbook, not the reality as it is perceived, experienced and faced by line executives who have the real problem of managing.

The managerial reaction to conventional marketing can be summarized by one executive's remarks to me at a Director's Workshop which I ran for a particular company. After my predictably masterly exposition on the tools of strategic auditing and market strategy models, this particularly ungrateful individual said something like this:

'That is great. I have no quarrel with what you say, there are some things I have learned. But you have told us *what* marketing plans and strategies are, and *what* the tools and techniques are, but not *how* to do it in practice, and definitely not *how* to make it happen in *this* company!'

He was right and this book is an attempt to build a systematic attack on precisely the problems he foresaw – the problems of making the things that matter in the market happen in a company. Such are the seedy origins of what follows.

The core of this book is the Strategic Pathway in Part III. This leads us through the stages of developing a market strategy: implanting customer focus and learning capabilities in companies; making critical market choices; developing a value proposition to our customers based on our differentiating capabilities; untangling the key relationships that we have to manage because the market strategy depends on them. The real key is a customer-focused market strategy based on offering value, that we are good at delivering, to a customer who wants it.

However, there are a couple of significant changes since the last edition of the book. These do not reflect my brilliance and insightful superior understanding of

> **'The real key is a customer-focused market strategy based on offering value'**

the business universe (though now I come to think of it like that . . . well, maybe they are[1]). In fact, the chapters leading up to the Strategic Pathway have grown out of the issues raised by executives in real companies, concerned with enhancing their companies' performance. These issues are:

- *Value* as the emerging issue in achieving and sustaining competitive success, and particularly how this relates to branding[2] and customer relationship management, with aggressive and sophisticated customers (see Chapter 3).
- The *Internet*, developing from a cumbersome electronic shop window into a powerful new marketing channel and creating completely new types of businesses on the way, as well as some financial catastrophies (see Chapter 4.com).
- *Total integration* of all the company's resources and capabilities to deliver solid customer value (even if it does mean our

precious marketing executives actually having to talk to the spanners in the production department) (see Chapter 5).

- *Strategizing and creativity* as the key to effective performance, replacing traditional concerns about structures and the bureaucracy of formal planning (see Chapter 6).

Some readers may wonder why I have dropped the use of the word 'marketing' in many places in the book and in my work with executives: 'going to market' instead of 'marketing', 'market strategy' instead of 'marketing strategy', 'market-led' instead of 'marketing-led', and so on. The reason is simple. It is not a ploy to save paper and ink (unless you are a green marketing fanatic – in which case, that's really what it is). It is simply because markets are more important than marketing, and it helps if we say so. It is also because markets and customers are the responsibility of *every* manager in a company, not the 'property' of marketing specialists[3].

'basically traditional marketing is dead in the water'

There is another reason also – basically traditional marketing is dead in the water. The days of the large corporate marketing department, with its market research surveys and brand managers and obsession with advertising, have gone – if indeed they ever existed for most companies. In a prize-winning paper in 1995, Antony Brown of IBM observed:

'There are now two types of corporation: those with a marketing department and those with a marketing soul. Even a cursory glance at the latest Fortune 500 shows that the latter are the top performing companies, while the former, steeped in the business traditions of the past, are fast disappearing.'[4]

Instead, he says, new marketing will be a corporate philosophy driven by clusters of teams building alliances inside and outside the organization, based around customers and supported by IT.

'if "marketing" is what traditional marketing departments do (or did), then "going to market" is what companies do (and always will)'

My view of this is that if 'marketing' is what traditional marketing departments do (or did), then 'going to market' is what companies do (and always will). 'Marketing' may have belonged to marketing specialists, but 'going to market' is a process owned by *everyone* in the organization – the 'part-time market-ers'[5], the chief executive[6], cross-functional teams[7] – and that is how we have to learn to manage it. More of this in Chapter 5.

The process of going to market

What do I mean by the 'process of going to market'? The model in Figure 1.1 explains.

The logic of the model is as follows. Frederick Webster suggests that we should think about how we design and bring together all the business processes that: *define customer value* (e.g. market research, analysis of our core competencies, economic analysis of customer use systems); *develop customer value* (e.g. new product development, design of distribution channels, selection of partners, develop price and value positioning), and *deliver customer value* (e.g. logistics, sales, transaction processing, after-sales service, applications engineering, customer training)[8]. Figure 1.1 shows these processes of value definition, development and delivery as making up the process of going to market and the creation of customer value. However, these processes have several dimensions which we must manage consistently[9]. Each value process has: an *analytical/technical dimension* (e.g. information for value definition, operations management for value development, and logistics and supply chains for value delivery). However, the processes also have a *behavioural dimension* (e.g. interpretation and understanding in value definition, motivation and commitment in value development, and attitudes and behaviour in value delivery). The challenge is not just to manage techniques but also

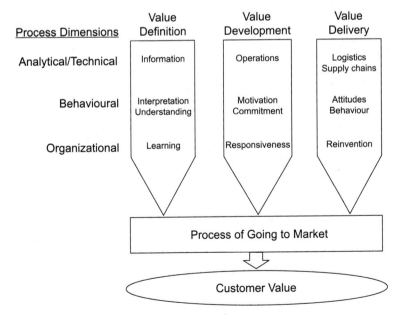

Figure 1.1 The process of going to market

people – many of whom will not be in marketing departments or even our own company, because we will see that processes span traditional functions and organizational boundaries. Processes also have an *organizational dimension* (e.g. learning capabilities in value definition, responsiveness, the ability to change in value development, and reinvention in value delivery to meet new customer demands). We have to manage processes in their organizational context[10]. Hold on though – this is all getting a bit theoretical for me – does this matter?

Where this model leads us is in identifying some important practical differences in managing the process of going to market, instead of just 'marketing'. These are:

- we base our strategies on our customers and markets – we are market-led or market-driven;
- our internal programmes of change and our external actions in the marketplace are driven by that strategy;
- we concentrate on getting our act together around the things that matter to delivering our customer-focused strategy into the market – the 'ownership' of activities by functional departments, the existence of 'specialists' in professional disciplines, and conventional organizational structures are all secondary to this;
- boundaries between traditional functional departments, and even between organizations, are crossed by teams and processes focusing on the creation of value for customers;
- new types of relationships – with customers, collaborators, competitors and co-workers – are more fundamental than contracts and transactions; and
- new ways of doing business are underpinned by information technology, as the infrastructure supporting complex relationships inside and outside the organization.

Now that is a pleasingly pompous set of platitudes, is it not? Actually, the perspective of the process of going to market instead of traditional marketing has very practical implications.

'who cares about conventional views when they are demonstrably out-of-date?'

Certainly, this viewpoint does not sit happily with many conventional views of how things should be done. But who cares about conventional views when they are demonstrably out-of-date?[11].

In fact, I would go still further. If you look at the many cases of market success studied in this book, in almost no case can you put the success down to structured marketing programmes with great planning, and the application of advanced theories of market behaviour by traditional marketing departments and executives. They are more often about managers with a sense of what will go with a particular type of customer, putting together a deal that will attract that customer, and driving that strategy through the internal and external obstacles.

That is really the difference between managing marketing and managing the process of going to market. Of course, marketing activities – new product development, branding, pricing, distribution, marketing communications, and so on – are a part of the process of going to market, and often a vital part. The difference is that the context for marketing should be the process of going to market, not the marketing department.

It is also why most of what follows comes out of what companies and consultants are *having* to learn to achieve superior market performance, not out of academic theories about marketing.

In fact, I would go yet further – if you look at the companies that *achieve* superior performance in the market and *sustain* that superior performance, the route they take is by managing better how they go to market, not by excellence in conventional marketing terms. Peter Doyle summarizes this nicely by urging us:

> 'to reject the notion of "quick-fixes", whether these be rationalisation, acquisition or marketing gimmicks. Sustained growth depends upon hard work and continuous investment in strategy, systems and staff over a long period. World class competitiveness depends upon delivering products and services which offer better value over rivals in the market.'[12]

In short, superior performance comes from going to market better than competitors, not from just having marketing departments or spending money on publicity. The focus of going to market is choosing and managing a strategic pathway involving superior market understanding and customer focus, appropriate market choices, a robust and sustainable value proposition to customers, a set of key relationships that underpin the value proposition, all based on superior customer and market understanding.

'superior performance comes from going to market better than competitors, not from just having marketing departments or spending money on publicity'

So, what do managers need to know?

I have said that this is a book about the process of going to market. This leaves the question of who it is for. The content of this book is chosen with two very simple questions in mind. Those questions may be simple, but they seem to have been somewhat neglected recently. The guiding questions are:

- What does a manager really need to know to improve the company's process of going to market, to change the way things are done, and to attain superior performance in the marketplace?
- What does a manager need to see when s/he stands back from day-to-day operations to see the big picture of going to market, to find ways of doing it better?

These questions suggest that the things a manager really needs to get a handle on, in the process of going to market, are:

- *Customers* – understanding customers and focusing on the market offering we make to them and what it produces in superior customer value.
- *Market strategy* – choosing market targets and building a strong market position based on differentiating capabilities to create a robust and sustainable value proposition to customers, driven by networks of critical relationships.
- *Implementation* – driving the things that matter through the corporate environment to the marketplace.

We are pretty short on technical details – pricing theories, new product development programmes, market research techniques, advertising theory, buyer behaviour models, and so on. There is a reason for this. Managers do not need to get involved in technical detail. We can underline this point.

What managers do not need to know

I sincerely believe that managers should focus on the process of going to market and they (probably) do not need to know much about:

- *Market orientation* – in recent years, academics have been obsessed with market orientation because someone finally figured out a way to measure it[13] – seeing what it relates to, who has it and who does not[14], and so on. The pioneer of market orientation studies, Bernie Jaworski, said some time ago that this stuff was past its sell-by-date. I agree. Also, it is very, very boring and of little practical significance to anyone except academics who write papers about it. This book is for managers not academics, so we will talk about customers instead.

- *Marketing programmes* – surely we need to know all about product policy and pricing and advertising and promotion, and all that stuff? Maybe – but really that is a job for marketing executives and agencies, not managers (and you can get chapter and verse on these topics in conventional textbooks). We need customer focus and a market strategy first, or none of the technical marketing expertise makes sense. The harsh truth is – customers could not care less about impeccably planned and structured marketing programmes. They are only concerned with the value of what we offer them, so that's where we start.

'*We need customer focus and a market strategy first, or none of the technical marketing expertise makes sense*'

- *Consumer behaviour theory* – why don't we just let the psychologists have fun doing their laboratory experiments and studies on rats and students[15]. They have been doing this quite happily for decades and have yet to produce anything of practical significance that was not blindingly obvious in the first place. If the situation changes I will let you know[16].
- *Market research techniques* – managers need to know how to understand customers and markets better, not how to: design questionnaires, develop sampling frames, collect data, analyse and model data, and all the rest of it. The manager needs to be better at market 'sensing' or market understanding – not running surveys and building databases – that is a job for technicians or research agencies.
- *Postmodernism in marketing* – conventions of decency in language and the laws of libel preclude me from making any comment whatsoever about the practical contributions of postmodernism to marketing[17]. I just wish postmodernists would stop taking themselves so seriously, and try to get a life.

That should make life easier?

Admittedly, the things managers do not need to know listed above knock out about 95 per cent of most conventional training and education courses in marketing. However, all we are doing is putting the *easy* stuff on hold, to focus on the *difficult* things that really matter: customer focus, market strategy, and effective implementation in the process of going to market. These are the tough issues, and the ones we cannot afford to run away from. This has just made life a lot harder. Sorry.

Market-led strategic change?

This brings me to the question of the possibly somewhat pretentious title of this book. The label 'market-led strategic change' (MLSC) is one we have applied to the research into market strategy implementation, which we have done over the past several years, together with the associated consultancy and in-company development work. The MLSC approach makes the following assumptions and assertions:

- that ultimately *all* organizations are forced to follow the dictates of the market (i.e. the paying customer), or go out of business when someone else *does*;
- in this sense we can pursue organizational effectiveness by being 'market-led' and focusing on the customer's needs, wants and demands – as well as using what we learn from customers as the foundation for creating new markets and finding new spaces in existing markets;
- many of the barriers to doing this do not come from ignorance of customer characteristics, lack of information, inflexible technology, competitive threats, and so on, they come from the way we run our organizations;
- being 'market-led' may require substantial and painful upheaval in the way our organizations are structured, the way decisions are made, the key values we communicate to employees and managers, how we all do our jobs, and how we look at the outside world;
- this amounts to a programme of deep-seated, fundamental strategic change in organizations, not just hiring a marketing executive or doing more advertising or any other short-term tactical ploy.

The key to effective strategic change is quite simply that we put the pursuit of superior customer value (and thus our organization's goals and survival) back where it should be – at the top of *everyone's* list of priorities.

'none of us have any right to prosper unless we provide the fickle, disloyal, but paying customers with what they value most'

The truth is that none of us have any right to prosper unless we provide the fickle, disloyal, but *paying* customers with what they value most, and we keep on doing that (or pay the consequences). We come to the market-led strategic model not in a spirit of altruism, but one of survival in the harsh reality of the customer marketplace of the twenty-first century.

But why upset the applecart?

. . . because if you don't, someone else will. The more you think about your company's process of going to market, instead of conventional marketing, you are likely to become aware of two quite frightening things:

- customers and markets have changed – radically and forever;
- the manager's job has changed – radically and forever.

I will expand on these points in the next two chapters, because they represent a reality from which there is no escape.

> 'A long habit of not thinking a thing wrong,
> gives it a superficial appearance of being right.'
>
> Thomas Paine (1737–1809), writer and revolutionary.

So, what does all that mean?

The purpose of this chapter was scene-setting – to clarify our goals and the approach being taken. This will not be to everyone's taste.

In fact, some people will probably be deeply offended. They will probably not have lasted to this point in the chapter, so there is no point in apologizing[18]. If you are still with me, then this chapter has tried to do the following things:

- to turn our attention away from traditional roles of 'marketing' towards the fundamental *process of going to market* that is critical in every organization – marketing departments may disappear, the process of going to market remains critical to success;
- to put three issues centre stage for the manager's agenda: *customers, market strategy,* and *implementation and change* – because sorting out these issues seems to be what distinguishes the winners from the losers just about everywhere you go;
- to highlight the *new context* for market strategy – the escalation of market demands for value in customer terms, the pervasive impact of e-commerce, the need for total integration, and the quest for putting creativity back into strategy;

- to focus on the process of going to market, and the central issues of customer, market strategy and implementation as the basis for creating and *managing market-led strategic change*;
- getting these things right is urgent, and means abandoning many of our traditional ways of doing things to cope with *new challenges* in the marketplace and how we do business and how we manage – that is why more and more people are talking about 'new marketing' that abandons the assumptions and inflexibility of the past.

Ten steps to transform the process of going to market

This book is designed to help managers who want to understand the ways in which companies can and should focus on improving the way they understand and manage the process by which they go to market. We will address the following critical issues to provide a framework and tools for action around customers, market strategy and the implementation of strategic change. We will do the following things:

- The remainder of Part I is concerned with the fundamental issues of *customers* (Chapter 2) and *value* (Chapter 3).
- Part II concentrates on three major areas of concern in how we respond to customer demands for value: the impact of *electronic business* (Chapter 4.com), the need for *totally integrated marketing* not 'marketing specialists' (Chapter 5), and the need for *creative strategizing* instead of unimaginative 'me-too' responses to every problem and opportunity (Chapter 6).
- Building on these foundation issues, Part III turns to defining a *Strategic Pathway* for a company to go to market – the development of customer focus and market sensing capabilities (Chapter 7); the *key market choices* that are made and how we define and segment markets around the things that matter to customers (Chapter 8); then we turn to developing a *value proposition* based on our market mission and our ability to differentiate against the competition based on our capabilities and key marketing assets like brands (Chapter 9); next we examine the *key relationships* with customers, co-workers, collaborators and competitors, which underpin our market strategy (Chapter 10); and lastly, we provide a framework for turning our strategizing into a *plan* (Chapter 11).
- Then, Part IV turns to the issues we face in driving market strategy through the corporate environment – the gaps emerging between our *strategic intent and reality* as market strategies are turned into marketing programmes (Chapter 12); and the critical opportunities for *managing key processes* like

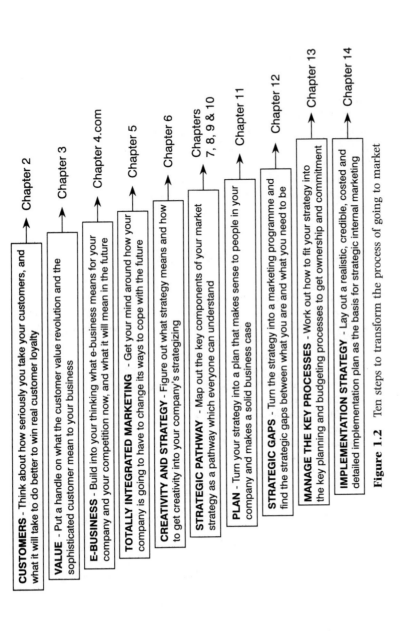

CUSTOMERS - Think about how seriously you take your customers, and what it will take to do better to win real customer loyalty → Chapter 2

VALUE - Put a handle on what the customer value revolution and the sophisticated customer mean to your business → Chapter 3

E-BUSINESS - Build into your thinking what e-business means for your company and your competition now, and what it will mean in the future → Chapter 4.com

TOTALLY INTEGRATED MARKETING - Get your mind around how your company is going to have to change its ways to cope with the future → Chapter 5

CREATIVITY AND STRATEGY - Figure out what strategy means and how to get creativity into your company's strategizing → Chapter 6

STRATEGIC PATHWAY - Map out the key components of your market strategy as a pathway which everyone can understand → Chapters 7, 8, 9 & 10

PLAN - Turn your strategy into a plan that makes sense to people in your company and makes a solid business case → Chapter 11

STRATEGIC GAPS - Turn the strategy into a marketing programme and find the strategic gaps between what you are and what you need to be → Chapter 12

MANAGE THE KEY PROCESSES - Work out how to fit your strategy into the key planning and budgeting processes to get ownership and commitment → Chapter 13

IMPLEMENTATION STRATEGY - Lay out a realistic, credible, costed and detailed implementation plan as the basis for strategic internal marketing → Chapter 14

Figure 1.2 Ten steps to transform the process of going to market

planning and budgeting to build ownership and commitment market-led change instead of writing plans that change nothing (Chapter 13).

- Lastly, in Part V we turn attention to the need to build *implementation and internal marketing strategies* inside the organization to put our market strategy into effect in the customer marketplace (Chapter 14).

To make it easier for those who want to pick out issues rather than starting at the beginning and working through, I have outlined these ten steps to transform the process of going to market in Figure 1.2, which indicates where to go in the book to examine a particular issue. This figure also tries to make the logic of the book clear. Bear in mind, this agenda is contentious and controversial and it is not traditional 'marketing'. However, it is the agenda that matters in doing things better. So, let's get on with it . . .

Notes and references

1. Although it behoves us all to recall the experience of the hapless American politician Dan Quayle, who having been awarded a plaque as an 'All Time Great American', on the way home made the mistake of asking his wife how many 'All Time Great Americans' she thought there were, only to receive the reply 'One less than you think, Buddy'.
2. And we should all be aware that successful branding is extremely difficult, and frequently rather painful for the cow . . .
3. I have come to hate the expression 'marketing specialist', and frequently cite the definition of the specialist as one who knows more and more about less and less, eventually knowing everything about nothing. It may not be original, but it sure is true.
4. Antony Brown (1995), 'The Fall and Rise of Marketing', *Marketing Business*, February, 25–28.
5. Evert Gummesson (1990), *The Part-Time Marketer*, University of Halsted Research Report 90:3.
6. 'High-Tech CEOs Plugged Into Marketing', *Marketing News*, 2 June 1995.
7. George Day (1990), *Market Driven Strategy – Processes for Creating Value*, New York: Free Press.
8. Frederick E. Webster (1997), 'The Future Role of Marketing in the Organization', in Donald R. Lehmann and Katherine E. Jocz (eds), *Reflections on the Futures of Marketing*, Cambridge, MA: Marketing Science Institute, pp. 39–66.
9. The multidimensional process is discussed in greater detail when we look at planning and budgeting processes later (pp. 577–630).
10. This model has been developed from an earlier version. Nigel F. Piercy (1998), 'Marketing Implementation: The Implications of Marketing Paradigm Weakness for the Strategy Execution Process', *Journal of the Academy of Marketing Science*, **26** (3), 222–36.

11. For example, see: Sergio Zyman (2000), *The End of Marketing As We Know It*, New York: Harper Collins.

12. Peter Doyle (1997), 'Go For Robust Growth', *Marketing Business*, April, 53.

13. Bernard J. Jaworski and Ajay Kohli (1993), 'Market Orientation: Antecedents and Consequences', *Journal of Marketing*, **57**, July, 53–70. Ajay Kohli and Bernard J. Jaworski (1990), 'Market Orientation: The Construct, Research Propositions and Managerial Implications', *Journal of Marketing*, **54**, April. John C. Narver and Stanley F. Slater (1990), 'The Effect of a Market Orientation on Business Profitability', *Journal of Marketing*, **54**, October, 20–35. Stanley F. Slater and John C. Narver (1994), 'Does Competitive Environment Moderate the Market Orientation–Performance Relationship?', *Journal of Marketing*, **58**, January, 46–55.

14. . . . how much it weighs, what colour it is, what it smells like, and so on – you get the picture?

15. And sometimes you have to use students in experiments, because some people like rats and are concerned for their well-being.

16. Some people question whether I really mean the bad things I say about consumer behaviour people? Well, aside from the consumer psychologist's uncanny ability to operate both eyes independently like a lizard, I would raise some questions about their field and profession:

    Question 1: What is black and brown and looks good on a consumer psychologist?

    Answer: A Dobermann Pinscher.

    Question 2: Do you know how to save a drowning consumer psychologist?

    Answer 1: Take your foot off his head. *Answer 2*: No? Good.

    Question 3: How can you tell when a consumer psychologist is talking nonsense?
    Answer: His lips are moving.

    Question 4: What is yellow and looks good on a consumer psychologist?
    Answer: A JCB earthmover.

    Question 5: What is the difference between a consumer psychologist and a catfish?
    Answer: One is an ugly bottom-dwelling creature that dredges up scum and feeds off it. The other is just a fish.

    I hope that may have made my feelings on the subject of consumer psychologists somewhat clearer.

17. However, if you are intrigued by this topic, at least Stephen Brown makes it funny: *Postmodern Marketing*, London: Routledge, 1995.

18. 'Never apologize, son, it's a sign of weakness', John Wayne, *The Yellow Rose of Texas*, 1926.

CHAPTER 2

The customer conundrum:

Service, servility, satisfaction, and then what?

The customer conundrum is that everyone *says* they believe in customers, but when you look at what they *do*, they really do not take the customer issue seriously at all. Service is seen as servility, satisfaction is confused with loyalty, and when our customer care programmes and customer satisfaction measurement systems do not help us – we are lost for what to do next. So we will start by looking at how companies treat their customers and why they need to do better.

Remember, the customer is always right-handed[1]

Why is it when you look around in most markets, companies treat their customers so badly? Is it because they don't care, or they just can't help themselves? Or, don't they know what they are doing?

REALITY CHECK

JUST WHO'S KIDDING WHO AROUND HERE?

Question: The new Severn Bridge between England and Wales is a £50 million a year sales revenue business, part-owned by the French company GTM. Adrian Evans of Cardiff is a commuter, who has paid about £7000 in bridge tolls over ten years. One day he forgot to take his wallet to work, and when he got to the Bridge, they refused to let him cross, causing him substantial inconvenience and aggravation. Why was this – did they think he was going to steal the bridge if they let him across without paying first? No, says the bridge company spokesman 'It is not our policy …'.

Question: To check into most international flights from Heathrow, there is a mandatory two hours extra added to check-in times. This leaves most passengers hanging around the airport for about three hours. Does anyone really believe that this is for security reasons (the official excuse)? Or could it have something to do with the fact that airport profits increase by 20 per cent for every extra ten minutes that passengers are kept waiting, evidenced by the fact that sales in Heathrow's airport-shops have risen five times faster than those on the high street, and contribute nearly half the British Airport Authority's profits? Who do they think they are kidding?

Question: Why do companies like Toshiba, Canon and America On Line offer fantastic technology in their products and services, and back this up with customer help-lines which are useless – do they think their wonderful products are more important than their customer?

Sources: 'Unlucky Severn for Driver With No Cash', *Daily Mail*, 28 March 1997. Joshua Miles (1996), 'Helpline Callers Left Hanging on the Phone', *Sunday Business*, 18 November.

It is telling that a survey of UK Marketing Society members by Taylor Nelson Sofres[2] in 1999 found that: some 40 per cent of board members felt that the customer voice was rarely or never represented at board level, rising to 60 per cent for smaller companies; while 93 per cent of companies regularly report to the board on profitability, 68 per cent on cash flow, but only 35 per cent regularly evaluate customer satisfaction levels. If boards demonstrably do not care about customers – why should we expect better from the rest of the company?

In fact, more generally, if you ask around most consumers and business customers will tell you that with most of the companies that sell to them – the people have bad attitudes and service stinks.

Customer service is bad all over

The critical importance to business survival and success of customer service and providing value to our customers is hardly news to anyone. Just about every sector you go to, companies tell you about their customer care policies and their focus on customer satisfaction. Who are we kidding? Just look at examples of how organizations treat their customers:

REALITY CHECK
THE REALITY OF CUSTOMER SERVICE

Example: The National Health Service has a 'patients' charter' and boasts slogans like 'Putting Patients' Interests First' as well as a management policy of 'positive customer care'. John Spiers, chairman of Brighton Health Care NHS Trust – an £801 million business – decided to put this to the test. He got into a wheelchair and visited the Royal Sussex County Hospital in the guise of a disabled outpatient. On arrival, the hospital porter took 40 minutes to respond to his bleep, leading to the conversation:

Patient: Where's your name tag?
Porter: What's it to you, mate?
Patient: You're supposed to wear one, it says so in the patients' charter and I'm a patient.
Porter: F*** off!

Other surprises for Spiers were: getting into a hospital in a wheelchair is difficult when there are no automatic sliding doors; hospitals like this one are full of discarded litter and are very grubby, and the roof leaks when it rains; there were no pillows on the trolley; he was told to expect a five-hour wait to see a doctor; there was no patient alarm to call help in an emergency; staff gave him incorrect directions, and stripped away his dignity in how they treated him – publicly humiliating him, for example, because he had failed to memorize his 'patient number'. Spiers concluded: 'If I had really been a frail and elderly patient in pain, I would have been scared and bewildered ... whatever happened to privacy and dignity?'. Two points spring to mind: how can service standards be so appalling in an expensive 'caring' business; and, why is it so unusual for a chief executive to sample his or her own customer service?

Example: Retail business in Britain routinely promises service and value to its customers. Customers find a slightly different reality all too often. A recent survey found that most retail staff will look the customer in the eye, but there is a good chance they will not smile, and while shop assistants were generally perceived by customers as polite, they were less likely to be helpful or friendly. Len Berry lists common customer complaints about retail staff as:

- *True lies* – blatant dishonesty or unfairness, such as selling unnecessary extra services or misquoting costs.
- *Red alert* – customers are treated harshly or disrespectfully because they are assumed to be stupid or dishonest.
- *Broken promises* – careless, mistake-prone behaviour, or no-shows at appointments.
- *I just work here* – powerless employees who lack the authority or desire to solve basic customer problems.
- *The big wait* – being made to wait in a queue because checkouts or service counters are closed.
- *Automatic pilot* – impersonal, emotionless, no eye-contact, going-through-the-motions non-service.
- *Suffering in silence* – employees who do not bother to communicate with customers who want to know what is happening.
- *Don't ask* – employees unwilling to make any extra effort to help customers, or seeming put-out by requests for assistance.
- *Lights on, no-one at home* – clueless employees who do not know, and will not take the time to learn, answers to customers' common questions.
- *Misplaced priorities* – employees who chat with each other or conduct personal business while the customer waits, or refuse to assist a customer because they are on a 'break'.

Example: Britain has an important tourism and leisure industry. Research by Coopers & Lybrand for the Department of National Heritage concludes that British hotel and restaurants are characterized by a 'self-perpetuating vicious circle' in which staff are poorly educated and trained, badly paid and take little pride in their work. They do not understand and cannot deliver good customer service. In fact, things are so bad that the British Hospitality Association has had the unmitigated gall to publish a survey accusing hotel *guests* of being ill-mannered, shouting and swearing, and complaining about 'trivial things', suggesting that 80 per cent of hotel owners say guests are making their lives a misery! I'm sorry, run that by me again, Basil Fawlty, everything is horrible, and it is the *customers'* fault … ?

Example: Why do airlines believe that treating passengers like inanimate objects to be processed in batches and held waiting in queues is good customer service? For example, Dan Jones enumerates the activities involved in a family trip from England to Greece:

> Total travel time: 13 hours
> Time actually going somewhere: 7 hours (54 per cent of the total)
> Queuing and waiting time: 6 hours
> Number of queues: 10
> Number of times luggage was picked up and put down: 7
> Number of inspections (all asking the same questions): 8
> Total processing steps: 23
>
> Jones raises some very direct questions which would totally change
> the customer experience, but to which no airline seems to have a
> sensible answer: why can't the person at check-in do security,
> customs and check-in tasks, so you pass them and walk straight onto
> the plane; why can't the ticket from the travel agent include baggage
> tags, boarding passes, taxi voucher, bus tickets and hotel registration
> to be read automatically at each point; why can't the customs
> authorities have your passport scanned in at check-in and use the
> long hours while you are en route to decide whether you can enter
> the country (instead of making a planeload of passengers queue
> while the custom officials look at everyone's papers – why do they
> seem so surprised that you arrived, do they know something about
> the planes that we don't?)? The underlying answer is that no-one
> really cares enough to go back to basics and look at the product or
> service through the consumer's eyes. It is much easier to make
> passengers do things in the way that is convenient to airlines.
>
> **Sources**: Susan Clark (1994), 'Vulnerable, Afraid and Humiliated', *Sunday
> Times*, 24 April. *The Front Line Survey*, The Grassroots Group plc, 1994. Len
> Berry (1996), 'Retailers with a Future', *Marketing Management*, Spring. Paul
> Marston (1996), 'Poor Staff Threatens Tour Trade', *Daily Telegraph*, 31
> October. 'Fawlty Manners, and That's the Guests', *Daily Mail*, 15 April 1997.
> James P. Womack and Daniel T. Jones (1996), *Lean Thinking: Banish Waste and
> Create Wealth Within Your Corporation*, New York: Simon & Schuster.

No-one ever said that dealing with customers and creating
customer satisfaction is *easy* to do. In many ways, from the
internal corporate viewpoint, customers are a bit of a problem
because all too often they do not think 'like we do', and they are
unreasonable in a number of significant ways. So, we end up
saying things like the following.

'We know better than the customer'

To begin with, customers are demonstrably completely unreasonable because they persist in behaving as though *their* needs and
their problems, and the things *they* think are important, are more
central than our superb products and services, and what we
think and know really matters most.

REALITY CHECK
WHO KNOWS BEST?

I worked a couple of years ago with a project team, in a high-technology computer business, tasked by their company with generating a new strategy to gain market share in the UK water industry. The key target product-market was that for management information systems (MIS), rather than the more traditional operating and engineering systems. I was amazed to find that a group of computer professionals (including incidentally sales/marketing executives as well as technical specialists) could not cope with the simple fact shown by their market research that there was one piece of data the chief executive of a water business wants every day – the level of the water in the reservoirs. This *is* in many ways apparently quite irrational – chief executive officer or not s/he can do nothing about rainfall. S/he would be far better off, in managing the business, with all the financial, resource and productivity data the sophisticated MIS product can provide. Unfortunately, what our sophisticated MIS product could not provide was the one thing the irrational, emotional, unreasonable customer actually wanted. In fact, in this case the customer was not being totally irrational. The truth is, of course, that to be comfortable in getting on with running a water business what you really want to know is that you have got some water (because if you haven't you can expect immediate pain from everyone from the local MP whose image is at stake, to the local hospitals whose kidney dialysis machines won't work). It may or may not be irrational, but it is what matters to the customer that determines your success. In this case the computer company's whole marketing strategy began to unravel at this point: to tell the CEO what the level of water is, you have to interface with the operating systems that run the water network, and dominance of the operating systems market had been gained by another supplier, because we were so concerned with technical superiority in MIS, and so on.

'Customers are stupid'

We believe that our customers are emotional and irrational and in some cases just stupid in their buying behaviour. This probably merits a few more words. It has been said that nothing is ever really irrational – there are simply cases where we do not understand people's motives. Take a case in point.

REALITY CHECK

JUST WHO IS THE STUPID ONE HERE?

An R&D director of a high-technology manufacturing company complained bitterly to me, in a new product review meeting, that in spite of the company's massive spend on developing and launching a new electronic measurement instrument, the unreasonable, complaining customer was causing problems by turning the product down, because the on/off rocker switch on this marvel of high-technology was located at the *back* of the cabinet – not on the front where the operator could reach it without standing-up from his/her seat at the workbench. He received little sympathy from me (or his customers). If the customer wants the switch on the front, there is really only one answer – move it (or better yet, put it where the customer wants it, in the first place).

An NOP survey makes the telling point that the most disloyal are frequently the most valuable, but also the most demanding and least tolerant of bad service[3]. Their overwhelming reason for taking their business elsewhere is dissatisfaction with customer service:

- Reasons why customers change suppliers: 44 per cent – service mistake/billing error; 34 per cent – indifference, rudeness, ill-informed service; 30 per cent – price too high/increased; 17 per cent – poor response to complaints[4]; 10 per cent – better service from competitor.
- How their loyalty could have been retained: 82 per cent – better customer service; 69 per cent – better price; 48 per cent – loyalty bonus; 35 per cent – an apology; 25 per cent – compensation.

Does it have to be like this?

The answer is emphatically not. In most cases we actually have the technology and knowledge to do better, and some companies use it[5].

On the first point, for example, Dan Jones[6] the airline complainant in an earlier example, has a vision of perfection for a new entrant to the airline business which would overturn all the conventional barriers to customer service and value. His advice is:

- Start with small and mid-sized cities that currently only feed hubs, and think of ways for travellers to fly direct in small aircraft to other small and mid-sized cities, thus bypassing the current system.
- Rethink the terminal, so the passenger can drive or be driven very near the gate, and walk quickly to the plane, rolling specially-designed luggage straight onto the plane.
- Make reservations by phone or computer – including the taxi, hire car and hot reservation or the same ticket or plastic card, which gets you on the taxi, on the plane, and opens the hotel room door.
- Baggage handling would be eliminated and there would be no need for staff at the gate.
- You save money, and the customer gets less hassle and thus better value.

This is a great recipe for powerful competitive differentiation in the airline business. It could be done, but there is little sign that it is.

The picture is not altogether bleak. Some companies have established new and better levels of customer service, and as we will see, they are reaping the rewards.

But what is it like dealing with our company?

The quickest way to find out is to pretend to be a customer. If this does not appeal, then the Service Encounter Diary provides an incredibly simple (and often quite entertaining), but very effective, eye-opener for executive groups and employee groups in companies. What we do is ask people to do these things:

- to identify buying situations where they have received out-standingly good or bad service and rate them on a scale where '1' means it was appallingly bad and '10' means it was truly outstanding and excellent;
- then to summarize the things that made the experience really good or horribly bad; and
- to discuss what they have found and see what the situations they have experienced tell us about managers and employees who build service and value, and those who do not – you can list the characteristics of good and bad service providers and it will nearly always come out as a list of things like reliability, employee attitude, friendliness, trustworthiness, making extra effort, exceeding expectations, providing good value, and treating the customer as someone special.

The real crunch then comes – you ask people which of these characteristics sound most like *our* company and what they think *our* customers would say. If you are overwhelmed by feelings of smugness and complacency (as you may well be), the answer is simple – go and ask customers to tell you their stories about what it is like to deal with your company, and bring the stories back to the company.

'things have got so bad for many companies that the challenge is to identify the "customer sacrifices" – i.e. what customers are forced to put up with to do business with your company'

In fact, one view is that things have got so bad for many companies that the challenge is to identify the 'customer sacrifices' – i.e. what customers are forced to put up with to do business with your company – and get rid of them[7].

Often, the starting point for solving problems is simply to get people to accept that we have got problems. This may be the starting point for your company. But, does it really matter what customers think . . .

Customer satisfaction and customer loyalty

The conventional response is – of course it matters what customers think, because satisfied customers are loyal customers, and loyal customers bring us repeat business, a higher share of their expenditure, and referrals and word-of-mouth recommendations to other customers. That sounds pretty convincing. Unfortunately, it may be wrong more often than it is right. Management disillusionment may explain why in 2000 a Marketing Forum report revealed that, among large British companies, the majority emphasize customer relationship management in their marketing strategies, but less than one in ten allocate more than half the budget to customer retention – marketing spend remains focused mainly on growing customer numbers[8].

From customer satisfaction to customer loyalty

The conventional argument is that satisfied customers are loyal. This means that an important goal is customer retention, because the financial gains can be huge. This is a well-trodden path, but to recap, the advantages of high customer retention are:

- *Profitability* – customer loyalty reduces costs and improves profits. Frederick Reichheld of the consultancy Bain & Co.

writes 'customer loyalty appears to be the only way to achieve sustainably superior profits', and using an example from the life insurance business concludes 'a five percentage point increase in customer retention lowers costs per policy by 18 per cent'[9]. The Bain & Co. work suggests that the average company loses 10 per cent of its customers each year but a reduction in loss of customers by only 5 per cent could increase profits by 25–85 per cent[10]. This reflects increased productivity and reduced new customer acquisition costs (see below). Also, at its simplest, if we keep a customer longer – the simple arithmetic suggests we make more profit from that customer.

- *Productivity* – gains in profitability from customer retention come because: acquiring new customers to replace those we lost costs five times more than the cost of maintaining existing customers; the longer the 'life' of the customer the higher the sales volume over which acquisition costs can be spread; and the return in investment in marketing to existing customers can be seven times higher than with marketing to prospective customers[11].
- *Sales volume* – to hold sales volume constant, with an 80 per cent annual customer retention rate, the customer base will need renewing every five years, but if retention is increased to 90 per cent, the base needs to be renewed only every ten years. Also, the evidence is that not only do loyal customers take less marketing effort, they buy more of the company's products. Research suggests that, in retailing, loyal shoppers spend up to four times more in their first-choice store, than those who are 'promiscuous' in their shopping habits[12]. Calculating 'customer lifetime value' is a powerful way of concentrating minds on the significance of customer retention.
- *Actionability* – customer retention is one of the things you can measure and evaluate, and build development programmes to improve. This is underlined by evidence that most of the customers we lose do not take their business elsewhere because of poor product performance, they switch because of our poor service and how badly we treat them[13].

The case for focusing on customer retention has proved overwhelming, and has spawned huge numbers of customer loyalty programmes and the like. This is exciting stuff, but tends to miss a couple of important truths: customer satisfaction and customer loyalty are not the same thing, and you cannot buy real loyalty that easily.

'customer satisfaction and customer loyalty are not the same thing'

Whoever told you that customer satisfaction and customer loyalty were the same thing – because they lied to you

Put crudely: customer loyalty or retention is about how long we keep a customer (or what share of their business we take), while customer satisfaction is what people think of us – our quality, service, value, and so on. These are different things.

For example, Figure 2.1 suggests four possible links between customer satisfaction and loyalty:

- *Satisfied Stayers* – this is the situation that is assumed by the customer retention argument above: if you satisfy customers through your quality in product and service, then they will remain loyal, so you reap all the advantages of customer retention. But, in reality, how often do we get lulled into a false sense of security because we confuse these customers with the next type?
- *Happy Wanderers* – these customers show every sign of being satisfied with what you do and how you do it, but they do not (or maybe cannot) give loyalty in return. They may choose to buy elsewhere because: tempting new products and services attract them; they want things they can only get from a competitor, so they transfer their business; or a technology innovation takes them to the competition. Alternatively, in business-to-business markets, you may lose the satisfied customer because: there is a change in key personnel; corporate purchasing policies change; the purchasing company starts a supplier base reduction strategy; or, the company stops outsourcing and produces the product itself. Or maybe the customer just wants a change for the hell of it. These customers will always give you great ratings on the customer satisfaction questionnaire – they just leave when they feel like it.
- *Hostages* – it is possible that some of our most loyal customers may be highly dissatisfied ones. They may be tied to us by: product compatibility (e.g. only our product works in their machines); loyalty incentives (e.g. accumulating enough frequent flyer miles with the same airline, to get the free flight); the costs of switching – economic or psychological (e.g. the complications for most people in switching bank accounts are substantial, and some customers are just lazy); corporate policy (e.g. central purchasing tells you where to purchase certain products); or even a form of monopoly if your brand or product is close to unique for the time being. These customers are not satisfied – but they are retained (at least for the time being).

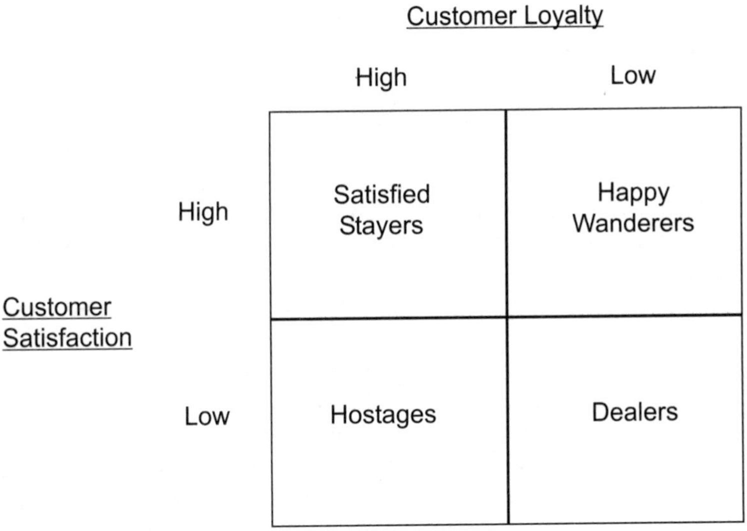

Customer Loyalty

	High	Low
High	Satisfied Stayers	Happy Wanderers
Low	Hostages	Dealers

Customer Satisfaction

Figure 2.1 Customer satisfaction versus customer loyalty

- *Dealers* – These customers are not satisfied and move brands and suppliers frequently. Often they will be the buyers most attracted by low prices and the best 'deal' on the market.

This model is not just speculation. It comes out of a project with a well-known company which is discovering that as its markets open up to new competitors, customer satisfaction (theirs is very high) is really not the same thing as customer loyalty or retention (theirs is falling rapidly). They are not alone in worrying about this issue. British Airways has found that the defection rate among their 'satisfied' customers was 13 per cent – *exactly* the same as with dissatisfied, complaining customers[14].

Why aren't customer satisfaction and loyalty the same thing?

Some managers object to the model in Figure 2.1 – since many have spent fortunes on improving customer satisfaction to build customer loyalty, it is not really surprising that they are not amused to have it suggested that their underlying assumption was at least partly wrong.

The difference between satisfaction and loyalty is straightforward: satisfaction is an attitude (how a customer feels about our company, product, service),

'*satisfaction is an attitude (how a customer feels about our company, product, service), while loyalty is a behaviour (do they buy from us more than once)'*

while loyalty is a behaviour (do they buy from us more than once). Using satisfaction (an attitude) to indicate loyalty (a behaviour) does not work particularly well – 90 per cent of car buyers are satisfied or very satisfied when they drive away from the showroom, but way less than half will buy the same car next time[15]. The chances are that some satisfied customers will defect – not least because there is a big difference between customers who are just 'satisfied' and those who are 'completely satisfied'[16].

One way of thinking about this is to distinguish between behavioural loyalty (what the customer does) and attitudinal loyalty (how the customer feels about us and our products/ services). The point of this is that considering only attitudinal loyalty (measuring satisfaction, intention to repurchase, and so on) leads us to make bad marketing investments, because the chances are that only a small proportion of the behaviourally loyal are actually attitudinally loyal as well. There are many non-attitudinal factors that impact on behavioural loyalty to a greater extent:

- *Committed loyalists* – place a high value on what we offer them, tend to be willing to pay a price premium, and not to switch – they are the Satisfied Stayers of Figure 2.1.
- *Feature loyalists* – place a high value on one or two 'must have' features of the product or service – they may be Satisfied Stayers or Hostages.
- *Convenience loyalists* – stick with the present option for an easy and convenient life: I may hate my bank but it's just not worth the hassle of changing – these are Hostages.
- *Channel loyalists* – place a high value on the channel of distribution: I prefer Pepsi, but if I eat lunch in McDonalds every day, I am going to be a loyal Coke consumer because that is all McDonalds sells – another form of Hostage.
- *Lack of choice* – have no alternatives: I believe Toshiba laptop computers are the best in the world, but I use a Research Machines laptop, because that is what my employer buys – another form of Hostage.
- *Price loyalists* – want the best price for basic product performance – the Dealers in our model[17].

'the key to understanding loyalty is value and choice, not satisfaction or attitudes'

William Neal of SDR Consulting is clear – behavioural loyalty is driven by perceived value, so the key to understanding loyalty is value and choice, not satisfaction or attitudes.

In fact, not all those investments in customer care and customer service to build customer satisfaction are wasted. Although customer satisfaction is a poor predictor of customer loyalty, customer dissatisfaction is a good predictor of customer defection – the happy customer may or may not stay, but it seems the unhappy customer will make every possible effort to leave if they can. A high level of customer dissatisfaction probably takes you out of the game altogether – you are no longer one of the alternatives the customer considers acceptable. (This is why satisfaction and dissatisfaction are probably different constructs, not either end of a single scale.)

The bottom-line on this is that you need to explore and understand better why some of your customers defect, and some of your customers are retained, and to avoid making simplistic assumptions about customer satisfaction and customer loyalty. This is the real basis for making effective decisions about investments in customer satisfaction, relationship marketing and loyalty programmes. (It is also a pretty good basis for deciding if you are retaining the customers you want to retain – see pp. 497–8.)

This also helps explain why someone like Sandra Vandermerwe talks not about customer satisfaction and loyalty, but about 'customer lock-on' achieved through superior value in relationships, intangibles like information and knowledge, networks, expanding customer bases, innovation, and reducing costs[18] – her message is clear: if you want the benefits of customer retention, it takes a lot more than winning questionnaire-based popularity polls.

'if you want the benefits of customer retention, it takes a lot more than winning questionnaire-based popularity polls'

But where does that leave 'loyalty programmes'?

Of course, this throws up an interesting question about the wastefulness in investing in loyalty programmes for customers who are Hostages, Happy Wanderers or Dealers (because those investments are unlikely to pay off), and what are the distinguishing characteristics of the Satisfied Stayers in our business. In particular, doing things to attract the Happy Wanderers and Dealers may actually undermine our position with the Satisfied Stayers – special offers and new services offered only to attract the low loyalty customer but which are not offered to the loyal customer can have this disastrous effect.

There is another problem also in confusing satisfaction and loyalty: some of the gains from customer retention do reflect attitudes as well as behaviour, particularly in word-of-mouth recommendations to others, referrals, and speaking well of the company to enhance its market reputation and standing. If customers are not satisfied (attitudinal loyalty), you get none of those 'soft' benefits, even if people continue to buy from you out of habit or lack of choice (behavioural loyalty). While we should not expect attitudinal loyalty always to translate into retained business, there may be other benefits we should factor in.

But, who said you can buy loyalty, anyway?

The strong case for leveraging customer retention led to what some call 'a mad dash back to the dark ages of marketing'[19] in a 'lemming-like rush'[20] to customer loyalty programmes – plastic loyalty cards from financial services firms, motor manufacturers and leading retailers like Tesco and Sainsbury; customer magazines; regular customer discounts; collectable vouchers for free flights from petrol stations; the 'Air Miles' scheme where purchases in various places using various payment methods earn points towards air travel or gifts; and the 'frequent flyer' programmes operated by the major airlines (offering the business traveller who flies a lot the chance to save points so that s/he can fly some more[21]). In fact, the proliferation of loyalty programmes is such that Datamonitor estimated that by the year 2000 there were 3.8 *billion* cards in circulation, and one commentator notes 'there is only so much loyalty to go around'[22]!

As sales promotion devices some of these schemes have been highly effective – the Tesco Clubcard is seen as one of the main reasons why Tesco took market leadership from Sainsbury in the UK grocery market. They are particularly effective if they focus on the customers who are most important to us – the big spender, the potential customers for new products; or the most profitable customers.

'There is, however, one problem that should be noted about customer loyalty programmes – they have very little to do with customer loyalty'

There is, however, one problem that should be noted about customer loyalty programmes – they have very little to do with customer loyalty. As Christopher Hapton, head of the customer loyalty practice at Bain & Co. noted some time ago: 'Loyalty is not developed by simply bribing someone to come back next time'[23]. George Day summarizes the critical point succinctly: 'Repeat behaviour is for sale, whereas customer loyalty can only be earned'[24].

In terms of Figure 2.1, what most companies seem to be doing is investing in developing Hostages, not building Satisfied Stayers. Is this because 'buying' a period of repeat purchases from a customer is easier than taking customer satisfaction seriously? If so, then conventional loyalty programmes are no more than short-term sales promotion, and will have little long-term effectiveness.

REALITY CHECK
THE PROBLEMS WITH PLASTIC LOYALTY CARDS...

Problem: they are easy for competitors to imitate – if all the supermarkets offer similar loyalty cards, and all the airlines offer frequent flyer programmes, the sophisticated customer is likely to be a member of them all (for example, in 2001 50 per cent of Sainsbury Reward card holders also had a Tesco Clubcard and 42 per cent of Tesco card holders also had the Sainsbury card), take the benefits on offer, and purchase where s/he wishes; i.e. our Hostages turn into Dealers (Figure 2.1).

Problem: they are easy for new entrants to attack – in the early days Asda did damage to the Tesco Clubcard simply by announcing at Christmas of the first year of operation that Asda stores would honour the Tesco discount vouchers, thus getting the sales promotion gains with none of the overhead costs of the loyalty scheme.

Problem: they can get really expensive. The airlines have created a situation where frequent flyer 'air miles' are the third largest currency in the world, after the US dollar and the Euro. Analysts estimate that in the US there are two trillion air miles outstanding. At the going rate of two cents a mile, this represents a $40 billion liability for the industry.

Problem: smart customers can and will play games: in the UK in 1997 a Tesco supermarket ran a bananas promotion involving extra Clubcard points – one customer worked out that if he spent hundreds of pounds buying the fruit he would get enough Clubcard points to get the bananas free. He did just this, and then gave the bananas away free outside the store, and made the national newspaper headlines. In the US one supermarket gives regular customers vouchers offering discounts off the next purchase trip. Most of the vouchers are for 5 per cent or 10 per cent off, but some are for 50 per cent off. They now get people outside the store with placards saying things like '$200 given for a 50 per cent voucher'. When asked why, one couple pointed out that most people were buying groceries, so the 50 per cent voucher would be worth $100 to them at most. They, on the other hand, wanted to buy a refrigerator costing $5000. By buying the voucher: the voucher is worth twice as much to the grocery buyer, they get $2500 off the refrigerator and the store loses all round. The loyalty voucher has actually become a tradable commodity in its own right.

These are amusing stories – what do they have to do with customer loyalty? Not a lot.

Problem: the big risk is that crude customer loyalty incentives will undermine the long-term value of the brand, by substituting price incentives for brand values.

These problems have led to some major rethinking about the 'plastic card syndrome' as a route to customer loyalty in recent years. Signs are that the cards have not impacted on loyalty to the degree expected, and the 'hassle factor' of carrying them annoys some consumers[25]. By 2000, in the grocery market, supermarket chain Asda had long since given up on the idea, Safeway had abandoned its ABC loyalty card scheme, blaming its £50 million a year running costs[26], and even Sainsbury was rumoured to be looking for ways to withdraw from its loyalty card scheme[27]. It seems the issue really is managing customers not loyalty programmes[28]. (We will discuss later the real issue in loyalty programmes – the customer information which is available.)

'the issue really is managing customers not loyalty programmes'

REALITY CHECK

THE ISSUE IN LOYALTY PROGRAMMES IS CUSTOMER INFORMATION

The information advantage from knowing more about your customers than anyone else does is the great unexploited potential – it comes simply from linking the customer information on the membership database with the purchase behaviour of that member. For example, if in week 1 you buy a dog lead and in week 2 you buy a dog bowl. There is a pretty good chance we can deduce that you have a dog (or that there is something very strange going on in your marriage), and that you are in the market for dog food (either way). There is, of course, a danger we get carried away with stereotypes. For example, let us say that an affluent customer of my acquaintance runs her own business and shops in three ways: a mega-monthly stock-up of household goods at Tesco; pot noodles and snacks for lunch at Sainsburys; and occasional posh shops at Waitrose for expensive dinner parties. She finds that Tesco keeps sending her coupons for disposal nappies (they are convinced that a household that buys as much as hers must have small children – unfortunately for them she loathes children); Sainsburys assumes that her small lunchtime purchases indicate she is a poor elderly person and keep sending her details of the free bus to the local store; while Waitrose believes she must be a member of the landed aristocracy, and keeps writing with special offers on Bolly. Nothing is perfect – as we will see the issue is becoming about understanding customers not just collecting information about them.

There is value for us in focusing on customer loyalty and customer retention, but this really is not the same thing as customer satisfaction. Customer loyalty programmes are no protection against the competitor who delights the customer, offers something new that attracts customers and offers better value in the customer's terms, or simply cares enough about the customer to build trust and commitment, i.e. to work for a relationship built on something more lasting and stable than sophisticated bribery!

'Customer loyalty programmes are no protection against the competitor who delights the customer'

Once again it seems we may be in danger of missing the point – do we really care about customers?

So, what's the real customer problem?

Rationally speaking one would probably believe that if a company does its best to offer high levels of service and to provide the best possible level of quality in all its dealings with customers, then it would be likely to prosper. In many cases this is true because of the lack of competition on precisely those things in all too many markets.

In fact, the easy assumption that *maximum* service and quality pays is not necessarily true for two reasons: we may not understand what service creates customer value and delight, and even if we do we may not be able to deliver it. We will see later that these are key issues underlying the strategic choices of markets and segments we need to confront in building a strong market strategy (see pp. 431–5).

REALITY CHECK

WAL-MART'S EUROPEAN ADVENTURE

American-owned Wal-Mart is the world's biggest and most service-conscious supermarket retailer. As part of its global expansion, in January 1998, Wal-Mart arrived in Germany, with sweeping price-cuts. However, this is a country where the rules of retailing seem to be 'the grumpier the better', the 'customer comes last' and 'shopping is boring', and the emphasis is on efficiency. Wal-Mart arrived determined to pamper every customer in sight. Wal-Mart's 'ten foot rule' states that if a customer comes within ten feet of an employee, the latter must smile and offer to help. Complaints/requests must be dealt with 'by sundown' (the sundown rule). In fact, the result has been a major culture clash. The Wal-Mart tactics have infuriated consumers and aroused their suspicions – if someone takes hold of their purchases at the checkout (to pack them in a bag), they think someone is trying to steal from them. Locally-employed shop-workers have been found hiding in the lavatories to avoid the embarrassing but mandatory morning Wal-Mart chant – 'Give us a W ... Give us an A' ... (swivel the hips at the hyphen) ... 'Wadduya get' ... 'Yeah, Waaal-Mart'.

By late 2000 Wal-Mart's losses were running in excess of £150 million a year in Germany from its 95 stores, and the company had been ranked bottom of all retailers in Germany in an annual customer satisfaction survey. Analysts blamed Wal-Mart's reluctance to adjust its retail model to the demands of German customers. In April 2001, the company announced it was scrapping its expansion plans in Germany and would not be launching the planned 50 new stores by the end of 2002. The German problem is starting to raise questions about Wal-Mart's entire international strategy. Being great at the wrong service is very expensive.

Sources: Toby Helm (2000), 'Service with a Smile Frowned on by Germans', *Daily Telegraph*, 28 October. Tony Major (2001), 'Wal-Mart Shrinks Plan for German Expansion', *Financial Times*, 24 April.

Do we know what service to maximize?

The first point is that customers are perverse, emotional, awkward, unreasonable people who want things done on *their* terms not ours. Providing service and quality which is not valued by the paying customer, however well-meaning, is unlikely to gain the business that we want, and, in fact, is a good route to 'servicing' and 'total qualitying' ourselves right out of business. Perhaps we should call this the 'RB211 syndrome'. Even if you are the greatest engineering firm (e.g. Rolls-Royce), designing-in quality and technology which the customer does not want enough to pay for (e.g. the RB211 aero-engine) does not pay off (e.g. bankrupts the company).

Consider the case of an industrial equipment supplier of my acquaintance, whose engineering-led managers were committed to producing the 'best' machines on the market. They dismissed the selling problem – 'we are the best, we are out on our own, there is no problem in selling ... '. The customer agreed that their machines were the 'best'. Unfortunately, what the customer wanted in this market was 'cheaper, and sufficient for our needs'.

Even more unfortunately, the manufacturer's management would not believe or accept this, and the company started down the slippery slope of believing that they knew better than the customer, with the inevitable disastrous results.

Often the problem really does come down to simply not understanding what things really *matter most* to the customer. For instance, the management of one garage chain offered customers a free 'courtesy car' while their own cars were being serviced. They were infuriated to find that customers who only worked a few hundred yards away still took a courtesy car and left it sitting outside the office all day in sight of the garage. Management then instituted a charge for the 'courtesy car' to get rid of this 'abuse' of the service. Customers still did the same thing, but now paid for it. The motor car addict will *pay* for the personal comfort of not being cut off from transport, whether s/he actually uses it or not. Possibly irrational – but if that is what the customer wants and values, the conclusion is clear.

'the problem really does come down to simply not understanding what things really matter most to the customer'

The point is that customer service and care can create satisfied customers, from which we then get the things we want (profit, growth, value of investment, and so on). Too many of us forget it.

However, in the real world we should never forget that when we are customers we are likely to be not simply harsh but also highly unfair in the judgements we make. For example, in the airline business people talk about the 'olive factor' – if you forget to put the olive in the martini, the customer thinks you will forget to put the wheels down when you land the plane, and this is not regarded as a good idea.

In a similar way, British Airways did a massive amount of expensive and sophisticated hard-nosed market research into the requirements of the short-haul air traveller, and what influenced airline choice. This led to the BA strategy of courtesy and sympathy and 'putting people first', with some considerable success. Even then they made a mistake with the critical business traveller market – they *believed* that the business traveller was mainly influenced by factors of timely arrival, availability of phones and faxes, and other 'rational' factors. The glamorous and sophisticated British Airways lost substantial market share to a small airline called British Midland because of the 'sausage factor'. The 'rational' business traveller wanted a free breakfast sausage and would change airlines to get it. British Airways had to respond with the Super Shuttle, including free breakfast.

Customers can be very unfair in the judgements they make – but at the end of the day it is allowed – because it is their *money.*

Maximizing the wrong service and quality (as far as the customer is concerned) is expensive and unproductive (as far as we are concerned).

Anyway, can we deliver what we promised?

The second point is that offering the customer service and quality and responsiveness which we cannot really deliver is also potentially a route to disaster. The point is that raising unrealistic *customer expectations* (in terms of what we can really deliver) will create dissatisfied customers just as surely as poor product marketing and service delivery.

For example, one technically superb UK advertising campaign in the 1970s was the 'Wonder of Woollies' campaign, which transformed the image of Woolworths chain stores from seedy, second-choice suppliers of cheap commodities from old-fashioned somewhat tacky outlets, to a clean, friendly, welcoming, service-oriented retailer with modernized stores. The campaign was an outstanding winner in all the usual marketing terms – consumer recall, attitude and belief change, rebuilding store image, and the like. Unfortunately, the company rebuilt store image, but did not rebuild the stores. The Woolworths of the 1970s in the UK was in reality much more like the seedy, second-rate position than the friendly, modernized image of the ads. The campaign was a triumph for the marketing people but a disaster for the company. To be second-rate is bad. To convince people you are first-rate, then let them find you second-rate, means they will write you off as third-rate, and you are worse off than when you started. Disappointed customers are vindictive and have long memories. Raising unrealistic expectations is a dangerous business.

'To convince people you are first-rate, then let them find you second-rate, means they will write you off as third-rate'

Of course, managing customer expectations is a neat trick if you can do it. The car hire chain Rent-A-Wreck is a good example of managing customer expectations *down* instead of up. They advertise the offer – as the company name suggests – that they will hire you an old, beaten-up wreck of a car, for a very low rental charge. In fact, when you get to the rental office – the cars are not wrecks, certainly they are not brand-new and they may have a few scrapes, but they are fine. So you end up with a much better car than you expected and a low price. Most people seem quite pleased with this.

Ultimately, customer service and quality should be *consistent* with all the other aspects of the total offering that we make to the customer.

REALITY CHECK
GARDENING TIME

One of the most successful and dynamic businesses I have worked with in the past few years is a family-owned wholesale nursery supplier, whose core business is supplying independent gardening shops and centres with plants and seedlings. This company has a very clear product and market position with its customers: you do not get service. This company does not deliver products, once they are outside the gate they are the customer's problem. They do not wash, label, package the plants in polythene tubs and wrappers, sort, or provide information leaflets – they offer no value-added services of this type. What they do offer is a good product at a rock-bottom price. Their customers are small independent retailers, not the big chains or sheds, and their customers' major need is low-priced products to survive the competition provided *by* the chains and sheds. Of course, the managers of this company suffered from the major disadvantage that they had not read the books or been on the management courses that would have told them that the *only* way to compete successfully in their market is on service and quality. This is perhaps fortunate because they have created a market position which does three significant things: it offers a particular kind of customer the one thing which is *most* important to them – low prices; it keeps customer expectations of what they will get closely in line with what they actually get, and the strategy is one that this company can deliver consistently, properly and profitably. The signs of this last point are noteworthy: if you ask the MD for his business card, he laughs and offers to write his name down for you if you cannot remember it (most people can), because the business does not pay printers for such frivolous things; very few employees have company cars and when they do the vehicles bought are second-hand Rovers; the people in the company are proud of each thing they do to cut costs and save money – and they brag about these things because the culture is driven by cost-efficiency. This capability and culture is supremely appropriate to delivering the company's market strategy – even though it would be a huge barrier to implementing a different strategy.

The conclusion to which I am drawing is that we should think in terms of *appropriate* service and quality strategies, that match the most important needs of our target customers but also our ability to deliver.

For example, one way of looking round at our competitors and how well they are doing, and comparing their performance to ours, is shown in Figure 2.2. Before we jump to easy conclusions about what works and what does not, why not see what the distribution and spread of competition is – is high customer satisfaction achieved through service and quality or other issues, is low customer satisfaction associated with high or low service provision, or is there no clear relationship? Indeed, we might then look at which types of firms are doing best in market share and profitability terms, and see what conclusions that leads us to.

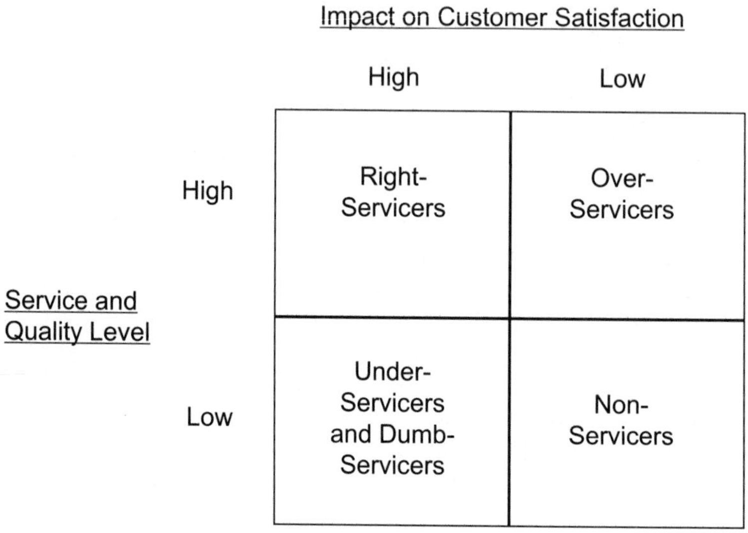

Impact on Customer Satisfaction

		High	Low
Service and Quality Level	High	Right-Servicers	Over-Servicers
	Low	Under-Servicers and Dumb-Servicers	Non-Servicers

Figure 2.2   Service and quality versus customer satisfaction

Whatever else we may find, it would be good to decide whether we are currently over- or under-servicing, or if we have got it about right, and whether there are low-service opportunities in the market as well as high-service niches. There is actually some truth in the saying 'There's riches in niches' (see p. 296).

So, what's the real problem?

The real problem is two things: *first*, the very real danger that we end up becoming obsessed with the *trappings* rather than the substance; and, *second*, the issues we have raised seem symptomatic of something deeply wrong in our organizations that may be hard to get close to. Let us consider these points, in turn, because they are quite important and warrant a little further thought.

Trappings or substance?

The worry is that by and large it is actually a lot easier to adopt customer care programmes, to train operatives in customer service, and so on, than to actually *care* about customers in the real sense, and to provide the services they want. Certainly I remain unrepentantly sceptical about top managements who foist such things as customer care programmes on their organizations, without themselves being committed, visible participants. At worst this smacks of lip-service and lack of real commitment where it matters most in the organization, and at best of top management going for the latest 'quick fix' (shortly to be replaced by the next fashionable panacea).

REALITY CHECK

WHAT WE DO VERSUS WHAT WE SAY

An extreme example of lip-service to customers rather than real commitment comes from a well-known Volkswagen distributorship in the UK. The Managing Director bought the quality and service message in a big way. On the appointed day he toured all the garages in the distributorship delivering a carefully prepared and emotionally-loaded customer service message; all staff were issued with plastic cards for their wallets bearing the customer mission message, to be carried at *all* times; every single member of staff was personally briefed by the MD on that person's individual and vital role in creating quality for the customer, regardless of the effect of greasy boots and overalls on his office furnishings. No expense or inconvenience was spared to deliver the customer service message. The effect was somewhat spoiled by the fact that on the same day the MD was seen to have an abusive public row with a customer, culminating in the MD telling the customer to f**k off! The *signals* we send to our people are remembered long after our *words* are forgotten.

This may sound unfair and over-critical – and it may be just that. But it strikes me as interesting that if you talk to managers in companies pursuing quality control programmes, total quality management, and so on, they may talk a lot about the excitement and the internal changes, or even the key values of quality and the like. They rarely seem to get round to talking about what the external, end, paying customer actually *wants*, and what he/she gets that is better in his/her terms. I wonder if this is because it is a lot easier, and perhaps more fun, to introduce such programmes than to deal with the less palatable realities of customer priorities and judgements (such as those we discussed earlier and will go on discussing).

Tokens or truths?

Perhaps what is most worrying is that many tools and techniques to improve our customer service are misused on a wide scale. They are being used to treat the symptoms not the sickness. They are token, very visible, efforts to cover up, but not solve, the underlying problem. Consider the following case.

REALITY CHECK
POWER AND THE PEOPLE

A little while ago, one of the regional companies of the UK power industry managed the interesting act of shooting itself in the foot by the very act of launching a massive customer care campaign. The top management group of this large, labour-intensive business conceived, resourced and implemented a customer care campaign, consisting mainly of a large TV and press spend, inviting the customer to voice his/her complaints, because the company now 'cared' (presumably by implication admitting that to date it had not given a damn about the customer). The advertising campaign was accompanied by a household questionnaire and leaflet drop, reinforcing the message. Some two weeks before the campaign went live and there was no way back, management finally decided to let its staff in on the big secret. At this point, things started to go wrong. Operational staff reacted with some considerable hostility – people said unreasonable things like 'we think its great that you care about the customer – why don't you care about us?' Management's response was to start issuing staff with hastily-produced glossy brochures about the customer care campaign – which did not cut much ice with staff, but at least meant that management did not have to talk to them anymore. The operational staff perceived that management expected them to bear the brunt of the new campaign, since quite evidently top management did not have the slightest intention of changing its behaviour or the way it runs the business. The net result is consumers who are urged to complain (who are quite reasonably not pleased when those complaints are ignored), operational staff who bear this new pressure with some lack of grace, and a well-meaning top management group who do not know what has hit them or even why. Tokenism is a dangerous game to play.

The point is twofold. First, if we just treat the symptoms (of poor customer service and low satisfaction) without getting to grips with the real underlying problem (of management attitudes and behaviour as well as those of operatives), then we will achieve little of lasting value, and may do considerable harm to our businesses. Second, if we only adopt the trappings of these tools, then the effect may be in the wrong direction in spite of the best intentions, and any beneficial effect will be short-lived.

This brings us to the fundamental issue to be confronted and tested – our *real* attitude towards customer satisfaction as the focus for our whole organization.

Measuring customer satisfaction[29]

About the most popular way of dealing with customer satisfaction has been the boom in customer satisfaction measurement. So, do you want the good news or the bad news? Try separating out two issues here:

- how we measure customer satisfaction; and
- how we use it once we have measured it.

How do you measure customer satisfaction?

The world and his uncle want to sell you systems and methods for customer measurement (CSM). There is a massive technical literature available to support moves towards formalizing the measurement of customer satisfaction. This supporting base is concerned with such issues as:

- developing different concepts of customer satisfaction which can be evaluated[30];
- designing effective customer satisfaction data collection and reporting systems, varying in sophistication[31];
- adopting methods for institutionalizing customer satisfaction measurement into organizational control systems[32];
- developing systems for responding effectively to customer dissatisfaction and customer complaints[33].

In fact, customer satisfaction measurement has proved to be one of the most successful products for market research agencies through recession and better times. Certainly, the market research industry offers a full range of products in this area: customer satisfaction survey methodologies; focus groups to study customer satisfaction issues; standardized packages for monitoring customer satisfaction; and the computer software needed to analyse and report customer satisfaction data to management.

'the real issues for managers are not so much about the data collection, but what happens to the information after it is collected'

However, the real issues for managers are not so much about the data collection, but what happens to the information after it is collected.

But what do we do with it?

A good question – but do we know the answer? Well, one source of insight into what happens in companies that measure customer satisfaction comes from exploratory workshop discussions held with managers. Simply looking at the themes emerging from what managers say about customer satisfaction measurement raises some very serious concerns about what effects are achieved. The themes emerging from those discussions are as follows:

- *Companies which trivialize CSM* – many say that in practice CSM becomes a superficial and trivial activity, which is significant only at the customer service level. They suggest that CSM is not related to market strategies and strategic change in their companies, but rather is about monitoring customer service operations and responding to customer complaints (sometimes quite disproportionately and inappropriately to boot).
- *CSM and interdepartmental power struggles* – some executives describe CSM as little more than a weapon used in the power struggles between functional areas, in attempts to 'prove' to management that other departments are responsible for losing market share and declining customer satisfaction.
- *The politics of CSM* – others describe CSM as characterized by gaming behaviour by company personnel to 'beat' the system, and to avoid being 'blamed' for customer complaints, often resulting in behaviour not anticipated by management and not supportive to customer satisfaction polices and market strategies – for example, sales and distribution personnel giving price and service concessions to customers, simply to win 'brownie' points in the CSM system. Others describe CSM as a 'popularity poll' for the salesforce, where 'popularity' is rewarded and 'unpopularity' is penalized.

- *CSM as management control* – some see the implementation of CSM in a negative way, as a crude control device used by management, to police the lower levels of the organization and allocate 'blame' for customer complaints. Others describe CSM systems as wholly negative and focused on criticism, with no balance of positive feedback or praise for what is good. In some cases the data are seen only by management and only the 'conclusions' are communicated to employees – often in a negative and critical way. Others see CSM as a crude attempt by management to coerce employees to change their behaviour in the ways desired by customers (or at least the desire of those customers who have complained most recently and most vociferously).
- *The isolation of CSM* – many executives talk about situations where CSM data are collected and stored but not disseminated in the organization. For example, in some cases CSM information is collected by the marketing department but not shared with the production or even the quality departments.
- *Poorly diffused CSM* – in some cases people describe a general lack of acceptance of CSM.

REALITY CHECK
WHAT DO WE REALLY CARE ABOUT?

In one high-tech company a monthly management information report is circulated with sales, profit and CS results summarized, for the use of all senior managers. The executive responsible describes how every month there were numerous queries and arguments and protests about the accuracy and validity of the sales and profit figures, but no-one had ever questioned the CS data – they simply did not matter to managers. Another company described how they knew that distributors completed CS questionnaires themselves, because they did not see the point of the exercise and did not want to 'bother' their customers.

These findings reflect only exploratory discussions with executives. However, they do appear to offer some novel insights into the reality of the operation of CSM systems in organizations, which are largely ignored when we talk about CSM.

In fact, we went deeper into this issue, and did a survey of several hundred British companies using CSM. The results of the survey are summarized in Figure 2.3, which shows the managerial uses of customer satisfaction measurements, the internal processual barriers found, and the market strategies managers identified:

- *Managerial uses of customer satisfaction measurement* – managers were asked to evaluate the degree of use of CS measurements in a number of decision-making areas, which were reduced by factor analysis to the use of CS measurements in: *quality/ operations management*, which linked the use of CS data to monitor and manage quality, to guide R & D, and to manage production; *staff pay and promotions*, linking pay and promotion decisions for operational and management staff; *staff training and evaluation*, linking the training and evaluation of both operational and managerial staff; and *strategic management control*, linking the development of company-wide strategy, control of the business, and the management of customer service and marketing programmes.
- *Internal processual barriers* – the central issue in the study related to the characteristics of the CS measurement process in terms of the perceived beliefs and attitudes of the people involved and the organizational context provided by the company in question and its management. A list of statements were evaluated by respondents and their responses factor analysed to produce the following structure – *internal politics*: CS measurement is believed to generate internal conflict and political squabbles, to produce a 'hostage to fortune' and brings increased management control, areas of customer complaint are politically sensitive in the company, CSM undermines management, and people cheat in the CS system; *market simplification*: word-of-mouth recommendation by customers is believed to be unimportant, customer loyalty is thought to be non-existent, repeat sales do not matter, the company is not believed to be a service and quality provider, the company cannot change to respond to complaints, people do not believe that CS matters; *customer fear*: if asked about satisfaction customers think something is wrong, asking about CS reduces satisfaction, it raises unrealistic customer expectations, it invites unwelcome complaints, it is badly received by people in the company; *corporate culture*: a lack of management support for CSM, a perception that CSM is not appropriate to the company or the market, a lack of attention to the results, a lack of a customer service policy, a low priority for CSM; *market complacency*: beliefs that the company already knows what matters in the market and what customers think, the belief that what matters is having the best product, CSM is believed to be difficult and to invite unwarranted criticisms

from customers; *resources/capability*: CSM makes excessive demands for technical expertise, systems, people and time; *logistics*: beliefs that identifying the real customer is problematic, and that it is a role for the distributor not the manufacturer; *cost barriers*: links the finance and expense implications of CSM; *perceived market drivers*: links beliefs that the market is driven only by technical specifications and price; *credibility*: people do not believe the results of CSM.

- *Market strategies* – respondents were asked to prioritize their market strategies, and factor analysis revealed the following imperatives: *service and quality*, linked goals of achieving the highest perceived quality in the market, providing excellent customer service and achieving high buyer loyalty; *competitive differentiation*, links issues of managing distribution networks, building brand image, and differentiation by design and technical specifications; *high profit/volume*, links goals of sales growth, higher market share and improved profitability; *low price/cost*, links strategies of being price competitive and minimizing market costs.

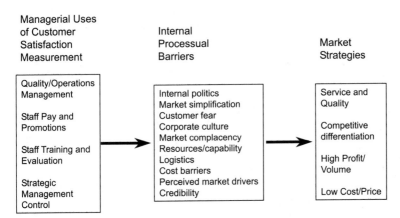

Managerial Uses of Customer Satisfaction Measurement	Internal Processual Barriers	Market Strategies
Quality/Operations Management	Internal politics	Service and Quality
	Market simplification	
Staff Pay and Promotions	Customer fear	Competitive differentiation
	Corporate culture	
Staff Training and Evaluation	Market complacency	High Profit/ Volume
	Resources/capability	
	Logistics	
Strategic Management Control	Cost barriers	Low Cost/Price
	Perceived market drivers	
	Credibility	

Figure 2.3 The customer satisfaction measurement process

This model, based on what we found in companies, suggests we need to think about a hidden management agenda to be addressed by executives in organizations adopting and using customer satisfaction measurement approaches. Conventionally, the agenda is concerned primarily with data collection, measurement techniques and reporting formats. Our findings suggest that, to realize the promises for CSM, this approach is inadequate.

First, the findings from the workshops and the survey underline the need for clarity regarding

'the need for clarity regarding customer service policies and customer satisfaction targets'

customer service policies and customer satisfaction targets. It is not enough to pay the usual lip-service to these ideals and to expect success in attaining them. The starting point must be to identify what has to be achieved in customer satisfaction to implement specific market strategies, and to position the company against the competition in a specific market. It is unlikely that achieving what we want will be free. We need to take a realistic view of the time needed and the real costs of implementation.

Second, the internal processual barriers uncovered here suggest the need to consider both the internal and external markets faced in implementing customer satisfaction measurement and management systems. To ignore the internal market is to risk actually damaging the company's capacity to achieve and improve customer satisfaction in the external market. If, for example, management uses CS data in a negative and coercive way, then it may reduce employee enthusiasm for customer service, or create 'game-playing' behaviour where people compete for 'brownie points' in the systems, at the expense both of the company and the customer. This said, we have also to recognize not just the complementarity between internal and external markets, but the potential for conflict of interest. Achieving target levels of customer service and satisfaction may require managers and employees to change the way they do things and to make sacrifices they do not want to make. This may take more than simple advocacy or management threat.

'target levels of customer service and satisfaction may require managers and employees to change the way they do things and to make sacrifices they do not want to make'

Third, and related to the above argument, recognizing the internal market suggests that there may be a need for a structured and planned internal marketing programme to achieve the effective implementation of customer satisfaction measurement and management. This has been described elsewhere as 'marketing our customers to our employees'[34], and can be built into the implementation process to address the needs of the internal customer and to confront the types of internal processual barrier we have encountered.

Fourth, also related to the recognition of the internal market, is the need to question the relationship between internal and external customer satisfaction. This was discussed with one company using the structure shown in Figure 2.4. This suggests four possible scenarios that result when internal and external customer satisfaction are compared:

● *Synergy*, which is what we hope for when internal and external customer satisfaction are high, and we see them as sustainable

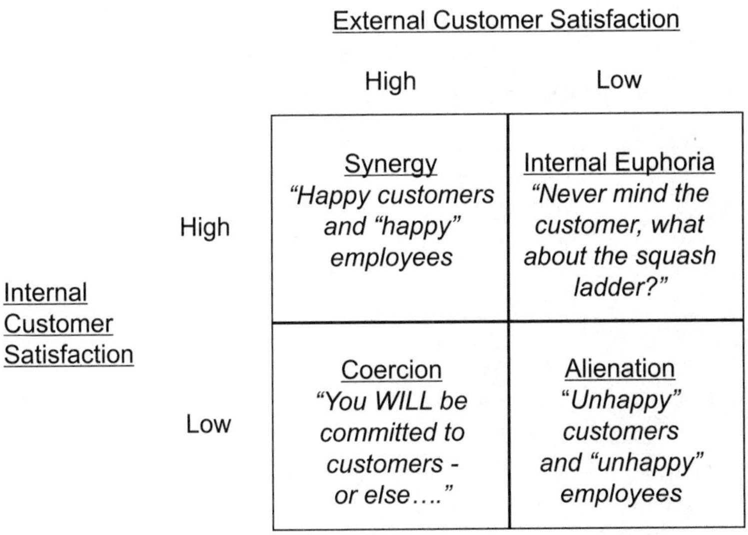

External Customer Satisfaction

		High	Low
		Synergy *"Happy customers and "happy" employees*	Internal Euphoria *"Never mind the customer, what about the squash ladder?"*
Internal Customer Satisfaction	High		
	Low	Coercion *"You WILL be committed to customers - or else...."*	Alienation *"Unhappy" customers and "unhappy" employees*

Figure 2.4   Customer satisfaction and the internal market

and self-regenerating. As one hotel manager explained it: 'I know that we are winning on customer service when my operational staff come to me and complain about how I am getting in their way in providing customer service, and tell me to get my act together!' This is the 'happy customers and happy employees' situation, assumed by many to be obvious and easily achieved.

- *Coercion* is where we achieve high levels of external customer satisfaction by changing the behaviour of employees through management direction and control systems. In the short term this may be the only option, but it may be very difficult and expensive to sustain this position in the longer term, and we give up flexibility for control.
- *Alienation* is where we have low levels of satisfaction internally and externally, and we are likely to be highly vulnerable to competitive attack in the external market and low morale and high staff turnover in the internal market.
- *Internal euphoria* is where we have high levels of satisfaction in the internal market, but this does not translate into external customer satisfaction – for example, if internal socialization and group cohesiveness actually shut out the paying customer in the external market. These scenarios are exaggerated, but have provided a useful way of confronting these issues with executives.

REALITY CHECK
THE EMPLOYEE–CUSTOMER–PROFIT MODEL

When it is focused on customers, employee buy-in can be a powerful competitive weapon. The US retailer Sears is attempting to turn its struggling business around with a new marketing strategy and a different relationship with its employees and customers. The company developed a business approach to track success in changing employee attitudes through to improvements in customer satisfaction and financial performance – the Employee–Customer–Profit Model. According to the company 'A five point improvement in employee attitudes will drive a 1.3 point improvement in customer satisfaction, which in turn will drive a 0.5 point improvement in revenue growth.'

Source: Anthony B. Rucci, Steven P. Kirn and Richard T. Quinn (1998), 'The Employee–Customer–Profit Chain at Sears', *Harvard Business Review*, January/February, 83–97.

'a critical mistake is to ignore the real costs and challenges in adopting customer satisfaction measurement'

Last, and simplest, we suggest that a critical mistake is to ignore the real costs and challenges in adopting customer satisfaction measurement as a management approach, and the limitations which may exist in a company's capabilities for improving customer satisfaction levels. While advocacy is widespread and the appeal is obvious, achieving the potential benefits requires more planning and attention to implementation realities than is suggested by the existing conventional methodological literature.

So customer satisfaction measurement may not be the answer to all your customer problems. It has great potential value, but used badly it can do more harm than good. If you do it – do it for the right reasons, and do it carefully.

REALITY CHECK
THE AWKWARD QUESTIONS ABOUT CUSTOMERS

Do we know what it feels like to do business with our company as a customer? Do our colleagues know? What are we doing to make the experience of buying from our company better for the customer in his/her terms than any of our competitors?

Do we understand the difference between customer satisfaction and customer dissatisfaction and what drives these outcomes for different customer groups?

Do we understand the difference between customer satisfaction and customer loyalty? Do we understand the factors that drive customer loyalty for different types of customer in our markets? Do our market strategies treat customers differently based on their loyalty drivers?

How well do we focus on superior service in the areas that we know matter most to different customers and enhance their perceptions of value? How often do we waste resources providing services that do not matter much to customers? Do we deliver against our promises?

Does our company truly get beyond just paying lip-service to customers, or do we really care? How do we ensure that we get beyond token efforts to achieve real customer focus?

Do we measure customer satisfaction validly? Do we then use the results to achieve positive improvements across the whole company, or just play games with the information?

The story so far

This chapter has tried to do some scene-setting and hopefully establish a few home-truths: the evidence that in spite of lip-service to customers, real service and real attitudes to customers are appalling and few of us can afford to be complacent on this issue – try the service encounter diary and see what it uncovers about your company's treatment of its customers when it matters; let's not confuse customer satisfaction with customer loyalty and think that customer retention statistics measure customer satisfaction – they don't; let's think in terms of customer service and customer satisfaction as part of a market strategy, not something we do for its own sake; and let's get past the trappings of customer care to how we really treat our customers.

'let's get past the trappings of customer care to how we really treat our customers'

However – if this chapter hurt, be advised: you ain't seen nothing yet. Taking customer issues seriously is a good start. But the nature of those issues – what customers demand from us – is changing fast, and we can see the start of a far more demanding era of value-based strategy, where the rules are even more stretching than before. This is the topic of the next chapter.

Notes and references

1. And according to Dilbert, if we could remember even that much, it would be an improvement in most companies!
2. 'Customer Disservice', *Marketing Business*, April 1999, 7.

3. 'Voting With Their Feet', *Financial Mail on Sunday*, 14 December 1997.

4. I do beg your pardon, I have just been told by one of my relationship marketing colleagues that there is no such things as 'customer complaints' in the brave new world of relationship marketing, we merely have 'unsolicited customer feedback' . . .

5. Nikki Tait (1999), 'Rewards of Making the Consumer King', *Financial Times*, 8 July. Peter Marsh (1999), 'At Your Service', *Financial Times*, 12 May. Rosie Murray-West (2000), 'Respond to Customers or Risk Failure, Retailers Told', *Daily Telegraph*, 25 April.

6. James P. Womack and Daniel T. Jones (1996), *Lean Thinking: Banish Waste and Create Wealth In Your Corporation*, New York: Simon & Schuster.

7. Christopher W. Hart (1999), 'Sacrificial Offerings', *Marketing Management*, Fall, 6–7.

8. Laura Mazur (2000), 'Booking Skills for the Future', *Marketing Business*, April, 33.

9. Diane Summers (1993), 'Rewards for the Loyal Shopper', *Financial Times*, 2 December.

10. Frederick J. Reichheld and W. Earl Sasser (1990), 'Zero Defections: Quality Comes to Services', *Harvard Business Review*, September/October, 105–11.

11. Laura Mazur (1996), 'Accountability', *Marketing Business*, July/August.

12. Diane Summers, op. cit.

13. Alan Mitchell (1994), 'What Makes a Defector', *Financial Times*, 4 August.

14. Alan Mitchell, op. cit.

15. Frederick F. Reichheld (1996), *The Loyalty Effect*, Boston, MA: Harvard Business School Press.

16. Thomas O. Jones and W. Earl Sasser (1995), 'Why Satisfied Customers Defect', *Harvard Business Review*, November/December, 88–100.

17. William D. Neal (1997), *Observations on Loyalty*, Atlanta, GA: SDR Consulting. William D. Neal (1998), *Satisfaction Be Damned, Value Drives Loyalty*, Atlanta, GA: SDR Consulting.

18. Sandra Vandermerwe (1999), *Customer Capitalism: Increasing Returns in New Market Spaces*, London: Brealey Publishing.

19. 'Paying Lip-Service to the Loyalists', *Business Age*, 1 April 1996.

20. Laura Mazur (1997), 'Brands', *Marketing Business*, April.

21. In fact, there is a rumour that in the US there are some business travellers who, in theory, will never have to pay for another flight, hotel rental or hire car for the rest of their lives, because of all the air miles they have accumulated. The paradox is that these tend to be the last people in the world who want to travel more and stay in another hotel away from home!

22. Laura Mazur, op. cit.

23. 'The Databases of the Argument', *Marketing Week*, 18 November 1994.

24. George Day (2000), 'Tying in an Asset', in *Understanding CRM*, London: *Financial Times*.

25. Louise Jones (1999), 'Cards Fail to Command Undivided Loyalty', *Daily Mail*, 6 May.
26. Teena Lyons (2000), 'How Disloyal Shoppers are Killing off the Loyalty Card', *Financial Mail on Sunday*, 11 June.
27. Teena Lyons (2000), 'Sainsbury Set to Axe Loyalty Card', *Financial Mail on Sunday*, 11 June.
28. Don E. Schultz (1999), 'Manage Customers, Not Loyalty Programmes', *Marketing News*, 4 January.
29. This section is based on: Nigel F. Piercy (1996), 'The Effects of Customer Satisfaction Measurement', *Marketing Intelligence and Planning*, **14** (4), 9–15; and Nigel F. Piercy and Neil A. Morgan (1995), 'Customer Satisfaction Measurement and Management: A Processual Analysis', *Journal of Marketing Management*, **11**, 817–34.
30. Abbie Griffin and J. R. Hauser (1992), *The Voice of the Customer*, Cambridge, MA: Marketing Science Institute.
31. E. McQuance and S. McIntyre (1992), *The Customer Visit*, Cambridge, MA: Marketing Science Institute.
32. M. M. Lele and Jagdish Sheth (1988), 'The Four Fundamentals of Customer Satisfaction', *Business Marketing*, June, 80–84.
33. M. L. Richins (1987), 'Negative Word-of-Mouth by Dissatisfied Customers', *Journal of Marketing*, January, 68–78.
34. Nigel F. Piercy (1995), 'Customer Satisfaction and the Internal Market: Marketing our Customers to our Employees', *Journal of Marketing Practice: Applied Marketing Science*, **1** (1), 22–44.

CHAPTER 3

The revolution in market demands:

From transactions to brands to relationships to value

The last chapter made the case that so far many of us have not done too great a job in taking customers seriously. The other side of the coin is that our customers are taking us very seriously indeed. We are in the midst of what can only be called a revolution in the types and levels of demands that customers are making[1]. Many of our traditional marketing approaches simply cannot cope.

'if you read the last chapter and still thought the answer was a bit more customer servility and a plastic loyalty card – boy, are you in for a surprise!'

I want to describe an evolution from marketing which is primarily about transactions (selling stuff), to our obsession with brands and relationships, to arrive at value-driven strategy as the inevitable response to escalating and diverse customer demands. Basically, if you read the last chapter and still thought the answer was a bit more customer servility and a plastic loyalty card – boy, are you in for a surprise! However, better you get that surprise now, than when your business meets the smart customer.

Value-driven strategy

What I want to underline is the evolution of market processes from transactions to value – what some people call **new marketing**. However, the driving force in this transition is not clever marketing people – it is sophisticated, demanding, invasive, angry, vengeful, unreasonable customers. The driving force of new marketing is the **new customer**. The challenge is to keep up with the sophisticated customer.

The sophisticated customer

Three words which chill executive souls in just about every company I visit are 'the sophisticated customer'. If those words do not keep your marketing and sales executives awake at night, then you probably need to get smarter marketing and sales executives.

'Three words which chill executive souls in just about every company I visit are "the sophisticated customer"'

The single most devastating factor, which is a time-bomb under traditional marketing, is that customers everywhere have wised-up. Whether you are in consumer marketing or business-to-business, you simply have to change the way you do things because your customers know exactly what you are up to. The consequences of not making this transition can be dire. It was summarized nicely by Stephen Bayley, one-time Creative Director for the disastrous Millennium Dome in London (he wisely resigned two years before it opened). Bayley concludes that while the Dome got many things wrong, quite simply the Dome 'failed after treating the public like morons'[2]. The cost to the taxpayer of the Dome fiasco approached a billion pounds.

Customer awareness of marketing activity and expectations of better value have escalated dramatically, increasing market volatility and unpredictability in their wake. Indeed, Simon Buckby noted a couple of years ago: 'Predictions of consumer behavior are being thrown into disarray by the chaos that this new freedom is creating'[3]. Quite simply, traditional marketing consistently underestimates the intelligence and street wisdom of the customer[4]. If you go on making assumptions about the future based on the compliant, deferential and easily satisfied customer, you are heading for a nasty surprise[5].

'If you go on making assumptions about the future based on the compliant, deferential and easily satisfied customer, you are heading for a nasty surprise'

What people used to say about customers . . .	What they should probably be saying now . . .
You never lost money by underestimating the intelligence of the housewife . . .	You will never lose money by underestimating the intelligence of people who underestimate the intelligence of the housewife . . .
Let's get down on all-fours and look at things from the customer viewpoint . . .	Let's get down on all-fours and pray that the customer never finds out what we used to say . . .

Sophisticated customers know more and they want more – 'Expectations spiral as our customers gain experience of world-class service'[6] – the better you get at delivering superior products, service and value, the more will be demanded from you. What is more you will be judged against the standards of the best everywhere, not just against your immediate competitors – new customers demand answers to questions like these:

- Why is it that Federal Express can 'absolutely, positively' deliver a parcel overnight, but most airlines have trouble getting your bags on the same airplane as you – do they think you don't care about your clothes?
- Why is it that it takes only a few minutes, and no paperwork, to drop off a rental car at Hertz, but twice that time and an annoying name and address form to check into a Hilton Hotel – are they afraid that you will steal the room?
- Why is it that Swatch can produce an inexpensive watch that will run accurately for years, but Rolex cannot or will not do the same for a hundred times more money. Don't they know that times have changed?[7]

The 'new world' in which we all have to compete is one rich in information – but information owned by the customer – the transition we are seeing is from old marketing which said 'here we are, this is what we have to offer', to new marketing, serving customers who say 'here we are, this is what we want'. The information age means there has been a fundamental shift in power between sellers and buyers[8].

It is worse than just customers with higher expectations though. Sophisticated customers are also increasingly cynical and hostile towards business and marketing in particular.

> They said: 'Smile, it could be worse'. So I smiled.
>
> They were right. It got worse.

For example, many consumers are increasingly sceptical about advertising and see only 'brainwashing and lies'[9], and they complain increasingly loudly about advertising images that are unsubtly based on sex and violence[10]. The challenge to the advertising industry is to drop the tired approaches of the 1960s and start 'with the fact that you know nothing about people, because all the old certainties are gone'[11] – many consumers may, for example, be less impressed by pictures of Michael Jordan wearing Nike sportswear, and more interested in the fact that Nike is not using sweatshop labour in developing countries. Excuses about why British consumer goods prices are 50 per cent higher than those in the US are wearing a bit thin too[12].

At the extreme, pressure groups abound – more than 1000, ranging from Greenpeace to 'Surfers Against Sewage' – actively campaigning to change business policies. In 1995, Des Wilson, a former campaigner, predicted 'The militant citizen is becoming an increasing proportion of the population. The tide is still rising'[13] – oh boy, was he right! The UK has even seen the emergence of career-radicals, earning their livings as 'professional troublemakers'[14] – both 'spikies', who indulge in violent protest, and 'fluffies', who peacefully give away veggie-burgers outside McDonalds. Mid-2001 one survey suggested that British business leaders are now more frightened of the Consumers' Association and Greenpeace than they are of trade unions or government ministers[15].

'British business leaders are now more frightened of the Consumers' Association and Greenpeace than they are of trade unions or government ministers'

The 'new consumers' have evolved from being conformist and deferential and prepared to trust mass advertising, into free-thinking, highly individualistic people, who are sceptical of figures of authority. They have exhausted the things they *need* to buy, and are now concentrating on what they *want* to buy. They are short on time, attention and trust[16]. Certainly, US advertising agencies are fearful of a consumer rebellion in which consumer disinterest may mushroom into frustration, distrust and hostility – brands seen as tolerable today may be the 'enemy' of the consumer tomorrow[17]. A recent study describes the new British consumer as 'an autocrat in a bad mood', where consumer restlessness and dissatisfaction are part of a long-term social trend[18].

Some companies have already responded to the fact that new customers want more than low prices and brands, and compete on the basis of 'a sense of purpose that goes beyond profit': at IKEA 'We are a concept company' or 'We're on your side' at Virgin. Values and standing for something may be the only way to build a competitive edge in the eyes of the sophisticated customer[19].

We will spell out the implications of the new customer in more detail shortly, but first let's deal with the question of why 'new marketing' and why 'value'. The changes in the process of going to market are driven by the sophisticated customer and the need for customer loyalty along the lines shown in Figure 3.1. This suggests phases in the development of our approach to marketing:

- *Transactional marketing* – with relatively unsophisticated customers when loyalty is low, traditional marketing responses have been low-quality products, backed by excessive advertising and promotion, and the 'hard-sell', where the complaining customer is treated as the 'enemy'.
- *Brand marketing* – as loyalty becomes more important (because of its potential impact on profitability, not because we like customers), we still see customers as pretty stupid, and marketing stresses brand and image, anything except price and real value, and complaining customers are bought off, e.g. with free products. In protected markets or industries dominated by a few companies, customers are loyal because they have no choice (or think they don't), and have to be thankful for what they get.
- *Relationship marketing* – when we find that as our customers get smarter, loyalty disappears, we respond with 'relationship' marketing – customer satisfaction surveys, loyalty schemes, complaint response systems, customer care programmes, and so on.
- *Value-based marketing* – the trouble is what we see now is the challenge of building and sustaining high loyalty with smart customers who demand openness and transparency, and the 'picky, fault-finding, hard-nosed, sophisticated customer'[20] forces us towards continuous improvement in the things that matter most to customers. This is the era of value-based marketing, and we are only just starting to realize what it means for how we manage the process of going to market.

Let's consider each of these approaches to marketing in turn.

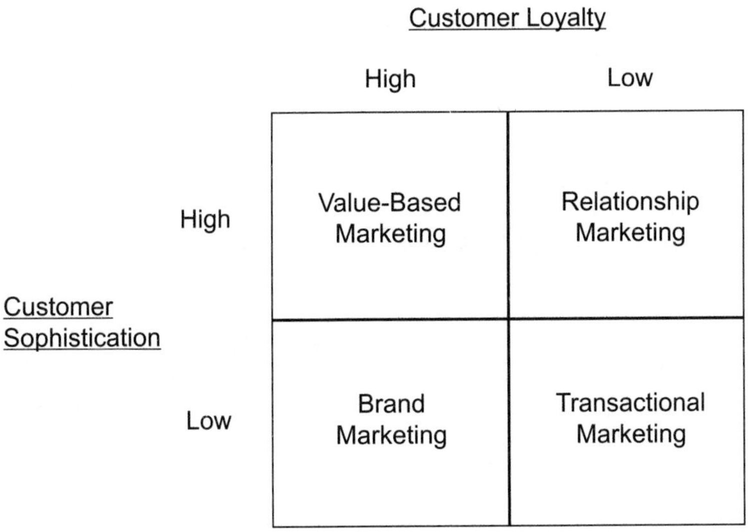

Customer Loyalty

		High	Low
Customer Sophistication	High	Value-Based Marketing	Relationship Marketing
	Low	Brand Marketing	Transactional Marketing

Figure 3.1 The evolution to value-based marketing

Transactional marketing

The issue in transactional marketing is the sale, the deal, the contract, and the immediate revenue and profit. This sounds old-fashioned. It is. It is still alive and well in some sectors like the retail car trade.

REALITY CHECK
EVEN IN THE CAR TRADE . . .

A long-time bastion of traditional, transactional sales approaches, even the car trade is having to wake up to what new customers want and demand. It seems that car showrooms are full of smarmy, arrogant, conniving and downright crooked people. At least, that is how some car dealers describe their enemy – the customers.

In January 2001, Toyota released the findings of a pilot scheme at its showrooms in Bristol and Grimsby. In particular, they had found that female customers found the macho and patronizing manner of staff to be objectionable and unacceptable. Female customers (or more importantly non-customers) disliked the atmosphere of car showrooms, the dirty toilets, the machine-brewed coffee, and being ignored by salespeople. The fact is that female consumers make or influence about 80 per cent of car purchases, and 60 per cent of company fleet managers are women.

Their findings matched those of Daewoo in the late 1990s – they designed car showrooms where: the floors were soft (so high heels do not click and attract unwelcome looks); there was enough space between cars to push a *double* baby-buggy without scratching the cars; the cars could be bought off a touch screen computer without talking to salespeople; children could be dumped in a playroom.

By contrast, traditional sales approaches are clear and reinforced by conventional sales training: (1) when a couple enters the showroom, sideline the woman (after all, what do girlies know about cars?); (2) find out what the man wants to buy; (3) explain carefully to the man that this is not really what he wants to buy because he is basically a good bloke, who you would like to have as a mate, but he is a bit stupid; (4) show him that what he *really* wants to buy is coincidentally the very car that you have available to sell ... Let's not forget that this is the sector that has invested serious money in training by hypnotherapists to try and hypnotize customers, and trains salespeople to play 'good cop and bad cop' to manipulate customers. Is it really surprising that current estimates suggest that the majority of car purchases will very soon be partly or wholly Internet-based?

At least Toyota has responded to the changed marketplace (maybe belatedly, but it is a start). It now gives interested customers a choice of brochures, Internet purchasing, or if all else fails, talking to salespeople. Salespeople are being put in separate offices, and will stay away from the customers unless they are asked for advice. The sad truth is that many people would rather buy a car from a computer screen than talk to the people employed to sell cars.

Sources: Ray Massey (1997), 'Would You Sell a Brand New Car to These People?', *Daily Mail*, 21 July. Giles Chapman (1998), 'Auto Suggestion', *Daily Telegraph*, 23 May. Ray Massey (2001), 'Why Female Buyers Hate Macho Car Men', *Daily Mail*, 17 January.

Indeed, the former chief marketing officer of Coca-Cola advises us that: 'When you can't genuinely add value for your customer (compared to what your competitors are offering) pull the wool over their eyes instead'[21]. Oh yes, I think transactional marketing is still around.

Indeed, Douglas Rushkoff has recently argued that corporate selling has moved on from being merely intrusive and misleading, to become coercive in a very negative sense, observing that 'Coercion is much more debilitating than persuasion or even influence ... Coercion seeks to stymie our rational processes in order to make us act against – or at the very least, without – our better judgment'[22]. He describes how the complaints department of one Japanese department store is scented to induce feelings of dread in consumers. And this, incidentally, from a man who reverse-engineered the recruiting practices of religious cults, so that an advertising agency could apply them to selling products.

REALITY CHECK
SELLING BLUE JEANS

Douglas Rushkoff describes the techniques used to sell in retail locations like clothes stores. They often depend on sex. He quotes the techniques used by one female salesperson to sell jeans: 'I kind of tilt my head to one side and stare at the guy's butt. Then, as soon as he notices I'm looking, I quickly glance away and pretend to be caught. I can hold my breath and get my face all flushed. It works every time.'

Source: Douglas Rushkoff (2000), *Coercion*, New York: Little Brown.

Transactional marketing is also about things like revenue enhancement through customer penalty policies:

- Airlines who make you pay the full price for a new ticket, if you happen to lose yours (notwithstanding the fact that your booking is in their computer system), with a possible refund later, naturally less a large administration fee deduction.
- Insurance companies who charge you penalties, commission and administration fees, if you cancel an insurance policy early.
- Banks who charge you a penalty if you withdraw your own money too frequently, or at a time they don't like, and then charge you for the letter they send to tell you they are fining you.
- Hotels who charge you for the room you booked, unless you give them 72 hours notice that you can't make the trip, presumably on the grounds that you should have known you were going to be ill and stay at home.
- Amtrak, the American railway, has a $20 penalty for a returned ticket, coincidentally the same fee as for changing a ticket[23].

MANAGEMENT TRAINING

There are two essential rules in management:

One. The customer is always right.

Two. They must be punished for their arrogance.

(Attributed to Dogbert)

'Is it really surprising that as customers have wised up, they are getting their own back?'

Is it really surprising that as customers have wised up, they are getting their own back?

Brand marketing

Branding products, services and companies is so central to conventional views of marketing, it is hard to imagine a time when brands would not be the central part of any marketing organization. Brands were the way we would improve over transactional marketing and build customer loyalty. However, the power of branding as the single sole answer to the marketing strategy problem is on the wane.

When I was brought up in marketing, we were always shown lists of the 'world's greatest brands'. These were the leading examples of the pinnacle of marketing's achievement, they were the models from which we should learn what marketing was really about, if we could ever aspire to the giddy heights of a brand manager job. These lists are still around, and some people (many of whom should know better) still believe the mythological power of the big brand. Unfortunately, if you look at the recent history of some of those brand icons, the reality is a little different. The brand bubble has burst.

'if you look at the recent history of some of those brand icons, the reality is a little different. The brand bubble has burst'

REALITY CHECK
THE DEMISE OF THE BRAND ICONS

Coca-Cola

Thirty years ago, Coca-Cola ran one of the most famous ad campaigns of all times – they stood 200 multi-ethnic young people on a hilltop in Italy and had them sing 'I'd Like to Buy the World a Coke'. Former CEO, Roberto Goizueta, said he would never rest until the 'C' on the cold tap in English-speaking countries stood for Coke. The company enjoyed pointing out that while the annual consumption of soft drinks in the US was 376 drinks a head, in China it was only six drinks a head, and the market was five times as large. The CEO said he was not selling a drink, but a 'piece of genius'. Coca-Cola had become the second most understood word on the planet – they even invented the modern Father Christmas in 1931 Coca-Cola advertising! By 1999, Coke had more than half the world soft drink market. The power of the global master brand, supported by global advertising of some $1.6 billion, seemed unchallengeable.

Coke's share prices fell from $85 in June 1998 to $47 two years later. In 2000, Coca-Cola announced the cut of 6000 jobs – one-fifth of its global workforce – and heavy costs being incurred in withdrawing large stocks of unwanted Coke concentrate from its global supply chain. Incoming CEO, Douglas Daft, announced cuts of 7–8 per cent in Coke's volume targets, and 15–20 per cent in earnings. Coca-Cola has tried to keep up with the fragmenting soft drinks market by producing local brands – its best-selling cola in India is Thumbs Up not Coke – and by launching products to meet growing demand for bottled water, flavoured water, juice-based drinks, flavoured iced tea and coffee drinks, and high energy drinks. None of these new products carry the Coke brand name. In 2000, Coca-Cola planned the launch of milk-based drinks for children, and the extension of the Coke brand onto fashion and sports clothing, and was partnering with Nestlé, the Swiss goods group, to market 'new beverages', such as health drinks, teas and ready-to-drink coffee. A joint venture with Procter & Gamble took Coke into the juices and snacks market, plus an agreement with Disney to sell children's drinks under the Disney brand. By 2001, the company had more than 200 brands. Weak sales and profit falls continued into 2001. When the company's CEO invested in developing a system to mix Coke in the house and deliver it by tap in the kitchen – the financial press could not resist the temptation to call this the latest 'Daft idea'.

Levi-Strauss

Levi denim blue jeans were a symbol of youth and rebellion – the symbol of the macho Old West, the connoisseur's brand of choice. People used to say proudly 'Just bury me in my 501s'. The baby-boomers of the 1960s wore their Levi 501 blue jeans as the uniform of rebellion. The trouble is the baby-boomers are still wearing their Levi's to do the family shop in Sainsburys and to wash the Volvo on a Sunday afternoon. To the young buyer of blue jeans, there is nothing cool about Levi's – they are indeed the jeans your Dad wears – their uniform is chinos and combat trousers (and definitely not Levi's Docker brand chinos, because your Dad wears them too after he has finished washing the Volvo). Denim jeans have become old people's clothes – even Prime Minister Tony Blair wears blue jeans. The only jeans acceptable to the 15- to 24-year-old market in 2001 come from design houses like Donna Karen, Tommy Hilfiger and Calvin Klein, not from Levi's. The blue jeans market is now driven by fashion not by brands like Levi. 1999 saw Levi-Strauss closing half its US factories and laying off 6000 staff, because of a 13 per cent fall in sales, with the closure of overseas factories following close behind.

McDonalds

The 'Big Mac' was launched by Ray Kroc in 1968, and the McDonalds brand is almost the definition of fast food throughout the world. By the late 1990s, McDonalds had reached sales of £20 billion, employing 1.5 million people in 25 000 outlets in 116 countries. The 1990 opening of a McDonalds in Moscow was an enduring symbol of the triumph of capitalism over communism. Lack of successful product innovation and loss of market share led to 1999 sales falling by 5 per cent, and profits failing to grow – in 2001 McDonalds reported consecutive quarters of falling profits for the first time in its history. The world seems to be getting bored with the Big Mac. Past attempts to diversify have been high-profile flops – Arch Deluxe, McPizza, Big Xtra. However, faced with a saturated and competitive market for its burgers in the US, McDonalds has gone on an acquisition spree to build growth – Boston Chicken, Donatos Pizza, Chipotle Mexican Grill chains in the US, the Aroma coffee house chain in the UK, and in 2001 a 33 per cent stake in Prêt a Manger, the sandwich and sushi chain – none of these acquisitions carry the McDonalds brand name. In the US, McDonalds announce plans for a chain of coffee shops – McCafes – to challenge Starbucks in the latte business. Early in 2001, the company issued a profits warning, reported zero sales growth in Europe, and cuts in its plans to open new restaurants.

Marlboro

Marlboro, the Philip Morris brand, is the most widely-recognized cigarette brand in the world. The lonely 'Marlboro Cowboy' has ridden everywhere. Marlboro was one of the first of the global brands to signal that an era of brand-based competition might be coming to an end. This signal was sent on 'Marlboro Friday'.

'Marlboro Friday' was 2 April 1993. Philip Morris faced a tough situation in the US cigarette market – market share was being eroded by sales of low-price, unbranded, generic cigarettes in supermarkets and filling stations across the US. Philip Morris did the one thing that brand-owners are not supposed to do – they took the huge gamble of cutting the price of Marlboro by 20 per cent (40 cents a pack). They then extended deep price-cutting to other premium cigarette brands.

This desperate attempt to hold market share immediately drove their share price dramatically down and impacted on the value of brand-based company stocks across the world. Investors took the view that if the only thing you can do when times get tough is to cut the price of a brand – then the brand is not worth much after all. The term 'brand equity' has never seemed quite the same ever since.

Sources: Richard Tomkins (2000), 'Fallen Icons', *Financial Times*, 1 February. Rupert Steiner (2001), 'Coke Chief's Latest Daft Idea – A Cola Tap in Every House', *Sunday Times*, 18 March.

The sad truth is that to survive now, you may need a brand, but you need *more* than a brand. You need *value*. When markets change, and new types of competition emerge, having the greatest brand in the world will not help you. You need more and you need to change. If all you can do when times get tough for a brand is to cut prices, then really your brand is not worth much. Brands are certainly one way of delivering value to customers, but only part of the requirement.

'to survive now, you may need a brand, but you need more than a brand. You need value'

And incidentally, playing games to keep brand prices high is not fooling anyone. In January 2001, leading designer brands stood accused by a *Sunday Times* investigation of manipulating anti-counterfeiting laws to keep British prices 50 per cent higher than the rest of Europe – telling customs and trading standards authorities that genuine goods being sold cheaply were counterfeit, to get them seized; using private investigators to exploit police intelligence to trace price-cutters and cut off their supplies; selling surplus stock into markets like Russia and condemning those items as fakes if they find their way back to Britain. The highly plausible claims by Levi-Strauss that Tesco should not be allowed to sell Levi jeans, because sales staff need 'special training', has the merit at least of being side-splittingly amusing. The world has changed – play these games and get caught, and you will have to live with your customers' anger[24].

The symptoms of problems for brand-based companies are several. While branded goods companies continue to launch new products, it is becoming more and more difficult to repeat the success of the blockbuster brands of the past – Procter & Gamble, for example, lost a third of its market value in March 2000 when it issued a profit warning, reflecting the fact that while it has continued to launch new brands like Febreze, a deodorant spray for clothes and furnishings, and Dryel, a home dry-cleaning kit, it is decades since the last major brand success, with Pamper's disposable nappies[25]. Rival detergent brander, Unilever, announced in 2000 a service called 'Myhome', offering to clean people's houses and do the laundry, while denying that this move smacked of desperation.

Indeed, 'brand culling' has become the name of the game for many. Unilever, for example, is going through the process of reducing its 1600 global brands to 400. The reason is that less than 20 per cent of its brands contributed 80 per cent of sales and 90 per cent of profit. There are just too many minor brands reducing production efficiency and cluttering supermarket shelves[26].

'"brand culling" has become the name of the game for many'

Meantime, advertising agencies are running around claiming that 'brands are the new religion', as if nothing had changed[27]. I think the boys and girls in adland should get out a bit more into the real world.

One visionary even claims that the real problem is that brands are becoming less a way of reaching out to customers and more of a barrier to getting closer to them. Alan Mitchell argues that the problem is that brand-building may be a distancing process that creates a rigid set of pre-packaged products and brand images or values, policed by the brand manager, which cannot respond to changing customer processes. He argues that increasingly we are in a world where customers seek the right to specify their own bundles of attributes and to create and manage their own 'brands'. Interactive marketing and radical one-to-one product and service customization may have made the traditional concept of brand obsolete[28].

So, is the brand dead? No, of course it isn't. What has reached the end of the road is *'blind branding'* – believing that the brand alone will create superior customer value. The challenge is *focused branding* that creates customer value in the customer's terms. It may have to be a lot different. Brands are always going to be important (see pp. 468–80 for a discussion of brand strategy issues in building value propositions), but you need more to succeed with new customers than a neat brand name, slick packaging and spurious brand values built through advertising.

'What has reached the end of the road is "blind branding"'

Along these lines, Peter Doyle[29] has recently suggested that we should be auditing brands for their value-enhancing characteristics:

- Is there any effective proposition to the customer – does the brand offer some unique benefit not offered by other brands and not easily imitated by them?
- Is the brand effectively integrated into business processes to sustain its proposition – for example, quality control, service and delivery performance?

- Is the brand in a market environment where it can prosper – or will strong competitors and low price players destroy its chances?

His conclusion matches ours – just to have a brand achieves little, this is 'blind branding' – the issue is whether the brand delivers value to customers (and hence to shareholders).

In essence, we may have to learn to see brands as less of a goal and more as what results from good marketing – John Deighton of Harvard Business School suggests 'Marketers are a little too desperate to build brands, but if they build strong customer relationships, the strength of the brand will follow' [30]. And lo, the answer to the problem became 'relationship marketing'.

Relationship marketing

So, what is the deal with relationship marketing? The 1990s saw just about everyone telling businesses that they had to get with relationship marketing as the only way to do 'new marketing' in modern markets – a major 'paradigm shift' for marketing theory and practice[31]. The difference between conventional marketing and relationship marketing is the move from emphasis on the transaction (the single sale of a product or service) to a focus on the continuing relationship with the customer. Critical differences between the two approaches are summarized in Table 3.1.

But, what did relationship marketing do for us?

In fact, relationship marketing is an exciting and major force which has helped to revitalize marketing in many companies. It can do the following types of thing for us:

'relationship marketing is an exciting and major force which has helped to revitalize marketing in many companies'

- it tells us that what matters most is the *relationship* we build with the customer, because this is the real source of enduring competitive strength;
- it tells us that we have to have a broader perspective that recognizes that we have more than one type of customer and market – Martin Christopher and colleagues[32] point to the importance of *five markets*: supplier, employee, referral, influence and internal markets, and this means relationship marketing involves all employees across traditional boundaries, in building and sustaining customer relationships – the role of the 'part-time marketers'[33];

Table 3.1 Transaction marketing and relationship marketing*

	Traditional transaction-based marketing	New relationship-based marketing
Focus	Individual sale to a customer	Total sales to a customer in the long term
Evaluation	Sales volume Market share Overall customer satisfaction	Customer retention Share of customer Individual customer satisfaction
Time perspective	Short-term	Long-term
Marketing dominated by	Marketing mix	Interactive marketing (supported by marketing mix)
Price sensitivity	Customers tend to be more sensitive to price	Customers tend to be less sensitive to price
Quality issues	Technical quality of product/service dominates	Quality of interactions with customer becomes more important
Customer information	Surveys of customer satisfaction	Continuous customer feedback system
Integration of marketing, operations and personnel	Limited importance	Strategic importance
Internal marketing	Limited importance	Strategic importance

* Source: Adapted from Christian Gronroos (1994), 'From Marketing Mix to Relationship Marketing', *Management Decision*, **32** (2), 4–20.

- because we focus on relationships in all these areas – customer and partners – instead of just transactions, then we turn from competition and conflict to *mutual co-operation and mutual interdependence*[34];
- our market strategy has also to be into the broader setting of *networks* of interdependent firms linked by strategic alliances, joint ventures and new types of joint trading agreements[35] – some now use the term 'viral marketing' to describe the web of relationships spreading to our customers' customers[36];
- it focuses our attention on *customer retention* – the efforts we make to build a lasting relationship with the customer, not just selling a product or service in a one-off transaction;
- it offers competitive strength from *micro-segmentation and customizing* – using our enhanced knowledge of the customer to take our value proposition down to the segment of one customer with customized or adapted offers and products[37].

Academics and consultants wax lyrical about the emergence of relationship marketing as a new approach. It is actually incredibly valuable in practical terms as well. What relationship marketing gives us is a framework and a rationale for doing the following things:

- focusing everyone's attention on our total offering to the customer and the value it creates for that customer – this is a greatly superior basis for building strategy than wonderful products (we think) *or* clever advertising programmes (the advertising agency thinks);
- it is the closest we have got so far in most companies to recognizing the need to manage the whole of the process of going to market, instead of just 'marketing' in the conventional sense;
- it gives us leverage against bean-counting accountants who want to see a margin on every transaction – everyone does some deals where they lose money, the point is whether we make money from the customer relationship through its life cycle;
- it gives us a logic for breaking free of traditional functional departmental boundaries, to build focus on value for the customer all the way from production to sales and distribution;
- it is exciting and innovative and offers us the chance to revitalize marketing processes in companies – because, let's be honest, in some firms marketing departments are looking a bit tired and bureaucratic (we will discuss Customer Relationship Management systems as a powerful approach underpinning market strategy in Chapter 10).

However, there is one thing that relationship marketing certainly is *not*. It is not *new*.

What do you mean – of course it is new!

If you want to be precious, you can probably trace the relational exchange approaches to doing business back several thousand years in the eastern cultures[38] and certainly to the industrial revolution in Britain[39].

Certainly the label 'Relationship Marketing' emerged as common terminology in the 1990s, and depending on your perspective was either pioneered by the Swedish and European academics led by Christian Gronroos and Evert Gummesson, or by a group of US academics led by Jagdish Sheth at Emory University[40]. However, if you look at the content of relationship marketing, there is little here which has not been known about for a long time:

'even now most forms of customer retention and loyalty programmes are little more than sophisticated attempts to take customers hostage'

- We have actually known about the importance of customer focus and retention for quite a while – this is not news, and even now most forms of customer retention and loyalty programmes are little more than sophisticated attempts to take customers hostage not build relationships or partnerships (see pp. 26–35).
- The importance of building a total market offering to the customer that involves service employees, technical specialists, purchasing experts, and so on, to sell to the customer may be a new idea to some marketing executives, but salespeople could have told you about it a long time ago, and it is what most successful firms have always done.
- Another name for 'mutual co-operation and mutual interdependence' with customers and collaborators is key account selling, and it is not a new idea for anyone dealing with multiple retailers, for example.
- Much of what passes for 'microsegmentation and customizing' is simply exploiting new computer stores of customer data to make direct contact – linking customer information to sales promotion is also not new, it used to be called (and still is) direct marketing, or database marketing, or even mail order marketing – it is simply using technology to do better what we have always done. This is about an IT revolution, not a marketing revolution. It is an incredibly important development in marketing practice – but a new paradigm or theory of marketing? I think not.

We also need to be very cautious about making promises we cannot keep in the guise of Relationship Marketing. Speaking as a 'segment of one' – is British Airways really going to give me more leg-room in an economy seat and let me smoke on the flight because I tell them this is what I want; is the Sainsbury Bank actually going to give me a different account to anyone else's; is Marks & Spencer going to use its database to stock trousers that are long enough for me; is BMW going to change more than the marginal extras on the vehicle to retain me as a customer? I really do not think so. All the evidence is that what they all actually want to do is to sell me financial services. Great relationship from a customer perspective (not).

In fact, a 1997 survey by Harris International Marketing[41] found that notwithstanding loyalty cards, relationship managers, customer service strategies and so on, shoppers continue to report that: retailers' customer service is poor, shopping is boring, all the supermarkets are very similar to each other, and overwhelmingly they buy groceries at the closest supermarket (i.e. the most convenient measured in distance and time). Perhaps consumers are trying to tell us something about relationship marketing?

Part of what they are saying may be that some customers simply do not *want* to have a relationship with you. A conundrum for the financial service sector – where many of the firms see relationship management as their salvation – is that many of their most attractive, affluent customer care saying things like: 'Do not telephone me to tell me that you are my personal banker and that you have some wonderful new products. Stop sending me letters and leaflets about your products. I do not want to have lunch with you, play golf with you or go to the races with you. I just want you to leave me alone!' Now that puts a different perspective on relationship marketing!

There does seem a danger that because marketing people have discovered relationship marketing, they assume that relationship strategies will be greeted with open arms by their customers. The evidence suggests that this is not the case. Before getting carried away – ask the question: are we embracing relationship marketing because it is a better way to meet our customers' needs, or because it meets our needs inside the company? If the answer is the latter – there is nothing necessarily wrong with this, just don't expect your customers to get excited about it.

'because marketing people have discovered relationship marketing, they assume that relationship strategies will be greeted with open arms by their customers'

It is also strange that enthusiasts for relationship marketing make so little of the negative side of relationship marketing – our goal with our database analysis, customized product, direct marketing communications, and retention and reward systems is to *break up* relationships, i.e. the existing relationships customers have with their present suppliers. The reality is not quite as cuddly as the theory in this respect, so let's drop the 'holier than thou' stuff.

On the other hand, when we find it is our customers who *demand* a relationship focus, then we really are talking about incredibly powerful leverage for competitive advantage. This pressure comes mainly in business-to-business marketing – either to distributors or industrial end-user customers. Here there is a major change in customer priorities that puts relationship management high on the agenda.

One neglected idea that arises from the above is that relationship requirement is potentially a very revealing way of *segmenting* markets. If we genuinely seek to distinguish important differences between customers, then maybe one way is to look at what they want from us in terms of a relationship (both type and degree of involvement). At least then we could focus on the customer groups where we are best able to deliver the relationship that they want. For example, Figure 3.2 suggests that if we look at the customers in our market in terms of whether they want a long-term relationship with their suppliers, and the closeness of the relationship they want, we may find very different types of buyer:

- *Relationship Seekers* – the type of customer becoming a major force in industrial marketing, who wants a long-term relationship with the supplier and a high degree of closeness or partnership in things like developing new products.
- *Relationship Exploiters* – customers who will take every advantage they can get from relationship offers for whatever they can get, but at the end of the day shop around, and your investment in the relationship does not buy you customer loyalty or retention.
- *Loyal Buyers* – customers who want a long-term relationship, but not a close one. Think of the financial services example above.
- *Arm's Length Transaction Customers* – will shop around for the best deal, will probably buy on price, and do not want a close relationship with the supplier. An example might be buyers of staple chemicals for industrial applications.

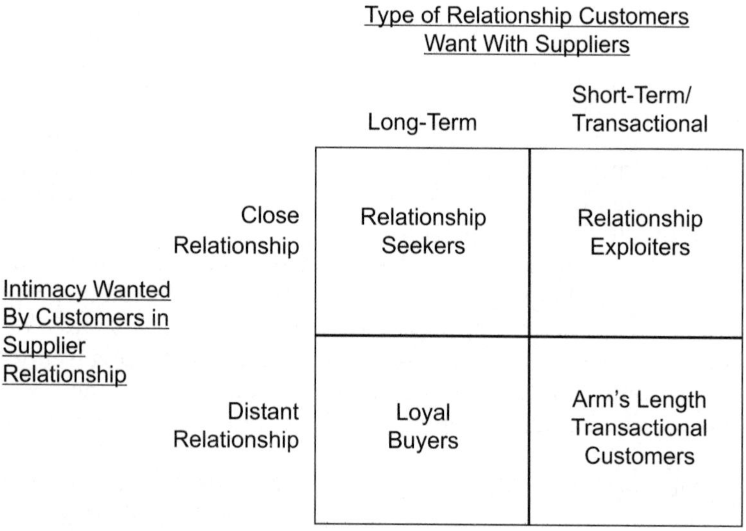

	Type of Relationship Customers Want With Suppliers	
	Long-Term	Short-Term/ Transactional
Close Relationship	Relationship Seekers	Relationship Exploiters
Distant Relationship	Loyal Buyers	Arm's Length Transactional Customers

Intimacy Wanted By Customers in Supplier Relationship

Figure 3.2   Segmenting markets by customer relationship requirements

---

REALITY CHECK
WHO SAYS I WANT A RELATIONSHIP WITH YOU?

In one company in the advertising business, at the height of the relationship marketing boom, top management bought into the idea of relationship marketing big time (I think someone had foolishly let them go on a management short-course). They cascaded this idea down through the company until it reached the salesforce. Salespeople were now to be coached in building customer relationships. In reality, they were selling directory advertising mainly to small and medium-sized enterprises, booked on an annual basis. The result was top management waxing lyrical about customer relationships, but customers who were saying: 'Go away and leave me alone. I do not want to have lunch with you, or sit and drink coffee with you. I am too busy. You are just not that important to me. Let me place the order on the Internet, and stop trying to waste my time', or words to that effect. The other result was severely irritated customers and a very unhappy salesforce.

This is not particularly profound. However, executives may find it is a good way of rethinking our priorities in investing time and effort in building customer relationships, and it may be a useful balance to the consultants' euphoria over relationship marketing as the solution to any problem you care to name.

So, where does that leave us with relationship marketing?

Actually, what all this means is that relationship marketing is the most fantastically useful thing for executives – it gives a new life to marketing and market strategy in particular, but you don't have to learn anything new! We probably should not dismiss relationship marketing as a fad (which it may turn out to be) or 'putting old wine in new bottles' (which it probably is) or 'academic theory' (which it certainly is) – take the opportunity to *use* relationship marketing to build customer focus in the company, to involve the people you need, and to drive market-led strategic change. You get this for free – it would be churlish not to take advantage!

The opportunity is to use relationship marketing to help in:

● putting the marketing process (not the marketing department) back on centre-stage in companies which have been looking elsewhere for leadership;

- getting the management focus back to the customer;
- involving every part of the company in concentrating on value for the customer; *and*
- put the customer higher on the agenda than advertising and marketing programmes.

'believing that relationship marketing is the killer approach because it guarantees customer satisfaction and loyalty is where it all goes wrong'

For most of us, this is just too good to miss out on!

However, believing that relationship marketing is the killer approach because it guarantees customer satisfaction and loyalty is where it all goes wrong. As we saw in Chapter 2 (pp. 28–31), customer satisfaction (the attitude) is a poor predictor of customer retention (the behaviour). The argument emerging is that value, as perceived by the customer, is what predicts and drives loyalty – *value* is what links satisfaction and retention[42].

Relationship rhetoric versus relationship reality

The situation we have reached is that 'relationship rhetoric' has reached the end of the road – believing that investing in customer relationship-building has value in its own right. In looking to prevent the 'premature death' of relationship marketing, Susan Fournier and colleagues are forced to concede that as it is currently practised, relationship marketing has not generally brought us closer to customers, it has forced us further apart – consumers have begun to view companies as enemies, not allies, and they are fighting back[43].

'"relationship rhetoric" has reached the end of the road'

My friend Malcolm McDonald takes a somewhat stronger and more cynical view about relationship marketing as yet another management fad:

> 'Remember "relationship marketing"? The domain quickly became occupied by happy-clappy, touchy-feeley, weepy-creepy, born-again zealots without any underpinning process. Apart from which, "delighting" or "exciting" all customers is the quickest way to bankruptcy!'[44]

The point is that relationships are important only as a route to learning and delivering superior value in the customers' terms. We will come back to relationship marketing, when we look at the network of relationships which have to be managed in developing our strategic pathway. However, for the moment, we can say that alone relationship marketing is not a sufficient answer to evolving market demands. Increasingly, we are looking for better ways to address what really constitutes value for our customers.

Value-driven strategy

Where many companies now find themselves is desperately pursuing customer retention and profitability goals, as a route to enhancing shareholder value, but at a time when branding strategies and relationship marketing programmes seem to have run out of steam. This is an era of value-driven strategy.

'This is an era of value-driven strategy'

Stan Maklan and Simon Knox hit an important nail right on the head when they wrote about the new challenge of competing on value, because we have to find ways of 'bridging the gap between brand and customer value'. They write that:

> 'Marketing has focused on creating brand value, particularly in the brand-conscious eighties, rather than exploring customer value and translating this into a value proposition through branding . . . Creating a unique selling proposition for product brands and exploiting them through predictable stimulus–response tools falls short of the modern customer's level of sophistication . . . Today's marketing challenge is to bridge the widening gap between brand and customer value, which is increasingly generated through supply chain leadership, networks of relationships and individualized customer service.'[45]

They are not alone in underlining the need for value-based strategy. Noel Capon and James Mac Hulbert describe as one of their fundamental principles of strategic marketing, the principle of customer value:

> 'success in targeted market segments is directly related to the firm's ability to provide perceived value to customers . . . A corollary of this principle is that although firms develop, produce, and deliver products and services, customers perceive value only in the benefits that these products and services provide.'[46]

A similar, if not stronger, statement of the importance of value in shaping management thinking about marketing has been made by Peter Doyle:

'The essential idea of marketing is offering customers superior value. By delivering superior value to customers, management can in turn deliver superior value to shareholders. Indeed this formula – customer value creates shareholder value – is the fundamental principle of capitalism.'[47]

'real value innovations are what changes the structure of an industry'

There is substantial and growing evidence that real value innovations are what changes the structure of an industry, creates a new market space for the pioneer, and opens up a gap between them and the competition[48].

However, there is a big difference between value-based strategy in the process of going to marketing and traditional marketing – what Philip Kotler has called 'neanderthal marketing'. Marketing has always been about innovation – new products, new services, new advertising and promotion – but weak at real innovation that abandons the 'rule-book'. Too much so-called innovation has been replacing existing products with updates or variations of the same thing. An *Economist Intelligence Unit* report in 1999 interviewed executives from leading companies throughout the world about their approaches to innovating for the benefit of their customers and shareholders:

'What counts, conclude the participants, is *value innovation*. This is defined as creating new value propositions . . . that lead to increased customer satisfaction, loyalty and – ultimately – sustainable, profitable growth . . . Market leaders are just that – pioneers.'[49]

'what is frighteningly new is the incredible and paradoxical challenge of building customer value with the new customer'

Obviously, there is nothing much new in talking about value and marketing. But what is frighteningly new is the incredible and paradoxical challenge of building customer value with the new customer. Value-based strategy is not straightforward, and it does not provide the 'single answer' – any more than brand or relationship strategies did.

For example, Michael Treacy and Fred Wiersema[50] underline the fact that value does not have a single meaning in any market – customers determine what creates value, and different customers buy different value. They argue that market leaders are those who focus on delivering superior customer value in line with one of three 'value disciplines':

- *Operational excellence* – providing reliable products and services at competitive prices, delivered with minimal difficulty or inconvenience; for example, the superb Federal Express courier service.
- *Customer intimacy* – segmenting and targeting markets precisely so as to tailor offerings very precisely to match exactly the demands of those niches; for example, retailers like Nordstrom.
- *Product leadership* – offering leading-edge products and services, such as Johnson & Johnson's Vistakon disposable contact lenses that caught competitors off guard, making it difficult for them ever to catch up.

One of the dangers that these writers warn us about is the simple-minded managerial assumption that 'value' means cheap, i.e. if you get unit costs down faster than your competitors, then you can have lower prices and dominate the market. It really is not that simple. Don't get me wrong – sometimes superior customer value is exactly about having low prices, like the 'no frills' airlines.

REALITY CHECK

**RYANAIR – ALTITUDE AND ATTITUDE
CREATE VALUE**

Ryanair is one of the successful 'no frills' airlines operating in Britain and Europe – it offers very low fares but provides no 'frills', like airport lounges, frequent flyer rewards, or free meals and drinks for passengers. The airline operates 'open seating' – if you fly with them you fight for the seat you want, there are no allocations. Ticket sales are increasingly direct over the Internet to avoid travel agent commission – now 40 per cent of ticket sales. The aircraft are worked hard and productively to give extremely low fares compared to existing airlines. In 2000, Ryanair advertising compared its fares with British Airways:

	Ryanair From	BA From
London to Frankfurt	£69	£374
London to Genoa	£129	£560
London to Biarritz	£99	£534

Ryanair is also fond of having sales – in October 2000, the company offered half a million return flights from the UK to Europe for £5 (plus airport taxes). This is not an easy sector in which to prosper – by 2000 competitors AB Airlines and Debonair had gone out of business, and loss-making Virgin Express was in deep trouble.

Ryanair was originally a conventional, full-service airline started by Tony Ryan to compete with Aer Lingus, by offering lower fares. The result was a disaster – Ryanair lost £18 million in four years and went through five CEOs. Current CEO, Michael O'Leary, adopted the 'no frills' approach pioneered by Southwest Airlines in the US and extended routes from Dublin to London to other parts of Britain and Europe. By 2000, Ryanair had become Europe's largest 'no frills' airline, reporting profits of around £70 million. Market value of £3.2 billion makes Ryanair the fourth largest airline in Europe by market capitalization.

O'Leary is a truly aggressive competitor – and stands accused by the Irish premier of 'tooth and claw capitalism'. For example, when British Airways decided to open a low-cost airline to compete with the 'no frills' carriers, O'Leary commented ' … they must be smoking too much dope … If BA wants a fares war, they have come to the right place', and lowered fares below cost – £16.99 from London to a string of European destinations. Incidentally, he also works check-in or baggage handling duties at least four times a year. In 2000, British Airways sued Ryanair for its advertising claims that BA fares were too expensive – adverts provocatively headlined 'Expensive Ba****ds'. Ryanair won the case.

O'Leary has taken Ryanair into substantial profitability, and his airline is renowned for its constant 80 per cent load factors. O'Leary comments 'We make money with falling airfares. And we make stinking piles of money with rising fares. It's scary.' Ryanair has skilfully avoided direct competition with other carriers, and expensive and congested national airports, by developing underdeveloped routes from Dublin to UK regional cities. Ryanair has also grown its market instead of just competing for market share – in 1985, when it started flying from Dublin to London, the route carried one million passengers a year; by 1998 this had reached four million passengers a year, some paying fares as low as £19.99.

The Ryanair value proposition allows people to fly when otherwise they would have travelled by sea and road, or simply stayed at home. Even more surprising, the 'no frills' passengers are not only leisure travellers and tourists – it is estimated that as much as 50 per cent of those carried by 'no frills' airlines are travelling on business. Large companies are cutting travel budgets, small companies can travel internationally when previously they could not afford it. In 2000 American Express reports that nearly two-thirds of business travellers are being asked to go 'no frills', to reduce corporate travel costs. Early in 2001, Ryanair announced seven new routes into Europe with fares as low as 60 per cent of the full service carriers.

Sources: Rupert Howell (2000), 'Whatever They Say in the Ad, Don't Call the Lawyers', *Sunday Business*, 10 December. Peter Cunliffe (2000), 'The Pilot Behind the Ryanair Takeoff', *Daily Mail*, 21 December. Dominic O'Connell (2000), 'Gaining Altitude by Rewriting the Rules', *Sunday Business*, 13 February. Gillian O'Connor (2000), 'Business Opts for No-Frills Flights', *Financial Times*, 13 March.

But, the lean, low-price business model of the 'no frills' airline is *not* the only way to create value[51]. Going from one extreme to the other, consider the Starbucks phenomenon.

REALITY CHECK
WAKE UP AND SMELL THE COFFEE

If value were concerned only with low prices, or even higher quality than competitors at the going market rate, then the Starbucks coffee house chain and its many imitators would not exist. They certainly would not be able to charge £3.00 or more for a cup of coffee which costs a few pennies to make – even if it is called a 'decaf triple grande skimmed no whip wet mocha'. In particular, they would not have been able to charge these prices in a market where the big coffee companies had fought for years to increase sales by reducing prices.

In fact, Starbucks has grown from a small Seattle-based coffee house for born-again hippies, into a profitable $1.3 billion business, operating 2500 shops worldwide and concession areas in many stores and other locations. This achievement has not been through low prices, but by finding an area of value creation which had been ignored by conventional coffee providers: Starbucks 'created an entire experience, almost a therapeutic quality, out of going into one of its stores and drinking coffee, and created almost unheard-of profit margins around that experience' (Eric Almquist, Mercer Management Consulting). It also helps that they sell very fine coffee, which makes it hard for consumers ever to return to the disgusting concoctions offered in many restaurants, let alone the indescribable glop produced by office vending machines, which may be why so many people are now seen on British streets carrying a Starbucks take-away cup.

Starbucks has not only become an American cultural icon, it is also an international retail phenomenon – even taking its coffee houses into Italy, the home of the café. It is estimated in 2001 that in Britain 60 per cent of the population will visit a new-style coffee shop at some point during the week.

Sources: John Willman (1999), 'Brands on the Run', *Financial Times*, 29 October. Catherine Wheatley (1999), 'Starbucks Wakes Up and Smells the $68m Profits', *Sunday Business*, 17 October. Dan Bilefsky (2000), 'The Rich Blend of a Caffeine Culture', *Financial Times*, 14 August. Quentin Letts (2001), 'The Great Coffee Con', *Daily Mail*, 2 May.

'the more you consider what creates customer value, the more are the paradoxes and surprises you encounter'

In fact the more you consider what creates customer value, the more are the paradoxes and surprises you encounter. But, finding new ways of creating value may offer direct impact on profits:

- Although derided as 'un-English' for doing so, the Alton Towers theme park has introduced an 'X-Celerator Pass', which costs £65 for adults (compared to the normal £21 entrance ticket). The X-Celerator Pass lets you do all the bad things you always wanted to do: you can park in the 'wrong' place closer to the rides, you can enter the rides at the exit gate, and most importantly you get to jump the one-hour queues for the rides and attractions[52]. This is such a wonderful idea, it is almost evil.
- Dinnerbooker offers a website and phone booking system for restaurant tables. The difference is that they work under the banner 'Twenty Quid And You're In', because they provide the online equivalent of tipping the *maître d'* to get a table. Their customers pay £20 extra for a booking to eat in expensive restaurants at the most popular times (i.e. after 8.00 p.m. in exclusive restaurants like Le Gavroche and Tante Claire in London). They are 'touts' for restaurants and proud of it. They have found a new service that creates value around a traditional product[53].
- In 2000 in the US, H. J. Heinz announced that its EZ Squirt Ketchup would be available in 'Blastin' Green' as well as the conventional tomato colour, in a cone-shaped bottle to encourage children to draw pictures on their food with the ketchup. The idea is to make mealtimes more interesting for the foul 6- to 12-year-old. It may sound weird, but stuck in a mature market with little growth, this product variant took 6 per cent of the $500 million US market in seven weeks, and its annual sales target in 90 days[54]. Making boring

food fun looks like value creation as far as children are concerned. Now available in the UK!

- EatZi's is a rapidly-expanding US food store which calls itself a 'suppermarket' not a supermarket, and celebrates 'the joy of not cooking'. EatZi's and its emerging competitors sell fresh ready-meals, slightly undercooked, to be taken home and finished off in the oven or microwave. In a typical store 100 chefs work to produce a choice of 1800 ready-meals. To busy time-pressed working people, value looks like being able to eat fresh food at home without having to cook it[55].
- Cyber-courier firms have started in major cities across the world, with such offers as 'mouse to house in half an hour', attracting cash-rich but time-poor consumers who are prepared to pay for fast delivery of anything from pizzas to videos and CDs, rather than collect things themselves[56]. Some say 'laziness', some say 'value' . . .

In fact the only certainty is that if your target customers do not think you are providing them with value, they are going to let you know about it.

REALITY CHECK
WHEN WE SAY 'VALUE' WE MEAN IT . . .

In January 2001, Nicholas Griffin, a sex shop owner, offering 'hardcore' pornographic videos, was fined £5826 by York magistrate's court. The reason was that the pornographic films he sold were not explicit enough. Customers of Little Amsterdam, in York, and The Adult Shop, in Grimsby, complained at paying £50 for 'hardcore' films, that turned out to be too tame, containing old films that could be seen on normal television. Mr Griffin was prosecuted under the Trades Description Act. Said Mr Griffin: 'I am amazed that people have the audacity to complain about things like that.' Said the head of York Trading Standards: 'They felt embarrassed and reluctant to come forward, but also felt *cheated* . . . '

Sources: 'Sex-Shop Boss Fined Because His Porn Wasn't Hard Enough', *Daily Mail*, 19 January 2001. Sally Pook (2001), 'Sex Shop is Fined Because its Videos Are "Too Tame"', *Daily Telegraph*, 19 January.

The paradoxes abound. Look at the British High Street. In the grocery business, it is clear that we all want more from supermarkets than low prices – if this were not true the market leaders would be the discounters Aldi, Lidl and Netto (who together account for less than 10 per cent of total sales), not Tesco, Asda and Sainsbury. On the other hand, in the clothing shops – at one end of the market value is successfully created by discounters like Matalan, Primark and TK Maxx, at the other end of the market sales of designer fashion clothes in stores like Next and Debenhams are booming by creating a different sort of value, but the tough place to be is in the middle where your clothes are seen as poor value because they are too expensive or poor value because they are unfashionable (this is the position occupied by Marks & Spencer at the moment).

Jim Maxmin, Chairman of Global Brand Development, summarizes nicely the types of challenges that an era of value-based strategy pose for us all:

> 'The real challenge for marketers now is the creation of real value in an environment where e-commerce is rapidly commoditizing products and services. Perception of value has changed. Technology has made the corporation transparent. How do you embrace this marketplace when your customers know more than you do? How do you embrace loyalty when your customers are just one click away from leaving?' [57]

The real issue is new customers not new marketing

'It is actually frightening to try to enumerate the types of demands that are being placed on us by new customers'

It is actually frightening to try to enumerate the types of demands that are being placed on us by new customers, and how these demands are escalating in size and complexity, but here are my suggestions of what to anticipate.

Who are you calling fickle? – I just changed my mind

New customers are allowed to change their minds, and they do. In 2000, for example, Germany's environmentalist Green party decided after years of battling against motorways, petrol-guzzling motorists, and anything faster than a bicycle, that maybe cars were a good thing after all: 'The car is not an atomic power station on wheels that has to be decommissioned' [58]. It would have been very helpful if they could have decided that in the first place!

Closer to home, 'alcopops' provided a roller-coaster for the cidermaker Merrydown. Merrydown's Two Dogs (alcoholic lemonade) product launched a craze in the UK for alcopops in 1995. Within two years the public decided that, though cute, alcopops were a 'bad thing' because they encouraged young people to drink, which is very naughty – because presumably teenagers had never imbibed alcohol before. Merrydown saw Two Dogs sales collapse from £20 million to £11 million in the space of six months, and the company moved into a loss-making position, putting itself up for sale[59].

Incredibly, it even starts to look like the extended American love affair with burgers and fried chicken is on the wane, not least because Eric Schlosser has pointed out *exactly* what people are eating in burgers, and it is not very pleasant reading for the squeamish[60].

Your excuses are wearing a bit thin ...

Many customers are getting thoroughly fed up with having their views ignored by service providers. Writer Bill Bryson comments 'Most big companies don't like you much. Hotels are an exception. They despise you almost as much as airlines.'[61]. It really is not surprising that smarter customers are getting ruthless in demanding what they want and punishing those who do not supply it.

'Many customers are getting thoroughly fed up with having their views ignored by service providers'

And, if you think training your employees to say 'have a nice day' is going to make customers think you care about them[62] ... pleeeese!

REALITY CHECK
HOW TO ADD INSULT TO INJURY

Early in 2001, a company manager spending £20 000 a year on postage was furious about continual late deliveries. He complained to the Royal Mail that its poor service was costing his company money – letters containing cheques were not arriving until after the banks had closed, and so on. The response of the Royal Mail was to send him a letter of apology and a booklet containing four 27p first-class stamps. They appeared surprised that the customer's anger had now been translated into incandescent rage, and that their 'gesture of goodwill' made the national press and attracted the attention of the local MP.

Source: 'As an Apology to the Boss Hit by Months of Postal Delays ... Four 27p Stamps', *Daily Mail*, 9 February 2001.

Value is what we say it is . . .

The next time you and colleagues are debating product quality and technical standards, and all the other things we know and love, and believe represent quality, remember the Spice Girls.

REALITY SPICE

VALUE VERSUS QUALITY

In the Spice Girls' film, *Spice World*, having heard the eponymous talents produce their inimitable sounds, someone comments 'that was perfect, girls, without actually being any good'.

'One more time – value is not defined by the factory or the supply chain – value is defined by the customer'

One more time – value is not defined by the factory or the supply chain – value is defined by the customer. Look around at the examples of those who have established new areas of value and profit creation, and you can only reach one conclusion – the customer says what is value in his/her terms, and he/she knows it.

The traditional approaches of going to market with 'confusion marketing'[63] – such as 'confusion pricing' to make it so complicated to compare prices that customers stay with you – are really not clever with sophisticated, value-seeking customers. Those customers are liable to become very angry if you do not provide them with value in their terms.

By the way, 'free' is one of my favourite prices . . .

Sometimes value is about the price sticker, if that is what customers choose. In 1999 the UK car trade experienced a 'buyers' strike' – inflamed by media and consumer group campaigns about 'rip-off Britain'[64], consumers held back from buying new cars. Car manufacturers were forced to respond with cash-back offers and price cuts[65]. Spookily, by late 2000, an overall 10 per cent cut in car prices saw an upsurge in new car sales to private buyers[66].

Bear in mind, the first mobile telephones cost $2500, and a few years later only $100, and increasingly are given away free with the connection contract, and Encyclopedia is now a free online service (funded by advertising), not an expensive set of books[67].

It is unavoidable that new customers will demand things 'free', for which previously they paid money. Look at Internet access for your example: at one time we were happy to pay a subscription and for phone call charges. Now we want the access free (thank you, Freeserve). Now we want the phone calls free (thank you, AOL). And by the way, if Freeserve and AOL could

'It is unavoidable that new customers will demand things "free", for which previously they paid money'

get together that would be an excellent value offer – no subscription or call charges. The next stage is that I want to be 'paid' in some form for visiting your web pages . . . Lest you think this overly fanciful – there are already web sites, like AllAdvantage.com, that will give you 'credits' to buy their products, if you agree to have their advertising running along the bottom of your screen.

Indeed, a revolution is underway in the computer software industry, where 'open source software' (i.e. free) is challenging the position of companies like Microsoft, who cling to the idea that they own intellectual copyright in software and make you pay for it. The open source Linux operating system has already taken about 9 per cent of the market, posing a growing threat to the supremacy of Microsoft's operating systems. In fact, OSS is even more revolutionary than just being free – online users amend, refine and develop the programs on their own initiative. Internal Microsoft documents note that the 'ability of the OSS process to collect and harness the IQ of thousands of individuals is simply amazing'[68]. Free *and* evolving faster!

Perhaps yet more stunning is the response of some revolutionary companies to the customer's predilection for 'free'. In May 2001, Ryanair announced plans for free seats on some of its off-peak flights (lest you think that Michael O'Leary has lost his interest in profit, be assured he plans to make money from passenger entertainment services instead). O'Leary says: 'The other airlines are asking how they can get fares up. We are asking how we can get rid of them.'[69]. And before you dismiss the idea out of hand – have another look at Ryanair's track record (see pp. 77–9), and wonder if they have got a business model that can get rid of fares . . .

Loyalty is for sellers not buyers . . .

'Smart customers know that we want them to be loyal – increasingly they are demanding that we should be loyal to them as well'

Smart customers know that we want them to be loyal – increasingly they are demanding that we should be loyal to them as well. Customer relationship is going to have to mean more than giving your business to a supplier in return for the right to be sold more. Also, bear in mind that customers who think you have been disloyal and treated them badly may be vindictive:

REALITY CHECK
SMART CUSTOMERS HAVE LONG MEMORIES

In the autumn of 2000, Britain faced a major fuel crisis when protesters blockaded ports and distribution depots to attempt to force the government to reduce its astronomical rates of tax on fuel. The crisis lasted some days and caused major disruption to travellers and food shortages as deliveries could not be made, but failed to win any significant concessions from the government.

However, the temporary fuel shortage provided opportunities for some. Paul Gizzonio of Normanton, Derby was condemned as Britain's greediest profiteer when he more than doubled his petrol prices during the fuel crisis – charging £1.99 a litre for unleaded petrol (about £9.10 a gallon) and £2.50 a litre for super unleaded (about £11.42 a gallon). The Automobile Association accused him of going 'way over the top'. He defended himself, saying that he had to 'ration by price' to stay in business, and put up a sign saying 'Petrol Prices Dictated by National Shortage'. At one stage he had to call the police to calm angry customers on his forecourt. In reaction, his supplier, Texaco, demanded that he remove their name and logo from his forecourt, or face legal action.

In January 2001, the 'Gizzonio UK' filling station in Normanton, Derby was declared bankrupt. Other stations he ran in the area were in the hands of insolvency agents. After the fuel crisis, his customers remembered the profiteering and simply took their custom else-where ... Many are reported to be more than happy with the result of their boycott, and smiling sweetly as they drive past the defunct petrol stations.

Sources: Maurice Weaver (2001), 'Petrol Profiteer Ruined by Drivers Who Steered Clear'. *Daily Telegraph*, 23 January. James Tozer (2001), 'Customers' Revenge', *Daily Mail*, 23 January.

'Has it ever occurred to anyone that strong customer relationships (to which all aspire) mean we should actually trust our customers?'

It works both ways though. Has it ever occurred to anyone that strong customer relationships (to which all aspire) mean we should actually trust our customers? If you want to know if I have a relationship with you as my supplier, maybe the test is whether you trust me to pay you – perhaps if you can't bring yourself to trust me, I should not trust you either? Some people have actually tried it, and incredibly it seems to work:

REALITY CHECK
TRUST MY CUSTOMERS – ARE YOU MAD?

An honesty box scheme for buying newspapers started by W. H. Smith began as an experiment at Heathrow airport to save travelling buyers from queuing at a counter. The experiment was an unqualified success: no increase in theft, higher sales and dramatic reduction in queues. The company is expanding the scheme to appropriate sites nationwide.

The supermarket Safeway pioneered its 'Shop and Go' system, in which customers scan and pay for goods without using a cashier. Safeway does regular spot checks and says there has been no increase in theft. Operated in 170 Safeway stores, the system has been imitated in some Waitrose and Sainsbury stores.

Boots the Chemist is piloting the same concept in fast-moving city centre stores (for holders of its Advantage loyalty card), where customers scan their own products in a specially designed till – the Self Pay Point.

Sources: Jack Grimston and Clive Entwhistle (1998), 'Honesty Pays for Store That Trusts Customers', *Sunday Times*, 5 April. Teena Lyons (2000), 'Honesty is on the Shopping List', *Financial Mail on Sunday*, 9 April.

Quality or cheap – both, please . . .

In many consumer sectors, price discounting has become the norm. However, it is important to understand that this is not because consumers are short of money and therefore only able to buy cheap goods. A Henley analyst notes: 'From the consumer's point of view, it's not so much trying to save money because we have to. It's trying to save money because we want to beat the system'[70]. We are starting to see in the UK the well-established inverse price snobbery of the tough US consumer – people who used to brag about how much they spent on an item, now brag about how much they have saved, and the question 'What? You paid retail?' has become an expression of universal contempt for those foolish enough to pay full prices. Stores like TK Maxx, Matalan, New Look and Wal-Mart do

'people who used to brag about how much they spent on an item, now brag about how much they have saved'

not just offer discounted prices, they provide high-quality products as well (often discounting the brand leaders, for example)[71]. While for the time being holding a modest share of total UK retail trade, factory outlets offering branded goods and designer products at low prices (frequently surplus or end-of-line stock) showed a 700 per cent growth in Britain between 1995 and 2000[72] – amazingly, even the ailing Marks & Spencer is trying out factory outlets. The cost to companies of not recognizing the implications of the demand for quality and low price can be substantial:

REALITY CHECK
ANOTHER DINOSAUR DISAPPEARS

The Dutch-owned clothing store C&A announced in June 2000 the closure of all its 109 stores in the UK, after 75 years trading. One of Britain's best-known retailers was effectively transformed into no more than a property company.

Nicknamed 'Cheap & Abysmal' by some consumers, the company's owners faced a harsh reality – that their product no longer met the needs of UK consumers. Edge-of-town retailers like Matalan and George at Asda can offer lower prices for basic clothing because the economics of their business models are quite different. Just being a retailer of cheap clothes is not sustainable. You have to be really cheap, or offer something else – like the design superiority and fashion innovation at Next and Debenhams. Being stuck in the middle is not a good place to be.

Sources: Richard Fletcher (2000), 'Discounters Get Ready to Fill the Gaps', *Sunday Business*, 18 June. Susanna Voyle (1999), 'Flight From the Middle Ground Benefits Value Retailers', *Financial Times*, 11 November. Kate Rankine (2000), 'Never Mind the Width, Quality Sells, Says Next', *Daily Telegraph*, 13 September.

Let's play the waiting game and see what happens . . .

In times of high price inflation, consumers want to buy quickly (before prices go up again). In times of stable or falling prices, waiting to see if a better deal will come along becomes a lot more attractive. Smart customers know this.

At Christmas 2000, consumers decided to play the waiting game with British retailers, with consumers holding off from Christmas shopping, until retailers' nerves broke and they started discounting prices. A Debenham's store spokesperson said 'Customers seem to have cottoned on to the idea that there's no point in buying a cashmere jumper at full price on Christmas Eve, when you can get it for half the money 48 hours later' [73]. It seems new customers are aware that we may need to sell things more than they need to buy them, and have no hesitation in exploiting that situation – why would they? Incidentally, the same Christmas trading period saw those customers demanding serious discounts in the sales – anything less than 50 per cent did not impress them.

'seems new customers are aware that we may need to sell things more than they need to buy them'

Make life simpler . . .

Providing greater consumer choice was a central part of marketing – more brands, new products, new services, and so on. Providing new choices which give greater value because they make people's lives easier is no problem, even if sometimes a bit strange:

REALITY CHUCK
THE PROBLEM WITH PEAS

The problem with peas is how to eat them. Using a spoon, which would be rational, is regarded as uncouth. The approved methods are (1) to spear a few at a time with a fork and mush a few more onto the back of the fork (which is not very pretty), or (2) to turn the fork over and scoop the peas onto the fork, with the assistance of the knife.

However, a generation of children has now grown up eating mainly fast food and television dinners and lack the cutlery skills required to eat peas (other than the mushy version which sticks to chips). Many children now arrive at school completely unaccustomed to a knife and fork, and schools have to teach them how to use cutlery.

The supermarket firm Tesco has become concerned. They sell 30 000 tons of peas a year, but they are eaten mainly by adults. Tesco has asked food scientists to solve the problem by developing a larger pea, with which young people will be able to cope, alongside their burgers and chicken nuggets – the 'grands pois'.

You really could not make this up. But responding to the needs of new customers is going to lead us all into actions and approaches that would previously have seemed bizarre and absurd.

Source: Tom Robbins (2000), 'TV-Food Kids Forget Art of Eating Peas', *Sunday Times*, 17 December.

The problem is when too many product choices make life more complicated not simpler – we are in danger of making the purchase of a toothbrush or a bottle of shampoo into an unnecessary life-changing drama for the customer. A 1999 study, by the product development agency CLK, underlines just how bewildered and extremely irritated consumers are becoming with the flood of product variants (mostly only marginally different to others), and they coin the term 'choice fatigue' to describe this[74]. The simple fact is that proliferation and duplication make shopping more difficult and many people have had enough of it – it annoys consumers and increases their cynicism. It also obscures the genuine innovations which we launch.

'proliferation and duplication make shopping more difficult and many people have had enough of it'

. . . But not too simple . . .

Paradoxically, however, consumers still want a degree of choice. One analyst describes the problem as 'selling to the sated', where the issue is that people's basic needs are just about met and are boring, but the higher level needs now being met are interesting and innovation and choice matters more[75]. The new customer wants to be teased, titillated and intrigued (and they may still not buy the product).

'The new customer wants to be teased, titillated and intrigued (and they may still not buy the product)'

REALITY CHECK
I DON'T KNOW WHAT IT IS, I JUST KNOW I WANT IT

At the beginning of 2001 an innovatory new product made headlines across the world, as the latest project of Dean Kamen, inventor of the world's first portable insulin pump, and a wheelchair that climbs stairs. This is noteworthy because no-one knew what the product was (and at the time of writing still don't) – including Harvard Business School Press, who had immediately commissioned a book about it for $250 000. Codenamed 'Ginger', the latest project of US inventor Dean Kamen was billed as potentially 'revolutionizing the planet'. A few people were in on the secret. Steve Jobs, of Apple fame, said cities would have to be redesigned because of it. Jeff Bezos of Amazon said 'It is a product so revolutionary, you'll have no problems selling it. The only question is are people to be allowed to use it.' The inventor claimed that Ginger will be an alternative to products that 'are dirty, expensive, sometimes dangerous and often frustrating, especially for people in the cities.' The tease mesmerized America and much of the rest of the world. Speculations were that Ginger might be a personal transporter of some kind (some suggest an emission-free hydrogen-powered scooter), or an energy cell, or indeed a giant hoax. The point is the global excitement about something just because it was new – one of the first worldwide examples of the gadget people were desperate to have, even though they didn't know what it was.

Sources: Andrew Cave (2001), 'The Gadget You Must Have Whatever It Is', *Daily Telegraph*, 13 January. Tom Robbins and Andy Goldberg (2001), 'Is This the Revolution the World is Waiting For?', *Sunday Times*, 14 January.

. . . But, I don't like change

The challenge imposed by new customers seems to be: innovate and improve, but don't change the things I like! In 1998, angry consumers forced cereals manufacturer, Kellogg, to admit defeat in its wholly rational attempt to standardize the size of cornflakes boxes throughout Europe. They said that increasing the height of the box by $1\frac{1}{2}$ inches made it too tall to be stored in British larders. There is actually no evidence that British larders are smaller than those in other countries. Kelloggs preferred not to reveal the costs of two box size changes in four months[76]. Anyone can get caught out:

REALITY CHECK

ORGANIC WHAT? NO, THANK YOU VERY MUCH

One of Britain's retailing success stories of the late 1990s was Iceland, the frozen foods and grocery chain, which pioneered low price deals and home delivery, before larger competitors got on the bandwagon. The 1990s also saw a ten-fold increase in sales of organic food – a billion pound market by 2001.

It is unsurprising that chairman Malcolm Warner, a Greenpeace member, should have taken a policy decision in 2000 to move totally into organic vegetables in its own-label products. This was Iceland's 'Food You Can Trust' campaign, which also involved banning genetically modified ingredients and artificial colourings. The strategy was to take organic foods out of their middle-class niche and to make them part of everyday, mass market grocery shopping. The initiative is estimated to have cost £8 million, and anticipating a 30 per cent increase in sales, involved long-term contracts with organic food suppliers.

In January 2001, following a 5.5 per cent fall in sales, and a Christmas trading statement that wiped a fifth off the company's value, Iceland reversed its pledge to go 100 per cent organic, and to sell organic products alongside its other own-label products. The plan is a 'one-for-one' strategy – an organic alternative to conventional lines.

Iceland customers were simply not prepared to support the company's policy, even with Iceland's low prices for organic vegetables. Consumer reactions to the new organic ranges were 'I don't want these, where are the ordinary ones I buy?', but the ordinary ones had gone. It seems Iceland's older, less affluent consumer profile consists of consumers who buy frozen food not fresh, for whom the organic issue is not a big deal, but prices are. It is also apparent that consumers do not appreciate having the choice taken away from them. Says new CEO Bill Grimsey: 'customers will not be dictated to'. Ending long-term contracts with organic farmers cost Iceland a one-off charge of £20 million in 2001, with a further £14 million cost over the next three years because of the cost of continuing organic vegetables contracts.

Iceland had the courage to swallow its pride and back off from the unsuccessful strategy instead of forcing it down their unreceptive customers' throats.

Sources: Alison Smith (2001), 'Frosty Reception Kills Off Iceland Organics', *Financial Times*, 23 January. Sean Poulter (2001), 'Why Iceland Went Cold on the Organic Food Crusade', *Daily Mail*, 23 January. James Robinson (2001), 'Organic Products Prove Cold Comfort for Iceland Chief', *Sunday Business*, 28 January. Maggie Urry (2001), 'Iceland Warns Again on Profits', *Financial Times*, 16 March.

Make it specially for me

In many sectors we are already seeing the customer demanding something different – customized products and services, not the mass-produced version that everyone else gets, and being treated individually. Pioneers of 'one-to-one marketing', Don Peppers and Martha Rogers[77], have founded a business to spread their philosophy of establishing a learning relationship with each customer, to tailor the product and how it is positioned to the needs of the individual. They argue that there are four steps: identifying your customers, differentiating among them, interacting with them, and customizing your product or service to meet their needs. The payoff is higher profit margins, greater customer loyalty, and a higher share of the customer's total spending, though they acknowledge that implementation is a huge barrier to achieving these payoffs.

However, whether it is the designer fruit juice (you specify the flavours and the proportions, and watch while it is mixed), the Dell computer (you choose the specifications and the machine is made to order), or the individualized package of financial services (for example, Halifax's Intelligence Finance product), there is huge power in treating customers as individuals.

'there is huge power in treating customers as individuals'

Instant gratification is just not fast enough . . .

But, I want it NOW! In many consumer sectors the truth is that waiting in line has been replaced by waiting online, and even that is not good enough. At one time, buying a book from an online supplier took two or three minutes instead of a trip to the shop and manual search. But you still had to wait days or weeks to get the book. New York now has one-hour delivery services – Kozmo.com and UrbanFetch.com – delivering books, videos, and even food and snack products. Sadly, however, the consumer one-hour delivery services have been unable to make a living – the consumer arm of UrbanFetch and BagsofTime.com in the USA, and ZapitOver.com in London, have gone out of business. The trouble is – I want it now, but I don't want to pay more – go back and re-read the section entitled 'Free is one of my favourite prices'.

A US writer, stunned by the absurdly long waiting times for those who try to buy furniture in Britain, and shocked to be asked to wait fourteen weeks for the delivery of a sofa, writes: 'Fourteen weeks is a period of time an American shopper simply cannot conceive. To an American shopper, there are just three spans of time: now, tomorrow at the very latest, and we'll look elsewhere. The idea of waiting fourteen weeks for anything, other than perhaps a baby, is unknown' [78]. But, of course, that is the US, or so it seems:

REALITY CHECK
WHEN I SAY 'NOW' . . .

In November 2000, Yates's Wine Lodge, Britain's oldest pub chain, was fined £1500 for delivering a £3.50 burger six minutes late. Actually, it was fined for refusing to honour its advertisement that offered refunds if it failed to serve food within fifteen minutes of an order being taken. The server's excuse that the offer did not apply when they were 'busy' did not cut any ice with the customer, or as it turned out with the judge.

Source: Paul Stokes (2000), '£1500 Fine for Burger That Was Six Minutes Late', *Daily Telegraph*, 30 November.

For countless years people buying houses have had to wait weeks and sometimes months to get a mortgage loan offer. The lenders' excuses were: we have to survey the property, we need to have legal searches done, there is much paperwork to be prepared, and so on. The reality is that what actually happens is that the paperwork sits on someone's desk for six weeks, while you are unable to buy your house without the mortgage. The 'survey' seems in reality to consist of little more than the surveyor driving past the house on his/her way to lunch. I have had many conversations with financial services executives, who tell me that they can agree a mortgage 'in principle' in a matter of days, and expect me to be impressed. They laugh at my view that there is no rational reason why I should not be able to choose the house in the morning, have the loan and conveyancing done from a standing start by lunchtime, and move into the new house in the afternoon. We are a long way from achieving that ideal, but things are starting to move.

In 1999 the online brokerage emfinance.com launched a service allowing housebuyers to arrange a mortgage in *eleven minutes*. By 2001, even NatWest was promising mortgage decisions in *six minutes*. Now let's sort out the surveyors and lawyers ...

Source: Clare Hall (1999), 'A Mortgage in Minutes on the Net', *Financial Mail on Sunday*, 31 October.

But don't make me angry[79] ...

Recent years have seen excessive use of the word 'rage' – as in 'air rage', 'store rage', 'trolley rage', even 'desk rage', to describe how angry and unpleasant new customers can become if they feel uncomfortable. The responses of airlines and retail stores have not been helpful – having air passengers arrested and refusing to fly them again, training shop assistants in self-defence, and so on. Time for a quick reality check, I think.

REALITY CHECK
CUSTOMER RAGE

Advice to airlines on 'Air Rage'

'Air Rage' will become a thing of the past if:

- you stop talking to the majority of your passengers as if you despised them, and treating them accordingly just to reinforce the impression;
- you stopped suffocating your passengers and making them ill because you can save money on the air used (and do not believe that we are so gullible that we believe you banned smoking on planes for health reasons – we know you did it to save money on cleaning and air supplies[80]);
- you stop turning the heat up on the plane to make people go to sleep, because it is so much more convenient for your cabin crew, because it makes us crabby;
- you stop cramming more seats in and expecting people to be happy with less and less leg room, and who cares about the occasional deep vein thrombosis;
- you finally get the idea that you are bus drivers and waiters in fancy suits, and start being a little nicer to the people who pay your wages.

Advice to retailers on 'Store Rage'

There are hundreds of thousands of reports of customer aggression towards shop employees each year. This is very sad. It is even sadder that it is not the managers (who are responsible for making customers angry because of the way they are treated) who get it in the neck, but their employees. The managerial response of issuing staff with security alarms and sending them on self-defence courses somewhat misses the point – why not spend the money improving the horrible shopping experience so that customers are less inclined to become angry?

There is no doubt that new customers are increasingly uninhibited and passionate in their complaints about bad service and poor value. For many years, British business was lulled into a false sense of security by the claim that British customers do not like to complain. In fact, this is no longer true. Evidence from the Henley Centre suggests that

'new customers are increasingly uninhibited and passionate in their complaints about bad service and poor value'

British consumers now complain more than American consumers. Film-maker, Michael Winner, who lists his hobby in Who's Who as 'being difficult', suggests 'The reason the British are complaining is that they have more to complain about, like the surly and unhelpful attitude in shops'[81]. However, the Somerfield supermarket's idea of banning a customer from their stores because he 'complains too much' is illustrative of how well some of us are responding to the demands of the new customer (not)[82]. And while we are talking about retail stores, a personal plea:

REALITY CHECK
SOME FREE ADVICE TO RETAIL MANAGERS

You may have a public address or tannoy system in your store. You may like speaking to your staff and/or customers. If so, then the rules are:

1 Shout if you really, really must.
2 Use the public address system if it pleases you.
3 **DO NOT DO BOTH AT THE SAME TIME!** It is extremely irritating to your customers.

By the way, it is not just consumers who get angry. In 2000, when Luton Airport announced plans to increase landing charges, easyJet's Stelio Haji-Ioannou was far from amused. His angry response was launched through Internet sites and press advertising and accused not just Luton Airport, but also Barclays Bank (Luton's major shareholder) of profiteering at the expense of easyJet's passengers.

And now entertain me . . .

'So now, the challenge is to manage the customer's experience as well'

In January 2001, a Mintel report underlined the apathy, lack of enthusiasm and indifference felt by British consumers towards shopping – and this at the peak sales season[83]. Chairman of the British Retail Consortium, Sir David Sieff, stated 'shopping must be more fun'[84]. So now, the challenge is to manage the customer's experience as well:

REALITY CHECK
THE NEW EXPERIENCE ECONOMY

Pine and Gilmore have described the 'experience economy' as one we are now entering. Companies should realize that they make *memories* not just products, and create a *stage* for generating greater value, not just deliver services. They believe that 'work is theatre and every business a stage'. In other words, successful companies do more than just sell goods and services, they create experiences that engage customers in a highly personal and highly memorable way – this is how you prevent your product or service becoming a commodity. Their examples are widespread:

- At theme restaurants like Hard Rock Café and Planet Hollywood, the food is no more than a prop for 'eatertainment'.
- At stores like Niketown, consumers are engaged in fun activities and events as 'shoppertainment' or 'entertailment' – Niketown is a show not a shop.
- The Rainforest Café chain has created a jungle representation with streams and jungle noise, and mist rising from the rocks, and its safari-suited servers announce 'Your adventure is about to begin' not just 'Your table is ready'.
- A Minneapolis computer installation and repair company is called the Geek Squad. Its 'special agents' are costumed in white shirts with thin black ties, carry badges, drive round in old cars, and turn a boring activity into a memorable encounter. So much so, that customers of this distinctive and memorable computer-repair experience buy Geek Squad T-shirts and lapel pins from the company's website.
- Silicon Graphs has a 'Visionarium Reality Center' in California, bringing customers and engineers together in real-time, three-dimensional product visualizations – customers can view, hear and touch product possibilities.

In this sense, experiences are a distinct economic offering, and one from which companies may in future gain revenue – in Israel, the 'Café Make Believe' is where people go to be seen and to socialize, so the café serves empty plates and mugs and charges for the social experience. Pine and Gilmore warn, however, that experiences offered must be 'refreshed', or they will cease to attract customers in the same way.

Sources: B. Joseph Pine II and James H. Gilmore (1998), 'Welcome to the Experience Economy', *Harvard Business Review*, July/August, 97–105. B. Joseph Pine and James H. Gilmore (1999), *The Experience Economy: Work is Theatre and Every Business a Stage*, Boston, MA: Harvard Business School Press.

'The joy of thinking about the experiences we provide for our customers and how memorable they are is the paradoxes it identifies'

The joy of thinking about the experiences we provide for our customers and how memorable they are is the paradoxes it identifies. For example, Alton Towers theme park has actually found that queuing can enhance the customers' enjoyment of a visit. Queues are designed to twist around so that the length is not intimidating, but also so that those waiting are exposed to those coming off the ride, to raise the level of anticipation. Closed circuit cameras spot queue jumpers, and invite them to rejoin the end of the line – but only just before they get on the ride. The park has found that customer enjoyment scores are actually lower on quiet days when they can get straight on the rides, than on busy days when they have to wait 15–20 minutes. Queuing appears to be part of making the experience memorable and enjoyable[85]. The challenge is to create and manage the experience, to entertain customers:

REALITY CHECK
AMUSING SHOPPERS

The Japanese retailer Don Quixote has abandoned the traditional orderly store layout and polite service on which Japanese retailers traditionally pride themselves. Instead, the stores are packed with shoppers shoulder-to-shoulder in narrow aisles packed with goods, and section changes are frequent. The busiest time is midnight (the stores are open 22 hours a day), when a carnival atmosphere builds up. Visiting the store appears to be almost addictive for some young consumers, as an alternative to visiting karaoke clubs and bars. Sales and profits are growing dramatically, in contrast to most recession-hit Japanese stores.

Takao Yasuda, president and founder, says the company does not think of itself as a retailer, but as 'an imaginative provider of space where young people can amuse themselves, especially at night ... I think it is going to become increasingly difficult for retailers to concentrate on selling things, especially in a traditional way. In the future, shops will need to have a strong amusement factor to keep people interested.'

Source: Naoka Nakamae (1999), 'Keeping Shoppers Amused is the Key to Success', *Financial Times*, 21 December.

In a similar way, Bernd Schmitt talks about 'experiential marketing' as turning away from traditional features and benefits and focusing on customer experiences[86]. He says, for example, that experiential marketers do not talk about product categories like 'shampoo', 'shaving cream' or 'hair dryer', they think about the consumption situation and 'grooming in the bathroom', and look at how goods and services can enhance this experience.

While marketing has long talked about the importance of the 'moment of truth' when the customer judges the product and the company, and things like the 'brand experience' or 'shopping experience', the new challenge is to develop new perspectives on how the experience can be enhanced to add value from the customer's perspective. This will require a completely new mind-set. The results may be revolutionary or just common-sense:

REALITY CHECK
BEAN-COUNTERS AND COFFEE

In 2001, Abbey National followed a successful pilot scheme with the development of 60 of its branches into sites run jointly with Costa, the coffee bar chain. Competitors immediately rubbished the move as one stage removed from branch closures (except Halifax, who have entered discussions with Starbucks!). There are two models: Costa taking space in Abbey National branches, or in sites where the bank no longer wants a full branch, Costa operates a coffee shop and Abbey National leases a corner of space. The bank is solving its unwanted branch problem, but more importantly creating a different environment. Increasing customer 'dwell time' and making branches a social meeting place, to impact on selling opportunities as well.

Source: Patrick Jenkins (2001), 'Abbey Banks on a Caffeine Injection to Perk up its Branches', *Financial Times*, 17/18 February.

And, believe it or not, Ford in Germany actually has a 'Head of Smells' – the smell of a new car is an important part of the experience to customers, so Ford tests whether the smell is right or needs adjusting. Consequently, Ford in Britain has a £35 000 electronic nose to test cars before they leave the factory.

'Ford in Germany actually has a "Head of Smells" – the smell of a new car is an important part of the experience to customers'

And now peel me a grape . . .

One extension of the experiential marketing trend is seen in the efforts that many companies are having to make to positively pamper their customers. The new customer seems to lay down the challenge: 'make me like you!'

David Freemantle argues that companies that prosper across many sectors and countries seem to do so in part by winning competitive advantage simply because their customers like them[87]. The argument is that companies like Nordstrom, Carphone Warehouse, and Marriott add emotional value to their businesses. A great deal of attention has focused on Daniel Goleman's books on 'emotional intelligence', which underline the need to unlock employees' emotions[88]. This suggests that adding emotional value to a business requires three things from front-line employees: emotional connectivity (the ability to make people like you); integrity or trustworthiness; and creativity to break the rules when necessary to provide excellent service.

'companies like Nordstrom, Carphone Warehouse, and Marriott add emotional value to their businesses'

But customer pampering is going far further than unlocking employees' emotional intelligence. For example, the developers of the Bluewater shopping mall in Kent took a 'total sensory design' approach to the retail environment, including 'male crèches', simplified road access to avoid stress, bigger parking spaces to avoid feeling 'crowded', and non-shiny floors because shiny means slippery and increases worries about falling over[89]. Designing retail environments extends to smells, noise levels and types, colours, lighting, traffic flows, to shape the customer's shopping experiences and perceptions[90]. In 2001, we even saw the London Underground perfuming its stations to relax the atmosphere – however, in this case the hoped-for increase in customer satisfaction may be a long time coming, as one passenger remarked in disgust: 'I would dodge dead rats and litter, if this would make the trains arrive on time'[91]!

People are making a living now out of showing retailers how to build customer 'amenability' into their stores: a 'landing strip' – space just inside the shop where shoppers can acclimatize without being bombarded with information; leaving enough space between fixtures to avoid the dreaded 'butt brush' (people jostled from behind move away from the products); providing seating, because 'a chair says "we care"'[92]. The thinking is clear – if your shops are not nice places that make customers comfortable, they will not stay long, they will buy less, and they certainly will not come back.

And make me feel good about buying things from you . . . make all the bad stuff in the world go away

Apart from excellent service and enhanced environments, part of being liked by customers seems to be increasingly about much bigger issues too – we are being held responsible for the woes of the world and being required to do something about them.

Al Dunlap was a chief executive of the old school – he worked for Sir James Goldsmith and Kerry Packer, and at various times managed Scott Paper and Sunbeam. He was known as 'Chainsaw Al' because of his ruthlessness in managing companies. In his book *Mean Business*, Al rubbished what he saw as sentimental approaches to business: 'The most ridiculous term heard in the boardroom today is stakeholders. Stakeholders! Every time I hear that word, I ask "How much did they pay for their stake?"'. His most famous comment on business was 'If you want a friend, get a dog' [93]. If only life were that simple . . . [94].

In the new world, we are required to be seen to behave ethically and to display high levels of social responsibility. Bear in mind – behaving ethically and being socially responsible will not guarantee commercial success, but it may be an important part of survival. It is already very clear that media attention, Internet sites, the spread of organized lobby groups, and enhanced sensitivities mean that if you get caught behaving unethically or offending against human rights, you will have no place to hide:

> *'we are being held responsible for the woes of the world and being required to do something about them'*

> *'if you get caught behaving unethically or offending against human rights, you will have no place to hide'*

REALITY CHECK
THE NIKE EXPERIENCE

Sports clothing and footwear company Nike grew from Phil Knights' $37 investment to establish one of the world's most recognized brands, and $9 billion sales in 2000, making it the leader in its field. Nike was seen as a prototype of the hollow company – outsourcing its production globally.

Since the mid-1990s, Nike has been fighting attacks on its record in human rights and employee abuse. In 1995, Christian Aid attacked pay and conditions in Nike's Asian factories – they estimated producing a $100 pair of shoes cost Nike only $3 – and there were media reports of knife attacks on a Nike factory employee for attempting to organize labour and establish an independent trade union. In 1996, CBS broadcast a programme about Nike factory workers being subjected to physical abuse, illegally low wages, and excessive working hours in Vietnam. While the CBS programme was never re-aired (Nike was a large sponsor of CBS Olympic Games coverage), accusations of brutality towards factory employees continued to emerge. The Worldwide Day of Action Against Nike was declared as 18 October 1997.

A leaked Ernst & Young audit in 1997 reported serious violations of Vietnamese environmental and labour laws, and the flow of public attacks on Nike continued. In 2000, an Oxfam report produced further evidence of verbal and physical abuse of workers in Indonesia Nike factories. The same year, Phil Knights withdrew sponsorship deals worth $30 million from US university sports teams, where there had been protests against sweatshops. In the autumn of 2000, a BBC Panorama programme exposed Nike as using child labour in a Cambodian sweatshop. The early part of 2001 saw the sackings of Nike workers at Mexican plants for organizing labour strikes for better conditions and less abuse.

Nike claims to have the industry's most elaborate system of internal and external monitoring, and that their strict code of conduct is enforced by internal and external audits of its 700 factories. The company is a member or founder of more than a dozen human rights organizations. Oxfam and others say this is a sham, and that Nike is more concerned about silencing its critics and undermining their credibility, than actually improving its human rights practices.

Energetic consumers have not ceased in their attempts to link Nike's brand to exploitative working conditions. In 2001, Nike offered a service where the buyer of their sports shoes could have a name or message printed on the shoes alongside the Nike logo to personalize the product. Large numbers of consumers asked for the word 'Sweatshop' to be printed next to the Nike logo on their sport shoes.

Source: Niall C. Piercy (2001), unpublished working paper, Cardiff University, February.

Nike is not alone in this dilemma. For example, Wal-Mart has also been attacked for the working conditions found in its supplier factories in China, and was dropped by two major investment groups as a result[95]. The situation emerging is almost that you will be held responsible for the human rights and social responsibility standards of your suppliers. This goes deeper than 'public relations'.

For example, the response to the attacks on its competitor Nike has stimulated the German sports clothing manufacturer Adidas to appoint a global director of social and environmental affairs.

Adidas sees its social affairs policy as a defensive tool to be used cautiously: 'We see our human rights policy as a natural part of being good corporate citizens. Emphasizing it would only detract from the brand'[96].

This gets to the heart of what is being called 'strategic corporate philanthropy' – the goals are to enhance corporate image and to build trust in the company and its brands. So much for being nice guys!

Indeed, in 2001 the Co-Operative Bank, which has long aggressively promoted its green and ethical stance in its advertising, claimed that it made an additional £14–17 million in pre-tax profits because of those policies. They also suggest that as many as one in five of their customers joined them because of their ethics and green stance[97].

But it goes further. Aside from avoiding situations that tarnish the brand, management faces new types of demand to solve problems in the world, that have not previously been thought to be the responsibility of commercial organizations. For example, early in 2001 the 1000 largest companies in the world were 'invited' to donate $500 000 each to a new trust fund to alleviate poverty in developing countries, under a proposal tabled by the Italian government for discussion by the Group of Seven (G7) leading industrial companies[98].

'Aside from avoiding situations that tarnish the brand, management faces new types of demand to solve problems in the world'

Even further, Oxfam accuses the pharmaceutical industry of defending its drug patents only to 'conduct an undeclared drugs war against the world's poorest countries'[99]. The pressure to renounce patent rights in selected countries does nothing less than to ask commercial companies to assume governmental responsibilities at the expense of their shareholders. While protesting that 'the industry cannot act as the National Health Service to the World', in March 2001 the US drugs group Merck agreed to provide AIDS medicines to developing countries at cost, and published those prices to allow competitors to equal them[100], and the following month a group of leading companies dropped their legal action against the South African government to protect AIDS drug patent rights[101]. The issue has become protecting the trust people have in your company and its brand. In 2001, GlaxoSmithKline came under pressure from institutional investors in alliance with Oxfam to make some drugs available in Africa at lower prices, and a company spokesman remarked: 'If millions of Africans are dying of preventable diseases and one reason is that drug companies are charging too much, you have a serious reputational risk.'[102].

What we are seeing is the emergence a kind of 'focused responsiveness', with companies watching, learning, retreating in places, modifying policies where needed, because public opinion impacts on customers and investors. The supermarkets did not remove genetically modified food from the shelves because of the environmental lobby, they did it because it was what their customers wanted (and besides it was the biotech companies like Monsanto that took the real financial hit). Pepsico did not cease trading with Burma because of that country's appalling human rights record, but because they judged the risk of damage to their brand outweighed the financial gain of staying in Burma[103]. What it comes down to is that smart companies watch and respond to public opinion to avoid being damaged.

'smart companies watch and respond to public opinion to avoid being damaged'

In fact, the May day protestors in London in 2001 seem to have a grudge against everyone – just about any company you can name is accused of exploiting workers, wreaking havoc in the Third World, or polluting some aspect of the environment[104]. In fact, it has almost got to the stage that if you are not on someone's hate list, you start to wonder if you are doing something wrong! Just imagine the day you get a phone call from your CEO saying 'I am embarrassed in front of my peers – our company is so insignificant that no-one is protesting against us. Do something!' Never fear, help is on its way:

REALITY CHECK
A NEW ANTI-BUSINESS PROTEST GROUP IS FORMED

I wish to announce the formation of a new anti-business protest group: the International Domain for Ideological Opportunities to Terrorize Someone (IDIOTS). The target is all companies who are not exploiters, polluters, environmental damagers, or guilty of any other such behaviour. You, we find guilty of denying hard-working activists the right to protest against you, and this is a flagrant and cruel abuse of our human rights. You have been warned!

However, I would hate for anyone to think that these issues do not matter – a YouGov Opinion survey on corporate responsibility in 2001 found that 72 per cent of shoppers claimed that their decision to buy from a company would be influenced by whether they believed it to be socially responsible[105]. However, they really do have to believe it, and they will check:

REALITY CHECK

TELLING THE TREE-HUGGING HIPPIES PORKIE-PIES DOESN'T WORK ANY MORE EITHER

In its summer 2000 re-branding, BP launched the slogan 'Beyond Petroleum ... ' and a new sunburst logo. The intention was to signal its broad vision of the energy business. Later CEO Sir John Browne said 'beyond petroleum just means that we are giving up on the old mindset, the old thinking that oil companies had to be dirty, secretive and arrogant'. Of course, it also helped that it suggested a new environmental awareness and socially responsible stance in BP's global operations. By the 2001 AGM, campaigners had started to use the slogan to beat BP over the head for its environmental and human rights record. Greenpeace was demanding timetables for BP to cut greenhouse gas emission, invest in renewable energy, and phase out production and sale of fossil fuels, and to live up to its 'Beyond Petroleum ...' promise. Attacking BP's investment in Tibet, campaigners suggested that far from standing for 'Beyond Petroleum ...', BP actually stood for 'Beijing's Partners' or 'Backing Persecution', and demanded BP withdraw from China. Together, Greenpeace and the Free Tibet Campaign had mustered more than 11 per cent of the proxy votes at the AGM and they had to be heard. Adamant that BP was not actually giving up the oil and gas business, or withdrawing from PetroChina, Sir John admitted somewhat ruefully that the time had come to ditch the slogan. The reality is that an enterprise whose main job is to extract hydrocarbons will never really be beyond petroleum, even if it does embrace cleaner energy sources. Making promises you cannot keep is not smart, because people will not let you forget them.

Sources: David Buchan (2001), 'BP Driven to the Back of Beyond', *Financial Times*, 20 April. Sophie Barker (2001), 'Browne Hails BP Oil Strategy Amid Logo Row', *Daily Telegraph*, 20 April. Alex Brummer (2001), 'BP's Wrong Shade of Green', *Daily Mail*, 20 April.

And there will be no secrets any more . . . now, get in that goldfish bowl and stay there while I keep an eye on you, because I'm in charge now!

The new customer demands to know what we are doing and why, and if they don't like it, they want us to stop. The new watchword is transparency, and it is going to be difficult for us to live with – see the next section where we consider the management challenges in this new era.

Patricia Seybould argues that the net result is that the customer takes control of an industry and reshapes it from outside – as in the music business and its current struggle to control music downloading from the Internet (see pp. 179–82). She says that managers no longer determine the destiny of a company – customers do. Her advice to companies is fight the customer revolution if you want, but you will lose – better to start practising 'sweet surrender' to the inevitable[106].

'fight the customer revolution if you want, but you will lose'

And clear up after yourselves!

The new economy increasingly imposes additional responsibilities and costs on business to pay for the implications of the consumption of their products, in ways that would simply never have occurred before:

REALITY CHECK

WHO PAYS FOR GETTING RID OF OLD CARS?

The European 'end-of-life vehicles' directive will force car manufacturers to cover the costs of recycling old vehicles, as well as ensuring that recyclable components make up 85 per cent of each vehicle's weight. The deal is that even though you thought you sold the car to someone else – you still pick up the tab for disposing of it when it becomes old. Although not in force until 2007, 2001 saw Volkswagen setting aside £330 million as ELV compliance costs, with BMW and DaimlerChrysler setting aside around £150 million each in 2001. Industry analysts estimate the ELV directive costs at £115 per vehicle for the twelve million cars scrapped in Europe annually, costing the industry around £1.4 billion annually. The German car companies campaigned unsuccessfully against the ELV directive. General Motors and Ford are now waiting to see if US authorities may seek to adopt similar regulations. The EU is also pursuing similar policies against manufacturers of electrical goods – from refrigerators and televisions to toasters – and other sectors are likely to be pursued later.

Sources: Tim Burt (2001), 'VW is Set for £330m Recycling Provision', *Financial Times*, 12 February. Jonathan Guthrie (2001), 'Industry Left to Bear the Burden', *Financial Times*, 19 March.

What is really intriguing is where this line of thought goes next. Should the breweries be made responsible for public conveniences? Should the chocolate companies have to pay for free dentists? I know it sounds silly, but who knows? Certainly, the role of the Environmental Manager has become established in many companies and is expanding[107].

What did you just call me?

New customers are also less than amused when they find out what some service providers call their customers behind their backs. For example, consider the 'secret' acronyms scribbled on hospital charts by doctors – 'secret' until one of them ratted, that is[108]:

To be found where?	Acronym	Translation
Patient's notes	SIG	Stroppy Ignorant Git
Patient's notes	PAFO	P(drunk) And Fell Over
Child patient's notes	FLK	Funny Looking Kid
Patients' notes	GROLIES	*Guardian* Reader Of Limited Intelligence in Ethnic Skirt
Patients' notes	FAS	Fat and Stupid
Patients' notes	NFH	Normal for Here
Female patients' notes	TUBE	Totally Unnecessary Breast Examination
Discharge letter	TF BUNDY	Totally F*****. But Unfortunately Not Dead Yet

This is wonderful laddish humour. Terribly amusing, until you may reflect that this is you and me they are talking about. Maybe such attitudes towards your paying customers by doctors helps explain why there are now more alternative medical practitioners in the UK than doctors, and private medicine is booming?

The challenges of the new era of value

Enough said, I think, to make the point that the sophisticated customer is going to be tough to live with. Indeed, the underlying challenge for

'the sophisticated customer is going to be tough to live with'

management is summarized beautifully by a group of Cranfield writers as 'creating a company for customers'[109], where market-driven processes pervade the whole of a company. The change involved for most companies is massive. Not changing is not an option. Gary Hamel nicely summarizes why not: 'Those that live by the sword will be shot by those who don't'[110]. But the demands for survival in this era are getting tougher by the day.

Integrity

For a start, a growing number of 'stakeholders' – customers, suppliers, staff, shareholders, the community and interest groups – have assumed the right to make moral judgements about us[111], which can have huge impacts throughout the business and on our freedom to operate:

REALITY CHECK

IT'S NOT OVER UNTIL THE FAT CAT RESIGNS

Malcolm Walker is the man who built the Iceland chain as an innovative and dynamic national food retailer from a single store selling unpackaged frozen peas and fish fingers in scoopfuls from plastic washing-up bowls. Late in 2000, Mr Walker was planning to step back from line responsibilities to allow new CEO Stuart Rose to run what had become a £5.5 billion business. Mr Rose left the company unexpectedly in November 2000. At about this time, Mr Walker sold £13.5 million of Iceland shares at an average price of 339p. When the company issued a profits warning, after a bad Christmas trading period, share prices collapsed to just over 100p. Shareholder and media reactions to news of Mr Walker's share dealing was furious and persistent.

At the end of January 2001, Mr Walker returned early from holiday to resign from his company, with the statement 'In view of the intense media interest and speculation of the last few days, I have decided it would be in the best interests of the company, its employees and its shareholders for me now to resign completely, to allow our new chief executive to get to grips with running the business without unnecessary distractions.'

The costs of being accused of having behaved badly had a severe effect, in spite of 30 years creating a major business from nothing. The issue is not simply transparency, but external perceptions of management integrity.

Sources: Maggie Urry (2001), 'Walker Quits Amid Iceland Slide' and 'A Bizarre End to an Extraordinary Career', *Financial Times*, 1 February. Kate Rankine (2001), 'Grimsey Sees Frost-Hard Times Ahead for Iceland', *Daily Telegraph*, 1 February.

Those moral judgements may spring up at any time and from anywhere, and they can tarnish our reputation and brand strength in profound and lasting ways:

REALITY CHECK

... AND THERE IS NO STATUTE OF LIMITATIONS ON MORALITY

In 2001, IBM stood accused of complicity with Nazi Germany in the 1930s and 1940s. Lawyers involved in the Holocaust-era cases are looking into the records of 100 US companies. IBM is accused of knowingly supplying punch-card technology, which was used by the Nazis to organize their campaign of genocide. The goal appears to be to force IBM to contribute further to the $5 billion compensation deal for slave- and forced-labourers, agreed in 2001 with German industry.

The trigger for this action against IBM was provided by the publication of a book *IBM and the Holocaust* by Edwin Black in 2001. Black claims that IBM punch-card sorters were used to facilitate all aspects of Nazi persecution – from the identification of Jews in censuses to the management of concentration camp slave labour. He writes: 'For the first time in history an anti-semite had automation on his side. Hitler didn't do it alone. He had help.' Indeed, Nazi demand for IBM technology was great enough to require an IBM factory be built near Berlin. IBM creator and then chairman, Thomas J. Watson, is said to have openly expressed admiration for Hitler and was awarded a medal by him. Certainly, an IBM Hollerith D-11 card sorter takes pride of place in the Holocaust museum in Washington. There are suggestions that IBM's German subsidiary continued to receive covert support from other parts of the company, even after the US and Germany were at war.

IBM stands to lose not just money in additional compensation payments, but damage to one of the world's most famous brands, bad enough to raise entry barriers to some markets, like Israel. The bottom-line is at the start of the twenty-first century a multinational company is being damaged by accusations about actions of company executives 60 years earlier – it is unlikely that the executives in question are still alive, there is no proof that there was anything illegal in their actions at the time; there is no real question that the IBM goal was profit not the support of ideology. Nonetheless, the problem for IBM management is very real and very contemporary.

Sources: Richard Wolffe and John Authers (2001), 'IBM Legal Bombshell Threatens Landmark Holocaust Deal', *Financial Times*, 15 February. Edwin Black (2001), *IBM and the Holocaust*, Little Brown. Tom Rhodes (2001), 'IBM Link to the Final Solution Revealed', *Sunday Times*, 11 February.

'cries of "hey, we're in marketing, we don't DO integrity" no longer carry any weight'

Issues of integrity, probity, and clean have been elevated to strategic importance for companies – and cries of 'hey, we're in marketing, we don't DO integrity' no longer carry any weight.

Transparency

This new era is also one of transparency – people demand to know what we have done, how we have done it, and what we are planning to do. Generally, they do not want to know these things out of idle curiosity. They want to know, so they can stop us doing things they do not like. The movement towards transparency has gone so far that some people get very angry with us if we do not share commercial secrets with them.

REALITY CHECK

EVER HEARD THE PHRASE 'MIND YOUR OWN BUSINESS'?

In February 2001, the Anglo-Dutch steelmaker CORUS announced job losses in the UK of 6000, to try to stem losses of more than £1 million a day. Government ministers led a blistering attack on the company, and its chairman Sir Brian Moffat, not so much because of the job losses, but because the company had refused to inform them of their intentions. The government expectation was that they had a right to know the plans of a commercial organization before its employees and shareholders.

It subsequently became clear that Sir Brian had been pressured by Prime Minister Tony Blair and Trade and Industry Secretary Stephen

Byers, to reveal the plans, and had even experienced the wrath of Blair's abrasive 'minder', Alastair Campbell. The company chairman took the view that steel is not a nationalized industry, and there was no good reason why he should tell the government his plans; Sir Brian commented: 'We were not prepared to go into detail with the government before first talking to our employees. Leaks from the government have been all too prevalent in the past'. CORUS share values rose as the market reacted favourably to its actions.

What is amazing is that this CEO's refusal to give in to these demands made headline news. What is illustrative is the expectation of ministers and media that they have the right to know company plans first, and the likelihood that this mood will continue. It is revealing that subsequently government MPs published a detailed criticism of CORUS's business strategy, as well as criticisms of the company for 'excessive secrecy' – it seems they wanted to make the company's strategic decisions for it! Incidentally, their credentials for making business decisions seem somewhat suspect.

Sources: 'The Man Who Refused to Entertain Blair Project Chorus Line', *Daily Telegraph*, 2 February 2001. Roland Gribben (2001), 'The Man Who Would Not be Bullied by Blair', *Daily Telegraph*, 2 February. Peter Marsh (2001), 'MPs Attack Steelmaker's Business Strategy', *Financial Times*, 15 March.

The critical truth is that the pressure for transparency comes from those who want to *change* what we do. The consequences of open information are only just beginning to be realized. Senior managers are only just beginning to see aggressive investor hostility towards their generous bonuses – and have been shocked by the willingness of investor groups to manipulate public opinion through the media, figuring that if there is one thing that frightens directors more than their shareholders, it is their customers[112].

'the pressure for transparency comes from those who want to change what we do'

At a whole different level, the case of Huntingdon Life Sciences underlines how big an impact transparency and openness can have on management and customers (see pp. 125–9). Many anticipate that similar pressures will spread to other sectors where people disapprove of how we do business.

Nonetheless, the pressure towards greater transparency continues to grow at an unprecedented rate. It seems we are not allowed commercial secrets any more: government proposals include forcing companies to publish complete details of directors' earnings alongside information about performance against competitors[113]; in 2000 British supermarkets were screaming 'rape' at proposals that they should be obliged to show what they paid suppliers for goods next to their retail prices on products on the shelf[114], notwithstanding the launch in France of just such a (admittedly problematic) system for fresh fruit and vegetables[115]; British car distributors are fighting a rearguard action against being obliged to show what they paid for the car, as well as their selling prices on used and new vehicles (as commonly occurs in the US).

Some of these proposals are actually pretty good ideas – the point is that good idea or not, the chances are you have no choice any more: you will tell all, whether you want to or not.

E-Literacy

This is an era where managers will have to be genuinely literate in information technology. With the Internet transforming the way businesses operate and e-business redefining whole industries (see Chapter 4.com), you will no longer be able to survive without an effective information technology strategy. The issue is becoming 'e-business or out of business'[116] – it is as simple as that.

'The issue is becoming "e-business or out of business" – it is as simple as that'

Manage long-term

Taking a long-term view has always been advocated and paid lip-service in management. Evidence is emerging that there is great competitive strength in managing for longevity. Arie de Geus argues that companies should not measure success by short-term returns to shareholders but by how long they survive in the face of constant change[117]. His research found that companies in Europe, the US and Japan lived on average little longer than 12 years. The biggest companies lasted only 40 years, yet some companies survive for centuries; for example, Sumitomo in Japan was 400 years old. De Geus' observation was that nowhere in the natural world would you find such a gap between average and potential life span.

A similar conclusion is reached in a study by James Collins and Jerry Porras of 'most admired' companies[118]. They concluded that the most successful companies have a purpose beyond making a profit, and sometimes act in ways that damage their short-term profits, because they believe that to do otherwise would go against their business philosophies, but they generate higher shareholder returns in the long run.

Manage talent

Managers know about managing hierarchy – this is what we have been trained to do. In the new era, the challenge is to manage talent, as possibly the most important company resource of all.

Market strategies ultimately depend on human talent. In future, they will depend on new kinds of talent – in technology, in managing ambiguous relationships inside and outside the company, in 'sensing' market change and understanding new types of customer, in coping with 'empowerment' and team-based working, in building flexibility and propensity to change, in leading into new areas and working in new ways that do not depend on formal authority[119]. The challenge to managers is how to find, nurture and retain these new talents, and it is not likely to be easy to do any of these.

New economy visionaries, such as Ridderstrale and Nordstrom, whose philosophy is 'funky business', argue that the only unique asset a company has is the brainpower of its employees – in that sense, employees' ideas and imagination *are* the company and that is how we have to lead[120].

'employees' ideas and imagination are the company and that is how we have to lead'

Traditional managers may have to learn to bite their tongues in the face of the demands from talented people, who know about skill shortages and what they can do to a firm's competitiveness[121]. Required employee benefits may now include minding the baby or walking the dog or planning holidays in 'lifestyle management' packages[122] – or 'napping rooms' at work. Indeed, one US company recently found itself arranging to exhume an employee's dead dog to move it to his new address[123]. The power of the new 'internal customer' who used to be called an employee was reinforced by published polls on the best companies to work for in the UK[124] – out of interest, the top five were: Cisco Systems, Microsoft, Capital One, Timpson and Asda. The issue has become one not of offering jobs to people, but of 'competing for talent'[125] – one manager describes the issue: 'We must think of our company less in product-market terms and more as collectors of great people'[126]. This is why one of the richest men in the world – Microsoft's Bill Gates – who is feted by presidents and prime ministers, sees no activity as more important than meeting superior employment candidates to convince them they should join Microsoft[127].

One of the tasks companies face increasingly is making themselves perceived as good places to work, to attract and keep staff, and also to benefit reputation and relationships with customers[128]. This is likely to place yet more emphasis on internal marketing to parallel external marketing (see Chapter 14).

Indeed, even once you have the talent, the problem becomes keeping it. The average tenure of chief executives of the FT 100 companies in the UK and the Fortune 100 companies in the US is four years and falling[129]. This explains why some companies have established the post of chief morale officer – though admittedly at McKinley Marketing Partners, the post is held by McKinley 'Mac' Boggs, a golden retriever who attends all corporate meetings, has his own business cards and authors a column in the company newsletter[130].

Manage surprise

'Managers have to be prepared to be surprised when the unpredictable or unlikely happens'

Managers have to be prepared to be surprised when the unpredictable or unlikely happens. You cannot predict when your airplanes are going to crash, but you know it is a risk, so you can have a response ready – you will be judged by how well you cope[131]. You cannot predict product tampering (such as cyanide pills into headache capsules in the supermarket) but if it happens you can respond, if you are prepared (Johnson & Johnson regained product leadership for the cyanide-contaminated Tylenol product by launching the first tamper-proof packs). These are the moments in a company's life that can build or destroy reputations and brands[132]:

REALITY CHECK
CLASS 'A' DISASTER

In 1997, Daimler-Benz was in its worst crisis for 50 years because of an imaginary elk. This was the occasion when the new Mercedez 'A Class' – the Baby Benz – was forced off the market, after Swedish motoring journalists conducted the 'elk test' (violent swerving to simulate avoiding a head-on with a stupid moose). Although most modern cars pass the test, the Baby Benz rolled and landed on its roof. Pictures of the crumpled car (and many 'elk jokes') spread rapidly. The company responded by offering new tyres with the car (at a cost of DM50 million) and an electronic stabilizing system as standard (at an additional cost of DM100 million a year), but after 3000 cancelled orders they were forced to take the car off the market for three months to undertake chassis modifications.

Rumours circulated that the company had stretched itself too far too quickly to get into the mass market. Further damage to reputation ensued when the company delayed the launch of its new Smart car because of similar safety concerns – it rolled too – at an estimated cost of DM300 million. Interestingly, the Trabant (the East German car derided as a mechanical joke) did pass the 'elk test', leading a German TV station to end its news bulletins for a while with film of a Trabbi driving at high speed with a stuffed, and somewhat startled, elk in the passenger seat. Daimler-Benz executives were allegedly unamused.

Sources: Rufus Olins and Matthew Lynn (1997), 'A-Class Disaster', *Sunday Times*, 16 November. Haig Simonian (1997), 'Daimler Delays Smart Car Over Safety Worries', *Financial Times*, 19 December.

It may lead you into some outlandish areas of thought. Cannabis is an illegal drug in Britain – though estimated to be a £1.8 billion industry. There is a remote possibility that cannabis could be legalized. Part of strategic thinking in the UK brewing industry is to do with the substantial implications for product marketing if cannabis were legalized – and they are more than open about this[133].

On the other hand, who would have expected Gerald Ratner, chief executive of Ratners, to repeatedly rubbish his company's jewellery products by comparing them (disadvantageously) to prawn sandwiches in front of City audiences – which led to the effective collapse of the company and the end of his career. Worse, in 2000 Antisoma, a small UK biotechnology company, lost 40 per cent of its market value in a single day, when an obscure Ph.D. student published a report that cast doubt on its main product[134]. Anyway, did anyone really expect to see a $10 disposable mobile phone, or self-cleaning windows, or washing machines with no water, or toothbrushes that work without toothpaste (all of which are on the way)? Learn to live with it – some things are always going to be a surprise!

'Learn to live with it – some things are always going to be a surprise!'

Manage paradox

The days of clarity and stability for managers in a largely predictable world have gone. The organizations in which we work create ambiguity and paradox:

- you have to focus and specialize (on key customers and market targets) but still be all things to all people (to protect company reputation);

- you have to collaborate and build relationships with suppliers and customers, but still compete 'fairly' to avoid offending the Mergers and Monopolies Commission or consumer interest groups;
- you have to deal with other companies, while a single company may be your supplier, your customer, your collaborator *and* your competitor all at the same time – I have this wonderful picture in mind of an executive from a branded goods firm sitting down with an executive from Asda because they are *collaborating* on supply chain management, but Asda is also a major *customer* for the brand and a *competitor* because they have an own-label version, and meantime the brand leader is *suing* Asda because the own-label infringes their brand's packaging copyright, now do they shake hands or hit each other?;
- you have to get better at going to market – but quite possibly without a marketing department;
- you have to manage a 'balanced scorecard' [135] – shareholder interest, customer interests, employee interests, and so on – but find a way through conflicts of interest;
- you have to build trusting and close relationships with customers and suppliers – but you can only do that by breaking relationships (the ones your competitors have with those same customers).

This is matched by paradox in the marketplace too:

REALITY CHECK
WHERE ARE WE?

Situation: A large direct mail campaign is to take place at a company. You find the direct mail pieces piled up in the mail room after they should have gone out. The reason is that the company will not send the material out until it has been blessed by a local religious leader and he cannot be found.

Question: Where are you?

Likely Answers: The developing world, the Far East, Outer Mongolia.

True Answer: You are at the prestigious headquarters of a sophisticated health insurance company in the mid-West of the USA, where they take their religion very seriously.

Coping with complexity, unpredictability and conflict within and outside the organization is one of the major challenges to managers.

Manage change and innovation

We are repeatedly told that the sign of successful companies is their capacity for change – particularly radical transformational change[136] – and for innovation in products, processes and structures[137]. This is fine but what it actually means is that we, as managers, have to find better ways of managing turbulence and sustaining change (as opposed to surviving the latest 'initiative' or 'project' and going back to the way things used to be). We will have much more to say about this challenge later.

'we, as managers, have to find better ways of managing turbulence and sustaining change'

And do it all cheaper!

And, if you expect more resources to do all these new things you are probably out of luck. You are going to get less resources to do more!

REALITY CHECK
THE AWKWARD QUESTIONS ABOUT BRANDS, RELATIONSHIPS AND VALUE

How well do we understand the sophisticated customer in our markets? What are the new demands that are surfacing that will change how we do business? How soon will the demands of the sophisticated customer be the demands of all our customers?

How much of our marketing is still stuck in the transactional era – spend some time with the salesforce, the telephone salespeople, and the Internet 'help desk' before answering?

How much of our thinking still relies on 'blind branding' – investing in a brand because it is what we have always done, instead of asking how the brand creates value for customers?

Have we been seduced in our company by 'relationship rhetoric' so we believe that the answer to every problem is to spend more money on building customer relationships? Do we actually know if our customers want to have a relationship with us, and what type of relationship?

Are we ready for an era where the focus is customer value? Do we know what drives customer value for different customers and what value means to them?

How many of the demands of 'the new customer' have surfaced in our marketplace, and how many more are on the way? How well are we prepared for these changes in how business is done?

How well are we set-up to manage profitably and sustainably in the new era which is opening up?

Who needs to be addressing these issues in our company, and how do we share these ideas with them?

So, what next?

What I have tried to do is to frighten you. What I hope I have also done is to communicate just how exciting and amazing the new world is, and how much fun it is to abandon old ideas and build new and better ways of doing things. The challenge of delivering value consistently to the sophisticated customer is awesome. Being a successful manager in this new era will be demanding, and it will be different.

'The challenge of delivering value consistently to the sophisticated customer is awesome'

Now, the next stage is to add some additional dimensions to these challenges: I want to look at the e-revolution; the route to total integration of efforts around customer value in the process of going to market; and then we can look at what it takes to get the creativity and innovation back into market strategy. Then we can lay out the strategic pathway.

Notes and references

1. I have colleagues who refer to the new way of things as the 'customer as tyrant' – my response is to ask that if the customer has become a tyrant, who made him/her become like that?
2. Sarah Womack and David Millward (2000), 'Dome "Failed After Treating Public Like Morons"', *Daily Telegraph*, 29 December.
3. Simon Buckby (1998), 'Consumer Choices for Marketers', *Financial Times*, 11 November.
4. Robin Wensley (1997), 'The Customer Knows Best', *Marketing Business*, May, 61.
5. Alan Mitchell (1997), 'Evolution', *Marketing Business*, March, 29.
6. Ron Zemke (1997), 'Quality Is Not Dead: Consumers Just Expect a Lot More of It', *Marketing News*, 31 March.
7. Michael Treacy and Fred Wiersema (1995), *The Discipline of Market Leaders*, London: Harper Collins.

8. Alan Mitchell (2001), 'Discovering the New World', *Marketing Business*, February, 29. Alan Mitchell (2001), *Right Side Up: Building Brands In the Age of the Organized Consumer*, London: Harper Collins.
9. Luke Johnson (1996), 'Advertising May Not be Good for Business', *Sunday Business*, 4 August.
10. Sean Poulter (1997), 'Bad Taste Billboards', *Daily Mail*, 15 April.
11. Marcus Fernandez, creative director at Myrtle, quoted in Tom Leonard (2000), 'Don't Mention the A-Word, We Are Media Neutral Now', *Daily Telegraph*, 17 March.
12. Robert Shrimsley (1999), 'Consumer Power Will Help Tackle "Rip-Off Britain"', *Daily Telegraph*, 23 July.
13. Des Wilson, quoted in Matthew Lynn and Rufus Olins (1995), 'Under Pressure', *Sunday Times*, 10 September.
14. Geraldine Bedell (2001), 'Radicals Required', *The Business*, 28 April, 29–32.
15. Robert Shrimsley (2001), 'Business Leaders Dread Consumer Group's Wrath', *Financial Times*, 17 April.
16. David Lewis (2000), *The Soul of the New Consumer*, London: Nicholas Brealey Publishing.
17. Joan Voight (2000), 'The Consumer Rebellion', *Adweek*, 10 January, 46–50.
18. Caroline Chandy (2001), *The Dissatisfaction Syndrome*, London: Publicis Trends Group.
19. Robert Jones (2000), *The Big Idea*, London: Harper Collins Business.
20. Alan Mitchell (1997), 'Evolution', *Marketing Business*, March, 27.
21. Sergio Zyman (2000), *The End of Marketing As We Know It*, New York: Harper Collins.
22. Douglas Rushkoff (2000), *Coercion*, New York: Little Brown.
23. Eugene H. Fram (1997), 'The Customer Penalty Box', *Marketing Management*, Fall, 60–63. Eugene H. Fram and Michael S. McCarthy (1999), 'The True Price of Penalties', *Marketing Management*, Fall, 49–56.
24. 'Brand Names "Use Dirty Tricks" To Keep Prices Up', *Sunday Times*, 21 January 2001.
25. Richard Tomkins (2000), 'Selling to the Sated', *Financial Times*, 22 March.
26. John Willman (2000), 'Brands on the Run', *Financial Times*, 29 October.
27. Richard Tomkins (2001), 'Brands are the New Religion, says Advertising Agency', *Financial Times*, 1 March.
28. Alan Mitchell (1997), 'Evolution', *Marketing Business*, July/August, 39.
29. Peter Doyle (2000), *Value-Based Marketing: Marketing Strategies for Corporate Growth and Shareholder Value*, Chichester: John Wiley.
30. John Deighton, quoted in Alan Mitchell (1997), 'Evolution', *Marketing Business*, July/August, 39.
31. Christian Gronroos (1994), 'From Marketing Mix to Relationship Marketing', *Management Decision*, **32** (2), 4–20.
32. Martin A. Christopher, Adrian Payne and David Ballantyne (1991), *Relationship Marketing*, Oxford: Butterworth-Heinemann.
33. Evert Gummesson (1990), *The Part-Time Marketer*, Karlstad: Centre for Service Research.

34. Jagdish N. Sheth and Atul Parvatiyar (1995), 'The Evolution of Relationship Marketing', *International Marketing Review*, **4** (4), 397–418.
35. Frederick Webster (1992), 'The Changing Role of Marketing in the Corporation', *Journal of Marketing*, October, 1–17. David W. Cravens, Nigel F. Piercy and Shannon H. Shipp (1996), 'New Organizational Forms for Competing in Highly Dynamic Environments: The Network Paradigm', *British Journal of Management*, **7** (3), 203–18.
36. Penelope Ody (2000), 'Focusing on Customers', in *Understanding CRM*, London: *Financial Times*.
37. Don Peppers and Martha Rogers (1997), *Enterprise One to One: Tools for Building Unbreakable Customer Relationships in the Interactive Age*, Piatkus.
38. Kenichi Ohmae (1989), 'The Global Logic of Strategic Alliances', *Harvard Business Review*, March/April, 143–54.
39. Philip Clegg (1956), *A Social and Economic History of Britain 1760–1955*, London: Harrap.
40. This conflict has no practical significance whatever, but it is always fun to see distinguished academicians squabbling in public.
41. Teena Lyons (1997), 'They're All the Same to Us, say Bored Shoppers', *Sunday Business*, 16 March.
42. Bradley T. Gale (1994), *Managing Customer Value: Creating Quality and Service That Customers Can See*, New York: Free Press. William D. Neal (2000), 'A Rebuttal: "Loyalty Really Isn't That Simple"', *Marketing News*, 14 August.
43. Susan Fournier, Susan Dobscha and David Glen Mick (1998), 'Preventing the Premature Death of Relationship Marketing', *Harvard Business Review*, January/February, 43–51.
44. Malcolm McDonald (2000), 'On the Right Track', *Marketing Business*, April, 28–31.
45. Stan Maklan and Simon Know (1998), *Competing on Value: Bridging the Gap Between Brand and Value*, London: Pitman.
46. Noel Capon and James Mac Hulbert (2001), *Marketing Management in the 21st Century*, New Jersey: Prentice-Hall.
47. Peter Doyle (2000), *Value-Based Marketing – Marketing Strategies for Corporate Growth and Shareholder Value*, Chichester: John Wiley.
48. W. Chan Kim and Renee Mauborgne (1997), 'How to Leapfrog the Competition', *Wall Street Journal*, 6 March. 'Pioneers Strike it Rich', *Financial Times*, 11 August 1998.
49. Laura Mazur (1999), 'Wrong Sort of Innovation', *Marketing Business*, June, 39.
50. Michael Treacy and Fred Wiersema (1995), *The Discipline of Market Leaders*, London: Harper Collins.
51. Although there is good reason to believe that it can be transferred to other sectors like car rental and hotels.
52. Maurice Weaver (2000), 'Step Aside, I've Got a Ticket to Ride', *Daily Telegraph*, 18 August.
53. Robert Uhlig (2000), 'Dinner At Eight? That Will Be £20 Extra, Sir!', *Daily Telegraph*, 27 October.
54. Andrew Edgecliffe-Johnson (2000), 'Children Learn to Love their Greens', *Financial Times*, 10 December.

55. Laurel Ives (1999), 'Have Your Cake – And Reheat It', *Daily Telegraph*, 6 August.
56. 'Cyber Couriers Ride into London', *Sunday Times*, 23 April 2000.
57. Quoted in Mandy Thatcher (2001), 'Defining Strategy in a Digital Age', *Marketing Business*, March,13.
58. Ralph Atkins (2000), 'German Greens Learn to Love the Motor Car', *Financial Times*, 29 May.
59. David Blackwell (1997), 'Alcopops Dog Merrydown', *Financial Times*, 2 December.
60. Laurel Ives (2001), 'Uncle Sam Turns His Back on Burgers', *Daily Telegraph*, 6 March. Eric Schlosser (2000), *Fast Food Nation: The Dark Side of the All-American Meal*, New York: Houghton-Mifflin.
61. Bill Bryson (1998), 'Notes from a Big Country', *Night & Day*, 19 April.
62. Suzamme Chetwin (1998), 'Smile Sir, You Won't Have a Nice Day', *Sunday Times*, 21 June.
63. James Curtis (2001), 'Clear as Mud', *Marketing Business*, February, 16–18.
64. British prices for a wide range of goods were demonstrated to be higher than those in other countries for the same goods; see: Nigel F. Piercy, 'Treasure Island', in Nigel F. Piercy (1999), *Tales From the Marketplace*, Oxford: Butterworth-Heinemann, pp. 122–45.
65. Thorold Barker, John Griffiths and Tim Burt (1999), 'Now Streetwise Buyers Drive a Hard Bargain', *Financial Times*, 11/12 December.
66. John Griffiths (2001), 'List Price Cuts Drive Upsurge in New Car Sales to Private Buyers', *Financial Times*, 7 February.
67. Jeremy Rifkin (2000), *The Age of Access: How the Shift From Ownership to Access is Transforming Capitalism*, London: Allen Lane.
68. Ed Platt (2001), 'The Revolution Starts Here', *The Business*, 17 February.
69. 'Ryanair Plans Free Off-Peak Flights', *Sunday Times*, 13 May 2001.
70. Quoted in Richard Tomkins (1999), 'The Power of Price Cannot be Discounted', *Financial Times*, 14 May.
71. Richard Fletcher (1999), 'Cut-Price Stores Upstage Giants on the High Street', *Sunday Business*, 10 October.
72. Rachel Unsworth (2001), 'Sales Sewn Up at Designer Shops', *Financial Mail on Sunday*, 22 April.
73. Quoted in Ben Laurance (2000), 'Just When the Clothes Stores Were Thinking That Things Couldn't Get Any Worse', *Mail on Sunday*, 31 December.
74. Virginia Matthews (1999), 'Simplicity is the Consumer's Choice', *Financial Times*, 10 December.
75. Richard Tomkins (2000), 'Selling to the Sated', *Financial Times*, 22 March.
76. David Graves (1998), 'Kellogg is Outboxed by Shoppers', *Daily Telegraph*, 3 October.
77. Don Peppers and Martha Rogers (1997), *Enterprise One-to-One*, New York: Doubleday. Don Peppers, Martha Rogers and Bob Dorf (1999), 'Is Your Company Ready for One-to-One Marketing?', *Harvard Business Review*, January/February.

78. Bill Bryson (1998), 'Notes From a Big Country', *Mail on Sunday*, 23 August.
79. To quote the Incredible Hulk: ' . . . you won't like me if you make me angry!'
80. The consolation for the disconsolate smoker destined to fly the world without a cigarette is that because airlines can now drastically restrict the fresh air supplies they provide, encouraging bacteria and viruses to spread, now everyone will get off the plane with the hacking chest cough, to which smokers are already so well accustomed!
81. Lynn Eaton (1999), 'Britons Become Top Complainers', *Sunday Times*, 5 September.
82. Nigel Bunyan (1998), 'Stores Tell Grumbling Customer to Check Out', *Daily Telegraph*, 11 November.
83. Richard Alleyne (2001), 'Shoppers Stay at Home as Sales Lose Their Sparkle', *Daily Telegraph*, 6 January.
84. Martin Essex (2000), 'Shopping Must Be More Fun', *Sunday Business*, 16 January.
85. 'A Day Out With All the Fun of the Queue', *Daily Telegraph*, 17 July 1997.
86. Bernd H. Schmitt (1999), *Experiential Marketing: How To Get Customers To Sense, Feel, Think, Act, Relate To Your Company and Brands*, New York: Free Press.
87. David Freemantle (1999), *What Customers Like About You: Adding Emotional Value*, London: Nicholas Brealey Publishing, 1999.
88. Daniel Goleman (1996), *Emotional Intelligence: Why It Can Matter More Than IQ*, London: Bloomsbury. Daniel Goleman (2000), *Working With Emotional Intelligence*, London: Bantam Books.
89. Charles Clover (1999), 'Persuading us to Shop Until we Drop', *Daily Telegraph*, 2 January.
90. Teresa Boyle (2000), 'Tricked You!', *Daily Mail*, 10 March.
91. Astrid Wendlandt (2001), 'It's Sure to Get up Travellers' Noses', *Financial Times*, 24 April.
92. Paco Underhill (1999), *Why We Buy: The Science of Shopping*, London: Orion.
93. John Kay (1998), 'The Chainsaw Falls on Instrumentalism', *Financial Times*, 24 June.
94. A cruel irony is that, by 2000, Sunbeam was in a 'cause related' marketing deal with the American Medical Association, paying the AMA for use of its logo on company products.
95. Nancy Dunne(1998), 'Wal-Mart Attacked for Supplier Labour Standards', *Financial Times*, 31 July 1998. Graeme Beaton (2001), 'Wal-Mart Hot by Sweatshop Row', *Financial Mail on Sunday*, 22 April.
96. 'Adidas Human Rights Policy Back on Track', *Financial Times*, 21 December 2000.
97. James Mackintosh (2001), 'Coop Advises "Green" Policies for its Rivals', *Financial Times*, 8 May.
98. James Blitz (2001), 'Big Companies Asked to Help Poor Countries', *Financial Times*, 24/25 February.
99. David Pilling (2001), 'Patents and Patients', *Financial Times*, 17/18 February.

100. David Pilling (2001), 'The Price of Health Without Frontiers', *Financial Times*, 9 March.
101. David Pilling and Nicol degli Innocenti (2001), 'A Crack in the Resolve of an Industry', *Financial Times*, 19 April.
102. Quoted in Alan Mitchell (2001), 'It's Now a Matter of Trust', *Marketing Business*, April, 33.
103. John Humphreys (2001), 'Corporate Man Controls All, and the Mob Won't Stop Him', *Sunday Times*, 29 April.
104. Ben Taylor (2001), 'The Household Names the Mob Loves to Hate', *Daily Mail*, 2 May.
105. 'Altruistic Approach is Good for Business', *Financial Times*, 7 March 2001.
106. Patricia Seybould (2001), *The Customer Revolution*, New York: Random House.
107. Roger Cowe (2001), 'Green Finds a Primary Role in the Boardroom', *Financial Times*, 12 April.
108. 'Alive and Well, the Sick Jokes Doctors Use at Your Expense', *Daily Mail*, 20 December 1997.
109. Malcolm McDonald, Martin Christopher, Simon Knox and Adrian Payne (2001), *Creating a Company for Customers: How to Build and Lead a Market-Driven Organization*, Hemel Hempstead: Financial Times/ Prentice-Hall.
110. Gary Hamel (2000), *Leading the Revolution*, Boston, MA: Harvard Business School Press.
111. Michael Skapinker (2000), 'In the Line of Fire – From All Directions', *Financial Times*, 31 March.
112. Simon Targett (2001), 'Boards get the Message on Bonus Culture', *Financial Times*, 21/22 April.
113. Andrew Sparrow (2001), 'Boardroom Law to Embarrass "Fat Cat" Directors', *Daily Telegraph*, 8 March.
114. Richard Fletcher (2000), 'Stores Fight Demand', *Sunday Business*, 6 August.
115. Robert Graham (1999), 'French Products to Display Two Prices', *Financial Times*, 15 August.
116. Louise Kehoe (2001), 'Time for Chief Executives to Become E-Literate', *Financial Times*, 31 January.
117. Arie de Geus (1997), *The Living Company*, Cambridge, MA: Harvard Business School Press.
118. James C. Collins and Jerry I. Porras (1997), *Built to Last*, New York: Harper Business.
119. Stratford Sherman (1995), 'Leaders Are Learning Their Stuff', *Fortune*, 27 November.
120. Jonas Ridderstrale and Kjell Nordstrom (2000), *Funky Business*, Hemel Hempstead: Prentice-Hall.
121. Kevin Brown (2001), 'Skills Shortage Leads List of Business Concerns', *Financial Times*, 17 January.
122. Stephen Hoare (2001), 'Allies on the Home Front', *Sunday Business*, 4 February.
123. Richard McClure (2001), 'Central Perks', *Sunday Business*, 13–15.
124. '50 Best Companies To Work For, 2001', *Sunday Times*, 4 February 2001.

125. Michael Skapinker (2001), 'The Competition for Talent', *Financial Times*, 15 January.

126. Quoted in Sumantra Ghoshal and Christopher A. Bartlett (1998), *The Individualized Corporation*, Heinemann.

127. Sumantra Ghoshal and Christopher A. Bartlett (1998), 'Play the Right Card to Get the Aces in the Pack', *Financial Times*, 28 July.

128. David Sumner Smith (2001), 'A Winning Strategy', *Marketing Business*, May, 26–28.

129. Alison Maitland (1999), 'It's Tough at the Top, Say Leading Companies' CEOs', *Financial Times*, 10 June.

130. Michael Skapinker (2001), 'Hail to the Corporate Chieftains', *Financial Times*, 14/15 April.

131. David Burnside (2000), 'How to Handle a True PR Nightmare', *Financial Times*, 30 July. Robin Cobb (2000), 'Disaster Moves', *Marketing Business*, June, 26–27.

132. Richard Tomkins (1998), 'Moments That Build or Destroy Reputations', *Financial Times*, 29 September.

133. Tom Rubython (1996), 'Brewers Prepare for Legalisation of Cannabis', *Sunday Business*, 4 August.

134. Francesca Guerrera (2000), 'Student Wipes 40% Off Antisoma as Doubt is Cast Over Lead Product', *Financial Times*, 23 May.

135. Robert S. Kaplan and David P. Norton (2001), *The Strategy-Focused Organization: How Balanced Scorecard Companies Thrive in the New Business Environment*, Boston, MA: Harvard Business School Press.

136. Vanessa Houlder (1997), 'Keep the Change', *Financial Times*, 3 April.

137. 'Innovation is the Key to Success', *Marketing Business*, January 1995, 3.

Case 1   Huntingdon Life Sciences*

Founded in 1952, Huntingdon Life Sciences (HLS) is Britain's leading drug testing company. HLS describes itself as 'one of the world's most successful contract research organizations for product development and safety testing for the pharmaceuticals, biotechnology and chemicals industries'. Much of its product testing work involves the use of live animals as subjects.

Early in 2001, HLS was brought to the brink of collapse by animal rights protesters, who have fervent objections to the testing of drugs on animals. HLS uses animals in about 50 per cent of its work, and around 70 000 animals including beagles and monkeys are 'used' a year; estimates suggest that 500 animals a day are killed. Their testing does not involve cosmetics, but medicines, food additives, veterinary products and dyes.

Problems started for HLS in 1997, with the British change of government. The incoming Labour Party government had received a £1 million donation from an animals rights group (the largest ever single donation from an outside body in the Party's history). Government support for HLS during its difficulties has been conspicuous by its absence, and HLS CEO Brian Cass reportedly refers to the Labour Prime Minister as a 'bastard'.

'Government support for HLS during its difficulties has been conspicuous by its absence'

An undercover television report led to a Home Office inquiry in 1997 revealing shortcomings and cruelty in the company's animal handling practices. Guilty staff were prosecuted. HLS shares fell from 124p to 54p in a matter of weeks, while the company struggled to restore its reputation.

In May 2000, four cars were set ablaze in the Cambridgeshire village of Sawtry. The vehicles were owned by employees of Huntingdon Life Sciences. At that time the 1200 HLS employees had been under siege for six months by protesters organized by a group called 'Stop Huntingdon Animal Cruelty' (SHAC). SHAC does not fall in the category of protesters dismissed by cynics as simple 'bunny huggers'. Staff going to work are spat at and sworn at, and taunted with banter like 'We know where your kids go to school'. One executive has received a direct death threat (resulting in the jailing of the protester in question), employees have been subjected to ammonia spray attacks, and hate mail has become routine – addressing HLS staff, for example, as 'animal-abusing scum'. An HLS director has been beaten up by men in balaclavas in front of his child. The MD has been sent a mousetrap primed with razor blades, and in February 2001 he was attacked and injured by attackers in balaclava helmets with baseball bats,

---

* This case material has been prepared on the basis of discussions with industry executives and published secondary sources.

who also sprayed gas in the faces of bystanders who came to his aid. Ronnie Lee, founder of the Animal Liberation Front, commented that: 'This serves Brian Cass right and is totally justifiable. In fact, he has got off lightly'. To date, no arrests have been made in connection with any of these attacks on HLS personnel. In addition, directors of companies with investments in HLS have found protesters outside their homes, after SHAC published HLS shareholder addresses on the Internet. The company describes this as a campaign of 'financial terrorism'.

'The company describes this as a campaign of "financial terrorism"'

Financial institutions began to abandon the company – Philips & Drew sold a 20 per cent stake, the Bank of New York and Schroders severed ties. At the beginning of 2001, the company's main financial backer, the Royal Bank of Scotland, after being subjected to protests and a SHAC campaign to crash its computer systems, chose to call in a £23.6 million loan, forcing HLS to the edge of bankruptcy. In fact, RBS was so desperate to distance itself from HLS, it wrote off an £11.6 million loan for a token payment of £1. Although worth more than 300p at the start of the 1990s, HLS shares fell to 1.75p in January 2001, and by mid-2001 had settled at around 3p.

The company was saved from the receivers by intervention from a US bank, which unsurprisingly opted to remain anonymous, providing £11 million funding. SHAC remains committed to closing HLS down, and mounted a legal challenge to the Financial Service Authority's decision to keep the name of the US backer secret. SHAC vows to uncover the name of the backer and take its protests to the US. Indeed, within days of the rescue bid, the US investment was revealed to be led by an Arkansas-based investment group called Stephens Group, an existing HLS shareholder, which had already been visited by SHAC representatives who asked the group to withdraw its investment. A SHAC spokesperson announced 'We know where all their sites are ... Stephens will very soon be suffering for helping HLS'. HLS and Stephens subsequently used US laws originally designed to tackle the Mafia to seek injunctions and damages against SHAC in the US. Later in 2001, investment banks Dresdner Kleinwort Wasserstein and Winterflood Securities declined to continue as HLS' market makers, in reaction to their executives' homes being targeted by protesters. By mid-2001, almost all HLS financial backing was based in the US.

However, in May 2001, Allfirst Financial, a US subsidiary of Allied Irish bank, withdrew from the consortium of lenders supporting HLS, after Allied Irish was threatened with SHAC protests outside its branches in the UK and Ireland, and hostile mail-shots to its staff and customers.

The Royal Bank of Scotland faced calls from SHAC to its customers to close their accounts with RBS (and NatWest) because of their association with HLS, and at the same time calls to its customers from the press to close RBS accounts because the bank had caved in to the protesters. By March 2001, disingenuous Home Secretary, Jack Straw, he of the government that hung HLS out to dry, denounced Barclays and RBS as 'pusillanimous' for abandoning HLS, suggesting they had neglected their 'wider social and business responsibilities'. Indeed, HLS itself has seen anti-animal rights demonstrators at its gates with placards reading 'Better the Life of a Rat, Than the Life of a Human'.

Indeed, having severed ties with HLS after being targeted by protesters, the bank HSBC started to lose its large medical charities account, because the trusts did not believe that HSBC could be relied upon to support them if they were in turn attacked by protesters, accusing HSBC of 'caving in to the extremists'.

By April 2001, the Home Secretary was urging business to 'stand up to the bullies', and the Treasury announced plans to safeguard the anonymity of financial backers and shareholders. Coincidentally, this was a period when the government in question was overseeing the slaughter of more than a million cloven-footed beasts (many not infected) to contain a foot-and-mouth epidemic in the British farming industry. That same month, the Home Secretary announced the formation of a new police team within the National Crime Squad to target the ringleaders of criminal activities by extremist protestors, reporting to a new government committee to co-ordinate government action against the activists. Critics suggested that these actions were a little late in the day, and might be motivated more by the government's problems than by those of HLS.

'By April 2001, the Home Secretary was urging business to "stand up to the bullies"'

HLS called on the government to adopt US-style anti-racketeering laws to combat animal rights protesters, and the Bio-Industry Association demanded laws to make it an offence to organize a campaign purely to cause the demise of a legitimate business. Shortly afterwards, the Association of the British Pharmaceutical Industry, the industry's trade association, threatened that Britain's drug industry could withdraw its business from banks and financial institutions that gave in to threats from animal rights activists.

Meanwhile, HLS faces the problem of persuading customers and investors that the company is financially viable. The company has received little or no public support from the pharmaceutical companies that use its services, although Glaxo stated it would continue to use HLS. Other customers like British Biotech have walked away.

HLS has conducted several advertising campaigns to explain its business – emphasizing its role in developing new medicines, improving agricultural crop yields, protecting the environment and ensuring product safety. These campaigns have been met with organized complaint campaigns to the Advertising Standards Authority (which have not been upheld). HLS's Website offers 'Mythsheets – Popular Misunderstandings' concerning its work and the need for animal testing, but the surfer going to the 'Huntingdon Laboratory Services Information Website' will actually find an animal rights protest site.

The dilemma is that, under British law, pharmaceutical companies are effectively obliged to test drugs on animals before they can be used on humans, and yet while most people want the benefits of the drugs and medical treatments, animal testing is unpopular. Indeed, extreme protesters remain committed to the financial destruction of companies associated with animal testing.

While HLS survives for the moment, investors question who will be the next target for protesters. SHAC has declared its continuing campaign against HLS will be pursued against HLS customers – claiming several pharmaceutical companies had already promised not to use HLS for contract research. SHAC has already linked to a US animal rights organization to pursue a campaign against Merrill Lynch's directors and corporate events in the US, because it claims that the investment bank owns a nominee agency protecting the identity of HLS investors. Financial backers with even tangential links to HLS have been targeted by protesters – demonstrations outside head offices, abusive phone calls in the middle of the night. HLS customers, such as Yamanouchi, the Japanese pharmaceuticals company, now face protest action by SHAC – in the UK and Japan. British police advice seems to be to cave in, since they can provide no protection. Speculation is that now activists have found a methodology that works, they will find other targets – possibly the horse-racing industry.

'**extreme protesters remain committed to the financial destruction of companies associated with animal testing**'

The HLS dilemma is that new drugs currently require animal testing according to the government's Medicines Control Agency. Drug researchers and producers generally regard animal rights as secondary to human rights, and insist that animal testing is essential. The overwhelming majority of people want new and better medicines. Many choose to ignore the fact that this requires animal testing. A vocal and passionate minority regard animal testing as, at best, unethical, and many regard it simply as 'murder'.

By the end of 2000, HLS was seeing orders falling, with pre-tax losses increasing from £6.6 million to £10.9 million, on turnover of £63 million, and share values sitting at around 5p. The management of HLS has to find a way through this minefield, or go out of business, and it has to do so while its opponents watch every move they make. It seems almost inconceivable that they can devise a strategy which will satisfy all parties, yet this is the challenge for management. A company spokesperson in April 2001 noted: 'This could happen to anyone ...'. The company's financial situation is weak:

'**A company spokesperson in April 2001 noted: "This could happen to anyone ..."**'

	1996	1997	1998	1999	2000
Sales turnover (£m)	73.6	63.7	52.6	58.2	63.3
Pre-tax profit (loss) (£m)	9.35	(7.16)	(25.4)	(6.64)	(10.9)
Earnings per share (p)	6.31	(3.41)	(10.7)	(2.57)	(3.49)
Dividend per share (p)	–	–	–	–	–
Cash, securities (£m)	3.04	0.44	14.1	5.26	2.20
Market capitalization (£m)	99.9	53.0	32.0	30.6	6.55

Finally, in July 2001, the Government assisted HLS, by making the Bank of England HLS's banker.

Points to ponder

1 HLS is in an unusual business, but all the signs are that what they do provide a high level of value for their customers – their testing services are necessary to get drugs and pharmaceuticals to market, and they have specialized expertise in this field. They have, however, certainly been prevented from delivering value to shareholders, and their financial position is precarious. The most urgent question is what else can they do to survive?

2 The HLS situation also suggests a network of relationships at work – the protesters targeting those of whom they disapprove, but also their suppliers and customers, leading to anti-protestor customers abandoning suppliers who 'cave in' and so on. This is a new phenomenon that many other companies may face in the future. Can anyone see a way out of this vicious circle?

3 The HLS experience underlines the reality of protest in the new era. Protesters are no longer a few disgruntled people at the AGM waving ballot papers at you – they are organized groups prepared to break the law to stop your operations continuing. They are also Internet-literate and can exploit information transparency to identify your managers, your investors and your customers, to include them in the battle. What defences are there for a company against organized, determined and violent opponents?

Sources: Francesco Guerrera, James Mackintosh and Andrew Parker (2001), 'Huntingdon Set to Tackle Investor and Client Fears', *Financial Times*, 23 January. Richard Alleyne (2001), 'Scientists Defend Animal Tests', *Daily Telegraph*, 20 January. Sylvia Pfeifer (2001), 'Animal Lab's Biggest Test Yet to Come', *Sunday Business*, 21 January. Jon Ungoed-Thomas and Jonathan Carr-Brown (2001), 'Dangerous Species', *Sunday Times*, 21 January. Sylvia Pfeifer and Frank Kane (2001), 'Revealed: Huntingdon's American Saviour', *Sunday Business*, 28 January. Benjamin Wootliff (2001), 'Cool Captain Survives His Toughest Test', *Daily Telegraph*, 27 January. Juliette Jowit (2001), 'Huntingdon Rescuer has Links with Clinton and Bush Administrations', *Financial Times*, 29 January. Robert Shrimsley and Francesco Guerrera (2001), 'Straw's Ire Over Animal Lab Loans', *Financial Times*, 13 March. Ross Hawkins (2001), 'Glaxo Stands Firm Behind Huntingdon', *Sunday Business*, 1 April. Sylvia Pfeifer (2001), 'Huntingdon Weighs UK Delisting', *Sunday Business*, 15 April. Francesco Guerrera (2001), 'HLS to Take Legal Action in US Against Animal Rights Groups', *Financial Times*, 20 April. Francesco Guerrera and David Firm (2001), 'HSBC Loses Charities Customer', *Financial Times*, 23 April. Francesco Guerrera (2001), 'Hit Squad to Tackle Animal Rights Activists', *Financial Times*, 27 April.

Synergizing customers and employees to create competitive advantage

'We try harder' is the slogan that captivated the American public in the early sixties. It created one of the ten most famous advertising campaigns of all time and encapsulated the competitive edge that was to turn Avis from a tiny American company with an unbroken record of financial losses, to a global service leader with over 333 000 vehicles, operating through 5000 locations in 163 countries, and characterized by one of the most powerful corporate cultures in the world.

Avis Europe was created in 1965 as a separate operating division to spearhead international expansion into Europe, Africa and the Middle East. With the singular vision of building the best and fastest growing company with the highest profit margins in the business of car rental, and boosted by the impetus of 'We try harder', the company climbed from 'greenfield' start to market leader in just eight years, and has remained there ever since. The company has gone through a number of changes in ownership structure, including three years as a highly successful plc in the late 1980s. Since 1989, Avis Europe has been privately owned and whilst legally separated from its former parent, Avis Inc. in the USA, it retains strong and cohesive operational links with the rest of the Avis system, presenting a global brand and customer service image to the world's travelling public. Its operating revenues this year will be in excess of £500 million, representing a growth of over 40 per cent since 1994.

'boosted by the impetus of "We try harder", the company climbed from "greenfield" start to market leader in just eight years'

This case describes how Avis Europe has built its organization and management processes around those early principles of 'We try harder', and taken its famous slogan from an 'underdog' strap line in an advertising campaign, to a market leadership strategy in a highly competitive industry.

The 'We try harder' story

In 1962 Avis was a small American company, with an unbroken record not of service excellence, but of financial losses in the previous six years. The newly appointed President of that time, Robert Townsend,

---

* This case study was prepared by Lesley Colyer, Vice President – Personnel, Avis Europe Ltd.

took a number of actions to turn the company around, including hiring a new advertising agency. He went to Doyle Dane & Bernbach, a prestigious Madison Avenue house. Townsend didn't have much money to spend on advertising – in fact, he had only one-fifth of the funds spent by Avis' major competitor, Hertz. He struck an unusual deal with the owner of the agency, Bill Bernbach. Bernbach's deal was: 'If you want five times the impact, give us 90 days to learn enough about your business to apply our skills…then run every ad we write, as we write them and where we tell you. Agree to this and we have a deal.' Townsend did.

'Avis did not do anything better than its competitor – the only difference was the Avis employees – they seemed to try harder than the rest'

The agency began their research to find a positive differentiating factor between Avis and its competitor. They concluded that there wasn't one! Ninety days of research revealed that Avis did not do anything better than its competitor – the only difference was the Avis employees – they seemed to try harder than the rest, but probably because they had to!

From this remark, a revolutionary campaign was born – revolutionary because it was the first time in history that *any* company publicly admitted that it wasn't the best…but it was trying to be. None of the Avis executives liked the campaign but Townsend honoured the deal and ran it anyway. The rest is history.

'We try harder' now holds the distinction of being one of the ten most famous advertising campaigns of all time. The slogan appealed to people's natural inclination to support the underdog – they tried Avis once to see if the ads were true. Having tried Avis once they came back

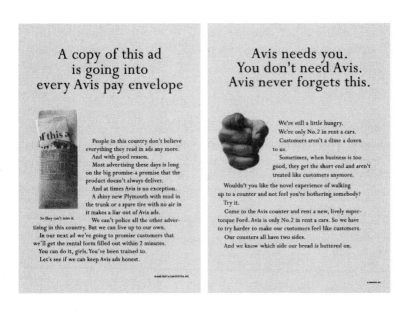

A copy of this ad is going into every Avis pay envelope

People in this country don't believe everything they read in ads any more.
And with good reason.
Most advertising these days is long on the big promise–a promise that the product doesn't always deliver.
And at times Avis is no exception. A shiny new Plymouth with mud in the trunk or a spare tire with no air in it makes a liar out of Avis ads.
So they can't miss it.   We can't police all the other advertising in this country. But we can live up to our own.
In our next ad we're going to promise customers that we'll get the rental form filled out within 2 minutes.
You can do it, girls. You've been trained to.
Let's see if we can keep Avis ads honest.

Avis needs you. You don't need Avis. Avis never forgets this.

We're still a little hungry.
We're only No. 2 in rent a cars.
Customers aren't a dime a dozen to us.
Sometimes, when business is too good, they get the short end and aren't treated like customers anymore.
Wouldn't you like the novel experience of walking up to a counter and not feel you're bothering somebody?
Try it.
Come to the Avis counter and rent a new, lively super-torque Ford. Avis is only No. 2 in rent a cars. So we have to try harder to make our customers feel like customers.
Our counters all have two sides.
And we know which side our bread is buttered on.

– again and again – not because of the ad campaign, but because of its most remarkable impact on the employees. 'We try harder' literally inspired the Avis people to deliver new heights of service. It turned good people into star performers because of the onus placed on the individual to excel.

Each ad was distributed in every employee's pay packet before being launched externally – and we mean every employee – from managers to front-line staff and those who washed and delivered the cars. Each ad told customers and employees what the car was to be like, what the service was to be like, and how the company was to perform. 'We try harder' created a charter of standards and expectations that became the company's new birthright. And most important, within three years the Company was solidly in the black and sales had tripled.

'We try harder' recognized that we could not take customers for granted and that each employee, no matter what their role in the company, would try harder to make sure that customers would come back again, and all this in an era before the concept of customer service and satisfaction was embedded in the USA or, indeed, anywhere else in the world.

From these early years Avis Europe developed a set of beliefs and values that remains at the heart of our organization and management processes. At the core of these is the 'We try harder' ethos:

> 'We believe that sustainable competitive advantage comes from our ability to continuously innovate ahead of the competition. In achieving this we look for continuous improvement, no matter how small, in everything we do and at the same time quantum improvement in the way we do business. We will never hesitate to adapt to new and more profitable ways of working provided that the honesty and integrity we apply to our business is not compromised. We actively encourage a "try harder" and "can do" mentality and operate a climate of trust at all levels. The only mistake is not to try something.'

'continuous improvement will not increase shareholder value or long-term profitability, unless it focuses on what matters to the customer'

One of the key lessons we learnt all those years ago is that no matter how successful an organization becomes, it must seek to continuously improve, if it is to compete in tomorrow's marketplace. However, continuous improvement will not increase shareholder value or long-term profitability, unless it focuses on what matters to the customer. It is all too easy to lose track of this in times of business success. We have tried very hard to avoid this trap and to translate those same customer philosophies and principles we employed as a small loss-making company, with a handful of employees in one country, to a global enterprise at the leading edge of service delivery, with 21 000 employees in 163 countries.

Continuous Improvement Cycle

Listening to customers

A company cannot know what matters most to customers, unless it asks them. In 1989, we took a quantum leap forward in the way we 'listened' to customers, by leveraging our technological advantage. Since the 1960s, Avis has invested over $1 billion in developing the most advanced global computer network and information processing systems in our industry, which today links more than 350 000 terminals around the globe. This has given us a major competitive edge in many areas and not least in the area of customer satisfaction. Through our technology we capture virtually every single customer transaction and obtain a wealth of data that can be linked to customer and employee opinion and used to drive improvements in areas that most affect customer satisfaction and loyalty.

We began this process by launching a significant piece of pan-European research. We talked to thousands of our customers in eleven countries, asking them what they thought of their experiences with Avis, and what they wanted from car rental. At the same time, we surveyed every one of our employees, asking them the same questions as the customers in addition to specifics about working practices and company processes.

The results of this baseline research formed the basis of a number of initiatives that we have implemented in the last five years...many of which have already reaped additional customer loyalty, additional profits and more awards for service excellence than anyone else in the industry.

The Avis baseline research

The key findings of the baseline research were:

● The research showed that only a very small percentage of our customers ever communicated about service issues...good or bad. Of those who had an enquiry or service issue, only 6 per cent actually contacted the customer service department. Each one of these contacts, handled to the satisfaction of the customer, resulted in a retention factor of over 90 per cent – almost as high as customers who were happy with the service they received in the first place!

Customer Contact Iceberg

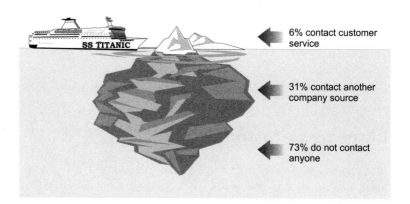

● Of the remaining customers who had an enquiry or service issue, 31 per cent contacted someone else in the organization – usually front-line staff. This was valuable customer data, not captured or fed into the Company's continuous improvement and root cause improvement processes. Moreover, service issues dealt with at the front line generated a lower level of satisfaction, some of which resulted in a second contact being made by the customer, usually to the customer service department. This 'escalation' phenomenon is costly in terms of customer retention and profit for a number of reasons:

 – negative word of mouth advertising occurs between the first and second contact;
 – the second contact may not happen at all...leaving a dissatisfied customer, unlikely to come back;
 – between the first and second contacts, the problem is likely to escalate in the customer's mind and become more costly for the company to resolve.

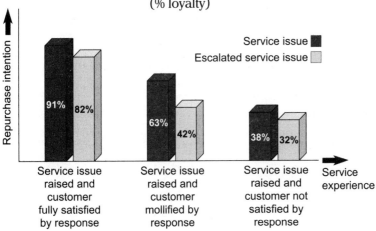

Service Issue Escalation and Impact on Customer Loyalty
(% loyalty)

- The vast majority of customers with enquiries or service issues did not contact anyone at Avis, but they did however tell other people! We call this 'negative word of mouth advertising' and we know from research across many industries that unhappy customers tell three to four times as many people about their experiences as happy customers do. Even worse is that these customers take their business elsewhere the next time. Research showed that only 78 per cent of these customers would use Avis again, compared with 92 per cent of customers who were satisfied with their service encounter. This difference of 14 per cent represents lost customers, lost revenues, lost profits and lost reputation.

Customer Loyalty vs. Service Experience

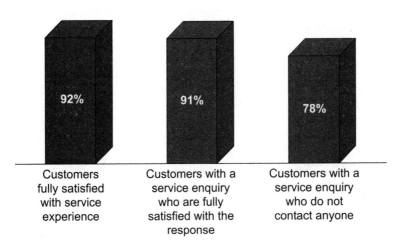

- The employee research indicated a 'positive morale' problem! Employees were committed to delivering excellent customer service, and wanted to resolve customer queries, but found insufficient flexibility to do so in some company processes.

The key actions that resulted from this research involved:

- making customer service a profit centre;
- transferring ownership of the service encounter to employees;
- aligning training processes with this strategy; and
- continuously tracking both customer and employee satisfaction with Avis.

Customer service as a profit centre

The research clearly showed customer service departments were key to customer retention and should be profit centres in their own right. Customers with service issues, who are satisfied with the way their query is handled, are the most loyal, give repeat business, and champion the company with positive word of mouth advertising to others. Since it costs a company at least ten times as much to solicit a new customer as it does to retain an existing one, investment in our customer service units became a priority. Our approach involved the following:

'it costs a company at least ten times as much to solicit a new customer as it does to retain an existing one'

- We invested substantially in state-of-the-art call management systems, linked directly to customer transaction data and receivable and billing systems.
- We fully empowered and trained our customer service employees to do whatever it took to resolve a customer issue, there and then on the telephone, and to action the resolution of the problem directly into the billing systems.
- We implemented a complainant satisfaction tracking system to assess effectiveness at retaining customers.
- We made it easier for customers to contact our customer service centres, publishing the telephone number on all rental material, and providing dedicated and unique numbers for major customers.
- We implemented a process of root cause analysis, to identify and resolve service issues at source, and a monthly feedback system to rental locations, giving them customer feedback – good and bad – about their specific location, thus providing a mechanism for root cause resolution at all levels in the company.
- Customer service representatives began to regularly attend meetings with major customers, along with operational employees, to ensure service requirements are understood and any issues quickly resolved.

These actions have had a significant impact on customer retention. Some of the key achievements of the UK customer service centre are: (1) today, over 90 per cent of customer service calls are resolved live, while the customer is on the phone and on the first call; (2) overall complainant satisfaction levels this year are running, on average, 10 percentage points above last year; (3) a multifunctional task team developed substantial process improvement programmes to address the top three service issues in 1995 – all of these are now in the process of implementation; (4) a new complainant satisfaction tracking system fully integrated with Avis technology and enhanced to reflect state-of-the-art contact measurement is under development.

Employee ownership of the service encounter

Responsiveness to customer needs is key to the longevity of any business. Our research re-emphasized the critical role front-line employees play in customer retention, and the need for us to remove any organizational obstacles to delivering good service. Today, this is fashionably called *empowerment*, **'Responsiveness to customer needs is key to the longevity of any business'** and to many it is simply devolving responsibility to the lowest possible level in the organization, to prevent escalation of customer problems – something that can be instilled in a two-day training course. To us, it means much more than this. It means creating an organizational and management climate that encourages responsiveness to customer needs. It means employees who are both willing and able to make exceptional service the norm, rather than the exception. It means employees who are willing to give a little extra: to create customer value every time – not just when there are problems; and everywhere – not just at the front line and the interface with the customer.

This is an extract from a customer letter about Dawn Swadling, a front-line employee at Heathrow:

> 'I had to travel to the UK to attend my father's funeral. I required a small auto...had to wait...she tried her utmost to solve my dilemma. I marvelled at her professionalism, courtesy and kindness...carried my suitcase to the car and put her arm around me in a very tender and consoling manner as she wished me well. My company requires all its 30 000 employees to attend "Customer First" training. Whenever examples of the ultimate in customer care were given, Dawn always came to mind. She could have written the book!'

Dawn is what we mean by empowered – customer retention through total responsiveness to customer needs. You cannot buy Dawns ready-made or from an advertising agency.

At Avis we had most of the necessary organizational characteristics and management processes in place, including, most importantly, as the research told us, a workforce that actually wanted to do it! The challenge was to adjust and implement the necessary mechanisms to develop total employee ownership of the service encounter.

Alignment of training processes

The first thing we did was to critically reappraise our training processes, to ensure we were delivering high levels of competence and clarity. As a result, we set up a project to develop a completely new and innovative training process for front-line staff, that would lead to customers experiencing a unique level of value and service that would not be experienced with any other service provider. The project team comprised operational management, the training manager, and rental sales agents – those who actually do the job! We believed that a programme conceived, designed and written by actual end users would be far more effective than one solely devised by 'training professionals'.

'In excess of 140 competence statements were produced to cover all the key elements of service excellence'

It took the team three years to produce a competence-based distance learning programme. In excess of 140 competence statements were produced to cover all the key elements of service excellence in our environment and grouped into five stages. The programme was designed to be completed in the workplace and takes a new recruit between 18 months and two years to successfully complete. The programme has BTEC accreditation and the successful completion of the final stage requires completion of a business improvement project. The programme was officially launched in the UK in 1993 by Alun Cathcart, Chairman and CEO, Keith Dyer, UK Managing Director, and Sir Geoffrey Holland.

Since its inception, more than 500 employees have been enrolled on the programme, 30 per cent of whom have successfully passed stage 3, which makes them fully competent as professional rental sales agents. The majority are now taking the optional stage 4 and 5 levels, designed to promote a greater understanding of the business and prepare individuals for supervisory and management positions. Forty per cent of those who have finished stage 5 have already been promoted, and some substantial business improvement projects have been presented. This is the world's first formal standards-based front-line employee training programme in the car rental industry and, whilst it is too early to offer proof of impact on employee turnover and customer satisfaction, it is clear that this programme is having a positive influence in both of these respects.

Continuously tracking customer and employee satisfaction

From what our customers and employees told us in the research we conducted, we developed comprehensive and *meaningful* customer and employee satisfaction tracking systems. Customer expectations are constantly changing and increasing. What the customer perceived as excellent yesterday is mediocre today, and will be unsatisfactory tomorrow. It is therefore critical to continuously listen to customers and to have ongoing customer and employee satisfaction and retention measure- *'Customer expectations are constantly changing and increasing'* ments integrated with the key business monitors of the organization. This ensures improvements are focused on what matters to the customer and avoids the trap of 'customer arrogance' into which otherwise successful companies can fall.

Customer satisfaction tracking system

We have developed one of Europe's most extensive independent measure-ment systems for tracking customer reaction to the service they have just received from Avis. Each month, over 13 500 customers are randomly selected from the total number of customers who rented in the previous month. These customers are contacted and asked to record the level of satisfaction they have experienced with our service, our product and our people for a particular rental. There are two important points here.

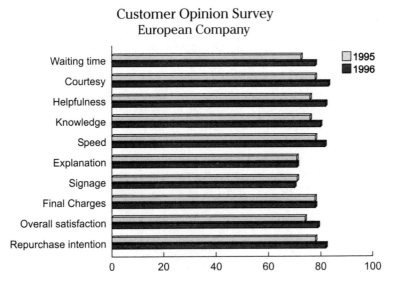

Customer Opinion Survey
European Company

First, the service attributes measured are those that have the greatest impact on satisfaction and retention in our particular operating environment, as identified in our baseline research. Second, *all* of the attributes measured can be directly influenced and affected by our employees.

Customers are also asked to express their overall satisfaction, and how likely they are to use our service again. Therefore, we are not asking a generic set of questions but what they thought about our service on a particular occasion. Our technology links each response to a specific rental contract, containing substantial data that we do not need to ask the customer for.

From the responses we receive from customers, comprehensive information is produced, which is filtered from Board level to every single rental location in our network. Each location receives regular and recent feedback from *their* customers – not just a set of average numbers but individual customer scores, together with the contract number. Local teams are, therefore, not only able to look at the survey results, but also to view the full details of the transaction on their computer screens. This is very powerful because it helps each team to identify what likely actions, circumstances or behaviours were responsible for the specific customer feedback. Continuous improvement is thus driven at local level by those who deliver the service and is in absolute response to *their* customers' feedback.

'Continuous improvement is thus driven at local level by those who deliver the service'

An example of local initiatives is the launch of 'full-service return' in the Scottish district, to improve performance on 'accuracy of billing'. This meant using the Wizard system real-time with the customers to calculate the rental charges and explain and agree them with customers. The district improved its accuracy of billing scores from customer opinion by five points in a six-month period. The District Manager responsible for this initiative is, today, the Director of Training for the Avis Group.

But customer feedback is not just used in our operations. It is used by every function, to continuously improve what matters most to the customer. Our marketing functions are able to track satisfaction by product, by day of the week, by location and by nationality, enabling improvements in product development. Our fleet functions are able to track satisfaction by make and model. As we are the largest purchaser of fleet cars in Western Europe this is of significant importance, not only to us as a factor in fleet purchase decisions but also to the vehicle manufacturers in terms of their fleet design and model acceptability. Our training and customer service functions are able to identify where changes are needed to processes and procedures, what are the root causes of customer dissatisfaction, and what new knowledge and skills need to be emphasized.

In addition, we use the data externally in a number of ways. We are able to assess and improve partnership products such as frequent flyer programmes. We also produce customer satisfaction reports for our major customers regarding the satisfaction of their travelling employees. This process forms a key part of contract negotiation and acts as a powerful tool, to demonstrate that service standards are being achieved and to agree service guarantees. This has undoubtedly created a competitive advantage for Avis.

A truly effective customer quality process is not just an internal and insular activity. Its ultimate success depends very much on the extent to which it also recognizes and integrates the interests and needs of customers, suppliers and partners alike.

In the spirit of continuous improvement, the customer satisfaction tracking system itself underwent significant enhancements last year to ensure it continued to reflect what matters most to our customers and that it remained at the leading edge of customer opinion measurement systems. The key changes were:

- An updated customer communication vehicle creating a more customer-friendly image and encouraging greater response levels.
- A substantial reduction in the process cycle from mailing to customers, to results being received by rental locations, together with increased frequency of rental location reporting (the latter being an enhancement requested by operations themselves!). Cycle times have been reduced by over 71 per cent, providing more meaningful and timely data for operational action.
- A broader base of questions on service and rental processes together with customer buying patterns and perceptions on competitor performance.
- The development of an exception reporting process on a routine basis to continuously focus attention to key areas.

Whilst only operational for a few months, we are already reaping substantial benefits from the new survey: response rates have increased by 15 per cent with an average pan-European response rate of 30 per cent; significant volumes of 'white mail' have been received, providing a valuable source of customer feedback, and a substantial improvement in quality of name and address capture at the time of rental.

Employee satisfaction tracking system

The linkage between customer satisfaction and employee satisfaction is very strong. This was bought home to us back in the 1960s. It is a lesson we have never forgotten.

We used our baseline research to develop an employee satisfaction tracking system to provide linkage with our customer satisfaction data. This survey embraces all employees

'The linkage between customer satisfaction and employee satisfaction is very strong'

in all parts of the organization, and measures the 28 attributes that customers and employees told us were essential to delivering excellent service. The data are fed to countries, to functional teams and directly to employees, and, when linked to customer satisfaction data, they provide a powerful information base for local action and continuous improvement initiatives.

The chart below shows the cumulative increases in employee satisfaction in one of our countries, Spain, over the last two years. It is no coincidence that over the same time-frame overall customer satisfaction in Spain increased, with satisfaction increasing on five service attributes and exceeding 90 per cent in two key areas. During this same period, the Spanish company grew its customer base by 45 per cent.

Employee Satisfaction Survey, Spain
(% Change FY96 vs. FY94)

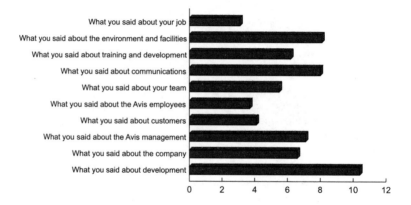

Employee satisfaction results at the headquarters of the Avis Europe Group in the UK have led to the development of a number of corporate initiatives over the last two years, which we are in the process of rolling out and integrating into our operating units:

- A new performance and development review process, linked to an employee development programme, providing both Avis-specific and professional training opportunities and qualifications.
- Bi-annual business awareness initiatives featuring 'hands on' experience of the latest developments in the business for all employees – examples are:
  - *Global branding*: Prior to externally relaunching our global branding this year, we invited employees to attend workshops to understand the external positioning and enter a team competition by creating designing and making brochures themselves using the new Avis guidelines.

- *Internet*: Avis established the industry's first World-Wide-Web site on 12 April this year. All employees had the opportunity to 'surf the Avis site' and view the Avis features offered to millions of customers worldwide.

- Opportunities for all newly-recruited HQ clerical staff to 'hear the tills ringing' with some time spent at a rental location.
- Bi-annual business performance briefings by the Chairman and Chief Executive.
- Social events, giving all employees regular opportunities to meet the directors and discuss anything they wish to raise.

Maintaining the momentum through people

Today, the satisfaction tracking systems are closely integrated with our key organization and management processes, and fully aligned to a strategy of customer retention.

'satisfaction tracking systems are closely integrated with our key organization and management processes'

All of these issues are important, but we firmly believe that the single most important factor in sustaining our momentum, and the competitive advantage of 'We try harder', lies with our people: the way we recruit, train, develop and manage them. We look for people who have a strong orientation to working with other people, who like a 'hands on' approach, and also know how to enjoy themselves and have fun in their jobs.

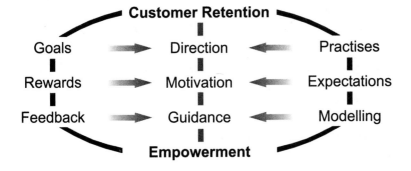

We have evolved an operating structure that minimizes bureaucracy and encourages initiative. Our vertical lines are short, with a maximum of six levels between the Chairman of the company and a car washer in downtown Rome. We operate a philosophy of decentralized management and a high degree of local autonomy, underpinned by strong support

Avis Europe corporate beliefs and values

The following statements encapsulate our beliefs and values and our approach to doing business throughout our operating territories

Business ethics

We believe it is in the interest of our shareholders, our customers and our employees that we maintain a highly acceptable public image supporting a progressively profitable company. Honesty, integrity and fairness in dealings must and will be absolute and an integral basis of our total philosophy.

Customers

We believe in providing consistently high standards of integrity, service, quality and value in satisfying customer needs. This operating ethos maintains our industry leadership and retains the loyalty and respect of our customers.

Employees

We aim to stimulate duty, mutual loyalty and a sense of pride in working for Avis through employee involvement at all levels, continuous updating of knowledge and skills and attractive and competitive recognition and reward systems. We believe that employees should be actively encouraged to grow and develop their careers with Avis and we always seek first to appoint candidates from within the Company to fill positions at every level - both nationally and internationally. To this end, we will provide the environment to help employees improve and develop themselves.

Management and leadership

We believe in local autonomy, working within broad guidelines and underpinned by strong support services at the centre. We are committed to professionalism in leadership; clear direction, clear team work development, clear communication, clear and sensibly quick and consistent decisions based on 'what' is right rather than 'who' is right. We recognise that excellence and professionalism amongst Avis management and employees is a key marketing tool. It gives customers confidence and competitors an inferiority complex.

'We try harder.' ethos

We believe that sustainable competitive advantage comes from our ability to continuously innovate ahead of the competition. In achieving this we look for continuous improvement, no matter how small, in every thing we do and at the same time quantum improvement in the way we do business. We will never hesitate to adapt to new and more profitable ways of working provided that the integrity and honesty we apply to our business is not compromised. We actively encourage a 'try harder' and 'can do' mentality and operate a climate of TRUST at all levels. The only mistake is not to try something.

Community

We operate as responsible members of the community and within the laws of the countries within which we do business. We recognise and respect the attitudes, characteristics and customs of local populations.

Environment

We recognise our corporate responsibility to the community at large for public health and safety and environmental protection. We fully comply with all legislation in this respect and actively pursue environmental and safety initiatives on a local, industry wide and global basis.

Suppliers

We ensure integrity and professionalism in all dealings with suppliers and expect the same in return. We seek economic quality and efficiency of service in all supplier relationships and, where possible, 'added value' to the mutual benefit of both. We continuously foster strategic alliances and partnerships with major travel industry organisations who share a mutual respect of the customer, a commitment to quality and a desire to maximise and enhance the reputation and value of the brand.

Costs

We regard efficiency as central to our whole business philosophy and we continuously search for means to reduce the cost of delivering a better product for the customer.

services at the centre and a shared vision of beliefs and values. We have achieved significant continuity and longevity in our workforce:

- We are only 30 years old as a company, but over 50 per cent of our employees today have more than five years' service with us – next year almost 15 per cent will achieve a long service award.
- Over 90 per cent of the 200 most senior managers in Avis today came up through the ranks – many began their careers serving Avis customers and they continue to do so today. Visible management is the

oldest corporate management process in Avis. For 25 years, and long before Tom Peters popularized 'walk the talk', the Chairman and managers across the network regularly set aside days to work at the rental counter, wash cars, take reservations and handle complaints. This is not stunt management, it is a key process for listening and staying close to customer and employee opinion – continuously.

● Cross-functional and cross-border appointments are a regular feature of Avis Europe's management development programme, minimizing the trap of 'functional' mind set and inter-departmental politics.

The future

We believe 'We try harder' is a unique organizational capability and a primary source of competitive advantage for us. Looking to the future, we have undertaken a comprehensive review of our reward and recognition processes, and developed a holistic programme for all employees in each of our operating territories to encourage and recognize the 'We try harder' service values and to tap the creativity of our workforce in a way that, we believe, will see Avis continue to thrive and be successful well into the next century.

'"We try harder" is a unique organizational capability and a primary source of competitive advantage'

Known as 'The Spirit of Avis', the first element of the programme is a recognition process for delivering the promise of 'We try harder'. A customer, supplier, partner or fellow employee can nominate anyone in the company for recognition for giving a little extra. There are various levels of recognition within the programme – for teams as well as individuals – culminating in a gold award from the Chairman and CEO. The programme is explained to all new employees at the time of their induction into the company and includes a 15-minute silent movie, made in the early 1970s, which demonstrates what the 'We try harder' promise means on a day-to-day basis. This recognition process is very powerful in perpetuating the cultural behaviours that drive responsiveness to customer needs – internal and external.

The second element of the programme is about putting 'We try harder' into action and bringing the 'We try harder' operating ethos of innovation and continuous improvement to life – permanently. Essentially, it actively encourages idea generation and provides reward for it. Each Avis territory has a multifunctional team, led by a member of the senior management team, which receives and rewards ideas generated in their country. A unique automated process is designed to capture the input from more than 90 countries to a multifunctional team at Group headquarters who, in addition to capturing ideas from Group headquarters' employees, are responsible for disseminating and progressing ideas from different territories across the Group. This new process will be fully implemented in all our countries by the end of 1996, when it will become the system that captures improvement ideas from many other company measurement systems and, critically, those described in this case study: customer satisfaction tracking, employee satisfaction tracking and complainant satisfaction tracking.

Evidence of success

How successful have we been with our approach, our management practices and measurement systems, and how valid are our presumptions that service values will continue to provide a competitive advantage in the years ahead? We have given specific locations and country results as illustrations throughout this case. For the total company, there is substantial external recognition of our approach: more innovation in product development than our competitors; more service awards than any other car rental company; and the only car rental company to receive site visits in major quality awards, spanning three continents. We could point to sustained market leadership, a profit record that consistently outstrips our competitors, growth in shareholder value and many other indicators of success.

In 1997, Avis Europe announced its intention to refloat on the stock market with an expected value of £700 million, leading to the buying-out of minority shareholders and gaining access for Avis Europe to the whole of Asia, as well as funding expansion into Central and Eastern Europe. In March 1997, market enthusiasm for the Avis share offer was shown by the fact that it was oversubscribed fivefold. After the float in 1997, shares rose from 124p to a peak of 293p by the end of 1998, following a profits increase of 44 per cent that year, and reached a peak of 318p in 1999/2000. In 1999, Avis Europe started its Asia expansion with a licensing deal with Japaren, one of Japan's largest independent car rental groups.

Innovation continues in the UK operation also. In 2000, Avis unveiled plans to sell used cars over the Internet in a joint venture with Navidec, a Nasdaq-listed provider of e-business solutions. The Internet strategy also includes online booking services. In 2000 also, Avis Europe became one of the first British companies to use Microsoft's new Pocket PC in a new damage tracking system. The goal is to allow rental drivers to scan their credit cards through the device and sign the bill, after staff have assessed the vehicle for damages. Avis estimates that the damage tracking system will save customers between three and 13 minutes when cars are checked in, and potentially reduce costs by £8 million.

'the most important indicator is what our customers think'

For us, the most important indicator is what our customers think, and we would like to leave the final word on 'service' to a customer – the Chairman of a major plc who sent us this letter just a few weeks ago. It demonstrates that the service values inherent in the 'We try harder' promise are as fresh as ever and as relevant today as they were in the 1960s.

'I can't tell you how enormously impressed I have been with the efforts of your operation at Derry airport. It is the epitome of "We Try Harder" in action. A recent example is that I arrived in Derry at 5.30 p.m. on Friday 3 May, without having booked a car (by mistake). Martin Hankin not only came up trumps immediately with a car, but was then kind enough to deliver to my address in Ireland a more suitable car much later that evening. I can tell you that it is rare to receive that kind of help from an organization and I am deeply impressed and thankful for it. If it represents your quality of service around the world then your competitors have a lot to be frightened of.'

Points to ponder

1 What does the Avis experience tell us about the power of customer focus?
2 What are the lessons we can learn from Avis about what it takes to actually achieve and sustain customer focus?
3 What are the barriers to other companies achieving the things that Avis has achieved?

Case 3   Barclays Bank*

There are only two real problems with being deeply unpopular: everything you say and everything you do

The retail banks in Britain are not popular – 'bank bashing' almost qualifies as a national sport, and attacks on the industry guarantee a few column inches in the financial and popular press – with particular customer aggression reserved for the big four high-street banks: Barclays, HSBC, Lloyds TSB and NatWest. In 2001, it is estimated that the top twelve UK banks will make a record £25 billion profit, and a government minister accused them of 'leeching off' their customers.

Criticisms of the banks are varied and numerous. They stand accused of making excessive profits, overcharging by exploiting the power of the Big Four Cartel to stifle competition, providing poor service, and indulging in a variety of 'dirty tricks' to make it difficult for customers to switch banks and of increasing charges to customers through subterfuge and sharp practice. Recent cases show customer complaints stalled for up to six years, and customers who complain too loudly having their accounts closed.

'the banking sector has attracted government attention as one where regulation and intervention may win popular acclaim and win votes'

As it has contrived to replace estate agents at the top of the public's hate league table, the banking sector has attracted government attention as one where regulation and intervention may win popular acclaim and win votes. Investigations by government 'watchdogs', and support for the 'people's universal bank' have ensued. The Competition Commission has recently slated the big banks for the anti-competitive behaviour in the small business sector – accusing the banks of operating a 'complex monopoly' with artificially high charges and borrowing rates, and a lack of transparency in charges, making it impossible for customers to compare banks. The Commission has floated ideas about a windfall tax on excessive bank profits, and possibly price controls, following its investigation into bank charges for small business customers, as well as the possibility of forcing the dominant banks to 'divest' branches to smaller rivals, to break 'local monopolies'.

While the existing players in the sector are mainly obsessing about mergers and alliances, the supermarkets have entered the banking field, direct Internet banking is gaining customer acceptance, and manufacturers, like Volkswagen and Sony, are seeing control of financial services and retail banking as attractive ways to leverage their profitability.

---

* This case material has been prepared on the basis of discussions with industry executives and published secondary sources.

However, among the Big Four high-street banking 'villains', Barclays appears to have unwittingly elected itself to be the scapegoat in the public eye, in the financial press, and with politicians and lobby groups.

'Barclays appears to have unwittingly elected itself to be the scapegoat in the public eye'

The Barclays leadership dilemma

Of all the banks in Britain, Barclays was widely regarded as the most hidebound by tradition. Many management mistakes over several decades – including the botched sale of BZW, one of the few successful UK investment banks – left Barclays judged by some City commentators as 'an injured dinosaur with no strategy'. Worse, there were suspicions that change would not happen because of layers of cultural inertia dating back to an era when Barclays was still run by an obscure group of founding families. Nonetheless, the sixth largest bank in Europe, in 1999, 'Barclays Bank' was judged to be the most valuable brand in Britain, by Interbrand, the agency that specializes in valuing brands, at £5313 million, substantially ahead of other banks and high-street retailers. A problem is that Barclays now finds itself challenged in every strategic move it makes and its freedom of manoeuvre increasingly restricted.

The CEO changes

Confidence in Barclays was not enhanced by its problems in holding on to a CEO. Martin Taylor vacated the post in November 1998, amid boardroom disputes about heavy losses in Russia and future strategy, with chairman Sir Peter Middleton taking over on a stop-gap basis. US banker, Michael O'Neill, was appointed CEO, with much publicity on his background as a US Marine, and a cost-cutter and deal-maker. In the event, O'Neill was forced to resign by diagnosis of heart disease on his first day in the new job. After a search process, Matthew Barrett was appointed from the Bank of Montreal – greeted by newspaper headlines 'The £7 million bonk manager', reflecting not only his pay package but also the circulating soft-porn pictures of his estranged wife.

Shareholder confidence was dented by these events, with many comments about Barclays losing its status as a first-division bank. City commentators focused on the huge pay deals needed to attract American bankers to the UK, and the need for Barclays to seek a merger – Halifax and Royal Bank of Scotland as the favoured candidates. Barrett's first task was to restore Barclay's credibility in the City and with shareholders.

Barclay's new strategy

Barrett addressed the City in February 2000, with the outline of his strategy for the future. His intention is to put Barclays back at the top of the British banking league. His speech mainly featured moves towards cost-cutting and profit enhancement, the move towards electronic Internet-based banking, and doubling the bank's mortgage business, largely through cross-selling to existing customers. His vision for Barclays is as a 'financial supermarket' rather than a group distributing only its own products. He also announced restructuring and performance-related bonuses for executives. Barrett faces the problem of coping with the remnants of the old Barclays culture. For example, the hierarchical nature of the old Barclays is reflected in its 54 Lombard Street headquarters, where security passes are needed to move between floors – Barrett is known to favour a move to open-plan offices at Canary Wharf, where senior executives can come down from their ivory tower and see what is going on in the business.

'Barrett faces the problem of coping with the remnants of the old Barclays culture'

Barclays and its customers

Barrett also faces what can only be described as a customer relationship crisis. In October 2000, a leaked internal document demanded 'nothing less than a complete overhaul of everything we do for customers', because Barclays products were expensive and uncompetitive, the bank was 'hated' by its customers, and relied on 'customer laziness' to make profits:

'The group is seen…as the ringleader of anti-consumer measures.'

'Negative perceptions include generating excessive profits – a culture of greed.'

'…selling expensive products to consumers who don't bother to shop around.'

'Being "big" means not caring.'

'Many of the group's products and services do not meet the demanding requirements of today's competitive financial services industry.'

'It is felt that the group has become idle internally…and been too hooked on premium pricing and customer inertia.'

'Being media-trained is not sufficient quality to qualify as a media spokesman…'

Sources: A leaked internal Barclays Bank document, reported in Paul Nuki (2000), 'Secret Report Tells Barclays it has Become "Hated" Bank', *Sunday Times*, 8 October. James Mackintosh (2000), 'Barclays "Needs Complete Overhaul"', *Financial Times*, 9 October. Simon English (2000), 'Our Greedy, Uncaring Image, by Barclays', *Daily Telegraph*, 9 October.

The immediate response by the bank was to plan a spend of £1 million on setting up a network of regional PR representatives to communicate with MPs and local businesses – dubbed 'the smoothies' by bank insiders – and to provide regular media training for executives. Barrett wrote to a select group of executives in May 2000, 'I feel very strongly that there is an urgent need to change the management of communications to help facilitate a more positive image'. Barrett's early months with the bank were said to be characterized by the phrase 'We did *what?*', as he uncovered bank policies and actions.

This crisis of confidence had been building as Barrett attempted to drive his cost-cutting and repositioning strategies through the business. Recall that the foundations for Barrett's strategies are the existing customer base and various forms of cross-selling to it.

Strategy 1 – Slimming the branch network

Barrett says 'banks don't close branches, customer behaviour does'. Following record profits in 1999, and a £1.3 million payment to Matthew Barrett for his first three months in the Barclays job, in April 2000, more than 400 000 Barclays customers received letters notifying them that their branches were among the 172 being closed the same week. In around half the closures, the Barclays branch was the last bank in the area concerned. This was a further stage in closing more than 723 branches over a ten-year period – more than a quarter of the original branch network – and progress towards Barrett's goal of cutting £1 billion in costs. The closures brought the loss of 7500 jobs in their wake. As protests mounted, Barclays defended its decision on economic grounds, and in an attempt to avoid a public relations disaster, offered to arrange for rural customers to cash cheques and make deposits at Post Offices.

'banks don't close branches, customer behaviour does'

The flood of protests grew. A government minister accused Barclays of abandoning any sense of social responsibility, the chairman of the All Party Parliamentary Group on Community Banking claimed 'Profits are going through the roof and the branch network is being systematically butchered', and Help the Aged called for urgent action to protect the elderly unable to reach a bank.

Barclays chairman, Sir Peter Middleton, defended Barrett's strategy as protecting shareholder interests by not subsidizing uneconomic branches from profits. Unfortunately, at the April 2000 shareholders meeting, Barclay shareholders demonstrated against the branch closures and labelled Matthew Barrett the 'Montreal Mauler'. The same month, angry Barclays branch managers went public with accusations that the bank was alienating many long-standing loyal customers and closing branches that had met all performance targets. Competitors were reported to be deluged with business from disaffected Barclays customers, and the Nationwide expressed interest in taking over closed branches and reopening them. Soon, NatWest had launched an advertising campaign claiming its branches would remain open as a service to customers.

The same month saw Chris Mullins, Environment Minister, urging Barclays customers to 'vote with their feet', and Kim Howells, Consumer Affairs Minister, saying 'I hope people will be much more choosy about what banks they use'. They emphasized that they were not actually calling for a 'boycott' of Barclays. Furious reactions by Barclays did not lead to the withdrawal of these statements.

Barclays continued to defend itself, saying that they were investing £100 million in the branch network to provide customers with 'better facilities and branding'. Pressure groups continue to operate – in January 2001 Barclays reversed its decision on closure of its Watlington branch in response to local business complaints and a press campaign. There have been few other signs of the closure policy being reversed.

However, in April 2001, Barclays announced that most of its branches would be opening longer hours – in the evenings and at weekends – creating 4000 new jobs (mostly part-time). Barrett suggested this was a response to consumer demand for increased convenience. Other banks have abandoned evening opening hour experiments because they failed to attract customers. Most analysts saw Barclays announcement as part of a drive to reduce the continuing negative publicity regarding branch closures, and to raise staff morale, bruised by job cuts.

Strategy 2 – Enhancing profits

Much of Barrett's strategy rests on cost-cuts and profit margin enhancement in several areas.

Charges for using ATM machines

As a route to leveraging greater profit from the use of cash machines, Barclays decided to introduce a 'disloyalty charge'. Mid-1999, Barclays announced its intention to charge competitors' customers for using Barclays cash machines – £1 a transaction from November that year. Other members of the Link cashpoint network threatened to exclude Barclays if it did so. Blocked by Nationwide in September, Barclays was forced to delay its November plan until February the next year. Enraged Barclays executives referred to smaller competitors as the 'rinky-dink banks', who were getting unfair advantage from free access to Barclays cash machines. Accusations of profiteering from politicians, pressure groups and the press continued. Barrett moved to centralize control over publicity, integrating press offices across the group. After a year of arguing, £1 million in consultancy fees and a lot of bad press, in July 2000, Barclays gave in to what seemed inevitable – it climbed down and agreed to scrap all charges on withdrawals from its machines by non-customers, but also to cease charging its own customers £1.50 for using competitors' ATMs. John Varley, Barclays retail CEO, sulked and threatened to scale back plans for new ATMs.

Profit enhancement

Barclays plans to double profits over four years through value-based management in Project Simon, a memo from Matthew Barrett stating 'We have to align our culture and day-to-day behaviour with the principles of maximizing value creation for our shareholders'. A 50-page report for Barclays directors revealed that British customers already paid substantially more than their European counterparts for basic services like current accounts, credit cards and loans – producing bank profit margins fully 40 per cent higher than banks in France, Germany, Spain and Holland. The report identifies ways of leveraging profit higher from customers – taking an extra £50–60 a year from each account while reducing the services provided. Methods to be used include: pricing out unprofit- able customers, widening the gap between interest rates paid to savers and interest rates charged to borrowers; introducing higher charges for those judged likely to put up with it; banning branch staff from showing goodwill by waiving one-off fees; incentivizing staff to sell low-interest accounts to savers (only offering higher interest-paying accounts as a last line of defence to avoid losing the customer altogether). The Barclays whistle-blower who leaked the above information to the financial press claims these methods have already been implemented. Further charges of profiteering and exploitation were laid at Barclays door. The price row refused to go away, and in May 2001, Barclays cut its current account overdraft rates for the first time in five years (though remaining one of the most expensive on the market). Unfortunately, any positive effect on Barclay's image was dissipated by revelations that, while reducing overdraft charges on current accounts, the bank had quietly reduced the rates it pays on cash ISAs – making a 1.25 per cent reduction at a time when base rates had fallen only 0.5 per cent. The financial press accused Barclays of 'cynical tactics' in reducing its ISA rates, as soon as they had attracted a few hundred thousand customers.

> *'The report identifies ways of leveraging profit higher from customers'*

> *'Further charges of profiteering and exploitation were laid at Barclays door'*

Strategy 3 – A 'big bank for a big world'

In March 2000, Barclays embarked on a £15 million advertising campaign to position itself as a 'big bank for a big world', featuring stars like Sir Anthony Hopkins and Tim Roth. It was unfortunate that the campaign coincided with public furore over the branch closures and job losses, and the 300 per cent pay rise for the chairman, and attracted much adverse commentary on this basis. The repositioning effort, as a platform for global expansion, lost much of its force.

Strategy 4 – Market segmentation

Financial services retail head, Martin Varley, is committed to differentiating everyday retail customers from the more wealthy, as a way of concentrating resources on the better-off as a market for added-value financial services. For example, 2001 saw the launch of Barclays' Premier Banking for customers with an income above £60 000, with specialist centres, special areas within branches, advisory services and special interest rate deals.

By mid-2000, Barclays was again in the headlines for its plans to discriminate between customers on interest rates for loans, offering better rates to less risky customers, for otherwise identical products. This contrasts with the traditional 'one-rate-for all' interest payments. Accusations of 'social exclusion' and discrimination against the disadvantaged began immediately after the plans were announced. The Consumers' Association waxed lyrical about higher prices for the poor. Competitors – Abbey National, HSBC, Lloyds TSB and NatWest – immediately and coyly claimed the moral high ground by denying that they had plans to follow Barclays (it is expected that they will imitate Barclays strategy when they are able to do so).

'Accusations of "social exclusion" and discrimination against the disadvantaged began immediately after the plans were announced'

Strategy 5 – The mortgage business

Barrett's strategy for building a stronger position in the mortgage market was advanced by the August 2000 takeover of the Woolwich (former) building society, in a deal worth £5.5 billion. The Woolwich has four million savers and borrowers. Barclays said it anticipated that the takeover would generate 'cost savings'. Shortly afterwards, Barclays confirmed that 100 Woolwich branches would close, with 1000 job losses from the 6000 Woolwich workforce. However, the Woolwich brand is to be retained and become the brand name for all Barclays mortgage products. The group predicts an annual £90 million income benefit from cross-selling between the Woolwich and Barclays customer bases.

In January 2001, Barclays and Legal & General put paid to rumours of a £40 billion take-over, when they announced a strategic alliance. In the alliance, Barclays will sell L&G pensions and investment products, and close its own life assurance operation and retail fund manager. This is a classic 'bancassurance' strategy. L&G anticipated increasing life and pensions business by 20 per cent and doubling unit trust sales as a result of the alliance. Barclays anticipates 250 job losses in London and the south-east.

In May 2001, in response to Lloyds TSB making a £17 billion unsolicited bid for Abbey National, and following the announcement of the Halifax/ Bank of Scotland merger, Barrett was looking at making a 'white knight' friendly bid for Abbey National.

Strategy 6 – Online banking

Barclays has made considerable inroads into Internet banking – adding more new Internet customers a month in 2000 than Smile (the Co-op internet bank) has in total. Industry analysts believe that Barclays has a more credible e-commerce strategy than its competitors. Two years into Internet banking, Barclays had 800 000 online accounts.

The present position?

Barclays' 2000 profits climbed 42 per cent to £3.5 billion, a 41 per cent increase on 1999 profits, notwithstanding a consultants' bill of £2.3 million a week, exceeding analysts' predictions, largely as a result of branch closures. Barrett announced his ambition to make Barclays a pan-European bank, through take-overs and mergers in Continental Europe – the aim is to raise overseas earnings from 20 per cent to 50 per cent of total group income. The City welcomes Barclays' profitability, while consumer groups leapt into action to accuse Barclays of milking its customers and manipulating interest rates to boost profits. Barrett's pay and bonus reached £1.7 million for 2000, and Barclays' share rose from £15 to £20 in the period June–December 2000.

However, one City commentator raised the question: 'The City loves Barclays. Does anybody else?'. The PressWatch 2000 survey shows Barclays attracted more negative press comment than any other organization (including even Railtrack, Camelot and the New Millennium Dome company).

'The PressWatch 2000 survey shows Barclays attracted more negative press comment than any other organization'

Points to ponder

1 Does all this customer satisfaction and customer loyalty theory fall over when confronted by Barclays' financial performance?
2 Is managing your image with customers the same thing as managing the substance of your value proposition?

3 Why are Barclays staff sending confidential documents to the press?
4 Will a brand-based strategy for hostages survive, in an era of value and transparency?
5 Are there lessons about customer relationship management in the story of Barclays' last couple of years?
6 Is there a long-term vulnerability in building strategies which rely on customer goodwill (cross-selling, Internet banking, and so on), at a time when that goodwill would seem to be an illusion?
7 If you have been elected the industry's whipping boy – how do you resign from that position, before the government competition commission decides to join in?

Sources: Helen Dunne (1999), 'Barclays Chief Quits on First Day', *Daily Telegraph*, 14 April. Andrew Alexander (1999), 'Jinxed Barclays Loses its Second Chief in Six Months', *Daily Mail*, 14 April. Helen Dunne (1999), 'Barclays Abolishes "Disloyalty Charges"', *Daily Telegraph*, 12 October. 'Secret Barclays Report Exposes How Banks Rip Off Customers', *Sunday Times*, 20 February 2000. Jeff Prestridge (2000), 'Barclays Staff Hit Out Over Closures', *Financial Mail on Sunday*, 2 April. David Ibison (2000), 'High Street "Villain" takes Flak for the Big Four', *Financial Times*, 5 April. Helen Dunne (2000), 'Barclays Defends Branch Cull', *Daily Telegraph*, 27 April. James Mackintosh (2000), 'Barclays Learns a Lesson in Keeping Customers Satisfied', *Financial Times*, 4 July. 'Revealed: Banks' Plot to Hike Profits and Cut Choice', *Sunday Times*, 9 July 2000. James Mackintosh (2000), 'Barclays Takes Loan Risk into Account', *Financial Times*, 14 July. Helen Dunne (2000), 'Barclays and Woolwich to Tie the Knot', *Daily Telegraph*, 10 August. Dominic White (2001), 'Barclays and L&G in Deal to Sell Branded Products', *Daily Telegraph*, 17 January. Ruth Sutherland (2001), 'Barclays Rides Profit Wave to Expansion on Continent', *Daily Mail*, 9 February. Jeff Prestridge (2001), 'The City Loves Barclays. Does Anyone Else?', *Financial Mail on Sunday*, 11 February. Simon English (2001), 'Barclays Chief Pockets £1.7m', *Daily Telegraph*, 8 March. Melanie Wright (2001), 'Two-Tier Banking Plan by Barclays', *Daily Telegraph*, 19 March. Robert Shrimley and James Mackintosh (2001), 'Banks "Leeching Off" Business Says Minister', *Financial Times*, 20 April. Roland Gribbens (2001), 'Barclays to Open Branches in Evenings', *Daily Telegraph*, 27 April.

PART II

New Millennium: New Realities

The e-volution of e-verything into e-business:

The e-ra of e-market-led strategic change

> 'The Internet changes everything for some businesses, and some things for all businesses'[1].

It was not long ago that I wrote about the Internet as the arena of the computer nerd's chat pages with messages like 'Hi there, I'm Dave. I'm into Country and Western and Airfix'[2], and I sympathized with John Dvorak's view that the Internet is 'an overhyped plaything destined to disappoint all but the most masochistic technofreaks . . . Web, schmeb!'[3]. However, times change . . .

> 'Learn from the mistakes of others,
> for you will never have time to make them all yourself.'

Jack Welch, chairman of General Electric, and one of the world's most admired managers, summarizes the situation nicely:

'We thought the creation and operation of websites was mysterious Nobel prize stuff, the province of the wild-eyed and purple-haired . . . [but] Any company, old or new, that does not see this technology as important as breathing, could be on its last breath.'[4]

> Everything you know is wrong.
>
> (Lit sign displayed at U2 concerts in the 1990s to unnerve audiences)

It is now impossible to talk sensibly about market strategy without the Internet. For better or worse, this is not just an era of customer sophistication and customer value, it is also one of e-market-led strategic change[5]. These things are, of course, distinctly related to each other.

However, you really do have to allow for the fact that blasé though we may be about buying a book off the Internet – this is all relatively new. Microsoft and Apple were only founded in 1976. It was only in 1989 that the World-Wide Web was developed by Timothy Berners-Lee for information to be shared among scientists at CERN in Geneva, thus providing the platform for software development and the growth of the Internet. The Internet probably did not enter the commercial arena until 1994, when Yahoo! was founded as an online directory for websites. Amazon did not sell a book until 1995. So, it is not surprising that we are still learning what the Internet and e-business really mean.

So, I want you to do two things with this chapter:

'it is not going to go away, and you need to understand what it means for your business'

- get your mind around the quite amazing things that the Internet represents, and particularly the outpouring of creativity to create new business models and new ways of doing things – it is happening right now, it is not going to go away, and you need to understand what it means for your business and where the competition is going to come from;
- then get *real* – people have lost fortunes by being seduced by the magic of the Web, and we have a lot to learn about what it takes to build and implement sustainable Internet-based business propositions.

However, the one thing you cannot do with the Internet is to ignore it, because it is unlikely to ignore you. For example, Craig Barrett, Intel's CEO, says that in the future there will be no such thing as 'Internet companies' because *all* companies, whatever their business, will be Internet companies[6].

This chapter will look at the vision behind the Internet and the business revolution it has created. We can examine the dot.com madness and its consequences, and what we now see as the power of 'bricks and clicks' strategies[7]. We can look at the disillusionment now surrounding Web-based ventures, and the hidden impact of the Internet on business-to-business channels, as opposed to business-to-consumer deals. Lastly, we can review what the Internet means for developing market strategies and creating new types of transformations in the process of going to market. This is organized in the following fashion:

- first, the boring stuff about where we are now, Web pages and Internet visionaries, and all that;
- then we can look at the exciting stuff – the Internet providing us with new ways to go to market and new ways of doing business;
- next we can get real again – the crash of the 'new economy' and many of the dot.coms is a harsh reality, but it should not be allowed to blind us to the real potentials of the Internet;
- finally, we can look at what we are now learning about the impact of the Internet on strategy and the process of going to market.

Much of this is in the form of stories about the fate of companies and industries in the era of e-business, rather than yet more theorizing about a way of doing business that most of us have barely started to understand. Be assured – we are at day 1 of the new era, no more than that.

'Be assured – we are at day 1 of the new era, no more than that'

The glorious anarchy of the Web

Don't forget though, that perhaps the greatest joy of the Internet is that it does not belong to anyone, and it is almost impossible for the forces of boredom, tedium and repression (e.g. MBA-trained managers) to control it. It is also almost unbelievably powerful. For example, in late 2000 when a young lady called Clair Swire sent a rather rude e-mail to a boyfriend at a London law firm, complimenting him on certain aspects of his personal perform-ance, he was proud enough to copy the message to friends, who copied it to their colleagues, and so on. It is estimated that by the time they had finished, to Ms Swire's great embarrassment, some *ten million* people throughout the world had read the scurrilous message. People in London were getting messages from small towns in the middle of China asking them if they had seen Ms Swire's e-mail.

REALITY CHECK
YOU DID WHAT IN YOUR BEDROOM . . . ?

In 2001, Raphael Gray was charged with hacking into corporate websites to access thousands of names addresses and credit cards details, by exploiting a security weakness in certain Microsoft products. Styling himself the 'Saint of E-Commerce', he was apparently motivated by the mission to highlight the dangers of Internet shopping. This must explain why he stole the credit card details of Bill Gates, head of Microsoft, and used them to send Mr Gates a consignment of Viagra. It is estimated that Mr Gray caused millions of pounds worth of damage to dot.com companies – Visa International alone spending £250 000 on reissuing credit cards. The most stunning and frightening facts of this story are actually twofold: first, it took the combined might of the FBI, the Canadian Mounties, British police, and a team of computer experts to track Mr Gray down; and, second, the basis for this international criminal campaign of destruction was a £700 home computer in Mr Gray's bedroom in a house in Pembrokeshire, Wales.

Source: Richard Savill (2001), 'Teenage Hacker Sent Gates Sex Pills', *Daily Telegraph*, 21 April.

'traditional managers seem to have trouble getting their minds around the fact that it is very difficult to control what happens on the Internet'

Certainly, traditional managers seem to have trouble getting their minds around the fact that it is very difficult to control what happens on the Internet. The difficulty of control is illustrated by the frustrating experiences for managers at the Disney Corporation regarding their employees' e-mails. Management sent a command that they did not like their employees referring to the Disney company as 'Mousewitsch'[8] and they were to desist in this minor amusement (a little bit of a managerial sense of humour failure where Mickey lives). The immediate response by employees was to comply, and instead to refer to their company as Duckau[9]. Trying to censor the Internet is a fast way to look very silly[10].

However, more seriously, individual websites – e.g. CompanyXSucks.com – can say things about your business which are potentially damaging, and notices posted on bulletin boards (often untrue rumours) can seriously impact your share value[11]. Indeed, 2000 saw Currys threatening legal action against the price comparison website Pricerunner.com for publishing their prices in disadvantageous comparison with competitors[12]. At the very least you should be aware of what people can do to your business by exploiting the freedom of the Web. It has reached the stage where some people will judge us by our website – comments like 'I knew your company was in trouble when I saw how bad the Web pages were . . .' are going to hurt.

It can get worse. In 1999, innocent Web surfers using some search engines got surprising results when they searched Rolls-Royce, Harrods, Manchester United and Land Rover:

- the false Harrods site had large pictures of the Knightsbridge store, and advice on the best places to find and use cocaine; the amusing fellow who thought of this did so because he claims that Harrods did sell cocaine in the nineteenth century (when it was a legal medicine);
- the counterfeited Land Rover site provided 'The Top Ten Reasons Why My Land Rover Discovery Sucks', thoughtfully translated into five languages, and with a clever graphic showing the vehicle dropping its exhaust and bumpers;
- the falsified Manchester United and Rolls-Royce sites were more routinely pornographic[13].

Similarly, in 2000, a hacker broke into supermarket firm Safeway's UK website and sent its customers an e-mail warning of price increases and urging them to shop at Tesco or Sainsbury[14]. I hate to be a miserable old killjoy[15], but this isn't actually very funny when it is *your* brand or company being vilified by the witty, wacky Web pranksters, and *your* customers being inconvenienced for the sake of someone else's warped sense of humour – because they are likely to blame *you*, not the cyber-moron responsible.

Dubbya dubbya dubbya dot WHAT?

'many of the things that have been produced by the Internet can only be described as seriously weird'

However, many of the things that have been produced by the Internet can only be described as seriously weird. It is pointless to try and surprise or shock readers with examples of 'wacky' websites, so I am not going to try. If you need convincing – get a technofreak to show you his or her bookmarked websites . . .

But there is an important point. Just about everyone who has tried to define the areas of business where the Internet would probably not have an impact have had to go back later and change their minds. People said no-one would buy their fresh food over the Web – tell that to the online grocers. People said that industries like dairy farming and construction would not be fundamentally changed by the Internet – both those sectors now have highly efficient business-to-business online exchanges in the US. It starts to look like the impact really is going to be on all businesses.

So, what has changed?

A 1999 Booze Allen & Hamilton report suggests that there are seven major 'megatrends' associated with the Internet that affect businesses:

- new channels of distribution that revolutionize sales and brand management;
- the balance of power shifting to the consumer;
- competition intensifying across all dimensions;
- the pace of business fundamentally accelerating;
- companies transforming into extended enterprises (linked electronically to partners);
- companies re-evaluating how they add value; and
- knowledge is becoming the key asset.

Their report concludes that:

> 'To thrive in the internet-enabled world, companies must reinvent themselves, their business models and processes, their interactions with customers, suppliers, intermediaries and alliances, and how they capture and leverage knowledge as a strategic asset.'[16]

The challenge for us is to ask how true this is of our company, our channels, markets and customers – right now and in the near future. To which the answer will probably be 'Well, yes and no'. Then we may be able to track what the Internet means for developing our market strategy and transforming our process of going to market.

First – theboringstuff.com[17]

In 2000, a MORI survey found Britain to be in the grip of 'e-apathy' – 93 per cent of consumers questioned did not want to be part of the new economy, nor did they feel they were missing out[18]. So maybe there is some way to go before e-business dominates everything? This said, Verdict, the retail consultancy, still predicts that, by 2005, the online shopping marketplace (i.e. business-to-consumer only) will be worth £12.5 billion, or around 5 per cent of all retail sales[19] – they predict this will include more than half of all computer software purchases and 20 per cent of all music, video and book purchases. Certainly, by Christmas 2000, the US was looking at a $10 billion online consumer market, standing at 3 per cent of total retail sales[20].

'In 2000, a MORI survey found Britain to be in the grip of "e-apathy"'

There have already been quite dramatic impacts on established companies. For example, in 1998, when the Automobile Association closed its 120 shops, the reason was 'People now prefer to buy their travel services over the phone, fax, or Internet, so our high-street stores are no longer viable'[21]. By 1999, major companies like Boeing and Motorola were warning suppliers that anyone not making the transition to Web-based commerce would be locked out of their businesses[22]. In 2001, the Prudential insurance company announced the phasing out of the 'man from the Pru', in the form of its direct salesforce, because 90 per cent of customers now do their transactions by post, telephone or Internet – the 'virtual' man from the Pru is to take over[23].

'There have already been quite dramatic impacts on established companies'

REALITY CHECK

THE BORING STUFF CAN MAKE A DIFFERENCE

The Teddington Cheese Company is a small specialist retailer established in south-west London in 1995. It sells cheeses, pickles, biscuits, wine, cider, port and hampers. The company established a website containing details and pictures of its products and hampers, offering delivery all over Europe in 24 hours. The costs of setting up www.Teddingtoncheese.co.uk were £8000, and by the end of 2000 the site was generating 1000 hits a week. Turnover has increased by 10 per cent a year as a result of e-mail orders, mostly from the UK, and the initial costs of the website were met within a year. The company also reports more visits to the shop from those who have viewed the website.

Source: Virginia Matthews (2000), 'Britain's Company Chiefs are Lost in Cyberspace', *Sunday Business*, 31 December.

The e-revolution or e-what?

'while visionaries pontificate, and sceptics snipe at them, businesses have to try to make sense of what e-business means to them'

However, while visionaries pontificate, and sceptics snipe at them, businesses have to try to make sense of what e-business means to them. The Web only became a significant business tool in the 1990s, and Figure 4.1 suggests the stages that we have seen so far are somewhat less than revolutionary for most of us:

- *Electronic directory* – At one level, a Web page is nothing more than an information source for prospective contacts. For many small businesses the Web page is still just a dumb picture with the name, address and telephone number. This is very boring, but may get some hits from people trying to find you. This seems to be a minimal requirement – it is hard to imagine any company not having a Web address on its letterhead these days.
- *Electronic advertising* – More sophisticated are websites where goods are displayed and listed. For example, The Gap's website will let you look at pictures of the clothes, but not buy them (unless you live in the USA)[24]. Harrods' site shows you around the store, but does not expect you to want to do something as tacky as buy things over the Internet.
- *Interactive advertising* – Some sites let you ask questions and try things out. For example, on the Rolex watch site you can specify different watchbands and faces and see a picture, but you cannot buy a new Rolex on the Web.
- *Interactive channel* – Cleverer yet are sites which will let you search for a product, buy it, and then guide you towards further purchases. The Tesco grocery site lets you place orders, but also reminds you about your 'favourites'. The Amazon.com site will use its information about your purchase history to suggest what 'other people like you' have bought, and link you to partner sites as needed, so you can make additional purchases.
- *Integrated processes* – The most sophisticated sites make decisions with you and for you. Most common in business-to-business applications, the seller adapts to the buyer's purchase process. For example, Dell Computers acts more like a company's outsourced Information Technology department than a simple direct seller of computers – keeping stock records, providing technical tools, loading the customer's software before delivery, planning for future IT needs, all via the Web pages (see pp. 202–4).
- *?* – What next depends on which visionaries you believe. Some suggest that 'peer-to-peer' computing will be the next

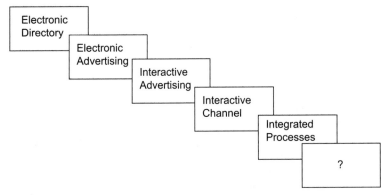

Electronic Directory

Electronic Advertising

Interactive Advertising

Interactive Channel

Integrated Processes

?

Figure 4.1   Evolution in the Internet

significant driving force (see pp. 179–82). Amazon.com's Marketplace product – putting sellers of used books in touch with buyers – is an attempt to exploit the power of peer-to-peer networks with an established online retailing brand.

I have some sympathy with those who think that e-business and the dot.coms may have been over-hyped by some people. But before any of us get too cynical just compare my recent experience in replacing the print cartridges in my laser printers:

REALITY CHECK
BUYING A REPLACEMENT PRINTER CARTRIDGE

1 *Replacing a laser printer cartridge at Cardiff Business School* – The cartridge runs out, the printer is knackered (fortunately experience in this organization has taught me to keep a spare cartridge locked in a secret place in the office, contrary to financial regulations). I ask Secretary to get me a replacement. Secretary asks Technician for a replacement. Secretary returns to ask me to specify the printer details and code number for the print cartridge, notwithstanding the fact the original request contained this information. I give her the information again. Secretary contacts Technician. Technician tells Secretary there are none in stock. Secretary tells me (in cowardly fashion by e-mail, to avoid temper tantrum, for she does not know about the secret stockpile). Technician completes order request form, after pondering for

some days about whether the wind is in the right direction. Form goes to Finance Office. Form sits in Finance Office festering for several days. In fullness of time, form goes to Director of Business School, who seemingly has nothing better to do with his time than check small purchase orders, and query why people need things like printer cartridges. After very boring phone conversation about laser cartridges, order form is eventually signed and returns to Finance Office. Form is photocopied, and photocopy is filed. After some days, when enough orders have accumulated, the order is mailed second-class to supplier. Some seven to ten days later printer cartridges are delivered to Business School. Documentation is checked against Order Form and photocopied, and the copy is filed. Cartridges go to Technician. Technician thinks things over, and the strain obliges him to take immediate sick-leave. Eventually, out of goodness of heart, Technician gives cartridge to Secretary. Secretary considers all possible alternative beneficiaries of this munificent bounty, before eventually giving in and delivering cartridge to me, around four weeks after it was requested.

2 *Replacing the laser printer cartridge in home office* – Log on to www.dabs.co.uk. Complete online order form in approximately three minutes. Cartridge arrives by first class post two days later.

Now think hard about this – which do you think is the more rational approach to getting simple, routine things done for customers? Which approach do you think is going to work in leaner, results-oriented organizations of the future? You are allowed three guesses and the second two don't count. How shall I put this – you would have to be clinically insane, or as stupid as the Director of Cardiff Business School, to prefer the first approach.

In the early stages, the Internet really is about little more than communications – e-mail on speed – and brochure-ware, but the challenge laid down is much bigger. This challenge is to remodel businesses around the Net and to integrate the Net into business processes. For some of us, survival will depend on how well we respond to that challenge. Apart from anything else, the Internet channel may be the only route to effective mass customization for many companies – 'build to order' products where the product is built to the specification chosen by the customer.

'This challenge is to remodel businesses around the Net and to integrate the Net into business processes'

> ## REALITY CHECK
> ## THE 'BUILD TO ORDER' POTENTIAL ON THE WEB
>
> To buy shirts from Shirtmaker.com, the customer chooses the fabric, pocket type, cuff design, and monogram if required. The chosen design is examined on the computer screen. The shirts are made to order by eleven tailors in Seoul, each responsible for one step in the process. The shirts cost about the same as a ready-to-wear shirt from a normal retailer, but are bespoke. Global textile industry sales are stagnating but the made-to-measure sector has grown 30 per cent from 1996 to 2000. Some forecasts are that within a few years a third of all clothing will be bought on the Web.
>
> In the car industry, it was estimated in 1992 that the statistical probability of a customer finding the right model and exact specification s/he wants by a daily visit to the same showroom was once in 19 years (notwithstanding there is frequently 60 days of stock spread between manufacturers and dealers at the same time). Car manufacturers like Volkswagen, Toyota, Ford and General Motors are investing heavily to establish e-commerce sites that will allow the assembly and delivery of customized cars within one or two weeks. In December 1999, DaimlerChrysler's Smart car (a two-seat city car) became the first car that could be configured and ordered online.
>
> **Source**: Chris Tighe (1997), 'Lean Sales Machine', *Financial Times*, 25 June. Christiane Schilzki-Haddouti (2001), 'Up Close and Personal', *Connectis*, May, 25–26.

Probably the first practical question is still, if you plan to invest – what exactly do you expect the Internet to do for your business? Right now, for many of us, the Internet issue is whether it fits our publicity plans, and whether we want to open up a direct channel that competes with our salesforce and distributors. However, in the longer term there are much bigger strategic issues to confront. To keep it real, however, a recent study – *E-Business 2001* – underlines the fact that, while an Internet strategy is a prerequisite for modern business, more than half the companies surveyed reported no increase in sales as a result of e-commerce investments, and two-thirds had not succeeded in reaching new markets via the Internet – lack of objective advice and consultants' hype were blamed for many unproductive e-investments[25]. Many of us may be still in the very earliest stage of the Internet revolution.

'the first practical question is still, if you plan to invest – what exactly do you expect the Internet to do for your business?'

> 'Embrace the Net. Bring me a plan of how you are going to transform your business beyond adding an Internet site.'
>
> Jack Welch, CEO, General Electric

Some of us may want to stay in those early stages for a while too. For example, one rule in building an effective transactional website is that the customer should never be more then 'three clicks away' from the information they need, because they are always 'one click' away from giving up on you. At Gateway, the company had to make the transition from an ordering system that took its staff three to five weeks to learn, to an online selling process that a first-time customer who has never seen the site before could understand and place an order correctly without making a phone call or seeking help. Those who achieved this note that 'this is really hard to do'![26]. It is also time-consuming and expensive.

The visionaries

So, what is the vision for the e-future that is going to change so much?

Somewhat belatedly, Microsoft decided to take the Web seriously, and in 1999 Bill Gates declared 'The internet changes everything', and argued that companies should put the Net at the centre of their strategic plans. Gates uses the phrase 'frictionless capitalism' to describe consumers' ability to shop around on the Web. Gary Hamel argues 'The Web will fundamentally change customers' expectations about convenience, speed, comparability, price and service', in ways which mean that it will become increasingly difficult for companies to make money using traditional business models[27].

However, this probably does no more than state what is now self-evident. There are many other ideas that start to suggest that the age of the Internet is fundamentally different in ways that we are only just starting to grasp.

For example, Jeremy Rifkin[28] suggests that the essence of the 'new economy' is that the ownership of physical assets is becoming less important than access to ideas and services. He gives an appealing example. In the old economy, the Pacific island Nauru made its living selling guano (accumulated bird droppings) as fertilizer. Today, in the new economy, its near neighbour, Tuvalu, is experiencing even more remarkable good fortune, because its internet domain (.tv) is in great demand from television companies. More pragmatically, Vinod Khosla, one of the founders of Sun Microsystems, makes the point – the new economy is about the power of ideas, and smart people can make more money and wield more influence with a bright idea and a new business than they ever could running a large corporation[29].

Thinking about guano though, a landmark publication was Bill Gates' book *Business @ The Speed of Light*[30], in which he predicts an era in which all businesses will use technology to accelerate the flow of information, making data instantly accessible and enabling knowledge workers to reach decisions and act as fast as they can think. He predicts three fundamental business shifts:

- Most transactions (between businesses, consumers and government) will become 'self-service digital transactions, with the result that traditional intermediaries will evolve to add value, or go out of business'.
- Customer service will become the main added-value function in every business, but human involvement in service will shift from routine tasks to high-value, personal attention to important issues or problems for the customer.
- The pace of transactions and the need for more personalized attention to customers will drive companies to adopt digital processes internally.

For consumers he describes an emerging 'Web life-style' for consumers, based on using the Web to get news, to learn, to be entertained, and to communicate, as well as a 'Web work-style'.

But the e-reality right now?

However, there may be a few barriers left in the way of embracing the e-future in your business transformation.

Access

The e-vision relies on a level of access to the Internet which does not yet exist. The Martini three As – Internet access will be 'Anytime, Anywhere, Any place' – is still no more than a vision of the future. Current estimates are that around a third of the UK population has access to the Internet (at home or work), although this is well over 50 per cent in the US and Sweden[31].

'e-vision relies on a level of access to the Internet which does not yet exist'

This said, one recent survey highlighted the fact that nearly half of British employees admit to surfing the Web for at least three hours a week (when they are supposed to be working)[32]. Certainly, there are all sorts of attempts to make Internet access easier – BT Multi.Phone kiosks; mobile access in taxis; Internet cafes; PhotoMe kiosks with Internet terminals; access through cable TV services; mobile phone access; and so on. However, right now access remains relatively limited. Mind you, with their infinite wisdom, European Union psychologists have decided that anyone who surfs the Internet for more than four hours a day is clinically ill and needs medical treatment[33], so don't say you haven't been warned.

The worldwide wait

'even if you have got access, it is so, so slow'

Let's be honest, even if you have got access, it is so, so slow. We have been promised all kinds of technological advances to increase speed of access, but at the moment for most of us they are just that – promises.

Security

Confidence in the 'new economy' was shaken when even Microsoft's own systems proved accessible to hackers. Even the mighty icon Amazon.com had the credit card details of 98 000 customers stolen late in 2000 (discovered four months after the event). Also in 2000, Barclays shut down its online banking when a software bug allowed users to see other customers' account information and Powergen advised 7000 customers to cancel their credit cards, after the company cleverly revealed their banking details through the website[34]. The reality seems a little short of perfect high technology security.

'The reality seems a little short of perfect high technology security'

Cost

Outside the US, most people have to pay for access to the Internet. You either pay for the Internet Service Provider (e.g. BT, AOL) or you pay for the phone calls, or you may pay for both (e.g. Microsoft Network). There is a lot of resistance on the ground (mainly from telecoms companies – surprise, surprise) to free unmetered access to the Internet.

However, none of this withstanding, potentially, the underlying power of the Internet is more than just providing a medium for communications, entertainment, or consumer commerce. It is the power to reinvent and revolutionize the way business operates.

Second – theexcitingstuff.com

More interesting than Web pages and brochureware is the potential for using the Internet to build new ways of doing business.

New business models

Perhaps the prototype for all that followed was the launch by Jeff Bezos of Amazon.com in 1994. Many managers threaten to vomit if they have the Amazon.com example thrust down their throats yet again. However, there are still interesting lessons to be learned from Amazon – they just aren't the lessons we used to think they were.

'there are still interesting lessons to be learned from Amazon – they just aren't the lessons we used to think they were'

REALITY CHECK

AMAZON. COM OR AMAZON.TOAST?

One of the earliest virtual businesses operating on the Internet with an innovative business model, Amazon.com, remains the largest online retailer, way ahead of the rest in brand recognition, international spread and product breadth. Amazon.com was started by Jeffrey P. Bezos in 1994 on three floors above an art gallery on a seedy Seattle street, named after the river with the greatest volume of water, and has a goal of building a $10 billion business. Amazon.com used its Internet site to sell books from more than 3 million available titles. It moved into selling music, and has quickly become the leading online music retailer, as well as videos. With 4.5 million customers in 1998, and sales of around $540 million, by 2001 Amazon.com had 20 million customers and sales forecast at $3.5 billion.

The Amazon.com business model has redefined the book business. Amazon.com made it incredibly easy for customers to buy books, and has built a 'community' of book buyers – reading reams of reviews about books, receiving e-mail notifications of new books and related purchases, who also participate in book reviewing, have online chats with authors, and suggest endings to short stories started by major authors. After the information collected in the first purchase, further buys involve just a mouse click – Amazon's unique and patented 'One Click' feature. While traditional booksellers offer discounts on the top hundred titles or so, Amazon discounts

400 000 titles. The strength of the model lies in its advantages over the traditional book distribution channel. For example, compared to the major US book retailer Barnes & Noble in 1998:

Amazon	Versus	Barnes & Noble
1 website	Number of stores	1011
3.1 million	Titles per superstore	175 000
2 per cent	Book returns	30 per cent
306 per cent	Sales growth (1998)	10 per cent
1600	Number of employees	27 000
$375 000	Sales per employee (annual)	$100 000
24 times	Inventory turnovers per year	3 times
Low	Long-term capital requirements	High
High	Cash flow	Low

Amazon was the first Internet trader to use 'collaborative filtering technology' to analyse customer purchases and visits on the site to suggest purchases (based on what people with similar interests have bought). This provides very accurate targeting of marketing. It also provides a database of customers and indications of what they might buy in the future.

The technology also facilitated Amazon's partnering with 'Amazon Associates' – other Internet sites providing links to Amazon.com for their visitors, and paid a commission on resulting sales. (Amazon has around 140 000 sites in the Associates programme.) This model has been patented as a business process. Bezos sees a future in becoming a broker who helps people find things being sold elsewhere on the Web, and takes a commission from those sellers as reward for putting them in touch with buyers. Ultimately, the purchases of partner companies' products may be made through the Amazon site where the customer's information is stored. The business model also has advantages in cash flow. Amazon carries only about 15 days worth of stocks (high volume titles only) and is paid almost immediately by credit card, so getting about a month's use of interest-free money.

As well as product expansion – e.g. toys, hand-held computers – and geographically – local websites for the UK, France, Germany and Japan – Amazon has expanded into an auction service, and a service called zShops allowing small businesses to sell from Amazon's site (and pay a 1–5 per cent commission on sales), and most recently into acting as an intermediary between buyers and sellers of used books (to the significant displeasure of new book publishers) as Marketplace Sellers. The Amazon Commerce Network provides space for smaller e-tailers on the Amazon site in return for stock and commission.

At its initial public offering Amazon.com shares were valued at $9, but by the end of 1998 the shares were trading at around $209, giving a market value of $11.1 billion. In December 1998, an analyst at CIBC Technology forecast a $400 price over the following twelve months, which drove the stock up to $243 (going through the $300 barrier for a short time). This made Amazon twice the value of Barnes & Noble, America's largest conventional bookstore chain.

The company has yet to make a profit. Bezos says this is a conscious decision to develop the business. By 2001, the company had accumulated $2.3 billion of losses, and sales growth in the core books business was slowing. Explosive sales growth had been followed by the same rate of growth in the company's losses – selling more books means losing more money. The company is carrying $2.1 billion of debt – more than is owed by some poor Third World countries. The twelve months from March 2000 to 20001 saw share price fall from $75 to $10. Bezos is amused that some critics suggest the company should be renamed Amazon.org – because it is clearly a not-for-profit organization.

A critical metric is customer retention and cross-selling. This defines when Amazon will be able to reduce customer acquisition spending and move into profit. In 1998, 64 per cent of sales were from repeat customers, and Amazon was gaining an average of 9000 new customers a day. By 2000, only 52 per cent of Amazon customers made a purchase in the following year. Mid-2000 saw a £2.2 million UK advertising campaign evidencing the continued costs of customer acquisition.

If there is a major flaw in the model, it is that it is relatively easy for conventional competitors to open their own websites, and this is exactly what has happened – the entry costs are low and the technology is easily accessible. In fact, there are now estimated to be some 500 online booksellers. In 1997, CEO of Forrester Inc., George F. Colony, promised that the Internet revolutionary would soon be made 'Amazon.*toast*'.

Amazon's marketing and promotion costs are high. This places pressure on profitability unless revenue per sale can be levered upwards. Fulfilment costs are also problematic.

While it is the world's largest e-tailer, Amazon.com was not spared in the dot.com crash. By early 2001 Amazon.com stock had fallen more than 80 per cent from its December 1999 peak, reaching $10, and many believe it is still overvalued. Bezos himself advises small investors and short-term investors not to hold Amazon stock, which has not stopped lawsuits being filed in the US claiming Amazon misled investors over crucial financial and business information. The company is taking action to reduce its cost base – 2001 saw 1300 jobs cut, and distribution and service centres being closed in

Georgia and Seattle. Amazon announced at this time that they would charge publishers for promoting their books in the e-mails sent to the 29 million customer base. However, in April 2001, Bezos reported sales gains and substantial reductions in losses, predicting pro-forma profit by the end of the year – the core US business of books, music and videos was making operating profits.

The Amazon business model is about much more than selling books and related products. In the US, Amazon sells a wide range of products – home electronics, pharmaceuticals, DIY products. Bezos says his mission is to sell 'anything, with a capital A – bar animals and armaments', and to be 'the place where people come to find and discover anything they might want to buy online'. Some have called this the 'Wal-Mart of the Web strategy'.

Important alliances are also being made to extend the business model. In 2000, Amazon.com signed a ten-year alliance with Toys 'R' Us, to sell toys through a co-branded website. This combines Toys 'R' Us purchasing and stockholding muscle with Amazon's superior Web model and fulfilment expertise. Bezos is actively searching for additional alliances with 'bricks and mortar' retailers. Less dramatic but also illustrative, in 1999 Amazon and the auction house Sothebys formed a joint venture to market collectibles and memorabilia on the new sothebys.amazon.com website. In March 2001, Amazon was reported to be in talks about a strategic alliance with Wal-Mart (operating as Asda in the UK), to combine Amazon's online and delivery skills with Wal-Mart's purchasing strength and low prices. In 2001, Amazon took over the online operations of Borders, the second largest US bookstore chain.

Frequently and wrongly called the 'Internet bookseller', Amazon.com is a new business form, for which we do not yet have a name. In 2000, Jeff Bezos was challenged at a public event by the question: 'I have 100 shares of Amazon.com. What do I own?'. His reply was:

> 'You own a piece of the leading e-commerce platform … The Amazon.com platform is comprised of brand, customers, technology, distribution capability, deep e-commerce expertise, and a great team with a passion for innovation and a passion for serving customers well.'

Sources: Randell E. Stross (1997), 'Why Barnes and Noble May Crush Amazon', *Fortune*, 29 September. Richard Waters and John Labate (1998), 'Brought to Book', *Financial Times*, 10 November. Andrew Edgecliffe-Johnson (2001), 'Amazon Loses Power Over Main Business', *Financial Times*, 1 February. Tim Jackson (2000), 'In Praise of Amazon', *Financial Times*, 1 August. Tim Jackson (2000), 'Amazon and Toys 'R' Us Rewrite Rules of Game', *Financial Times*, 15 August.

New types of alliance

One characteristic of e-business is that it encourages and facilitates collaboration between companies – even if they are rivals – for example, in product development[35]. The Internet supports the concept of the 'extended enterprise', by allowing companies to link together electronically far-flung constituencies – customers, suppliers, partners – in spite of organizational, functional or geographic boundaries[36]. This is particularly important in recognizing the massive impact of the Internet on business-to-business relationships (see pp. 202–5).

'characteristic of e-business is that it encourages and facilitates collaboration between companies – even if they are rivals'

However, what is more revolutionary yet is the start of alliances and mergers which span the new economy and the old, for example Amazon plus Toys 'R' Us has already happened and Amazon plus Wal-Mart has been predicted. However, the AOL/Time Warner merger is a bigger story.

REALITY CHECK

THE AOL/TIME WARNER MERGER: NEW MEDIA SWALLOW THE OLD

Investors were initially baffled by the January 2000 announcement of a merger between America Online (AOL) and Time Warner (TW), and share values suffered. In fact, they were witnessing the start of the biggest corporate merger in history and a groundbreaking alliance between the old economy (TW was Ted Turner's conventional media company) and the new (AOL was a 14-year-old net company). It was the first large-scale merging of content (films, news, music) and context (Internet access) to create a new type of business. It represents a new type of convergence between industries, driven by the Internet. AOL's $163 billion all-share takeover of TW was to create the world's seventh largest corporation. The new company combines AOL's 18 million Internet access subscribers with the Time publishing empire, Warner Brothers' movies, Warner Music, Home Box Office pay-TV services and the cable TV giant Time Warner Cable, and has combined revenues of more than $40 billion and more than 100 million regular subscribers worldwide, spanning print, cable TV, the Internet, music and news.

The underlying rationale for this new type of business is that as more TV programmes, music and movies become digital, then television and the Internet will merge into one, e.g. people may watch TV on the computer, or access the Internet from the television set. For example, in 1998, A. C. Nielsen Meal reported that most evenings there were as many Americans logged onto AOL as there were watching CNN or MTV. As this process continues, companies will need access to the ways in which people reach the Internet or watch television. AOL Time Warner is positioned to do both, by operating television and satellite networks as well as Internet access. In other words, the merger is a bet that content providers (such as Time Warner) and online distributors (such as AOL) will converge to dominate the home entertainment business. At its simplest, the new company can distribute AOL services through a huge cable network, and provide Time Warner films, music and magazines to Internet subscribers. Indeed, EMI tried to join this party but the attempt was blocked by the European regulators on competition grounds. One key success factor will be the spread of 'broadband' access to the Web, i.e. fast enough access to the Internet that a consumer can download an entire feature film in seconds, currently in its infancy.

In many ways this is the first test of whether an Internet company can prosper in the 'real' world of traditional business. It is telling that the dominant partner in the merger is AOL – the smaller partner, but the one in charge. AOL's chairman and CEO, Steve Case, said at the announcement: 'This is a historic moment in which new media truly come of age. By joining forces with Time Warner we will fundamentally change the way people get information, communicate with others, buy products and are entertained ... this is the first time a major Internet company has merged with a major media company and the possibilities are endless.' Speculation is that the third part of the new business will be a telephone (and especially a mobile telephone) company for enhanced access to new media, and Vodafone has already shown interest.

The merger survived the US and European regulators'objections, gained shareholder approval and went live in January 2001, facing the task of integrating two very dissimilar organizations, and starting with job cuts at TW's CNN news network and sidelining Ted Turner from an executive role. Facing a hostile environment of economic slow-down, weakening advertising spending, and loss of investor confidence after the dot.com crash, the company was looking for rapid cost-cuts in the former Time Warner empire. By mid-2001, AOL Time Warner, the world's biggest media company, was in discussions with NTL, the world's biggest cable operator, with a view to forming an alliance to give AOL access to NTL's networks in Europe. Whether with NTL or another cable operator, AOL Time Warner needs a European partner to distribute and market its content to European consumers.

Sources: Richard Waters(2000), 'A New Media World', *Financial Times*, 11 January. Richard Waters and Louise Kehoe (2000), 'Fight for the Future', *Financial Times*, 15/16 January. Garth Alexander (2000), 'The Man Who Dreamt Up the Biggest Merger in History', *Sunday Times*, 16 January. Dawn Hayes (2000), 'Net Comes of Age With Merger', *Sunday Business*, 16 January. Christopher Grimes (2001), 'AOL Time Lays Out Ambitious Growth Targets', *Financial Times*, 1 February. Andrew Cave (2001), 'AOL Links With Time Warner', *Daily Telegraph*, 13 January. Christopher Grimes and Richard Waters (2001), 'Pittman's Progress', *Financial Times*, 19 March.

We are also seeing the formation of industry-based online exchanges between competitors, as a new form of collaboration. For example, Ford, General Motors and DaimlerChrysler collaborate in an online exchange for their combined $240 billion a year expenditure, estimating prospects of 20 per cent reductions in costs (see pp. 204–5).

In fact, strategic alliances may be the most effective way of resurrecting the failing dot.coms. For example, Nutravida, a health and beauty e-tailer, has struggled to survive on modest funding, but has used an alliance with a bricks and mortar retailer to get the website close to break-even and to grow sales – the website takes the orders while the store holds stock and processes the orders[37].

'strategic alliances may be the most effective way of resurrecting the failing dot.coms'

Revolutions in how industries operate

There can be few better illustrations of the Internet creating a revolution in an established industry than the music business. Initially, the Internet provided no more than an additional channel of distribution selling the conventional products – Amazon, CDNow, and so on. However, what we are seeing now is an industry that is reshaping and restructuring to survive the fact that its basic product – the recorded CD or tape – is becoming obsolete in the face of music downloading from the Web.

REALITY CHECK
HAS THE FAT LADY SUNG YET?

The music industry has struggled to come to terms with what the Internet means for their sector. When selling recorded tapes and CDs over the Internet was the big issue in the 1990s, aside from the difficulties this posed for relationships with traditional retailers, the multinational record companies were just about able to cope. However, this was before they had understood the power of MP3 technology, and peer-to-peer computing in the form of the dreaded Napster. The record companies have responded to these threats, but the structure of their industry will never be the same again, and we wait to see how well the film companies will do, because it is probably their turn next.

The MP3 movement

MP3 is the technology that makes it possible for consumers to download music from the Web and to play it on a portable device, and to send it to other people, thus avoiding the need to buy tapes and CDs to access new music. In 1999 it is estimated that around one billion songs were downloaded and MP3 overtook 'sex' as the most frequently searched word on the Web. Also by 1999, forecasts in the UK were that within five years, 80 per cent of the singles chart would be downloaded from the Net, and Artists like Alanis Morrissette and Tori Amos were signing deals to put their music out on My.MP3.com, the most popular MP3 website. That year, MP3.com claimed 38 million song downloads.

The record companies tried to ban the manufacture of MP3 players, and then to establish 'secure' digital formats (i.e. ones you pay to download). In April 2000, in a dubious legal decision, MP3.com was found guilty of infringing the record companies' copyrights. However, MP3.com merely used the technology, it did not own it. Four of the five large record companies settled with MP3.com out of court – MP3.com paid each $20 million in damages and agreed to reform its services, and in return the record companies started to make their music catalogues available to MP3.com. Having initially dismissed digital music downloading as a cult phenomenon, the record companies are making large investments in commercializing digital distribution. It is becoming clear that digital music downloads to a variety of playing devices will be a major part of the music business. By mid-2001, the record companies were back in court trying to stop the operations of MP3Board.com, that explicitly searches the Web for pirated music, and defends itself under the rights of 'free speech'.

Music moguls caught napping

The next devastating factor to emerge was Napster, the online file sharing resource, established by 19-year-old Shawn Fanning – i.e. one person posts a music track on the Napster website, and another Napster customer downloads it. Napster has no central store of songs, just software allowing people to find music that other people have loaded from CDs onto their computers. One user's words capture the real threat: 'I love Napster – I'm never buying another CD again'. Opened in 1999, by 2000 Napster had 40 million users worldwide, rising to 65 million by 2001. The Recording Industry Association of America blamed Napster downloading for a 40 per cent drop in shipments of CD singles in 1999, and 46 per cent in 2000. This is one of the first times the world has seen the power of peer-to-peer computing, connecting millions of computers, and capable of transferring any form of digital information files, as well as pooling computing power. Napster was soon followed by Wrapster – allowing the copying of digital files as diverse as software, computer games and films. Of course, Napster did not generate any income in this form.

Sued for copyright infringement by the record companies, in November 2000 Napster signed a deal with Bertelsman – the German group investing $100 million to turn the free music community into a subscription-paying membership paying royalties for music downloaded. Bertelsman wanted to turn Napster into a platform for downloading and selling its entire catalogue of media products. The idea seemed to be to take over the online renegade, rather than to rely on the courts closing him down. Napster promised the record company $1 billion in additional revenues, once it was a fee-paying service. Vivendi and Sony announced they were planning to establish their own rival version of Napster.

However, the other music companies subsequently won their legal assault against Napster. On 6 March 2001, a US judge ordered Napster to remove all unauthorized music from its site within 72 hours, but allowed the company to stay in operation. Within two weeks the record companies were back in court claiming that Napster was using an ineffective screening device that its members could get around rather easily, and were doing so.

But what next?

Napster may be struggling to prevent its members freely trading copyrighted songs, but if Napster dies, music users will not stop downloading, they will migrate to other free-music sites – rival file-sharing companies like Aimster and LimeWire are already signing up Napster refugees – or maybe something worse: maybe AOL Time Warner might decide to leverage its membership to rock the music business? This would be a stronger appeal than any of the pay-for-downloading sites being developed by the record companies. The first move was an alliance between AOL Time Warner, Bertelsman and EMI and software group RealNetworks to build a business offering songs from their catalogues to websites for downloading – MusicNet. Their goal was to make buying music as easy as stealing music. EMI had already announced its intention to cease manufacturing CDs (outsourcing their production). At the same time, Yahoo! linked with Vivendi Universal and Sony to deliver music over the Web as Duet.

The biggest problem is probably the record companies 'bunker mentality'; one industry analyst says: 'They want to clamp down and protect existing assets rather than thinking creatively about new types of revenue streams and relationships with customers'. The real Napster issue was not free music – it was about providing music listeners with choice, convenience and flexibility that the record companies never even tried to provide. The entertainment industry should now be worrying about software called Gnutella (interestingly an 'unauthorized' project at an AOL subsidiary which escaped onto the Web), which is a purely peer-to-peer filesharing and can cope with films as well as music, and sites like FreeNet, which lets people share music but offers encryption so they cannot be traced, as well as the hackers who can decode their own CD and DVD encryption and give the information away free on the Web. The record companies are up against people who copy films and music as a matter of pride, not for money. The challenge is to devise a music distribution system that gives consumers what they got from Napster, but which makes money as well, accepting that it will be impossible to generate the same level of income from downloads as from over-priced CDs.

Sources: 'Technology May Prove Better Than the Law in Defeating Music Piracy', *Financial Times*, 1 May 2000. Wendy Grossman (2000), 'Music Business Records a Victory', *Daily Telegraph*, 11 May 2000. Ashling O'Connor (2000), 'Harnessing the Power of the Web', *Financial Times*, 15 September. Christopher Parkes and Christopher Grimes (2000), 'Life After Napster', *Financial Times*, 26 September. Andrew Cave (2000), 'Music Industry Caught Napping', *Daily Telegraph*, 4 November. Christopher Grimes (2000), 'Napster Still Has a Case to Prove', *Financial Times*, 8 November. Thomas E. Weber (2001), 'Why Gutting Napster Won't Cure the Blues of the Music Industry', *Wall Street Journal*, 26 March. David Kirkpatrick (2001), 'In Napster's Void: You've Got Misery', *Fortune*, 2 April, 144–46.

And don't let's kid ourselves – some people made a lot of money out there

At a time when dot.coms have been crashing almost on a daily basis, it is easy to assume that everyone lost everything. Not so. Indeed, Jeff Bezos points out that if you had bought Amazon.com shares at launch for $1.50 in 1997, they were worth $10 in 2001, which is not a bad return – he concedes that the problem for investors is that they peaked at more than $300 in 1998, and that's where the disappointment clicks in.

REALITY CHECK
THE HOTMAIL STORY

Sabeer Bhatia is one of the originators of Hotmail – the free e-mail service now provided by the Microsoft Network. He took Hotmail from a daydream to a $400 million buyout in two years.

When Bhatia's co-worker, Jack Smith, called him from his car phone to brainstorm the thought that was to become Hotmail, after one sentence, Bhatia said 'Oh my! Hang up that cellular and call me back on a secure line when you get to your house! We don't want anyone to overhear!' Bhatia subsequently stayed up all night writing the business plan. The concept originated because when they were looking for new business ideas, they were nervous that their bosses at Apple might read their e-mails and accuse them of spending working hours on personal projects (actually quite true). This frustration led to the idea – free e-mail accounts that can be accessed anonymously over the Web. In just over two years Bhatia built Hotmail's user base faster than any media company in history, and by 1998 had 25 million active e-mail accounts and was signing up users at the rate of 125 000 a day.

The idea had been rejected by twenty venture capital firms, before Draper, Fisher, Jurvetson put up $300 000 for a 15 per cent stake. After getting a bank loan without collateral, a PR firm willing to work for stock, and employees given shares not wages because he was almost out of money, Bahtia launched Hotmail on 4 July 1996.

Late in 1997, Microsoft came calling. They made offers to buy Hotmail, which Bhatia rejected – he had been brought up in India, and therefore knew how to bargain. The Microsoft team came back every week for two months. Then, they took Bhatia to meet Bill Gates. Microsoft offered $200 million, so Bhatia asked for half a billion. Bhatia turned down $300 million, and the Microsoft negotiator pounded the table and walked out, and then offered $350 million. Hotmail's management team was in favour of accepting – on his own Bhatia turned the offer down. Said one colleague in frustration: 'Why don't you just wait until you're big enough to buy Microsoft, instead of them buying you?'. New Year's Eve 1997, the deal was announced – Hotmail was sold for 2 769 48 Microsoft shares, then worth $400 million. More than sixty Hotmail employees instantly became millionaires on paper. Eight months later, Hotmail had tripled in size, and the price looked like a bargain. The Microsoft logic was clear – free e-mail was a necessity, and they wanted to own the market leader.

Sources: Andy Reinhardt and Heather Green (1998), 'Microsoft and Hotmail: It's About Capturing Eyeballs', *Business Week*, 19 January. Po Bronson (1999), 'What's the Big Idea?', *Stanford Magazine*, September/October. Jat Gill (2000), 'Shopping: I'll Make It My Heart's Desire', *Financial Times*, 14 May.

Third – gettingrealagain.com

If you tear a £10 note in half, you do not get two £5 notes.

What you get is an urgent need for sticky tape.

The much-publicized e-revolution we have just experienced was mainly about the quite amazing expansion in dot.com businesses, and then the collapse of many soon after – leaving many disillusioned about the whole thing.

The dot.com disasters – dot.com today and dotgone tomorrow?

REALITY CHECK
THE DOT.COM CEO'S DILEMMA

Dot.com CEO to executives: 'We have no profit now and we never will have. You're all laid off'.

Dot.com Executive 1 to colleagues: 'Hey guy, does anyone know what "laid off" means?'

Dot.com Executive 2: 'No. It must be a compliment!'

Dot.com Executive 1 to CEO: 'Thanks, man. You're pretty laid off yourself, Dude!'

The late 1990s saw the launch and collapse of many dot.com businesses – for these purposes the 'dot.coms' are Web-based businesses that started with no physical sales locations, i.e. virtual businesses. Fortunes were lost and fortunes were made – losses were mainly experienced by investors, egged on by investment analysts, who were desperate to get the astronomical earnings promised by dot.com entrepreneurs; the main bene-factors were investment banks and analysts, and dot.com entrepreneurs who sold out while the going was good. This was an investment 'bubble' – company valuations driven ludicrously high by an investor 'feeding frenzy', with the bubble bursting when the lack of profitability of most dot.coms became apparent, and investor confidence evaporated. Many small investors saw their stakes reduced to almost zero value overnight. The world economy may yet pay the price for the bursting of the dot.com bubble.

'The world economy may yet pay the price for the bursting of the dot.com bubble'

Bad Ideas Don't Get Better Online

The first chapter of e-business was an emotional one.

The second chapter of e-business will be a wiser one.

(*IBM's Book of e-Business*, 2001)

However, once the hype and hoopla about dot.coms and the great 'dot.con' is at an end, maybe we can take a more sensible view about the development of new business models that use the Internet to find new ways of developing customer and shareholder value? Maybe then we will understand why so many of these ventures failed, and possibly avoid making the same mistakes again?

'once the hype and hoopla about dot.coms and the great "dot.con" is at an end, maybe we can take a more sensible view about the development of new business models'

The crash of the dot.coms

The headlines in the late 1990s and the early 2000s were dominated by the spectacular crashes of the dot.coms that had promised so much. Killed by brutally high customer acquisition costs and lack of value creation, many of the plans were not sustainable. Many of us had to learn the hard way that even new business models have to live with the same basic rules of business as everyone else.

'even new business models have to live with the same basic rules of business as everyone else'

The market crash in 2000 saw £140 billion wiped off share values. In December 2000, the value of £100 invested in leading Internet companies at their 52-week highs was as follows[38]:

QXL (auctions)	£1
Oxygen (site for women)	£4
Interactive Investor	£5
Durlacher (investment)	£5
e-Xentric (invests in Internet firms)	£9
365 (sport, entertainment, lifestyle)	£11

Gameplay.com (computer games)	£11
Just2Clicks (business)	£12
New Media Spark (manages a range of dot.coms)	£13
Lastminute.com	£15
InterX (software company)	£18

Among the dot.com carnage, one of the highest-profile failures was Boo.com:

REALITY CHECK

BOO-HOO.COM: FROM BOO(M) TO BUST IN LESS THAN TWO YEARS

In 1999, 28-year-old Swedish model Kajsa Leander and two co-founders established the online fashion retailer, Boo.com, supplying designer sports and streetwear. In spite of the founders' lack of experience, the launch capital they raised reached £76 million – a record for a European Internet start-up. Investors included the Benetton family and Bernard Arnault, chairman of luxury goods retailer LVMH. The aim was for Boo.com to stock tens of thousands of products – including such brands as Puma, The North Face, New Balance and DKNY, as well as cult labels like Cosmic Girl and Fubu. This would make US brands available to European purchasers – sports fashion is global, margins are high, and consumers are young and online – at premium prices, not discounted. The impact of the start-up as an exciting, visionary and ambitious business model was phenomenal – the Swedish founders even featured on the cover of *Fortune* magazine. The company was almost a fashion statement itself, let alone its products – it was so trendy it hurt.

Their website was sophisticated and state-of-the-art. Customers were welcomed by 'Ms Boo', an electronic sales assistant, and offered a choice of languages and currencies to pay. Advanced graphics allowed customers to zoom in on product images and rotate them, and to dress a model in the clothes being considered. The founders' goal was 'We want Boo to be the number one brand.'

Following a huge amount of publicity surrounding the start-up, and an expensive 'off the wall' advertising campaign, Boo.com's launch was delayed until November by computer software problems. Around a third of Boo's marketing budget was spent in the six-month delay before launch. Another problem was that customers needed state-of-the-art computers, and some expertise, to access the sophisticated Boo.com site.

Labelled the 'Boo Crew', employees enjoyed first-class air travel, champagne receptions, and a daily supply of free fruit and chocolates, while working in expensive offices in Carnaby Street, next to Soho's smart bars and restaurants. A dot.com executive commented later: 'They were telling staff "you have to spend it like you have it'". Boo opened six offices around the world, and employed 450 people, in eighteen different countries – huge for an Internet company.

Sales in the first three months after launch were substantially less than £500 000. From the start, it was estimated that Boo was spending 75 per cent of turnover on advertising and marketing – double the amount in other start-ups. Financial information was scarce, but in a speech in February 2000, Ernst Malmsten revealed that on a single day that month Boo.com made gross sales of just £51 900 from 1078 orders. This was reckoned to be less than a third of the turnover needed to cover Boo's outgoings. Boo started reducing prices on some lines by 40 per cent early in 2000.

In May 2000, having burned up the capital in expenses and gone £17 million into debt, and like other ventures of Leander and Malmsten in Sweden, Boo.com went into liquidation, with the founders blaming the banks and investors for not providing further £20 million funding. The market was shocked by the failure of one of the highest-profile and best-funded Internet start-ups in Europe. CEO, Malmsten, was unrepentant: 'If we had got the money we would have turned the business around … The company had been very visionary and ambitious and we have built something fantastic. The hard facts, the numbers, show that the business was improving and working.'

The failure of Boo.com has been blamed on many factors: the founders' lack of experience; the lack of financial control and the 'spending frenzy' that ensued; crippling marketing and advertising costs (around £30 million) to acquire customers who did not spend enough; the business idea may have been flawed – the customers who buy expensive designer wear like to go to expensive shops and try the clothes on, not buy online; a lack of strategic advice from investors; a hopeless computer system that could not support the ambitious website adequately, and made purchasing difficult; and Boo may just have been ahead of its time – for example, Boo pioneered three-dimensional imaging on their site, which is now the 'must have' for all e-tailers – and too ambitious right from the start. But it did hold super parties.

In November 2000, Boo was resurrected by a US management team, with nine employees, and a simplified website, which provides a form of online fashion guide run by Boo's 'style scouts', with links to recommended retailers. The logic is that while the business model of Boo.com has been discredited, there is still value in the brand – it still stands for leading edge fashion and style. The only Boo employee to make the transatlantic trip was Ms Boo. The new Boo plans to make money from site advertising and sponsorship from certain products, and to develop own-label Boo products.

Sources: Alice Rawsthorn (1999), 'Online Fashion Retailer Sets European Start-Up Record', *Financial Times*, 10 May. Caroline Daniel and Thorold Barker (2000), 'Boo's Next?', *Financial Times*, 19 May. Dominic Rushe (2000), 'From Boo to Bust', *Sunday Times*, 21 May. Richard Fletcher (2000), 'Boo Founders Hit Back', *Sunday Business*, 21 May. Jonathan Fenby (2000), 'Bang Goes Boo – Could This be the End of the Beginning', *Sunday Business*, 21 May. Thorold Barker (2000), 'Miss Boo Makes a Fashion Return at Fashionmall', *Financial Times*, 7/8 October.

What is even worse, huge disappointment has been expressed with dot.coms that have survived and that may have sustainable value propositions – simply because they did not live up to the grossly inflated expectations of an hysterical investment community.

REALITY CHECK
LASTMINUTE.COM – MYTH AND REALITY

Founded by Martha Lane Fox, and partner Brent Hoberman (both consultants in business strategy), in November 1998, Lastminute.com aims to use the reach of the Web to offer reduced prices direct to the consumer – at the start, mainly theatre tickets, flights and hotel reservations. Suppliers included 30 airlines, more than 500 hotels, 75 holiday providers, 400 entertainment suppliers, 60 restaurants and 120 gift providers. By June 1999, Lastminute had added its 'Lifestyle Services' portfolio, aimed at the cash-rich, time-poor urban consumer – comprising cleaning and laundry services, taxis, hairdressers, childminders and assorted other services. Plans are to extend into interactive television and other Internet-accessible devices like mobile phones, and there are partnerships with the phone company NTL, and the cable companies Telewest and Cable & Wireless Communications.

The business model could not operate without the Web – it provides a last-minute marketplace (said to have been conceived by Hoberman because of his inability to organize anything in advance), linking buyers and sellers, but with no involvement in fulfilment. The business is a 'Web brand' – it provides information and customer service, not products, taking a commission from suppliers. Start-up funding was a modest £600 000, supplemented later by $10 million of venture group funding in 1999. Advertising was almost completely offline: London Underground posters, print and billboard advertising, and promotional tie-ups with other companies, as well as Fox's 'Blonde Ambition' PR tour, and much TV and press publicity for the 'Web babe'. Lastminute achieved unprecedentedly high profile for a small dot.com, largely as lifestyle journalists alighted on Lane Fox and Hoberman as icons for the Internet age. After its first year, Lastminute had almost 600 000 registered users, rising to 2.1 million by August 2000, but did not anticipate profitability until 2004.

Surrounded by an unprecedented level of hype and publicity, Lastminute went public in March 2000, in a badly-managed launch, and was valued at £732 million on its debut, towards the end of the European dot.com frenzy. The issue was heavily oversubscribed, and many angry investors received only small allocations of shares. By the beginning of April, the market was experiencing a crash in technology shares, and Lastminute stock had halved in value – down from 560p to 240p. By November 2000, Lastminute shares were trading at just 120p, and Lane and Hoberman were labelled 'Bonnie and Clyde' by some journalists. The December 2000 share value was around 76p, and Robin Geffen of Orbitex suggested they were actually worth about 7p.

In August 2000, Lastminute bought France's leading online travel agency, Degriftour, for £59 million, to increase revenue and scale, reducing its cash pile to £100 million. Allan Leighton, formerly Wal-Mart's European head, joined Lastminute as non-executive chairman in October 2000 – paid wholly in share options. The end of 2000 saw Lastminute unveiling a gross profit of £3.2 million – almost 20 times the figure of a year earlier – but a pre-tax loss of £36 million on sales of just £3.7 million. The French acquisition brought the anticipated time of profitability forward to end-2002. City commentators were impressed with Leighton's assurance that the company was perform-ing 'ahead of plan'.

At Christmas 2000, Lastminute made its first venture into offline trading with a Christmas gifts catalogue, based on state-of-the-art voice-recognition software allowing customers to place telephone orders 24 hours a day. Lastminute also held stock of the product range to ensure fast delivery.

At the end of 2000, Hoberman commented: 'The investment business is a fashion business. If we continue to execute and do what we said we were going to do, the valuation will take care of itself. We're not in the fashion business, we're in a real business. We're not frustrated by the share price. But if it gives the impression that we're not delivering as we said we would, that is frustrating.'

The early part of 2001 saw Lastminute with sites in France, Italy, Spain and Holland, and a new Web-based alliance with Thomas Cook to attract new customers. Announcements in April 2001 started to show Leighton's influence. Lastminute was increasing its focus on the core markets of UK, France and Germany, and looking at ways to cut costs – shedding a tenth of all staff and reducing advertising expenditure – and placing emphasis on revenue growth instead of just acquiring more customers. Quarterly results showed turnover of £2.9 million and losses of £15.4 million, but with growing revenues and falling costs, predictions were for break-even in the core UK and France markets by the end of 2002. In May 2001, with cash reserves of £62 million and spending of £3 million a month, Lastminute is liable to run out of cash by November 2002, unless things change. They are testing the belief that while a traditional business cannot expand from a declining cost base, an Internet business can.

Sources: David Murphy (2000), 'The Last Minute Waltz', *Marketing Business*, February, 22–24. Catherine Wheatley (2000), 'First of the Dot.com Casualties Makes a Lastminute Recovery', *Sunday Business*, 20 August. Guy Dresser (2000), 'Lastminute Suffers From Net Malaise', *Sunday Business*, 3 December. Elizabeth Rigby (2000), 'Lastminute Says it is Ahead of Plan', *Financial Times*, 5 December. Alex Brummer (2000), 'High-Flier Keeps Orbitex Soaring', *Daily Mail*, 28 December. Andrew Davidson (2001), 'The Andrew Davidson Interview', *Management Today*, January, 58–63. Thorold Barker (2001), 'Is Lastminute Online to Profitability and a Decent Valuation', *Financial Times*, 16 April.

The dot.com killers

If you look at the factors that led to the devastation of the dot.coms, that we should now be smart enough to avoid, then you should include the following.

Investor insanity

'Many start-ups were founded on a commercial model of short-term greed'

The desperation of (mainly small) investors to get a share of the Internet action, added to the inability of analysts to place values on Internet 'assets', led to a frenzy of investment. Many start-ups were founded on a commercial model of short-term greed. However, even worse, in spite of venture capitalist assurances that the smart thing for a dot.com to do was to raise money in stages (once you are successful money is cheaper and easier to get), when the dot.commers came back for the next instalment, it frequently wasn't there. The growing conclusion is actually that, in spite of the global losses incurred by the dot.com movement, very few Internet companies were able to raise enough money to see them through to the point where they might be self-financing[39]. Investors first threw money at dot.coms, then lost confidence and declined to invest further – neither side of this investment hysteria was particularly productive.

Distorted market signals

Michael Porter argues that investment in Internet ventures has been based on distorted market signals[40]. Revenue figures were unreliable (subsidized purchasing exaggerates market value; buyers are temporarily attracted by novelty of a new way of buying; 'revenues' are often stock not cash). Similarly, cost figures could not be relied upon (suppliers eager for dot.com business discounted prices, sometimes to zero, and accepted stock instead of cash in payment; capital needs were understated). Porter suggests that the result was that the attractiveness of some industries and ventures was grossly exaggerated by the metrics used.

'investment in Internet ventures has been based on distorted market signals'

Value

In this frenzy, it is not surprising that many dot.com-mers and technofreaks had difficulty in distinguishing between services that are technologically feasible, and those that people actually need or want. Their claims to provide customer value were frequently stupid.

'Their claims to provide customer value were frequently stupid'

First-mover advantage

Part of the frenzy of dot.com spending was driven by the total belief that you had to follow Amazon's model and achieve a first-mover advantage – market share is what matters, because once you dominate the market, you can 'monetize' the advantage later[41]. This was a fatal fallacy for many dot.coms. First movers do not always have an advantage. It only works under four conditions:

● First, the market served must be ready for rapid development – you aim to start in a niche ignored by competitors, which then expands rapidly, so a small lead in a small market turns into a big lead in a big market.

- Second, you have to be able to erect or exploit barriers to entry – distinctive technology or expertise that others cannot easily imitate.
- Third, you have to have all the skills needed to exploit the market.
- Fourth, it helps if you do not face capable competitors[42].

'it all went wrong when we allowed ourselves to believe that the rules for success in the new economy were somehow completely different to those in the old economy – they were not and they are not'

The trouble was that: many of the markets that attracted dot.coms have remained small because consumer habits have not changed fast enough; the dot.coms generally had no distinctive advantage that could not be copied or bettered by competitors; they often were poor providers of customer service or order fulfilment (see below); and they often took on strong and capable competitors with too much to lose not to respond strongly – see the comments on the 'e-fightback' below. Some are suggesting that it all went wrong when we allowed ourselves to believe that the rules for success in the new economy were somehow completely different to those in the old economy – they were not and they are not[43].

The virtual myth

One of the big attractions of the dot.com organization was that it would not need to bear the costs of physical facilities – factories, warehouses, shops, and so on – and would exist only as a website. There are companies around which are to a large extent already virtual – for example, at Cisco a growing proportion of customers place orders electronically and these orders are fulfilled automatically by third-party contractors that build the equipment to Cisco's specification, and then ship the order direct to the customer[44]. Many of the dot.coms found it impossible to operate like this and thereby lost one of their major advantages – troubled eToys looked at its first e-Christmas from behind warehouses full of toys, which was the only way they could get the products out to customers in time for Christmas. eToys was one of the first dot.coms to find that its low online prices, designed to take business from Toys 'R' Us, simply could not support the cost of dealing with 5000 small suppliers and operating conventional warehouses and distribution centres – they filed for bankruptcy in February 2001.

'many of the e-tailer dot.coms that have failed simply were not very good at what they were doing'

Customer service

Sadly, it has to be said that many of the e-tailer dot.coms that have failed simply were not very good at what they were doing. For example, an A. T. Kearney survey of Internet shoppers in Europe, the US and Japan in 2000 suggested that e-tail websites were so bad that would-be shoppers give up eight times out of ten, while a third of transactions require a phone call[45]. Indeed, I have a colleague who swears that she found BMW's early website so slow and cumbersome that she e-mailed the company pointing out that her phone charges were getting high because of their slow site. The company's reply that if she was worried about phone costs she was not likely to be a customer for their expensive cars, led to her immediate e-mail that if the cars were as slow and unreliable as their website, they could keep them! BMW has since decided to shun the Internet as a consumer sales channel. Another study deplores the customer services practices of some of the hottest e-tailers, and suggests that the issue is simply an absence of retail thinking[46]. It may also have been lack of preparation – a PricewaterhouseCoopers survey suggests that seven out of ten e-tailers fail to test their service before offering, with the unsurprising result that nearly all experience significant customer service disruption[47]. Evaluation of US dot.coms finds that with a few exceptions like Amazon.com, customer satisfaction with Internet shopping is low[48]. In the US, the turnover of customers unhappy with the service they receive from online banks has reached more than 50 per cent a year, leaving the online bankers desperately searching for profit[49] – no-one can live with churn like that.

Customer acquisition costs

The costs of acquiring customers for dot.coms was often nothing short of brutal, and without high customer retention stayed that way. From the start, for example, Amazon.com was looking at marketing and promotional costs of $29 a sale compared to $2.50 a sale for its conventional bookstore competitors. A 1998 Boston Consulting Group study concluded that

'The costs of acquiring customers for dot.coms was often nothing short of brutal'

typical e-tailers were spending 65 per cent of revenues on marketing and advertising, compared to 5 per cent for conventional retailers. There was an illusion that dot.com start-up costs were very low – after all, you just needed a computer and an Internet connection. The reality, of course, is that the costs of acquiring customers are potentially astronomical, and for many dot.coms, they did not get less (because they failed to retain customers or establish an enduring brand identity). At one point in the US in 1999, it was estimated that annual dot.com advertising expenditure had reached $7.5 billion. In part this was also driven by investors – if the dot.com could not show customer numbers growth, it would not get the next round of funding, so the pressure was to spend every penny available on customer acquisition through advertising (because no-one seemed to care about profitability). The 'burn rate' (the amount spent in excess of income) to acquire customers was higher than most anticipated and failed to slow down. For many, their average customer acquisition cost was higher than the average lifetime value of their customers[50], which is suicidal.

Customer retention costs

In online transactions, taking your business elsewhere requires a simple click of the mouse. Yet in the middle of 2000 a survey of dot.coms found that only one in ten actually identified and welcomed returning customers with any attempt at personalized service – less than half even had the technology to recognize returning visitors to the site[51]. The 'stickiness' of websites was greatly overestimated. It sort of sounds like many of the dot.coms had missed the message about the impor-tance of customer retention to profitability[52]. In fact, the evidence is not that Web customers are inherently disloyal – just that we have failed to establish the relationship that retains their e-business[53].

'many of the dot.coms had missed the message about the importance of customer retention to profitability'

Fulfilment

The unavoidable truth also is that however glitzy the website may be (and some really were), there comes a point when the customer actually wants to receive the product. Unreasonable, but there it is. Getting this right can be expensive for a dot.com – Amazon's fulfilment costs average 14 per cent of sales, while traditional bookstore Barnes & Noble's are 6 per cent. Many of the e-tailers who have failed struggled to get the product to the customer even vaguely on time – this is the Christmas tree arriving in January scenario (well done, and goodbye Letsbuyit .com, we'll miss you). Research by DHL suggests that fully 20 per cent of Internet orders are delivered later than the customer expects[54]. Similarly, Andersen Consulting suggests that 45 per cent of goods ordered over European Internet sites fail to arrive within seven days, and one-fifth of those ordered from new start-ups never arrived at all[55]. The strength of a company like Lands' End, the largest US catalogue and Web clothing retailer, is that they have 38 years experience in mail order, and get 99 per cent of their orders delivered on time[56].

Some new e-tailers have tended to be better at taking orders (and money) than delivering the goods. Incidentally, it looks like this is also one of the big barriers to conventional businesses exploiting the Internet too – BT estimates that four-fifths of organizations cannot make e-business work for them because their purchasing and distribution systems are not adequate for online business[57]. One report into e-tailers' performance in fulfilling orders simply concluded that things were so bad that: 'Online vendors need to grow up. Until customers receive what they want, when they want it, online shopping will remain unfulfilling to customers and profits will remain elusive to vendors'[58].

> *'Some new e-tailers have tended to be better at taking orders (and money) than delivering the goods'*

The revenge of the competition

Even the most enthusiastic dot.commers must have known that conventional competitors would fight back? Did they really understand so little, that they did not anticipate the 'e-fightback'? As the aggressive chairman of Airtours notes: 'We are not in the business of helping dot.com entrants to establish themselves on the back of our investment in assets'. If the traditional players have the brands, the trust, the technology, the customers and the expertise, the dot.com has to have something unbeatable or impossible to imitate to sustain a market position. The established firms also tend to have the muscle to cut prices in the face of intrusive competition. They can also play dirty – Volkswagen told its dealers it would dump any of them that supplied Internet traders with their vehicles[59].

> *'Even the most enthusiastic dot.commers must have known that conventional competitors would fight back?'*

Certainly, as the value of dot.com start-ups plummeted, they became quite attractive things for conventional companies to buy, to get the online expertise on the cheap[60]. Having seen its mail-order clothing profits plunge by 80 per cent in 2000, in 2001, Great Universal Stores paid a paltry £1.4 million to the liquidators for the assets of Breathe.com (the bankrupt Internet retail portal, valued the previous year at £100 million), to acquire the Internet e-tailing expertise and technology that otherwise GUS would have had to develop on its own[61].

While direct Internet-based sales channels have led to some 'disintermediation', i.e. loss of business for the middleman, it has not always been in the predicted way. The big pressure on estate agents is not from free-standing dot.coms advertising houses for sale, but by the consortium of house builders and mortgage banks looking to establishing a presence in e-commerce selling houses[62].

REALITY CHECK

WHERE DID IT ALL END . . .

'Thank you for making Checkout.com one of the most popular entertainment destinations on the Net.

Our site is now closed.

(Message on defunct dot.com site, April 2001)

What about the 'wanna-dots'?

If you look at the underlying reasons for the shake-out and the demise of so many of the dot.coms, and conclude that it is down to conventional business pragmatics – e.g. the strange idea that a retail business should sell goods for more than it paid for them – then consider also the frantic struggles of some conventional companies to get in on the Internet gold-rush. Rosabeth Moss Kanter has labelled these the 'wanna-dots'[63]. Her conclusion is that when the wanna-dot's e-ventures fail it is not usually anything inherent to the Internet that causes that failure – it is because they have proved inept at managing the organizational change involved:

REALITY CHECK

HOW TO ENSURE THE FAILURE OF AN INTERNET VENTURE

1 Spread Internet responsibilities far and wide in the company, as long as they stay small and unthreatening.
2 Form a committee to create the new Internet offering, preferably full of bored people with no experience or interest in the Internet.
3 Find the simplest, least-demanding thing you can do on the Web – the 'yawn application' – then cross the Internet off your 'to do' list.
4 Find an abusive agency, which thinks you are a bunch of dinosaurs, to design the website, then ignore their advice.
5 Make sure what you do on the website is exactly the same as what you do offline.
6 Demand that the Internet venture conforms to all established corporate standards, controls and policies.
7 Offer no incentives to business units to collaborate in the Internet venture – better to keep them apart.

8 Only compare your company's performance with traditional industry competitors, not those Internet upstarts.

9 Launch the e-venture by giving people in the organization tools they are unable to use, requiring changes they are confused about making – then criticize them for their resistance to change.

10 Make sure the company not the customer stays in the driver's seat – the issue is us communicating with them.

Strict adherence to these guidelines should guarantee the failure of your online venture.

Source: Adapted from Rosabeth Moss Kanter (2001), 'Ten Deadly Mistakes of Wanna-Dots', *Harvard Business Review*, January, 91–100.

Perhaps the biggest gap of all was that so many e-business ventures have lacked a coherent strategy for building a sustainable competitive advantage. Along these lines, Michael Porter has recently concluded that:

'Many of the pioneers of Internet business, both dot.coms and established companies, have competed in ways that violate nearly every precept of good strategy. Rather than focus on profits, they sought to maximize revenue and market share at all costs, pursuing customers indiscriminately through discounting, giveaways, promotions, channel incentives, and heavy advertising. Rather than concentrate on delivering real value that earns an attractive price from customers, they have pursued indirect revenues from sources such as advertising and click-through fees from Internet commerce partners.' [64]

The era of disillusionment

The bursting of the dot.com bubble in 1999/2000 destroyed millions of pounds worth of share value that momentarily resided in the super-inflated share prices of Internet-related companies. As many dot.coms curled up their toes and died, the result has been much disillusionment about the 'new economy'. It is a great opportunity for the cynical to claim the moral high ground, suggesting that they were right all along, and the Internet is just another over-hyped fad. This is probably just as stupid as the greed and 'feeding frenzy' among investors that inflated the bubble in the first place. Let us recall the informed

'As many dot.coms curled up their toes and died, the result has been much disillusionment about the "new economy"'

opinion of Janet Street-Porter, then editor of the *Independent on Sunday*:

> 'Forget the superhighway, get a life. The future isn't wired. In fact, historians will look back on the 1990s and the current surge of techno-hype and net-euphoria as a bizarre blip, a meaningless cul-de-sac in the cultural story of the 20th century.' [65]

I have no idea what ever happened to Ms Street-Porter, but I bet the words 'I told you so' were heard in her proximity as the dot.coms crashed.

'if there is any positive outcome of the debacle maybe it is a more pragmatic view of how the Internet provides business opportunities'

In fact, if there is any positive outcome of the debacle maybe it is a more pragmatic view of how the Internet provides business opportunities, instead of some mad belief that if you put 'dot.com' next to a business idea, then the magic will somehow rub off and everyone will become rich.

However, all is not disaster anyway. In May 2001, McKinsey produced the latest results in their 'e-performance report', suggesting that 20 per cent of the dot.coms they monitor were in profit by the end of 2000, and Internet retailers (particularly those which are off-shoots of established retail firms) were opening up a performance gap against 'pureplay' ventures (Internet-only companies)[66]. We may have overdone the disillusionment and scepticism the same way we overdid the enthusiasm for dot.coms.

But, what if you add bricks to the clicks?

What many have discovered is that, contrary to the hype, there is a major strength in having bricks and mortar (e.g. retail shops) behind the dot.com, mainly because it makes it so much cheaper to fulfil your customers' orders (i.e. every retail shop is a 'warehouse' from which you can cheaply deliver products to local customers). The grocery business is a prime example of the power of 'bricks and clicks'.

REALITY CHECK
THE INTERNET GROCERY PHENOMENON

The British grocery market is worth around £95 billion, and estimates are that nearly 30 per cent may eventually involve online buying. Most of the virtual 'Internet grocers' launched in the US in the

1990s have fallen by the wayside, like Streamline.com, which closed in 2000. However, in 1998, a sceptical British public saw the launch of Tesco.com by the country's leading grocery supermarket firm. Ridicule was aimed at Tesco.com's low-tech approach:

1 Customers log on and enter a shopping list.
2 The list goes via Hertfordshire to Dundee, to be printed out and retyped into a second computer, a copy is filed and the list is sent to the customer's local store.
3 At the store the list is printed again and a 'picker' goes round the shelves compiling the order before queuing at a designated checkout.
4 The shopping is taken by van to the customer's home.

It may have started out as a cumbersome low-technology way of doing things, but by the national roll-out in 2000 (after almost five years preparation and piloting), Tesco.com was leading the Internet quality measurements published by the Chicago-based Gomez company, and was regarded by US companies in this field as a world leader. Tesco.com is now the world's largest e-grocery business.

By the end of 2000, Tesco.com was handling 60 000 orders a week with 750 000 registered customers and a sales target of £200 million, and claimed to have reached break-even point. The target is to burn £400 million to reach £500 million a year profitability by 2005. By mid-2001, weekly sales had reached £6 million, suggesting annual sales of around £300 million, and Tesco was suggesting that the grocery component of online sales had reached profitability (estimates suggest margins of 10–12 per cent over operating costs).

The service also delivers electrical goods, baby clothes, videos and some home furnishings – the target is to get half of online sales in higher-margin non-food goods. The company believes its model is robust because their Internet shoppers use the Tesco.com service for the basic shop (the boring household necessities), but still visit the store for other things (the fun stuff like cream cakes and delicatessen). The model integrates online and offline business – online sales are part of branch sales and feed into store-based replenishment systems – and it does not breach the integrity of the tight supply chain, because bulk is not broken until the retail store level. The value proposition is convenience and time-saving, but also greater personalization – the software remembers previous purchasing and gives 'reminders', and can also warn those vulnerable about things like nut allergies and food choices. The relatively low start-up costs (£35 million) and fast national coverage reflect using the conventional stores as 'mini-depots' where pickers can make up to six online orders a time using a special trolley. The expansion of Tesco Direct created about 7000 new jobs. Although the delivery charge is a standard £5 (covering about two-thirds of the picking and delivery costs), average order sizes are around £100. Company estimates are that the average online shopping order is 2 or 3 per cent more profitable than the average in-store order, because Internet shoppers tend to select the higher margin products on offer.

However, the formulation of Tesco Direct's value proposition and business model was based on close study of what customers wanted from Internet grocery shopping. Contrary to expectations that online shoppers would want to abandon traditional stores, they found customers liked to visit stores to examine fresh produce personally and to see what new products were available, and trusted their local stores to provide quality goods at fair prices. Most customers did not see online shopping as a substitute for traditional shopping, but as a complement. For this reason the online shopper uses the same store that they visit in person, choosing from the same regional product selection and buying at the same prices. The proposition was to 'shop on-line from my store'.

Tesco.com secured a substantial first-mover advantage – at the end of 2000 they were claiming that 50 per cent of Internet turnover was new turnover, won from rivals' offline stores, but this may not last once competitors impact on the market. Tesco does not have this market to itself. Iceland was the first in the online market in October 1999. Sainsbury and Asda have both unrolled online ordering sites, though opting for picking in warehouses rather than from stores – analysts believe this is a more credible long-term approach to efficient order fulfilment – and Waitrose offers delivery to the workplace instead of the home. Marks & Spencer is trialling an Internet delivery service, though Somerfield has ended its home shopping business because of the high costs. Mid-2001 saw both Waitrose and Sainsbury investing heavily to upgrade their online services, to attempt to close the gap with Tesco, while Tesco was teaming with ITV Digital to provide grocery shopping through digital television. The next battle is expected to revolve around improving the 'last mile' of delivery to the consumer – secure boxes outside the home or in the garage, collection from local garages or the Post Office, to avoid the customer having to be home for the delivery.

Sources: David Rudnick (2000), 'Supermarkets Fight for Online Shoppers', *Daily Telegraph*, 27 January. Susanna Voyle (2000), 'Food E-Tailers Struggle to Get the Recipe Right', *Financial Times*, 15 February. Alan Mitchell (2000), 'How to Get Shoppers to Click', *Financial Times*, 15 March. Richard Longhurst (2000), 'Fill That Basket Without Car Park Queues', *Daily Telegraph*, 6 July. Peggy Hollinger (2000), 'E-Shopping Profits for Tesco and Sainsbury by 2005', *Financial Times*, 4 September. Jonathan Lambeth (2000), 'Tesco Envied by US Shops for Online Service', *Daily Telegraph*, 12 October.

Certainly, in the US, by Christmas 2000, the fastest growing websites in traffic volume at peak selling time were the bricks and clicks operators – Wal-Mart, Eddie Bauer, RadioShack, Nordstrom, and so on[67].

It works both ways though – while John Lewis, the department store group, has bought California-based Buy.com's UK operations to pursue its online ambitions[68], we see that Lastminute.com is considering opening high street stores for its service and product offerings, after its use of print catalogue selling at Christmas 2000[69]. Indeed, both Microsoft and AOL have taken the fight for Internet customers into traditional retail stores – Microsoft in RadioShack consumer electronics stores and AOL in Circuit City – to establish 'stores within stores' selling their Internet services[70]. Also in the US, dot.coms like Expedia.com and e-trade.com have now started to expand into conventional retail stores and launching magazines to supplement their online presence[71]. Late in 2000, Richard Branson announced plans to turn his Our Price music stores into 'V-Shops' including a wall of touch-screen computer kiosks gaining access to all Virgin's products from music to cars, in a virtual store inside the real one[72] – now dubbed 'clicks and mortar' retailing.

There seems to be growing evidence that the real competitive strength comes from the hybrid operations that combine online and offline resources effectively[73]. For example, ThinkNatural, a health and beauty e-tailer, launched first as a dot.com, then four months later started a mail order channel, and then started selling its branded products in Kingfisher's Superdrug stores, and other retail outlets. Increasingly, the hybrid model looks like becoming the norm in business development, not the illusion of the purely 'virtual' dot.com model. *'the real competitive strength comes from the hybrid operations that combine online and offline resources effectively'* Even sneakier is the approach of Matalan, the highly successful clothes and houseware discount retailer – customers can buy off the website or from a print catalogue, but they have to collect the order from the store, thus opening up an Internet sales channel at minimal fulfilment cost and increasing store traffic at the same time!

These observations fit with the findings of Oxford University's 'Virtual Society?' research programme, which concludes that, although the Internet has revolutionized how some people work, generally new technologies tend to supplement rather than substitute for existing practices and forms of organization[74].

The hidden world of business-to-business e-business – the quiet revolution

You should also bear in mind that most of the dot.com disasters were associated with business-to-consumer business models, and the business-to-business (B2B) models have proved far more robust and enduring. It is likely that the business-to-business use of the Internet will be worth ten times more than consumer e-commerce. For example, Forrester, the IT consultancy, estimates that 85 per cent of all electronic purchases are made by businesses not consumers[75]. Goldman Sachs estimates that B2B commerce will grow, in the US alone, from $39 billion in 1998 to $1500 billion by 2004, and business e-markets will take 44 per cent of all business-to-business revenues worldwide by 2004[76]. Online exchanges remove the inefficiencies involved in traditional ways of matching buyers and sellers, by locating suppliers quickly and removing the need for expensive intermediaries.

'It is likely that the business-to-business use of the Internet will be worth ten times more than consumer e-commerce'

However, some of the euphoria has disappeared here as well in the wake of the dot.com crashes. The spread of online exchanges has been plagued by the difficulty of getting diverse IT systems to work together, problems in settlement systems and lack of expertise, and estimates suggest far fewer online exchanges will succeed.

But, it is important to understand that in this context, the Internet is far more even than just a sales channel – a Booze Allen & Hamilton report summarizes this point:

'The opportunity to deal with customers in a new channel is only the most visible aspect of a much larger phenomenon. The ability to network more efficiently and effectively with customers, suppliers, intermediaries, employees and partners is changing the underlying basis of competition.'[77]

Perhaps the most widely-recognized prototype is Dell Computers.

REALITY CHECK
THE DELL INTERNET REVOLUTION

Michael Dell founded his company in 1984, and from a zero-base built a Fortune 500 company that is the leading world supplier of personal computers, with sales of around $30 billion. Dell's business model from the outset was to deal direct with business customers

(mainly) and to cut out computer distributors. From the outset –
relying on telephone ordering and later a salesforce for major
accounts – Dell's direct business model offered: more powerful
systems for the price than competitors, because of eliminating
resellers from the channel; customization – computers were built to
order; tailored customer service and support; and the latest
technology into the market faster, because of no stock in the reseller
channel.

However, the real transformation of Dell into a market leader came
from the 'rocket boost' of the Internet. The Dell website went live in
June 1997, and later that year Dell became the first company to sell
$1 million of products on the Internet in a single day – followed
quickly by a couple of $6 million days, which even Dell described as
'pretty scary'. The individual customer specifies the computer
configuration on-screen and orders, while major customers have
their own 'Premier Pages' – each is a site dedicated to the specific
customer with details of orders, pricing and deliveries as agreed with
the account. The Premier Page acts as an interactive catalogue for
customer employees to select approved equipment and order
(frequently with Dell loading the customer's own software before the
computer is delivered), and records orders and deliveries direct into
the customer's own systems.

The underlying strength of Dell's direct business model on the
Internet comes from what Michael Dell has called 'the power of
virtual integration'. Web-based links with suppliers, sharing databases and methodologies, means that customers 'pull' products
through the supply chain, giving less variability in orders (which are
now a steady stream), less stockholding in the supply chain, and
consequently lower costs and risks. The critical issue for Dell is
inventory velocity – not how much inventory is held, but how fast
it moves through the supply chain. With some suppliers, Dell holds
no stock at all – e.g. Airborne Express collects monitors from
Sony's Mexico factory on a daily basis determined by customer
orders received, and picks up the same number of computers from
Dell's Austin plant, matches up the monitors and computers on the
plane, and delivers them to customers. Dell's global operation runs
on around six days' stock. Similarly, Dell is linked by the Internet to
its major customers, almost as an outsourced IT department rather
than a supplier, analysing and forecasting the customers' IT needs,
and providing Dell's own tools for diagnosis to the customer on the
website. Perhaps Dell's greatest strength is that it has learned more
from suppliers and customers than any competitor, creating a new
type of competitive advantage, which is difficult for any competitor
to imitate.

The PC marketplace has become tough for all suppliers – in 2001 Dell is able to leverage its 15–20 per cent cost advantage in aggressive price cutting to take market share gains, and Michael Dell suggested 'We like to think we are taking over our competitors, one customer at a time'. In 2001, Dell's direct competitor Gateway moved into loss, and Hewlett-Packard reported sales well below plan. In mid-2001, Dell overtook the traditional leader, Compaq, in PC sales, having pushed market share from 9.9 to 12.8 per cent. Shortly afterwards, Compaq planned 5000 job cuts to try to save costs and get prices closer to Dell's, while Dell was looking at reducing logistics and product design costs yet further to control costs.

Sources: Nigel F. Piercy (1999), 'Dell Computers: The Dell Direct Business Model', in *Tales From the Marketplace: Stories of Revolution, Reinvention and Renewal*, Oxford: Butterworth-Heinemann, pp. 59–77. Andrew Heavens (2001), 'Investors Gasp at Dell News', *Financial Times*, 6 April. Duncan Hughes (2001), 'Upbeat Dell Sparks Rally on Wall St.', *Sunday Business*, 8 April.

Many others are looking to exploit forms of 'virtual integration' in their own operations: in what may become known as D.e.troit, General Motors, DaimlerChrysler and Ford have established an online exchange called Covisint, for their $200 billion a year components business, linking tens of thousands of suppliers. Renault and Nissan have since joined. Initially seen as the 'mother of all exchanges', providing a prototype of 'industry-led' electronic exchanges, Covisint has had to cope with supplier hostility, IT systems incompatibility and Federal trade Commission anti-trust investigation. Certainly, in Europe, the evidence is that the majority of 'tier one' components suppliers have no strategy for using Net-based procurement or exchanges. Closer to home Sainsburys has joined Germany's Metro, Sears Roebuck in the US and Carrefour in what is being described as the world's biggest supply chain on the Internet – GlobalNetXchange. Estimates are that procurement through the Net may cut 30 per cent off costs[78].

'Estimates are that procurement through the Net may cut 30 per cent off costs'

REALITY CHECK

THE ABB OF BUILDING A NEW BUSINESS MODEL

ABB is a Swiss–Swedish organization with sales of $20 billion and 160 000 employees, and is a pillar of the European business establishment. Along with General Electric and Siemens, it is one of the three largest electrical engineering companies in the world. Late in 2000, having moved the company away from its traditional base in heavy engineering towards industrial automation, CEO Gran Lindahl resigned because he was convinced that the company should be led by someone with an information technology background, not an engineer. The reason is that rather than just using the Internet as a means to support the purchase of goods and services, ABB is trying to use the Web as a communications pathway to feed its technology expertise and knowledge of industrial trends to its corporate customers. In return the Internet provides the means for the customers to share their ideas and plans. The intention is to become one of the world's biggest users of e-business in its broadest form. ABB products are drives, electrical power systems and computer codes that are buried inside other companies' products, and it sees this deep and rich connection with customers as one of its major assets. The Internet provides the means to add another level to these connections, by linking customers to ABB's 'brainpower' – the knowledge of its employees. The Web provides the basis for knowledge sharing within the company – a technician working on controls for a 'clean room' in an electronics plant in Brazil can have instant access to the ideas of a colleague who has done a similar task in Europe. But information sharing is also with customers – the Swiss chocolate company, Lindt, uses an ABB Web page to see how other companies are using 'preventative maintenance' to run factories efficiently. In the US, DuPont can interrogate a secure ABB website to learn about new types of control software for its chemical plants. These sites can also host an interactive 'chat room' where a customer can discuss product needs with ABB personnel, but also people from other ABB customers. ABB already has about 45 'customized' websites tailored to specific large customers, and is planning more. ABB's e-business model is also about increasing the effectiveness of its R&D 'lifeblood' – its ten research centres are linked by an internal 'intranet' called Pipe to each other and also to the business divisions. The results have been to speed up the commercialization of technology and to reduce the overlap between research projects at savings estimated as tens of millions of dollars.

Source: Peter Marsh (2000), 'Welding Metal to the Internet', *Financial Times*, 30 October.

E-Market-led strategic change

It is almost impossible not to be excited about the innovations and rethinks that the Internet allows in the way business is done. The crashing of the dot.coms around our ears does not mean that

Internet-based business is doomed, just that we have a lot left to learn about e-business. Now that things are getting real again, there are some major questions for you to ask about how the Internet is affecting your industry and markets, and how you will integrate electronic business into the way you go to market.

'the challenge is to think about how we exploit the Internet in developing our market strategy, and in managing our process of going to market'

The single most important thing that has changed most is this. A few years ago the question for companies was *whether* or not to become involved in Internet technology. This is no longer the issue. The question now is *how* to use the Internet. The alternative is to become uncompetitive and suffer the consequences. So, the challenge is to think about how we exploit the Internet in developing our market strategy, and in managing our process of going to market.

Strategy is redundant

In a 'speed of light economy', how can strategy be relevant or possible? When things change that fast, who has time to make strategic decisions?

Phillip Evans, a senior vice president with The Boston Consulting Group, argues that many traditional views of strategy have been outpaced by the Internet and the economics of information. He says that the controls and policies devised to minimize the probability of getting things wrong are made obsolete by the overarching goal of getting things right (not the same thing), when risk has to be embraced, speed matters more than accuracy, and innovation matters more than control. He also reckons that traditional competitive analysis is undermined because the Internet destroys traditional definitions of the company's boundaries, who are the competitors, and so on. He says that resource-based theories of the firm are fundamentally undermined by open business models, open standards, technology sharing between firms, strategic partnering, and fluidity of people and ideas transferring between companies. He concludes we should redefine strategy as the art of surviving rapid transition: success is survival into the next round of the game, successful strategies generate options[79].

However, when you come down to it, all this really says is that we have to get better and smarter at figuring strategy, not that we do not need one. Even Andy Grove, chairman of Intel, has despaired of what he calls 'Internet bigots' who see e-commerce as the cure for everything without really knowing what they are doing[80].

Those who believe strategy is redundant are advised to return and re-read the section on the demise of the dot.coms and many wanna-dot e-ventures (pp. 184–97). Now do you see? It is becoming apparent that one of the fastest ways to lose money is to plunge into an e-venture without a clear sense of strategic direction based on a profound understanding of what has changed and what has not. Strategy may be (probably should be) different, but not having one does not look any smarter online than it does offline.

'Those who believe strategy is redundant are advised to return and re-read the section on the demise of the dot.coms and many wanna-dot e-ventures'

In fact, there is an even stronger case that can be made for the old rules of strategy coming back into focus.

An antidote to the e-hysteria

Michael Porter provides a powerful antidote to those who tell us that strategy does not matter in the 'new economy':

> 'The time has come to take a clearer view of the Internet. We need to move away from the rhetoric about "Internet industries", "e-business strategies", and a "new economy" and see the Internet for what it is: an enabling technology – a powerful set of tools that can be used, wisely or unwisely, in almost any industry, and as part of almost any strategy.'[81]

His case is that, once the bubble bursts, we have to return to the fundamentals of business strategy because the old rules regain their currency: industry structure determines the profitability of competitors, and only sustainable competitive advantage allows a company to outperform the average competitor.

Put another way, the issue is that you need a strategy – you need to know your goals for being on the Web and plan how to achieve those goals, including working out how the website will relate to the rest of the company's marketing, and how you will measure the site's success[82]. Porter's view is that 'In our quest to see how the Internet is different, we failed to see how the Internet is the same'[83].

'Porter's view is that "In our quest to see how the internet is different, we failed to see how the internet is the same"'

And let's be clear about something else – having a website never did automatically provide you with an 'e-business strategy' – the strategy is what you do with it once you have it. These days, having the website is just about street credibility. The people who think the website is the strategy are probably the same ones who thought that marketing was just about a glossy promotional brochure.

Integrating the Internet into the business

Porter argues that even the terms we have begun to use have been destructive – 'e-business' and 'e-strategy' suggest we should see Internet operations in isolation from the rest of the business, when the real challenge for most companies is the most advantageous way to use the Internet as a complement to established ways of doing business. We are already seeing major bricks-and-clicks corporations, like US office supplier retailer Staples, rethinking the policy of separating their dot.com operations from the core business, and bringing them back into the main operation[84]. The real issue is tailoring the way we use the Internet to support our business strategy, not buying 'out of the box' packaged applications for an 'instant e-business'.

'The real issue is tailoring the way we use the Internet to support our business strategy, not buying "out of the box" packaged applications for an "instant e-business"'

The fear that e-business will cannibalize a company's existing sales base may be ill-founded. The US pharmacy Walgreens' website allows customers to order prescriptions online – but 90 per cent of those ordering online prefer to visit the store to collect the order, rather than have it sent to them. W. W. Grainger is a distributor of maintenance products and spare parts to companies, with a print catalogue and outlets all over the US. Grainger's Internet approach was to closely coordinate aggressive online efforts with its traditional business. They found that customers online continue to purchase in other ways as well – Graingers estimates a 9 per cent sales growth for customers using the online channel. The Grainger experience suggests that Web ordering actually increases the value of its physical locations to customers – they have combined the efficiency of Web taking and processing of orders, with the traditional distribution system. They have also found the traditional print catalogue promotes the website and stimulates its greater use[85].

'established companies with established business models have the opportunity to build stronger competitive advantage by the way they exploit the Internet to extend the established business model'

It is becoming increasingly apparent that established companies with established business models have the opportunity to build stronger competitive advantage by the way they exploit the Internet to extend the established business model. The idea that all established businesses would disappear at the hands of the dot.coms seems to have been a mite exaggerated. However, the issue is integration – not just bolting a website onto the existing business. Porter concludes: 'Only by integrating the Internet into overall strategy will this powerful new technology become an equally powerful force for competitive advantage'[86].

The critical e-customer issues

From the outset we noted that one anticipated impact of the Internet was that the balance of power would shift towards the customer – and we saw that there is evidence this is true in some situations. We also saw that the dot.coms and wanna-dots have done a remarkably poor job in offering superior customer service and satisfaction. This suggests that we face some big questions about what matters to customers who deal with us online (whether for information or purchase itself), and how well we can cope with these demands.

The potential of the Internet and the integrated digital enterprise (e.g. see the Dell example, pp. 202–4) is to 'expand the customer relationship', through fast response and customization, enhancing the customer's experience and loyalty[87]. However, there appear to have been a few problems in realizing that potential so far.

For a start it is clear that not all customers – particularly consumers – are ready to buy products and services online. Are your customers primarily 'habit-bound die-hards' who will not change how they shop, or 'frenzied copers' and 'experimenters' who are likely to find online shopping an attractive alternative to conventional purchasing?[88].

'it is clear that not all customers – particularly consumers – are ready to buy products and services online'

It is important to evaluate how and why your customers are prepared to adopt technology. Recently, US researchers Parasuraman and Colby have introduced the concept of 'Technology Readiness' as a measurement of customers' predispositions to adopt new technologies – based on their fears, hopes, desires and frustrations about technology. They identify five types of technology customers: *Explorers* – highly optimistic and innovative; *Pioneers* – the innovative but cautious; *Sceptics* – who need to have the benefits of the technology proved to them; *Paranoids* – those who are insecure about the technology; and *Laggards* – those who resist the technology. This approach starts to provide us with a mechanism for assessing the readiness of a particular market for the technology, and targeting Internet efforts better towards those who are most receptive. This is a big move forward on assuming that everyone is the same in their readiness to trade over the Web[89].

'key determinants of success are not just having a Web presence or even low prices, but delivering higher levels of service quality'

More significant is the recognition that the key determinants of success are not just having a Web presence or even low prices, but delivering higher levels of service quality – gaining customer loyalty will require a shift in focus from e-commerce (the transactions) to e-service superiority. Groundbreaking research from the Marketing Science Institute, for example, suggests four common 'disconnects' between consumers' expectations of a website and their experience in using it: a *marketing information gap* – insufficient or incorrect information in the e-tailer's operation regarding website features desired by consumers, and about consumers' perception of the e-tailer's e-service quality; a *design gap* – even complete and correct knowledge about consumer preferences may not be reflected in the site's design and operation; a *communications gap* – lack of understanding among marketing personnel about the website's features, capabilities and limitations; and a *fulfilment gap* – when, for example, the communications gap leads people to make promises to customers (delivery dates and the like) which cannot be kept, so the promises are broken[90]. While this research programme is in its early stages, the findings start to suggest a framework of issues that we have to address to achieve superior e-service quality.

The e-value imperative

'Internet-based trading is viable only to the extent that we can use it to improve the value we offer to customers'

Internet-based trading is viable only to the extent that we can use it to improve the value we offer to customers.

In his useful attempt to make 'business sense' of the Internet, Shikar Ghosh suggests that the challenge to managers is to determine what opportunities and what threats the Internet creates, and they should focus systematically on what new things the Internet allows their particular organization to do. Ghosh identifies four types of opportunities:

- establishing a direct link to customers (or suppliers and distributors) to compete transactions or exchange information more easily – adding to convenience for the customer, personalizing interactions with the customer, and developing new services;

- the technology lets companies bypass others in the value chain – e.g. distributors;
- the Internet may allow the development and delivery of new products and services to new customers;
- a company can use the Internet to become the dominant player in the electronic channel of a specific industry or segment[91].

The flip-side of this, of course, is that you also need to be aware of the potential threats to your position from others establishing the direct links, shutting you out of the supply chain, or coming into your marketplace from outside.

Another recent study has suggested that the two main strategies for creating added value through the Internet are: make transactions more efficient and make websites 'stickier'. The first strategy aims to: strengthen the supply chain by reducing supplier costs; offer a larger array of products and services; make buying more convenient for the customer; allow the customer to save time; and provide customers with better market information. The second strategy involves: rewarding customers for their loyalty; personalizing or customizing the product or service; building virtual communities of customers; and establishing a reputation for trust in the transaction[92].

Similarly, Peter Doyle suggests that there are seven ways in which the Web can create value for customers:

- *Customization* – in how products are presented to different customers, in allowing customers to make product choices, or in collaborating with the customer to design the product or service.
- *Greater choice* – through your own site, or in collaboration with partner sites, you can offer more choices than a conventional trader.
- *Lower prices* – unless offset against higher fulfilment costs, online operations may have lower costs and offer lower prices than conventional competitors.
- *Greater convenience* – since websites offer 24/7 access, customers can buy when and where they want.
- *More information* – the Web provides almost unlimited free access to product and service information and comparisons.
- *Greater assurance* – more personalized approaches, automated processes and feedback of information (e.g. order tracking) can reduce customer uncertainty.
- *Entertainment* – real-time bidding on auction sites, supplementary website features and the like can be used to enhance the customer experience[93].

'unless you know how you are going to deliver superior value to consumers (in their terms) and do so without bankrupting your business, you really have not got very far in figuring how to exploit the Web in transforming the process of going to market'

Put more simply – you can only justify large technology investments if they give you major cost savings, new money-making opportunities, or 'convenience plays', i.e. making life easier or better for customers[94]. The point is that however you choose to list or categorize the ways in which Internet trading can enhance your value proposition – unless you know how you are going to deliver superior value to consumers (in their terms) and do so without bankrupting your business, you really have not got very far in figuring how to exploit the Web in transforming the process of going to market.

This all suggests that most of us need to answer some searching questions about the impact of the Internet on our businesses before we get any further towards developing our market strategy.

REALITY CHECK
THE AWKWARD QUESTIONS ABOUT OUR E-STRATEGY

Where are we now? Is our existing Internet investment achieving the things we wanted, or has the result just been an ineffectual website and another half-hearted initiative? Should we be improving what we do already, or looking to do more?

Are we ready for e-commerce? Is the goal to move from e-communications to taking orders through the website? Do we have the capabilities to support this trading or can we acquire them? Do we have the ability to capture customer information and to use it to develop and extend the relationship? Do we have any choice – or are major customers already demanding that we trade with them on the Web?

Cost reduction possibilities? Are there opportunities to reduce costs as e-customers perform services for themselves instead of us – e.g. Web-based order tracking instead of telephone call centres? Are there advantages in tighter supply chain integration? Are there opportunities for by-passing intermediaries to form direct relationships with e-customers – what will that do to the rest of the business?

How do we attract e-customers? What will be our customer acquisition strategy and costs – how do these costs compare with average transaction values and average customer lifetime value? Should we emphasize the website, or other aspects of our offer?

How do we retain e-customers? What approaches will we take to build e-customer loyalty and a long-term relationship (at least long enough to get a payback on the acquisition costs)?

How do we maintain and enhance e-service quality? How well do we understand the factors that impact on e-customer perceptions of service, and how well do we manage them? Can we use the information we get about e-customers to make it easier for them to do business with us? How can we enhance the e-customer's experience of buying from us? Can we enhance service by reducing the number of members of the supply chain the customer has to deal with?

Do we have a value proposition for the e-customer? What advantages can we offer the e-customer that distinguish us from the rest? Can we sustain that difference? Can we keep the promises? Can we extend the value we provide through affiliate programmes and alliances with others to create a unique offering?

Do we have to keep up with the competition? How much will we lose if we lag behind our major competitors in developing direct Web-based trading?

How do we integrate the Internet with our existing business? How do we achieve complementarity between our online activities and our existing business – e.g. in marketing communications, in distribution and order fulfilment? Does it make sense to cannibalize our own sales base – i.e. 'transfer' some customers onto the Internet to make savings in transactions costs? Where is there a sustainable competitive advantage in a 'hybrid' clicks-and-bricks business? What will be the impact on our people, e.g. the sales force, and how do we manage that impact?

How do we make money? How quickly can the investment costs be recovered? What is the trade-off between customer acquisition and retention costs on the Web, and average customer transaction size and average customer lifetime value?

So, where does that leave us?

Hopefully this chapter has built on our foundation of the customer value imperative the fact that the Internet will be part of how we deliver value to some customers in some markets. In some cases, this will be a whole new way of doing business – a new business model. In other cases, it will involve the integration

'It would be unbelievably dumb to ignore the Internet as some kind of fad, when there is the opportunity to make it part of our market strategy and transforming our process of going to market'

of an Internet channel of communication and sales into our existing business model. The hysteria about the dot.com revolution should be finished by now. The disillusionment should have abated. Perhaps we can now be sensible about seeing how e-business impacts on our business and make smarter decisions. It would be unbelievably dumb to ignore the Internet as some kind of fad, when there is the opportunity to make it part of our market strategy and transforming our process of going to market.

The next issue to confront – which is in part related to the Internet – is the total integration of marketing in our process of going to market.

Notes and references

1. This sounds so smart it should have been said by someone important. Actually I made it up.
2. 'Encyclopedia, Yellow Pages, or Kook's Refuge', *Daily Telegraph*, 13 March 1997.
3. Quoted in Bob Donath (1997), 'No "Web Schmeb" for Business Marketers', *Marketing News*, 14 April.
4. Quoted in John Waples and Dominic Rushe (2000), 'E-Fightback', *Sunday Times*, 14 May.
5. OK, I know a bandwagon that's worth jumping on when I see it!
6. Quoted in Paul Taylor (1999), 'Business Urged to "Get a Connection" as Web Turns Out to be More Than a Fad', *Financial Times*, 6 July.
7. As we will see later, the addition of Internet channels to existing businesses, e.g. Tesco's direct grocery business.
8. In case you don't geddit – the somewhat unkind allegory is the World War II concentration camp at Auswitsch, linked to Mickey Mouse's name.
9. ... another World War II concentration camp reference, this time to Dachau, linked to Donald Duck.
10. Many computer-illiterate bosses have paid the penalty for this shortcoming, when people have set up automatic replies to all the boss's incoming e-mails, saying things like: 'I'm sorry, but I'm too stupid to use e-mail. Thanks for trying though.'
11. Jane Croft (2001), 'Lies, Damned Lies and Web Rumours', *Financial Times*, 18 January.
12. Jonathan Lambert (2000), 'Currys Warns of Legal Action Over Website', *Daily Telegraph*, 14 October.
13. 'Seek and You Will Find Sex, Drugs and Rocking Rolls', *Sunday Times*, 16 January.
14. Simon Goodley (2000), 'Tesco Plans Web Attack', *Daily Telegraph*, 17 August.
15. ... but why change the habits of a lifetime?

16. Quoted in Paul Taylor (1999), 'Business Urged to "Get a Connection" as Web Turns Out to be More Than a Fad', *Financial Times*, 6 July.
17. I am just showing off how 'webbed-up' I am by not leaving spaces between words any more, a skill we must all acquire to impress our technofreak colleagues, it seems.
18. Cited in Richard Fletcher and James Robinson (2000), 'Boo Founders Blame Investors for Collapse', *Sunday Business*, 21 May.
19. Susanna Voyle (2000), 'Demand for Groceries "Will Fuel Sharp Rise in Online Shopping"', *Financial Times*, 12 July.
20. Garth Alexander (2000), 'Christmas Brings Little Joy for American E-Tailers', *Daily Telegraph*, 24 December.
21. Michael de Kare-Silver (1998), 'Shopping on the Net is Poised to Change Face of Retailing', *Sunday Times*, 8 November.
22. Weld Royal (1999), 'Death of Salesman', www.industryweek.com, 17 May, 59–60.
23. Jane Croft (2001), 'Insurer Bites the Bullet and Moves to Phase Out "Man From Pru"', *Financial Times*, 17/18 February.
24. And yes, the reason is that they are terrified that you will want to buy the products at the US prices, i.e. $25 for the jeans instead of £25.
25. Carlos Grande (2000), 'Companies Fail to Reap Rewards via the Internet', *Financial Times*, 6 April.
26. Daniel Marowitz, Jon Lowry and Michael Drapkin (2001), *Three Clicks Away: A Manager's Guide to Winning on the Web*, London: John Wiley.
27. Quoted in Paul Taylor (1999), 'How the Internet Will Reshape Worldwide Business Activity', *Financial Times*, 5 May.
28. Jeremy Rifkin (2000), *The Age of Access: How the Shift From Ownership to Access is Transforming Capitalism*, London: Allen Lane.
29. Quoted in Roger Taylor (1999), 'Shaping the Future With Nothing But Ideas', *Financial Times*, 19 July.
30. Bill Gates (1999), *Business @ The Speed of Light: Using A Digital Nervous System*, London: Collins Hemingway.
31. 'E-Index', *Connectis*, February 2001, 6–7.
32. Tom Teodorczuk (2001), '44pc of Staff Surf Online at Work', *Daily Telegraph*, 19 April.
33. John Harlow (1999), 'Health Experts Say Net Nerds Are Sick People', *Sunday Times*, 22 August.
34. 'Hackers Break into Amazon Site', *Daily Mail*, 9 March 2001.
35. Andrew Baxter (2000), 'Internet Heralds a New Era of Collaboration', *Financial Times*, 1 November.
36. Paul Taylor (1999), 'Online Revolution Set to Overthrow Many Established Practices', *Financial Times*, 19 July.
37. Hugh Fraser (2001), 'Dotcoms That Came Back From the Dead', *Daily Telegraph*, 22 March.
38. Darren Behar (2000), 'The Dotcom Disaster', *Daily Mail*, 30 December.
39. Matthew Lynn (2000), 'The New-Economy Undertakers', *Sunday Business*, 20 August.
40. Michael E. Porter (2001), 'Strategy and the Internet', *Harvard Business Review*, March, 63–78.
41. Matthew Lynn (2000), op. cit.

42. Charles Leadbetter (2001), 'Fallacies and First Movers', *Financial Times*, 1 February.
43. John Kay (2000), 'Competing Under the Same Old Rules', *Financial Times*, 11 August.
44. Paul Taylor (1999), 'Online Revolution Set to Overthrow Many Established Practices', *Financial Times*, 19 July.
45. Brett Arends (2000), 'Net Fails to Woo Shoppers', *Daily Mail*, 7 November.
46. Catherine Wheatley (2000), 'Retailers' Websites Are "Hopeless"', *Sunday Business*, 2 April.
47. Nuala Moran (2000), 'Frustration and Delay can be Everyday Experiences', *Financial Times*, 5 April.
48. Patrick Barta (2000), 'Web Firms Underwhelm', *Wall Street Journal*, 28 November.
49. James Mackintosh (2000), 'If Only Halifax's Much Hyped Online Service Had Been Ready On Time', *Financial Times*, 15/16 July.
50. Donna L. Hoffman and Thomas P. Novak (2000), 'How to Acquire Customers on the Web', *Harvard Business Review*, May/June, 179–88.
51. Penelope Ody (2000), 'Why are Dotcoms so Bad at Customer Relations?', *Financial Times*, 7 June.
52. David Kenny and John F. Marshall (2000), 'Contextual Marketing: The Real Business of the Internet', *Harvard Business Review*, November/December, 119–25.
53. Frederick F. Reichheld and Phil Schefter (2000), 'E-Loyalty: Your Secret Weapon on the Web', *Harvard Business Review*, July/August.
54. Elaine Cavanagh (2000), 'Losing Out on Delivery', *Financial Mail on Sunday*, 19 March.
55. James Robinson (2000), 'Christmas is Coming But Your Gift Isn't', *Sunday Business*, 22 October.
56. Carlos Grande (2000), 'Delivering the Goods on Time is Far From Easy', *Financial Times*, 6 September.
57. Jonathan Guthrie (2000), 'Traders "Failing to Reap Internet Rewards"', *Financial Times*, 5 December.
58. 'Dotcom Retailers "Need to Grow Up"', *Daily Mail*, 3 May 2000.
59. Ray Massey and Peter Cunliffe (1999), 'VW Warns Over Cut-Price Cards on the Net', *Daily Mail*, 2 June.
60. John Waples and Dominic Rushe (2000), 'E-Fightback', *Sunday Times*, 14 May.
61. Susanna Voyle and Thorold Barker (2001), 'GUS Buoys E-Business Side With Breathe.com', *Financial Times*, 9 January.
62. Ruth Sutherland (2000), 'Builders Home in on Net Selling', *Financial Mail on Sunday*, 2 April.
63. Rosabeth Moss Kanter (2001), *E-Volve! Succeeding in the Digital Culture of Tomorrow*, Boston, MA: Harvard Business School Press.
64. Michael E. Porter (2001), 'Strategy and the Internet', *Harvard Business Review*, March, 63–78.
65. Quoted in Paul Taylor (1999), 'Business Urged to "Get a Connection" as Web Turns Out to be More Than a Fad', *Financial Times*, 6 July.
66. Thorold Barker (2001), 'E-Performance Report Offers Boost to E-Tailers', *Financial Times*, 10 May.

67. Louise Kehoe (2000), 'Christmas Cheer for Off-Line Brands', *Financial Times*, 20 December.
68. Thorold Barker (2001), 'John Lewis to Beef Up Internet Side', *Financial Times*, 3 February.
69. Robert Uhlig (2000), 'Internet Use is Heading Offline for Most of Us', *Daily Telegraph*, 26 December.
70. Richard Waters (1999), 'Microsoft Moves Into High Street', *Financial Times*, 12 November.
71. Jonathan Lambeth (2001), 'Smart Money Moves onto the High Street', *Daily Telegraph*, 4 January.
72. Christopher Field (2000), 'Browse it, Touch-Screen it, Kiosk it', *Financial Times*, 7 December.
73. Ranjay Gulati and Jason Garino (2000), 'Get the Right Mix of Bricks & Clicks', *Harvard Business Review*, May/June, 107–17.
74. Sara C. M. Daw (2001), 'The Reality of the Virtual Society', *Marketing Business*, May, 40–43.
75. Quoted in Paul Taylor (1999), 'Businesses Urged to "Get a Connection" as Web Turns Out to be More Than a Fad', *Financial Times*, 6 July.
76. Annie Counsell (2001), 'To B2B Or Not To B2B', *Connectis*, May, 22–24.
77. Quoted in Paul Taylor (1999), op. cit.
78. Jonathan Fenby (2000), 'B2B, Or Not To Be?', *Sunday Business*, 26 March.
79. Phillip Evans and Thomas S. Wurster (2000), *Blown to Bits: How the New Economics of Information Transforms Strategy*, Boston, MA: Harvard Business School Press.
80. Quoted in Dominic Rushe and Claire Oldfied (1999), 'E-Mania', *Sunday Times*, 19 September.
81. Michael E. Porter (2001), 'Strategy and the Internet', *Harvard Business Review*, March, 63–78.
82. Bruce H. Clarke (1997), 'Welcome to My Parlor', *Marketing Management*, Winter, 11–23.
83. Quoted in Michael Skapinker (2001), 'Death of the Net Threat', *Financial Times*, 12 March.
84. Andrew Edgecliffe-Johnson (2001), 'Staples Brings Dotcom Back into Fold', *Financial Times*, 4 April.
85. Michael E. Porter (2001), op. cit.
86. Michael E. Porter (2001), op. cit.
87. Adrian J. Slywotsky and David J. Morrison with Karl Weber (2001), *How Digital is Your Business?*, London: Nicholas Brealey Publishing.
88. Michael de Kare-Silver (1998), *E-Shock: The Electronic Shopping Revolution*, London: Macmillan.
89. A. Parasuraman and Charles L. Colby (2001), *Techno-Ready Marketing: How and Why Your Customers Adopt Technology*, New York: Free Press.
90. Valerie A. Zeithaml, A. Parasuraman and Arvind Malhotra (2000), *A Conceptual Framework for Understanding E-Service Quality: Implications for Future Research and Managerial Practice*, MSI Report No. 00–115, Boston, MA: Marketing Science Institute.
91. Shikhar Ghosh (1998), 'Making Business Sense of the Internet', *Harvard Business Review*, March/April.

92. Christoph Zott, Raphael Amit and Jon Donlevy (2000), 'Strategies for Value Creation in E-Commerce: Best Practice in Europe', *European Management Journal*, **18** (5), 463–75.
93. Peter Doyle (2000), *Value-Based Marketing: Marketing Strategies for Corporate Growth and Shareholder Value*, Chichester: John Wiley.
94. Daniel Marowitz, Jon Lowry and Michael Drapkin (2001), *Three Clicks Away: A Manager's Guide to Winning on the Web*, London: John Wiley.

CHAPTER 5

Total integration:

Processes and teams take over from departments

So far we have placed the following issues on the strategic agenda for transforming the process of going to market: the customer imperative, the value priority, and e-business as the new technology surrounding and reshaping what we do.

The next big issue[1] is the organizational questions we have to address in transforming the process of going to market. We can do this in two stages: first, let's look at how we have traditionally organized marketing, and the problems this has caused, but then let's look at the need for total integration of everything we do that impacts on customers, and how this can be achieved. The move is from thinking about specialized functions in a company – marketing, sales, production, and so on – to thinking about the need to coordinate absolutely everything and everyone in the company and in partner organizations around the value offering we make and deliver to the customer.

The thinking is simple – the chances are that improving our process of going to market is probably not going to involve building bigger and bigger marketing departments; instead we have to think about how to get better at marketing processes, with or without a marketing department[2].

'The move is from thinking about specialized functions in a company – marketing, sales, production, and so on – to thinking about the need to coordinate absolutely everything and everyone in the company and in partner organizations around the value offering we make and deliver to the customer'

The rise and fall of the marketing empire

For a long time it looked like the smart thing to do to make marketing effective was to organize it. There is a lot of theory that suggests we need to have marketing departments: if we want to implement marketing strategy we need marketing structure; how we organize marketing may be at least part of how we differentiate ourselves from our competitors[3]; the way we organize reflects how we divide up the market; the way we structure determines how information flows in the company; structure determines resource control; and so on. If you want chapter and verse on this stuff, you can find it elsewhere[4].

Organization has practical significance too though. In 1994, part of Lou Gerstner's amazing change strategy at IBM was to build greater customer focus and change the culture of the company by moving from geographical structure to industry-based structure[5]. In the detergents business, we have seen Unilever replacing global product units with regional divisions, and its rival Procter & Gamble trying to differentiate itself by moving in the opposite direction – forming global business units based on product lines, and abandoning its geographical units[6]. More recently, in the wake of Bill Gates' resignation from his CEO role, Microsoft has been through a company-wide restructuring to reinvent itself as a customer- rather than product-focused company[7].

'where it all started to go wrong was with the myth of the all-powerful corporate marketing department'

Organization is a significant competitive weapon, and it can be a way of changing important things. However, where it all started to go wrong was with the myth of the all-powerful corporate marketing department. People began to assume that everyone would and should have a textbook marketing department:

- *A marketing department* – it was assumed that there would be one, and that it would be formally organized and resourced around the market entities that matter most – geographical areas, customer types, product groups, specialized marketing functions, and so on.
- *A Chief Marketing Executive* (CME) – it was assumed that there would be one – not only this, it was assumed that s/he would be a powerful figure in the company, controlling significant resources and directly managing the customer interface.
- *Integration of marketing functions* – this view of the CME implied that all the 'customer-impinging' activities would be integrated by the Marketing Department, so they could be welded into a

consistent total offering to the customer, and this would be reinforced by the marketing programme structure as the basis for planning and managing marketing. The presumption is that the CME controls not simply advertising and selling, but also product policy, pricing, distribution, and so on.

- *Powerful* – it follows from all the above that the CME would be recognized as a powerful figure in the company, controlling many critical resources and activities.
- *The voice of the market in the company* – by controlling the company interface with the customer and the distributor, by collecting information on marketing performance and market change, the CME and the Marketing Department would provide corporate decision makers with guidance in lining-up company resources to achieve what the customer values.
- *Structure follows strategy* – besides, since we all believed in the 'marketing concept' (don't we – because we all said we did?), then it followed logically that to implement marketing we would naturally organize marketing along the lines above.

What is even worse is that the people who wrote textbooks and designed executive education and training in marketing went along with these assumptions – because if we assume that the structure is sorted out, then we can talk about more interesting things like new product development and advertising, and so on. The trouble is that for most companies these assumptions come from cloud cuckoo land – they simply are not true, and in most cases they never were.

In fact, experiences with a variety of organizations suggest that one of the things that went wrong in many UK companies was that we simply did not organize ourselves properly to make marketing happen. Indeed, in some cases we organized to make it virtually impossible for it to happen effectively! And that is before we even think about how the process of going to market will fit the new types of organization which are fast emerging (see pp. 234–7). Along with collaborators, I did a number of research studies of how companies in different sectors organized for marketing[8]. We found in a large number of companies there were *no* structures or systems whatsoever for implementing marketing. In many others marketing structures were weak token gestures with no real chance of changing anything. We had to conclude that generally speaking companies did *not* organize to make marketing happen in any real way – even if they *thought* and *said* that they did.

What is most worrying is that marketing organization and the growth of marketing departments may have been a token

'one of the things that went wrong in many UK companies was that we simply did not organize ourselves properly to make marketing happen'

response to the problem of matching what we do to what the customer values most, rather than real commitment, and that is why the marketing department is currently in disgrace in many companies. However, the issue now is probably not reorganizing marketing. Superficial restructuring and the creation of job titles never was good enough to achieve real market-led strategic change. Certainly, some companies do actually regularly reorganize as a *substitute* for having a market strategy – they work hard, they feel good, but all too often they achieve nothing other than disruption. Indeed, some reorganization fanatics cause even more substantial harm by actually making life even *more* difficult for the paying customer than it was to begin with. Think about the kind of constant organizational restructuring which results in: breaking customer relationships by moving salespeople around; pestering customers with frequent announcements about our internal organizational arrangements; leaving the customer uncertain about even who to contact and how to place an order, and generally feeling unloved and unwanted. This is not overly smart.

'some companies do actually regularly reorganize as a substitute for having a market strategy – they work hard, they feel good, but all too often they achieve nothing other than disruption'

In fact, the paying customer is probably not that interested in how we choose to organize marketing, or not as the case may be (although as we saw above, they may well care about the effects on them). Agreed, people who are really committed to market-led goals may achieve them by hook or by crook, whatever the personnel people put on the organization chart or in the procedures manual. But organization still matters for a number of reasons, not least because it defines the 'Monday Morning' reality that our marketing executives experience, and routinely have to cope with, in trying to get things done. Consider the following 'Monday Morning Reality' pictures[9]. These are all composites put together from a variety of sources, but just consider for a moment which sounds most like *your* company, because then you will understand better what the problems are in getting things done better.

Monday morning in Company A

Fiona Stewart, Marketing Manager, arrives in her small cubicle office, in a corner of the order processing room. Most of the available space in the office is occupied by product package dummies, printers' proofs of sales brochures, artists' layout boards and models of point-of-sale displays. It is 9.30 and she finds taped to her chair, by the secretary she shares with the

Purchasing Manager and the Office Supervisor, a list of phone calls to be made and e-mails to be returned. The messages are urgent – the printer has major problems with the new sales brochures and wants to change the layout, which means Fiona will have to obtain permission for the changes from her boss, Roy Burgess the Sales Director, and then arrange for some new typesetting, and then get back to the printer. The Regional Sales Managers are calling to complain about delays in the arrival of the new retail point-of-sale displays, and Fiona has to sort out the supplier and negotiate a new deadline for the promotion campaign (she knows this will have to be explained and defended to Roy, who will not be pleased). The local university is doing a 'free' piece of market research for Fiona, but needs authorization for some travelling expenses for the student researchers, which will have to be arranged by the Finance Director and counter-signed by Roy (who is not the world's greatest fan of market research, and will object that the annual Sales and Marketing Plan is already written, so why bother?).

The chance of Fiona offloading any of this work is zero, because her one-and-only Marketing Executive, James Blackwell, is out with the salesforce attempting to find out why the new sales area report cards are not being completed properly. Fiona knows that the real reason is that the Regional Sales Managers think that the report cards are a waste of precious selling time, and are highly suspicious of what will happen to the information anyway. This, however, is not an explanation acceptable to Roy, who persuaded the Board to invest £25 000 in a proprietary sales reporting system. Roy selected James to undertake this job, because he believes that James will have to join the salesforce soon anyway, to develop his career, and might as well gain some field experience now.

Fiona makes a cup of instant coffee from the kettle in the corner, but smiles briefly when she sees a direct mail advertisement in her in-tray for a short course on Strategic Marketing. This reminds her that Roy is presenting his Sales and Marketing Plan to the Board on Wednesday, so she can expect a series of urgent requests from him for extra information, figure-checking and proof-reading. She reflects that at least this means she may get to see the Plan, which will make a nice change, but then the phone rings . . .

Monday morning in Company B

Frank Hurst has progressed in Company B from Technical Sales Manager to National Sales Manager, and now Marketing Director.

His Monday is carefully scheduled by his secretary, because the rest of the week will be taken up by making sales visits with the new salesmen in the field, and a day with the Board of a national key account to pitch for the next year's business. Today, however, is mainly devoted to clearing up the aftermath of Friday's presentation of next year's Strategic Plan to the annual sales conference.

Frank is aware that the sales managers and area representatives are unhappy with the targets for the next year, and about the lack of consultation with them, when the Plan was formulated. Unfortunately, this has coincided with the Transport Manager's decision to remove car phones from company vehicles of all staff below senior management grades, and the Personnel Director's launch of a new company-wide Job Evaluation Programme. Memos of complaint from the sales managers are already on Frank's desk. Frank's problem is to defend the Strategic Plan, in which he really had little role himself, and in which he secretly has little faith, while heading off the impending crisis on salesforce terms and conditions of employment. The major fear is that he will lose some of his key sales staff to the competition, which will disrupt his sales plan, strengthen the competition, but also create major problems in recruitment and training, which is a nightmare in the company's specialized technical field.

His first task for the day is to make a case to the Managing Director for the reinstatement of the car phones for sales staff, to delay the application of Job Evaluation to the salesforce, and to set up a series of regional meetings with the salesforce. Frank has built enough slack into his operating budget that, if need be, he can run a salesman incentive campaign to overcome some of the immediate problems of sinking morale, but he knows that this is an 'elastoplast' solution. However, 'right now', he tells himself, 'elastoplast is better than bleeding to death!' Funnily enough, he has just received the same direct mail shot as Fiona. He frowns and throws the leaflet unread and crumpled into his waste bin with some irritation, before starting his first memo to the Transport Manager.

Monday morning in Company C

Michael Lucas is 27 years old and an MBA, and he worked previously as a Product Manager and then Group Product Manager for a national branded goods manufacturer, after brief experience with a management consulting firm. Last year he joined Company C as Marketing Manager. Michael was away from the office the previous week, attending a five-day course on strategic marketing. This is, strangely enough, the same course being offered to Fiona and Frank, but as a regular customer for such programmes, Michael went on an earlier running of the programme. He is delighted to see that the computer software he ordered to apply the new strategy screening matrix covered in the course is already sitting next to his personal computer. His secretarial work is handled by Viv Croxford, the Managing Director's PA. Michael had initially been worried about the arrangement, but has found Viv delighted to produce his reports, because it gives her the chance to use the graphics package on her word processor, and the new colour printer which Michael purchased.

In the centre of Michael's empty desk is a typed note from Viv to let him know that 'JBC', the Managing Director, would like a word about the marketing plan. This is no problem since JBC's office is opposite Michael's, and they frequently chat informally over coffee about the development of the business, long-term market changes, and new ways of doing things in the company. He is aware that the salespeople call him the 'MD's poodle', though he is unsure if this refers to his relationship with JBC or his hairstyle.

Michael's week is clearly structured in his personal organizer: he has two days work on the computer to reconcile the figures in the five-year plan, and to design the appropriate visual displays for JBC to present to the Board next month; he has one day to catch up on the reports and journal articles in his in-tray, and to meet a lecturer from the local university business school to discuss new developments in computerized 'expert systems' for allocating salesforce resources, and one day to prepare his presentation to the national salesforce.

The only dark spot on the horizon is that on Friday he has to attend and make a presentation of the Marketing Plan, at the sales conference, and he anticipates a rough ride. He has not recovered yet from his first meeting with the National Sales Manager, who took him, in his very first week with Company C, to meet a major client in the North East of England. The client and the National Sales Manager spent two hours badgering Michael into conceding a new discount structure. Afterwards, in a local pub, while the client ordered pints of beer for himself and the National Sales Manager, he looked at Michael, laughed and said: 'and how about you, bonny lad, a Snowball?' Michael no longer wears baggy Armani suits, or carries his Gucci document case with shoulder strap, on trips into the field. Michael arranges lunch with JBC, and turns to his computer and the long-term sales forecasts with considerable relish.

Monday morning in Company D

Geoff Kearsley is 45, an engineering graduate, and has spent 20 years in sales and marketing management, prior to obtaining his present post as Sales and Marketing Director at Company D. His department has more than 100 staff, covering sales, sales support, product planning, advertising and promotion, marketing research and planning, order processing, and exporting. It is a busy time of year because in four weeks' time the Marketing Plan must be presented to the Board, and then Geoff leaves for a three-week trip, meeting distributors in Europe and the Middle East, to investigate the feasibility of establishing sales subsidiaries as joint ventures.

His Monday diary consists of a set of meetings with small gaps between. First, the Sales Manager needs to see him to discuss short-listing candidates for two senior vacancies in the sales support section. However, the bulk of the morning will be devoted to the monthly Interdepartmental Executive Committee. The IEC agenda looks innocuous, but Geoff suspects that there is to be a renewed campaign to relocate order processing from Marketing to Accounting. He also has a series of problems to do with the pricing discretion given to salesmen, which the Internal Audit Committee wants to reduce effectively to zero, and the lack of tight liaison between his order processing system and the despatch of goods by the warehouse (controlled by Operations).

The afternoon starts with a meeting with the section heads in Marketing to discuss progress with the annual Marketing Plan, and a meeting with the Managing Director to discuss the company's current advertising spend and the new 'value-for-money' campaign in the company. Geoff has also to evaluate and authorize a pile of price adjustment forms on his desk, and a request for a non-standard product for a major customer, which he anticipates will go down like a lead-balloon with Operations. At the back of his mind is the worry that he needs to stay up-to-date with the gossip about the new restructuring plan being formulated by the Personnel Department. He too opens the same direct mail shot for the course on Strategic Marketing, and decides to send one of the new Product Planners, who is junior enough to be spared from the office. It is time for his first meeting of the day.

So what? – we all have problems

Just consider those Monday Mornings again. Does this really look like a good way to develop customer focus and deliver a superior value offering to the customer? Look at the pressures towards 'short-termism', inertia, navel-gazing, 'not invented here', organizational in-fighting, and complete lack of customer-orientation that we created for ourselves, simply by how we organized marketing. In fact, perhaps we should start again, because most of what we have got so far does not look like an effective way to create and drive market strategies.

'Look at the pressures towards "short-termism", inertia, navel-gazing, "not invented here", organizational in-fighting, and complete lack of customer-orientation that we created for ourselves, simply by how we organized marketing'

The reality of the corporate marketing organization

The 'Monday Morning' scenarios sum up much of the reality of corporate marketing as it has been described to us by a variety of different marketing executives, but we have harder evidence as well. Our research studies of marketing organization in UK companies are revealing.

For a start, in what we believe to be a reasonably representative sample of the heart of British manufacturing industry, about half the companies did not have a marketing department or a Chief Marketing Executive. This is not to say that having a marketing department is a 'good' thing and not having one is a 'bad' thing – far from it, because life is rarely that simple. It does mean that the conditions assumed as 'normal' in how we have all been trained in marketing simply do not exist in many companies, and that is a major cause for concern.

Where we did find marketing departments they were typically very small in headcount. Where we found marketing organizations, we asked – what are these Marketing Departments actually responsible for? The astonishing conclusion was that many had formal responsibility only for advertising and market research. Very few had any serious integration of even a very partial listing of 'marketing' responsibilities. In fact, we found that in large numbers of the companies, 'marketing' areas like sales, distribution, customer service, exporting and trade marketing *did* exist, *were* formally organized, but were organizationally *separated* from the Marketing Department and the Chief Marketing Executive.

'as more and more companies recognize the critical importance of customer service, they tend to take this responsibility away from marketing'

Indeed, one interesting insight was gained by looking at marketing 'critical success factors' as perceived by executives. Basically, the more important the critical success factor was thought to be, the less likely it was to be handled by the marketing department! (This observation is underlined by the fact that other studies reveal that as more and more companies recognize the critical importance of customer service, they tend to take this responsibility away from marketing.)

We decided to dig deeper and look at what decision areas Marketing Departments played some kind of role. In fact, there seemed to be five broad areas of involvement of marketing departments: *selling, product policy, marketing services, corporate strategy,* and *physical distribution.* Now this is a little closer to the conventional view of what marketing is about, but the results do not mean that *all* CMEs are responsible for *all* these areas, simply that these are how responsibilities fall into groups. It was clear that the responsibility factors above were not shared equally by all the CMEs and Marketing Departments, so we took each company's scores on the responsibility factors, and grouped the companies according to their scores. The result is shown in Figure 5.1.

What we found was that, in terms of responsibilities (shared as well as formally 'owned'), we could identify four quite different types of Marketing Department:

- *Integrated/Full-Service Marketing Departments* – These were the closest we found to the 'textbook' model, and they showed a relatively high degree of integration of marketing functions and personnel. These organizational units had high scores on

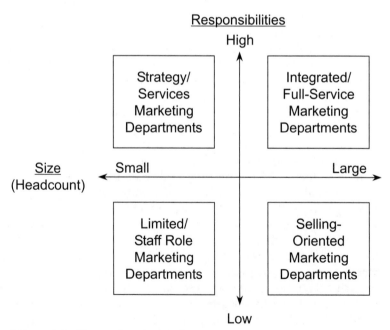

Figure 5.1 Types of marketing department

all the responsibility factors, so they controlled or influenced the major marketing decisions, and they are large units in terms of headcount in the company. Make no mistake, these departments have 'clout' – they have a high *power* ranking in their companies.

- *Strategy/Services Marketing Departments* – These marketing departments showed a much lower degree of integration, their high responsibility rating coming from Product Policy, Marketing Services and Corporate Strategy, not from Selling or Physical Distribution. They were also much smaller units – in some cases only two or three people. However, they were powerful. This power came not from involvement in line marketing activities, but from being close to strategic issues and planning, and thus close to top management. Small, non-integrated units, but high-powered with 'clout' and influence.

- *Selling-Oriented Marketing Departments* – These were large departments in headcount, but scored far less in terms of integration and had relatively low scores in the strategic areas – Corporate Strategy, Product Policy, and so on. They were dominated by the Selling responsibility. They were, however, generally relatively powerful in perceived rank within the business.

- *Limited/Staff Role Marketing Departments* – These were small departments, with the lowest scores on all the responsibility factors, and were mainly involved with staff services like market research and sales promotion. They were not powerful. Indeed, they seemed largely peripheral to the main business of the company – token gestures towards the marketing concept.

We have by now shown this model to, and used it as a diagnostic with, several hundred executives and almost as many different companies, and with few exceptions most executives have recognized the situations described as relating to their own companies. Indeed, one of the exercises we have used with executives is to ask them to judge which type of marketing department they have in their companies, and to describe what it is like to work in such a department – what are the problems, the barriers, and so on. Responses fall into the following pattern:

What is it like to work in a Strategy/Services Marketing Department?

The most common complaint here is (and I quote one executive, for whose sentiments I take no responsibility): 'the meat-heads in

'people describe the problems of being isolated from the field operation, the problems of communication with the sales and distribution operations, and the lack of line authority over people in the field'

the field, who just won't listen, who can't think past today, and don't understand what we are trying to do with the business!' Less emotionally, people describe the problems of being isolated from the field operation, the problems of communication with the sales and distribution operations, and the lack of line authority over people in the field. People also describe being uncomfortable with reliance on only informal influence and advocacy, and on top management sponsors, for the credibility and acceptance of the sophisticated marketing strategies and plans they produce.

What is it like working in a Selling-Oriented Marketing Department?

The real answer is, just the same as working in a Sales department, because there is a lurking suspicion that these are repackaged, relabelled sales operations, rather than marketing departments as such. One executive (for whose articulations I also disclaim responsibility, but include for balance) suggested somewhat forcibly to me that the real problem he faced was 'the MBA fairies at head office, who have never met a customer or done a deal in their lives, and should get their hands dirty before they try and tell us about marketing strategy!' You will understand that people get a bit heated about issues such as these. What people describe is isolation from centralized decision making, and lack of involvement or consultation about major strategic marketing decisions. They describe how intelligence from the field is apparently ignored, and their problem

'People describe the domination of short-term, urgent issues over longer-term marketing questions'

is to 'sell volume not quality'. People describe the domination of short-term, urgent issues over longer-term marketing questions. These executives describe company views of marketing as purely high-pressure selling, razzmatazz and hype, and lavish executive entertainment expenses.

What is it like working in a Limited/Staff Role Marketing Department?

People in this situation gain sympathy from most audiences as the great unloved of the marketing community. These are the purveyors of sales brochures, the organizers of sales promotions and sales conferences, the doers of market research (who are almost always ignored by decision makers), the progress-chasers.

People here describe their role as the marketing 'go-fers', as being peripheral and powerless at the edge of things – isolated both from the field and strategic levels. The only problem is that every so often, someone turns round and holds you responsible for

'People here describe their role as the marketing "go-fers"'

declining sales and market share, poor strategic positioning or the like, because you *are* the Marketing Department, aren't you?

What is it like working in an Integrated/Full-Service Marketing Department?

Maybe marketing executives are just natural whingers, but any expectation that executives from this type of marketing organization will be evidencing smug smiles and happy dispositions compared to their less fortunate peers is quickly dashed. Executives here describe the effects of bureaucracy – committees to co-ordinate the disparate parts of the marketing operation, inter-departmental committees about budget, production issues, staffing and training, etc., memos and reports and jurisdiction disputes, and so on. They describe interdepartmental conflict – with finance, with operations, with corporate planning. They describe the intervention of top management and interdepartmental committees in 'marketing' issues like advertising and promotion – where everyone is an 'expert'. They describe having token control of resources, where allocation decisions are really made by others. They describe the pressure to 'disintegrate' marketing in the perpetual 'empire-building' game in their organizations.

'They describe the pressure to "disintegrate" marketing in the perpetual "empire-building" game in their organizations'

If we put together these various pieces of evidence, what emerges is a list of fundamental things that seemed to go wrong in how we organized ourselves for marketing. Even with what we have found so far we can ask ourselves the following questions: Is this *really* the way to effective implementation of market strategies? Is this *really* how we are going to achieve the focus on customers and customer satisfaction in the companies that we said we wanted? Is this *really* how we are going to pack together our strategies and marketing programmes to create a distinctive differentiated total offering to the customer, or is this where some of the worst strategic gaps originate?

Just consider what we are really saying about how companies have tried to organize for marketing.

Isolation of strategy from operations

In many of the real situations we find, companies have developed marketing organizations, apparently designed purposefully and specifically to drive an impenetrable wedge between strategies and operations in marketing.

Reactive, short-term marketing

Given the choice between thinking long-term and going for short-term results in income, and demonstrably solving urgent operational problems, most of us will probably plump for the latter most of the time – it is easier, more comfortable, more familiar, it is what we are good at, and in many of the organizational situations we have described above it is apparently what the company seems to *want* us to do.

No direction or mission

It follows from the last two points that by separating strategic marketing issues from the operational level of doing things, with the resulting dangers of short-termism and reactive marketing, then we may well have organizationally created for ourselves a headless monster stumbling from crisis to crisis. If that is how you are running your marketing, then the achievement of a strategic direction, or the drive of a customer-oriented mission, is likely to be just a little bit elusive.

No market leadership in strategy

'If you organize marketing around sales brochures, or short-term selling operations, or keep the marketing organization weak and peripheral, then you have already made your choice about marketing's voice in long-term strategy'

In many of the real marketing organizations we have studied, those wonderful visionary concepts of the marketing department as the voice of the customer in the corridors of power, the constant provider of the discipline of the marketplace, are simply cloud-cuckoo-land. If you organize marketing around sales bro-chures, or short-term selling operations, or keep the marketing organization weak and peripheral, then you have already made your choice about marketing's voice in long-term strategy. The question is – did you mean to make that choice? And indeed, did you realize you had made it?

Weak implementation of marketing

If you follow the conventional logic, then how you organize something is how you implement what you are trying to do. For reasons not unrelated to those above, if you look at how companies actually organize for marketing, then it is not a bad indicator of just how serious they are about actually making it happen – or not, as the case may be.

Strategy follows structure

What we have seen and been told about by executives all too often can be described as the exact reverse of the rational, conventional logic. Far from the strategies chosen leading to the adoption of appropriate organizational structures to implement marketing, we see the existing structures (because of what they stand for) as a prime determinant of what goals and strategies are actually adopted by a company. This may sound perverse, unless you dig a little deeper and ask what organizational structure *really* represents. When you get past the 'rational' explanations, structure is about:

- *Power* – the organization chart is a snapshot of who runs the organization (and who doesn't).
- *Inertia and the status quo* – because structure tells us about who runs things, it also tells us what are the vested interests in the present position, and it is not hard then to figure what they are likely to buy in terms of strategic change (and what they won't).
- *Status* – issues of organizational level and position, relative departmental size, recognition in key memberships of decision-making committees, and so on, are about status or perceived power and sponsorship (or the lack of it).
- *Culture* – or simply 'the way we do things here' is partly shown by organization positions, and the 'share of voice' that different parties have in making important decisions (or the lack of it).
- *Information* – information is the other dimension of organizational structure, because structure shows us how the information flows – or perhaps more revealing yet, what information does *not* flow.

It seems impossible to avoid concluding that many of the problems we have faced in getting the marketing act together have been because we missed the point about marketing being more than just another specialized function. But before anyone starts running around demanding that marketing should be reorganized, I think we may have missed the boat on that one. The reality is increasingly that we have to forget about marketing departments and look at what new types of structure we need to focus on customers, to develop new strategies, to deliver the service that matters, to integrate, to collaborate, to manage partnerships, and to manage change. The good news is that the role of marketing is becoming much more strategically important – the bad news is that this means marketing *processes* not marketing *departments*.

> **'many of the problems we have faced in getting the marketing act together have been because we missed the point about marketing being more than just another specialized function'**

The issue of the type of marketing department may still be important in some companies, along with the questions about its effectiveness in driving market strategy – you need to have a look at what you have got, and use that as the basis for identifying the real implementation problems you face in getting things done. See where your marketing department falls in the model in Figure 5.1, and see what that tells you about the real problems.

But one of the implications of the developing focus on the process of going to market instead of conventional organizational structures is that the future is even more complicated. In fact, the question is rapidly changing to '*What* marketing department – where has it gone?'

What marketing department?

'the traditional marketing department is a thing of the past' There has been vocal opinion for some time which suggests that the traditional marketing department is a thing of the past, as market strategy moves to a relationship focus instead of transaction, and that centralized marketing organizations are 'dinosaurs'[10]. Popular commentators say top management considers marketing departments to be 'a millstone around an organization's neck'[11] and that 'marketing departments are in top management's sights'[12]. Others point to the business process re-engineering technique being applied to marketing[13], with the resulting demise of traditional ways of organizing around processes like order generation and order fulfilment. Indeed, a Marketing Society survey of senior marketing executives at the end of 1998 found that 57 per cent of companies with over £1 billion turnover had no board-level marketing director[14].

REALITY CHECK

NEW MARKETING STRUCTURES

The Unilever-owned toiletries company Elida Gibbs (now Elida Fabergé) has radically revised its marketing structures. In effect, the company divided the traditional brand manager's job into three, and abolished the job of 'marketing director'. A process perspective suggested that their marketing was partly operations and partly the development of new initiatives. Instead of forcing these processes to fit with established functional boundaries, they were separated. The company divided day-to-day operating and tactical marketing from longer-term issues of brand development, creating three centres of expertise: one for the consumer/brand, one for the category, and one for the retailer/customer. Category managers bridge the gap with sales as well as taking over operational marketing to the retailer, and report into sales. The former sales director became customer development director and the former marketing director became brand development director. The brand manager's job for the big brands divides into two responsibilities: consumer directed communications and innovation management.

Similar developments are apparent in other consumer goods companies like Procter & Gamble, Colgate Palmolive and Heinz, particularly in the adoption of category management (see pp. 478–9). Indeed, category management is just one part of the move towards 'trade marketing', through which suppliers and retailers 'co-market'. The role of its traditional marketing department has been in decline in this type of channel for some years now.

At the end of the day – if there is a better way of going to market than having a traditional marketing department, then they will disappear. As one commentator puts it: 'Theoretically, the marketing department should have been "the voice of the customer" within the corporation. But in practice, over the past few decades, that voice seems to have been all but silent.'[15].

'if there is a better way of going to market than having a traditional marketing department, then they will disappear'

Catching up with the rest of the organization

At a time when channels of distribution have become more complex and demanding, buyers are increasingly cynical, and database marketing is pushing towards micro-segmentation, the predicted pressures for change in how companies go to market are:

- *Breaking hierarchies* – the speed and flexibility we need comes from reducing the number of organizational levels and numbers of employees, creating smaller business units, and empowering line management to manage key business processes.
- *Self-managing teams* – the critical changes in how we respond to customers will be managed by groups with complementary skills, in the form of high-performance multifunctional teams to

achieve the fast, precise and flexible execution of programmes, possibly organized around market segments and categories, and possibly temporary in duration, like a task force.

● *Re-engineering* – critical organizational processes will be radically restructured to reduce cost and increase spend and flexibility, and to increase responsiveness to customers.

● *Transnational organizations* – competing globally requires more complex structures and new skills to manage in networks and alliances.

● *Learning organizations* – organizations will require the continual upgrading of skills and the corporate knowledge base, leading to the adding of value for customers through knowledge feedback, to create competitive advantage through enhanced capabilities.

● *Account management* – achieving customer focus may require new structural mechanisms built around key accounts[16].

'much emphasis is being placed on the role of teams that cross functional boundaries to deliver value to the customer, or "pancompany marketing"'

As we will see shortly, currently much emphasis is being placed on the role of teams that cross functional boundaries to deliver value to the customer, or 'pancompany marketing'. This raises many questions over the need for the traditional marketing department. To that, add the new scenario created by going to market through networks of partners held in place by strategic alliances (see pp. 508–19). For the moment, the point is that new ways of going to market mean a new way of organizing for marketing.

New ways of going to market

Fred Webster's view is that as the focus of marketing changes from transactions to relationships, and then increasingly to managing strategic alliances among independent organizations, there will be blurring in traditional external boundaries between the firm and its market environment, which will be paralleled by less distinct boundaries between functions inside the organizations. His key conclusions are:

● At the *corporate* level, in the network organization the role of marketing will be to help design and manage strategic partnerships with suppliers and technology partners.

● At the *business* level, the key task facing marketing managers will be deciding which marketing functions and activities are to be purchased, which are to be performed by strategic partners, and which (if any) are to be performed internally.

- At the *operating* level, there will be more emphasis on relationships with customers, and less on customer manipulation and persuasion, and this may lead to dominance by the sales organization[17].

A more detailed view of how alliances and partnerships may affect the role of the marketing organization is provided by Ravi Achrol[18]. He proposes two innovative marketing organizational forms: the marketing exchange company and the marketing coalition company. Both the models are of organizations acting as hubs of complex networks of functionally specialized firms, where emphasis is on managing transorganizational boundary-spanning.

What Webster and Achrol tell us is how the development of such strategies will impact on the location and organization of marketing. It is a long way from the traditional textbook model of a marketing department. But they tell us something more as well – they underline the fact that the role of marketing is to create and sustain a value offering to the customer which does not fall apart because of gaps between marketing and production, or internal disputes between sales and customer service, or conflicts of interest between alliance partners. The big issue facing us is whether we can create and manage totally integrated marketing.

'the role of marketing is to create and sustain a value offering to the customer which does not fall apart because of gaps between marketing and production, or internal disputes between sales and customer service'

The goal is totally integrated marketing[19]

The comments above about catching up with the rest of the organization and new ways of going to market lead to a clear conclusion. We have to focus on integrating and co-ordinating everything in the company that goes towards identifying, meeting and delivering the customer's value requirements – we have to pull together all the activities and processes in the company that impact on customer value, by the way we manage the process of going to market (see Figure 5.2). The critical question in the new ways of delivering superior value to customers is marketing as a process, not marketing as a department or function. This is a bigger challenge than just reorganizing marketing departments – expressions about rearranging the deck chairs on the *Titanic* spring to mind. It suggests one or two problems too.

'The critical question in the new ways of delivering superior value to customers is marketing as a process, not marketing as a department or function'

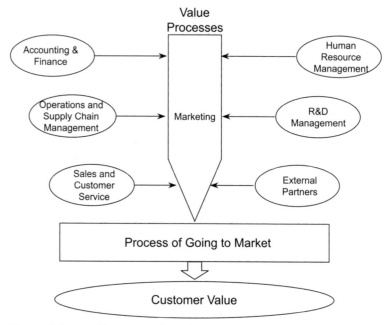

Figure 5.2 Totally integrated marketing

The trouble is that traditional 'command and control' organizations appear to have been established precisely to prevent us integrating and coordinating things around the customer. Rigid, hierarchical organizations do not permit the merging of systems, activities, people or anything much else. People and what they do have been put in boxes, and the boxes have been put in divisions, and lines have been drawn between them – those lines have become a straitjacket preventing movement, change or integration, and resisting the challenges of those who try to achieve these things[20]. Organizational theorists say these are the organizations of the past, that will fast disappear, so we have nothing to worry about. If you spend more than five minutes in most companies, you have to conclude that organizational theorists are blind as well as stupid, and to speculate what planet they inhabit.

'marketing people appear to be pathologically unable to avoid upsetting everyone else in the organization'

Everyone hates marketing

One of our earliest findings about marketing organization was that marketing people appear to be pathologically unable to avoid upsetting everyone else in the organization. Part of this may reflect their obnoxious personalities, but it is also because, as Philip Kotler pointed out some thirty years ago, one of the problems with being a conscientious marketing executive is that to do your job well in the *customer's* terms, you are likely to have to persuade other people in the company to do their jobs less well in *their terms*; for example:

Marketing wants	In order to get	Which causes	To perform less well in
More variants on standard products and 'one-offs', complete flexibility to vary the product's characteristics to customer specifications	Specialized offers for different market segments, and customized product offers	Production and Operations	Controlling operations costs and minimizing re-tooling and machine changes
Many price lists	Exploit customer differences in sensitivity to price	Accounting and Finance	Controlling administrative costs and maintaining average unit revenue
Multiple channels of distribution – direct selling, Web-based sales, different intermediaries	Maximum reach into the market, reaching different segments with different sales channels	Sales Department	Maintaining sales revenue, forming stable customer relationships, developing key accounts
Instant delivery of products and spares	Customer satisfaction and competitive advantage	Transport and warehousing	Scheduling delivery vehicles and controlling stock levels
Customer-care trained staff at point-of-sale	Customer perceptions of care and service	Personnel/ Human Resource Management	Training costs and standardization of training across the company

The result of differences in perspective and departmental goals and objectives is *conflict* – hidden or open, but conflict nonetheless. And when push changes to shove in companies under pressure, weak, non-powerful marketing departments lose the internal battles. The trouble is, it may be the most important battles they lose, because things like managing to achieve customer satisfaction and value and making market strategies work are the *most* likely to cause discomfort elsewhere in the organization.

'the result is that marketing executives are frequently not the most loved individuals around'

It is perhaps less than surprising that the result is that marketing executives are frequently not the most loved individuals around. A study by Synesis for the Marketing Forum found that the majority of executives in other functions (Finance, Human Resource Management, Logistics, Sales/Customer Service, Production, and IT) rated their marketing team's effectiveness as adequate at best and often poor. HR Directors commented 'Marketers should be more communicative . . . more pragmatic and less egotistical', while finance directors described their marketing peers as 'brash . . . wide-boys . . . flash . . . uncontrollable . . . into freebies . . . never in the office . . . over-enthusiastic' [21].

Never argue with stupid people.

They drag you down to their level and then beat you with experience.

More recently, Susan Baker, at Cranfield School of Management, has reported her research into what non-marketers think of marketing people – they want to have the best of everything, make heavy use of statistics and incomprehensible terminology, and insist on taking long lunches when everyone else is cutting back. More specifically, non-marketers' messages to their marketing colleagues are:

- *You're not accountable* – marketing people consider themselves the 'chosen ones', deserving quick promotion, with little company loyalty, and incur high costs without demonstrating value (and take the credit for other people's work when things go right).
- *You're (a touch) arrogant* – marketing people get what they want by using (and abusing) market research and jargon.
- *You hold meetings over lunch* – marketing people are seen to operate off-site and have long lunches, and to have a general air of 'busyness' with no apparent purpose.

- *You're always in meetings* – marketing people do nothing but hold meetings, lack structure in their work, and show a heavy internal orientation.
- *You work a shorter day* – marketing people swan around while others do the real work.
- *You're unaccountable, untouchable, slippery, expensive* – marketing people are out of touch with their colleagues[22].

'OK, so what if the spanners in the factory, the bean-counters in accounting and the bleeding hearts in HRM don't like us much?'

OK, so what if the spanners in the factory, the bean-counters in accounting and the bleeding hearts in HRM don't like us much? Well, it gets worse . . .

No-one listens to us any more

One potentially disastrous outcome of the low esteem in which many functional specialists appear to hold marketing is that they stop *listening*. Research by Elliot Maltz and Ajay Kohli suggests that when marketers try to share insights and information with other departments, they are frequently ignored or misunderstood – often the fight now is actually to get marketing's voice heard in the company[23]. Part of the problem is that marketing may make insufficient or weak efforts at communicating with other departments – more of this below. However, there is more to it than that.

'Part of the problem is that marketing may make insufficient or weak efforts at communicating with other departments'

For example, in studying the integration of marketing and R&D, research findings suggest that it is interfunctional rivalry and political pressures that severely reduce R&D's use of information supplied by marketing personnel[24]. It seems it's not just that they don't like us – they won't believe what we say either.

REALITY CHECK
PEOPLE IN R&D?

They are the ones who can tell you the volume of a jar of jam, and the viscosity and specific gravity of the jam. They just can't get the lid off the jar.

R&D executives are like a lighthouse in the desert – brilliant but of no practical use.

Fragmentation of marketing

'there is growing evidence that the functions we used to assume would belong in the marketing department are being dispersed yet further across the organization'

We saw earlier in the chapter that formal integration of marketing has always been hard to find in real companies – most marketing departments had very limited direct control over so-called marketing issues. But over and above this question, there is growing evidence that the functions we used to assume would belong in the marketing department are being dispersed yet further across the organization[25]. As marketing priorities are changing to cope with the new marketplace, marketing is fragmenting across the company – the competition to 'own the customer' and to control the business processes that drive customer value appears to be one that conventional marketing has lost. The signs of this are numerous:

- Market research was always the last refuge of the marketing executive – surely we control this? In fact, increasingly technology means that information is a by-product of operations, not a marketing fiefdom – Customer Relationship Management programmes span departments and systems to integrate customer knowledge (see pp. 493–9); point-of-sales scanning systems operated by retailers replace many traditional market research needs; key account management changes who has close contact with the customer to account teams and senior management; websites operated by the IT people or a partner organization have the insights and information about customer behaviour.
- Finding new products is increasingly about leveraging R&D capabilities faster than the competitor, not trying to do conventional surveys to 'find out what people want' – sorry about that all you 'market researchers'.
- Many of the people and processes that impact on the customer/company interface are the responsibility of human resources and operations, not marketing or sales.
- In many situations, the driving force behind product quality, price and availability is supply chain management not marketing.
- Increasingly, the key to adding customer value may be through alliances and networks (see pp. 508–19) – and these are not traditionally associated with marketing.
- The move in many companies from product branding to corporate branding means that managing a brand has moved upwards and beyond the traditional marketing area of influence[26].

- As the company website has moved from just being 'brochure-ware' towards real interactive marketing and e-commerce, the control of the website has moved from marketing to IT or specialists in the new type of business[27].

Indeed, a Marketing Forum report in 2000 found that in less than a third of the companies they examined did marketing even oversee customer service[28].

The overwhelming priority of integration

There is not much new in suggesting that getting the real marketing job done – i.e. delivering superior value to customers – requires working with other functions better and more effectively. For example, interfunctional coordination is central to how people understand what makes an organization market oriented[29], and to the attainment of customer service goals and customer value[30]. The trouble is the fact that people have to keep saying it, kind of suggests we may not be too good at doing it.

What all this suggests is that integration is actually now the main challenge facing marketing, and it is not likely to be achieved by rebuilding the departmental bureaucracies of the past (or worse starting them for the first time). It is not just me. For example, Northwestern University's guru of integrated marketing, Don Schultz, tells us that in the customer markets that we now face:

> '*integration is actually now the main challenge facing marketing, and it is not likely to be achieved by rebuilding the departmental bureaucracies of the past*'

> ' . . . integration of the entire organization becomes critical. Everything must work together, fit together, and appear together for the customer . . . increasingly it is viewed as a way to develop and implement the critical customer's view of the organization. An organization can no longer consist of a group of unrelated activities and work groups because customers won't accept that.'[31]

Indeed, one view is that the issue of better alignment between brand and business strategy is becoming the major concern of general management[32].

The most critical weakness of conventional marketing?

The trouble is that marketing has generally not been very good at managing out-of-the-box and across boundaries. For example, a Cranfield University

> '*marketing has generally not been very good at managing out-of-the-box and across boundaries*'

research study underlines the fact that while organizations are increasingly thinking across traditional departmental boundaries to build customer value, the initiatives have mainly originated in manufacturing, IT, or from external partners, not from marketing[33].

However, this is not just about a 'mid-life crisis' for marketing, it is about a lot of breast-beating in other functions too, concerned with how they add value to the company. Finance people know they are called 'bean-counters' only concerned with history, the operations people know they are accused of being inflexible and inward-looking, the HR people know that they stand accused of being mindless bureaucrats, concerned only with paperwork and working conditions – the difference is that in each of those areas we have seen huge efforts to change and refocus. In marketing we thought we had got it right, because we 'owned' the customer, so we sat back and watched while the old models just ran out of steam[34].

'to build a new agenda for totally integrated marketing, how about considering the potential for conflict (which needs to be managed) and the prospect of shared interests and partnership (which should be exploited), with each of the main functions in the company and beyond'

So, to start to build a new agenda for totally integrated marketing, how about considering the potential for *conflict* (which needs to be managed) and the prospect of shared interests and *partnership* (which should be exploited), with each of the main functions in the company and beyond – and maybe we should do this before everyone consigns marketing to the corporate rubbish bin? Marketing folks really are going to have to learn to play nicely with the other boys and girls, or face the harsh consequences of not doing so.

Marketing and finance

There is pretty clear evidence that improving marketing's interaction with finance is important to getting a better handle on the allocation of resources to marketing initiatives[35]. Try telling that to the marketing executives who describe the 'hassle factor' in getting the resources they need to do things (see pp. 579–81). However, there is an interesting new idea around that may help marketing and finance people work better together – in 2000, the failure of BT's American market strategy led to the culling of headquarters *finance department* staff[36] (including eventually the Finance Director); in the same year, the problems of convenience goods retailer W. H. Smith in holding market share led to the simultaneous departure from the company of the retail arm's marketing director *and* finance director in June[37]. In fact, there are signs that in struggling US companies, the first neck on the boardroom chopping block is likely to be the one attached to the chief financial officer[38]. Now that's what I call being in this thing together – when things go bad now finance people can get busted just as easily as marketing people. That may help concentrate a few minds among the corporate dinosaurs.

There are several typical areas of disagreement between marketing and finance, reflecting different priorities. Probably the biggest is that finance usually wants to cut costs and increase reported short-term profit, while marketing wants long-term investment to build brands and market share. Indeed, a recent KPMG/Institute of Practitioners survey reports that the vast majority of Finance Directors complain they cannot measure the effectiveness of marketing efforts, and fully one-third admitted the marketing budget would be the first thing to be cut when business costs were under pressure[39]. The two areas also tend to get upset about each others' different views of pricing – cost-plus to recover overhead conflicts with market-based pricing against customer value criteria.

'There is potentially a great synergy between the roles of marketing and finance which can be exploited'

However, it does not have to be this way. There is potentially a great synergy between the roles of marketing and finance which can be exploited, if we can get finance people to stop acting like the 'corporate police', and marketing people to understand the financial implications of their proposals.

REALITY CHECK

MARKETING AND FINANCE MEET AT NATIONWIDE

Nationwide Building Society is one of many companies that have made progress in building productive bridges between marketing and finance, to work across traditional functional boundaries. Cross-functional teams from Marketing and Finance hold regular meetings – at least once a month, but more frequently when needed – supplemented by quarterly events off-site to see how well things are going. Social links are encouraged and facilitated by Nationwide's self-contained site, with its own restaurant, shop, gym and other facilities. While Finance maintains its independence, it has appointed managers to specialize in different parts of the operation, including one to keep in touch with marketing. One major gain has been speed in developing and launching new services. For example, a year's extended warranty as a credit card feature took less than three months from inception to launch, as a result of the high degree of cross-functional working.

Source: Mark Whitehead (1999), 'Building Bridges', *Marketing Business*, May, 34–39.

Marketing and operations: supply chain management

Next, consider the advent of 'lean thinking' in the operations area, and 'supply chain management' in particular, and what these new management approaches do to conventional ideas about marketing – i.e. blow them out of the water.

Jim Womack and Dan Jones[40], in their deservedly influential book, tell managers how to 'banish waste and create wealth' in their companies – this is one very seductive pitch to senior executives. Their approach to creating the 'lean enterprise' rests on four principles:

- Define *value* in the product or source from the end-customer's perspective – for example, they say value for the airline passenger is convenient, hassle-free travel, yet airlines invest in large aircraft to take hundreds of passengers to 'hub' airports (i.e. places they do not wish to be) with the result that 'passengers are miserable (this is not what they meant by value, the aircraft producers make little money because airlines can't afford new planes), and the airlines . . . have flown a decade-long holding pattern on the vicinity of "bankruptcy"'[41].
- Identify the *value streams* for each product (i.e. the activities which add to customer value) and eliminate *muda* (waste) – they use the example of the can of cola soft drink where some three hours of actual processing of package and product requires nearly eleven months of storage in the traditional supply chain, in which all companies are organized for mass production not around the value stream. A collaboration between supplier and retailers can reduce this to a few weeks, as it has done for Tesco.
- Organize around *flow* instead of batching and queuing everything – they illustrate this with house construction where investigations in one firm showed that five-sixths of the typical house construction schedule was occupied with *waiting* (for the next set of specialists to do their work) and *rework* (to correct work done incorrectly or out of sequence).
- Respond to the *pull* of the product through the supply chain to eliminate stocks – they give the example of Toyota's 'Daily Ordering System' for replacement car parts, where orders are placed for parts as cars come in for repair, and are met on the same day.
- The pursuit of *perfection* in all things.

This is truly impressive and will exercise senior management's minds for some time to come yet, as indeed it should. However, there are a couple of problems here – they are in danger of substituting supply chain efficiency for market strategy and not telling anyone.

For example, they see value only as measurable technical product quality and price – we know that value to customers is more complex than this, but production engineers are not interested in 'irrational' consumer requirements (until it loses us market position and then they blame 'marketing'). They also believe that supply chain efficiency will increase customer value and satisfaction. In a 'rational' world it might. In the real world, who really believes that the fact that the can of Coke has been on the shelf for three weeks instead of eleven months is of any interest to me whatsoever as a consumer, let alone increases value to me – I could care less? I actually asked a detergent company executive if he believed that the fact the detergent was a few days old when I bought it, instead of a few months, was seriously going to increase my satisfaction and loyalty – and his honest reply was a definitive 'yes ... because it is fresher!' I believe the sky is very pink on the planet where he lives. The lean supply chain gurus also believe that branding is irrational, and in a sensible world we would all drink a generic cola – which would make the supply chain much more efficient.

They believe that consumer demand is inherently stable, and chaos is only created by bad marketing people advertising and promoting products to win market share, and this should stop. They say 'level scheduling needs level selling'[42]. They believe totally that the centrally planned and coordinated supply chain is a better way of doing business. They are persuading many senior executives and major companies that this is the way to do business in the future.

'They believe that consumer demand is inherently stable, and chaos is only created by bad marketing people advertising and promoting products to win market share, and this should stop'

What a marketing executive may see is the potential rebirth of production-orientation – the last time we tried that, it did not work too well, why should anyone think it will work now? And yet that is the reality in many companies right now – if you don't think so, then have a look at the Efficient Consumer Response movement (pp. 514–17).

That is the basis for conflict between marketing and supply chain management. In case you are interested, it looks like a conflict where the score in most companies is: supply chain management 1, marketing 0 – or, if you prefer: supply chain management 1, marketing lost. This is very silly, because it obscures the most fantastic potential for better coordination of marketing capabilities with supply chain strength to define competitive superiority in new ways.

For a start, supply chain capabilities are likely to place a large part in: reducing costs and thus impacting on prices; determining the speed of availability of the product to the customer; influencing the degree of product customization possible; impacting on customer choices; capturing and sharing information with suppliers and customers; and negotiating critical aspects of the relationship with distributors and key accounts. If that is not the basis for dialogue with marketing, then I don't know what is.

Then, for example, consider the model in Figure 5.3. What this suggests is that a major source of competitive advantage comes from the *combination* of supply chain advantage with marketing/brand advantage – these are the *Market Leaders* in most sectors. But supply chain strength that is not linked to marketing/brand advantage leaves us competing on price and availability and fighting to hold onto the *Cheap Generic* position in the market. Conversely, superior marketing/brand strength coupled with lack of supply chain strength positions us as an *Expensive Brand*, with all the market size and potential limitations and vulnerabilities this implies. Competitive inferiority in both supply chain and marketing/brand almost certainly destines us to be a *Market Loser* – we cannot equal the low prices of the efficient or the added value of the strong brands.

'a major source of competitive advantage comes from the combination of supply chain advantage with marketing/brand advantage'

The dialogue then possible is about which competitors are positioned where on the model, how competitors are moving

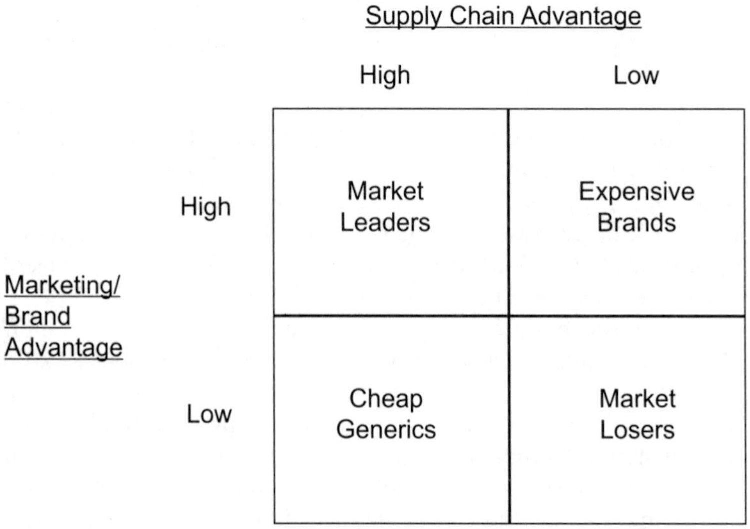

Supply Chain Advantage

	High	Low
High	Market Leaders	Expensive Brands
Low	Cheap Generics	Market Losers

Marketing/ Brand Advantage

Figure 5.3 Marketing and the supply chain

within the model (as marketing/brand strength and supply chain advantage vary compared to the competition), and the relative investments we need in marketing and supply chain to improve our competitive position. For example, in the UK grocery sector, there is little doubt that the Market Leader box is dominated by Tesco – formidable supply chain strength combined with a strong corporate brand. Sainsburys, on the other hand, is probably now in the Expensive Brands box – they have conceded they cannot equal Tesco's prices, but are trying to rejuvenate their brand through wider product choices and high service levels, even though this adds to their already substantial supply chain disadvantage against the market leader. The Sainsbury alternative is dropping into the Market Losers box – traditionally inhabited by firms like the ill-fated Kwik Save and Somerfield. At the same time, Asda is fighting its way out of the Cheap Generics in an attempt to challenge Tesco in the Market Leader category. The Cheap Generics box is the preserve of Aldi, Netto and the like. The critical strategic trade-off we are seeing is between relative supply chain strength and marketing/brand advantage. There is a major opportunity for integrating company thinking around this issue – try applying the model to your industry and see what it tells you, and what you should be discussing with your supply chain managers.

Marketing and R&D

There is also sound evidence that new product development effectiveness relies on the quality of the interaction between marketing and R&D[43]. In many companies R&D is the 'engine for growth', because that is where the new technologies and processes are created[44]. And yet the outcome in profitable products has often been disappointing – Jan Leschly, architect of the massive GlaxoSmithKlein merger, points out that in the R&D-intensive pharmaceuticals industry, over the last fifteen years, the entire industry has brought only 137 products to market, while thousands of other projects have failed despite the investment of billions in their development[45]. However, the whole rationale for the GlaxoSmithKline merger was that the new company would have an R&D spend of $4 billion, creating a product pipeline superior to any competitor's. The trouble is that the product pipeline must not just produce innovations, it must commercialize products better than competitors. The simple truth is that R&D spend on its own is worth nothing – until it is linked to a customer through effective marketing processes.

'In many companies R&D is the 'engine for growth', because that is where the new technologies and processes are created'

Similarly, the Dutch company, Philips, has 1500 'creative' research staff with a budget of $300 million a year, and owns 65 000 patents, but has regularly failed to successfully commercialize its inventions. A commentator suggests that 'the company's research establishment has been inward-looking and arrogant', and the company has failed to link its researchers to the marketplace[46].

The challenge for R&D lies in new customer-oriented research management methods that translate technical advances into new business options and profitable products. This is why we are seeing companies like Xerox and IBM bringing lead-customers into the R&D labs. Those new approaches – championed by R&D innovators – rely on close liaison with both marketing and manufacturing. Conversely, in some high technology businesses R&D is emerging as a major component of relationship marketing – the ability of R&D to work with suppliers and customers on technology innovation is becoming a defining part of the buyer–seller relationship, and may create a new type of marketing capability[47]. There is opportunity number 1 for better integration for you – maybe the stick the R&D Director has been beating you with turns out to be an olive branch?

'in some high technology businesses R&D is emerging as a major component of relationship marketing – the ability of R&D to work with suppliers and customers on technology innovation'

There is a broader scenario too. In industries characterized by an accelerating rate of innovation, the lack of tight and effective integration of marketing and R&D is a force driving down customer loyalty, and hence ultimately long-term profits. When an innovation is developed, the pressure is to get it in the market, regardless of commercialization and technology readiness, in case a competitor gets there first. Marketing turns into the hard-sell, and quality and service, as perceived by customers, take a back seat. Customers may buy the innovation, but in the absence of superior quality and service they are likely to migrate to the next supplier with the next 'big idea', and the cycle starts again. The trick seems to be to balance innovation and quality in such a way that customers respond with loyalty[48]. Sounds like opportunity number 2 for a dialogue between marketing and R&D to me.

Marketing and human resource management

Old-style personnel management was concerned with systems and procedures and enforcing bureaucracy, and all that stuff. Personnel Managers were the ones who told you what you were not allowed to do. The same is not true of the developing role of strategic human resource management, and its primary concern with aligning the skills and capabilities of employees and managers with the requirements of business strategy. In fact, the time is ripe, if not downright overdue, for building positive and value-creating relationships between executives (who lurk in marketing departments, if they still exist) concerned with people called customers and executives (commonly located in human resource management departments) concerned with people called employees. Our joint interest is to make the company a better place to work at, a better place to buy from, and a better place to invest in – the 'employee–customer–profit chain'[49].

It is nearly a decade since Glassman and McAfee proposed the full-scale integration of the marketing and personnel functions – largely on the grounds that they were working on two sides of the same people issue, and seemed unable to effectively link their activities together[50].

The challenge is really quite simple: the goal is to align the values and behaviour of employees with the values that we want in the brand and that achieve customer value[51]. Specialists in HRM have skills in recruitment and selection, evaluation and reward systems, training and development, and manage many of the things that impact on corporate culture. The process of going to market will be enhanced if those skills are deployed and exploited to the full, instead of being ignored. A start would be to consider talking to HRM about:

'the time is ripe, if not downright overdue, for building positive and value-creating relationships between executives (who lurk in marketing departments, if they still exist) concerned with people called customers and executives (commonly located in human resource management departments) concerned with people called employees'

- Aligning employee and manager training processes with customer issues.
- Tracking and comparing both employee satisfaction and customer satisfaction and looking for the relationship between them.
- Establishing linkages between customer satisfaction and loyalty measures and training, reward and employee evaluation processes.
- Looking at linking internal communication programmes to external market strategies (see pp. 670–3)[52].

If you could make some progress on those basic issues, then you might stand a better chance of genuinely unleashing the abilities and enthusiasms of people in the organization to support your competitive strategy.

Marketing and sales

You would think that sales and marketing would quite naturally work well together – but the evidence is often of rivalry and hostility (perhaps particularly in companies where sales has taken over many operational marketing responsibilities, for example in key account management structures; see p. 499). It is a sign of how far we have fallen when even these two functions seem more concerned with fighting political battles with each other than delivering sustained customer value into the marketplace. The signs of poor alignment between sales and marketing are there to be seen in too many companies:

'The signs of poor alignment between sales and marketing are there to be seen in too many companies'

- the failure of market strategies devised in the corporate ivory tower to have any real impact on sales operations, other than achieving derision among salespeople;
- market strategies being produced that ignore the intelligence and learning processes in the salesforce – who actually meet and work with customers;
- misunderstanding about what sales can and should achieve (perhaps mostly among managers who think the only measures of sales effectiveness are sales call numbers and reduced expenses);
- acrimonious conflicts of interest between sales and marketing managers – for example, when the new product launch kills off sales of maintenance services for the old product;
- massive problems in salesperson retention and high replacement costs;
- ludicrous mis-matches between how salespeople are organized, evaluated and rewarded, and the tasks marketing wants them to perform to implement the market strategy;

REALITY CHECK
MARKETING WANTS WHAT?

Let me clarify the real world a little. I am one of your salespeople, I work in a geographic territory, a substantial part of my income is commission on sales volume, and my manager mainly appraises whether I hit sales targets or not. Do not talk to me about the need for customer specialization – you can't do that and cover all customers in the sales territory, end of discussion. Do not talk to me about customer relationship-building and service quality – I get paid by volume and I will give you volume, messing around with the rest

> of that stuff will cost me money. You want me to spend time troubleshooting for customers and providing 'seamless service', then you pay me for that instead (and tell my manager as well, because he says the issue is sales targets and he fixes my annual bonus). Now, is there anything else I can do for you?

- undercurrents of burnout and emotional exhaustion among salespeople as they try to cope with the conflicting demands of their customers and their companies and the ambiguous roles we have created for them;
- salespeople enraged to find that their main competitor is their own company – for example, now operating an Internet-based direct sales channel alongside the salesforce, which mops up the easy, routine reorders that used to provide commission to salespeople;
- weakening customer relationships, at a time when this is most damaging, as companies provide little assistance to salespeople in making the transition from order-taker to order-maker.

Business-to-business customers have made it clear what they expect from salespeople: manage our satisfaction personally; understand our business; recommend products and applications expertly; provide technical and training support; act as our advocate in your company; solve logistical and political problems for us; find innovative solutions for us – become our 'outsource of preference', because if you don't someone else will[53]. This sounds good, but my observation is that senior managers in many companies appear to have dedicated their lives to making it as difficult as possible for salespeople to do the things that customers say they value most.

'senior managers in many companies appear to have dedicated their lives to making it as difficult as possible for salespeople to do the things that customers say they value most'

REALITY CHECK
WHO DELIVERS CUSTOMER VALUE?

The head of marketing from a sophisticated medical diagnostics company was unhappy. His complaint was that he had become aware that members of the salesforce were 'in cahoots' (his words) with customers, to reduce product prices and undermine his product profitability. In fact, the company had developed a complex pricing approach for its medical products, which tried to have highest prices at the time of maximum demand (i.e. when hospitals have patients they need to test), and lowest prices at other times (i.e. when customers did not need the products because they had no patients to test). This scheme had largely been devised by the Finance Department as a way of improving profitability. So, for many products used by hospitals to test for patients' illnesses, prices were highest for Monday deliveries to service clinics, and lowest on Fridays, because clinics rarely work over the weekend. The products deteriorate rapidly, and can only be stored for a few days. Salespeople were advising customers to order higher than needed specification products for Friday delivery, because over the weekend they would reach the lower specification and be ready for the Monday clinics. By doing this, the customers would get the products at much lower prices. Ignoring how clever (or otherwise) it may be to have pricing schemes that annoy customers, what appears to be happening is salespeople working with customers to enhance value and lock them in to the company. Their efforts to achieve this result in a direct conflict with marketing management. Fortunately for them, in this case the CEO thought the salespeople had a point and supported them.

Working with sales to overcome the internal company obstacles to delivering customer value sounds like a pretty good start for marketing executives who want to be partners with sales instead of antagonists. Then we might be able to focus more effort on integrating sales operations with market strategies.

'to many customers your brand and its value is determined by the salesperson they meet, not your clever advertising'

It may be stating the obvious but: to many customers your brand and its value is determined by the salesperson they meet, not your clever advertising; in many cases the strongest impact on whether the customer will do business again is their relationship with the salesperson, not our strategy; the people who know most about customers are frequently the salespeople, not the market researchers and account planners. Rebuilding the marketing/sales relationship is a priority for many of us.

Routes to totally integrated marketing

There is no perfect solution that fits all situations to achieve better integration, but there are a lot of things that can be adapted and tried out. Some perspectives on achieving total integration are considered briefly below.

Pan-company marketing for real this time

The words 'pan-company marketing' have been around a long time, and many managers have paid lip-service to them, before retreating back into their functional silos. If it is real, then pan-company marketing is about aligning every-one on the organization around the same customer commitment and market focus – everyone from the CEO to the telephone salesperson. This is about achieving a customer-centric philosophy for the whole company to be embraced by everyone, and needs the support of knowledge management, relationship man-agement and supply chain management. It is about 'creating a company for customers' [54]. This is why we have used the phrase 'Everybody Markets!' as a signal of

'If it is real, then pan-company marketing is about aligning everyone on the organization around the same customer commitment and market focus'

what we believe that managers in all functions need to understand and put into practice[55]. Put another way, if everyone knows what the brand stands for, it helps determine investment and new product priorities, the choice of business partners, distribution strategies, the risks worth taking, the areas to 'lean', and so on[56]. My friend, Peter Doyle, has said that 'Re-engineering the whole company around satisfying customers is not a marketing department problem'[57]. I think he has missed the point – the issue is not the marketing department, it is marketing processes; the issue is not customer satisfaction, it is customer value; the issue is re-engineering; and if we don't do it, who will?

To some the issue is the brand, and the idea that keeping the brand promise to the customer involves everyone from the boardroom to the shopfloor 'living the brand', so the manage-ment task is to create the climate where this is possible[58]. For example, Don Schultz argues:

> 'In short, the brand is the integrating factor around which all marketing and communication should be built. It is the glue that keeps the organization, its customers, and its stakeholders together. It is the unifying force in the marketplace.'[59]

REALITY CHECK
THE BMW BRAND

BMW acquired the problematic car producer, Rover, in the UK, in a search for greater scale of operation and efficiency, but failed in its attempts to use its brand identity to transform Rover – a company so beset with problems that the attitude tended to be 'get the basics sorted, and then we can worry about things like brand strategy'. In 2000 BMW gave up on its 'English patient'. What is less well known is that, 40 years ago, BMW was also a basket-case, on the brink of bankruptcy, with an unfocused business including limousines at one extreme and bubble cars at the other. The arrival of the Quandt family as long-term investors allowed BMW to define what it stood for, to convince the outside world of this statement and to unite the company. Now, everyone in BMW – engineers, accountants, designers – knows exactly what BMW stands for. The company's whole product range defines 'BMW-ness', and each new offering fits with this. Brand strategy and business strategy are completely aligned.

Sources: Alan Mitchell (2000), 'Dancing to the Same Tune', *Marketing Business*, September, 30. Chris Brady and Andrew Lorenz (2001), *End of the Road: BMW and Rover – One Brand Too Far*, Hemel Hempstead: *Financial Times*/Prentice-Hall.

If that is the ideal, then the issue remains – what are the tools we can use to get there (or at least closer than we are now)? One thing we have surely learned by now is that sending people memos about being a 'customer-centric' company, or standing up on platforms to tell them, does not rate very high on a scale of effectiveness (slightly below zero sounds about right).

Leadership and vision

Certainly, the advocacy of pan-company marketing and the fully customer-centric company has got to be about more than running around telling people that 'Marketing is everything and everything is marketing'[60], which seemed to be the approach last time around. Something which is 'everything' is liable to become 'nothing' pretty quickly. We have argued elsewhere that for a totally integrated marketing effort to be effective, then the core strategy of the organization needs to be the driver of all the functional activities that affect the customer[61].

'customers will accept nothing less than totally integrated marketing (about which they could care less) to deliver them superior value (about which they care quite a lot)'

Making this real requires building the vision among leaders and an effective network of interaction between functions and collaboration between them. The degree of change required by many companies will be severe, and the process will require careful management. There may, however, be no alternative to accepting that pain, because customers will accept nothing less than totally integrated marketing (about which they could care less) to deliver them superior value (about which they care quite a lot).

Communicating out of the silo

A start is to look at how well, how regularly and how effectively we have built channels of communication between marketing and the rest of the company. This is about interaction and its effects[62]. The paradox is that executives who pride themselves on skills and expertise in communicating with customers seem not to be able to flex those same skills and expertise inside the company. Research suggests that the reason why marketing insights are often ignored or misunderstood by other departments is how often and in what manner marketing communicates with other functions – marketers who communicate with colleagues fewer than ten times a week tend to be undervalued and ignored. Infrequent contact with other functions means that you never learn what information is needed by others in the organization or when and how it should be presented. However, too frequent communication also leads to being ignored, because the other functions become overloaded with information[63]. Assessing communication is difficult but these researchers suggest a good start would be just to count the number of formal and informal communications that a marketing executive has with each of the other functions in a typical week:

'executives who pride themselves on skills and expertise in communicating with customers seem not to be able to flex those same skills and expertise inside the company'

		Number of communications per week with department
Written	Memos and letters	_____
	Reports	_____
	Faxes	_____
Verbal	Formal group meetings	_____
	Planned face-to-face meetings	_____
	Impromptu face-to-face meetings	_____
	Planned phone conversations	_____
	Impromptu phone conversations	_____
	Voice mail	_____
	Teleconferences	_____
		_____
Electronic	E-mails	_____
	Electronic conferences	_____

They suggest that marketing managers achieve the greatest impact when they communicate between ten and 25 times a week with a non-marketing colleague.

Collaborative relationships

'what we really need to do is to build alliances and use the same skills inside the organization in partnering as we have tried to do outside the organization in inter-company and supply chain alliances'

Integration based on building collaborative relationships is mainly about informal processes, based on trust, mutual respect and information sharing, the joint ownership of decisions and collective responsibility for outcomes[64]. Some people suggest that what we really need to do is to build alliances and use the same skills inside the organization in partnering as we have tried to do outside the organization in inter-company and supply chain alliances. We have already highlighted some of the collaborative cross-functional opportunities just begging to be exploited.

Formal mechanisms for integration

Much has been written about formal mechanisms for integration, particularly in areas like new product development, although the evidence of what works in different situations is mixed[65]. The types of mechanisms for achieving integration include the following:

- *Relocation and design of facilities* – mainly concerned with using spatial proximity to encourage communication and exchange of information between people and to reduce conflicts. The advent of 'virtual organizations' makes this yet more problematic – electronic communications replace face-to-face meetings, 'hot desking' replaces permanent offices, on-site working places people semi-permanently with customers.
- *Personnel movement* – including all the opportunities for managers to learn about other functional areas: training in the other function; joint training programmes with other functions; job rotation; and so on. The goal is to help people understand and allow for the language, goals, perspectives, problems and priorities of other functions.
- *Rewards* – some suggest changing reward systems to pay people for achieving higher level goals not just functional objectives, e.g. company profits or earnings from a cross-functional project. The idea is to provide managers with incentives to interact more with other functions and bring their goals into line.
- *Formalization of procedures* – some take the approach that centralized control over procedures and systems is the route to achieving better integration across functions; for example, the project investment proposal documentation that requires

coordinated input from marketing, finance, operations and IT is one way to encourage working together around a common goal. It may also be a way to stifle innovation in bureaucracy.

- *Social orientation* – others suggest that part of the problem may be solved by providing people in the organization to interact in a social, non-work-related setting, as a way to let them understand each other better and want to avoid conflicts[66].
- *Project budgeting* – another approach is to centralize control over financial resources so that they are channelled to the project and its team, not to functional departmental managers[67].

Process focus

We noted earlier that many organizations are moving away from reliance on functional organizations – departments staffed by 'specialists' – to reorganize around processes, such as innovation, customer support, and so on (see pp. 234–6). In part, this reflects the weaknesses of functional organizations, but in part also the need to respond faster and more effectively to change – this demands that we work 'in parallel' not 'in sequence'. Marketers may have a number of specific skills to bring to the process party – identifying innovation opportunities; brand building capabilities; and experience in building networks and partnerships that can work together to deliver superior value[68].

Cross-functional teams

One of the trends we noted earlier is the use of teams drawing members from diverse functions and levels in the company. The main idea is to pool the talent needed to solve a problem or manage a project all the way through – focusing on the goals of the organization not the department or function – but the subsidiary benefits are reducing barriers between functions and the team members acting as 'translators' and mediators in interfunctional relationships on a longer-term basis. Some companies even include suppliers, distributors and customers in this type of team, to achieve integration across the organization's boundaries, as well as between functions inside the organization. The danger, of course, is that teams become a battleground for turf control, power plays and budget fights – see my views on managing teams as part of managing processes of planning and budgeting (pp. 601–5).

REALITY CHECK

THE SIX PHASES OF A NEW PROJECT

1 Enthusiasm.
2 Disillusionment.
3 Panic.
4 Search for the guilty.
5 Punishment of the innocent.
6 Praise, honour and rewards for the non-participants.

Vertical marketing

'One way of combining a process approach to integrating efforts and exploiting the power of cross-functional teams and collaboration may be vertical marketing projects'

One way of combining a process approach to integrating efforts and exploiting the power of cross-functional teams and collaboration may be vertical marketing projects. For example, some companies have adopted the approach of selecting key customer groups and forming teams – with people chosen for their commitment and relevant expertise, regardless of function, division, organizational level or strategic business unit. Those teams are then tasked with focusing the company's resources on developing achieving a stronger market position with the customer group in question. There is inevitably some conflict with established functions and strategic business units, but that may be the price you have to pay to improve integration from the customer's perspective.

Organization structure

Some major approaches to improving cross-functional integration bring us back to the issue of structure – and the management dictum 'if all else fails, let's reorganize'. Noel Capon and Mac Hulbert describe some of these approaches as follows[69]:

● *Inclusion organizations* – Early in the day, Pillsbury described how it grouped virtually all organizational activities under marketing, to brutally enforce a united, external perspective, though this was later abandoned. More recently, British Airways, recognizing that two of the most important factors affecting customer satisfaction were safety and schedule reliability controlled by operations, restructured to have operations report to marketing; the result was that 80 per cent of their employees had a marketing responsibility.

- *Business process organizations* – One outcome of the re-engineering movement has been the attempt to organize around business processes by some companies[70]. The company retains functional structures but much of the work is done by cross-functional process-based teams.
- *Customer management organizations* – Although it is a mixture of structural change and information technology, the current trend towards Customer Relationship Management systems is a form of this approach to integration (see pp. 494–9).

The problem with approaching the integration issue through structural change alone is that we may achieve no more than conformity, not genuine commitment across the company, and people will just keep their heads down until the latest management fad has run its course.

Internal marketing

As suggested earlier, one of the key tasks facing marketing in the future may be internal marketing – marketing the customer, the strategy and the marketing process to all parts of the organization. Increasingly, this responsibility may extend to developing and sustaining relationships with alliance partners and other organizations in the network, because they also impact on the value that we deliver to the customer. We will develop a practical framework for internal marketing strategy later (see pp. 675–82).

'one of the key tasks facing marketing in the future may be internal marketing – marketing the customer, the strategy and the marketing process to all parts of the organization'

A strategic approach to total integration

There are major limitations in thinking about the relationship between marketing and each of the other functions in the organization: first, there may be no marketing department, or if there is one it may fall far short of the 'marketing function' ascribed to it by the textbook (see back to pp. 220–1); and second, the key issue is probably about the network of relationships spanning functions, projects and interest groups in the organization – e.g. what is the point of marketing getting cosy with finance if this destroys its credibility with operations? The need is for a strategic approach to integration, not a piecemeal one.

A changing management agenda

'there may be more important organizational issues to worry about than developing a traditional marketing department'

The organizational issue is important in managing the process of going to market, and the ways organizations organize is increasingly diverse. Certainly, we can start by evaluating what marketing organization we have got now, particularly in terms of the problems we have created for ourselves in implementing our market strategy. However, we should be open to the conclusion that there may be more important organizational issues to worry about than developing a traditional marketing department (not least because that seems to be the conclusion reached by an increasing number of senior managers). Some companies believe that re-engineering marketing is the way ahead, and some companies believe that the process of going to market is managed better by multifunctional teams that cross functional boundaries and even organizational boundaries by including suppliers, distributors and customers in these teams. The agenda that matters then becomes how we reduce conflicts between functions and business units, and how we build collaborative relationships between them. The underlying issue is not marketing departments, but marketing processes. The goal is totally integrated marketing not functional specialization. This is a major challenge, which many of us will struggle to meet, but it is the one that matters.

'The underlying issue is not marketing departments, but marketing processes. The goal is totally integrated marketing not functional specialization'

REALITY CHECK
THE AWKWARD QUESTIONS ABOUT MARKETING AND THE ORGANIZATION

What type of Marketing Department have we got? Is it likely to stay in this form or are things likely to change? How many of the problems we encounter in managing marketing processes are traceable to the way we organize for marketing, and how can we improve on this situation?

How well does our company integrate all the factors and activities that impact on customer perceptions of service, quality and value – if we do not know, maybe we should ask customers?

What are the conflicts between marketing and other functions in our company? What are the most promising areas of common interest between marketing and other functions, which may be the basis for better collaboration? What senior management support can we build for achieving better cross-functional integration and collaboration? What integration approaches are most likely to work in our company?

If we rely on alliances and networks of other organizations to deliver value to our customers, what is the role of marketing in achieving integration with these partners?

So, does the organizational dimension of marketing matter?

The goals of this chapter were: to underline the hidden significance to customer-led market performance of how marketing is organized; to look at the gap between the mythology we have always assumed about the way marketing is organized, and the reality that marketing executives experience; and then to evaluate what type of marketing department we have in our own organizations and how things are changing. This is a basis for understanding some of the problems we face in changing the ways things are done to deliver superior value to customers. However, the second goal was to focus attention on the routes to totally integrated marketing – instead of worrying about reorganizing marketing, we should be looking at the network of relationships between marketing and other departments, functions, divisions or business units in the company. We should be looking at the conflicts that exist, but most particularly at the potentials for collaboration and interaction to build a better process of going to market. The reason is that, in the new era, marketing processes matter more than marketing departments (and if you don't believe me, try asking customers whether they prefer 'seamless service' that delivers value to them, or nice organization charts).

'try asking customers whether they prefer 'seamless service' that delivers value to them, or nice organization charts'

We have now examined two major aspects of the way marketing is changing: the impact of Internet-based buyer–seller relationships, and the need for total integration in marketing to deliver value to customers. The next issue to worry us is strategy and how we get the creativity and innovation back into strategic thinking.

Notes and references

1. And, that reminds me, next time some scruffy homeless person shouts 'Big Issue' at you while you are trying to do your shopping, why not take a moment out to ask them what they think the 'big issue' *really* is; they will not understand, but this way you can annoy them almost as much as they annoy the rest of us.

2. James M. Hulbert and Leyland Pitt (1996), 'Exit Left Centre Stage? The Future of Functional Marketing', *European Management Journal*, **14** (1), 47–60.

3. Theodore Levitt (1984), 'Marketing Success Through Differentiation – Of Anything', *Harvard Business Review*, January/February, 83–91.

4. Nigel F. Piercy and David W. Cravens (2000), 'Marketing Organization and Management', in Michael J. Baker (ed.), *The IEBM Encyclopedia of Marketing*, 2nd ed., London: International Thomson Press, pp. 186–207.

5. Bart Ziegler (1994), 'IBM Plans to Revamp Sales Structure to Focus on Industries Not Geography', *Wall Street Journal*, 6 May.

6. Garth Alexander (1998), 'P&G Gambles on Shake-Up to Beat Crisis', *Sunday Times*, 13 September.

7. 'Refocusing on the Customer', *Marketing Business*, March 2001, viii–ix.

8. See, for example: Nigel F. Piercy (1985), *Marketing Organization: An Analysis of Information Processing, Power and Politics*, London: Allen & Unwin. Nigel F. Piercy (1986), 'The Role and Function of the Chief Marketing Executive and the Marketing Department, *Journal of Marketing Management*, **1** (3), 265–90. Nigel F. Piercy (1989), 'The Role of the Marketing Department in UK Retailing Organizations, *International Journal of Bank Marketing*, **4** (2), 46–65. Nigel F. Piercy and Neil A. Morgan (1989), 'Marketing Organization in the UK Financial Services Industry', *International Journal of Bank Marketing*, **7** (4), 3–10.

9. These scenarios comes from simply asking a large number of marketing executives to describe what their typical Monday morning is like in the Marketing Department in their companies. The names are fictitious for obvious reasons, and the situations are composites – but the feeling is real.

10. Frederick Webster (1992), 'The Changing Role of Marketing in the Corporation', *Journal of Marketing*, Winter, 1–17. Ravi S. Achrol (1991), 'The Evolution of the Marketing Organization: New Focus for Turbulent Environments', *Journal of Marketing*, October, 77–93. Nigel F. Piercy and David W. Cravens (1995), 'The Network Paradigm and the Marketing Department: Developing a New Management Agenda', *European Journal of Marketing*, **29** (3), 7–34.

11. John Brady and Ian Davis (1993), 'Marketing's Mid-Life Crisis', *McKinsey Quarterly*, Summer.

12. Alan Mitchell (1993), 'Transformation of Marketing', *Marketing Business*, November, 9–14.

13. Alan Mitchell (1993), op. cit.

14. Marketing Society (1998), *Is British Industry Listening Hard Enough To Customers?*, London: Marketing Society.

15. Alan Mitchell (1997), 'The Future of Marketing', *Marketing Business*, September, 26–30.
16. Nigel F. Piercy and David W. Cravens (2000), 'Marketing Organization and Management', in Michael J. Baker (ed.), *The IEBM Encyclopedia of Marketing*, 2nd ed., London: International Thomson Press, pp. 186–207.
17. Frederick Webster (1992), 'The Changing Role of Marketing in the Corporation', *Journal of Marketing*, Winter, 1–17.
18. Ravi S. Achrol (1991), 'The Evolution of the Marketing Organization: New Focus for Turbulent Environments', *Journal of Marketing*, October, 77–93.
19. My thinking on totally integrated marketing and interfunctional coordination has been shaped and guided by working with Mac Hulbert and Noel Capon of Columbia Business School. The outcome of that project is: James M. Hulbert, Noel Capon and Nigel F. Piercy (2002), *Everybody Markets! A Guide To Total Integrated Marketing*, New York: Free Press. However, if they read this and feel I have nicked some of their ideas, I apologize – and plead that I stood on the shoulders of giants. On the other hand, if they don't, then I don't apologize at all, and instead I take all the credit!
20. Don E. Schultz (1999), 'Structural Straitjackets Stifle Integrated Success', *Marketing News*, 1 March, 8.
21. 'Marketers – Not 'Soft' Enough', *Marketing Business*, November 1998, 10.
22. Susan Baker (2000), 'What Non-Marketers Think About You', *Marketing Business*, September, supplement, v–vii.
23. Cited in Regina Fazio Maruca (1998), 'Getting Marketing's Voice Heard', *Harvard Business Review*, January/February, 10–11.
24. Elliot Maltz, William E. Souder and Ajith Kumar (2001), 'Influencing R&D/Marketing Integration and the Use of Market Information by R&D Managers', *Journal of Business Research*, **52** (1), 69–82.
25. Alan Mitchell (1998), 'New Directions', *Marketing Business*, October, 12–15.
26. Alan Mitchell (1998), op. cit.
27. 'Marketing is Losing Control of Websites', *Marketing Business*, October 2000, 4.
28. Laura Mazur (2000), 'Booking Skills for the Future', *Marketing Business*, April, 33.
29. For example, see: Stanley F. Slater and John C. Narver (1995), 'Market Orientation and the Learning Organization', *Journal of Marketing*, **59**, July, 63–74.
30. Michael D. Hutt and Thomas W. Speh (1984), 'The Marketing Strategy Center: Diagnosing the Industrial Marketer's Interdisciplinary Role', *Journal of Marketing*, **54**, April, 53–61.
31. Don E. Schultz (1997), 'Integration is Critical for Success in the 21st Century', *Marketing News*, 15 September, 26.
32. Alan Mitchell (2000), 'Dancing to the Same Tune', *Marketing Business*, September, 30.
33. 'Marketers Shamed', *Marketing Business*, June 1999, 7.
34. Alan Mitchell (1998), op. cit.

35. Rajendra K. Srivastava, Tassaduq A. Shervani and Liam Fahey (1998), 'Market-Based Assets and Shareholder Value: A Framework for Analysis', *Journal of Marketing*, **62** (1), 2–18.
36. Richard Wachman (2000), 'BT Finance Chief May Go in Shuffle', *Sunday Business*, 5 March.
37. Lisa Buckingham (2000), 'Bosses Fall in W. H. Smith Cull', *Financial Mail on Sunday*, 4 June.
38. Duncan Hughes (2001), 'Now Finance Chiefs Are the First to Go', *Sunday Business*, 13 May.
39. Rupert Howell (2000), 'Time for Business to Value the Brand', *Financial Times*, 18 February.
40. James P. Womack and Daniel T. Jones (1996), *Lean Thinking: Banish Waste and Create Wealth in Your Organization*, New York: Simon & Schuster.
41. James P. Womack and Daniel T. Jones (1996), op. cit.
42. James P. Womack and Daniel T. Jones (1996), op. cit.
43. For example: Robert J. Fisher, Elliot Maltz and Bernard J. Jaworski (1997), 'Enhancing Communication Between Marketing and Engineering: The Moderating Role of Relative Functional Identification', *Journal of Marketing*, **61** (3), 54–70. Ashok K. Gupta, S. P. Raj and David Wilemon (1996), 'A Model for Studying R&D–Marketing Interface in the New Product Development Process', *Journal of Marketing*, **50**, April, 7–17.
44. Clive Cookson (2000), 'R&D Proving to be an Engine For Growth', *Financial Times*, 15 September.
45. Quoted in Rosie Murray-West (2001), 'Can Drug Firms Kick the R&D Habit?', *Daily Telegraph*, 6 January.
46. Peter Marsh (2001), 'The Need to Harvest Homegrown Creativity', *Financial Times*, 22 March.
47. Nikolas Tzokas, Michael Saren and Douglas Brownlie (1997), 'Generating Marketing Resources by Means of R&D Activities in High Technology Firms', *Industrial Marketing Management*, **26**, 331–40.
48. Bob Donath (1997), 'Marketers of Technology Make Promises They Can't Keep', *Marketing News*, 13 October, 5.
49. Anthony J. Rucci, Steven P. Kirn and Richard T. Quinn (1998), 'The Employee–Customer–Profit Chain at Sears', *Harvard Business Review*, January/February, 83–97.
50. M. Glassman and B. McAfee (1992), 'Integrating the Personnel and Marketing Functions: The Challenge of the 1990s', *Business Horizons*, **35** (3), 52–59.
51. Leslie de Chernatony (1999), 'People Power', *Marketing Business*, May, 54.
52. Nigel F. Piercy (1998), 'Barriers to Implementing Relationship Marketing: Analyzing the Internal Marketplace', *Journal of Strategic Marketing*, **6**, 209–22.
53. The H. R. Challey Group (1996), *The Customer-Selected World Class Sales Executive Report*, Ohio: H. R. Challey Group.
54. Malcolm McDonald, Martin Christopher, Simon Knox and Adrian Payne (2001), *Creating a Company for Customers: How to Build and Lead a Market-Driven Organization*, Hemel Hempstead: Financial Times/ Prentice-Hall.

55. James M. Hulbert, Noel Capon and Nigel F. Piercy (2002), *Everybody Markets! A Guide to Total Integrated Marketing*, New York: Free Press.
56. Alan Mitchell (2000), 'Dancing to the Same Tune', *Marketing Business*, September, 30.
57. Quoted in Alan Mitchell (1998), 'New Directions', *Marketing Business*, October, 12–15.
58. Hamish Pringle and William Gordon (2001), *Brand Manners*, London: Wiley.
59. Don E. Schultz (1998), 'Branding the Basis for Marketing Integration', *Marketing News*, 23 November, 8.
60. Regis McKenna (1991), 'Marketing is Everything', *Harvard Business Review*, January/February, 65–79.
61. James Mac Hulbert, Noel Capon and Nigel F. Piercy (2002), *Everybody Markets! A Guide to Total Integrated Marketing*, New York: Free Press.
62. Kenneth B. Kahn and John T. Mentzer (1998), 'Marketing's Integration With Other Departments', *Journal of Business Research*, **42**, 53–62.
63. Regina Fazio Maruca (1998), 'Getting Marketing's Voice Heard', *Harvard Business Review*, January/February, 10–11.
64. Alexander E. Ellinger (2000), 'Improving Marketing/Logistics Cross-Functional Collaboration in the Supply Chain', *Industrial Marketing Management*, **29**, 85–96.
65. Elliot Maltz and Ajay K. Kohli (2000), 'Reducing Marketing's Conflict With Other Functions: the Differential Effects of Integrating Mechanisms', *Journal of the Academy of Marketing Science*, Fall, 479–92.
66. Those who rely too heavily on this solution have probably never witnessed the blood spilling at the average company interdepartmental football or cricket match, or the careers ruined at the firm's Christmas party!
67. Don E. Schultz (1998), 'Branding the Basis for Marketing Integration', *Marketing News*, 23 November, 8.
68. Alan Mitchell (1998), 'New Directions, *Marketing Business*, October, 12–15.
69. Noel Capon and James M. Hulbert (2000), *Marketing Management In the 21st Century*, New Jersey: Prentice-Hall.
70. M. Hammer and J. Champy (1993), *Reengineering the Corporation: A Manifesto for Business Revolution*, New York: Nicholas Brealey.

CHAPTER 6

Strategy and creativity:

Strategizing and reinventing

You would have to be the greatest Luddite in the world not to have been impressed by some of the e-business start-ups and new business models, described in Chapter 4.com. For sheer ingenuity, inventiveness, originality, perversity, and frankly creativity, you just have to admire the dot.com entrepreneurs. It would be helpful if some of them could make profits as well, though there is little doubt that those with a sustainable competitive advantage will do so. The creative force that they represent is underlined by

'People who can innovate and manage break-neck speed change are in demand'

the fact that when Boo.com collapsed, personnel headhunters were waiting outside Boo's Carnaby Street offices with job offers – in the windows of an office opposite, a handwritten poster read 'Dear Boo. Don't Jump. We've got jobs'[1]. People who can innovate and manage break-neck speed change are in demand, even when an enterprise turns its toes up.

But what I want to talk about is the issue of creativity in strategy, which is an issue for us all, not just companies with e-business models.

When did we forget about creativity in marketing and strategy?

In other words, before getting into the stages of the Strategic Pathway, I think we should look at the issue of creativity in marketing and in building strategy.

Personally, I am not a particularly 'creative' person – except when it comes to the important things in life, such as having a good reason for not eating salad or broccoli, and ensuring that whatever goes wrong there is always someone else to blame. However, what worries me is that the professionalization of marketing, and all us marketing people becoming respectable, has created a situation where we believe that strategic decisions can be programmed and routinized – made by planners, analytical models and computer software. This seems to be reinforced by the marketing literature and reflected in how marketing is presented to executives.

I have nothing against professionalization. Some of my best friends have MBAs[2]. But the truth is that winning strategies are smart, innovative and original, and break the rules, and most times there is someone somewhere who has seen through conventions and traditional assumptions to create a new business idea.

'But the truth is that winning strategies are smart, innovative and original, and break the rules, and most times there is someone somewhere who has seen through conventions and traditional assumptions to create a new business idea'

Like most people, my first training in marketing came from the seminal marketing management textbook written by Philip Kotler at Northwestern University and published in 1967[3]. Although there had been many other texts concerning marketing and related issues, Kotler was the first to produce a systematic and accessible approach to structuring marketing decisions, which shaped how we understood the discipline and how it has been taught to generations of MBA students and executives. That book has, over the following thirty years, been revised and developed into ten editions, and translated into many languages, and remains the global market leader.

My point is this – in that first edition in 1967, there was a chapter called 'Marketing Creativity', which did not appear in any subsequent editions. I have not asked Phil Kotler why this is the case. My suspicion is that the reason is simple – lecturers and professors using the textbook did not want it to remain, because they want to teach theory, structure and systems, not creativity. I repeat my question: when did we forget about creativity in marketing and strategy?

The trouble is that we seem to act as though 'creativity' were something only permitted in the advertising agency – among those wacky guys who think up those natty slogans and zany artwork, whose major contribution to marketing seems to be the insight that if you have nothing worthwhile to say about a product, you should sing it instead. Actually, I do have a certain fondness for people who can position a dishwasher as a sex product[4], and I admit to laughing out loud the first time I saw French Connection's 'FCUK' advertising[5], but who said people in advertising agencies were the real creative people? It is very telling that Saatchi & Saatchi removed the word 'advertising' from their company description some time ago, in favour of being 'the ideas business'[6].

'there is a huge difference between bright ideas in advertising and promotion, and developing a new business model that creates a new market, or wrongfoots traditional competitors by a new process of going to market'

The point is that there is a huge difference between bright ideas in advertising and promotion, and developing a new business model that creates a new market, or wrongfoots traditional competitors by a new process of going to market that creates superior customer value. For example, look at British Airways in 1997, obsessing over 're-branding' and spending £60 million to paint weird designs on the tail fins of the aircraft to represent 'cultural empathy', as well as creating a new set of advertisements (at £1 million a throw) to 'convey the universal joy of shared experience'. Then look at them dropping the whole idea little more than a year later. Compare that to the success in the same period of easyJet and Ryanair with a 'no frills' business model offering vastly superior customer value in fares, expanding the domestic flight market, and progressively taking market share from BA and the other conventional carriers (see pp. 77–9).

That is why I think we should be a lot more defiant in demanding creativity in marketing that goes a lot further than natty advertising campaigns and branding. Hence, the horrible words:

- *Tactivizing* – I have invented this word to describe the process of innovation and originality in marketplace tactics – in advertising, in sales promotion, in pricing, in packaging, in selling approaches, and in distribution. There is nothing whatever wrong with creativity in tactics. Far from it – positioning a brand in the customer's mind may be a critical element of competitive success; coming up with innovative ways of capturing the customer's attention may be vital to stand out from the competition. The danger is when we confuse the smart tactics with having a strategy.
- *Strategizing* – Most important is creativity in developing new ways of doing business and new processes of going to market. This is where reinvention comes in – it is about developing a new business model.

The importance of strategizing is underlined by a simple but very powerful quotation from the writings of Peter Drucker:

'A company beset by malaise and steady deterioration suffers from something far more serious than inefficiencies. Its "business theory" has become obsolete.'[7]

The goal here is to emphasize the crucial importance of creativity in building new strategies – strategizing – not just in new advertising and promotional ideas – tactivizing. Smart tactics follow smart strategies, not the other way around.

'The goal here is to emphasize the crucial importance of creativity in building new strategies – strategizing – not just in new advertising and promotional ideas – tactivizing'

REALITY CHECK
BUT YOU ARE ALLOWED TO BE WEIRD

Ben Cohen and Jerry Greenfield, a college drop-out and a failed laboratory technician, are the 'unreconstructed hippy' founders of Ben & Jerry's ice cream company. Founded in 1978, Cohen and Greenfield took a correspondence course in ice cream making, raised about £6000 and moved north from industrial New Jersey to rural Vermont, where they established their first factory in a renovated petrol station. Using highest quality ingredients including locally-produced milk from cows that had not been fed growth hormones, they sold their full-fat luxury ice cream in colourful containers, with unusual descriptions of flavours – such as Chunky Monkey, Cherry Garcia, Entangled Mints, From Russia With Buzz, Urban Jumble and Pulp Addiction. In every Ben & Jerry ice cream store, there were pictures of Ben and Jerry in tie-dyed T-shirts, peering out from behind glasses and facial hair. The distinctive products of the company quickly attracted a cult following – not buying just an expensive pudding, but making a statement about community values. In fact, Ben & Jerry's almost invented the 'super premium category' of ice creams.

From the start, the management style in the company was distinctive. For most of the company's life, the highest paid person could not earn more than seven times the salary of the lowest paid. Employees enjoyed the best healthcare, childcare and pension programmes in the country, along with perks like free massages and as much ice cream as they could eat. The company was a sponsor of the World Conker championship, and pursued ideas like 'Peace Pops' (ice cream bars sold during the Cold War), organized opposition to the 1991 Gulf War, and was associated with calls for stricter gun controls. The business always stressed social responsibility, and Ben & Jerry offer the recipe for success as 'leading with values': use values-led suppliers – develop products with ingredients that make a positive social impact; go for values-led finance – raise money from the community, invest in companies that make a positive social impact, use banks with ethical policies; adopt values-led retailing – use distributors at the centre of communities and work in partnership with ethnic minorities and disadvantaged communities; values-led marketing – tell people who you are, build long-term relationships and differentiate yourself from others; values-led human resources – help people do jobs well in line with the values of the business; and mix business and politics – take a stand on social issues.

Ben & Jerry's floated on the New York stock market in 1983 and built a market value of $150 million by 1999. By that time – bolstered by *Time* magazine's verdict that they sold 'the best ice cream in the world' – they were making profits of $6.2 million on sales of £209 million, employing 700 people in Vermont. When they needed capital for a new plant in 1984, they sold shares to the Vermont community only. The company gives 7.5 per cent of its profits to charity and 5 per cent to employees.

Late in 1999, rumours that Ben & Jerry's was to be bought by a multinational sparked protests on the streets of Burlington, Vermont, as angry dairy farmers formed the Vermont Public Interest Group to protect their beloved company from being taken over. This was soon followed by a 'save Ben & Jerry's' Web page and national petitions – the website warned that the big companies wanted 'to skin the company alive and use its gentle lambskin brand identity to fool unsuspecting consumers into purchasing their soulless profit-driven products'.

The decision to sell provoked a rift between Ben and Jerry. Cohen formed an alliance with a group of investors in an unsuccessful attempt to buy the company. The deal would have involved Cohen keeping a 36 per cent stake, Meadowbrook Holding (a group of investors including Anita Roddick of The Body Shop) would take 38 per cent, and Unilever would take the rest. Greenfield was shut out from this deal, and opposed any sell-out. With shareholders threatening to sue if the offer was turned down, Ben & Jerry's was sold in 2000 to Unilever, one of the world's biggest consumer products companies, for £200 million, promising to retain its uniqueness and social mission. Greenfield and Cohen held around 15 per cent of the business at this time.

Sources: Ben Cohen and Jerry Greenfield (1997), *Ben & Jerry's Double Dip*, New York: Simon & Schuster. William Lowther (2000), 'US in a Stir Over Ice Cream Hippies', *Financial Mail on Sunday*, 19 December. Philip Delves (2000), 'Ben & Jerry Sell Out as Hippie Ideal is Licked', *Daily Telegraph*, 13 April. Louella Miles (2000), 'Sleeping With The Enemy', *Marketing Business*, July/August, 17–19.

What you have to ask yourself is if Ben and Jerry had come to see you in 1978 to borrow a few grand for their new business – would you have believed in them? Now, I am not suggesting that every 'off-the-wall' idea that people have constitutes a new strategy. Nor am I suggesting that you can teach creativity (although some would disagree). Nor am I suggesting that managers instruct their employees to 'be creative', which is among the more futile of gestures known to mankind. I am suggesting that we should all respect new ideas, desperately seek them out whatever the source, and look for ways of exploiting them profitably – not come out with the usual reasons why new things won't work. When we talk about strategy in a company, our quest should be for the 'marketing revolutionaries' – not the frequent syndrome of reorganizing or hiring design consultants as an alternative to having new ideas[8].

'When we talk about strategy in a company, our quest should be for the "marketing revolutionaries"'

First, let's spend a little time looking at what strategy is, and what it is not, then let's look at some of the ideas that may jump-start your strategy process, and finally let's introduce the Strategic Pathway.

What is strategy?

The simplest possible view is as follows. While strategy may sound esoteric and academic and daunting (which is how strategic planners like to win their own personal turf wars), it is really about:

- being best at doing the things that matter most to customers;
- building shareholder value by achieving superior customer value;
- finding new and better ways of doing things to achieve the above.

That should get you out of a hole next time you get button-holed by someone who wants you to explain strategy to them. In fact, all the complex strategy stuff is just to help with these things (and if it isn't, maybe we should not bother with it). This too may be worth remembering next time your planners and analysts want to show you the latest techniques and computer software. There is also something to be gained from understanding what strategy is not.

What strategy is and what it is not

'*Strategy is not the same as* **strategic planning**'

Strategy is not the same as *strategic planning*. Tom Peters is famous for, among other things, offering $100 to the first executive who could demonstrate that a successful company strategy had resulted from strategic planning. He has yet to part with the $100[9]. The danger of the blind alley that we create by thinking that strategic planning is the same thing as strategy is underlined by Andrew Campbell and Marcus Alexander:

'The answer to developing a good strategy is not new planning processes or better designed plans. The answer lies in managers' understanding of two fundamental points: the benefit of having a well-articulated stable purpose, and the importance of discovering, understanding, documenting, and exploiting insights about how to create more value than other companies do.'[10]

Their sentiments are underlined by the *Financial Times* survey of the 'world's most respected companies', which asked 650 CEOs across the world which attributes will make a company most respected in the future. The top answers were:

1 Strong, well thought-out strategy.
2 Maximizing customer satisfaction and loyalty.
3 Business leadership.
4 Quality of products and services.
5 Strong and consistent profit performance.

'*The saving grace for strategic planning was that it has not done as much harm as it might have done, because no-one took much notice of the plans that the planners produced*'

This finding suggests that strategic clarity is what matters, leading through customer value and quality to profit performance and shareholder value[11].

If we think planning is the same as strategy, then we probably also confuse *analytical techniques* with strategy – matrices, models, expert systems, and so on – and hope the techniques will make the decisions for us. The saving grace for strategic planning was that it has not done as much harm as it might have done, because no-one took much notice of the plans that the planners produced[12]. But look at the sort of advice you would have got from them:

● Analysts and planners cling to models like the Boston Matrix to identify the appropriate strategy, which is dictated by relative market share and market growth rate – so Virgin Atlantic would have been advised not to get involved in the airline industry because they could only take a small market share in a mature slow-growth marketplace (and the company would have missed one of its most important successes).

- A company like Daewoo would have been advised by conventional analysts never to invest in the UK car market – they would have run a business screening model to prove beyond any doubt that this was a highly unattractive market in growth and competitiveness, where the company could only be a minor player – and we would have missed the treat of seeing Daewoo taking 1 per cent of the market in six months based on their innovative direct business model responding to customer needs.

- Conventional advice to Jeff Bezos starting Amazon.com would have been that there is no sustainable competitive advantage in selling books on the Internet, because anyone can imitate the operation, and Michael Dell would have been told much the same about the competitive madness of a direct business model taking on the likes of IBM and Compaq – if they had listened (which is highly unlikely) the world would currently have two less billionaires.

- Many traditional strategy models have obsessed about market share as the route to superior profitability. What we have learned by studying companies as diverse as Microsoft and the 'no frills' airlines is that the issue for them is not actually market share at all – it is their ability to drive up market growth rates that impacts their profitability most of all.

It is not before time that some of us are getting very sceptical about generalized 'rules' and prescriptive models as routes to developing strategy – hence the plea for creativity and strategizing to which we come shortly (pp. 287–313).

> *'The next confusion is that we think strategy is the same as operational efficiency. It is not'*

The next confusion is that we think strategy is the same as *operational efficiency*. It is not.

A lot of management thinking in recent decades has been dominated by the global pursuit of operational efficiency – total quality management, new technology for automation, business process re-engineering, value engineering, core competency focus, lean supply chains, agile manufacturing systems, and so on. This pursuit of operational efficiency has had enormous benefits in improving product and service quality and reducing unit costs in many industries.

However, one effect is that the rapid diffusion of 'best practices' achieved through benchmarking against competitors is that industries have become more efficient without individual companies becoming more profitable – because benchmarking and best practice make companies more similar, not more differentiated. Michael Porter clarifies the confusion:

> 'Operational efficiency means you're running the same race faster, but strategy is choosing to run a different race because it's the one you've set yourself up to win.' [13]

Superior operational efficiency may give you a short-term advantage over competitors, but it will be copied or bettered by them in the longer term. Strategy is about competitive advantage through differentiating against the customer's alternatives, continuous innovation to sustain that advantage, and organizing to achieve 'fit' in maintaining the advantage. Porter clarifies for us again:

> 'A company can outperform its rivals only if it can establish a difference that it can preserve. It must deliver greater value to customers or create comparable value at a lower cost or do both.' [14]

The fatal arrogance of success

Many managers turn off at this point in the strategy debate (though not my readers who have proved how smart and discerning they are by getting this far in the book, hopefully preceded by having purchasing it). When people say things like: why do we need this theoretical mumbo-jumbo – we're doing OK, look at last year's figures, we're the market leader, we're the industry standard, we just won the Queens's Award for Export, and so on, then that is the time to really start worrying.

'The trouble is that your moment of greatest strategic vulnerability is probably when you experience greatest success, because it is then that the seeds of complacency are sown'

The trouble is that your moment of greatest strategic vulnerability is probably when you experience greatest success, because it is then that the seeds of complacency are sown. It is when you are dominant and overwhelmingly successful that you are most likely to fail to make the changes needed to stay successful. This is the time when a company may think that it can do things its own way, and customers will get used to it. This is the moment of maximum smugness, complacency and arrogance.

Think of the arrogance with which British car manufacturers (yes, young reader, there used to be some) viewed Japanese cars with open disdain. Think of Marks & Spencer as the fallen icon of

British business. Think of Sainsburys supermarkets being overtaken not just by Tesco, but then by the much despised Asda. The more successful and dominant you are, the greater the risks of complacency. Peter Martin's analysis of the IT industry reaches a similar conclusion:

> 'If there is a long-term threat to Microsoft and Intel, it will come in the first instance from within. Just at the moment their dominance seems most assured, the curse of monopoly will be gradually eating away at the company's success. The desire to preserve compatibility with previous products at all costs; the belief in a divine right to market share; a profound mistrust of the bona fides of competitors – these are the penalties that the gift of monopoly brings.'[15]

The paradox of strategy is that you probably need to be making new strategic decisions at the time when you feel least inclined to do so.

Indeed, Robert Simons tells us that while success brings profits, growth and unbounded optimism, it also has a way of blinding executives to the many organizational dangers that creep in at the same time, and he suggests we should use an 'internal risk exposure calculator' to see how vulnerable we have become[16].

The importance of strategic clarity is underlined even more by the new era for business that we have been describing – achieving and maintaining competitive advantage is about revolution and reinvention, not incremental change from the past.

Revolution, reinvention and renewal

Colleagues and I have argued elsewhere in more detail that the key words to describe modern markets are revolution, reinvention and renewal[17]:

- *Revolution* – in the ways industries and markets operate and the sources of competition which become important, and consequently in the strategies that successful organizations pursue.
- *Reinvention* – in the creation of new business models that make traditional ways of doing business obsolete as routes to delivering and sustaining superior customer value.
- *Renewal* – in the strategies of change and repositioning by companies whose business models have become outdated, as they rebuild and respond to change. Increasingly the priority is not just short-term performance but building the robustness to bounce back, to change, to survive, to turn things around.

Managers are frequently sceptical about the use of emotive words like the trio of Rs above[18].

I have devised the competitive box shown in Figure 6.1 as a way to convince the non-believers that there are big things going on in most markets, which can destroy the incumbents if they do not open their eyes (yes, that is you). You can try this.

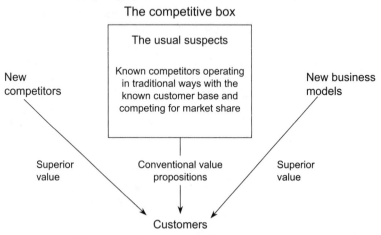

Figure 6.1 The trap of the competitive box

'**The competitive box reflects the pernicious tendency of managers to build a fixed mental map of the industry in which they compete**'   The competitive box reflects the pernicious tendency of managers to build a fixed mental map of the industry in which they compete. The competitive box puts a ring-fence around familiar competitors using similar technology to produce similar products and services for a shared customer base – these are the 'usual suspects' we mean when we talk about our competitors. We know these people well – we probably swap personnel with them every so often, we go to the same trade fairs and exhibitions as they do, we belong to the same trade associations, and so on. Competition is probably based on brand, and the measure of success is probably market share in the familiar customer base, with great excitement about percentage point changes in brand market shares. The fences we build – the boundaries of the competitive box – are what blind us to the real sources of competition and prevent us from developing appropriate strategies.

Indeed, recent research confirms this observation – studies suggest that when they identify their competitors managers tend to think of a relatively small number of firms and they use supply-based attributes (what firms are and what they do) rather than demand-based attributes (how customers see substitutes), and this determines which competitors they take seriously[19].

In fact, what you see in sector after sector is that the most deadly competitor is not the person you sat next to at last year's trade convention, it is someone you probably never even heard of (and if you did, you didn't take them seriously). The examples of managers being suckered by the competitive box are numerous: banks who simply did not believe that grocery retailers and Internet sites could be retail banks; booksellers who did not believe that anyone would buy books off the Internet; airlines who did not believe that business travellers would use a 'no frills' carrier with no 'free' food and drinks; a travel industry that did not believe that people would buy flights and holiday packages online or direct. Car distribution provides a nice example of this – traditional distributors under attack from new business models in manufacturing and distribution, and a range of new types of competitor, looking at taking their business away, while most of the established firms sit back and watch.

'what you see in sector after sector is that the most deadly competitor is not the person you sat next to at last year's trade convention, it is someone you probably never even heard of (and if you did, you didn't take them seriously)'

REALITY CHECK

CAR DISTRIBUTION: THE PRODUCTS OF THE TWENTY-FIRST CENTURY IN A DISTRIBUTION CHANNEL FROM THE VICTORIAN ERA

In the UK, and most of western Europe, new car sales are primarily made by dealers locked into partnerships with car makers. There are over 6000 franchised dealers in the UK, each selling new cars of only one brand. These partnerships fall under the European block exemption, introduced in 1985, revised in 1996, and looking for renewal in September 2002. The block exemption allows car manufacturers to avoid competition law by supplying only to captive dealers. Consumer groups claim that car manufacturers use the block exemption to charge higher prices in the UK than elsewhere – up to 40 per cent higher – while the manufacturers say that block exemption protects service levels, vehicle safety and residual values in used cars (expressions about turkeys not voting for Christmas spring to mind).

Car manufacturers have made it clear that while they are not enthusiastic about becoming retailers, they wish to exercise tighter control over their distribution channels, including dealing with fewer distributors. They are actively exploring new ways of getting cars to consumers. For example, Ford has bought major equity shares in some of its largest distributor groups, such as Pendragon and Dagenham Motors. Toyota has been following this lead and buying up dealer sites to get greater control over retailing, while Vauxhall already owns 30 per cent of its dealer network.

December 2000 saw Mercedes reducing its dealer network by 40 per cent at a potential cost of 2000 jobs, blaming cheap imports from Europe for undermining their British distribution system. Ford, Fiat and Volvo were also looking to prune their independent dealerships and create dedicated salesforces. Commentators speculate that one way for manufacturers to avoid losing control of distribution, if block exemption goes, is to own their own outlets, leaving only used car sales and maintenance to independent dealers.

Car manufacturers' online sites allow purchasers to buy cars, but currently the vehicles are still supplied by a dealer. However, Vauxhalls' price reductions for Internet buyers in 1999 made it clear that the intention was to use the dealers as little more than delivery drivers. Ford's website offers around a 5 per cent discount on dealers' list prices. The speculation is that the long-term intention is to use the Internet to bypass the dealer network altogether.

Smaller car manufacturers have already established direct sales channels with no dealer network. Daewoo pioneered this business model with its 'hassle-free' selling proposition, and Proton from Malaysia has followed this lead, as has Daihatsu from Japan. The signs are that a direct business model allows small car makers to expand sales quicker and cheaper than recruiting independent dealers.

By mid-2000, cheap 'grey' imports from Europe – purchased at lower European prices – had reached the level of about 140 000 a year, including individuals arranging their own purchases and those organized by independent traders. By the end of 2000, it looked like unofficial imports would account for 10 per cent of the British market.

In addition, the huge car supermarkets, such as Trade Sales and Motorpoint, had previously sold only used cars because they were not franchised dealers. Now, more than half their sales are new cars (obtained either from continental dealers or from British franchised dealers who have pre-registered new cars to achieve sales targets). These outlets sell on price only.

In January 2000, cross-channel ferry operator P&O announced plans to import large numbers of cut-price cars into the UK from Europe, offering a door-to-door service with no need for the purchaser to travel abroad and 18 per cent price cuts, as a way of filling their surplus car freight capacity. Ferry company, Stena, was already operating a similar but smaller deal with Broadspeed, said to have reached imports of 3500 vehicles a week.

In addition, a variety of independent Internet-based operations have emerged. In 1999, the Consumers' Association launched its own dealership service to import cheap cars into the UK – its website operation Carbusters.com attracted more than a million visits on its first day. Virgin.com/cars launched in March 2000, offering 40 per cent price reductions, a simple purchase process and the ability to pay online. The service package is provided by Virgin Cars. Direct Line, the insurance company, entered with Jamjar.com – again obtaining vehicles wherever they are cheapest. Early in 2000, OneSwoop.com was launched as a pan-European online car retailer, backed by a consortium including Marks & Spencer Financial Services and Anderson Consulting. Following large-scale success in the US, Autobytel offers an information service that links the buyer to a vehicle in a dealership signed up with Autobytel. Even the online book and video seller, Amazon.com, has entered the car distribution market in the US, again reducing the role of the dealer to that of delivering the vehicle to Amazon's customer. April 2001 saw Microsoft partnering with Pendragon to launch Carview through the Microsoft portal MSN.co.uk – with the intention of becoming the biggest car e-tailer in the UK.

If block exemption is removed, Internet providers may no longer be obliged to use existing dealers to obtain vehicles, and the way will be clear for new car supermarkets to emerge, like the 'category killers' seen in other sectors. There are rumours that some of the retail banks would also enter the market, as a way of gaining share in the car financing market. In 1999, Sainsburys supermarkets began selling cars on a lease-purchase deal, though the supermarket essentially sells the finance package and the vehicles are supplied by a dealer. Tesco and Asda are rumoured to be interested in entering the market with their own offerings.

Meantime, after aborted attempts by some to organize their own 'grey imports' in defiance of the manufacturers' wishes, British car dealers seem to be assuming that the block exemption will be renewed and all will continue much as it always has done. In fact, it looks increasingly unlikely that block exemption will be renewed – since the car manufacturers have flagrantly disregarded their promises to allow consumers to buy vehicles in any European country of their own choosing, and to keep price differences between markets at less than 12 per cent. Already in September 2000, as a result of the Competition Commission report, car makers no longer officially have control over retail prices – and the manufacturers are not legally allowed to stop UK dealers sourcing cars from other dealers in Europe at lower prices.

In fact, the car trade disparages its new competitors – in its first six months P&O only took 250 orders and only delivered 25 cars because of the problems for their European suppliers in obtaining right-hand drive cars; by mid-2000 Virgin's operation had delivered only 30 cars, with five-month lead times; price differences between the UK and Europe were falling; even Vauxhall had sold only 900 'dot.com cars' in its first nine months of operation. In a market where around 2.2 million vehicles a year are registered, the impact of Internet purchasing and direct selling business models is seen as trivial, and not really worth worrying about. Paradoxically, the success of manufacturers in restricting vehicle supplies to starve new competitors of vehicles may itself be the final nail in the coffin of block exemption.

In spite of the prevailing complacency, management consultants Cap Gemini estimate in 2000 that within three years dealers will retain only 60 per cent of car sales to private motorists, with Internet channels taking 15 per cent of the market and independent dealers (like the car supermarkets) holding 25 per cent of the market. Others point to the declining levels of brand loyalty and the rising 'commoditization' of mass market cars, further strengthening new channels and weakening manufacturers' control.

Sources: Tim Burt (1999), 'Deals Within Wheels', *Financial Times*, 16 August. Tim Burt (2000), 'Slow Traffic Forces Motor Dealers to Seek a New Route', *Financial Times*, 19 January. David Bowen (2000), 'Sites Trigger Alarm for Car Dealers', *Financial Times*, 3 March. David Litterick (2000), 'Online but Still off the Road', *Daily Telegraph*, 15 July. David Sumner Smith (2000), 'Car Market in a Tail Spin', *Marketing Business*, November, 14–16.

'by taking conventional advice and following industry rules, you see managers taking an operation that has developed an unconventional business model outside the competitive box, and forcing it back inside the box'

It gets worse too. In some companies, by taking conventional advice and following industry rules, you see managers taking an operation that has developed an unconventional business model outside the competitive box, and forcing it back inside the box. The 'rules' say you have to be a manufacturer or a retailer, so you have to choose one or the other; this way the stock market knows what to compare you with. The troubled Body Shop is a case in point. Body Shop was always one of the worst and most inefficient retailers in the world. It survived this shortcoming by virtue of its image of environmental responsibility but also a steady flow of exceptionally innovative new products. Competitors copied the image and the products and brought Body Shop down with a bump. Current management is determined to make Body Shop into a conventional retailer, which it never was, while weakening its image and watering-down its product innovation. They will probably succeed, and in so doing they will create a chain of quasi-conventional cosmetic shops, that they can sell to someone else.

The other side of the competitive box is, of course, even more interesting. That is about *becoming* the pioneering competitor that disrupts and revolutionizes the existing market – see the section below on creating market space (pp. 299–300).

What is strategy about?

So far, we have said what strategy is and is not, and the powerful need for strategic thinking illustrated by the competitive box. But we probably get further if we ask what strategy is about.

Strategy is about breaking free

To paraphrase two major milestone publications about strategy by Michael Porter[20] and Gary Hamel and C. K. Prahalad[21], strategy is about *breaking free*. It is about breaking free in the following senses:

- Breaking free from an obsession with *management tools* that are spectacular and seductive in improving operational efficiency but are not strategy – such as total quality management, benchmarking, time-based competition, outsourcing, re-engineering, lean supply chain management, efficient consumer response, and so on – on the grounds that while operational effectiveness and strategy are both essential to superior performance, operational effectiveness does not substitute for strategic direction.
- Breaking free of *industry dogma* – John Kay has pointed out that an industry is a group of organizations with similar capabilities and supply technologies, while a market is defined by customer needs and demands[22] – customers do not care about industries, just meeting their needs, as shown by the entry of supermarkets into banking and financial services (not their industry but definitely their market).
- Breaking free from the *industry 'rules'* – Gary Hamel says there are three kinds of companies in all industries: rule makers, who built the industry, rule takers, who follow and imitate, and rule breakers, like IKEA and Virgin, who implement revolution in the industry and reinvent the business[23], and he challenges us to recognize the 'nine routes to industry

Table 6.1 Ten principles for building revolutionary strategy*

Principles for revolutionary strategy	
Principle 1: Strategic planning is not strategic	Distinguish planning from strategizing, the first produces ritualistic plans, the second produces strategy
Principle 2: Strategy making must be subversive	Relax the fundamental beliefs shared by people in your industry, and see what new business opportunities appear
Principle 3: The bottleneck is at the top of the bottle	Senior management is often the repository of orthodoxy, not the source of radical innovation
Principle 4: Revolutionaries exist in every company	In middle management, at the operating level, muffled by the bureaucracy, but liable to leave and become competitors if they are denied a voice
Principle 5: Change is not the problem, commitment is	Strategy making process should give people the responsibility for creating change, not impose it on them
Principle 6: Strategy making must be democratic	Supplementing the hierarchy of experience with imagination and innovation
Principle 7: Anyone can be a strategy activist	Front-line managers and employees should be activists not victims in the strategy process
Principle 8: Perspective is worth 50 IQ points	Innovation in strategy requires a change in perspective
Principle 9: Top-down and bottom-up are not the alternatives	The strategy process should be deep and wide in the organization
Principle 10: You can't see the end from the beginning	The strategy cannot be set at the outset, or why would we go on a quest for it?

* Source: Adapted from Gary Hamel (1996), 'Strategy as Revolution', *Harvard Business Review*, July/August, 69–82

revolution', summarized in Table 6.1 – this list is a good way to figure out if we ever even take market strategy seriously in our company.

● Breaking free of *the present* to create the future, and particularly from trying to preserve the past – Hamel and Prahalad estimate senior managers spend only 1–3 per cent of their time looking at the future (see Table 6.2 to test that out – and be prepared for a shock, because few companies stand up well against these criteria).

Table 6.2 Strategies for the future*

How well does management in this company perform in the following areas:	Non-visionary management		Visionary management
Senior management's view of the future compared to that of our competitors?	Conventional and reactive	Versus	Distinctive and far-sighted
What absorbs more senior management time?	Reengineering core processes	Versus	Regenerating core strategies
How do competitors view our company?	Mostly as a rule follower	Versus	Mostly as a rule maker
What is our greatest strength?	Operational efficiency	Versus	Innovation and growth
What is the focus of our company's attempts to build competitive advantage?	Mostly catching up	Versus	Mostly getting out in front
What has mainly set our company's agenda for change?	Our competitors	Versus	Our foresight
Do we spend most of our time monitoring the status quo (the maintenance engineer) or designing the future (the strategic architect)?	Mostly as an engineer	Versus	Mostly as an architect

* Source: Adapted from Gary Hamel and C. K. Prahalad (1994) 'Competing for the Future', *Harvard Business Review*, July/August, 122–28

- Breaking free from *tactics* – 'strategy is revolution; everything else is tactics'[24]. Gary Hamel also challenges us to consider ten key principles in becoming an industry revolutionary, which are summarized in Table 6.3 – again these points are an excellent way to get started on a fundamental strategy debate in your company instead of just planning and budgeting for the same things every year.
- Breaking free from '*sameness*' – we saw earlier that Michael Porter argues that a company can only outperform its competitors if it establishes a difference that it can preserve, that delivers greater value to customers or creates comparable value or a lower cost (or both). Consider the impact of Virgin Direct on the financial services industry, attacking with a better value product sold direct. Or look at the impact of Matalan on the UK clothing market by a strategy of value and a differentiated channel of distribution – and in both cases, remember to ask what differentiated conventional insurance

Table 6.3   Nine routes to reinventing an industry*

Route	Methods	Examples
Reconceiving the product or service	Radically improve the value equation	Hewlett-Packard and Canon in computer printers
	Separate function and form	The credit card that opens the hotel door and acts as an international passport
	Achieving joy in use	Making shopping fun. Changing the razor from a simple artefact into an expensive adult toy (the Gillette Mach 3)
Redefining market space	Pushing the bounds of universality	Transforming the expensive camera into a cheap disposable product for any consumer (even children). Turning the child's scooter from a plaything to 'cool' adult transport
	Striving for individuality	Levi's 'Personal Pair' system to make jeans to the individual consumer's measurements
	Increasing accessibility	Twenty-four hour banking with First Direct
Redrawing industry boundaries	Rescaling industries	Increasing scale in a fragmented industry e.g. funerals Decreasing scales for specialized advantage, i.e. local microbreweries or bakeries
	Compressing the supply chain	Xerox plans to transmit information electronically to cut out freighters and suppliers of documents
	Driving convergence	A credit card from a car supplier. A bank account at the supermarket. A BT phone box that combines a videophone, a cash dispenser and foreign currency converter, a printer/copier, a keyboard to access the Internet, a rolling treadmill floor to walk through the virtual environment, and a transmitter allowing remote Internet access

* Source: Adapted from Gary Hamel (1996), 'Strategy As Revolution', *Harvard Business Review*, July/August 1996, 69–82

companies and cheap clothing companies from each other (and the answer will be 'not a lot').
- Breaking free from hostility to *change* – change is seen as unpleasant and is resisted mainly when it is something nasty imposed on us from above (and when it is a synonym for cost-cutting and downsizing), not when it is about growth, new ways of doing things and new activities that we choose for ourselves.

But these examples also show that strategy is about much more than breaking free of these constraints and burdens – it is about defining what we are going to be in the marketplace, or what Hamel and Prahalad have called building a 'strategic intent'[25]: a stable but stretching perspective of how to win based on our core competencies as an organization[26].

REALITY CHECK

PEPSICO'S 'POWER OF ONE' STRATEGY

Pepsi has always been perceived as Coke's main rival in the cola drinks market, and has always been the 'number two' player. Roger Enrico became CEO in 1996 and concluded that Pepsico was charging ahead with no real focus. He disposed of businesses like restaurants and bottling plants and focused the corporation on the two businesses that had created Pepsico in the first place: salty snacks (mainly Frito-Lay products) and soft drinks. The result is a company that is less dependent on Coke's successes and failures for its own performance. However, Enrico's strategy is driven by the fact that Pepsi has always been perceived as 'number two' – he insists that each business is 'run like number two' (even when it isn't). The gap between Pepsi and Coke widens as Pepsi concentrates on developing new snacks and Coke tries to become an all-beverage company. Enrico's strategy is the 'Power of One' – playing snacks and soft drinks off against each other – the rationale described to him by a previous CEO: 'You make them thirsty and I'll give them something to drink'. For the retailer, the soft drinks bring traffic, and the snacks give margin. The Power of One recognizes that Pepsi cannot beat Coke in cola sales, and the intent is to avoid head-to-head competition with Coke.

Source: Adapted from Betty Lui (2001), 'Cola Warrior With a New Recipe for Success', *Financial Times*, 23 January.

But, of course, the issue we then have to grapple with is – how do we develop strategic thinking that is revolutionary and creative in our organizations?

Jump-starting the strategy process

There are no simple 'plug and play' solutions to how we develop our strategic thinking into revolution and reinvention, but there are many ideas and insights discussed below, which provide some basis for you to jump-start the strategy process in your organization. What we are learning from research is that the myths that large organizations cannot innovate or reinvent businesses are just that – but that long-term growth, like that shown by GE, depends on continual 'breakthroughs' in every area[27]. The challenge is to 'put innovation back into strategy'[28]. This raises the major issue – how do we get beyond talking about new strategic ideas and actually create them?

'The challenge is to "put innovation back into strategy"'

Managing creativity and innovation breakthroughs

Clayton Christensen says that one of the biggest challenges managers face in developing effective strategy is to ensure that the strategy is not a product of the biases (and possibly the ignorance) of the management team – those biases are likely to be rooted in the organization's past successes not its future needs[29]. This provides us with a managerial mandate for creativity and innovation.

Do creativity and innovation matter?

'conventional strategies will, at best, produce conventional results'

At its absolute simplest, it has been clear right from the start of talking about marketing, that conventional strategies will, at best, produce conventional results[30]. Some believe that one of our greatest failures in marketing has been to hide behind piles of numbers, using market research as a crutch to support us, and we have forgotten that the goal is distinctiveness in the marketplace, while the same information processed on the same software just produces 'me-too' ideas the same as everyone else's – Peter Dart, chair of the Added Value Company, concludes:

> 'I think Western companies have lost the art of creativity. Growth is coming from areas such as cost-cutting, reengineering management and fine-tuning the supply chain, but it's not coming from great ideas. There doesn't seem to be any time for marketers these days to actually do any marketing.'[31]

Similarly, a learning consortium formed by the Performance Group to share ideas about innovation and change confirms that companies tend to play to their traditional strengths and fail to recognize or value new ideas[32]. The picture of what it is like in many companies is of continuing 'steady-as-she-goes-incremen-talism', when what the world wants is leaps in customer value[33]. One study into product innovation carried out by IMD in France and the PIMS group concludes along similar lines that:

'Producers tend to think of innovation as what they have tweaked in the product or done to the process, but if you look at what actually works . . . real innovation, as defined by the customers, is something that makes a big difference to them, which changes their behaviour and which offers them something they can use in a way that hasn't previously been possible. It seems that this whole mind-set has still to go through some companies.'[34]

Increasingly, we desperately need to see innovation as part of a broader strategy of change, not something locked away in the R&D department, because research suggests the most profitable companies are those placing most emphasis on innovation[35]. At the same time, we are beginning to realize that for successful innovation the key drivers are creativity and management leadership[36] – the challenge to managers has been laid down: 'build an innovation factory'[37].

Creative processes

The trouble with the word 'creativity' is that we then start talking about creative people as some kind of breed apart from the rest of us – the more awkward, idiosyncratic and unruly the better. They are the ones who wear jeans instead of suits, refuse to wear ties, and come to the office late because they have been having an idea. Indeed, psychologists who measure these things do indicate that 'creatives' share informa-tion processing patterns and other characteristics with psychotics[38]!

'The trouble with the word "creativity" is that we then start talking about creative people as some kind of breed apart from the rest of us'

In fact, Ken Robinson, Professor of Creativity at Warwick University, tells us that we face three challenges in making the most of our creative resources in an organization:

- understand the real nature of creativity – everyone has creative capacities, different in all of us, and related to the nature of our intelligence;
- implement a systematic strategy for developing creative capacities in people – giving people the environment, col-leagues, culture and opportunity to be creative in their work;
- facilitate and reward creative output at all levels of the company[39].

Some stress the role of creating problem-solving groups to achieve these things[40], while others emphasize the need to find ways around the 'dominant logic' that prevails in a company.

However, realists also suggest that it is not that easy. Researchers suggest that, in some companies, being innovative can positively damage your career – the rewards of success may be small, while the risks of being pilloried if the project fails are substantial – and innovators may be seen as an 'irritating virus' that should be subtly discouraged, and in one project:

'in some companies, being innovative can positively damage your career – the rewards of success may be small, while the risks of being pilloried if the project fails are substantial'

'The usual organizational antibodies were applied in an attempt to neutralize it: withholding of funding, general naysaying and subtle signals that it might not be "career smart" to associate with the project.'[41]

'Innovators need to be sensitive to organizational politics and the need for top manager champions as well as creative!'

Innovators need to be sensitive to organizational politics and the need for top manager champions as well as creative!

In fact, organizations are often unaware of just how constrained they are by their assumptions and the beliefs of the powerful. For example, during its war games in the 1980s, the US Navy refused to allow the hypothetical sinking of any of its aircraft carriers – it was simply unthinkable. In another case, a consultant demonstrated to a hotel company a computerized prototype that could predict demand for rooms in different locations, based on demographic data and information about competing chains. The company objected to the model because it included the rooms of another hotel chain that they refused to accept as a competitor because its rooms were 'inferior'. The barriers to innovation may be deeply entrenched in the organizational psyche[42].

Fostering creativity in the organization

Stimulating and rewarding creativity and innovation is mainly an issue of leadership. There are lots of views on what form that leadership should take. For example, Paul Horn, Director of IBM Research, suggests the guidelines:

- Under-define jobs – so people have the time, space and freedom to develop new things without being totally constrained by a defined role.
- Brainstorm with people who use what you sell – customers bring problems, but also give you credibility in pursuing change.

- Do not over-map the journey – being over-analytical and demanding to know the outcome at the start can kill creative thinking.
- Pair visionaries with implementers – to cultivate both sets of skills.
- Encourage the flow of ideas outside work – social interaction can facilitate new ideas.
- Evaluate the process not the short-term result – ask how things are moving and what is happening, not where's the result?[43]

Others suggest that the role of the manager is to protect those working on innovative projects from attack and criticism from the rest of the organization – particularly the 'brand police' with their vested interests in existing brands not innovations[44], and the importance of designing and leading supportive cultures[45]. Bringing in outsiders, partnering with customers and establishing separate organizational units are all described by companies as part of their attempts to provide a useful setting for creativity and innovation[46]. In this sense, the manager's role is to remove the obstacles and barriers to creativity and innovation.

'the manager's role is to remove the obstacles and barriers to creativity and innovation'

REALITY CHECK
NURTURING THE NEXT BIG IDEA

The fear in companies like IBM of missing out on new technologies and new opportunities, as the company has in the past, has changed the way it identifies and pursues promising new ideas. Because new ideas fall between organizational boundaries and sometimes conflict with existing business units, they are managed differently. 'Horizon Three' businesses, as opposed to Horizon One businesses (mature businesses like mainframe computers) or Horizon Two businesses (current growth businesses), are protected from the rest of the organization. They are put in separate organizational units with dedicated teams, providing visibility and management sponsorship. The young Horizon Three business units are insulated from traditional management methods and performance yardsticks – efficiency measures can squeeze the life out of a promising new idea. There is a clear understanding that Horizon Three businesses benefit from personal sponsorship by senior managers, to prevent middle managers using their power to block new developments that might not fit their personal agendas.

Source: Adapted from Richard Waters (2001), 'Never Forget to Nurture the Next Big Idea', *Financial Times*, 15 May.

'it is one of the prime duties of managers everywhere to build companies where creativity and innovation flourish and achieve results'

The chances are that no-one can tell you exactly how to do this in your company – you have to look at what other people try and match it to the way your organization operates. The important thing at this stage is that you accept it is one of the prime duties of managers everywhere to build companies where creativity and innovation flourish and achieve results.

Breaking the 'rules'

Not least of the reasons why fostering creativity may be one of the most important things a manager does is that one of the things that a lot of us have learned (often the hard way) is that many of the old 'rules' about strategy are just no longer the right ones. We need the people and the processes that will challenge those old assumptions, and maybe build the new 'rules' (possibly indicating that 'Rule 1' is that there are no longer any rules). The goal is to avoid the potential disasters that happen when competitors in an industry all converge like lemmings on the same strategies and the same courses of action, convince themselves that this is the only way to do things, and simply slug it out in the middle of the market[47].

The innovator's dilemma

The failure of many major organizations to innovate and change is in some important ways explained not because managers are complacent or necessarily stupid, but because they do what the textbooks tell them to do. Clayton Christensen describes what he calls the 'innovator's dilemma'[48]. He was puzzled why seemingly smart companies so often get it wrong. Why, he asked, when the computer market moved from mainframes to mini-computers was IBM left behind, and then when the market moved again from mini-computers to personal computers, were the makers of mini-computers (Digital, Wang, Nixdorf, and the rest) left behind in their turn? Could it be that these companies were too stupid and too blinkered to see how the market was changing? Or was there something else at work?

Christensen argues that the PC is an example of a 'disruptive technology'. Generally, new technologies tend to do things better from the customer's viewpoint – these are 'sustaining technologies' because they allow us to sell similar things to current customers, but better, cheaper and faster. The distinguishing characteristic of the disruptive technology is that it does the job *worse* than the existing technology – but it is cheaper. But as disruptive technologies improve over time, and get to do the job adequately, then their lower prices drive the existing technology out of the market. Disruptive technologies are fundamentally different to conventional or 'sustaining technology'.

REALITY CHECK

DISRUPTIVE TECHNOLOGY IN THE EXCAVATOR MARKET

Until the 1920s, the established technology for excavators was the steam shovel. This was followed by the machines powered by the internal combustion engine, which did the job better, and was a sustaining technology. Most large steam shovel excavator manufacturers made the transition successfully. In 1947, J. C. Bamford developed the hydraulic shovel, or backhoe. This did a poor job – it could only handle small bucketfuls of earth, far smaller than was demanded by the big contractors in mining and sewage construction. The JCB was, however, cheap, because it worked off the back of a tractor. Initially its market was restricted to digging narrow trenches in the street. As its technology became more robust, backhoes attacked the main excavator market. Few of the traditional manufacturers survived.

Source: Clayton M. Christensen (1997), *The Innovator's Dilemma*, Boston, MA: Harvard Business School Press.

Established manufacturers are bad at coping with these break-throughs *because* they are so good at serving their customers. These companies knew about the innovations in question, the reason they did not adopt them was that their customers did not want them. The new technology appeals to less sophisticated, lower margin customers. The product is not as good as what went before. It is not what our (currently) most profitable customers want.

In other words, sticking to tried-and-tested strategies with our major customers may blind us to changing market needs and competitors with new technologies. The risk we face is that established firms, excelling in the core competencies that keep their biggest customers happy, fail to see the threat of disruptive innovation in time because their customers do not see it, need it, want it, or ask for it[49].

'sticking to tried-and-tested strategies with our major customers may blind us to changing market needs and competitors with new technologies'

It gets worse too – while the disruptive innovation undermines some business models, it may at the same time be a sustaining technology for others. The Internet, for example, disrupted Compaq's distributor-based approach to computer marketing, but was an important sustaining technology for the direct marketers Dell and Gateway – the Web allows them to serve customers in the same way they always did, but faster and cheaper.

Christensen also tells us that few established firms succeed in adapting to disruptive innovation. The best hope is to create an independent business with a completely new business model designed to attack the competition including its parent company. It also has to ignore the wishes of existing major customers – he calls this 'agnostic marketing'.

But this throws up the spectre of competing with ourselves, which is anathema to the conventional marketer.

Cannibalization[50]

One of the strongest traditional arguments against radical innovation is that we simply compete with ourselves – we cannibalize our own sales to our existing customer base. Executives often believe that it is unproductive for a company to compete with its own products and services, rather than targeting those of competitors – it risks under-exploiting existing investments for no gain in sales (or probably profits).

'the idea of "proactive cannibalization" has taken grip of many strategists' minds'

However, the idea of 'proactive cannibalization' has taken grip of many strategists' minds. At its simplest the logic is compelling – someone is going to compete with you and attack the sales of your products and services, so you might as well do it yourself and retain the customer. More elegantly expressed:

'What causes some firms to be radically innovative over long periods of time, whereas many others ossify and perish? We suggest that the answer lies in the extent to which firms are prepared to give up the old and embrace the new. Firms must break out of the natural human trait that propels them to use yesterday's bag of tools to solve tomorrow's problems. They must do so today, while they still have options, not tomorrow, when they will have nothing left but a useless bag of tools. They must be willing to cannibalize before there is nothing left of value to cannibalize.'[51]

These researchers conclude that, although it is counter-intuitive for many managers and organizations, willingness to cannibalize is one of the most powerful drivers of radical product innovation[52].

Of course, in some cases you may have little alternative anyway, but even then you have to be careful:

REALITY CHECK

BRITISH AIRWAYS' 'GO'

Faced with the invasion of the British and European internal flight market by 'no frills', low-price operators like easyJet and Ryanair, BA needed to respond to stop the decline in market share. Having looked at buying their new competitors or putting them out of business (the full extent of BA's competitive strategy repertoire from time immemorial), and being prevented by the European regulators from doing either, BA's response was to establish its own 'no frills' airline – Go. However, from the start Go was priced substantially higher than the 'no frills' operators, but offered less service and convenience than BA's regular flights. Predictably, the major effect of Go was to cannibalize sales of BA flights, with little impact on the 'no frills' operators, who continue to expand. By 2001, BA was in the process of selling Go (for much less than the original asking price). The end-result seems to be the conclusion that a conventional full-cost airline lacks the will or the ability to operate a 'no frills' operation, and BA has simply established a new competitor for itself. It appears to be a case of the biter being bit.

Defensive cannibalization – or at least cannibalization resulting from defensive strategies – is different to proactive cannibalization, when the price of innovation is to compete with your own products. For example, Intel's continuous improvement of computer chips and Gillette's continuing introduction of improved shaving technology show proactive cannibalization that has positive benefits.

REALITY CHECK

VOLKSWAGEN'S MULTI-BRAND STRATEGY

Volkswagen in the late 1990s displaced Fiat as the domestic market leader in the European car market. The basis for their market share gains was a 'multi-brand strategy'. In the mass market, VW markets

> vehicles under the VW, Audi, Seat and Skoda brands. Many vehicles share the same platform – VW has cut its number of platforms to four. The same platform carries the VW Golf, the Audi A3, the Audi TT Roadster, the VW Jetta and New Beetle, the Seat Toledo, and the Skoda Octavia. Seeing the similarities between these models, it is inevitable that some price-conscious buyers will trade down – in 2000 Skoda new car registrations in western Europe grew 19 per cent, and VW dropped by 6 per cent. The VW strategy rests on customers trading up and down, and switching between brands, but remaining within the VW group.

Many of us may have to accept that accelerating cannibalization to the detriment of our existing products and services may be an inevitable consequence of the innovation we undertake to survive.

There's riches in niches

Another of the old rules was that market size and market share were the dominant issues that should shape our strategies. What we have seen is that niche companies can use technological advances and the Internet to build profitable and fast-growth 'sliver' companies or 'micro-multinationals'. Sliver companies are 'small participants in the industries of giants' – they make themselves valuable to large corporations willing to pay for their innovations[53]. For example, Biorobotics in Cambridge makes high-technology machines to analyse DNA samples for pharmaceutical companies – it sells a narrow range of highly-specialized products, but to customers throughout the world. Many of these businesses devise wholly new ideas and subcontract manufacturing – such as Prolien, responsible for half the world market in robotic milking equipment for cows. These are what Hermann Simon has called the 'hidden champions'[54] – little-known world market leaders in niche markets. Small and flexible, niche players may lead the way in taking advantage of technological, social, economic and legislative change. They have taken advantage of such phenomena in the US as: the increased movement of women into the workforce (growth in demand for pre-packaged meals); the growth of mass long-haul travel (travel agents offering customized holidays); privatization (offering commercial services to former state-owned industries)[55].

'niche companies can use technological advances and the Internet to build profitable and fast-growth "sliver" companies or "micro-multinationals"'

REALITY CHECK
IS THERE A THIRD WAY?

The IT industry has given us one of the most basic pieces of guidance in market strategy. That advice is:

Get big.

Get niche.

Or get out.

The thinking is that there are no half-measures, you either have to be huge enough to dominate rivals or find an unexploited vein of value to excavate – but a vein too slender or difficult to attract the industry giants. If neither of those is available to you in a market, you should not stay there.

What niche players show us is that most markets have new, uncovered opportunities waiting to be exploited. Think about that when we examine the process of creating market space (pp. 299–313).

> '*What niche players show us is that most markets have new, uncovered opportunities waiting to be exploited*'

The unavoidable imperative for innovation

No-one disputes that innovation and change is a reality of business and effective strategy. The norm in international markets is now intense 'hypercompetition'[56], and a recent *Forbes ASAP*/Ernst & Young research initiative ranked innovation top of eight value drivers, while use of technology (ranked 7) and customer satisfaction (ranked 8) were not significant drivers of market values[57]. The issue is increasingly, however, about what sort of innovation and change?

Certainly, broad-based innovation is critical – extending far beyond new products and services to include ideas, processes, business practices and designs[58] – and is not just concerned with marketing's traditional preoccupation with new product development and minor brand extensions. Gary Hamel is critical, for example, of the type of product-led, incremental change led by marketing departments in the past – his challenge is that we should be creating radical new products, concepts and business models or face the alternative of 'crash and burn' – he says 'Radical, non-linear innovation is the only way to escape the ruthless hyper-competition that has been hammering down margins in industry after industry'[59].

'it is no longer possible to beat the competition by making incremental improvements and changes, because they will be instantly copied, and in modern markets you quickly reach the point of diminishing returns'

For example, in one major research programme, the study of 100 major new business launches found that 86 per cent were 'me-too' launches, or incremental improvements, but these generated only 62 per cent of launch revenues and 39 per cent of profits. By contrast, the other 14 per cent of launches – those radical enough to create or recreate markets – generated 38 per cent of revenues and a massive 61 per cent of profits[60].

Quite simply, the reality is that as products tend to converge and become more similar, it is no longer possible to beat the competition by making incremental improvements and changes, because they will be instantly copied, and in modern markets you quickly reach the point of diminishing returns[61].

It is for this reason that Seth Godin talks about 'unleashing the ideas virus' and says 'ideas aren't a sideshow that make our factory a little more valuable. Our factory is a sideshow that makes our ideas a little more valuable' – at its best, Nike, with no manufacturing capacity of its own, markets ideas, says Godin: 'It's the idea of the Air Jordan sneakers, not the shoe, that permits Nike to sell them for more than $100. It's the sizzle, not the fit'[62].

One additional insight comes from the work of W. Chan Kim and Renee Mauborgne at INSEAD (to which we make more detailed reference in the next section). Their observation is that, between 1975 and 1995, 60 per cent of the Fortune 500 companies disappeared. The reason was that in industry after industry, companies building innovative businesses raced ahead by replacing established firms who were focused on improving existing businesses. Their research suggests that the really high-performing companies in every sector are those who achieve 'value innovation' – they do not just imitate competitors or invest for competitiveness against established rivals, they innovate in new value for customers. They suggest that one useful exercise is to assess our portfolios of products and service on their 'Pioneer–Migrator–Settler' map, because innovation linked to value determines our real growth prospects (see Figure 6.2). Their categories are:

'the really high-performing companies in every sector are those who achieve "value innovation" – they do not just imitate competitors or invest for competitiveness against established rivals, they innovate in new value for customers'

- *Settlers* – these offer 'me-too' value, based on equalling what their competitors do, usually in the same way that they do it.

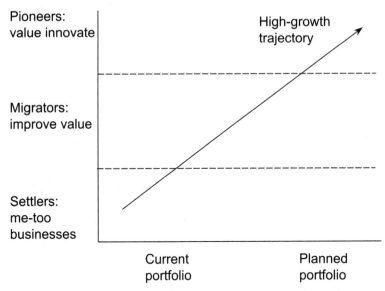

Figure 6.2 The Pioneer–Migrator–Settler map. Source: Adapted from W. Chan Kim and Renee Mauborgne (1997), 'Value Innovation: The Strategic Logic of High Growth', *Harvard Business Review*, January/February, 102–13

- *Migrators* – these offer value improvements over competitors.
- *Pioneers* – these are the businesses that represent real value innovations, e.g. the Sony Walkman (see pp. 302–3), the Dyson vacuum cleaner (see pp. 331–40) and the Swatch watch (see pp. 306–7).

A portfolio that is heavy with settlers leads to a company's decline. One dominated by migrators offers some growth potential, but is vulnerable to the strength of a value innovator. The issue is whether we are gearing our planning towards pioneers, or merely settling for the status quo. The challenge is to continuously shift the portfolio away from settlers. This may produce very different conclusions to those based on just looking at current numbers like market share, sales revenue, customer satisfaction and profitability – because these numbers all represent the past not the future[63].

Creating new market space

As we saw earlier, people like Gary Hamel talk about breaking free from the 'industry rules' that prevail in our markets, and redefining markets. Managers are frequently highly sceptical about the practical significance of such remarks. They ask us for something more useful than advice to develop more creative strategies or to 'think outside the box'. They ask for evidence and practical tools.

A compelling case that successful companies reshape their industries and sometimes create new ones comes from a ground-breaking body of research compiled by W. Chan Kim and Renee Mauborgne at INSEAD[64] over the last decade. What they describe is how managers in high-performing companies across the world have succeeded in systematically looking outside the conventional boundaries and structures to find the unoccupied territory that represents a real breakthrough in value. This section leans very heavily on their work and the companies they have studied.

'managers in high-performing companies across the world have succeeded in systematically looking outside the conventional boundaries and structures to find the unoccupied territory that represents a real breakthrough in value'

Kim and Mauborgne tell us that companies know that they must innovate to succeed, but too often interpret this as head-to-head competition with rivals for a bigger share of existing markets. This is the route to long-term decline. Successful growing companies innovate by creating new markets or reinventing existing ones. They identify six basic paths to creating new market space, applicable to all industries. The difference between conventional strategic thinking and that needed to create new market space is summarized in Table 6.4, and discussed below.

Looking across substitute industries

Conventional strategy focuses on competing directly with known competitors offering similar products and services to ours (refer back to the competitive box, pp. 278–83, to test that one out). However, actually companies do not just compete with each other within the industry – they compete with substitutes in seemingly unrelated industries. For example, e-mail competes with postal services, because both get messages from one place to another, but using different technologies. The founder of Intuit software, famed for its low-cost and easy-to-use personal finance software packages, did not see his competitor as other software producers. He saw the main competitor as the pencil, because it is cheap and easy to use. By focusing on ease of use and cheapness to compete with the pencil, Intuit created a new market space for personal finance software, and grew the market by a factor of 100. It is in the space *between* industries that opportunities exist for creating new markets. One way of breaking free of competition with rivals

Table 6.4 Creating new market space*

Conventional ways of looking at competition	Conventional head-to-head competition	Strategic thinking to create new market space
The industry	Focuses on conventional competitors and market share	Emphasizes looking across substitute industries for opportunities
The strategic group	Focuses on competitive position within a conventional group of competitors	Emphasizes looking across the strategic groups within the industry
The buyer group	Focuses on better performance with the conventional buyer group	Emphasizes redefinition of the buyer group
Scope of product and service offering	Focuses on improving the value of the product service offering within the conventional industry boundaries	Emphasizes complementary product and service offers that go beyond the conventional industry boundaries
Functional–emotional orientation of the industry	Focuses on improving price and performance in line with the functional–emotional orientation of the conventional industry	Emphasizes taking a different perspective on the functional–emotional orientation of the conventional industry
Environment	Focuses on adapting to external trends	Emphasizes participation in shaping external trends

* Source: Adapted from W. Chan Kim and Renee Mauborgne (1999), 'Creating New Market Space', *Harvard Business Review*, January/February, 83–93

in an industry is to find substitutes and to look at why buyers choose one substitute over another – the goal is then to concentrate on the strengths of both substitutes and eliminate everything else. An illustrative example is Southwest Airlines.

REALITY CHECK

THE REAL SECRET OF THE SUCCESS OF SOUTHWEST AIRLINES

Southwest is famous as the innovator of 'no frills' flying, on which the European airlines easyJet and Ryanair have successfully based themselves. Southwest has been consistently profitable for more than 25 years, in contrast with the performance of its traditional airline competitors, and has substantially grown the market on the routes it flies. The factors underlying Southwest's success go far beyond cost savings achieved by eliminating in-flight meals and drinks. While conventional US airlines were locked in head-to-head competition based on traditional tactics, Southwest sidestepped all of that and created a new market: short-haul air transport.

Southwest created the concept of frequent point-to-point flights – its average flying distance is only 425 miles – with fares up to 60 per cent below conventional airlines, using airports in smaller, less-congested cities.

The Southwest strategy was to move across substitute industries. For short-haul destinations, surface transport, i.e. the car, is a substitute for flying. They focused on the reasons why people choose to fly instead of driving – it is to save time, not to watch films, eat meals, let alone worry about multiple-class seating or designated seats. Southwest created point-to-point flights to make short-haul travel even quicker, and used secondary airports to avoid the delays in getting to and through congested major city airports. Their frequent flights counter the advantage to the car driver of leaving when they want. The other 'benefits' of flying were eliminated. The effect is that Southwest has created a market space between conventional flying and surface transport. This is encapsulated in their strategic principle, which is to: 'Meet customers' short-haul travel needs at fares competitive with the cost of automobile travel.'

Sources: W. Chan Kim and Renee Mauborgne (1999), 'Southwest Airlines' Route to Success', *Financial Times*, 13 May. Orit Gadiesh and James L. Gilbert (2001), 'Transforming Corner-Office Strategy Into Frontline Action', *Harvard Business Review*, May, 73–79.

Looking across strategic groups within the industry

'The Sony Walkman, Polo Ralph Lauren and Toyota's Lexus are all ideas that created new markets by breaking free of the conventional strategic groups in their industries'

The Sony Walkman, Polo Ralph Lauren and Toyota's Lexus are all ideas that created new markets by breaking free of the conventional strategic groups in their industries. Strategic groups are mainly companies pursuing similar strategies obsessed with improving their competitive position within the group. Existing industry players or new entrants can achieve major gains by changing the way in which they compete. For example, the Sony Walkman combined the transistor radio and the 'ghetto blaster' to create the personal stereo – combining convenience with 'coolness' took business from both the existing strategic groups and attracted new customers, varying from joggers to commuters, into the market. Similarly, in the US luxury car market, Toyota's Lexus was positioned between the high-end group of Mercedes, BMW and Jaguar and the low-end group of Cadillac and Lincoln. Polo Ralph Lauren created a market worth $5 billion for 'high fashion with no fashion' by combining the appeal of haute couture with classic designs. The critical issue is focusing on the factors that make buyers trade up to a higher price strategic group or trade down to a lower group, and eliminating everything else. Another example is the Formula 1 low-budget hotel chain.

REALITY CHECK
BREAKING FREE OF STRATEGIC GROUPS

In the mid-1980s, one- and two-star hotels in France were in trouble – no growth, low occupancy rates, poor profitability. Existing competitors competed by trying to improve against each other, creating more of the same. In creating the Formula 1 budget hotel chain, Accor asked the fundamental question of why people looking for cheap accommodation trade up to a two-star hotel or trade down to a one-star hotel. They found that two-star hotel customers trade up for the 'sleeping environment' – one-star hotels were dirty, noisy and had bad beds. The other amenities such as larger rooms and restaurants were irrelevant. One-star customers went there for the very low price – often half the rate of the two-star hotel.

Accor's strategy was to focus on the distinctive strengths of both strategic groups and eliminate or reduce everything else – its Formula 1 hotels offer cleaner, quieter rooms, with better beds than the conventional two-star hotel, but at the price of a traditional one-star hotel room. Its operating costs are lower than the traditional one-star hotel because it eliminated restaurants and lounges, and kept furniture, room size and other amenities to a minimum. It took custom from both strategic groups and expanded the market. By 1999, Formula 1 had a market share larger than the sum of the next five largest competitors. They had created a new market space in between the traditional strategic groups of competitors.

Source: W. Chan Kim and Renee Mauborgne (1999), 'Finding Rooms for Manoeuvre', *Financial Times*, 27 May.

Redefining the buyer group

In conventional thinking, competitors converge on a common and shared definition of the target customer – and then compete hard for a share of that customer's attention and business against each other. Separating members of the chain of customers – purchasers, users and influencers – with different concepts of what is good value. Opportunities to recreate the market can come from focusing on the buyer group neglected by conventional competitors. For example, in the industrial lighting business, traditional strategies focused on corporate purchasing managers who buy on the basis of how much light bulbs cost and how long they last – so all suppliers compete head-to-head on these value drivers. The Dutch company, Philips, understood that price and bulb-life do not account for the full cost of lighting – these lamps contain toxic materials that involve customers in high disposal costs (in which purchasing officers, quite reasonably, have little interest). Philips changed its focus away from corporate purchasing officers to chief finance officers and public relations departments. It launched Alto, an environmentally friendly bulb, to appeal to chief finance officers (on lower total user costs including disposal) and to PR departments (on environmental image issues). The Alto has replaced more than 25 per cent of the total market for traditional industrial fluorescent lamps in the US.

'Opportunities to recreate the market can come from focusing on the buyer group neglected by conventional competitors'

Look across to complementary products/services

Often the convergence of existing competitors on maximizing the value of their products within the boundaries of the industry's products and services makes them blind to the opportunities represented by complementary products and services (often from outside the conventional industry boundaries). For example, when the Bert Claeys Group in Belgium built Kinepolis in 1988, the world's first megaplex with 25 screens and 7600 seats, taking 50 per cent of the market within a year, one of the factors they addressed for customers was the cost and difficulty of getting a babysitter. In another example, Virgin Megastores combined CDs, videos, computer games, and stereo and audio equipment in a single store to solve their customer's complete entertainment needs. Compaq provides another illustration of the power of complementarity in creating new markets.

REALITY CHECK
COMPAQ'S SERVER STRATEGY

Compaq created the computer server industry in the early 1990s, but found that the speed of imitation in the computer industry meant they quickly faced many competitors. Rather than try to compete with the others on product improvements, Compaq tried to reinvent the market it had shortly before created. Compaq looked beyond the server itself to the network of complementary services that surrounded it – finding that 90 per cent of the customer's costs came from installing and maintaining servers, and only 10 per cent from buying the hardware. Suppliers were united in focusing on maximizing the price-performance of the server hardware, even though this was the least costly element for the buyer. Compaq's 1993 launch of ProLiant servers had some important differences. The Compaq product came with new software – to automatically configure the server hardware making installation simple and error-free, and to diagnose maintenance needs before components broke down. Compaq remains the leader in the server market, but it is a market which they have made attractive to many additional customers by reducing the costs of owning a server.

Source: W. Chan Kim and Renee Mauborgne (1999), 'Try Complementary Medicine', *Financial Times*, 3 June.

Rethink the functional–emotional orientation of the industry

Competition in industries tends to be on one of two bases of appeal. Some industries compete mainly on price and functional performance; the appeal of these industries is 'rational'. Other industries compete largely on emotions; for example, cosmetics. It is rare that there is only one way to compete in any industry. However, companies' strategies educate customers in what to expect, so rational industries become more functional and emotional industries become more emotional. Companies can create market space by breaking out of this convergence and shifting the functional–emotional orientation of the industry. The aim is to appeal to a different customer motivation by transforming a product or service whose appeal is functional into one which is emotional, or vice versa. These opportunities may be even more attractive as they allow the company to develop a simpler lower-cost business model (by removing the 'extras' that add to price in an emotion-oriented industry, or if it is possible to add emotion and pleasure of use to a previously functional industry). Swatch and The Body Shop provide good illustrations.

REALITY CHECK

MAKING THE FUNCTIONAL FASHIONABLE AND THE EMOTIONAL FUNCTIONAL

Until the early 1980s, budget watches were a functional item, sold cheaply, used solely to keep track of time. The industry leaders were Citizen and Seiko, competing by using quartz technology to improve accuracy and digital displays to make reading the time simpler. Low price was critical. Swatch's Swiss parent company, SMH, had a design mission to combine powerful technology with artwork, colours and flamboyance. Swatch created a market space by making the budget watch a fashion item – they transformed the industry's conventional functional orientation into an emotional one. They also grew the size of the market – traditionally people owned only one cheap watch, because that met the functional need to tell the time. Swatch achieved multiple repeat purchases from buyers encouraged to match the wrist watch they wore with their clothes, mood and social occasion.

The Body Shop created a new market in the cosmetics industry by shifting the appeal from an emotional one to a functional one. Unlike conventional cosmetics companies, the Body Shop did not sell 'glamour, hope and fantasy' in expensive packaging, it sold health and well-being in cheap, refillable plastic bottles. While conventional competitors spent heavily on R&D and image-creating advertising, the Body Shop used simple, natural products, at reasonable prices with no hype. The Body Shop created a new market space by shifting the appeal from emotions to functionality.

Both examples illustrate a further issue. Once you have created a market space, imitative competitors are likely to flood in (as The Body Shop found in particular), so the challenge is further reinvention. The Body Shop's market space was steadily invaded by direct imitations as well as 'natural collections' from large companies like Boots. The latest reinvention has come not from The Body Shop, but from one of its former suppliers – Lush. Lush is dedicated to producing effective personal care products out of fresh fruit, vegetables and cream, making the products freshly by hand, printing their own labels and making their own fragrances. They are vehemently opposed to animal testing and ingredients. Lush stores are laid out like 'beauty delis' with soap shaped like slabs of cheese and round 'bath bombs' piled high like apples. A fresh counter, like those used to sell fish, is piled with ice chips to preserve beauty products that must be used within 24 hours. Prices are by weight and products are wrapped in greaseproof paper complete with stickers with sell-by dates. Founder Mark Constantine says 'Our aim is to have the youngest, freshest products in the history of cosmetics'. Lush has created a new market space, which it is more difficult for competitors to enter. Started in 1995, by 2000 Lush had stores in ten countries, and in 2001 was rumoured to be considering the purchase of the troubled Body Shop.

Sources: W. Chan Kim and Renee Mauborgne (1999), 'Coffee Blended With Emotion', *Financial Times*, 20 May. Bernice Harrison (2000), 'Lush Cosmetic Chain for Grafton Street', *Irish Times*, 4 October. 'Market Miscellany', *Sunday Telegraph*, 6 May 2001.

Participate in shaping external trends

Industry changes can be important sources of new market space. The danger is that conventional company responses are incremental and passive as events unfold. The issue is how a trend will change the value that a company can deliver to a customer.

REALITY CHECK
THE CISCO KIDS ARE NOT KIDDING

Cisco Systems was quick to recognize that the world was hampered by slow data exchanges and incompatible computer networks, at the same time that demand for network computing was exploding – at that time the number of Internet users was doubling every 100 days. They could see that the data exchange and compatibility problems would only get worse, constraining the trend towards networking. Getting ahead of this trend, Cisco invested heavily in developing routers, switches and other networking devices that offered fast data exchanges and contributed towards achieving a seamless computing environment. By 1999, 80 per cent of Internet traffic flowed through Cisco products, and its margins in this new market were in the 60 per cent area.

Source: W. Chan Kim and Renee Mauborgne (1999), 'From Trend to Quantum Leap', *Financial Times*, 10 June.

But, will the big idea work?

Good ideas tend to find backers – but the question is: how do we figure out which ones will work and make money? Research at INSEAD suggests that there are four sets of economic conditions that successful business ideas have in common, and which we should evaluate before getting carried away with the creativity, innovativeness and technology[65]. This framework provides us with an excellent structure for asking the big questions about the 'big idea'. They suggest that the 'Winning Business Idea' index comprises:

- *Buyer utility* – what is the compelling reason why customers should buy the new product or service?
- *Strategic pricing* – how is the price approach going to attract the mass of buyers and grow the market?
- *Business model* – how can the company profitably deliver the new idea to the market; does it have the appropriate capabilities and cost structure?
- *Adoption hurdles* – are there any compelling reasons why the new idea may be rejected by employees, partners, or society/law makers?

The first two tests determine the new idea's potential to generate sales and win customers. The second two tests concern the ability to generate profitable growth.

These may seem very obvious questions to ask. Given the high rate of innovation failure – see back to the dot.com crashes (pp. 184–90) if you have any doubts about this – maybe we should see whether we really do ask and answer the obvious questions before we invest time and money in new business ideas? Quite simply, what the INSEAD research tells us is that it is not enough to have a wonderfully desirable product to attract large numbers of customers, or to have large numbers of customers – alone these do not guarantee success and profit.

'The novelty of the technology and the ideas it creates may blind us to the rudimentary question of the value of the innovation and whether there is a reason for people to choose it in preference to alternatives'

Buyer utility

The novelty of the technology and the ideas it creates may blind us to the rudimentary question of the value of the innovation and whether there is a reason for people to choose it in preference to alternatives. Technology innovation is not the same thing as buyer utility. Many failures score highly on technology, just not on buyer utility.

REALITY CHECK
PHILIPS' CD-I

The Dutch electronics group, Philips, invested the time of its world-class R&D staff and several billion dollars on developing CD-I – a video machine, music system, games player and teaching tool in a single package. The company's thinking was that this machine would be the most important innovation in the industry since the video player. The CD-I was promoted heavily as the 'Imagination Machine'. The product was a failure, in spite of its outstanding engineering and innovativeness. There was simply no compelling reason why the customer would buy it. The CD-I player did so many different things that customers could not understand how to use it. The product also lacked attractive software titles – while in theory it could do almost anything, in practice it could do very little.

Source: Adapted from W. Chan Kim and Renee Mauborgne (2001), 'How to Tell a Flyer from a Failure', *Financial Times*, 23 January.

The INSEAD research suggests that there are six 'buyer utility levers', and we should think carefully about which of these levers we can use in each stage of the buyer's experience: of purchasing, in delivery and use of the product, in supplementing and using the product, and in disposing of the product. The utility levers are:

- *Customer productivity* – how does the innovative product or service remove important barriers to the customer's productivity, e.g. Tesco's Internet grocery shopping saves the consumer time and effort in basic shopping activities and frees them from conventional shopping hours.
- *Simplicity* – how does the innovative product or service reduce the most significant sources of complexity for the customer, e.g. Intuit's Quicken personal finance software takes accounting jargon out of personal accounting.
- *Convenience* – how does the innovative product or service remove the hassle from a major inconvenience faced by the customer, e.g. Virgin's limousine service from home to airport and back for business class travellers removes one of the biggest sources of inconvenience for them.
- *Risk* – what does the innovative product or service do to counter the greatest uncertainties that buyers face, e.g. Daewoo's 'no haggle' car pricing removed discomfort from car purchase.

- *Fun and image* – how does the innovative product or service counter blocks to customer enjoyment by adding emotion and image, e.g. Starbuck's coffee shops are far more than a place to drink coffee (see pp. 79–80).
- *Environmental friendliness* – how does the innovative product or service reduce or eliminate the things causing greatest harm to the environment, e.g. environmentally friendly light bulbs use less mercury and eliminate the need for special disposal.

'Successful companies focus on the costs of alternatives and substitutes, not just prevailing prices in their own industries'

Strategic pricing

The INSEAD research suggests that successful innovations are also characterized by strategic prices that create demand and win customers not just from within the current industry, but also from other industries. Successful companies focus on the costs of alternatives and substitutes, not just prevailing prices in their own industries.

REALITY CHECK
STRATEGIC PRICING ACROSS INDUSTRIES

Corporate executives tend to buy first- or business-class tickets for air travel. These are expensive – a trip from London to the US may cost £2000. The cost of this level of travel accounts for the bulk of corporate travel budgets. An alternative is to use a corporate jet. These cost tens of millions of pounds and hold a tiny share of the total corporate travel market. Executive Jet, a Berkshire Hathaway company, devised a pricing model whereby companies got the convenience and cachet of private air travel, but at the price of the annual business-class travel budget. Their model consisted of selling shares of time in using a corporate jet. They took business from premium-ticket airline customers, and also from customers preferring a time share rather than continuing full ownership of their own corporate jet that would spend much of its time sitting in the hangar.

Source: Adapted from W. Chan Kim and Renee Mauborgne (2001), 'Now Name a Price That's Hard to Refuse', *Financial Times*, 24 January.

Profitable strategic pricing can take several forms: direct sales; renting or leasing; time share; 'slice share' (e.g. unit trust investment); 'equity for price' (e.g. Hewlett-Packard exchanges servers for a share of the customer's revenue). There are many options to straightforward price lists and payment on the purchase.

Business model

The successful start with a strategic price, allow for profit, and work back into what this makes the cost target. The business model then has to hit the cost target without losing utility or increasing price: replacing conventional raw materials with newer cheaper ones; eliminating or outsourcing low added-value activities in the supply chain; digitizing activities, e.g. Internet ordering and exchanges. Using partnerships to build and reinforce capabilities is also critical.

Adoption hurdles

Major barriers in understanding and attitudes towards the innovation may be of decisive importance to success.

REALITY CHECK

MONSANTO'S GENETICALLY MODIFIED SEEDS

Monsanto developed genetically modified seeds and created a completely new market. The new seeds had many advantages over traditional products for farmers – less risk of crop failure due to disease or bad weather, lower costs, less need for pesticides, a longer shelf-life for some products, a cleaner environment and food quality benefits to consumers. Most of these claims were scientifically verifiable. Yet the failure Monsanto experienced was severe enough that to survive it had to merge with the drugs group Pharmacia & Upjohn in 2000. Monsanto totally underestimated the acceptability of its innovation. The main adoption hurdle was posed by the green movement, and its media support, that claimed the company was defying the laws of nature for the sake of profit, as well as entrenched objections from supporters of organic farming. While the UK supermarket firm Tesco staged the grand gesture of removing all GM food from its shelves, it was Monsanto that paid the price.

Source: Adapted from W. Chan Kim and Renee Mauborgne (2001), 'Are You Sure the World is Ready?', *Financial Times*, 25 January.

Hurdles to adoption may come from: employees (threatened by the launch of the innovation and what it does to their role);

partners (e.g. distributors sidestepped by direct sales channels); or society at large. Obstacles should be identified at the outset and dealt with fairly and effectively. In fact, there is evidence that the best innovators turn their customers and colleagues into collaborators by presenting them with an idea they can improve on – not a fait accompli – so they have a stake in the innovation[66].

Evaluating new ideas

This framework is an excellent one, which we can use operationally to evaluate whether demand can be built for the innovation, and whether we have the capabilities to develop a business model to meet that demand and to overcome the obstacles to adoption which we face in the marketplace.

REALITY CHECK
THE IRIDIUM PHONE

Motorola and its partners spent $5 billion developing and $140 million launching Iridium – a satellite communications system – with the slogan 'Anytime, anywhere'. This product was launched in 1998 with the goal of redefining the world of mobile phones. It was the first mobile phone that could provide uninterrupted wireless communication anywhere in the world, regardless of country or terrain, via a global system of satellites linked to ground-based digital services. Demand estimates had been optimistic – more emphasis had been placed on solving technology challenges than evaluating global use potential and how to access it. For example, in many geographical areas rapidly expanding demand for ground-based digital wireless systems had reduced the need for global satellite systems. At its peak the Iridium venture attracted less than 100 000 subscribers, compared to the break-even figure of 500 000, and the company's forecast of 2 million users by 2002. In March 2001, Iridium closed, unable to find a last minute buyer; its 66 satellites are expected to crash into the sea, and the company took its place among the twenty largest bankruptcies in US history. The phone was heavy and it needed a range of attachments to work. It could not be used in cars or buildings (which tends to be where business people want to use mobile phones). It was expensive – $3000 for the phone and call charges of $7 a minute, compared to conventional $150 cell phones and competitive call charges. Iridium failed to provide a compelling reason why customers should buy, and its pricing was unattractive to target users. The company greatly overestimated customer take-up. While the technological capabilities were fantastic, Iridium faced problems in matching its cost structure to an acceptable price for customers. Hurdles to adoption were not considered until it was too late to do things to overcome them.

Source: Adapted from Christopher Price (1999), 'Iridium: Born on a Beach but Lost in Space', *Financial Times*, 20 August.

As ever, though, before we proceed further, we may want to ask ourselves and our colleagues some awkward questions about where we are on strategy and creativity in our company – and we may want to do this before we start making or assuming choices about our market strategy. It is likely that many of us will be alarmed at the answers.

REALITY CHECK
THE AWKWARD QUESTIONS ABOUT STRATEGY AND CREATIVITY

What efforts do we make to get creativity and innovation into how we think about the business and its future, rather than seeing creative input as just producing smart advertising – do we strategize or merely tactivize?

As a management group, do we understand that strategy is not the same as planning, or analytical techniques, or operational efficiency, but about breaking free from the trap of conventional thinking? Does the 'usual suspect' in the competitive box describe where we are trapped?

Are we prepared for revolution in our industry and to reinvent ourselves – even though last year's figures may encourage the 'fatal arrogance of success'?

Do we as managers in our company create an environment and a structure which welcomes new ideas about developing the business for the future? Do we challenge the 'rules' – about innovation, cannibalization and niche strategies?

Do we simply compete head-to-head with conventional competitors, or are we actively seeking to create new market space? Do we evaluate our new ideas against the criteria that really matter – buyer utility, strategic pricing, the business model and adoption hurdles?

Now, let's talk about the Strategic Pathway

This part of the book has attempted to build a foundation for what follows. My point is that it has become impossible to be effective in developing and sustaining the market strategies that deliver superior customer value, unless we recognize:

- that e-commerce and e-business is impacting on every marketplace and every customer to some degree and in some ways – you cannot ignore the Internet when you think about market strategy, because your customers and competitors will not, but you need a realistic and pragmatic appraisal of what you can do;
- that for many of us the challenge is not worrying about marketing departments and organization but finding ways to achieve real integration of traditional functions and resources around the process of going to market and delivering superior value to customers; and
- that the issue is strategizing and creativity, not programmed routine decisions that can be made by a staff planner, or that cute planning package we downloaded from the Internet.

That clears the way to examining the key questions we need to address in developing market strategy: customer focus and market sensing; market choices; value propositions; and the key relationships to be managed in the process of going to market. So, you may ask, why a 'Strategic Pathway'?

The search for strategy clarity

'The Strategic Pathway approach is intentionally a way of simplifying the market strategy issue to provide a basis for practical decision making'

The Strategic Pathway approach is intentionally a way of simplifying the market strategy issue to provide a basis for practical decision making. Strangely there seems to be a lot of virtue in making strategy simple. This paradox is described by Eisenhardt and Sull:

'When the business landscape was simple, companies could afford to have complex strategies. But now that business is so complex, they need to simplify. Smart companies have done just that with a new approach: a few straightforward, hard-and-fast rules that define direction without confining it.'[67]

Similarly, others suggest that we should physically 'map' our strategies as diagrams showing where we are going and the critical things we need to get us there, so that we understand our strategies better and can communicate them to others[68].

The reason for this is that the most common failure in developing strategy is not to make clear choices, and not to uncover simple, fundamental principles underlying the successful business strategy – indeed, it is argued, the only thing worse than having an elaborate strategy full of preconceptions and restraints is having no strategy at all (with the ensuing confusion and loss of purpose)[69].

The Strategic Pathway is a response to these needs.

> *'the most common failure in developing strategy is not to make clear choices, and not to uncover simple, fundamental principles underlying the successful business strategy'*

The search for strategy consensus

Simplicity in strategy is not quite the same thing as consensus in strategy[70]. The Strategic Pathway helps us clarify and agree what the process of going to market should be – our market strategy.

REALITY CHECK
CONSENSUS AND THE ABILENE EFFECT

Imagine, if you will, that there are six of us in New York. Three of us want to go to Miami. Three of us want to go to Los Angeles. Because we have been trained in management, we have a meeting and reach a compromise around which we can build a meaningful consensus. As a result, we all go to Abilene, which is actually where none of us wanted to go.

Restricting strategic thinking to only those things that everyone in the company agrees with may be very short-sighted. Strategizing is not necessarily a democratic process – being in a minority of one does not mean you are wrong, though it may make it difficult to get things done. Building consensus is about managing processes of planning, budgeting and internal marketing – but first we need a strategy.

> *'Strategizing is not necessarily a democratic process – being in a minority of one does not mean you are wrong, though it may make it difficult to get things done'*

Choosing the Strategic Pathway

'The Strategic Pathway is about getting from the challenges and open-endedness of the strategy issues and strategizing, to something more specific. It provides us with structure and tools to address the issues that matter in a practical way'

The Strategic Pathway is about getting from the challenges and open-endedness of the strategy issues and strategizing, to something more specific. It provides us with structure and tools to address the issues that matter in a practical way. The Strategic Pathway is a simple model of the market strategy process, as shown in Figure 6.3.

The logic is that market strategy issues can be grouped into four highly interrelated categories: our customer focus and how well we understand the marketplace through sensing; the consequent market choices we make; our value proposition to customers in the chosen markets; and the key relationships underpinning the strategy, which we have to manage to deliver the strategy to the customer. None of these sets of issues are self-contained, and we may have to make trade-offs between them – for example, we may have to rethink market choices on the basis of whether we have a superior value proposition for those markets, and whether we can manage the key relationships that matter.

Customer focus and market sensing are essentially about what we do to build, sustain and extend our market understanding. These processes are the foundation on which we make better and more innovative market choices, and innovate value for our chosen customers.

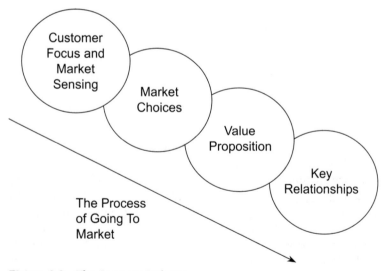

Figure 6.3 The Strategic Pathway

Market choices are about how we define our markets in terms of customer groups and products and services, and how we develop market segments to target, that are compatible with our capabilities. This is about making choices based on how attractive different markets or segments are, but also how well we can perform in those markets.

Linked to this, how well we perform and our choice of market targets should be informed by how we build a value proposition: what role do we want to play in the market (our market mission); how will we establish competitive advantage in the customer's eyes through differentiation and positioning; what intangible marketing assets and brands can we use to achieve this – what is our promise to the customer that represents value to the customer?

This links in turn to the key relationships in the strategy: with the customer, with collaborators and distributors, with existing and new competitors, and with our own employees and co-workers who have to deliver the real quality and service to our customers. In turn again, this leads back to the issue of which market targets we should choose.

This model is far from perfect. It does, however, provide a practical tool for defining strategic direction and positioning, and acts as a framework within which we can plan market strategy.

We will open up each part of this model in turn.

Notes and references

1. Dan Sabbagh (2000), 'From Boo(m) to Bust in Under Two Years', *Daily Telegraph*, 19 May.
2. Actually, that's not true, but I'm trying to be nice.
3. Philip Kotler (1967), *Marketing Management: Analysis, Planning and Control*, New York: Prentice-Hall.
4. The logic, before prurient minds get to work, is that if there is no family dispute in the evening about whose turn it is to wash up the dishes, then there may be more likelihood of other activities ensuing. Actually, all that happens is a family dispute about whose turn it is to load the dishwasher.
5. 'FCUK' stands for French Connection (UK), the rest is down to your imagination. However, it is perhaps not surprising that the Advertising Standards Authority took even more exception to their website promotion: www.fcukinkybugger.com and banned the posters. The company's response was, of course, posters saying simply 'Sorry, fcuk'.
6. Though, while we are on the subject, I have to mention that my favourite campaign in 2000 was the 'Bottle of Britain' campaign for the Spitfire beer produced by Shepherd Neame in Faversham. Their poster ads ran foul of European political correctness and were removed from

the London Underground. Apparently, there was some problem with copy lines like:

'German beer is pants'
'Have the sunbeds, we're off to the bar'
'Downed all over Kent, just like the Luftwaffe'
'No Fokker comes close'
'Votz zo funny about zeez posters?'

I really cannot understand what was the problem . . . not even with

'Rear gunners drink lager shandy'

said to be insulting to gay men as well. Interestingly, the Advertising Standards Authority agrees, and rejects calls that the posters should be banned!

7. Peter Drucker (1993), 'A Turnaround Primer', *Wall Street Journal*, 2 February.
8. Laura Mazur (2000), 'Creating Change That Counts', *Marketing Business*, March, 30.
9. This said, most of the problem is how planning has been managed. As we will see in Chapter 13, processes like planning can be made productive strategy-generators if they are managed better.
10. Andrew Campbell and Marcus Alexander (1997), 'What's Wrong With Strategy?', *Harvard Business Review*, November/December, 42–51.
11. *The World's Most Respected Companies*, London: *Financial Times*, 1998.
12. '. . . about as much use as a one-legged man in an arse-kicking contest' is how one CEO explained to me how much he valued strategic plans.
13. Quoted in James Surowiecki (1999), 'The Return of Michael Porter', *Fortune*, 1 February, 135–38.
14. Michael E. Porter (1995), 'What is Strategy', *Harvard Business Review*, November/December, 61–78.
15. Peter Martin (1998), 'Dangerous Gifts', *Financial Times*, 12 December.
16. Robert Simons (1999), 'How Risky is Your Company?', *Harvard Business Review*, May/June, 85–94.
17. Nigel F. Piercy (1999), *Tales from the Marketplace: Stories of Revolution, Reinvention and Renewal*, Oxford: Butterworth-Heinemann. David W. Cravens, Gordon Greenley, Nigel F. Piercy and Stanley Slater (1998), 'Mapping the Path to Market Leadership', *Marketing Management*, Fall, 29–39.
18. Some managers even suggest we may not know our 'Rs' from our elbows, though risking substantial personal injury in making such comments.
19. Bruce H. Clark and David B. Montgomery (1998), *Managerial Identification of Competitors*, Cambridge, MA: Marketing Science Institute, Report No. 98–127.
20. Michael E. Porter (1995), 'What is Strategy?', *Harvard Business Review*, November/December, 61–78.
21. Gary Hamel and C. K. Prahalad (1994), 'Competing for the Future', *Harvard Business Review*, July/August, 122–28.
22. John Kay (1995), 'Learning to Define Your Core Business', *Financial Times*, 1 December.

23. Gary Hamel (1996), 'Strategy as Revolution', *Harvard Business Review*, July/August, 69–82.
24. Gary Hamel (1996), op. cit.
25. Gary Hamel and C. K. Prahalad (1989), 'Strategic Intent', *Harvard Business Review*, May/June, 63–76.
26. C. K. Prahalad and Gary Hamel (1990), 'The Core Competence of the Corporation', *Harvard Business Review*, May/June, 79–91.
27. Tim Burt (1999), 'All Change for Profit', *Financial Times*, 29 June.
28. Constantinos C. Makrides (2000), *All the Right Moves: A Guide to Crafting Breakthrough Strategy*, Boston, MA: Harvard Business School Press.
29. Clayton M. Christensen (1997), 'Making Strategy: Learning by Doing', *Harvard Business Review*, November/December, 141–56.
30. Philip Kotler (1967), *Marketing Management: Analysis, Planning and Control*, 1st ed., New York: Prentice-Hall.
31. Quoted in Julian Lee (1997), 'Forget Research, Just Come Up With a Good Idea', *The Times*, 25 November.
32. Matthew Jones (2000), 'United in the Quest to Become Radical', *Financial Times*, 12 May.
33. Ty Francis (2000), 'Ideas and Lies', *Marketing Business*, April, 20–23.
34. Tony Clayton of PIMS Associates, quoted in David Murphy (2000), 'Innovate or Die', *Marketing Business*, May, 16–19.
35. *Going for Growth – Realizing the Value of Innovation*, London: PA Consulting, 1999.
36. Alison Maitland (1999), 'Strategy for Creativity', *Financial Times*, 11 November.
37. Andrew Hargadon and Robert L. Sutton (2000), 'Building an Innovation Factory', *Harvard Business Review*, May/June, 157–69.
38. Adrian Furnham (1999), 'A Rare Gift That Can Only Be Encouraged', *Financial Times*, 24 August.
39. Ken Robinson (2001), *Out of Our Minds: Learning to be Creative*, Oxford: Capstone.
40. Dorothy Leonard and Walter Swap (1999), *When Sparks Fly: Igniting Creativity in Groups*, Boston, MA: Harvard Business School Press.
41. Richard Leifer, Christopher M. McDermott, Gina Colarelli O'Connor, Robert W. Verzer, Lois S. Peters and Mark Rice (2001), *Radical Innovation*, Boston, MA: Harvard Business School Press.
42. Teresa M. Amabile (1998), 'How to Kill Creativity', *Harvard Business Review*, September/October, 76–88.
43. Paul Horn (1997), 'Creativity and the Bottom Line', *Financial Times*, 17 November.
44. Vanessa Houlder (1998), 'Keeping a Lid on Egos at Work', *Financial Times*, 26 January. Ty Francis (2001), 'Breaking Brand Barriers', *Marketing Business*, April, 26–27.
45. Ty Francis (2000), 'Divine Intervention', *Marketing Business*, May, 20–22.
46. Michael Skapinker (2001), 'Open Your Company to New Ideas', *Financial Times*, 16 January.
47. John Saunders, Philip Stern, Robin Wensley and Ros Forrester (2000), 'In Search of the Lemmus Lemmus: An Investigation Into Convergent Competition', *British Journal of Management*, 11, S81–S94.

48. Clayton M. Christensen (1997), *The Innovator's Dilemma: When New Technologies Cause Great Firms to Fail*, Boston, MA: Harvard Business School Press.

49. Bob Donath (2000), 'Big Customers May Cause Bigger Dilemmas', *Marketing News*, 11 September, 16.

50. This section leans heavily on David W. Cravens, Nigel F. Piercy and George S. Low (2002), 'The Innovation Challenges of Proactive Cannibalization and Discontinuous Technology', *European Business Review*, forthcoming.

51. Rajesh K. Chandy and George J. Tellis (1998), 'Organizing for Radical Product Innovation: The Overlooked Role of Willingness to Cannibalize', *Journal of Marketing Research*, November, 474–87.

52. Rajesh K. Chandy and Gerard J. Tellis (1998), *Organizing for Radical Product Innovation*, Boston, MA: Marketing Science Institute, Report 98–102.

53. Peter Marsh (2001), 'A Little Goes a Long Way', *Financial Times*, 4 January.

54. Hermann Simon (1999), 'Trumpet Accomplishments of "Hidden Champs"', *Marketing News*, 15 February, 13.

55. Sarah Gracie (1998), 'High Flyers Profit by Breaking Rules', *Sunday Times*, 27 December.

56. Richard D'Aveni (1994), *Hypercompetition*, New York: Free Press.

57. Geoff Baum, Chris Ittner, David Larcker, Jonathan Low, Tony Siesfield and Michael S. Malone (2000), 'Introducing the New Value Creation Index', *Forbes ASAP*, 3 April, 140–43.

58. Tasaddura Shervani and Philip C. Zerrillo (1997), 'The Albatross of Product Innovation', *Business Horizons*, January/February, 57–62.

59. Gary Hamel (2000), *Leading the Revolution*, Harvard Business School Press.

60. W. Chan Kim and Renee Mauborgne (1998), 'Pioneers Strike It Rich', *Financial Times*, 11 August.

61. Robert Jones (2000), *The Big Idea*, London: Harper Collins Business.

62. Seth Godin (2000), *Unleashing the Ideavirus*, New York: Do You Zoom Inc.

63. W. Chan Kim and Renee Mauborgne (1997), 'Value Innovation: The Strategic Logic of High Growth', *Harvard Business Review*, January/February, 102–13. 'Pioneers Strike It Rich', *Financial Times*, 11 August 1998.

64. W. Chan Kim and Renee Mauborgne (1997), 'Value Innovation: The Strategic Logic of High Growth', *Harvard Business Review*, January/February, 102–12. W. Chan Kim and Renee Mauborgne (1999), 'Creating New Market Space', *Harvard Business Review*, January/February, 83–93. W. Chan Kim (2000), 'Knowing a Winning Business Idea When You See One', *Harvard Business Review*, September/October, 129–38.

65. W. Chan Kim and Renee Mauborgne (2000), 'Knowing a Winning Business Idea When You See One', *Harvard Business Review*, September/October, 129–41.

66. Michael Schrage (1999), *Serious Play*, Boston, MA: Harvard Business School Press.

67. Kathleen M. Eisenhardt and Donald N. Sull (2001), 'Strategy as Simple Rules', *Harvard Business Review*, January, 107–16.
68. Clayton M. Christensen (1997), 'Making Strategy: Learning by Doing', *Harvard Business Review*, November/December, 141–56. Robert S. Kaplan and David P. Norton (2000), 'Having Trouble With Your Strategy? Then Map It', *Harvard Business Review*, September/October, 167–76.
69. Constantinos S. Markides (2000), *A Guide to Crafting Breakthough Strategy*, Boston, MA: Harvard Business School Press.
70. Christian Homburg, Harley Krohmer and John P. Workman (1999), 'Strategic Consensus and Performance: The Role of Strategy Type and Market-Related Dynamism', *Strategic Management Journal*, **20**, 339–57.

'Priceline has pioneered the reverse auction as a new form of e-commerce'

After Amazon.com, Priceline.com is one of the most recognized names on the Internet. Priceline has pioneered the reverse auction as a new form of e-commerce – customers submit binding bids for products and services (most notably air tickets and hotel reservations) to Priceline, which then shops these bids among sellers to locate a supplier willing to accept the price and terms set by the customer. The effect is that customers are changed from price-taking buyers into price-setting bidders.

The revolutionary and the new business model

The driving force behind Priceline is the founder, Jay Walker – Vice-Chairman of Priceline and CEO of Walker Digital, he was named in 1998 as one of Time Digital's 'CyberElite Top 50'. Now aged in his 40s, Walker has a lengthy track record of entrepreneurial ventures – some successful and others not. In one such venture, Walker came across new cryptography software that separated the locking and unlocking of codes, and true to form, saw this as an opportunity to create an online casino where cheating was impossible. In seeking to protect this idea, he researched patent law and discovered that it was possible to patent a business process, as long as it was new, useful and not obvious to someone with knowledge in the field. This led to Walker's key question: 'If I can patent this, what else can I patent?'

This question led to the establishment of Walker Digital – a think-tank business with the purpose of creating and reinventing business models, to be patented if feasible. By 1998 Walker's new business process development concept led to 250 patent applications, twelve of which had been accepted, including the reverse auction model to become Priceline – covering 'bilateral buyer-driven commerce'. This gives the right to licence the Priceline process to other companies, and Walker hoped that this would be a major source of income.

The Priceline idea came from the discovery that the airline industry flew each day with over 500 000 empty seats, and the observation that airline yield models had the effect that a ticket priced at £250 when purchased

---

* This case material has been prepared on the basis of discussions with industry executives and published secondary sources.

21 days in advance could cost as much as $1000 when purchased a few days before the flight. (Yield models attempt to increase the price of the ticket as demand increases or the day of the flight gets nearer – but generally the price will not decline in the week prior to the flight, regardless of the number of empty seats. The airlines cannot just cut the prices of excess inventory like other firms, because they rely on charging high prices to last-minute business travellers, and because many of the empty seats are on less desirable early and late flights.)

Walker's idea was to offer an airline $200 for the empty seat, and to sell the ticket to the consumer a few days before the flight, but at the 21-day advance purchase price (e.g. $250 in this example). In addition he applied the reverse auction concept to the deal – i.e. the customer sets the price instead of taking the going price. The effect would be that a customer would bid online or over the telephone and commit to purchase with a credit card number, and Priceline shops the customer's bid in a computer database – notifying the customer within an hour if the bid is accepted or refused. The service is free, with Priceline's income coming from the spread between what the customer bids and the price Priceline can buy the ticket from the airline. Since the airline's marginal cost of filling the empty seat is about $5 (the food, baggage handling, etc.), and the rest of the fare goes direct to profit contribution, even the reduced fare is attractive to them, as long as it does not undermine their ability to sell at higher prices to other customers.

'he applied the reverse auction concept to the deal – i.e. the customer sets the price instead of taking the going price'

This model is not the same as selling discount airline tickets over the Web, it actually changes the nature of the buyer–seller relationship by making the customer the price-maker not the price-taker. Some suggest that Priceline is part of the beginning of an era of 'dynamic pricing' in which a wide range of goods will be priced according to what the market will bear – constantly and instantly.

'Some suggest that Priceline is part of the beginning of an era of 'dynamic pricing' in which a wide range of goods will be priced according to what the market will bear – constantly and instantly'

Initially, Priceline was seen as little more than a clever way for airlines to sell empty seats, but investors were quickly persuaded that the hidden value in the Priceline model was the process it provides, rather than the specific markets in which it deals. Jay Walker noted at this time: 'It is an entirely new concept. We can get the consumer to tell us the trade-off he is prepared to make to get something.' *Fortune* magazine's Marshall Loeb commented: 'Jay Walker doesn't think out of the box, he thinks out of the Planet!'

'Jay Walker doesn't think out of the box, he thinks out of the Planet!'

The launch of Priceline.com

Walker had a hard time selling the Priceline concept to airlines – he had to give Delta a stock warrant and other protections to get its involvement in a 'sweetheart deal' that may give Delta so much control that it runs foul of anti-trust regulations – and some airlines simply refused to participate, but Priceline.com went live in April 1998, with a million visitors to its website in the first week. In its first six months Priceline received bids worth $244 million, and sold more than 67 000 air tickets for around $15.5 million – i.e. only 5 per cent of bids were successful. In this period, Priceline spent $15.9 million on advertising, mostly in the first month after launch – i.e. its marketing outlay was higher than total sales – and total losses over the first six months exceeded $38 million. The company also had negative gross margins – it was selling tickets for less than it paid for them, as a way of building customer loyalty, at an average loss of $30 on every ticket sold.

The amount of venture capital and private equity raised by Priceline in the last nine months of 1998 was well in excess of $100 million – investors were excited not just by the initial market (air tickets) but the prospect of extending the business model into other areas.

The bulk of trading (85 per cent) was Web-based, the remainder on a free phone line, but Priceline avoided the expensive anchor tenancies on portal sites or banner ads, favouring instead a large radio advertising campaign featuring William Shatner (Captain Kirk from *Star Trek*). This campaign made Priceline the second most recognized e-commerce site in America. By the end of 1999, affiliated airlines included Delta, Northwest, Continental, TWA, America West, Lufthansa and Singapore.

In March 1999, Walker took the company public and the share value quickly put his personal wealth at $10.2 billion. Priced at $16, Priceline shares reached $79.50 the following day, and peaked at $165 at the end of the month. By September 1999, Priceline had accumulated $157 million in losses, but had a market capitalization of more than $10 billion – bigger than that of any US airline – and a year after launch had a market value of $24 billion.

The extension of the business model

Quickly after launch Priceline added hotel rooms in 26 US cities to its site – customers specify the quality level of the hotel, and bid in the same way as for air tickets. By August 1999, Priceline was selling 10 000 room-nights a week. Rental cars followed quickly behind.

This was quickly followed by home loans and motor cars (on a regional basis only) – all operating as variants of the 'name-your-own-price' model. Priceline's home mortgage service filled more than $125 million in home loan offers in its first 90 days of operations, and the new car offer is part of an alliance with AutoNations Inc. (the largest US car distributor), under which AutoNations get first refusal offer on any bids. Later in the year, Priceline linked up with Ford, with Ford letting its website visitors bid for new cars through Priceline. Priceline had struggled for a year to extend the model to cars, but found problems in extending the process to high-price items like cars and trucks – insufficient information on the website, unco-operative dealers, confused customers.

Priceline also did deals with credit card issuers, First USA and Discover, Internet provider EarthLink and Net broker E*trade, to provide their services to its airline customers.

In October 1999, Priceline announced a deal with WebHouse Club to make groceries available through the Priceline model – the customer accesses the WebHouse site through Priceline and bids for groceries; if the bid is accepted the customer gets a printout to take to the store for fulfilment. A similar arrangement was operated for the sale of petrol to motorists. Later in 1999, Priceline announced the addition of long-distance phone calls to its products. Car and travel insurance also features in Priceline's plans.

Future areas include cruises and vacation packages. Walker is also looking to extend Priceline into business-to-business markets such as telecommunications, office supplies and IT equipment.

Geographic extension of the Priceline operation

In January 2000, Hutchinson Whampoa Ltd. announced it was partnering with Priceline to expand its services to Asia. Under the agreement both companies invest $10 million to form a company managed by Hutchinson using Priceline's bidding process. Priceline receives a licensing fee from the new company.

In mid-2000, the company announced the launch of Priceline in Europe, in partnership with venture capital firm General Atlantic Partners, with sites planned for Britain, France and Germany. Again the plan was for Priceline to take licencing fees from the new operations. Dennis Malamatinas announced his resignation as CEO of Diageo's Burger King operation to head Priceline.com Europe.

Priceline went live in the UK in February 2001, backed by a large TV advertising campaign, costing $10 million in the first two months, and achieving brand awareness second only to Lastminute.com by May 2001.

The problems

Notwithstanding the fact that it had amassed 6.8 million customers and handled 4 per cent of all airline sales, by mid-2000 Priceline shares had plunged in value – partly along with

'by mid-2000 Priceline shares had plunged in value – partly along with the loss of confidence in Internet shares generally, but also in response to the company's slowing growth'

the loss of confidence in Internet shares generally, but also in response to the company's slowing growth. Walker's 37 per cent stake had fallen in value from $6.7 billion to $1.6 billion. From a peak of $162 in April 1999, by September 2000 the shares were trading at $26.

In October 2000, Priceline announced it was abandoning groceries and petrol. Despite a 2 million customer base, WebHouse could not raise enough cash to become profitable, and did not have suppliers willing to absorb the discounts given to customers – WebHouse ended up in the business of selling dollar bills for 90 cents. In addition, Priceline could not cope with consumer complaints about the operation of the service – some consumers are now suing for fraud. WebHouse has burned up almost $400 million by its closure. The loss of licensing fees to Priceline drove share value down to $5.

The following month Priceline announced the lay-off of 16 per cent of its workforce. In addition, Walker started to lose some of the highly talented senior managers he had attracted to Priceline to manage growth, who wanted no part of a rescue operation – the loss of his star chief financial officer in November 2000 saw shares drop to $3.25. Further lay-offs were announced in December, as well as the abandon-

'Analysts started to urge the company to focus on the travel business and to stop trying to be a Wal-Mart, selling everything possible under its name-your-own-price approach'

ment of plans to open a Priceline site in Japan. Share value drifted down to around $2.00. From its peak value of $21 billion (incredibly $7 billion more than Coca-Cola), Priceline was now worth less than $500 million.

The November 2000 lay-offs included halving the staffing of its car services group, following disappointing results. Analysts started to urge the company to focus on the travel business and to stop trying to be a Wal-Mart, selling everything possible under its name-your-own-price approach.

The star of Priceline TV adverts in the US – William Shatner – had been paid in Priceline shares. As the value of the shares collapsed, Shatner grumpily withdrew from the advertising, saying that he never used Priceline anyway.

The tough questions

The tough questions relate to whether Priceline has a sustainable business model that can achieve profitability.

To begin with, much of Priceline's appeal to investors was its patent – giving it a form of monopoly. In September 1999, apparently not impressed by Priceline's patent protection, Microsoft announced plans to offer reverse auctions of hotel rooms on Expedia, its Web travel site. An analyst at Forrester research commented: 'It's only the patent that is holding the barbarians at the gate. If not for the patent, what would Priceline have to stand on?' Priceline filed a suit against Microsoft in

October 1999, anticipating a two-year wait until the case is heard. In fact, in January 2001, the two companies settled out of court, with Expedia agreeing to pay undisclosed royalties to Priceline. There are also new start-ups like Respond.com which searches travel agents and other suppliers against customer 'bids', but then offers the best deal found – i.e. sellers make an offer against what the customer specifies.

As early as 1999, the *Wall Street Journal* commented: 'Will Priceline shareholders really capture the benefits of this tweak to "yield management" (the well-established practices using information technology to fine-tune prices for maximum efficiency)? Or is it really just a demonstration project for methods that everyone will soon be using?'

There is an issue over whether the Priceline model really offers customers such a great deal on air tickets – you can pick the dates but not the times, so may find you have paid for tickets to fly at inconvenient times, the tickets are non-refundable, and you cannot bid again on the same ticket if you are rejected. The majority of bids are rejected – Priceline claims to complete 40–50 per cent of all 'reasonable' bids (i.e. no more than 30 per cent below published fares). However, because some airlines do not participate, there are growing suggestions that Priceline does not have any better access to cheap seats than a conventional travel agency, or Web-based discounters. Some now suggest that the 'revolution' in pricing really did not live up to its promise, and that 'name-your-own-price' was no more than a marketing gimmick with short-term appeal.

'Some now suggest that the "revolution" in pricing really did not live up to its promise, and that "name-your-own-price" was no more than a marketing gimmick with short-term appeal'

Indeed, it may be that the reverse auction will only work with 'perishable' items – if not sold, the air ticket or hotel room is worthless, but if the car doesn't sell, the dealer waits for another customer to come along. But this raises the question of whether the share that Priceline can take of this business is defensible and profitable. Further, there is a good chance that for most products and most customers, traditional systems of prices posted by sellers are seen as more convenient and fairer to all concerned. Price haggling for groceries and petrol offered slow service and little convenience. In January 2001, a Merrill Lynch Wall Street analyst concluded of Priceline's business that: 'It has become clear…that this is a much smaller business opportunity than we initially hoped'. It may be the real future for Priceline is as a small (but profitable) travel business.

Even then, the idea that the customer really sets the price is misleading. In reality, Priceline negotiates with participating airlines for access to unsold seats at special prices (which may actually not be that 'special'). Those prices, which the airlines can revise several times a day, go into Priceline's database, before any bid is received. When a bid arrives, the computer system checks for a match and accepts or rejects the bid. In other words, the bid is accepted only if it meets or exceeds a price previously specified by the airline. In this sense, customers may 'name' prices, but the airlines still 'set' them. Since Priceline keeps its prices of available tickets secret, the

'Some clients have renamed the business "Priceline.scam" on finding they could have got tickets cheaper from ordinary ticket consolidators'

real value proposition seems to be that the customer gets the chance to pay more than the asking price! Some clients have renamed the business 'Priceline.scam' on finding they could have got tickets cheaper from ordinary ticket consolidators, as well as enjoying the convenience of specifying the airline, the time of flying, avoiding stopovers, getting frequent flyer miles, and so on. Walker protests: 'It's never that we've got the "best" price, it's that it's "your" price.'

Maybe as a result, the University of Michigan's American Customer Satisfaction Index in 2000 rated Priceline very low, even among Internet companies. There may be traps inherent in the business model: most bidders do not get the ticket for which they have bid; many get a ticket, but at undesirable times; and many are likely to be dissatisfied with having to accept whatever ticket meets their price. If there are no ways of improving on these problems, Priceline may be highly vulnerable to new competitors who offer low-price tickets with more customer choice and freedom.

'Priceline may be highly vulnerable to new competitors who offer low-price tickets with more customer choice and freedom'

Late in 1999, there were signs of friction between the airlines affiliated to Priceline. Accusing Delta of limiting access to other airlines' tickets out of Atlanta flights on Priceline (Atlanta is dominated by Delta), Northwest started to offer cheap flights from Atlanta through its own website in retaliation. In fact, Priceline is increasingly vulnerable to the airlines launching their own excess capacity service and excluding Priceline. Certainly, by late 2000 the airlines in the US were offering large discounts direct to customers. The launch of Hotwire.com in October 2000, aiming to provide more choice than Priceline, was backed by six major carriers, including United Airlines and American. Hotwire finds the cheapest ticket and asks the customer if s/he wants it. Analysts suggest this is a much stronger value proposition than Priceline's. The airlines backing Hotwire are the same on which Priceline depends for its tickets. Similarly, in 2000, major hotel groups were actively examining ways to offer unbooked hotel rooms through their own collaborative Web page. Walker accepts that reaching secure profitability relies on developing out of the travel business, and its wafer-thin margins into other areas.

Lastly, in common with other dot.coms, Priceline has accumulated enormous losses in its first two years of operation, and has yet to deliver a profitable quarter. By September 2000, Priceline had accumulated losses of $1.2 billion, and was still postponing its first promised profitable quarter.

However, there is a chance that Priceline's air ticket business could still be profitable. On average, Priceline earns around $35 in profit and fees on a ticket selling for $215 – by comparison, a conventional travel agent earns $10 on the same ticket. In effect, Priceline buys heavily discounted tickets for unsold seats, and then marks them up, earning a gross margin of 9–12 per cent, compared to the travel agent's 5 per cent commission on a ticket sale. The main reason Priceline has failed to achieve a profit is that its expenses are too high – it has invested its gross profits from air tickets, and the hundreds of millions raised in stock offerings, into largely failed efforts to expand. To expand its business model into new markets, Priceline has bought expensive computer systems, hired software programmers and spent lavishly on advertising. The result is the following calculations:

Price of air ticket (example)		$215
Priceline gross margin		$ 35
Expenses:		
Credit card fees and outsourced		
customer service	$13.55	
Advertising	$ 8.93	
Employee costs	$14.70	
Total expenses		$37.18
Net profit (loss)		$ (2.18)

As the company cuts its workforce and advertising costs, it has a good chance of moving into profit on air tickets.

However, Chairman Richard S. Braddick remained committed to growth by adding new products not reducing costs further. By May 2001, the company was cutting back other activities to focus on its travel business.

Walker walks – the beginning of the end or the end of the beginning?

In January 2001, it was announced that founder and largest shareholder, Jay Walker, was stepping down from the board of Priceline, to focus on rebuilding his new-business incubator, Walker Digital Corp. – Walker Digital had laid off most of its staff at the end of 2000. At this stage, Priceline shares were trading at around $1. May 2001 saw the unexpected departure of Patrick Schulman, group chief executive, only months after the resignation of Heidi Miller, the chief financial officer.

Points to ponder

1 The big issue is whether Priceline really has a business model that will provide a secure market position and profitability, or whether it is just another dot.com that will disappear. A lot depends on whether you think the business model delivers customer value or not.

2 The conclusion reached about the robustness of the Priceline customer value proposition will probably depend on which customer and which markets you have in mind – can this business model extend or is it just a way of selling excess capacity for airlines?

3 Another question is whether Priceline points the way to a new type of value-based strategy – it is driven by price, it puts price choices in customers' hands (to a degree), it is anti-brand loyalty, and makes a nonsense of things like store, airline and hotel customer loyalty programmes (and the huge investments that have gone into them). Is this, perhaps, a perfect strategy for the 'Dealers' on our customer loyalty matrix (see p. 29)?

4 Is Priceline doomed to wither under the 'curse of the innovator' – having paid the cost of establishing a limited form of 'dynamic pricing', will the real benefits go to others who amend and refine the model, and take Priceline's market?

Sources: David Leonhardt (1998), 'Make a Bid, But Don't Pack Your Bags', *Business Week*, 1 June, 164. 'Business: It Was My Idea', *The Economist*, 15 August 1998. Leigh Buchanan (1998), 'A Business Model of One's Own', *Inc.*, November, 82–85. Denny Hatch (1998), 'Direct Marketer of the Year: Jay Walker', *Target Marketing*, December. Martha Brannigan and Carrick Mollenkamp (1999), 'Delta's Stake in Priceline Poses Challenge for Airline', *Wall Street Journal Europe*, 14 June. Peter Elkind (1999), 'The Hype is Big, Really Big, at Priceline', *Fortune*, 6 September, 193–201. Nick Wingfield (1999), 'Priceline.Com Brings Suit Over Patent', *Wall Street Journal Europe*, 15 October. Pamela L. Moore (2000), 'Name Your Price – For Everything?', *Business Week*, 17 April, 72–78. Adrian Michaels (2000), 'Knocked Down But Not Out', *Financial Times*, 23 August. Heather Green (2000), 'Letting the Masses Name Their Price', *Business Week*, 18 September, EB44. Andrew Edgecliffe-Johnson (2000), 'Priceline Under Pressure From Rivals, Clients', *Financial Times*, 3 October. Carol J. Loomis (2000), 'Inside Jay Walker's House of Cards', *Fortune*, 13 November, 127–38. Patrick Barta (2000), 'Web Firms Underwhelm – Survey Finds That Customer Satisfaction in the US is Moderate and Spotty', *Wall Street Journal*, 28 November. Andrew Cave (2000), 'Beam Me Up, Says Sore Shatner', *Daily Telegraph*, 13 December. Pamela M. Moore and Monica Roman (2001), 'Jay Walker: Walking Away From Priceline', *Business Week*, 15 January, 44. Dominic Rushe (2001), 'Dotcom Travel Agent Heads for Europe', *Sunday Times*, 21 January. Julia Angwin (2001), 'Is There a Way to Save the Web Wonders?', *Wall Street Journal*, 26 January.

Case 5   Dyson Appliances*
The man who cleaned up

James Dyson, 53, is famed as the inventor of the bagless vacuum cleaner, which carries his name, and he runs what has been one of the fastest growing manufacturing businesses in Britain. In 2001 his personal wealth was estimated at £700 million, mainly accounted for by his personal ownership of his two companies, Dyson Appliances and Dyson Research – in 1999, those two companies made profits of £47 million on sales of £381 million. In 2000, Dyson was paid £14.4 million in salary and dividends. He is regarded by many as somewhat eccentric – he works tie-less and sock-less surrounded by as much purple as possible, and there are two fundamental rules for his employees: no ties and no smoking.

Inventors rarely make money by setting up factories to manufacture the products they have invented, but this is exactly what Dyson has done.

The growth and development of Dyson's business is characterized by creativity and 'rule-breaking', but also a continuing struggle in his fight against his much larger competitors. Basically, Dyson has been successively laughed at, exploited, ripped off and sued by big business, along the route to his current success. He notes: 'Business is about people in suits whose main concern is to maximize profit and to shaft people'.

> 'The growth and development of Dyson's business is characterized by creativity and "rule-breaking", but also a continuing struggle in his fight against his much larger competitors'

Dyson's story

James Dyson graduated in design from the Royal College of Art in 1970, and his first job was with Rotork engineering in Bath, working on the design of landing craft, for a salary of £10 000. His first big gamble was to abandon this job in 1974 in favour of a product of his own design, the Ballbarrow – a brightly coloured plastic garden wheelbarrow with a big red ball at the front to replace the traditional wheel. (Even the Design Council had refused its sticker for this product regarding it as too garish for gardens.) The new venture quickly accumulated debts of £200 000, but moved into profitability, and in 1978 Dyson invented the Trolleyball – an innovative type of boat launcher with ball wheels.

---

*This case material has been prepared on the basis of discussions with industry executives and published secondary sources.

However, in 1979, jealous directors sacked Dyson from the company built around his inventions.

It was around this time, in the 1970s, that Dyson had seen a cyclone extractor on top of a sawmill – indeed, he broke into the sawmill at night to photograph and study the strange cone-shaped device. Impressed with the cyclone device, and with time on his hands after his sacking, Dyson experimented with fitting smaller extractors to carpet sweepers. The idea of a new type of vacuum cleaner came to him because he found that a new bag in his conventional cleaner clogged up with the first dust that went in, so even the most powerful motor achieved little suction after that point. He says that the design challenge was easy: 'Nobody had bothered to change the product for 100 years – the current vacuum cleaner has a fan motor, a cloth bag, and a nozzle – exactly the same as when it was invented in 1891'. In fact, he spent the period 1979–1984 developing the new cleaner – reputedly going through 5127 prototypes on the way. The result was the Dyson bagless, cyclone cleaner, and a £50 000 debt for Dyson.

THE DYSON CYCLONE VACUUM CLEANER

'The world's first bagless vacuum cleaner – 100 per cent suction, 100 per cent of the time'

With distinctive transparent bodywork and styling, the Dyson cleaner claims 'No bag. No loss of suction.' It uses powerful dual cyclone technology to suck dirt from carpets – essentially using centrifugal force – and filters the dirt from the air. Because there is no accumulating debris in a bag, clogging things up, the level of suction remains constant.

Traditional cleaners use an electric motor to drive a fan, which draws in air and dirt from the surface being cleaned. The dirt-laden air is then pumped into a bag – being porous, the bag allows the air through but traps the dust. However, as the machine is used, the pores in the bag become blocked with dirt, reducing airflow and the cleaner's efficiency, until the bag is changed.

By contrast, with the Dyson technology, the motor spins the air into two nested drums, creating a miniature artificial 'tornado' – the outer cyclone spins at 200 mph and the inner cyclone at 900 mph. As the air is spinning, heavy particles (dust and dirt) are forced to the edge of the drum. The air is passed through a shroud, while lighter particles are retained in the outer cyclone. The air then enters the inner cyclone, where the flow is reversed, accelerated and subjected to centrifugal forces to remove smaller particles of dirt. The user sees the dirt accumulating in the canister and can empty when ready. There is no bag to change or to be purchased, though the filter does have to be replaced.

However, Dyson then spent the years from 1982 until 1993 actually getting the product onto the market. Initially, he took the new technology to existing manufacturers – he was turned down flat. Hoover belatedly recognized that this was a serious mistake, but at the time the manufacturers were making large profits from selling the waste bags required by conventional cleaners, and were not attracted to the idea of killing off this lucrative market.

'at the time the manufacturers were making large profits from selling the waste bags required by conventional cleaners, and were not attracted to the idea of killing off this lucrative market'

At the same time, Dyson was approaching banks for funding to establish his own manufacturing company for the new cleaner, but was also turned down flat. The banks saw him as an impractical designer incapable of running a manufacturing business (notwithstanding the fact he had already done just that for the Ballbarrow).

'The banks saw him as an impractical designer incapable of running a manufacturing business'

Dyson took the gamble of getting patents registered in every country that he could afford, and then trawled the world looking for licensees to manufacture the product. In 1984, he made his first licence agreement in the US, followed by an agreement for Japan. Both deals brought in cash to clear debts. In the US, Dyson does not control the operation but takes 5 per cent of sales from the Fantom, Fury and Lightening cleaners. In the case of Japan, Dyson designed a special version of the cyclone cleaner, which now sells a quarter of a million units a year. The Japanese product started off retailing at an amazing price of £800, later increased to £1300 – it was positioned as a design object, a status symbol, for style-conscious Japanese buyers.

Finally, Dyson managed to impress a lender, and Lloyds Bank provided a £600 000 loan on the basis of little more than a promise. Together with sale of the perpetual rights to the patent in Japan for £1 million and putting his family home up as security, this provided the capital for Dyson to start his own manufacturing in Britain at Chippenham in Wiltshire.

Within two years of launch, and despite its high price tag – around £200 – Dyson's invention became the best-selling vacuum cleaner in Britain, leap-frogging the conventional manufacturers, such as Hoover, Electrolux, Panasonic and Miele. By the end of the 1990s, Dyson had more than half the British market by value and about one-third by volume. His manufacturing operation was set up to survive by moving 10 000 cleaners a year, and by this time was producing 9000 a day. Profits of £200 000 in 1993 had reached £20 million a year. In 1999, sales had reached £200 million, with a 2000 target of £280 million.

Cynics at the time said few consumers would pay the price for Dyson's machine, and at best the market would be small. Despite its high price and the maturity of the market, it was clear that the customer would pay more for a better designed product with better performance claims. Indeed, one of the earliest batches of Dyson cleaners was sold as a lifestyle item in the shops of Paul Smith, the fashion clothes designer.

By the late 1990s, Dyson had established his first overseas subsidiary in Australia (because he had a friend there), followed by operations in France and Germany, as well as distribution agreements in a large number of other countries.

Dyson's business has, however, been plagued by competitive actions, while he has succeeded in building a highly distinctive management approach and innovative new product development programme.

The competitive situation – a good clean fight or a dust-up?

In his book, Dyson summarizes the competitive problem as he sees it: 'It's a salutary lesson to learn that when you've overcome the problems of launching a new product and it meets with some success, you have only won the first battle in a war. Once you start to threaten the established multinationals, the big boys will come gunning for you.'

The British vacuum cleaner market had been dominated since the 1950s by the conventional technology of firms like Hoover and Electrolux. Hoover had for years held 50 per cent of the upright cleaner market, and saw this halved by Dyson. While tied to a technology which began to look obsolete, the established players' reaction to Dyson was, first, to try to keep him out of the channels of distribution – leaning unsuccessfully on retailers like Comet to persuade them not to stock the product, then attacking Dyson's product claims in court, and finally bringing out imitative products using a version of Dyson's cyclone technology.

Even at the outset, Dyson's business came close to being destroyed by an expensive court battle with the US direct-seller, Amway. Amway had ruthlessly reneged on a license agreement and secretly started manufacturing its own version of the cyclone cleaner, without paying Dyson royalties. After an expensive court battle lasting five years, Dyson settled out of court for an undisclosed cash sum. Amway profited from its actions, but Dyson could not afford to fight the case at that time. He also had a major battle with the US company Philips, contracted by Dyson to assemble plastic mouldings. Philips got government funding to build a new factory with Dyson as its only customer and then announced huge price rises. Dyson resisted and cancelled the contract. In retaliation, Philips tried hard to put him out of business. This affair stimulated Dyson's move to its own factory in Malmesbury in 1995.

Dyson has been sued by almost all the established manufacturers over its advertising, and claims of defamation, disputing the superior effectiveness of his product. In 1997, Dyson faced legal action by Philips, Electrolux, Bosch, Siemens, Miele and Nilfisk – all objecting to his advertising claims that their vacuum cleaners lose suction when the bag becomes clogged. Dyson threatened to counter-sue on the grounds his ads were telling the truth. By 1998, Miele, the Eurpoean market leader, had launched an aggressive advertising campaign to deny Dyson's claims, and demanded that Dyson's German ads be withdrawn. The battle continued into 1998, with Miele running tests on BBC's Watchdog. By this stage, the Advertising Authority had upheld 12 out of 15 complaints about Dyson's adverts, and Dyson had reached stalemate in its court case with Electrolux. However, the Advertising Standards Authority upheld Dyson's claims against Electrolux's advertising, and the German court found for Dyson against Siemens' advertising claims.

However, the most significant competitive attacks in the UK came from the displaced market leader Hoover. Hoover had problems other than Dyson, and was sold by the US owners Maytag to the Italian firm Candy in 1992. While joining others in attacking Dyson's advertising, in 1999 Hoover launched its own bagless cleaner – the Triple Vortex – accepting that Dyson had broken the mould for the industry. Dyson was not impressed by the suggestion that imitation is the sincerest form of flattery, and sued for copyright infringement, and in October 2000 was awarded £200 000 towards costs, and Hoover was ordered to stop sales of the product until Dyson's patent expires in two years. Dyson is looking for multi-million pound damages also, but Hoover is appealing. However, the court did not stop Hoover going to market with a single cyclone cleaner under the name Vortex, backed by a £4 million advertising spend. In the meantime, Hoover is advertising Vortex as 'the most powerful bagless cylinder cleaner', and other manufacturers like Rowenta are marketing their own bagless cleaners at lower prices than Dyson.

> *'the most significant competitive attacks in the UK came from the displaced market leader Hoover'*

An innovative management approach to managing innovation

James Dyson has won numerous awards for design, invention and entrepreneurship, and has a high profile in the UK – he was awarded a CBE in 1997, and throughout the 1990s and early 2000s he has rarely been out of the headlines as the defender of his product and critic of his competitors. Dyson does not like being described as a 'businessman', preferring to be seen as a designer, an inventor and a champion for British manufacturing industry. When people comment on his company's financial success, his response is 'Oh, vulgar, vulgar, vulgar, vulgar, vulgar', but concedes 'The beauty of making a lot of money is that it allows you to do more expensive research and development that will help you to make even better products.'

Dyson dresses casually at work, and likes as much of his surroundings as possible to be purple – he has actually found

> *'The beauty of making a lot of money is that it allows you to do more expensive research and development that will help you to make even better products'*

'I am totally product-oriented. If our product is wonderful and if we look after our people, including our retailers and our customers, the business looks after itself . . . This place isn't about making money. It is about making products'

somewhere that sells him purple desert boots. He prizes youth and new ideas – the average age of his staff is around 25, and he likes to recruit direct from universities not from other employers, to avoid people contaminated by conventional companies. His staff wear their own clothes to work – suits are the uniform of the enemy. He has upwards of 400 people working in R&D projects, out of a workforce of around 2000, and he elects to spend at least half his time with the R&D teams. His annual R&D spend is in excess of £30 million. Dyson's explanation and reasoning is that 'I am totally product-oriented. If our product is wonderful and if we look after our people, including our retailers and our customers, the business looks after itself . . . This place isn't about making money. It is about making products.'

All Dyson's staff, whatever their function, spend their first day assembling a cleaner, which they can then buy for £25. Dyson wants everyone to know how the product works. However, they all then get to eat at the company café – Dyson hates canteens – run by a former antiques dealer and serving food like rocket salad, pesto and fusilli, and smoked mackerel pate. They sit on £400 designer chairs while filling their faces.

Dyson summarizes his interest in a product-led manufacturing business: 'I am very interested in the holistic approach in which you have designers,

'I am very interested in the holistic approach in which you have designers, sales and production people all working alongside each other in a creative unit'

sales and production people all working alongside each other in a creative unit'. That, he believes, remains the route to turning plastic granules into household products that people find useful. He is unimpressed by advertising and brands in particular: 'Britain is obsessed by brands. I've never believed in all that. It is so depressing that people buy something because of a brand name.' Dyson's advertising is created in-house, not through an agency – though this does not prevent the company producing comparative ads to its competitors' displeasure (numerous complaints have been upheld against Dyson's advertising).

The company faces the problem of maintaining its culture while growing fast. However, when challenged that his informal, open, creative company will become a suit-wearing bureaucracy as it becomes bigger, Dyson says he will avoid this by sub-dividing the business into new sections around new products as they come along. However, he is prepared to take action to maintain the business the way he likes it – in 1995 he changed most of the board, bringing in directors from other businesses, and in 1999 the chief executive of Dyson Appliances was sacked after four months in that post, leading to an out-of-court damages settlement.

His experiences have left Dyson with a continuing grudge against the patent system. He points out that patents and renewals are expensive to obtain and enforce. For example, one patent in the US cost him $100 000, and to enforce it, you have to take the plagiarist to court. He pays nearly £1 million a year in patent renewal fees, as well as nearly £100 000 a year in application fees, and regards this as iniquitous. He has twice taken his complaint about patent fees as a tax on entrepreneurs to the European Court of Human Rights, on behalf of inventors, but without success. He plans a third attempt.

The Dyson new product trail

Dyson has invested heavily in teams of young designers investigating what other products he can introduce to make money by taking market share away from the multinationals. His policy is not to introduce a product unless he is confident that it will beat anything the competition has to offer, and he says 'Big appliances with a big price tag are a logical step for us'. Projects include the 'crumb-free' toaster. But he also believes that 'We won't succeed by emulating Panasonic, Sharp or any of the others.'

The first outcome of Dyson's R&D strategy was the launch in 1999 of the DC06 robot vacuum cleaner, involving an investment of £16.5 million. The goal is sales of £2 billion by 2005.

DYSON'S DC06 ROBOT CLEANER

The DC06 is less than nine inches high and fifteen inches long, but has 50 sensors and three on-board computers, and is pre-programmed to clean a room in an outward spiral, using its electronics to avoid obstacles (even pets). Its systematic coverage of the room offers superior cleaning compared to the human meandering around the main areas with a conventional cleaner. It runs on powerful rechargeable batteries, and uses the established Dyson dual cyclone technology. It has three coloured lights to indicate: blue, when it is happy and working as normal; green, when it has to move round an obstacle; and red, when it is distressed or threatened, e.g. by a pet or child. It is also smart enough not to commit suicide by plunging down the stairs. The machine is operated by five buttons, not a complex digital display. The launch price was £2500.

In spite of teething problems with the new product that delayed its full launch to 2000, Dyson argues that 'At the moment people vacuum their homes as infrequently as possible – only when there is some dirt to pick up. With the new robots, they will be able to use their cleaners virtually all the time, keeping their houses perfectly clean without breaking sweat.

In the same way as people are happier when they have clean clothes, the innovation will make people feel better about their homes and themselves.' Dyson's vision is that the robot cleaner will do to the conventional vacuum what the automatic washing machine did to the mangle and spin-tub washing machine. Dyson is clearly interested in more than an analogy about washing machines. In 2000, Dyson announced a twin-drum 'Contrarotator' washing machine.

The Dyson Contrarotator

The result of a £25 million four-year project, the innovative Dyson washing machine replaces the conventional single tub with two concentric drums rotating in opposite directions, to replicate the 'kneading' action of hand-washing in which clothes rub against each other – the research suggests hand-washing gets clothes cleaner than conventional automatic washing machines. The launch selling prices vary between £1000 and £1200, depending on model. The product reached the market in December 2000, after a £13 million expansion at Dyson's Malmesbury factory.

DYSON'S CONTRAROTATOR

The machine that does the washing 'by hand'

The Dyson machine replicates the action of hand-washing of clothes by having two sections of drum that rotate in opposite directions. The effect is that the washing is flexed rather than rolled, opening up the fibres to the detergent, allowing the washing cycle to be shorter. The drums are also larger than on conventional machines, allowing a shorter and more efficient spin cycle. The machine is constructed from polycarbonate, to avoid rust problems.

The Dyson innovation was greeted with a mixture of scepticism and hostility by the conventional suppliers in the £14 billion a year washing machine market. A spokesperson for Electrolux said: 'It's just another way of moving clothes through water ... But Mr Dyson will find he is entering a highly competitive business'.

There are certainly other new technologies underway in the washing machine business. Most of the large companies have invested large R&D budgets into new concepts like 'waterless' machines that clean clothes using ultrasound or liquid carbon dioxide – currently found to be less effective than water because they release dirt from clothes, but then let it back onto the fabric. General Electric's Wizard is a new breed of 'ultra-fast' washing action machine – from spilling coffee on your shirt to getting the clean dry shirt out of the machine in thirty minutes. Maytag's Neptune senses the load and adapts the washing programme accordingly. Monotag Industries announced their Titan washer at the same time as Dyson's machine – the Titan takes a 40 per cent larger load than conventional machines, can be opened mid-cycle without spilling water, and has a removable clothes basket, selling for around £600. However, the Titan has been plagued with technical problems and the launch delayed. Ariston, in Italy, has announced a washing machine that can be operated over the Internet or from a mobile phone, as well as having faults diagnosed through the Internet link.

Early in 2001, the Consumers' Association carried out tests suggesting that the Dyson machine did not perform as well as claimed – suggestions rejected by Dyson on the grounds of the inappropriateness of the tests used, which favour conventional machines. They claimed that a Bosch machine priced at £480 was superior to Dyson's £1200 machine. Dyson took out full-page ads in the national press in January 2001 to accuse the Consumers' Association of misleading the public.

Points to ponder

1 If James Dyson does not believe in advertising, marketing, business or profit, how come he is worth more than half a billion pounds? How come he was able to build this business with a premium priced product and almost no advertising?
2 Is Dyson an example of a company creating a new market space by breaking free from conventional competition?
3 Is Dyson an example of a value-based strategy, which casts doubt on the strength of conventional brand and relationship marketing?
4 What lessons can we learn from Dyson about the management of creativity in strategy and the integration of functions into a unified process of going to market?

Sources: Tom Rubython (1997), 'Whipping up a Storm with a Cyclone', *Sunday Business*, 28 June. Lucy Kellaway (1997), 'Sweeping Convention Aside', *Financial Times*, 31 July. James Dyson (1997), *Against The Odds*, London: Orion Business Books. Natalie Graham (1998), 'Inventor Cleans Up With Profits', *Sunday Times*, 1 March. Rufus Olins (1998), 'Dyson Aims to Clean Up With New Appliances', *Sunday Times*, 10 May. Jon Rees (1999), 'Hoover Aims to Sweep Aside Dyson Challenge', *Sunday Business*, 23 May. Catherine Wheatley (1999), 'The Man Who Cleaned Up', *Sunday Business*, 18 July. 'Who Cleans Up', *The Business*, 14 October 2000. Lucinda Kemeny (2000), 'Dyson and Strong Pound Put the Wind Up Hoover', *Sunday Times*, 15 October. Robert Uhlig (2000), 'Dyson Beats His Drum

For Washing Machine', *Daily Telegraph*, 3 November. Peter Marsh (2000), 'Back to Basics for a Washtub Revolution', *Financial Times*, 8 November. Peter Marsh (2001), 'Pioneer Hopes Robot Will Put Happiness Back Into the Housework', *Financial Times*, 11 July. Robert Uhlig (2001), 'Why *Which?* Won't Crown Dyson the King of Spin', *Daily Telegraph*, 4 January. 'Dyson Chief in Secret Settlement', *Financial Times*, 26 April 2001.

PART III

What Going to Market is About:

Defining the Strategic Pathway

CHAPTER 7

Market strategy:

Customer focus and market sensing

> If you can keep your head
> when all those about you are losing theirs –
>
> you are simply not aware of the real situation.

From the somewhat acid (though well-deserved) comments about how badly companies treat their customers, in Chapter 2, we established that there is a major imperative for management in all types of organization to focus better on customer needs – to be market-led, to care for the customer, to create the value that matters to the customer, and so on. For example, one report has recently suggested that 'customer-centric' companies are 60 per cent more profitable than those who are not, and have lower operating costs[1]. However, what is far less clear is how managers can evaluate and monitor, let alone change, the performance of their organizations, in terms of achieving effective and productive customer focus. That is, even if we agreed on what we should be doing about this issue, there remains the problem of how we can actually do it. The achievement of the much sought-after customer-focused organization has proved elusive (though not impossible). Two things are clear, however:

- Achieving real customer focus normally needs more than management 'say so' or edict – however exalted and prestigious the managers in question may be.
- No-one ever said it would be easy (or if they did, they never tried it themselves) – there are no 'plug-in' quick fixes for this issue.

'Customer focus is not just about better customer service and being more responsive, it is about understanding the customer and desperately trying to anticipate and meet customer needs'

There is another more important point that seems to escape people who scoff at 'customer care' and 'customer focus', and such like notions. Customer focus is not just about better customer service and being more responsive, it is about understanding the customer and desperately trying to anticipate and meet customer needs – how else can you know which services to improve and what adds value in the customer's eyes. That is why this chapter discusses these two related issues together – customer focus and market sensing – because they are both about our capacity to learn and provide superior value. I see this as the first step in developing a strategic pathway.

First, we can put on the agenda a number of ideas, things to try and approaches to consider, in the pursuit of customer focus. None of these are total solutions, but the evidence suggests that each can achieve some good things for organizations if used thoroughly and appropriately. Then we can turn to the market sensing or understanding issue.

The customer relationship scale

As a starting point, Figure 7.1 suggests that we can see customer focus and our ability to understand the marketplace varying on a

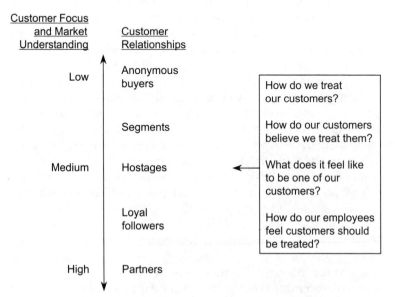

Figure 7.1 The customer relationship scale

scale, where different positions on the scale are associated with different types of customer relationships.

At one end of the scale, there is little genuine, real customer focus. In this situation, we talk of 'the market' or 'clients' or 'accounts' as some kind of anonymous entities who we hope will buy and consume our products and services. Unfortunately, anonymous entities and 'markets' are not what buy products and services – people do, and they are called customers, and that is normally how they wish to be treated.

You may get away with operating at this end of the scale – particularly if, for a time, demand outstrips supply in your industry, if you have a monopoly of some kind for a while, if you have a radical product/service innovation which only you can supply, or if you are just cheaper than anyone else can be at the time. But remember – never expect loyalty, commitment or real satisfaction from customers you treat badly, and do not expect them to stay when a better alternative appears.

The chances are that what you know about customers will come from market research – surveys, focus groups, and the like. It will be crude and out-of-date information, because that is the nature of market research.

> *Question*:   How do market researchers take their exercise?
>
> *Answer*:   They jump to conclusions.

One move down the scale towards customer focus is probably where we find most marketing companies today. Some effort is made to identify and target customers as members of key market segments and/or key accounts. At least here we have some idea who customers are, and introduce some degree of customer focus into sales and market operations, though often little more than that in reality. We probably do better market research into customer opinions and attitudes.

In the middle of the scale, we see what most modern marketing seeks to achieve – 'taking hostages'. We focus our efforts on winning 'loyalty' through customer 'satisfaction', but by doing our best to take away customer freedom. We saw in Chapter 2 that we can think of hostage-taking through: airline and credit card air miles programmes; consumer and trade 'collectables' and coupons; machines designed to work only with one supplier's materials; the invalidation of warranties and guarantees if the customer dares to use competitors' components or maintenance services.

This may make some sense in markets where volume is critical, switching costs are low for customers, and we really cannot think of any better way to win repeat business. But, ultimately, hostages want their freedom, and 'loyalty' is a temporary illusion. The saving grace is that we may start gathering information from these 'loyalty' schemes that is worth its weight in gold.

One further move down the scale suggests we are more focused on customers and see them as 'loyal followers'. This differs from hostage-taking in that we try to win our customers' hearts and minds, rather than shackling them to the product or service. The goal is similar, but the means are more subtle. Most 'lifestyle' or image-based advertising seeks to achieve this effect, as do many programmes of customer care and customer calling.

The extreme on the scale is where we see customers as partners. This approach has been widely advocated in relationship marketing and strategic alliance or network theories (see pp. 508–19), but has proved to have more limited appeal among practical managers who see little way of implementing this in their markets. The biggest attraction is that we start to 'know' our customers and how their needs are changing, instead of just collecting information about them.

'we are likely to need to accommodate different viewpoints in this evaluation; our views of how our customers are treated may be very different from customers' views of how they are treated!'

One starting point in getting to grips with the customer focus issue is to discuss this scale with people – colleagues, employees, distributors, even customers – to figure out where our organization is and where it would like to be. The critical questions raised in Figure 7.1 suggest we are likely to need to accommodate different viewpoints in this evaluation; our views of how our customers are treated may be very different from customers' views of how they are treated!

If the customer relationship scale is a way of putting a handle on the customer focus in a particular company, then the approaches from which we can choose the most appropriate include:

- learning to listen to customers and to respond to what they say;
- obsessing over customers – what some call building the 'cult of the customer' in the company; and
- building and sustaining a customer-focused culture in the company.

If we were able to successfully do all those things, we would indeed have a customer-focused organization. Some companies succeed in doing just this.

Listening to customers and learning

Perhaps one of the hardest things we have to do in building customer focus is simply to learn to listen better to customers. This is not about sophisticated surveys and tests or huge computer databases, just about listening and being prepared to learn. Besides, we saw in Chapter 2 that we get customer satisfaction scores at satisfied/very satisfied when we do the surveys, but the same customers still defect to the competition. Indeed, the issue is really market 'sensing' or understanding. If you can find better ways of listening to customers, the pay-off may be enormous. The surprise again and again is that customers will actually talk to you and help you learn how to be better if you are just prepared to listen.

'one of the hardest things we have to do in building customer focus is simply to learn to listen better to customers'

'the issue is really market "sensing" or understanding. If you can find better ways of listening to customers, the pay-off may be enormous'

Storytelling

Some major organizations have adopted storytelling as a way of listening and learning – not as silly as it sounds because it comes out of the insights of Gerald Zaltman at Harvard Business School. The goal is to find out the things that are missed by the conventional surveys and focus groups, and the method is to get real-life stories for customers about how they behave and what they really feel[2]. Some of the results are impressive:

- Kimberley-Clark has reinvented the baby's disposable nappy business. The paradox in this market is that every time a baby graduates to underpants from nappies, you lose the customer forever. The issue was would people buy 'training pants' – a transition product that looks like underpants but works like a nappy. K-C sent a small team of individuals (many themselves in the midst of the trauma of toilet training their own children) into consumers' homes to hear real-life stories. What they discovered was that the real stress in toilet training came from parents' feelings of failure, and dread of someone looking at their child in horror and asking 'Oh, is your child *still* in nappies? Nappies are an indicator of child development, not just a waste-disposal product. This is what really matters to young parents, but it is *not* what they say in conventional surveys and focus groups. K-C launched Huggies Pull-Ups training pants in 1991, and by the time the competition caught up they had a $400 million business.

- Intuit is a computer software company, whose worldwide success with Quicken personal finance software grew out of listening to customers' problems in balancing their cheque-book, let alone getting a computer to do it for them. Chairman, Scott Cook, says 'People don't buy technology. They buy products that improve their lives.' He concluded that personal finance software that could only be operated by the computer-literate 12-year-old in the family would just get turned off. They have gone to a lot of trouble to listen to customers. They have 'usability labs' where non-users come in and try to make the product work. They have a programme called 'Follow Me Home' – a kind of formalized stalking when employees go home with customers, have a tour of their cheques and bills boxes, and look over their shoulders while they use the Intuit software. They also leave a cassette recorder so when it all goes wrong the customer can hit the Record button and say what happened. Customer stories are the basis for product improve-ment and the creation of highly user-friendly software, and also new products – they found that small business owners were using Quicken home finance software to keep their business accounts. The product was not designed for this purpose, but people preferred it to conventional business accounting software that forces you to learn double-entry bookkeeping, when you don't need to. Today, Intuit's 'Quick-Books' is used in thousands of small businesses around the world.

- Even the mighty IBM is prepared to listen and learn – customer feedback showed one business unit that less than 1 per cent of customers preferred to make contact with the company by sales calls, but 82 per cent wanted more regular telephone contact. What customers said they wanted (and now get) actually saves IBM money.

'when was the last time anyone in your company came back with some "war stories" from customers and got taken seriously?'

This is not high technology stuff. But, when was the last time anyone in your company came back with some 'war stories' from customers and got taken seriously?

Watching customers

Other companies have discovered you can learn just by watching the people who set the standards. The fancy name is generating 'holistic customer insights', but it's really just about watching and learning:

- The power tools company Black & Decker achieves its innovative product designs and features by watching people using the tools and asking them about the experience and what would make it better (in the context, of course, of the well-known male bonding ritual with power tools).
- At Wiremold, a 'low-tech' producer of wire management systems (to route wiring through buildings), they have coined a wonderful phrase to describe how the voice of the customer drove their highly successful new product development and launch: they say 'we designed it with our ears' – their product design comes from listening and watching and learning.
- At Sony, marketing innovative consumer electronic products, they have an even simpler logic: they say our employees are our customers, so let's give them the product to take home and test, and then they can tell us about it.
- At Nike, the business is not really sports clothing, it is fashion – so they employ 'trend observers', to follow and observe the setters of trends in fashion – urban youth, sports stars, pop stars, and so on.

This is simple stuff, but the evidence is few of us do it, or do it well . . .

Meeting customers

There is actually a big learning experience for most of us not just in meeting customers, but meeting them in the real world, where the product or service is consumed; this is likely to tell you things you will not otherwise learn:

- Talking to passengers actually on the long-haul flight or waiting in the airport will tell you how angry and frustrated they are at their loss of control over the process and what really irritates them, more so than nice controlled interviews later when the flight is just a (bad) memory.
- Just talking to people walking round the supermarket will tell you more about what they like or don't like than questionnaire surveys will.
- One bank went for a glass-wall design for its offices for customer contact staff – the design won prizes, and was received favourably in market tests. The bank thought it made staff more approachable – in the actual event customers felt robbed of their privacy and were very uncomfortable, and were prepared to say so when asked[3].

- Computers for word processing are not used in quiet controlled laboratories, they are used in noisy, busy offices where interruptions are constant and people want things done fast – that is the environment where you can find out what value means to the customer!

More generally, many sales people will tell you that if you are going to do a deal with someone, then it is important to meet them socially, and to eat and drink with them. Many of us may be tempted to write this off as an excuse for sales to build a big entertainment budget! But if the people who earn their living by doing deals and building relationships tell us that socializing with customers matters – perhaps we should listen.

This may be most obvious in the business-to-business setting. For example, a key aspect of implementing a vertical marketing strategy with one manufacturer was that the company was not organized around markets, it was structured around products, and that was the way managers liked things. There was much resistance to an industry sector-based strategy which cut across different product departments, to put together the product range customers wanted. One of the most influential ways that this resistance was reduced was simply by organizing events and social functions around the target industrial sectors (actually in the form of training seminars and charity events). The effect of having senior managers meet customers informally and talk to them was fundamentally to shake the corporate belief that strategies were about products not markets.

The same thing can be done in consumer markets. In the US, the car manufacturer Saturn (a small GM subsidiary) achieved quite amazing things in customer loyalty and retention simply by meeting their customers. The company said 'Saturn cars are bought not sold', so the distributors run parties for customers, called 'familiarization' days, when new car buyers are taught the basic features and maintenance requirements of their cars, fed from a pit barbecue, treated as important, and sent on their way to spread the Saturn message. The factory in Georgia also holds events where large numbers of buyers visit and are fed and entertained, and made to feel like valued members of the 'Saturn family'. This may sound trite and trivial, but the effects are remarkable (particularly since publicizing the events is also the main platform of the company's advertising). If this sounds exaggerated, soon afterwards this small producer was the leading US brand in the J. D. Power Customer Satisfaction Index.

'maybe we should ask when we last talked to a customer in a social setting (and when did our chief executive) – and if the answer reveals that we never do, then perhaps we should, even if it is difficult to arrange'

Before we dismiss this as unworkable, maybe we should ask when we last talked to a customer in a social setting (and when did our chief executive) – and if the answer reveals that we never do, then perhaps we should, even if it is difficult to arrange.

However, do not expect 100 per cent success from the word go. Life is rarely this simple. In a medium-sized manufacturer of fire alarms, there was a major source of friction between the accounts office and customers – customers were being chased very aggressively for payment in the minimum time period (in at least one case before the product was delivered!). So the company was advised to take the head of accounts out to meet some customers and listen to what they had to say. This they did, over an excellent lunch at the customer's expense. On return to the office, the head of accounts said 'Well, if they can afford lunches like that, they can afford to pay our invoices quicker', and returned to harassing customers with renewed vigour!

Indeed, I made this point about managers visiting customers in an after-dinner speech to one prestigious company's senior management. These managers spent some four hours until 3.00 in the morning rehearsing all the reasons why it was not appropriate for managers from production and logistics and service to 'waste' time on visiting customers. They still do not visit customers.

Customer Days

Following the same logic, one very powerful way of getting customers taken seriously in the company is if we can get them to come to us – to enter the corporate lair and tell us what they think of us and our products.

'one very powerful way of getting customers taken seriously in the company is if we can get them to come to us – to enter the corporate lair and tell us what they think of us and our products'

The conclusions may be remarkable. For instance, in one high-technology company (which must remain nameless), customers visited to view a new machine, which dispensed a pharmaceutical product for injection into humans. The company was very proud of this machine, which was a new design and very sophisticated. Customers showed that by ignoring the instructions for use (as is the way of technical folk throughout the world), it was possible to use the machine to squirt a fine spray of the injectable material over a wide area. Since the material in question was radioactive, this was not unparalleled good news. It would have been far worse if the product had gone into the market and patients had been sprayed with the material. The company redesigned the product.

Although this is most obviously applicable to the business-to-business market, it can be done anywhere. For instance, CIGNA, a major health insurance organization in the US, has faced a process of strategic change from marketing to employers, to marketing to employees. One problem the company faced was that managers believed that what they knew about their old markets would apply to their new markets. It did not. The marketing vice-president confronted this problem in stages. First, he asked teams of managers to specify the key customer needs and preferences for the new market. Second, he organized Customer Days, when groups of customers visited the company to tell managers what *they* believed were their needs and preferences. Stage 3 was to wait a short period while managers licked their wounds. Stage 4 was to ask managers to compare the two lists and their recommendations of how the company needed to change its approaches to attack the new market. He says this was a brutal process but changed managers' minds about a few important issues.

Similarly, at Xerox's famous Palo Alto Research Center, R&D executives are required to spend a full 20 per cent of their time interacting and participating with customers. This is a very expensive investment. The measure of success is simple – 'what have we learned?'

Surveys and research reports may be excellent things – generally they do not seem as powerful a form of communication as real customers who come to spit in your eye, and tell you face-to-face what they really think of you. Put it this way, if Lou Gerstner can run IBM and still spend 40 per cent of his time talking to customers – what are the rest of us doing?

Building customer scenarios

'Another approach is to map out broader "customer scenarios", that identify the whole context in which customers buy, or meet the challenge to "get inside the lives of your customers"'

Another approach is to map out broader 'customer scenarios', that identify the whole context in which customers buy, or meet the challenge to 'get inside the lives of your customers' [4]. For example, two shoppers arrive at an electrical goods store looking for a refrigerator – they seem identical and probably get treated the same. In fact, the first shopper needs the new fridge to replace one that died the night before, to save the frozen food from melting, while the second is looking for a fridge for the house he is building that will not be finished for months. They have very different needs – the customer scenario of the first is 'emergency replacement', and of the second 'furnish a new home'. Treating them the same misses a major opportunity – e.g. to sell a whole kitchen to the home furnisher, and insurance to the emergency buyer.

The originator of the concept, Patricia Seybould, describes the basic steps of building useful customer scenarios as:

- Select a target customer set (as explicitly as possible, e.g. business travellers using company travel agents).
- Select a goal the customer needs to fulfil (e.g. changing travel tickets in the middle of a trip).
- Envision a particular situation for the customer (e.g. the exhausted traveller staying in a hotel).
- Determine the start and end-point for the scenario (the end-point is the customer achieving his/her goals).
- Map out as many variations of the scenarios as possible – mentally go through each step as if you were the customer.
- Think of the individual activities the customer performs and the information s/he needs at each step – ask what your company could do to support those activities, provide the information, or save the customer time and trouble.
- Ask how your marketing, distribution and service channels can be used and developed to support and improve the customer scenario.
- Test the scenarios with real customers to refine the scenarios and develop new ones.

It was this type of approach that underpinned the development of Tesco Direct's winning value proposition for Internet grocery shopping (see pp. 198–200).

Listening not evaluating

If we are privileged enough that our customers will tell us things, our role is not to evaluate and disagree because we know better. Our role is to keep quiet, listen and learn.

In fact, perhaps the single most difficult thing to confront in this whole area is that customers may see things differently to us. They may have very different ideas about what matters about our products and services. This is very unfair – we are the experts, after all. If we say the computer switch

'If we are privileged enough that our customers will tell us things, our role is not to evaluate and disagree because we know better. Our role is to keep quiet, listen and learn'

belongs on the back of the box, or you cannot have a TV rental delivered on a Sunday or in the evening, or the office has to shut at lunchtime so people can eat, or guests should not walk on the grass in front of the hotel, then surely people should bow to our superior wisdom and professional expertise? I think not.

One stunning piece of corporate arrogance was displayed in a recent edition of the *Wall Street Journal* by a leading computer manufacturer. The article in question reported the war stories collected in the 'Customer Service' department (the reason for the quotation marks will become apparent shortly). These stories concerned the pathetic inadequacies of customers, who surely do not deserve to own the manufacturer's fantastic products:

- the lady who could not get the computer 'foot-pedal' to work, and had to be told the computer was not a sewing machine, and to take the 'mouse' off the floor . . .
- people who feed computer disks through a manual typewriter to type nice neat labels on them, thus corrupting the disks and rendering them useless . . .
- people who phone up to complain that their software says 'Press any key', but the keyboard has no key marked 'any', so there must be something wrong with the keyboard.

Such instances lead to customer service reports of RTFM (the clean translation being: 'read the "flaming" manual').

This is terrifically amusing, and we may permit ourselves the self-satisfied smirks of those who know better. But how profoundly depressing that a major company like this can display such overwhelming arrogance and offensiveness to its paying customers, and what is more sees nothing wrong with doing this in the pages of the *Wall Street Journal*. What does this say about the attitude of these 'service' employees towards the people who pay their wages? What does it say about this company's inability to grasp the basic needs of customers for clear and unambiguous guidance in using the products? What does it say about the underlying beliefs of the managers of this company as far as customers are concerned? Does it give insights into why Dell is now the PC market leader?

'Taking the trouble to find out what matters to paying customers, respecting and not rubbishing those priorities, and doing something about them is likely to be a painful process for many of us'

Taking the trouble to find out what matters to paying customers, respecting and not rubbishing those priorities, and doing something about them is likely to be a painful process for many of us. It may be one of the most powerful sources of competitive advantage and real customer focus, and it may be staring us in the face.

But what about the complainers?

In an ideal world where we got everything right there would be no customer complaints. We do not live in an ideal world. If we do not receive any customer complaints it does not mean all is well – do not confuse silent customers with satisfied customers. It probably means our customers think so poorly of us they cannot even be bothered to tell us how bad they think we are.

'If we do not receive any customer complaints it does not mean all is well – do not confuse silent customers with satisfied customers'

The figures about dissatisfied customers and complaining behaviour are well known[5]:

- *Most dissatisfied customers do not complain to us – probably only 4–5 per cent bother.* One estimate is that for every single customer who brings us a complaint, another 26 probably also have problems, six of which are likely to be serious, and do not complain to us. The silent majority defect to a competitor, or put up with us being bad and then defect.
- *Dissatisfied customers tell everyone except us –* in consumer markets the estimate is the disgruntled customer tells around 14 others.
- *Dissatisfied customers buy less –* and seem to do their best to get others to buy less as well.
- Typically the *cost* of complaint resolution is 10–25 per cent of the cost of finding a new customer[6].
- Some evidence says that when complaints are *resolved satisfactorily –* these customers tend to be more loyal than those who never experienced a problem in the first place, although there are signs that this may be unduly optimistic and in the long-term the customer remembers the reason for the complaint longer than how you handled the complaint once it was made.

But why do so many customers not complain and give us the chance to do better? Conventional answers might be: they did not think it would make any difference, they did not think it was worth their time and effort, they did not know what they had to do to get help, or they just never got round to it[7]. Or maybe they thought we were so crass that we would make complaining a horrible and demeaning experience?

REALITY CHECK

HANDLING COMPLAINTS THE RIGHT WAY AND THE WRONG WAY

Consider the situation: a young lady buys an expensive, branded face cream in a well-known department store, having ascertained from the salesperson that it did not contain skin tightening agents to which she is allergic. Nonetheless, she was allergic to the cream and took it back for a refund. She explained this to the salesperson at the counter, whose attitude was immediately hostile, and who accused the customer of ignoring the instructions and buying the wrong product – all this takes place at the counter in a busy shop. A refund is not forthcoming. The customer asks to see a supervisor. The supervisor arrives, apologizes for what has happened, provides a chair in a private area and basically provides an instant refund, but also asks for the chance to work with the customer to find an alternative product that would be suitable. Now, that is the difference between someone who has been trained to handle customer complaints positively and someone who has not[8]. Which sounds more like your company?

In fact, the real question is how would you like to be treated the way your company treats customers who complain – *find out*. Act like a customer and *see* what it is like and what it *feels* like.

What you will probably find is that much of what loses us business is things which are trivial for us, but that turn customers off – how long it takes to get a reply to a letter, the time it takes to get the phone answered, whether the salesperson knows anything about the product (or the company), whether the sales literature tells you anything, 'company policies' that make sense to the company but not to the customer. That last one is a joy. When *you* are the customer see how *you* feel about being passed from salesperson to salesperson because you contacted the 'wrong' one, the corporate 'policeman' who does credit checking and billing, the queuing procedures, the routine attempts to disprove warranty claims, and all the other 'rules' that seemed to make sense inside the organization, but which are irritating obstacles and insults for the customer. The reality is that when *you* are the customer you want things done *your* way. Something as simple as this is

'The reality is that when you are the customer you want things done your way. Something as simple as this is a good start to getting to grips with the real customer satisfaction issue'

a good start to getting to grips with the real customer satisfaction issue, and the joy is that in practice so many of the problems and idiocies that you find can be solved instantly, and at little cost – it just takes the effort of taking them seriously.

In fact, if you look at things from the customer's perspective, you may find yourself amazed at how your company seems to have set out to positively irritate and annoy the paying customer, when it costs so little not to, and how astounding it is that so few customers do actually complain.

REALITY CHECK
CALL CENTRES DESTROY VALUE

Recently I bought a new lap-top off the IBM website – expensive, but incredibly light, weighing in at around 3 lb. So delighted was I with the new computer, I even forgave IBM the fact that they had not included a port replicator or floppy drive with the machine – so I ordered them off the website, plus a few little goodies like a nice new carry-case and so on. Disaster – the carry-case is just a standard shoulder bag, not something designed for my lovely new X20 Think Pad. Disaster – I must have clicked twice by mistake, so have received two floppy drives instead of one. No worry – this is Lou Gerstner's IBM, and I have every confidence they will recover this situation in five seconds flat. So, I phoned them. The call centre operator made her extremely abrasive views very clear: I was stupid; I should have ordered more carefully (yes, really!); and the administrative fee for each returned product would be £50 plus post and packing. Since the carry-case and the floppy drive each cost less than £50, this is not a great deal. In fact, I have just thrown the surplus products away. It was worth £100 to me, to get this story about IBM's inability to manage customer relationships successfully because of their obnoxious and rude call centre staff, and to understand better why Dell has stuffed them. Of course, my payback will be relating the story to every management audience I address throughout the world for the next five years, and I will ... oh, believe me, I will.

In fact, disgruntled complaining customers can offer us a marvellous opportunity. The research evidence is that it makes a big difference to the chances of doing repeat business with a complaining customer if we just *listen* to the complaint, although this pales into insignificance compared to the effects achieved if

'If we can find the unhappy customer we may have the opportunity to convert them into our most loyal customers of all time, by virtue of the way we treat them as individuals'

we listen to the complaint *and* do something about it. If we can find the unhappy customer we may have the opportunity to convert them into our *most* loyal customers of all time, by virtue of the way we treat them as individuals.

In fact, the results of pursuing these types of questions with customers who complain can be surprising as well as productive.

REALITY CHECK
UNDERSTANDING COMPLAINTS

In one Volkswagen dealership, in the UK, management had made determined, systematic efforts to regularly *listen* to what their customers thought about the level of service provided by the garage. Top management's message to staff in dealing with customers was 'you have two ears and one mouth, so use them in proportion'. All was going well except for one particular customer, who *every* quarter complained lengthily, bitterly and in detail about the poor quality of the servicing of his car and the intractability of the service people in acting on his complaints. The General Manager finally phoned him and said that clearly the company did not deserve to keep his business, but would he help them avoid the problem happening again. He was persuaded to visit the General Manager to tell the company how it could do better. He provided a list of service tasks which were *never* done on his car and which service staff refused to put right – greasing ball-joints, and the like. Further questioning showed that *all* his expectations were wholly based on the old 1968 owner's workshop manual. It was 1988 – ball-joints no longer *had* to be greased, and so it went on through his entire list of 'complaints'! The problem was solved by the free gift of the 1988 owner's workshop manual, and the customer was converted. Understanding expectations is as important as seeing how delivery of the service goes wrong.

In summary then, what is so special about complaining customers? Well, they are the ones who actually want to talk to us, which makes listening easier. The opportunities we face with complaining customers are:

- to *learn* about the areas were we need to improve the way we do business;

- to satisfy these customers by replacing the service or replacing the product and get the repeat business and refusals;
- to potentially build real customer loyalty (though many do think it would be better to avoid the complaints in the first place, than to be great at handling them).

There may be problems – if we see the customer as the enemy, then we probably do not like complaints or the people who make them. Indeed, dealing with angry customers or ex-customers can be tough. The example set by managers is critical.

Most organizations do have formalized procedures for reacting to complaints – but too often this is too low in the organization, and is no more than a tactical coping mechanism, which has little impact on the rest of the company.

One chief executive of a highly successful European company takes a different view of the complaints issue. He insists that all senior managers in the company take responsibility for investigating three customer complaints each month, and for one of these it is expected that a customer visit will be made. Incidentally, he includes himself in this rota. He says it is easy to do this, because when you go and ask Customer Service to give you three really bad complaints to deal with, they are delighted and give you really difficult ones! This is expensive, but a superb way to get customer complaints taken very seriously by everyone in the company. Besides, he says the things they have learned about how their products work in the real marketplace and what annoys customers is far more effective than all the market research surveys in the world, and this alone makes the policy worthwhile.

Be sure, though, that this is about developing ways for effectively listening to customers and responding positively. It should not be a police-action to punish people in the organization.

In fact, you have to learn to *trust* the people in the company and give them the power to solve customer problems. Easy to say, but often not so easy to do. For example, in one company managers said to this that you cannot trust front-line operatives to give refunds or replace products because 'the kids would give the store away!'. A test was set up: groups of managers and groups of front-line employees were given simulation exercises in handling customer complaints. At the end we compared who gave away most in solving customer problems – guess what, it was the managers. At that company, front-line employees are now trusted with handling customer complaints.

*'In fact, you have to learn to **trust** the people in the company and give them the power to solve customer problems. Easy to say, but often not so easy to do'*

A learning organization?

Many leaders in management thinking advocate the 'learning organization'[9]. This is ambitious. A start for most of us is to learn, to listen, to share the lessons throughout the company, and to retain the knowledge we are building for future use[10]. However, be aware of the other trap – learning is not the same as policing. Listening to customers, and particularly analysing customer complaints, can easily be turned into a managerial disaster. We can make the whole thing negative by:

- *Over-reacting to isolated, ad hoc criticisms* – a single isolated complaint may really not be enough evidence sensibly to take action in how we do things in the future (although this does not mean we should not do what we can to make the unhappy complaining customer happy).
- *Over-reacting to complaints about sensitive issues* – there is a risk that we only respond to complaints about the things *we* think are most important, not what the *customer* thinks are most important. This misses the whole point.
- *Under-reacting to major criticisms* – when we start we may well be shocked by the extent and spread of criticisms. This should provide an agenda for action, not a rejection of the results because 'we can't be that bad' (see the question of the elephant, p. 375).
- *Poor quality reaction because of defensiveness* – we may easily achieve disastrously negative effects if we simply use customer feedback as a big stick with which to beat up people in the organization. The idea is to help us all improve the way we do our jobs, not a ritualistic blood-letting.
- *Politicking* – finally, there is a substantial danger with some organizations that customer feedback becomes a political weapon in the interdepartmental vendettas and struggle for power. Management uses the results to criticize Marketing, Marketing uses them to attack Production, the Accountants use them to fight back budget requests, and so on. Certainly, some marketing executives have said to me that to publish customer views would simply be to create a 'hostage to fortune' – a basis for them to be attacked and sniped at by others in the company.

If we do it badly, then there is no doubt that customer feedback and complaints handling can be a disaster. However, note that most of the ways it can go wrong reflect how the results are *used* and *abused* – not something fundamentally wrong with doing it in the first place. The goal is to learn and improve, not to 'police' the company.

Obsessing over customers

In fact, if you look at companies that do focus on what is value to their customers, and who do listen and learn, it goes much further – they are obsessional and almost overpowering. International examples are well known, and centre on companies like Marriott, Disney, Delta Airlines and Dell.

But there are examples in successful companies closer to home. Tesco has won undisputed market leadership in the UK grocery sector. The man who has driven the transformation of Tesco from 'pile it high, sell it cheap' discount relating is Terry Leahy, Marketing Director under Ian MacLaurin, and in 1997 made chief executive. Behind the scenes, Leahy has driven major customer-focused changes by listening to customers, learning and doing:

- he drove a programme to make the stores nicer places to shop because customers wanted it – shorter queues, better decor, higher quality products, and new ways of shopping such as the Tesco Metro, providing a food store near the office that opens early and shuts late;
- he championed the Tesco Clubcard loyalty scheme, and is using it to target individual customers with special offers, such as the 'Babyclub';
- he is increasing investment in customer service – hiring 5000 new customer assistants, reducing the time employees spend on administrative work and encouraging them to spend more time with customers.

What they say about Leahy is things like this:

'Leahy's obsession is not the graphs that show good performance, but rather the customers who shop in the stores. Leahy's mantra is "customer". The word creeps into every sentence to the point of irritation. But to Leahy . . . it is the crux of the business and the focus'[11]

Maybe this is how you go from being a shelf stacker to the chief executive's job (which Leahy has)?

There is nothing like a true obsessive, is there? You may prefer to call it leadership (but 'obsession' works for me). Another view is that it is all about 'creating the cult of the customer'[12], where everything everyone does is judged by what it means to the customer.

Some of the obsession is about managing the symbols – managing rewards to give incentives, giving employees the power

'ask what we do to reward those who foster and develop productive customer relationships or, even more apposite, what we do to avoid the organization punishing those who do their best for the customer'

to do the things that matter, and to behave as though customers matter. One way of approaching this is to ask what we do to reward those who foster and develop productive customer relationships or, even more apposite, what we do to avoid the organization punishing those who do their best for the customer.

The best companies reward and value those who break the rules to do a better job for the customer. For example, in the Marriott hotel business, one valued manager diverted the budget for putting televisions in the bathrooms to providing ironing boards in all bedrooms. His thinking was very clear – customers repeatedly ask for ironing boards and there is a lot of time spent on taking them around and collecting them, and there are never enough to go around. No-one has ever complained of the lack of a TV in the bathroom. The solution was obvious, and the company applauded his decision.

Another well-known example is from a courier delivery business. This company promises its customers overnight delivery. A depot manager was faced with the problem that this promise apparently could not be kept for one customer's package, because of public holidays and uncompromising haulage schedules. The answer was obvious – he chartered a plane to take the parcel to its destination. Far from being punished, the manager has been rewarded and turned into a hero in the company (although it is rumoured that at his presentation the CEO did take him on one side and suggested that if the same thing happened again, could he possible find a *small* plane . . .).

'The question which arises is simple – if we know what matters to our customers, what are we doing to honour and reward those who do the things that win customers' hearts and minds, and to protect them from company systems set up to punish and sanction such actions?'

Conversely, how many times when we find customers being treated badly do we find the reason being that the organization rewards precisely this type of behaviour towards customers. One Japanese photocopier supplier understands this and has changed the way maintenance engineers are rewarded. Maintenance engineers get a bonus, which reduces as the number of customer call-outs increases. The logic is clear. If installation and maintenance is done thoroughly and effectively in the first place, there should be fewer call-outs for breakdowns. This is what is rewarded, not the number of calls made.

The question which arises is simple – if we know what matters to our customers, what are we doing to honour and reward those who do the things that win customers' hearts and minds, and to protect them from company systems set up to punish and sanction such actions? If the answer is nothing, then that is probably where we need to start in taking customers seriously.

This includes managing less tangible things as well. Radio Cornwall, a BBC local radio station, was widely criticized for one of its policies in 1996. That was very unfair because their policy was exactly right. The company's internal memo to staff using company cars read as follows:

> 'If you listen to anything other than Radio Cornwall in our cars you will be banned from using them. This is no longer a warning, it is a statement of policy. And if the station which is paying your money isn't good enough for your listening needs, go and work for another station. If you get in a car that isn't tuned to Radio Cornwall, then retune it pronto. Otherwise, you will be spending a lot of money on petrol. From today there will be spot checks on the cars – if they aren't tuned to Radio Cornwall, you are banned.'[13]

OK, marks out of ten: tact, diplomacy and internal communications skills, zero; obsessing with the customer, ten. The moral? Obsessing with customers may not always make you popular with your colleagues.

Don't forget that you attract new customers by honouring employees who go the extra mile to deliver excellent service to existing customers. For example, Marriott has run entire, international advertising campaigns based on what customers say about how Marriott employees treat them when the chips are down. The wording of one such ad reads as follows:

> 'There were no taxis and no chance of catching my plane until the Marriott receptionist took a *personal* interest in the matter. Without hesitation she made an executive decision. If she couldn't order a car in time to get me to the airport, she'd take me in her own. It was no stretch limo but thanks to her I made the flight. I believe, at Marriott, they call it Empowerment. It means that the staff see their roles as being more than just a duty. They're really sensitive to guests' needs and assume responsibility for attending to them. I needed to catch that plane and they ensured I did. It's been the same wherever I've stayed at a Marriott . . . '

Call me sentimental if you wish, but if your customers write your advertisements for you, you have to be getting something right.

If you believe in customers and want to do something about customer focus, it may take just such obsessive management behaviour. If our goal is to 'reach an interaction with the customer that so utterly distinguishes you from others that it is a brand in itself – a unique impression that sets your company apart from others', then every contact between the customers and the company must prove how much the company values them[14].

Building a customer-focused organization

What we have said so far is to achieve customer focus: look at your current relationship with the customer and see how it needs to change; focus attention on what creates value for customers; find better ways to listen to customers, learn from what they say and apply the lessons in the company; and obsess about customers – focus management leadership and efforts on the customer credo. But this leaves the question of packaging these things together and finding the key drivers to make it real – i.e. building a customer-focused organization. A number of things are worth considering.

Customer care programmes

This is often the first thing people try, when it should probably be the last. After all, it is a great way for managers to convince themselves they are taking customers seriously, while dumping the issue on their people instead.

'There is a lot more involved in genuine customer care and service than "slapping in some training and accompanying it with hype" or sending employees to "smile schools"'

There is a lot more involved in genuine customer care and service than 'slapping in some training and accompanying it with hype' or sending employees to 'smile schools'[15]. The results of trying to 'enforce' smiling and customer care are shown in the retail business: store operatives accepting their compulsory name-badges, but deliberately wearing them upside down; smiles which last as long as the video surveillance of the checkout; management policing of 'false smiles' and the use of *agents provocateurs* to test staff without warning, leading to predictably resentful staff[16]. These people are trying to tell us something!

On the face of things, customer care and customer service training programmes are a way to improve our performance where it counts most – at the place where the customer experiences what we do. Great things can be achieved by such efforts and they should not be ignored or denigrated. We may actually improve on the 'service with a snarl' that all too many customers get when they pay their money. However, there is a worry that how we actually use these things is as something we 'bolt-on' as an afterthought to cover up our real inadequacies and our real disregard for what matters to customers.

David Clutterbuck[17] has estimated that up to 90 per cent of customer care programmes have failed or are likely to. He points to the absence of objectives and evaluation, with companies viewing customer care as the latest, plug-in 'quick fix', and (the real point of significance) no real change in *management* behaviour.

The reality of customer care is about how we run the whole operation from top to bottom, not manipulating front-line employees, and what I have come to call the 'have a nice day syndrome'. Real customer care is not about building new bureaucracies and lip-service, it is about anarchic commitment to the customer. It is not about adding a bit of customer service training at the end of the process of going to market – it is about how we manage the whole process. It is about commitment at the top and customer care as an integral part of market strategy. The best customer care programmes recognize precisely this, but I am somewhat less convinced about others.

> *'The reality of customer care is about how we run the whole operation from top to bottom, not manipulating front-line employees, and what I have come to call the "have a nice day syndrome"'*

Customer care programmes *can* be used to manage change. But then they are likely to be 'root and branch' programmes of change, not afterthoughts. For example, UNISYS has used the word 'customerize' to describe this type of approach to customer care. Customerize is defined as '1: to make a company more responsive to its customers and better able to attract new ones; 2: to customerize an organization's information strategy, e.g. to extend systems capabilities to field locations and other points of customer contact and support.' The UNISYS customerizing process is linked to:

- Top management commitment – providing leadership and role models.
- Understanding customers.
- Setting customer-centred strategies.
- Cultivating pro-customer employees and service programmes.
- Focusing on customer retention.
- Gaining new customers.
- Using technology-enablers and measurement systems to achieve this.

Then, add to that something like Customer Management Teams[18], and we see something powerful coming together.

Now that adds up to a bit more than management lip-service and 'smile schools' for the employees. Look, for example, at the volunteer 'ambassador' programme launched at Southwestern Bell, the US telephone company, in 1995. Non-sales employees volunteer as ambassadors to establish relationships with their designated customers – a very powerful way of putting a face to the company and letting the customer know that the company really does care about them. The ambassador visits the customer quarterly, and gives out his/her office phone number for the customer to call with any query or problem. The company says it has stronger, smarter problem-solving employees as a result of the ambassador programme, and gives better service to more loyal customers. Indeed, some of the customers are paying the ultimate compliment – they are copying the ambassador programme for their own companies.

People buy from people

. . . or more probably they only buy from people they like (who are not rude, arrogant, offhand or unhelpful). It is the people in the company who are the 'value creators'[19], and it is the people in the company who can undermine any customer-focused market strategy you care to name.

One commentator all too rightly notes that 'too many employees who deal directly with customers are damaging the product, service or corporate brand every time they open their mouths'[20]. Karl Albrecht goes as far as to say that unhappy employees can work as 'terrorists' in the company[21]. Others go even further and say that company employees, not customers, have to be 'number one' if the company hopes to truly satisfy its customers[22]. Recent research underlines the fact that it is the beliefs of the individuals who work in our companies that determine real customer focus – at least far more than the posturing of managers. The issue has become 'implementing the marketing concept one employee at a time'[23].

But why don't our people do what we tell them, and be nice to customers? John Crump, of Kaisen Consultancy, works on these issue and his views can be summarized along the following lines. He says people do not always deliver the best possible service because of:

● The human factor – in the real world people make mistakes and become demotivated or have an 'off-day', and we often assume that they have knowledge and capabilities which they do not have.

- They do not always know what 'right' looks like – and why should they, unless we provide a model of what is good and bad in customer service.
- They do not always know if they are being effective – because we fail to give them regular feedback as customer satisfaction (and customer complaints!).
- They are not always rewarded for doing the right thing.
- Sometimes jobs have conflicting demands that cannot be met – time with the customer versus time doing administration, for example, because managers pass on paradox (see pp. 115–16) instead of simplifying, so people do the minimum they have to do to stay out of trouble.
- Sometimes they get stuck in the 'old way' of seeing things and we do not help them to change.
- They simply may not understand what we want from them, because we have failed to communicate properly[24].

For example, thinking about that last point, psychologists have been employed to try to teach Berlin's notoriously rude transport workers to be nice to passengers[25], with the following results:

We say . . .	They say . . .
Say 'please' when you ask passengers to stand back from the doors when they close	Why should we say 'please', it is an order!
Help passengers with their luggage	Why – if they can't carry it, they shouldn't expect others to do it for them
Look customers in the eye and speak slowly	Why – if they ask us questions, they should listen to the answer carefully
Wish people a nice day	We only say what we mean, and we do not care if they have a nice day or not
What matters is customer service	No, what matters is speed and efficiency

And you thought you had problems?

So, if the real problem in building a customer-focused organization is the people, who can help us? Maybe the Human Resource Management people can – see back to Chapter 5.

However, I said at the outset that customer focus was about more than customer care and service, it is about developing a continuous search for better understanding of the customer – developing and sustaining the learning capabilities to which I referred earlier. This brings us to the issue of marketing information and market sensing. Just in case you think I am exaggerating about the need to link customer focus and market sensing, just consider the following terrifying facts: recent research by the US agency Forrester Research found that approximately half the companies they surveyed did not, and did not plan to, use customer information in designing or implementing marketing or customer services processes; and nine out of ten companies surveyed did not have plans to use customer information to improve the results of their product development[26]. Now, tell me there is not a major issue here!

Information, sensing and intelligence for superior marketing

Of all the marketing areas in which I have worked with companies, I have no hesitation in saying that marketing information is the most difficult, because it is the area which is surrounded by most misconceptions and misunderstanding. It is the area where it is easiest to convince ourselves that the answer to all our problems is to do more market research, or collect more information and store it on a computer database – i.e. make a token gesture and ignore what really matters, so we can get on with doing things the way we have always done them. It is the area of marketing which sounds most academic, esoteric and theoretical (for which read: impractical, vague and useless in the real world). It is the part of marketing which is most easily and most defensibly 'delegated' to junior executives – after all, 'real managers' are too expensive and important to spend time digging up market information and processing it. The trouble is that the expensive managers then take no notice of what the information says.

This is a great pity. Experience suggests that the marketing information area is more significant than we normally think, but for different reasons. I would say that it is the single area where you can make the greatest and most significant differ-ence to market strategies, marketing programmes and customer satisfaction. Information offers us this leverage because it is not really about doing surveys and collecting facts and figures, or building computerized databases – these are just the trappings, the incidentals. Marketing information is about how we understand, think about and deal with the environment, i.e. the customer, the partner and the competitor. This is why information gives leverage – if you can influence how decision makers and operational staff *think* about the marketplace, then you have a good chance of influencing what they *do*.

We saw that customer focus is about much more than the trapping of customer care programmes – it is about learning. The issue of market sensing takes us further in this direction.

'Marketing information is about how we understand, think about and deal with the environment, i.e. the customer, the partner and the competitor. This is why information gives leverage – if you can influence how decision makers and operational staff think about the marketplace, then you have a good chance of influencing what they do'

From market research to market sensing

We are not going to discuss all the conventional technology of marketing information systems – marketing accountancy techniques, marketing research methods and things like questionnaires and sample design, sources of information, or building mathematical models and integrated marketing information systems. All that can come later if you need it.

Managers do not design questionnaires, collect data, build models, and so on (or they should not). Those are jobs for market researchers and technicians. What managers have to do is to *understand*. To understand the customer, the distribution systems, the partners in an alliance, the competitor, and the big changes in the marketplace that can make us rich or put us out of business.

Perhaps the greatest indication of the importance of superior market sensing is the surprises it uncovers for companies: one US record company was amazed to discover that the biggest purchasers of its rap and techno music were grandparents – they buy the records for young people, whose parents will not buy it because they do not want it in the house[27].

That is why I see the issue as *market sensing* – how those of us inside the company understand and react to the marketplace and the way it is changing. This is actually a more difficult issue than market research techniques, but it is more important too. Does market sensing make any difference?

REALITY CHECK

MARKET SENSING CAPABILITIES – THE NEW COMPETITIVE RESOURCE

The *Encyclopaedia Britannica* was first published in Edinburgh more than 200 years ago. By 1990, *Encyclopaedia Britannica*'s sales in the US had reached $650 million with profits of $40 million. However, during the early 1990s, CD-ROM technology gained acceptance in the consumer market for encyclopaedias, especially in the key US market. The management of *Encyclopaedia Britannica* did not respond to this threat – in spite of the fact they had CD-ROM technology in one of the company's divisions. The reason was management simply did not *believe* that CD-ROM technology could undermine their traditional market. The company's marketing advantage in the US was a 2300 person direct salesforce, each earning a commission of $300 on the sale of a $1500 encyclopaedia. In fact, by the early 1990s, the competitors' CD-ROM packages were available to 7 million US households, with computers with CD drives, at prices ranging from $99 to $395. By 1994, *Encyclopaedia Britannica*'s US sales had declined so far that the salesforce was halved in size, and the company was in serious financial trouble. To compete against CD-ROM competition would have required the company to change both its product and its direct selling strategy. Management simply did not believe that they had to change. By 1997, the US and European direct salesforces had been disbanded. By 1999, the content of the 32-volume tome was available free on the Internet as a portal, with income generated by advertising and hot links. An extreme example of where faulty market sensing can lead.

Royal Doulton is a premier brand of china – famed for its tea services and plates. The company has seen its sales falling at 20 per cent a year on the high street, and share prices down from £3 to 99p by 2000. The Chief Operating Officer explains: 'The problem has been … failing to understand consumer requirements and the fact that people have changed their dining and living habits'. The decline in formal dining has fundamentally undermined fine china sales. The company is struggling belatedly to find ways to provide products for the casual dining market, but without going downmarket (merchandising Royal Doulton in Wal-Mart and CostCo in the US proved a disastrous mistake, undermining the value of the Royal Doulton brand). The changes in how people organize eating was hardly news to anyone, but the company failed to understand and react to how its major market was developing.

Waterford Wedgwood plc, the Irish manufacturer of crystal and china, entered the 1990s with declining sales and growing competition from low-cost crystal makers in Eastern Europe. A key market is the US premium crystal market (items over $25), where there are 120 competing suppliers. Waterford's management believed there was an opportunity in the market for cheaper crystal products. This was not just 'hunch' – management's belief in the existence of price-conscious buyers who would be willing to pay a high but 'sensible' price for crystal products was tested and confirmed by focus groups conducted in three countries and 30 hours of taped interviews with consumers. Waterford designed the Marquis brand products to be different enough from traditional Waterford (in price and design) to avoid weakening the equity of the main brand, but to still gain from the Waterford brand identity. For example, a long-stem wine glass from Waterford is around $50, while the Marquis equivalent is $30. Marquis Crystal by Waterford was launched in 1990 – the first new Waterford brand for 200 years. By 1994, Waterford's sales were up by around 30 per cent and share of the US premium crystal segment was up by 7 per cent to 34 per cent, based on inspired market sensing.

Motorola is a $22 billion high-tech global enterprise that started as a six-person firm making and selling battery eliminators (wires to plug battery-powered radios into mains electricity). The Motorola case has been described many times because of the distinctive leadership and culture of innovation. However, another characteristic has been the constant search for new ideas and what they call 'sensing opportunity'. From the battery-eliminator business, the company moved into the expanding market for radios themselves and then televisions, and then into the diodes and transistors that underpin the embryonic worldwide electronics business. What they call 'sensing opportunity' is a form of market sensing that has driven the spectacular growth of the company, when it could have simply coasted in existing markets.

Sources: Gary Samuels (1994), 'CD-ROM's First Big Victory', *Forbes*, 28 February. Caroline Daniel and James Harding (1999), 'E-Britannica: A Free Encyclopaedia', *Financial Times*, 23/24 October. Judith Valente (1994), 'A New Brand Restores Sparkle to Waterford', *Wall Street Journal*, 10 November. Peter J. Flatow (1996), 'Managing Change: Learning from Motorola', *Marketing News*, 1 July.

These examples illustrate market sensing, or market understanding by managers, not sophisticated marketing research or technology-driven marketing information systems. If you want another illustration of the difference between market sensing and market research, consider the statements in Table 7.1.

Table 7.1 The silly things we say*

What did they say?	Who said that?
'I think there's a world market for maybe five computers'	Thomas Watson Chairman, IBM, 1943
'Computers in the future will weigh more than 1.5 tons	*Popular Marketing*, 1949
'I have traveled the length and breadth of this country and talked with the best people, and I can assure you that data processing is a fad that won't last out the year'	Business Books Editor Prentice-Hall, 1959
'There is no reason why anyone would want to have a computer in their home'	Ken Olson Chairman, DEC, 1977
'Who the hell wants to hear actors talk?	H. M. Warner, Warner Bros, 1927
'A cookie store is a bad idea. Besides, the market research says that America likes crispy cookies, not soft and chewy cookies like you make'	Response to Debbie Fields' idea for the Mrs Fields Cookies business
'We don't like their sound and guitar music is on the way out'	Decca Recording Company, rejecting the Beatles
'No'	Response to Steve Jobs, founder of Apple Computers, when he attempted to interest Atari in his new computer
'We don't need you. You haven't got through college yet'	Response to Steve Jobs, founder of Apple Computers, when he attempted to interest Hewlett-Packard in his new computer
'640K ought to be enough for anyone'	Bill Gates, Microsoft, 1981
'They couldn't hit an elephant at this dist . . .'	The last words of General John Sedgwick at the Battle of Spotsylvania, 1864

* Source: Adapted from C. Lloyd (1995), 'Towards the One-and-a-half Ton Computer', *Sunday Times*, November 12

Some of these statements look amusing, with the benefit of 20:20 hindsight. This is not the point. The point is that every one of those wholly wrong-headed statements could probably have been 'proved' to be correct at the time by extensive (and expensive) market research. It is just as true that *Encyclopaedia Britannica* could probably have commissioned market research in the 1980s to 'prove' that CD-ROM was a fad that would not affect the published encyclopaedia business and Waterford could have run surveys to demonstrate that a lower-priced brand would destroy the premium crystal market in the US.

> Any event, once it has occurred, can be made to appear inevitable by a competent market researcher.

Conventional marketing research is actually very limited in what it can really do – see the myths of marketing information below. It is also used and badly abused in many situations, and at the heart of the problem is that we have been brought up in traditional marketing to expect far too much from marketing research:

'at the heart of the problem is that we have been brought up in traditional marketing to expect far too much from marketing research'

- We expect market research to give us new ideas for products and services and to tell us which is the best advertising – but innovation is not democratic, so if one person in a thousand has a great idea, why do we bury it as '0.001 per cent of the sample said . . . ' or more likely ignore it as 'other responses'. The advertising legend in the US – George Lois – goes further. He says doing research is about being careful and 'Being careful guarantees sameness and mediocrity'[28]. He says his two best campaigns were the Braniff airlines 'If You've Got It, Flaunt It' ads of 20 years ago, and the 1990s poster campaign for the then unknown clothing designer Tommy Hilfiger, which listed the few 'great designers for men' as: R---- L-----, P----- C-----, C----- K---- and T---- H------[29]. These campaigns infuriated company lawyers, market researchers and competitors, and were outstanding successes for the companies concerned. The 'big idea' is not a votable issue – surveys of opinion about them are meaningless.
- We want to know things – so we ask people questions and call it market research. Why do we believe that people know, or will tell us the things we want to know? Scientific market research techniques have become much more sophisticated in the past 20 years, and still fail to produce the result of national elections, unless they are already a foregone conclusion. Those same sophisticated techniques were used to test the taste of Coca-Cola's 'new Coke' on 190 000 people prior to launch. The taste test results were positive. The product failed miserably. People do not buy the product for its taste –

new Coke just was not 'cool'. Bob Worcester of the MORI research agency says: 'Ten per cent of people believe ICI makes bicycles. You show them a list of products like paints and fertilizers, throw in bicycles as a dummy, and one in ten will tick it'[30]. Fifty years ago, a US academic surveyed Americans' attitude towards the Metallic Metals Act – 38 per cent said it should be passed. There was no such thing as the Metallic Metals Act.

- How often is it true that market research gives us the answers we want because it studies the segment of the market that gives the 'right result' – of course most existing customers say they are satisfied, why should they own up to being stupid and buying the wrong product; of course most existing customers say they are happy – do you want them to wear a sign saying 'I am stupid'?; what about the customers who left or never tried us? Marketing databases, like those created from the retailer loyalty schemes, are wonderful – but what about consumers who do not join the scheme, or only visit the store infrequently. Are they of no interest, because profiling them by recency, frequency and monetary value will tell you they do not matter (so do they starve to death, or shop elsewhere?)[31].

- When Disney transferred its Disneyland format to Europe – EuroDisney near Paris – the company lost $921 million in the first year. The decision to enter the European market was well-supported by research: figures showed the growing number of European visitors to the US theme parks. In the conventional Disney way, the location was based on modelling population figures – 17 million people live within a two-hour drive of the Paris site, and 109 million within a six-hour drive, which are much better figures than the US parks show. The figures were encouraging, but the launch of EuroDisney was an expensive lesson in the importance of market understanding not market research. The company ignored the failure of amusement parks in France, it dismissed anti-Disney demonstrations as insignificant, and it ignored the fact that European holiday patterns are completely different to those in the US – people in Europe have longer holidays and spend less on each. Myopia also led the company to ban alcohol from its park – you try telling the French they cannot drink wine at lunchtime and see what happens! Excellent research that ignores the things that really matter (because no-one asks the right questions) reinforces company myopia and costs a lot of money to put right.

- Research can provide you with the perfect justification for ignoring new market opportunities. Initial evaluations of tofu, organic tomatoes and alfalfa sprouts as food suggested they were for weirdos only. Organic food is one of the fastest growing categories in the fresh food sector. The future is not best predicted by opinion polls.

> Those who do not study the past will repeat its errors.
>
> Those who do study the past will find other ways to foul up.

You probably think this is just a petulant tirade against market researchers[32]. Well, try the following test on your own company.

The elephant in the market

When a family suffers a trauma – such as incest or alcoholism – it often refuses to acknowledge it, a syndrome known to therapists as 'the elephant in the living room', which everyone steps around and pretends is not there[33]. Well, maybe we should think about the elephant in the market, or maybe the elephant in the company. When you look at the things that are studied by our market analysts and researchers, published by our research agencies, and reported in our marketing information systems – are they really the things that matter to managers in understanding the market (or are they the things that we always measure because they are easiest to measure)?

'When you look at the things that are studied by our market analysts and researchers, published by our research agencies, and reported in our marketing information systems – are they really the things that matter to managers in understanding the market (or are they the things that we always measure because they are easiest to measure)?'

REALITY CHECK
IGNORING THE ELEPHANT IN THE MARKET

Retailer Marks & Spencer entered the 2000s with severe trading problems. Its profitability and share price collapsing – shares down from a 1997 peak of 650p to just over 150p in late 2000. The company is desperately working on a turnaround under new CEO Luc Vandevelde. While successful competitors, such as Next and Matalan, have spotted emerging customer needs and met them, M&S seemed to be hobbled by its history and its cumbersome management structure. However, in the late 1990s, confidential company surveys revealed that customers were losing faith with

M&S. But when M&S sales collapsed, the fall was completely unexpected and a shock to senior management in the company. Then-Chairman, Sir Richard Greenbury, claims that he was never shown the confidential surveys or informed of their findings. Whether they did not think the loss of customer faith in M&S service or ability to provide 'value for money' was important enough to tell the CEO, or whether they were afraid to tell him, management did not pass on the message from the customers. This appears to have been some kind of 'collective myopia' in the company – a refusal to face the really big challenge. Some suggest that M&S management had come to believe that they could not fail.

Sources: Kate Rankine (2000), 'Marks Ignored Shoppers' Fall in Faith', *Daily Telegraph*, 30 October. Michael Skapinker (2000), 'How to Bow Out Without Egg on Your Face', *Financial Times*, 8 March. Peter Martin (1997), 'Look Out: It's Behind You', *Financial Times*, 15 May.

Try this in your own company. Figure 7.2 suggests that any question of information differs in two respects: importance and urgency. Different types of research question are then:

- *Priorities* – important and urgent questions that need speedy answers to support management decision making. Issues like quality performance and brand performance would probably fall here – they are core issues for most of us and if things go wrong we need to react.
- *Time Wasters* – questions that do not really matter, they may be 'nice-to-know', but that is all. These should be ignored.
- *Short-Term Dilemmas* – urgent but unimportant questions that should be resolved by a judgement call not extensive study. Dwight Reskey of Pepsico calls these 'the curse of the brand manager' – issues like the colour of the package and the typeface for the logo. Reskey describes these as the 'tyranny of the in-box. People busy themselves with lots of tiny, immediate projects, winning momentary job satisfaction while avoiding bigger issues that are important to their business' [34].
- *Strategic* – questions which may not be important to the day-to-day running of the business, but which are critical to long-term direction. This might include questions like 'Are there limits to our growth potential in this market and what are they?'.

The challenge is simply this – look at what happens in your company and see where the efforts and resources go. How much of our information is truly strategic (i.e. vital to the long-term direction of the business) and how much goes on Short-Term Dilemmas and Time Wasters? You may be depressed by the

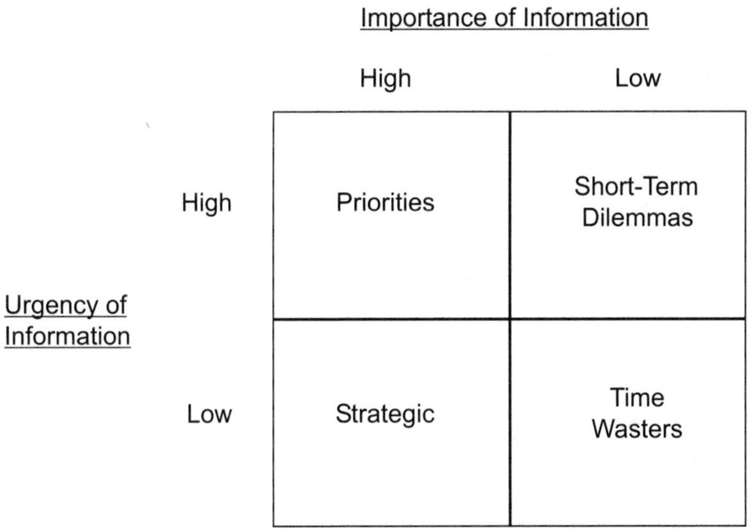

Importance of Information

	High	Low
High	Priorities	Short-Term Dilemmas
Low	Strategic	Time Wasters

Urgency of Information

Figure 7.2　Strategic and non-strategic marketing information

conclusion – typically 1–10 per cent of the effort goes into the Strategic area that generates 90–99 per cent of the value.

If we are to improve on this, let's consider a few fundamental issues: the difference between market research and market sensing; the mythology surrounding the information issue in marketing; the underlying role of information in market strategy; and managing the process of market sensing.

UNREALITY CHECK
A LITTLE KNOWN FACT . . .

It has recently been discovered why there are never any teaspoons in the kitchen when you want to make a cup of tea. It is because while you are out at work, teaspoons migrate upstairs and transmute into wire coat hangers in the wardrobes. Alright, it may be silly, but no worse than some of the things that market researchers come up with.

The difference between market research and market sensing?

Many managers will challenge this difference – they would. They have been trained to believe that precise information and immaculate information systems are the hallmark of professional management. The difference is actually very real. It is the difference between what we know and understand, and what can be measured scientifically and presented to us in research reports.

The easiest way to explain this difference is with Murphy's Law – the principle that if something can go wrong, it will. Many of the predictions of Murphy's Law have been denied by scientific, rational research. What we *know* is that Murphy's Law is right and the scientific researchers are wrong. Consider the following examples from the fascinating research of Robert Matthews[35], which actually demonstrates this:

Murphy's Law predicts:	Scientific research says:	The reality is:
When your breakfast toast falls on the floor it will land face down if it can.	Experiments show that if toast is tossed in the air a large number of times, it will land face down only half the time, as probability theory would predict.	Few of us toss our breakfast toast in the air – it normally slides off the plate because you are reading the paper. When this happens the toast will land face down most of the time, and this can be proved.
If your queue in the bank or supermarket can be beaten by the neighbouring one, it will be.	The mathematics of queues indicate that in the bank or supermarket queues are subject to random delays, and on average will tend to move at the same rate. Therefore all queues have the same chance of finishing first.	When you are in a queue you are not interested in averages, you just want to be out fastest. If there are, for example, three queues of the same length, the chances are only one in three that your queue will suffer fewer delays than the others – two-thirds of the time the other queues will do better and will finish before us.

This leads to three points of comment about research and management:

● If something is true and you know it to be true, having someone measure it and write you a report about it does not make it any more or less true – it simply stops you doing something about it, while you wait for the research to be done.

- Most research is crude and arbitrary in the assumptions it makes – this reflects technology and budgets, not competence – and measuring the wrong things badly is not an inspiring description of what we should use to make decisions.
- The real challenge is not making market research more sophisticated, it is trying to ensure that the things that managers 'know' and 'understand' are the right things and they are well understood. As we will see shortly, this is actually something we can work on. It also leads to identifying the important information needs, and the role that market research can usefully play.

REALITY CHECK
CONSUMER PSYCHOLOGY GETS RUDE

In 1999, the supermarket firm Tesco instructed its suppliers of melons to grow more small melons for them – no more than 1 lb 3 oz. The reason? Because it had received market research findings from its consumer psychologists suggesting that the fashionable preference for smaller female breasts – epitomized by the model Kate Moss and the actress Gwyneth Paltrow – explained why women shoppers were rejecting large melons in favour of small ones. Focus groups of female shoppers suggested that breast size was the most likely subconscious factor influencing the choice of a melon. The Tesco psychologist's report also dwelt on the idea that when choosing a melon, customers liked to feel around the blossom end of the fruit with its nipple-like scar ...

Is it just me, or does anyone else think that Tesco's market researchers should try and get out more, and perhaps get a life? I believe it was Robert Townsend who said of psychologists: 'I have nothing against 55-year-old bachelors who live with their mothers, until they set themselves up as arbiters of normality'.

Let me save Tesco a lot of money in further research. The reason people do not like big melons is that they crush the rest of the shopping, they are difficult to carry, they fall out of the shopping bag, they do not fit on the cool shelf in the fridge, and you end up throwing most of it away because it rots before you eat it all. I would guess that anyone who has worked in a supermarket for more than five minutes could have told you this.

Source: Peter Birkett (1999), 'Sales of Smaller Melons Go From Bust to Boom', *Daily Telegraph*, 3 May.

Myths of marketing information

At the risk of seeming perverse, perhaps we can build up to the issue of what marketing sensing is really about by flushing out some of the myths about marketing information which stand in the way of effective market sensing. Most of these myths are to do with our needs for information, and how we use it when we have got it.

Myth 1 – We need more marketing information

'There seems to be a built-in presumption in the minds of many market researchers and computer analysts that if you give managers more information they will make better decisions'

There seems to be a built-in presumption in the minds of many market researchers and computer analysts that if you give managers more information they will make better decisions. Much of this presumption rests on the 'scientific' model of decision making. Perhaps the clearest manifestation of this at the moment is 'database marketing' – where we aim to build a bank of information containing everything it is possible to know about our customers. However, to be fair, managers are also party to this conspiracy – the research evidence is that *however* much information they already have, when faced with a decision managers will demand *more* information.

Perhaps the greatest danger is that we simply create 'information overload' for our executives, such that they cannot cope with all the information we direct at them. The result is that instead of helping managers to understand the marketplace, we overwhelm them with facts, figures, reports, and so on. If anyone says they need more information, try asking them 'why?'.

Myth 2 – We need marketing information faster

One of the joys of listening to the disciples of technology and 'database marketing' is to observe their simple pleasure in how quickly they can get results on their desks – with scanning at the retail electronic point-of-sale, we can monitor sales and cash flow by the hour! This is impressive technology, but raises a couple of minor questions like:

- So what? What are you going to do with the information when you have got it? (Probably sit around waiting for some more.)
- What did you used to do with your time, instead of watching hourly results (run the business, perhaps)?

Certainly, one of the major uncertainties we all face is due to the fact that much of the information we get is out-of-date by the time we get it. No quarrel with that. But let's not be silly about this! More to the point are questions about what information we *need*, how *complete* it is, and what we *use* it for, than simple technology-driven speed of delivery.

Myth 3 – If we try hard enough, we can know everything

There is a seductive notion that if we just invest enough in market research, if we can just get enough computing power, if we can just crunch enough numbers, then we will know *everything* there is to know about this market – and then we cannot get it wrong.

There are a couple of problems here. The largest is the simple, unavoidable fact that you can *never* have the most important information because it does not exist when you need it. With the biggest market research budget in the world and the greatest computer, the most crucial uncertainties remain. On the things that matter most, we cannot reduce uncertainty to zero or anything like it. Anyway, this is why marketing is fun, and why some people do it better than others.

Myth 4 – We know what marketing information we want

Surely no-one still believes that managers know what information they want?

REALITY CHECK
SPOTTING THE MOST IMPORTANT INFORMATION

Picture the scene: A Royal Navy warship is proceeding across the ocean, when its radar detects a stationary vessel directly in its path, some miles distant. The Captain is informed, and immediately radios the message 'You are on a collision course with me, please steer 10 points South immediately'. Within minutes he receives the reply: 'You are on a collision course with me, alter course 10 points North immediately'. Somewhat rattled by such insubordination, the Captain radios 'I am a large vessel on urgent business, please steer 10 points South immediately'. The reply comes back: 'My business is also important, change your course immediately'. The Captain is now an interesting shade of purple, his fingers are twitching over the missile

> launch controls, collision is imminent, and he radios the message: 'I am one of Her Majesty's frigates, with nuclear arms, proceeding on Royal Navy business, you will steer South 10 points now!' There is a short delay before the reply which reads: 'I am a lighthouse, I suggest you steer 10 points North now!'
>
> *The moral*: Believing you have all the facts you need is risky, even if you have a nuclear missile with you.

Strangely enough, expecting managers to know (and thus to be able to tell us) what information they need, we are on a loser in most cases. If you ask managers what information they want, you are likely to get one of three responses (only one of which is absolutely frank, and that one doesn't help us much):

● Exactly what I get now (because I am right and who the heck are you to suggest I am not).
● Everything (because then I will be all-powerful and rule the world).
● Don't know (please help me).

What is even worse is that as we move to the most important decisions, the predictability of information *needs* approaches zero. The real truth is that we can only decide what we need to know when we can *model* our decisions. The idea that we model the decisions and then we know what our information needs are, comes directly from the notion that making decisions is 'scientific'. In this scenario: we know with certainty and can quantify our single, paramount goal; we can identify and isolate all the options open to us; the goal implies the quantitative criterion of choice; we input full information to work out the pay-off for each option; we apply our criterion to make an optimal choice. What could be simpler, and what better way to identify precisely our information needs?

'we actually know relatively little about how managers make decisions faced with unresolvable uncertainties, and we should at least avoid some of the sillier assumptions that people make'

In the real world, however, a few things get in the way: fuzzy, unclear, qualitative and multiple goals; the inability to identify all the options which exist; lack of information availability; and often the impossibility anyway of separating and isolating one decision from all the rest. That is why we cannot give simple answers about what information we want.

The truth is that we actually know relatively little about how managers make decisions faced with unresolvable uncertainties, and we should at least avoid some of the sillier assumptions that people make.

Myth 5 – We know why we want the information

This brings us back to the fairy tale of scientific decision making. Obviously we want information to make better decisions between the options open to us, to monitor performance, and so on. This sounds sensible, but it does not tie-up very well with the role information actually seems to play in organizations.

Two learned and prestigious American researchers[36] have examined the way managers use information in organizations and found that generally: much of the information collected has little *relevance* to decisions; information is frequently collected *after* the decision has been made; much of the information requested is subsequently ignored; regardless of how much information is available, *more* is requested; managers complain about the *inadequacy* of their organization's information resources, while ignoring what information is actually available to them; and the relevance of information requests is less conspicuous than their *insistence*.

These researchers concluded of this 'information perversity' that: 'It is possible, on considering these phenomena, to conclude that organizations are systematically stupid'. Equally, they note it may just be that we have a very limited understanding of why and how managers use information.

Certainly, the evidence is that managers search for marketing information for all sorts of reasons, including the following: to *justify* decisions already made; to provide managers with *reassurance* about decisions made; to *signal* to all concerned that something matters and that we are being 'rational' about it; to build *consensus* about something, so we all think about it in the same way; to provide a 'collective memory'; to *delay* decisions and 'take the heat off'; to *prevent* decisions being made (until the research is completed); to *reconcile* diverse viewpoints about an issue; to *ritualistically* recognize a problem area, even though we know there is nothing we can do about it; to provide the basis for *negotiation* about the issue; to provide *conciliation* between diverse viewpoints in an executive group; to establish 'ownership' of a particular issue or set of issues; to gain influence; or to build personal 'secret' files of our own on important issues for the future. These reasons for obtaining and using marketing information have precious little to do with the 'scientific' model of the rational decision maker.

However, there is something we should bear in mind about this. We have *no basis whatever* for assuming that there is anything wrong about this use of information. The simple truth is that we do not know enough about how organizations actually work to dismiss or condemn such information practices. Indeed, some people would say that these are the *most* important and valuable functions of information in organizations, because they provide decision makers with the comfort, reassurance and influence they need to make decisions and to get their jobs done.

Myth 6 – Well, we know what we don't need to know

Perhaps the fastest way into understanding the culture and dogma of an organization is to look at its information resources. However, don't just look at what information they collect – look at the information they choose *not* to collect; look at the information they *discard*; look at the information they receive but *discredit* and refuse to believe. Then you will start to put a handle on that organization's dogma, stereotypes and the critical strategic assumptions they make about the world, and thus about what works and what doesn't.

REALITY CHECK
MAKING ASSUMPTIONS AND PLAYING CHICKEN

One of the companies, which shall remain nameless, that designs high-speed railway engines and carriages has a major concern with driver safety as speeds increase. How can you test to see if the wind-shield will resist being struck by outside objects when the train is going at 150 miles an hour? They contacted Boeing, who know about testing wind-shields on aircraft. They borrowed Boeing's testing apparatus, which was flown in from America. The machine was essentially a catapult. The instructions were to load the machine with a chicken and fire it at the train wind-shield to simulate collision with a bird at high speed. This they did. The chicken went straight through the wind-shield, through the back of the driver's cab and stopped only at the back of the carriage. The engineers were distraught. Boeing flew over experts to assist. They repeated the test with the same results. The man from Boeing smiled quietly, and suggested that they might get a better result if they repeated the test, but this time maybe defrost the chicken ...

If this all sounds a bit brutal – then try asking anyone who has ever been a junior market analyst, business analyst, financial analyst or anything similar about how they used to do reports and analyses when they joined the company, but they always seemed to get it 'wrong', and had to do it again until they got it 'right'. (Where 'wrong' means 'not what we expected you to tell us', and 'right' means 'what we expected you would tell us'!)

REALITY CHECK
IGNORING COMPETITIVE INFORMATION

A dramatic example of managerial selectiveness, in what to pay attention to, comes from working with a group of executives from a large firm in the computer industry, who faced the task of building a new market position in a specific key account. One of the basic techniques we used was SWOT analysis (enumerating our Strengths and Weaknesses and the Opportunities and Threats in the market – see pp. 539–47 for a full description). The group did a SWOT analysis of their own current position, and the results were depressing – they saw the market as dominated by IBM and could find no way around this. We tried another tack – we said 'go away and pretend that you are the competitors and do the SWOT from their point of view, because their Threats and Weaknesses define our Opportunities'. This they did. They came back several hours later with a SWOT analysis of IBM's view of the market and they were pleased – they could actually see some chinks in the IBM armour. We then said 'great, now what about the other competitors?' They said 'well, we didn't do a SWOT for them, we don't know anything about them, and besides, they are not *real* players!'. This 'not real players' category, incidentally, included a few minor companies like DEC, Honeywell and the Japanese. That is not the real point. The real point is that the story shows how to go from being number 2 in a market to number 5 in the space of three years, because you did not take the competitors seriously enough to collect information about them. That is the real point.

I like to discuss cases like this with managers by asking them if they will accept that ultimately all organizations, including their own, tend to behave like the 'Ravenous Bugblatter Beast of Traal' from Douglas Adams' book, *The Hitch-Hiker's Guide to the Galaxy* (Pan Books, 1979). Readers may recall that the Ravenous Bugblatter Beast of Traal is 'a mindbogglingly stupid animal, it assumes that if you can't see it, it can't see you – daft as a brush, but very very ravenous'. The parallel is, of course, that we assume that if we keep quiet and hide from our competitors, then because they cannot see us, we won't be able to see them, which gets us back to organizations like the computer company described above.

Myth 7 – We measure what matters

One way to turn a blind eye to all the points above is to adopt the view that we have done OK so far, so we must be doing it right, i.e. we research and evaluate what matters, so let's talk about something else. The evidence is, however, that what most of us measure is not what matters, but what is *easiest to measure*.

Now there are two sides to this as well. The first is that we *literally* measure what is cheapest and least problematic to measure, for example: sales not customer satisfaction; marketing costs not the value of marketing assets; established competitors not new ones; and so on. This is one thing we can, and should, challenge.

At a deeper level, however, secondly, we measure what the culture of the organization *tells* us it is easiest to measure and what matters (usually because that's what we've always done, and it suits us just fine, thank you). That is more difficult to deal with, but needs challenging as well.

'we measure what the culture of the organization tells us it is easiest to measure and what matters (usually because that's what we've always done, and it suits us just fine, thank you)'

My all-time favourite (and true) story of looking the wrong way comes from the days when I worked in retailing. Our Head Office team was convinced that a particular manager's stock deficits could only be explained by fraud. They checked the goods-in at the back door, stock control and cash-in at the checkouts. But everything balanced perfectly – the store was being run beautifully, apart from the fact that every so often they seemed to lose an entire lorry-load of produce. The team sat and watched the checkouts for days, but could never find a discrepancy between till rolls and cash received. They had just about given up, when someone finally had the sense to *count* the checkouts – there were eleven instead of the ten for which they had books (ten for the company and one for the manager). It is a very easy assumption to make! It is the things we don't think we need to know that catch us out time and time again.

Or, consider the following account published in *The Sunday Times* in 1996, describing events at the Bloemfontein Pelanomi hospital:

'Every Friday over a period of months a couple of years ago, hospital staff found the patient occupying a certain bed in intensive care lying dead with no apparent cause. At first it seemed coincidental. Then doctors feared a "killer disease". Deaths continued. Finally, a nurse noticed the Friday cleaning lady doing her weekly chores. This maid would enter the ward, un-plug the life-support systems beside the bed, plug in her floor polisher, clean the ward and once again plug in the patient, leaving no trace of the cause of the patient's death. How many died in the South African Floor Polisher Massacre?'

None of us can ever afford to believe that we have all the relevant facts and can ignore new, unexpected information!

Myth 8 – We know what we know

There are two issues here depending on where you put the emphasis in the name of this eighth myth. We know what we *know* – all too often it would seem that we have a very limited view of what is actually available in the company, and who knows what. We can make progress by finding the internal experts and the undisseminated information, and conversely the blockages to information flows. Alternatively, we *know* what we know – do we really, or do we just accept what we are told?

REALITY CHECK

INFORMATION AND ANALYSIS VERSUS COMMON SENSE

During World War II, researchers were tasked with identifying the most important areas on aircraft which should be protected with additional armour. Conventional wisdom was that armour protection should be concentrated on the engines and the fuel tanks. The researchers therefore arranged to inspect bombers returning from actual raids over enemy territory shortly after they landed. The methodology involved identifying bullet and shrapnel damage and carefully assessing the concentration and severity of damage to each aircraft. Their findings were stunning – conventional wisdom appeared quite wrong. On the aircraft they examined there was little, if any, enemy damage to the engines and fuel tank areas, suggesting no need for additional armour plating in these locations. Fortunately, their report was quashed when one of the fliers pointed out that they were examining the planes which survived and got home, and maybe they should look at some of the ones that got shot down, mainly through hits in the engines and fuel tanks ...

Myth 9 – We know who decides what we know

Sounds reasonable, but let's just think that one through. If you consider some of the hidden effects of formalized information systems, you come up with factors like these:

- *Constrained data sets* – We cannot have information on everything. This selectivity in the information system determines what we know (and in large part, what we don't).
- *Skewed data sets* – The selectivity in what data we collect comes from the biases and prejudices of the systems designer, easy information availability, and the designer's understanding of the problems we face.
- *Static data sets* – Information systems become self-perpetuating and reinforcing, so we are stuck with the selectivity and biases.

Less technical, there is ample evidence that once information systems are formalized people become far more 'careful' in the data they put in, and what they communicate. There is more to it though. Consider the following situation.

REALITY CHECK
THE REAL POLITICS OF INFORMATION

A Market Analyst in a high-technology company needed to get data on advertising spend divided by product group, as part of a programme of evaluating the absorption of marketing costs by different products, markets and channels. This was a surprising but real information gap. The strategy was clear – to approach the Advertising Manager for the necessary data on advertising and sales expenses by product. The result was that the Advertising Manager was very difficult to get to see, hostile and very unhelpful. The information provided after much discussion was: incomplete, contained only budgeted figures not expenditure, was not split by product, and contained many 'mistakes' and 'errors'. There appeared to be something of a barrier. The Analyst concluded that the fact that no-one (including the Accounting Department) had *any* figures on advertising and promotional spending, other than in gross, total budget terms, might well be because the Advertising Manager did not *want* anyone to know. It started to become clear that there was significant 'slack' or discretionary spend built into the Advertising Manager's budget, which he had no intention of uncovering. Conversations with management accountants and the corporate planning unit showed they too were well aware of the problem, but they did not know what to do either. The only strategy open seemed to be to persuade the Marketing Director to *order* the Advertising Manager to provide the information. The persuasion was easy, because the Marketing Director had already given this 'order' numerous times, with no effect whatever. Not wholly insignificant was the fact that the Advertising Manager, though relatively junior in the hierarchy, was a long-term employee who had been around since the business started, had been to school with the Managing Director, and regularly socialized with the MD because their children were the same age, played at the same tennis club, and so on. The Market Analyst concluded that the only way forward was to get the information indirectly, or to remove the need for the information, at least for the time being. Besides, the MD and Advertising Manager would soon be retiring …

Now, let's ask the question again – do you *really* know who makes the hidden choices which determine how your organization understands the outside world?

Myth 10 – Well, we know what it means

Charles Hardy recounts the story of the Peruvian Indians in South America who suffered at the hands of Spanish invaders. The point of the story is that the Indians saw the sails of the Spanish ships on the horizon, but believed this must be some new phenomenon of the weather, and did nothing to prepare to defend themselves against the Spanish invasion.

The question is: how often are companies wrong-footed in the marketplace simply because they ignore important information for the reason that it is inconsistent with managers' past experience?

Even worse if we buy research to tell us only the things that are consistent with our past experiences, confirm our existing conclusions, and validate a 'no change needed' strategy? Impossible? Not impossible according to studies by the Center for Strategic Research in Boston. They found widespread beliefs among major users of market research that market research was biased and distorted to confirm views rather than to challenge them. They concluded: 'Market research is a very wonderful thing. It can support or deny any premise or allegation or lack thereof that you want'[37].

> *'how often are companies wrong-footed in the marketplace simply because they ignore important information for the reason that it is inconsistent with managers' past experience?'*

Now some of these myths about marketing information are just silly, because they represent a lack of understanding of what is feasible and what is not. However, in other ways, dispelling some of these myths is useful because it moves us closer to the reality of information in the organizational setting. One more time: the issue is customer focus, the issue is superior understanding of customers, so the issue is market sensing not market research. If you buy into the point – the next bit is important: you can do things to leverage and improve market sensing capabilities, and hence support real customer focus.

Enhancing our market sensing capabilities[38]

The difference between market sensing and conventional market research or information systems is that our focus is on managers' *understanding* of the market. Understanding is not the same as information. It is about developing new ways of looking at the outside world, to improve the way in which we develop our market strategies and deliver our marketing programmes. This is a process which we can *manage* for greater effectiveness in most companies. This is not something to be taken lightly. What we are building up to is no less than a challenge to the organization's culture.

REALITY CHECK
CHALLENGING THE STATUS QUO

An interesting story from the operations research literature of World War II illustrates the importance of challenging the way things are. Researchers made a film of the military drill used by soldiers to load and fire the big guns, looking for ways of improving efficiency. They found that in slow-motion the film showed that at the end of the drill, just before firing the gun, two soldiers who played no other role stood to attention behind the gun. No-one could explain what this was for, but assumed it was essential because that was how it was *always* done. Finally, a World War I veteran looked at the film and said 'Ah, yes, of course ... they used to hold the horses to stop them bolting!'

The underlying problem is that *telling* people what their problems are, and by implication to get their act together, has proved to be a singularly ineffective approach to winning people's commitment and achieving effective strategy implementation. This is for a number of reasons.

First, corporate culture may be such a barrier that they simply do not believe us. Culture has been defined in many ways, but a useful definition of culture is 'the way we see things here'. This includes the process of selecting the information we accept and what we reject, the issues we monitor and those we ignore, and all the assumptions we make inside the organization about the outside world – what works in this market and what does not, who the competitors are and how they respond to competitive challenges, what matters to customers, how the market is changing or not changing, and so on. The underlying point is that people in organizations develop simplified models, which become their shared understanding of the world. The problem arises when that shared understanding becomes outdated and inflexible, and yet we still cling to it – and, after all, we must be right because everyone around us agrees.

Second, 'telling' people what their problems are is unlikely to gain their 'ownership' of those problems – communication effectiveness demands that we recognize the importance of employee and manager perceptions of events and the strength of two-way communication to identify problems in those perceptions. Quite simply, it is naive to expect attempts at one-way communication to change people's minds about things.

Third, it is too easy to be simplistic in assuming that we know how managers search for information and use it when they have it for decision making. There is abundant evidence to suggest that the information search and use in organizations is complex and reflects many needs other than making better decisions.

It follows that a critical precursor to strategy implementation and change is that the people who have to change in a company see the need and reasons for change. But, just telling them does not seem to work.

This suggests the need for an approach to improving the understanding that managers and specialists have of their markets, which uncovers the problems to be solved and identifies the new challenges to be met, but which involves 'finding out' what matters, not just being told. In this situation the role of the marketing planner or analyst becomes one of managing the *process* of market sensing, not simply the provision of information and conclusions. The approach described below is a simple method of achieving some of these things.

'a useful definition of culture is "the way we see things here". This includes the process of selecting the information we accept and what we reject, the issues we monitor and those we ignore, and all the assumptions we make inside the organization about the outside world'

A structure for market sensing

This approach is simple and accessible to managers. The goal is simply to provide a structure for executives and planners to articulate what they know about changes outside the company, and to identify the most critical gaps in that knowledge.

There are two stages. *First*, we need to specify:

- which environment facing the company we are evaluating and the dimension of the environment to be analysed (see comments below on how to manage these choices for maximum effect);
- the time-frame (normally three to five years); and
- the market in question should also be specified.

The task then is to brainstorm the events in the chosen part of the company's environment which might take place or which are currently developing. The most important events are listed (and also mnemonic codes for ease of reference). However, the framework also requires that we identify specific effects on the company if this event takes place. If we cannot do this – the event is too broad and should be defined more narrowly, or it is unimportant to our analysis. For example, events like 'Single European Market' or 'Change of Government' are normally too broad. Then, we need to do two further things: assess the current view of the *probability* of the event happening (initially a subjective 'guesstimate' which we may want to test and evaluate further), and the *likely effect* of the event on the business if it does happen (the suggested scale runs from 1 = Disaster to 7 = Ideal, and again this is something on which we may want to take an initial view which can be refined at a later stage). We should try to build a full view of the most important aspects of the environment as they impact on the company.

Second, the events (or their codes) are then entered on the model in Figure 7.3 – positioned by the scores we have placed on the probability of each event occurring and the effect of the event if it does occur. The broad categories of event are categorized into:

- *Utopia* – events with a very good effect which are very likely to occur.
- *Field of Dreams* – events which are highly desirable but seem unlikely to happen the way things are at the moment.
- *Danger* – events which are very threatening to the company and which are very likely to happen.
- *Future Risks* – undesirable events that seem unlikely to happen, but which we may want to monitor in case they become more likely.

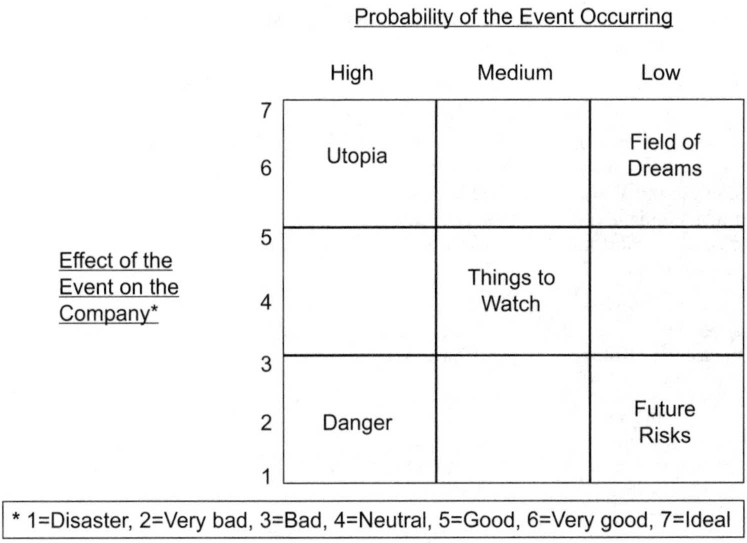

Probability of the Event Occurring

* 1=Disaster, 2=Very bad, 3=Bad, 4=Neutral, 5=Good, 6=Very good, 7=Ideal

Figure 7.3   A framework for market sensing

- *Things to Watch* – where we do not see the probability as very high and the impact is relatively neutral, but where monitoring is needed in case either of these changes.

What we now have is a model of the outside world, which we can use for testing the robustness of proposed market strategies, identifying information gaps and evaluating market attractiveness. However, making this truly effective is far more about how the process of market sensing is *managed*, rather than just filling in forms and building models.

Managing the market sensing process

The approach described above is very simple to implement. It is accessible and provides a structure for the information and intelligence in the company, and captures a picture of the outside customer and competitor world as it is currently understood in the company. This is, however, only a starting point in achieving our goal of building and sharing real market understanding so that it impacts on strategic decisions and implementation. There are a number of key issues to be addressed in managing this process, which are summarized as a checklist in Table 7.2, and discussed below. The first two points relate to how to focus thinking to the maximum advantage,

Table 7.2 Checklist for managing market sensing

Questions	Examples	Goals
What environment needs addressing to improve our market understanding, customer focus and market strategies?	Business, Market, Competitive, Technological, Legal, International Environments.	FOCUS on the area where our assumptions are weakest and our market understanding is poor.
How should we subdivide the environment to understand it better?	Business Environment: Political, Economic, Social and Technological.	FOCUS on the most critical aspects of the chosen environment.
How should we interpret the impact of changes we identify in the chosen environment?	Impact on customer relationships. Impact on market size and share.	LINK TO PLANNING by confronting the importance of changes to our strategies.
Who should interpret the picture built and what are the critical questions they should address?	Managers to specify: how are we exploiting the good things and defending against the bad things in our strategies, and how are we monitoring the most critical issues?	LINK TO PLANNING by challenging conventional views about strategies and information needs and use.
How do we link our new market understanding to decision making?	Plans must state explicitly how they reflect changes, opportunities and risks in the most critical areas of the environment.	LINK TO PLANNING by demanding that implications are addressed in detail and not ignored.
What information should be provided?	Published studies, reports, research studies, corporate intelligence, etc.	ENRICH THE SENSING PROCESS by stimulating 'out of the box' thinking.
Who should be consulted/involved?	Planning team, cross-functional representatives, line managers, suppliers, customers, outside experts.	ENRICH THE PROCESS by bringing more viewpoints to bear to challenge conventional company management assumptions.

the next three are concerned with linking market sensing to planning, and the last points address the issue of how to enrich the sensing process.

Choosing the environment

The first issue is what approach to the outside world is potentially most needed to confront change and influence behaviour in the company. The basic framework described above can be used to evaluate the Business Environment, the Market Environment, the Competitive Environment, the Technological Environment, the Legal Environment and the International Environment in different companies and to deal with different types of problems.

For example, in one clothing company we used the most general version of the model (the Business Environment), and the model produced by executives was 'Utopian' in the extreme – i.e. every event they could identify in the environment around their business fell into the Utopia cell of the model shown in Figure 7.3. This suggests that managers believe they know everything and everything is certain. When asked if they had considered renaming the company the 'Smug Corporation', the executives said things like 'You have to understand, we do not have competitors, only imitators'. When the scanning was refocused onto the competitive environment, their views started to change quite dramatically.

Subdividing the environment to focus attention

The second point of focus is how to subdivide the environment to ensure that people address the most important aspects, and highlight the gaps in understanding that are most critical.

For example, with one high-technology company, which was led by R&D and driven by scientific innovation in products, one glaring omission in management thinking was about competition – as evidenced by recent new product failures and as claimed by the company's marketing manager (who felt he was largely ignored). This problem was approached by asking teams of managers associated with new product projects to specifically address the Competitive Environment in their planning. This was subdivided into: *Direct Competition* (i.e. other companies in the same industry producing the same type of product); *Customer Competition* (i.e. the tendency in key markets for customers to develop their own materials and to substitute this for product purchase); *Generic Competition* (i.e. different technologies capable of serving the same customer needs). This has become a permanent and essential part of the company's new product planning, because their views on market positioning have changed dramatically, developing, for example, into deals with key customers to help them produce their own products and collaborations with companies outside the industry to use the newer technologies becoming available to meet customer needs.

Identifying the impact of environmental changes

If events that happen outside are of any importance it is because they influence something that matters to the company. There is advantage therefore in addressing at the earliest stage what these impacts may be. For example, in viewing the Market Environment, we could ask for each event to be analysed in terms of its impact on customer/supplier relationships, or with the Competitive Environment, the impact of each event on our market share. The aim is to encourage thinking to be very specific to the company and its goals.

Interpreting the model of the environment for strategy building

Probably the most important issue is how we interpret the model of the environment which has been built. Here there are three questions to stress and demand attention. Given that the model is a picture of the things happening outside which we regard as most important to the survival and prosperity of the company, then we should demand responses to the following questions:

- We have identified the changes in this market which are potentially very advantageous for our performance in this market, and which are likely to happen (Utopia in the model) – the question is: where, explicitly and realistically, are we exploiting those factors in our market strategies?
- We have also identified the changes in this market which are potentially major threats, and which are also likely to happen (Danger in the model) – the question is: where, explicitly and realistically, are we defending against these changes in our market strategies?
- If it has been done properly then the model we have produced shows the things that are most important to our position in this market – the question is: are we monitoring and evaluating these factors in our marketing information system?

It is amazing how often executives have to admit that their plans and strategies do not address the real changes in the marketplace where they intend to operate – this is the moment when new thinking about strategies may become possible for the first time, because managers are confronted with their own logic. Even more surprising are situations where managers are forced to admit that their information systems do not focus on the things that really matter to their performance – the systems report the figures and statistics that are easiest to report and that have always been reported.

For example, precisely this situation was found in work with a wholesaling company. The company essentially has a sophisticated telephone marketing system, selling specialized wooden furniture to schools and homes and training centres for the disabled. In undertaking a view of the Business Environment, at boardroom level, one conclusion reached was that just about the most significant factor for profitability was merger and acquisition activity in the furniture manufacturing sector, which led to increased pressure on the wholesaler's margin. The point is that nowhere in the company was there any monitoring or evaluation of this merger activity – every time a new merger came as a big surprise. Managers objected that it was not possible to have advance information on mergers and acquisitions. They are quite right. However, few such events take place without gossip at the exhibitions and trade events and without comments in the trade press and so on. The data may be soft, but maybe that is more use to the board than sitting back and waiting to be surprised again. People often suggest it is an exaggeration, but it seems all too often the case that we do not watch the things that really matter because the information does not fit the computerized information system.

'it seems all too often the case that we do not watch the things that really matter because the information does not fit the computerized information system'

There are also other types of question that can be raised around our model of the environment:

- Are there things we can do to reduce uncertainties around important issues, to improve the power of the model?
- Are there things we can do to change the position of events in the model?

An initial response to the first of these questions may be negative. This is not always necessarily true. For example, in work with a company targeting the water industry in the build-up to privatization, one major unknown at the time was the form that privatization would take, which was a barrier to developing market strategies. Clearly, the government is unlikely to provide such information ahead of time – but it was possible to go to a specialized agency in contact with senior civil servants and politicians and to get a pretty good idea of the plans, which is what the company did.

To some, the second question may appear even more out-landish – how can a company change the environment? Clearly, in the general sense it cannot. However, the point of making the whole exercise focused bears fruit here. If, for example, the largest issue in the 'Danger' area is competitive entry with a new product, then maybe the strategy to pursue is one of collaboration.

This is an area where creative thinking may become possible, as we ease people away from the status quo represented by corporate culture. For instance, in the USA, Hershey, the chocolate company, came very close to persuading the federal authorities to change the date of the change to daylight saving time into November, instead of being in October. The reason is – because parents do not like their small children making 'trick or treat' visits to houses after dark – an extra hour of daylight on October 31 – Halloween – is worth several million dollars worth of extra chocolate sales in the USA. The company failed in this attempt, but it remains surprising how creative thinking may be about 'unchangeable' events in the environment, given the chance.

Linking market sensing to plans

If the benefits of this approach are to be realized, then the conclusions reached by understanding the environment that matters should be linked to the decisions made about market strategies. This may take no more than agreement that strategic market plans must state explicitly how they reflect changes in the most critical aspects of the environment.

Providing information as a stimulus to thinking

Another decision requiring careful thought is what information should be provided to the executive and planning teams scanning the environment, through written reports, presentation by outside experts, and so on. The key to handling this seems to be not to overload people with new information but to provide enough that is new to help people break the mould. Certainly, it is disastrous at any point to suggest to people that they are wasting their time because everything has been done before by 'Corporate Intelligence' or by 'Market Research' departments. The aim here is to enrich the sensing process, not to truncate it.

Who should be consulted and involved?

Perhaps the most actionable lever for enriching the sensing process is consultation and participation. The argument is clear: it is that consultation with managers and employees and their participation is critical to determining their responses to market developments. This follows the principle that giving discretion to managers and empowering them to find solutions and innovations is a powerful lever for strategic change, which should not be underestimated.

'Perhaps the most actionable lever for enriching the sensing process is consultation and participation'

Clearly, the marketing analyst can use the framework provided here to undertake an appraisal of the market environment as an individual exercise, but this is unlikely to impact on the problems we set out to solve, and ignores a major opportunity to build consensus on the need and direction for change. The issues to consider in managing participation in this type of exercise are:

- *A team* – if we want 'ownership' and commitment, then we need to involve the key players in implementation in the analytical stage of planning, for how else can we get a 'buy-in' to new strategic directions?
- *Cross-functional representation* – one of the most powerful levers for change in major corporations is the use of the powerful and informed cross-functional team, which pools specialized expertise around a focused problem. At the simplest level, it may be that people from operations and R&D can contribute useful insights into market change. At a deeper level, if we expect co-operation and support across departments for market strategy implementation, then it makes sense to have them involved and consulted in the process.
- *Line and staff specialists* – similarly, managers from line roles and staff roles may bring very different insights and sources of intelligence to the table, and challenge conventional ways of addressing the market. There is also the question of gaining credibility and 'buy-in' from line management as a foundation for effective implementation of resulting strategies.
- *Outsiders* – in some situations it may be possible to gain from the involvement of outsiders who bring new information and understanding of the markets we are appraising. This might include suppliers, customers or experts from the relevant research institutes and universities.
- *Culture shakers* – it is sometimes good to include company 'non-conformists' to shake some of our conventional beliefs and assumptions. In looking at how people fit into corporate cultures, Vijay Sathe[39] suggests the categories in Figure 7.4. The question is how many of our market sensing group are Mavericks or Rebels, who will look at things in a new way, from which we can learn new insights?
- *Unhardening the categories* – Alan Kantrow[40] suggests that all humans suffer not just from hardening of the arteries, but also 'hardening of the categories' – the traditional ways in which we look at information in the company – and we risk becoming 'prisoners of our categories'. Part of our task is to break the information we have into different categories to see what we learn – new market definitions, different types of customer segment, different ways of comparing ourselves to our

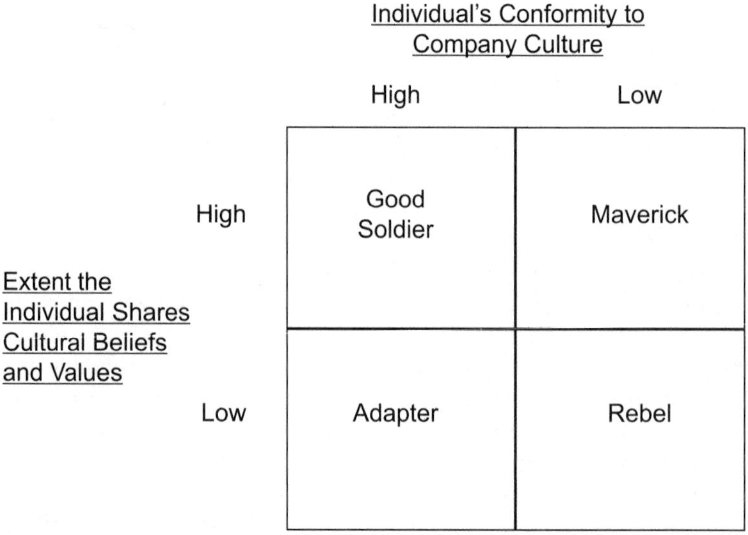

Individual's Conformity to
Company Culture

	High	Low
High	Good Soldier	Maverick
Low	Adapter	Rebel

Extent the
Individual Shares
Cultural Beliefs
and Values

Figure 7.4 Cultural conformity and non-conformity

competitors, different ways of grouping customer priorities, and so on. Remember the (alleged) quotation from US President Ronald Reagan: 'It is not interpreting the future that is difficult, the problem is predicting the past'.

It may not be possible to exploit all these sources of influence over the creation of market understanding in all cases, and it may not be necessary to do so. The principal points are summarized in Table 7.2 as a checklist for consideration in managing the process of building and sharing market understanding with managers.

'*the tools for building and refining market understanding have to be placed in the hands of the line managers and technical specialists upon whom we depend for the effective implementation of market strategies*'

The point of this is very simple – the tools for building and refining market understanding have to be placed in the hands of the line managers and technical specialists upon whom we depend for the effective implementation of market strategies. How can we expect people to commit to something when they do not see the reason for it? These market sensing procedures have been developed to work with line managers and planning teams to enrich and enhance their understanding of the most critical aspects of their markets, to use this as the basis for developing market strategies of which they may take 'ownership' and drive through to effective implementation, with all that is implied in terms of organizational change and disruption to the status quo.

A note of caution

However, a word of warning! These are fundamental issues not to be taken lightly – there are risks as well as opportunities. For the most part, people in organizations do not cling to the familiar way just out of perversity or bloody-mindedness (although there are exceptions to this!), but because it is a way of getting on with the things that we think matter. When we start to tamper with the flow and use of marketing information we have to run the risk of *reducing* performance in the short-term. For example, we can compare the opportunities and risks like this:

The problem	The opportunities	The risks
There is a too limited flow of customer and market information to put managers.	Increase the flow and amount of information to put more important issues on the agenda.	Information overload.
Key managers have adopted a simplified model of what works in the market and what matters to customers, which is invalid.	Force managers to confront and cope with a different view of the world, and to track the implications for marketing strategies.	Abandoning the accepted and assumed model of the world creates confusion, uncertainty and self-doubt which 'freezes' decision makers.
We ignore the impact of major changes in the marketing environment.	Develop new sensing approaches that change our view of what is happening out there, and how we need to change our strategies.	We make managers so fearful and intimidated by the speed and complexity of change in the outside world, they cannot make decisions – they just sit and watch the outside world in bemused wonderment.
Strong group consensus in our decision making, which means they will not look at new information or new ways of doing things.	Operate on the inertia and 'group think' by redesigning group memberships and the 'ownership' of critical information types.	We create resistance to change, conflict between groups, internal competition and in-fighting.

People do not adopt simplification mechanisms, group consensus, a false sense of stability, and so on, for the hell of it. These are mechanisms which allow us to make sense of things (however arbitrarily and inflexibly) and to get on with things (like making decisions and doing the work). We may *have* to change some of these things to get a new strategic direction – but slowly and with care!

Market intelligence

'it seems more likely that the most valuable inputs will be messy, qualitative, subjective and incomplete market intelligence, than neat research reports'

One of the things people say when they are introduced to market sensing is that you still need information to build the picture – so we are straight back to the conventional marketing research reports, and nothing is new. This is a fair point. However, while we may use marketing research reports in building a new picture of the market and a better understanding, it seems more likely that the most valuable inputs will be messy, qualitative, subjective and incomplete market intelligence, than neat research reports.

> In any organization, there is always one person who knows exactly what is going on – that little creep must be fired!

Indeed, many companies now have in-company intelligence units to co-ordinate and disseminate soft data and improve shared corporate knowledge[41]. If the issue is, for example, competitors' promotional activities, knowing what they are doing and responding is what matters, not having it written in a report with full statistics and graphics. The goal is to know something that you competitor does not, or if we all have the same information to use it more effectively than the competitor.

Intelligence is about knowing things. For example, when the Southwestern Bell Telephone Co. in the US heard rumours about new competitors entering the telephone market with special packages for home renters, they were able to counter this quickly by a programme of appointing apartment complex managers as Southwestern Bell sales agents. Similarly, feedback that new independent 'micro' phone companies appealed particularly to younger telephone renters led Southwestern to move resources into product offers and promotions based on college

companies[42]. This is about spotting patterns of change in the market and using that understanding to respond, not complex market research projects.

The issue of competitive intelligence is not new – as long ago as 1981 *Business Week* published *The Business Intelligence Beehive*, describing how Japanese companies had set up surveillance posts through the heartland of the US computer industry in Silicon Valley in California, to monitor US technology development by hiring American software experts. Competitive intelligence sources run all the way from readily available 'open sources' (like press clippings, government records, trade shows, industry reports) to observation of competitors' activities and interviews with competitors' suppliers, customers, former employees, present employees, and so on. This is not particularly sophisticated. Yet in 1995 a US survey was still able to divide US companies into:

● *Intelligence ostriches* – who did not use intelligence gathering, and did not believe their competitors gathered intelligence about them; compared to
● *Intelligence eagles* – who know these competitors are watching their every move, and do the same in return[43].

You might like to raise the issue of which category your company falls into. It might help if you know that an agency called OTA/Off The Record Research already claims to have intelligence informants in all the world's largest companies[44], and with the outbreak of peace, many spies have moved into lucrative corporate intelligence work[45].

The point is that while intelligence may be no more than a press cutting, a chat with a competitor's employee at a meal, a note from a salesperson about a rumoured new product coming out, compared to the beautifully-produced marketing research report complete with statistics and graphics, if our goal is understanding then it is probably a better source[46].

However, where it all comes together is in the question of how well we manage knowledge for competitive advantage with our customers.

Managing customer knowledge

Customer focus, market sensing and market intelligence are increasingly being brought together as key ways of building better understanding and developing better learning capabilities – the challenge is becoming to manage customer knowledge better than our competitors do.

Peter Drucker has pointed out, for example, that 90 per cent of the information that companies collect is internal – market research and the like only tells the company about itself. The challenge is to build knowledge about customers, about non-customers, about new markets they do not serve and new technologies that they do not yet possess[47]. We may yet see a new organizational role emerging – the Chief Knowledge Officer[48].

'We may yet see a new organizational role emerging – the Chief Knowledge Officer'

In case this sounds like an impossible dream which can never be realized, a recent study shows us four ways to improve the availability and use of customer knowledge so it impacts on our strategic choices[49]:

- *Creating 'customer knowledge development dialogues'* – for example, in the US, DaimlerChrysler's Jeep division runs customer events called 'Jeep Jamborees', attracting enthusiasts from far and wide. As well as observing customers using the vehicles in skills-related events, Jeep employees connect with customers through informal conversations and semi-formal roundtables. Jeep employs engineers and ethnographic researchers to build from this a better understanding of Jeep owners' relationships with their vehicles. This understanding drives changes to existing models and plans for new models.
- *Operating enterprise-wide 'customer knowledge communities'* – for example, IBM uses a collaborative Internet workspace called the CustomerRoom, focused on its major accounts, where individuals throughout the company's divisions and functions can exchange knowledge about particular accounts, including customer contacts and changes, proposals being developed, and research opportunities that can address a customer's emerging needs.
- *Capturing customer knowledge at the point of customer contact* – for example, one financial services company is already experimenting with call centres that focus on potential customer defections. Based on a combination of customer activity information and customized solutions that address customer dissatisfaction issues, customer service representatives can make product offers tailored to win profitable customers back to the company.
- *Demonstrating management commitment to customer knowledge* – management has a responsibility to invest resources, time and attention in maintaining customer dialogues and communities as a commitment to customer focus. For example, the Vice President of marketing at Ford's LincolnMercury division actively participates in, and encourages other employees to monitor, customer-related chat-rooms in the Internet.

Managing customer knowledge is about building understanding and better responses to customer needs and how they are changing.

'Managing customer knowledge is about building understanding and better responses to customer needs and how they are changing'

What it comes down to is this. You may cling to the idea that customer focus is about running the occasional customer care campaign, and that marketing information is about running surveys and writing reports, if you wish. However, market leaders across the globe are developing superior market understanding and sensing capabilities because they know that learning is the basis for developing superior strategies. You work out the difference and what it means for your company.

Now may be the time to consider the awkward questions again.

REALITY CHECK

THE AWKWARD QUESTIONS ABOUT CUSTOMER FOCUS AND MARKET SENSING

Do we know where we stand on the customer relationship scale – is this where we want to be?

What active and continuous strategies do we have to get better at listening to customers and learning from them and understanding what creates value for them – how should we extend and develop these activities? Do we listen to non-customers, former customers and new customers, as well as existing customers? What efforts are we making to respond by building and maintaining a customer-focused company – in terms that matter to customers not just management lip-service?

How well developed are our market sensing capabilities – at all levels in the company? Do we really know what the difference is between market information and market understanding – what can we do to enhance our sensing capabilities in this company? What efforts are we making to manage the knowledge we have about customers as a critical competitive resource?

How well do we link our customer knowledge and our market sensing to making strategic choices and decisions – should we do better?

So, where have we got to?

This chapter has tried to persuade you that the foundation for superior market strategies that deliver value to our customers is actually how well we understand those customers and how we use that understanding. We looked at customer focus as a continuous process of learning. We looked at market sensing as a way of extending that learning process and building our capabilities. The lynchpin is customer knowledge management – recognizing that customer focus and market understanding are the foundation for developing better market strategies and better processes behind them.

There are many challenges in putting this into practice in companies which still do no more than pay lip-service to customer focus, and see no need for any information other than what the agency produces in the occasional survey and focus group. No-one is saying it is easy. What we are saying is that it matters. It may be the single most important issue in revitalizing your process of going to market.

The next stage in building that strategy concerns the critical market choices that are faced. The logic of this progression should be clear – the authors of a study of the fastest-growing small and medium enterprises in the country summarize it nicely: 'Those that come out on top are ruthlessly exploiting the right marketplace by understanding what the customer wants'[50].

Notes and references

1. Deloitte Consulting (1999), *Making Customer Loyalty Real: A Global Manufacturing Study*, London: Deloitte & Touche.
2. Ronald B. Leiber (1997), 'Storytelling: A New Way to Get Close to Your Customer', *Fortune*, 3 February.
3. David Kay (1997), 'Go Where the Consumers Are and Talk to Them', *Marketing News*, 6 January.
4. Patricia B. Seybould (2001), 'Get Inside the Lives of Your Customers', *Harvard Business Review*, May, 81–89.
5. Peter Doyle (1997), *Marketing Management and Strategy*, 2nd ed., Hemel Hempstead: Prentice-Hall.
6. George R. Walther (1994), *Upside-Down Marketing*, New York: McGraw-Hill.
7. Peter Barley (1994), 'Looking for Trouble', *Marketing Business*, September, 21–24.
8. I must admit to a frisson of sympathy for the shop assistant in this particular case. The customer was my wife, Nikala – as formidable a consumer as any shop assistant is ever likely to meet! Expressions like 'customer from hell' spring to mind.

9. Stanley F. Slater and John C. Narver (1995), 'Market Orientation and the Learning Organization', *Journal of Marketing*, October, 63–74.

10. David W. Cravens, Gordon Greenley, Nigel F. Piercy and Stanley F. Slater (1998), 'Mapping the Path to Market Leadership', *Marketing Management*, **7** (3), 29–39.

11. Rachel Oldroyd (1997), 'Man With Plenty in Store', *Sunday Business*, 13 April.

12. Michael Treacy and Fred Wiersema (1995), *The Discipline of Market Leaders*, London: Harper Collins.

13. Hugh Muir (1996), 'Stay Tuned or Start Walking', *Daily Telegraph*, 30 September.

14. Pat Long (1997), 'Customer Loyalty: One Customer at a Time', *Marketing News*, 3 February.

15. Michael Thomas (1987), 'Coming to Terms With the Customer', *Personnel Management*, February, 24–28.

16. Jolyon Jenkins (1990), 'Say "Cheese"', *New Statesman and Society*, 20 April, 24–25.

17. David Clutterbuck (1989), 'Developing Customer Care Training Programmes', *Marketing Intelligence and Planning*, **7** (112), 34–37.

18. Robert Monaghan (1995), 'Customer Management Teams Are Here to Stay', *Marketing News*, 6 November.

19. William A. Band (1991), *Creating Value for Customers*, Toronto: Wiley.

20. Laura Mazur (1996), 'Accountability', *Marketing Business*, September.

21. Karl Albrecht (1988), *At America's Service*, Homewood, IL: Irwin.

22. Hal F. Rosenbluth and Dianne McFerrin Peters (1992), *The Customer Comes Second*, New York: William Merrow.

23. Chris T. Allen, Edward F. McQuarrie and Terri Feldman Barr (1998), *Implementing the Marketing Concept One Employee at a Time: Pinpointing Beliefs About Customer Focus as a Lever for Organizational Renewal*, Cambridge, MA: Marketing Science Institute, Report No. 98–125.

24. John Crump (1996), 'Changing the Culture', *The 8th UNISYS Life and Pensions Seminar*, Nice.

25. Mark Fronchetti (1996), 'Germans Learn to Grin and Bear It', *Sunday Times*, 7 April.

26. Eric Lesser, David Mundel and Charles Wiecha (2000), 'Managing Customer Knowledge', *Journal of Business Strategy*, November/December, 35–37.

27. John Thornhill (2000), 'The New Consumer is Always Right', *Financial Times*, 21 August.

28. Bob Lamons (1996), 'Research Won't Yield the Big Idea', *Marketing News*, 18 November.

29. Yes, OK, it took me a while too. They are: Ralph Lauren, Pierre Cardin, Calvin Klein and Tommy Hilfiger.

30. David Bowen (1996), 'There's No Safety in Numbers', *Independent on Sunday*, 20 October.

31. David Reed (1996), 'Information', *Marketing Business*, March, 56.

32. For reasons which wholly escape me, a junior colleague left this written on my whiteboard:
    Question: What's the difference between God and a professor?
    Answer: God does not think she is a professor.

33. Robert Harris (1996), 'Our Dance Around the D-Word', *Sunday Times*, 4 August.

34. Quoted in Ian P. Murphy (1997), 'Urgency of Strategic Research', *Marketing News*, 6 January.

35. Robert Matthews (1997), 'Murphy Really Does Sock It To Us', *Daily Telegraph*, 2 April.

36. Marta S. Feldman and James G. March (1981), 'Information in Organizations as Signal and Symbol', *Administrative Science Quarterly*, **26**, 171–86.

37. 'Respondents Assail the Quality of Research', *Marketing News*, 8 May 1995.

38. This section leans heavily on Nigel F. Piercy and Nikala Lane (1996), 'Marketing Implementation: Building and Sustaining a Real Market Understanding', *Journal of Marketing Practice: Applied Marketing Science*, **2** (3), 15–28.

39. Vijay Sathe (1988), *Culture and Related Corporate Realities*, Homewood, IL: Irwin.

40. Alan Kantrow (1989), *The Constraints of Corporate Tradition*, New York: Harper & Row.

41. Thomas A. Stewart (1995), 'Getting Real About Brainpower', *Fortune*, 27 November.

42. Pat Long (1995), 'Turning Intelligence Into Smart Marketing', *Marketing News*, 27 March.

43. Kelly Shermach (1995), 'Much Talk, Little Action on Competitive Intelligence', *Marketing News*, 28 August.

44. David Bogler (2000), 'Many Ears Kept to the Ground', *Financial Times*, 13 March.

45. Stephen Overell (2000), 'Masters of the Great Game Turn to Business', *Financial Times*, 23 March.

46. Kate Button (1994), 'Spies Like Us', *Marketing Business*, March, 7–9.

47. Peter Drucker (1998), *Peter Drucker on the Profession of Management*, Boston, MA: Harvard Business School Press.

48. Unpublished London Business School report, quoted in Richard Donkin (1998), 'Doing the Knowledge', *Financial Times*, 15 July.

49. Eric Lesser, David Mundel and Charles Wiecha (2000), 'Managing Customer Knowledge', *Journal of Business Strategy*, November/December, 35–37.

50. Katherine Campbell (1997), 'Steered by the Customer', *Financial Times*, 16 September.

CHAPTER 8

Market strategy:

Market choices

We took the first step in our strategic pathway as the development of customer focus and market sensing capabilities. The first area where superior market understanding should impact is on the market choices that we make and remake. This is the topic for this chapter, leading then to considering our value proposition and key relationships.

Market choices

A critical part of building and designing an effective market strategy is with the key choices we make about our markets (Figure 8.1):

- *Market definition* – how we select a piece of the marketplace and identify it as our market.
- *Market segmentation* – how we identify groups within the market as targets for our products and services.
- *Market attractiveness and market position* – what we decide makes a market or segment attractive to us and a position we take good or bad, and the choices we make about where to concentrate and to establish our marketing priorities.

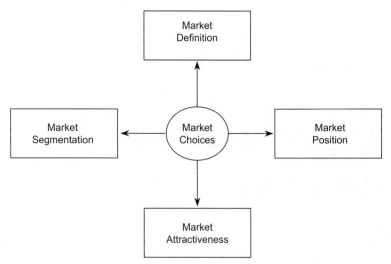

Figure 8.1 Key market choices in market strategy

Market definition

'in an era where the Internet is daily fuelling the blurring of traditional product–market boundaries, there is nothing fixed or static about the definition of the market where you hope to earn a living'

My first point is simple but dogmatic – in an era where the Internet is daily fuelling the blurring of traditional product–market boundaries, there is nothing fixed or static about the definition of the market where you hope to earn a living[1]. The first issue on which you can be trapped by the 'competitive box' is believing that markets stand still and the boundaries stay the same (see pp. 278–83).

Incredible though it may seem, there are valuable insights to be gained in most organizations by looking at, and frequently reviewing, the practical *definition* of our markets, in terms of specific products and services, and specific customer types. And yet very few people do this on a regular basis. This is silly. We know that markets change – so surely how we define the markets that matter to us should be constantly under review and revision? For example, see back to the reinvention of markets that lead to the creation of new market space and market growth (pp. 299–313).

To start with, there are obviously some basic parameters which should be defined so we know where we are competing, and planning, and so on: the geography of the market; the industrial sectors included; the type of consumer in demographic terms; the product/service applications or customer needs; the range of products/services which go into the market to meet these needs; and the broad types of customer within this need market. This can lead to a very productive analysis of the customer differences and thus potential segments within the total market.

But this is not about a conventional statistical analysis using traditional categories and measurements. Conventional market definitions reflect *industries*. We have already seen that industries are groups of companies linked by technology or product similarities. What we are interested in is *markets*. Markets are based on customer needs and demands. This is where market strategy must focus.

'industries are groups of companies linked by technology or product similarities. What we are interested in is markets. Markets are based on customer needs and demands'

The results of rethinking market definitions may be surprising. For example, one well-known whisky brand cut its price in response to a similar move by an own-label version. In fact, the own-label initiative had had no impact on the whisky brand because they were selling to different customer groups. By cutting price the company alienated its customers and ended up with weaker margins and sales, which also weakened its ability to respond to its real competitor for its customers – new white spirits. The truth is customers just do not fit traditional industry definitions of markets – you think you make crisps, the retailer thinks that the category is salty snacks, but the customer-defined market is lunch[2].

To open this issue up for a company, one practical approach, which is deceptively simple, but which has proved to have great leverage in helping to get executives to look at the market in a new way, is described below – the Product–Customer Matrix (Figure 8.2). This matrix is simple – all it asks us to do is to identify the five or six different types of product or service going into the market we have chosen, and the four or five types of different customer, which defines the total market. But there are some important angles here.

Let us consider *products* first. The initial reaction of most companies is that this task is *completely* impossible, unless we are prepared to give them a 20-foot wall for the matrix, because they have 500 products, or 5000, not five or six. This is the first catch – we are only interested in products as they are seen to be different by the *customer*, i.e. they meet different *needs*, as they are felt by the customer.

For instance, in attempting this exercise with managers from one of the retail banks, when the executives had finally finished falling off their seats laughing at the impossibility of the task, and the naivety of consultants, they produced a computer printout listing their retail bank products which was fully five inches thick,

Market:							
Products / Customers	1	2	3	4	5	6	Total
1							
2							
3							
4							
5							
6							
7							
Total							

Figure 8.2 Product–Customer Matrix

because they had some 600 or more different products. The task was self-evidently impossible.

In fact, if you think not about production or technology or our bank's back office operations, but what matters in the *front* office to the customer, there are only *six* customer benefits in the retail bank market and thus only six types of product. Quite simply, as a retail bank customer I want to:

● lay my hands on ready money when I need it;
● have my savings held safely;
● buy things before I have the money to pay for them;
● pay bills via cheques and debits;
● get income from my savings; and
● acquire some services like insurance, investment advice, and so on.

I do not really care how many different ways the bank has of giving me an overdraft, I just want to buy a car before I can really afford it! There are only *six* retail bank products – so that side of the matrix is done – impossible it is not!

Now we can talk about *customers*. This too is normally seen as impossible (we either have too many customers or not enough to make up five or six groups or types), or this is something which is so obvious we already know about it.

For example, in another case, working this time with a corporate bank (i.e. one dealing only with companies, not retail customers), on being asked to do this the bank executives were exultant, they said they had done this *before*. We pointed out that the object of this analysis is to group customers together according to their most important needs, their priorities, significant differences in their behaviour, and so on, so we can use them as distinct market targets. They said 'yes, yes, we've done it before'. We were astounded but pleased. We asked them to complete the matrix. The sum result of hundreds of years of combined banking experience, university-level education and professional qualifications was the following definitive list of customer types in the corporate banking market: *Small* companies; *Medium-sized* companies; and *Large* companies. (This incisive and deeply analytical model, incidentally, represents how most bankers traditionally view this market).

This was not very helpful. But we persevered – or tried to. If you then use the matrix to ask a couple of basic questions, the insight into customer needs, generated by the customer-base divided in the conventional way by company size, is almost zero:

We asked . . .	They said . . .
Which customers take which products?	They all take everything (or at least some in each category do).
Which are the most important products for each type of customer (i.e. the ones you have to get right to be a player in this market)?	Impossible to say, different products are the most important to some companies in each size category.
What are the critical success factors for each type of customer?	Impossible to say, it depends which customers you mean in each category.

In fact, this group of executives persevered manfully with the matrix and after much hard work, heart-searching and substantial cost in human suffering (theirs and ours), classified corporate customers according to the *strategy* the customer is pursuing – because that predicts the customer's need for financial services, and the critical products and success factors. For example, 'market share strategy' companies need good liquidity products, but companies pursuing a 'profit-reconstruction strategy' are likely to value most highly financial efficiency products, and so on. This provided them with a novel and creative way of choosing customer targets, and specializing the total 'offering' around the customer's needs.

Incidentally, if you try to use the Product–Customer Matrix and it really *is* impossible to group products and customers in the way described above, then you have probably not defined a market at all – i.e. a group of customers sharing a set of common problems buying products to solve those problems. The way round this is to split the 'market' up, and then try the matrix for each part. You are likely to find you are really talking about a number of markets and not just one. Perhaps the greatest value of this approach is that it is capable of generating new ways of segmenting the market, which we will consider in more detail in the next section.

Once the matrix is constructed though it can be used for a number of significant purposes:

- look at market size and trend, product by product, and customer by customer;
- look at the market and product life cycle stage, product by product, and customer by customer;
- look at our present strategic position product by product and customer by customer (see pp. 410–12), evaluate whether our real strength is in products or relationships with particular customers, and thus the best way to grow the business;
- find out where we make most of our profit in the market, i.e. from different products and services going to different customers;
- identify where we are achieving the highest levels of customer satisfaction and loyalty;
- isolate those parts of the market where we have the greatest competitive advantage over our competitors;
- identify the parts of the market in which we are actually doing business – the 'competed market';
- look at our real market share in the competed market.

On the last two points, for example, we were told by one medium-sized manufacturer of varnish products that they were part of a market worth about £1000 million a year, and since they only had 0.05 per cent of the market they saw no need to worry about market strategy. Actually, they had the figures wrong anyway, but this is not the point of the story. Completing the product–market matrix showed that the supposed £1000 million was *all* paints and surface coverings for industrial and consumer uses, not the market for small tins of varnish sold to the retail customer for use in the home. In addition, this firm was effectively in business only in the South of England and through only one type of retailer. In the *competed market* they had 10–15 per cent of a declining business sector. They had market strategy problems after all.

The value of this type of analysis is demonstrated by the performance of Federal Express – one of the most successful companies in the world – in a strategy of improving customer satisfaction and profitability, by defining the needs of different customer segments in a better way to offer customers in each target segment expertise and service tailored to their specific needs – the value proposition is different for each customer segment. For example, companies like Intel are offered a specialized international logistics support system because this is a critical customer need – the effect, for example, is that Intel does not have warehouses in China; the FedEx airplanes are the warehouses.

Incidentally, experience suggests that one of the main sources of company short-sightedness and inflexibility in how markets are defined is not lack of executive vision or understanding of customer differences – it is company information systems, which contain fixed and historical assumptions about what the market is.

'one of the main sources of company short-sightedness and inflexibility in how markets are defined is not lack of executive vision or understanding of customer differences – it is company information systems, which contain fixed and historical assumptions about what the market is'

The point of putting this analysis of market definition at the start is that it is a practical vehicle for rethinking segmentation as well, i.e. moving from the basic customer needs in our market, to ways of setting specific strategic targets for our marketing programmes. Let us move on to the question of market segmentation.

Market segmentation [3]

The biggest difficulty we face in working on market segmentation is that everyone thinks they know what it is, and no-one thinks it is strategic. They don't. It is.

The theory is simple. We divide a market into groups of buyers who make coherent targets – for example, by age, gender, geographic location, socio-economic group or lifestyle for consumers; or company size, industrial sector and the like for industrial buyers. Conventional thinking is that we can then develop consistent marketing programmes based on the important characteristics of the customers in a segment, with potentially different marketing approaches for each segment (see Figure 8.3).

To many operational marketing and advertising executives, market segmentation is quite simply about tactical issues like: where to advertise to get the best audience 'reach' for our

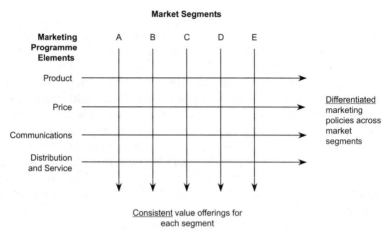

Figure 8.3 Consistency versus differentiation in market segmentation

promotional messages; which types of distributive outlet have the optimum customer profile; and where the salesforce can locate potential customers. This is one of the many reasons why markets are too important to be left in the hands of marketing executives. In fact, segmentation is a fundamental issue of market strategy with far-reaching effects – indeed, ultimately the only real logic for how we organize the whole company is our understanding of the structure of the market (i.e. market segmentation).

'segmentation is a fundamental issue of market strategy with far-reaching effects – indeed, ultimately the only real logic for how we organize the whole company is our understanding of the structure of the market (i.e. market segmentation)'

The other misconception about segmentation is that if you could simply collect enough statistical information about the market, then the 'right' segments would be identified automatically by the computer. In the real world, notwithstanding the wonder of database marketing, in most cases you cannot get 'enough' information anyway, but even if you could, approaching segmentation like this would miss the whole point about the power of creativity in segmenting markets to create competitive differentiation.

At the strategic level, segmentation is really about one thing and one thing only – the *customer benefit* from the product or service. This brings us right back to our central theme – what matters most to the customer.

Take the absolute classic example of segmentation – in the toothpaste market. A major piece of market research conducted by Haley[4] in the USA in the late 1960s remains the model for this marketplace, more than a quarter of a century later. Surely, if ever a product should rationally be an undifferentiated commodity product it is toothpaste. Functionally, the product is a grinding compound, chemically very similar to the compound used to remove surface blemishes on the paintwork of a car (although there may be differences in flavour).

However, the customer benefit segmentation of this market shows that it is far from being a price-led commodity market, as summarized in Table 8.1. In customer benefit terms there are quite different types of customer in this market – i.e. groups of customers to whom different things are the most important thing about the product. Maybe the strategy that drops out is one of developing separate brands for each customer, or maybe we attempt the trick of developing a multiple-benefit brand that has appeals matching the critical requirements of each customer, or maybe we do both. The real point is that if we focus on the *customer benefits* in the market, we are going to create a different model of the world and how it works, than if we simply think about prices and products.

> '*The real point is that if we focus on the* **customer benefits** *in the market, we are going to create a different model of the world and how it works, than if we simply think about prices and products*'

Table 8.1 **Haley's customer benefit segmentation of the toothpaste market***

	The sensory segment	**The sociable segment**	**The anxious segment**	**The independent segment**
Demographic characteristics	Children	Young adults	Families	Men with a higher level of education
Personality characteristics	Self-involvement, little interest in others	Sociable, looking for partners	Hypochondriacs	Autonomous
Lifestyle characteristics	Hedonistic – pleasure and sensation seeking	Active, gregarious, outward-looking	Conservative and security conscious	Value-oriented
Most important product benefits	Flavour Appearance	Cosmetic properties	Decay prevention promises	Price
Product features required	Specialist flavours Stripes Shaped extrusions	Promise of attractiveness	Promise of health care Reassurance of fulfilling family duty	Low price/no branding, e.g. retailer own-labels and special offers

* Source: Adapted from Russell I. Haley (1968), 'Benefit Segmentation: A Decision-Oriented Tool', *Journal of Marketing*, July, 30–35.

Lest it be suspected that this is all a bit theoretical and you can only get into customer-benefit segmentation if you have a king's ransom to spend on clever market research, consider the following case.

REALITY CHECK
AN EXHAUSTING MARKET

The General Manager of the Spares Division of one of the imported car firms in the UK had a beef about replacement exhausts. He could not understand why his potential customers for replacement exhausts were so 'irrational' – or, as he actually put it, 'stupid'. His case was that with the first exhaust replacement, in the majority of cases, only the back pipe needed replacing, costing on average £40, if purchased from the manufacturer's distributor. If the customer went to a high-street exhaust and battery outlet, s/he would probably be sold a complete new exhaust system for about £100. This appears to be economic madness to an engineer with expert knowledge of the motor business. We worked out a benefit-segmentation model in a couple of hours over discussions with him. The sort of segments that appeared were:

- the *Wealthy High Dependence Driver* – people like the self-employed, who rely on the car for income, whose primary product benefit is dependability;
- the *Impoverished High Dependence Driver* – people like single-parent families, or the elderly, whose lifestyle crashes if the car breaks down, and who also seek dependability above all else;
- the *Scared Driver* – who just wants the fear of mechanical breakdown taken away;
- the *Ignorant Driver* – who wants expertise to solve the problem; and
- the *Value-Seeking Driver* – whose main goal is value.

The model is probably not exactly right. What it does do is suggest why the majority of the car exhaust market is not driven by price. In fact, the conclusion reached was that whatever customer-benefit you identify, Kwik Fit has beaten you to it! The General Manager concluded that this was not a market worth the cost of fighting.

Markets may also look very different if we adopt *customer loyalty segmentation*. Think back also to the view we took of the relationship between customer satisfaction and customer loyalty –

we distinguished between the Satisfied Stayers, the Hostages, the Happy Wanderers and the Dealers (pp. 28–29). In fact, this model gives us a novel basis for thinking about the link between 'loyalty segments' and market strategy (Figure 8.4). This starts to suggest that appropriate strategies may be very different for each loyalty segment: with the Satisfied Stayers we should invest to reward and reinforce loyalty to stimulate referrals and continued retention; with the Hostages, the goal should be to focus on building positive commitment, instead of relying on inertia to retain the business; with the Happy Wanderers, we may emphasize innovations in the value offer to retain their interest, while being aware of the different balance between costs of retention and the benefits with this type of customer (they may not be retained long, however much we spend); while with the Dealers, investments in relationships and retention are likely to be unproductive, so we may emphasize transactional efficiency.

'there is much untapped potential in segmenting markets on the basis of customer relationship-seeking characteristics, as an antidote to relationship marketing myopia (treating all customers the same, in terms of how they want us to treat them)'

The exact characteristics of the satisfaction/loyalty segments will vary between companies, but loyalty segmentation provides a platform for developing market strategies that truly reflect important customer characteristics, not just demographics. This may be worth trying out for part of your business to see what you learn.

Going further in this direction, there is much untapped potential in segmenting markets on the basis of *customer relationship-seeking characteristics*, as an antidote to relationship marketing myopia (treating all

Loyalty Segments	Our Customers	Competitors' Customers
Satisfied Stayers	Committed to us and rate us highly, show little interest in competitors	Committed to competitors and rate them highly, show little interest in us
Hostages	Loyal customers, but may only be inertia, may be vulnerable to competitors	Repeat buyers for competitors, but may be interested in us
Happy Wanderers	Show little positive commitment, may become interested in alternatives	Little commitment to competitors, may be interested in our offer
Dealers	Show strong preference for the best 'deal' on the market, with low supplier loyalty	No commitment to competitors - open to superior offers

Figure 8.4 Segmenting by customer loyalty

customers the same, in terms of how they want us to treat them). Recall Figure 3.2, where we distinguished between customers on the basis of the type of relationship they want with suppliers and the intimacy of the relationship they want. This suggests the type of customer relationship-seeking segments shown in Figure 8.5, where the best strategies for our own and the competitors' customers differ substantially between segments. This time the logic is that the type of relationship that customers want to have with their suppliers is the major determinant of their receptiveness to different relationship marketing strategies.

Relationship Segments	Our Customers	Competitors' Customers
Relationship Seekers	Invest in customer relationship management and loyalty programmes to give a close relationship that is long term	Find ways to offer a relationship that is superior in the customer's terms to attract away from competitors
Loyal Buyers	Focus on retention through the value offering and not through relationship emphasis	Emphasize superiority in value offering and rewards for long-term retention superior to those of competitors
Relationship Exploiters	Control expenditures on loyalty incentives and provide economic contact, e.g. through Internet	Offer relationship-based incentives to switch suppliers, but control costs to allow for short retention
Arm's Length Transactional Customers	Emphasize value offering and avoid relationship investments unless can be converted to Loyal Buyers	Demonstrate superior value offering and lack of ties or barriers to switching

Figure 8.5 Segmenting by customer relationship-seeking characteristics

Again this is speculative, and the details of the relationship-seeking characteristics of customers will vary greatly between markets and companies. The point is that segmentation is about a lot more than descriptive customer demographics. Companies who have tried this model have found it insightful to say the least, and a fine antidote to the mindless dogma of the relationship marketing fanatics!

Where this is leading us is into another way of opening up the market segmentation issue, which is to distinguish between *strategic* and *managerial segmentation* issues – as suggested in Figure 8.6. Strategic segmentation is led by customer benefits and relates to broad issues like corporate mission and value, and strategic intent and market position. Managerial segmentation is the more familiar level of managerial planning and resource allocation and operational issues of sales and advertising

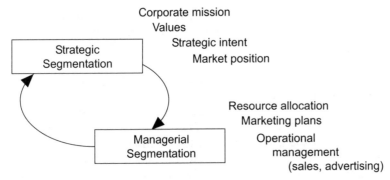

Figure 8.6 Strategic and managerial levels of segmentation

allocation. Most people only see the managerial aspects of segmentation and ignore its strategic significance. Let us consider the conventional view of segmentation and then get a bit more real about segmentation strategy.

Conventional views of market segmentation

The traditional view of segmentation is concerned with:

- the *methodology* of identifying segment targets – for example, dividing markets by geographic or demographic character-istics, or more sophisticated statistical clustering techniques;
- *criteria* for testing the robustness of the segments identified as marketing targets – are segments measurable, accessible, sustainable, actionable and stable enough to make good targets; and
- the *segmentation strategy* decision – do we develop separate products and/or marketing programmes for different segments (differentiated marketing), focus efforts on certain segments (concentrated marketing), or ignore segment differences and treat all customer groups the same (undifferentiated marketing).

The only problem with this conventional approach is that it largely misses the point. It is concerned only with the operational aspects of marketing. It ignores the strategic issues almost entirely. This may explain why there is growing evidence that companies do not use segmentation theory to much extent beyond targeting advertisements into media based on demographics.

'The only problem with this conventional approach is that it largely misses the point. It is concerned only with the operational aspects of marketing. It ignores the strategic issues almost entirely'

Indeed, the typical (but recurring) responses of managers in workshops to conventional segmentation are revealing. They say things like:

- Is the fact that we *can* segment markets any reason why we *should* segment markets?
- Should we allow our marketing strategies to be driven primarily by the availability of the information technology that facilitates sophisticated market segmentation?
- If, as competitors, we all pursue the conventional, mechanical approaches, using the same techniques, and often the same databases – surely we all end up with the same segments and no competitive advantage (indeed, maybe more competition in the critical segments because everyone goes after them)?
- What's the use to anybody of identifying and choosing market segments that nobody in the organization owns?
- Fancy segment labels are all well and good, but they do not fit the marketing plan and they don't get budgeted for.
- It is fine being imaginative about basing segments on customer needs and benefits sought, but how do you turn that into quantifiable targets with specific customers for the salesforce?
- Don't we have to revert to demographic and geographic segmentation anyway, because those are the only things we can easily measure, and see what we've got and where we're going?

Such responses have led us to build an extended model of segmentation to use with executives to work on market segmentation questions.

An extended model of market segmentation

Our extended model – which can be used as a diagnostic framework to sort out segmentation issues for a company – is shown in Figure 8.7. This model is based upon two important propositions: *firstly*, that there is a need to distinguish between strategic and operational organizational levels in dealing with the segmentation issue; *secondly*, that in order to address the issue of implementation it is necessary to examine the internal organizational context, as well as the external marketplace in considering segmentation. The suggestion is that in each of these areas the managerial agenda to be addressed is different, as suggested in Figure 8.7 and outlined below.

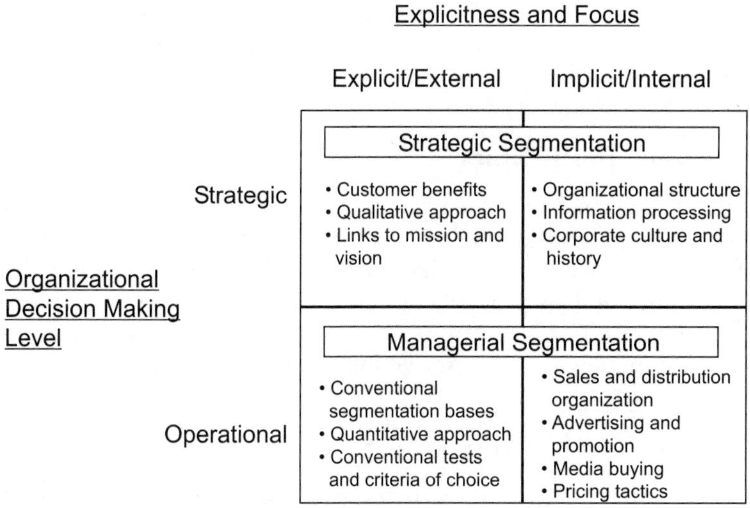

Explicitness and Focus

	Explicit/External	Implicit/Internal
Strategic	**Strategic Segmentation**	
	• Customer benefits • Qualitative approach • Links to mission and vision	• Organizational structure • Information processing • Corporate culture and history
Operational	**Managerial Segmentation**	
	• Conventional segmentation bases • Quantitative approach • Conventional tests and criteria of choice	• Sales and distribution organization • Advertising and promotion • Media buying • Pricing tactics

Organizational Decision Making Level

Figure 8.7 An extended model of market segmentation

Strategic, explicit issues

These issues relate to *Strategic Segmentation* and the goal is to focus on the fundamental customer benefits sought in different parts of the market, whether from physical product differences or from non-product attributes. It is quite possible that the conventional criteria of segment evaluation do not validly or usefully apply to what is built here. The pursuit of a strategic market vision may quite reasonably be judged by criteria other than measurability and the like.

At this level, segmentation models might be better judged by such criteria as: the ability to create and sustain competitive differentiation and advantage; innovativeness in how the market is attacked; the compatibility with mission; providing a coherent focus for thinking in the organization; and consistency with corporate value and cultures.

Indeed, the relevant techniques for generating 'strategic segmentation' in the first place are more likely to be qualitative and creative than quantitative and 'scientific'. This is arguably the practical link between corporate mission and the marketplace – it is where the broad concepts and ideas in the mission statement can be related to customer needs and benefits in a specific marketplace, or conversely where market insights provide feedback to those building mission statements. However, it is at this decision-making level that we must also recognize the other characteristics of strategic decision making: levels of uncertainty and ambiguity are high; information is scarce; and the market environment is enacted or constructed rather than objectively known.

Tactical, explicit issues

Here the critical issues are the most familiar ones: the choice of conventional segmentation bases and the application of quantitative methodology to identify segment characteristics. Here the conventional tests probably do apply, and the goals are primarily managerial in allocating resources, and operational in the tactical management of marketing programmes.

Strategic, implicit issues

This is where it gets more interesting. We refer here to a set of issues that have been largely neglected by conventional segmentation, although they are likely to be critical to successful implementation of segmentation strategies. These issues are concerned with the fundamental implications of market segmentation for the 'inner workings' of the organization. These issues are likely to include the following areas:

- *Organizational structure* – Strategic market vision may be incompatible with marketing organization structures (and the related organizational decision-making processes and information flows), raising a variety of practical questions which are central to the ability of an organization to implement a segmentation strategy: how well can existing organizational structures of departments, functions and divisions service the segments targeted; does mismatch between a segmentation model and the reality of the organization mean that segments are never 'owned' or taken seriously, because they fall between the jurisdictions of existing departments or SBUs?
- *Information and reporting* – Fundamental problems may be that: new segment targets may be incompatible with existing information processing systems (i.e. data collection and dissemination), and unfamiliar to managers and difficult to identify and evaluate in conventional terms; if existing reporting lines do not put sales and market achievements in terms compatible with the segmentation model, it may be very difficult to set targets, allocate responsibilities, monitor progress, or even have target segments taken seriously within the organization.
- *Internal decision-making process* – If segments are conceived and defined in a radically different way to the conventional market

targets, a major implementation barrier may arise concerned with whether the new segments will become a genuine focus in marketing plans and whether they will be recognized and gain resources in the budgeting process.

- *Corporate culture* – Here the issue is the acceptability of new segments to the people in the organizations in terms of values, ethos, internal rules, evaluation systems and the like. If new segments represent radical change and are potentially threatening to the status quo and the current distribution of influence and control, there may well be hidden barriers to implementation which are powerful. It is the neglect of issues such as these that really lies behind the observed failure of many innovative customer-benefit-based segmentation models, when this construction of the market produces segment targets that: fall between the responsibilities of different organizational units, so are not 'owned' by anyone; which are not easily measurable or monitored in the existing information system, and are not the focus of conventional reporting; which are not part of existing planning and budgeting processes; and in which the people in the organization have little belief or confidence.

Tactical, implicit issues

Here the concern is also with internal organizational issues, but now at an operational level:

- *Sales and distribution organization* – are the segment targets easily identifiable by salespeople and accessible through existing distribution channels and are they compatible with the way these processes are currently structured?
- *Advertising and promotion campaigns* – are the segment targets reachable as separate targets through our existing procedures and capabilities for marketing communications?
- *Market research* – do we have information organized around these segment targets to identify them, to size and measure opportunities, and to evaluate our performance?
- *Pricing tactics* – do we currently have the facilities to price differently to segment targets?

These issues, though frequently hidden and ignored, pose tactical problems in implementing segmentation: where segments cut across sales and distribution systems and cannot be adequately serviced by either; where marketing communications, pricing and market research systems are not set up to deal with, or differentiate between, segments of the type proposed.

Market Segment Attractiveness	Internal Compatibility: High	Internal Compatibility: Low
High	Attractive segments that match with company capabilities	Attractive segments but with poor match with company capabilities
Low	Unattractive segments but with match to company capabilities	Unattractive segments that do not match with company capabilities

Figure 8.8 Segment attractiveness and internal compatibility

'The critical implementation issue is compatibility and consistency between segment targets and organizational attributes, both overt and covert'

The practical conclusion is that we should screen segments not just in terms of 'market attractiveness' (the conventional criteria), but also in terms of 'internal compatibility', in the way suggested in Figure 8.8. The critical implementation issue is compatibility and consistency between segment targets and organizational attributes, both overt and covert. However, to identify such issues of internal compatibility may require more detailed analysis of the kind discussed below.

Consistency and integration

The argument above suggests that overall we can reduce the market segmentation issue to two critical questions to evaluate relevance and the practical usefulness of a given segmentation model, in terms of whether it can be implemented at all by a given organization. These critical issues relate to: questions of consistency, or the internal compatibility of segment targets with organizational characteristics; and questions of integration, or the relationship between strategic and operational aspects of segmentation.

Consistency is concerned with the 'fit' between the explicit/external and implicit/internal issues in segmentation, at both the strategic and at the managerial/operational levels. On the other hand, *integration* refers to the 'fit' between the Strategic Segmentation model and the Managerial/Operational level, and between internal issues at both these levels. To go about addressing these issues, stimulus questions for executives are:

- What is the existing or achievable 'fit' or internal compatibility between the 'strategic segmentation' model of the external customer marketplace, and the internal organization structure, information systems, processes like planning and budgeting, and corporate culture?
- What is the existing or achievable 'fit' or internal compatibility between the 'managerial/operational segmentation' model of the external customer marketplace, and the sales and distribution organization, advertising and promotion management, media buying, market research systems and pricing administration?
- How compatible is the strategic segmentation at the managerial/operational level, and can customer benefit groups be translated into accessible target segments?
- How compatible are the internal issues at the 'strategic' level with their counterparts at the 'managerial/operational' level – in terms of organization, information, planning, budgeting, people and so on?

Although it cannot provide easy answers, this framework provides a structure by which managers may evaluate the real nature of market segmentation for their companies and for identifying implementation barriers to segment-based strategies. In practical terms, this is a useful device for bridging the gap between the conventional theory of market segmentation and the implementation of segmentation strategies.

What happens if you stick to a narrow view of segmentation?

A no-brainer – it does not work. Also, the consequences may be painful.

REALITY CHECK
SEGMENTING A MARKET TO THE DEATH

Pursuing the corporate banking example cited earlier (pp. 413–14) – the strategic vision of top management was to target corporate customers for financial services according to the customer's own corporate strategy (which would predict customer needs and priorities for financial services), with product offering and marketing programmes built around, for instance, 'market share-driven' companies as compared to 'profit-reconstruction strategy' companies. As we saw, this defined an unusual and novel strategic segmentation model which offered considerable potential competitive advantage. However, many problems emerged in attempting to implement this segmentation model in the bank. The powerful branch network in the bank saw the new corporate market segmentation as a threat to their own business – they called it 'cherry-picking' – and lobbied against it, as well as effectively withholding co-operation. It was impossible to value or target the new segments because the bank's information system coded only customer size and industry type. The new segments did not 'fit' with the established planning system and were largely ignored when targets were set and when promotional resources were allocated. Lack of information meant that salespeople were given little support in how to identify corporate customers in terms of the new segments, and so largely ignored them. The new 'marketing' idea of segmenting the bank's customers by need and benefit found little support among management, who defended the status quo as 'prudent banking' practice. The strategy was a complete failure. This may be an extreme case, but it illustrates the pointlessness of market segmentation – however innovative – that ignores issues of integration and consistency inside the organization. The corporate banking operation was closed.

'There is a simple and obvious fact to bear in mind: if you do not have a competitive advantage in a segment, then it is not attractive – however big, free-spending and dynamic it may be. Segmentation strategies that cannot be implemented are dreams not strategies'

More publicly, the House of Fraser has struggled with the implications of segmentation in the women's fashion clothing market, in a traditional department store chain of fifty stores with declining performance[5]. The plan was based on attracting women clothes shoppers in three highly attractive, high spending segments: the '*Quality Classic*' buyer; the '*Smart Career Mover*'; and the '*Fashion Lover*'. They controversially rejected 'The Young Mother' clothes buyer as a target. However, the problem is that House of Fraser brands are not particularly appealing to these target segments – these consumers visit House of Fraser stores, but shop at concessions like Oasis, Mondi, Liz Claiborne and Windsmor. The target was 'the affluent woman with aspirations'; with the products positioned against Marks & Spencer, the operation has struggled to achieve the repositioning, even against the weakened competition. There is a simple and obvious fact to bear in mind: if you do not have a competitive advantage in a segment, then it is not attractive – however big, free-spending and dynamic it may be. Segmentation strategies that cannot be implemented are dreams not strategies.

Segmentation is a powerful strategic tool for focusing on customer needs and building competitive advantage from that focus. The Product–Customer Matrix analysis (Figure 8.2) provides a mechanism for identifying and evaluating market segments. But we have to be realistic and think segmentation through to the capabilities and characteristics of the organization as well, or we end up with a brilliant market strategy that does not work.

However, markets are dynamic . . .

Market segments that stand up and bite

Segmenting markets may not be so much of a choice as you thought it was. Ignoring the existence of distinctive segments in our markets may involve more risk than simply missing opportunities to build competitive strength. In sophisticated modern markets some segments are proactive – they judge us and attack us for not adapting our products and services to their needs!

There is a compelling argument, for example, that in Britain in the 2000s, ethnic or cultural identity is a powerful lever for analysing markets:

- ethnic minorities comprise 5.5 per cent of the UK population and the number will double in the next 50 years;
- ethnic minorities spend £10 billion annually;
- ethnic minorities include many socially mobile and increasingly affluent groups[6].

In the past, these groups were rarely targeted by companies, which was a missed opportunity. However, while they may be ignored, ethnic groups do not ignore companies, and their perceptions impact on brand equity:

- Brands perceived as *ethnically insensitive*: Persil (TV ad showing Dalmatian shaking off black spots); McDonalds (TV ad showing stereotype of young black man listening to very loud music while driving); TSB (ad showing two short planks with Irish accents).

- Brands perceived as *ethnically sensitive*: BT (radio ads in Hindi promoting long-distance calls); Persil (TV ad with black family); Sainsbury (catering for local ethnic minorities); W. H. Smith (stocking ethnic greeting cards).

Similarly, consumer attitudes towards 'green' issues remain on the agenda, even if we prefer to ignore them. The National Consumer Council identifies: *Affluent Greens and Young Greens* (36 per cent of the population) – committed to green consumerism; *Recyclers and Careful Spenders* (38 per cent of the population) – act in an environmentally friendly way, but do not usually 'buy green'; and *Sceptics* (26 per cent of the population) – determined not to buy 'green' under any circumstances[7].

As markets change, market strategies like segmentation have to evolve as well. Companies do not miss just market opportunities, they risk being judged and written off by significant parts of the market, if they do not stay in touch.

Indeed, some new segments may be both judgemental and hostile. 'Generation X' (the youth of the 1990s) consumers are not differentiated by age and gender but by attitude – disillusionment, knowingness and cynicism. Nike understands this market. A Nike sports shoe advertising insert in *Loaded* (a magazine for 'new lads') reads:

'We don't sell dreams. We sell shoes . . . Don't insult our intelligence. Tell us what it is. Tell us what it does. And don't play the national anthem while you do it.'[8]

In similar media, Hugo Boss' advertising for its male fragrance Boss reads:

'No fancy women, no passionate embraces. No silly sunsets. Just a great fragrance.'

This is a market where 'maverick' brands like Virgin and Benetton have enormous competitive advantage. This is a market where brands need 'attitude not platitude'[9]. How many other companies have taken seriously an anti-marketing, anti-advertising 'Generation X' market segment?

However, do not worry too much about 'Generation X'. It may be too late. The new challenge is 'Generation Y' – the 5- to 20-year-olds, who are actually living the 'web lifestyle' described by Bill Gates (see pp. 170–1) – whose values and aspirations are different again. They are rejecting the brands that were developed for 'Generation X' and responding to new types of value offers – says one consultant 'Think of them as this quiet little group about to change everything'. These are the consumers who hold Nike responsible for inhumane labour practices, and does not care that Michael Jordan endorses Nike sports shoes. These are the targets for Sprite's advertising that parodies celebrity endorsement with the punchline 'Image is nothing. Obey your thirst'. Companies ignoring the interests and obsessions of Generation Y are already encountering a wall of distrust and cynicism[10]. There is nothing fixed or static about markets or how they can be segmented.

'There is nothing fixed or static about markets or how they can be segmented'

And thinking forward

It should be remembered that we also have to think about our value proposition and the key relationships before we finalize our thinking about market segments – who said it was going to be easy?

Market attractiveness and position

Rethinking market definitions and market segments and targets is likely to very quickly confront us with choices. If we cannot pursue all the markets we have identified, if we cannot attack all the segments we can see – then how do we see priorities and decide where to focus? We have been warned of the strategic weakness in trying to be all things to all people – but how do we set our priorities?

The results of this type of focus can be surprising. ANI Bradken is a Scottish foundry which continued to improve profitability in its declining and highly price-competitive market. The firm was 'sacking' unrewarding customers. The role of the business development director was to sift through potential clients to choose which ones to do business with, and the salesforce interviewed prospective customers as though they were applying for a job. In this unusual way, Bradken took its customer base down from 212 to 25 and focused all its efforts on those customers[11].

At the larger corporate level, more and more strategy is driven by market focus in the fight for market leadership. The thinking is that focus creates a strong position in the minds of customer: Volvo owns safety, Xerox owns copiers, Kleenex owns tissues. One analyst suggests that the reason that Pepsi has failed to win

*'there is strong
evidence that one
key to sustained
performance and
the survival of a
company is
choosing attractive
markets and
entering early, but
also making a
timely exit from
industries where it
is no longer
possible to compete
profitably'*

market leadership over Coke, in spite of the fact that consumers prefer it, is that Pepsico lacked market focus until it started to divest businesses like its restaurant chains[12]. Indeed, there is strong evidence that one key to sustained performance and the survival of a company is choosing attractive markets and entering early, but also making a timely exit from industries where it is no longer possible to compete profitably[13]. We will see examples of such moves out of markets when we examine the core competencies argument in Chapter 9 (pp. 458–64).

But how do we confront the market choices important to our business? The world is full of portfolio models and decision aids. Perhaps the most straightforward is one that prioritizes by looking at:

● *Market (or segment) attractiveness* – the degree to which an opportunity fits with our goals and capabilities.
● *Market position* – how well we believe we can do in this market or segment.

Obviously, neither of these things is static. Market attractiveness can change. In 1997, Texas Instruments sold off its notebook computer business. The notebook computer market is large, growing and on the face of things an attractive market. They reasoned that margins were pressured by price-cutting and only Intel (supplying the computer chips) and Microsoft (supplying the software) made money – the suppliers of the boxes did not.

In the US telecoms business, costs of long-distance phone calls have declined dramatically. Five years ago they averaged 37 cents/minute, now they are 10–15 cents/minute unless you are a large corporation, when it may be as low as 1.5 cents/minute. The cost may soon be zero – a new service provider offers free long-distance calls, with revenue generated by 10- to 15-second advertisements during the phone call. As a profit centre this market is not attractive (though for telecom companies it is a strategic platform on which to build other things).

The term 'adjacency' has been coined to describe market choices like Ford's purchase of car distributors and exhaust and tyre replacement supplier Kwik Fit – Ford is trying to build a consumer services company that makes a profit from every stage of a car's life cycle from factory to scrapyard, and this strategic logic provides the rationale for its new market choices.

Bear in mind too that the factors that make markets attractive are not the same for all companies. For example, fast-moving fashions in clothes may make a market unattractive for some retailers, while a company like Zara has a different business model, designed to offer 'live collections' that change every week in response to short-lived fashion trends, and can produce a new fashion line in days[14]. In other words, high market volatility is extremely unattractive to one competitor, but highly attractive to another. Issues like how well buyers in this market will receive our value proposition and niche opportunities should also be considered[15].

The market position you can take will depend on what you do – the strategy, the value proposition, and so on. For example, the Body Shop International is expanding its branch and distribution network to channel its cosmetic products to new international markets – but in different retail formats depending on customer needs and behaviour in each market. While direct marketing operations are planned for Switzerland and Canada, the 'microstore' outlet is more suitable for expensive large city sites and markets like Japan.

Market position can change dramatically, and quickly too. The loss of market share by Marks & Spencer to competitors like Next and Matalan, the loss of the personal computer market by IBM to Dell, fashion turning against Laura Ashley, the world falling out of love with The Body Shop's fruit-flavoured lotions – all show how dramatic loss of market position can be.

Accepting that things change, our logic is shown in Figure 8.9 – assuming we grade a market or segment as high or low in attractiveness, and the position we take as strong or weak, then the options and priorities are:

- *Core Business* – areas where the market offers the potential for us to achieve our goals and which fits our capabilities and competence, *and* where we believe we can take a strong market position. Such areas are a high priority for investment.
- *Peripheral Business* – where the market is less attractive to us (there is no growth, competition is tough, margins are low, and so on), but we can take a strong position. These may be areas where we continue to do business, but unless they bring us other benefits they are not a high priority for investment.
- *Illusion Business* – these are highly attractive markets which offer everything we want, but where we can or do take a weak position. These markets and segments are an illusion because the market looks great – but we can never get a pay-off.

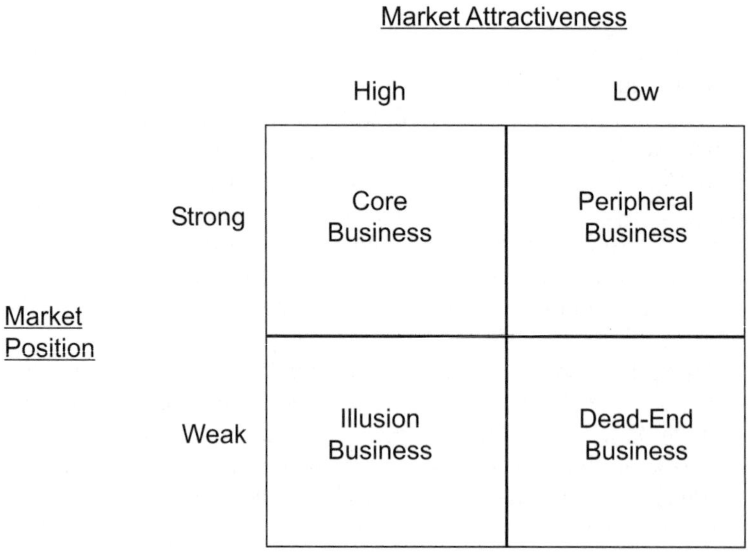

Market Attractiveness

		High	Low
Market Position	Strong	Core Business	Peripheral Business
	Weak	Illusion Business	Dead-End Business

Figure 8.9   Market attractiveness and position

- *Dead-End Business* – these are the lowest priority because the market is not attractive to us, and we can only take a weak position.

Clearly, this is a crude and often uncomfortable view of the markets and segments we have identified. It can be a very useful tool, because it forces us to face up to realities.

When we add to this our thoughts about our strategy – our competitive advantage with different customer groups, the sustainability of our market position, the robustness of our brand or value proposition, i.e. movement from one issue to another within the market strategy – then the picture may be even more valuable. Experience suggests we may flush out some interesting things:

- cases where all our thinking is about defending our market position in Peripheral Business – because it is where we have always been;
- executives who champion new markets and segments but can see no way of taking a strong position – they drive us into the Illusion Business;
- the deep-seated and vigorous defence of markets which are Dead-End Business, because we just refuse to accept that one of our traditional markets has become less attractive or that we have been overtaken by new competitors.

These are vitally important questions to confront before we commit to a market strategy. Do not forget, however, that we need to think also about the value proposition and key relationship components of market strategy in making these judgements – how else can we be sure about the strength of our market position, unless we know what it is based on and whether we can sustain it through collaborations and employees and defend against competitors?

Time to consider some awkward questions before we proceed:

REALITY CHECK

THE AWKWARD QUESTIONS ABOUT MARKET CHOICES

How recently have we tried to redefine the boundaries of what we understand to be the market – can we see the shape of the market changing and new market spaces becoming available? If not – go back to 'Creating Market Space' (pp. 299–313) and think again.

How do we segment our markets – do we ever get our heads around the natural segmentation by customer benefit and customer relationship requirements, or do we try to force our markets to fit our statistical models? Does our segmentation strategy impact on what we do for customers – where are the disconnects that prevent us achieving this, and what do we do about them?

How well and regularly do we reconsider our market choices? How well do we understand and communicate the factors that make markets attractive to us for the future, and market positions strong? Does the strategic logic of the choices we make impact on the strategies we implement?

How good are we at using our market sensing capabilities to define markets and market targets differently to our competitors as a way of avoiding the trap of never-ending head-to-head competition?

So, where are we now?

What we tried to do in this chapter was to develop our strategic pathway from its foundation in customer focus and market sensing, to assess our market choices: market definition, market segmentation, and making market choices based on market attractiveness and market position. These are incredibly important questions that underpin most of what follows. They are also difficult to sort out – which is why we often neglect them. Success in making smart choices will reflect our market sensing capabilities. However, it is clear that market choices are also informed by how we can compete – the value proposition and the key relationships to which we turn attention now, as the next stages in the strategic pathway.

Notes and references

1. David W. Cravens, Gordon Greenley, Nigel F. Piercy and Stanley F. Slater (1997), 'Integrating Contemporary Strategic Management Perspectives', *Long Range Planning*, **30** (4), 493–506.
2. Alan Mitchell (1996), 'Marketers Seek Oasis From Blur', *Marketing Business*, 27 September.
3. This section of the chapter leans heavily on Nigel F. Piercy and Neil A. Morgan (1993), 'Strategic and Operational Market Segmentation: A Management Analysis', *Journal of Strategic Marketing*, **1**, 123–40.
4. Russell I. Haley (1968), 'Benefit Segmentation: A Decision-Oriented Research Tool', *Journal of Marketing*, **32**, July, 30–35.
5. Kate Rankine (1996), 'Not a Happy House', *Daily Telegraph*, 5 October.
6. Robert Dwek (1997), 'Losing the Race', *Marketing Business*, March.
7. Charles Clover (1996), 'The Green Shopper is Alive and Well', *Daily Telegraph*, 11 December.
8. Robert Dwek (1997), 'Cool Customers', *Marketing Business*, February.
9. Graham Lancaster (2001), 'Attitude, Not Platitudes', *FT Creative Business*, 1 May, 15.
10. Ellen Newborne and Kathleen Kerwin (1999), 'Generation Y', *Business Week*, 15 February, 81–88.
11. Alan Mitchell (1997), 'Putting Customers First', *Marketing Business*, April.
12. Laura Ries (1997), 'Welcome to the Focus Generation', *Marketing News*, 14 April.
13. Geoffrey Owen (2000), 'The Secrets of Corporate Survival', *Financial Times*, 28 August.
14. Leslie Crawford (2000), 'Putting on the Style With Rapid Response', *Financial Times*, 26 September.
15. W. Chan Kim and Renee Mauborgne (1998), 'Pioneers Strike It Rich', *Financial Times*, 11 August.

CHAPTER 9

Market strategy:

The value proposition

Our progress along the strategic pathway so far has involved trying to put a handle on the things we can do to develop better customer focus, and to learn from the customer through our market sensing capabilities, and then to exploit this market understanding in the critical market choices that we make – which markets, which segments, which niches should we make our targets? But none of that makes sense unless we also have the capability to offer superior value to those customers in those markets. The third stage in developing our strategic pathway is concerned with our value proposition to our customers.

First, we consider what value is to a customer, and then look at the company issues we may need to work on to refine and articulate our value proposition. As pictured in Figure 9.1, these tools consist of:

- *Market mission* – what do we want to *be* and to *stand for* in this market, and how does this relate to corporate goals and mission (if it does), and to delivering customer value?
- *Competitive differentiation and positioning* – what do we have to do to build a difference between what we offer and what our competitors offer in the customer's eyes, and how do we use this to build a sustainable and profitable competitive position in the market based on superior customer value?
- *Marketing assets and brands* – what competitive advantages do we have, in intangible assets like company reputation, unique

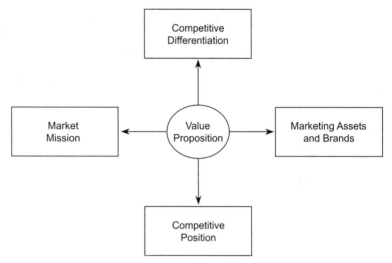

Figure 9.1   The value proposition in market strategy

capabilities and brand identity, that can be used to build our market strategy because these resources create value for customers?

'the most critical issue is whether we know what value means to our customers in the first place'

These are just the tools that can help us address the issue of customer value in the company. But the most critical issue is whether we know what value means to our customers in the first place.

What is value for our customers?

Because it is just about the most important issue for managers to confront, we spent a lot of time in Chapter 3 describing the value challenge we are facing, particularly as it is posed by the sophisticated customer. We saw that customer value is about much more than leaning the operation to get prices lower and quality higher. We saw that the new customer wants high quality and low prices, but that we face constant surprise and paradox in what creates customer value. We saw that value is defined by customers not companies, and that the most important drivers of value change dramatically over time and are different for different customers. We saw that value is influenced by how we treat customers, how we respond to them and how they judge our qualities, as well as products and prices. One of the greatest challenges we face in market sensing is identifying and tracking the value drivers for different types of customers (alright, segments if you prefer).

However, to backtrack, if we go back to basics, customers develop value expectations and make purchases based on their perceptions of a product's benefits compared to the total cost of the purchase (in price but also time, effort, difficulty, and so on)[1]. It follows that superior customer value is created when the buyer's total experience is very favourable compared to expectations, and compared to their perceptions of the equivalents provided by competitors. An overview of the sources of superior customer value, which we can exploit to meet the value demands of customers, is suggested in Figure 9.2:

- our *capabilities, skills and resources* – what we are good at doing and what we are able to do, that matters to the customer;
- our *organizational processes*, of service delivery and value creation, to do things the way the customer wants, not the way that happens to be most convenient for us;
- the *commitment and service* of our people – what the customer finds when dealing with us; and
- *innovation and change* – our ability to get better at doing the things that matter and to find new ways of 'delighting' customers.

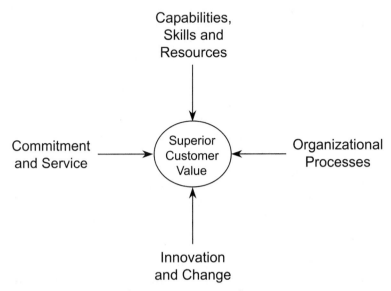

Figure 9.2   Sources of superior customer value

'we may just have to get better at listening to customers and learning from them, otherwise we have little chance of bringing our capabilities to bear on customer value'

As we suggested in looking at customer focus and market sensing, we may just have to get better at listening to customers and learning from them, otherwise we have little chance of bringing our capabilities to bear on customer value.

However, there is another point we really have to expand here, because it is the one that managers really struggle to capture – customer perception is reality.

Customer perception is reality

The hard truth is that value is not created in the factory or the back office, customer value exists only on the customer's terms and reflects the customer's priorities and preferences – look back to the illustration in Chapter 3 of the demands of the sophisticated customer if you need convincing all over again. You may say the customer is irrational, ill-informed, misguided, short-sighted and so on (and that is just what we do say – see back to Chapter 2, pp. 22–4), but value exists only when the customer decides it does.

Knowing what means value to our customers is therefore rather important. We may get nice surprises or we may get nasty surprises.

The Royal Mail was plagued by customers demanding that they cut the length of queues in Post Offices. So, they did just that. The trouble was that their customers believed the (actually shorter) queues were longer than ever. Managers found the quickest way to cut customer perceptions of queuing times was to repaint Post Offices. Customers in clean, redecorated Post Offices reported they had queued for a shorter time, even though it was not true.

'if we do not know what the value drivers are for our customers, we are likely to do the wrong things for the right reasons'

The issue is not just standing in line, it is queuing in squalor. Royal Mail managers' bonuses now depend in part not just on meeting performance targets, but on whether customers believe they are meeting those targets[2].

On the other hand, if we do not know what the value drivers are for our customers, we are likely to do the wrong things for the right reasons:

● One company believed speed of service was the key to customer value, so trained telephone staff to be quicker. They lost market share because in fact customers wanted time to chat and resented being hassled[3].

- When Federal Express went for faster delivery speed to please customers they also achieved the reverse. The extra speed caused more misdirections and errors. Customers actually value getting the parcel most of all!

There are a couple of additional complications to really knowing what value is to your customers:

- *Different customers buy different kinds of value*[4]. This is true both within the market (see market segmentation by customer benefits, pp. 416–21) and more surprisingly in different markets. Look, for example, at the portable clockwork radio, designed by a British inventor and manufactured in Africa, which is creating a sensation in the developing countries – where for large parts of the market, radio ownership is a high priority, but the cost of batteries is prohibitive.
- *Things change – value 'migrates'*[5]. This suggests that value propositions become less effective over time and unless you find ways to enhance or refocus the value in your product or service, buyers will migrate to alternative value concepts. British financial service companies have always offered trust-worthiness, prudence and financial expertise to the market, and were wrong-footed by firms like Virgin Direct offering simple products that were less complicated and easier to buy.
- *Even value is not enough.* The best companies positively 'delight' customers. In looking at its customer satisfaction data, Xerox discovered a simple truth – satisfying customers is good, but the truly delighted customers buy six times more than the satisfied customers. Delight may be additional product features or absolute guarantees of quality and price, but the winners seem to be the companies that dramatically exceed customer expectations on critical dimensions of value.

As we saw in Chapter 3 (pp. 92–3), Don Peppers uses the term 'one-to-one marketing' to focus on the value issues at the individual customer level, and to customize products and services accordingly. This sounds outrageous but it can be done:

- Value to young buyers of jeans is that they fit tight round the bum. The giant Levi Strauss & Co. developed a 'Personal Pair' customized tailoring service for its famous blue jeans. Custom-ized software is used to design tapered-leg jeans to the individual customer's body measurements, input by a trained sales assistant. The program identifies a 'prototype' which is closest to the customer's size, final adjustments are made to perfect the fit, and these measurements go by modem to the factory, from where the perfect fit individually-tailored Levi's go to the customer. The product is coded to allow easy reordering of an identical fit[6]. Their next move was to put touch-screen computers in the stores to allow customers to design their own jeans[7].

- Value to sophisticated computer buyers is to choose their own specifications for the machine. This is essentially what Dell Computers offers in its direct-selling channel (see pp. 202–4). From a standing start Dell got to a position in the top ten computer manufacturers in a decade. Virtually every computer with a Dell badge is built to individual order (see pp. 202–4).

'It may mean massive change in the process of how you go to market, but focusing on what creates value for customers is incredibly powerful'

It may mean massive change in the process of how you go to market, but focusing on what creates value for customers is incredibly powerful.

With those provisos in mind, let's turn our attention to the tools we have at our disposal to develop value propositions that will impress our customers, as suggested in Figure 9.1.

Mission analysis[8]

Perhaps the strategic analysis most demanded by companies and executives, but all too often the least rewarding aspect of working with companies on market strategy, is mission analysis. In theory, mission is where we start, because it tells us the broad purpose of the operation and gives us the framework within which to develop sets of specific objectives and programmes – as suggested by Figure 9.3. The logical sequence is that we start with basic purposes (mission), determine specific goals (objectives), figure out what we need to do to achieve these things (market strategies), and how we are going to do it in the marketplace (marketing programmes).

The results of mission analysis tend to be statements of varying length that state what we want our business to be. Examples include:

- *Pepsi* – 'We will be an outstanding company by exceeding customer expectations through empowering people guided by shared value'.
- *Kentucky Fried Chicken* – 'To provide families with affordable, delicious chicken-dominant meals'.

Figure 9.3 Mission and market strategy

- *Sony* – The 'BMW' slogan: 'Beat Matsushita Whatsoever'.
- *Littlewoods* – This troubled British retailer is trying to change its old-fashioned image with a statement of mission and value. The company's vision is to be 'the UK's most admired consumer business', and the mission statement talks about 'achieving our vision by being intimate with the lifestyles and aspirations of the average-income UK families who make up our customer base'. It defines its values as PRIDE: 'P' stands for 'pursue excellence for all our customers', 'R' for 'respect for everyone', 'I' for 'ideas galore', 'D' for 'deliver value', and 'E' for 'enjoy the journey'[9]. They have clearly had a lot of fun with this exercise – but can anyone see a difference in how the company operates?

Other mission and vision statements run to many pages and hundreds of words, and consume many hours of management time in their construction.

For a handful of companies, strategy is reduced to a single memorable phrase used to drive consistent action throughout the organization, such as:

AOL   Consumer connectivity first – anytime, anywhere
Dell   Be direct
Wal-Mart Low prices, every day

These phrases encapsulate the company's main strategic principle and for them it seems an effective way of communicating that principle as a basis for action[10].

However, for many others, the results seem mixed at best. McDonalds has the mission of existing to 'provide great-tasting food backed up by excellent operations and friendly service in a relaxed, safe, and consistent restaurant environment'. The effectiveness in creating service quality should be considered in the light of the (hopefully untypical) customer experience in Chester of receiving a printed receipt reading 'One regular Coke – no f***ing ice'[11]!

Chief Executive: 'Sales have gone through the floor, and we are trading at a loss. But I think our mission statement – "Frankly we couldn't care less" – has the competition worried.'

If mission statements are to contribute anything, then they must:

- reflect our core competencies and how we intend to apply them to creating customer value, and how we plan to sustain them;
- be closely tied to the critical success factors in the marketplace – the things we have to be good at to survive; and
- tell our employees, managers, suppliers and partners what contribution is required from them to deliver our promise of value to the customer.

If they do not do this – they are of no use in building market strategy. But, in reality, how often do they do these things? Often, they do not. Frankly, most of the time they do not.

'The trouble with talking about mission is that at the extreme it becomes top management ego-massaging and "holier than thou" posturing, and has little to do with running the business and providing value to the customer'

The trouble with talking about mission is that at the extreme it becomes top management ego-massaging and 'holier than thou' posturing, and has little to do with running the business and providing value to the customer. Indeed, I have been driven to suggest to some companies whose version of mission analysis is pure, non-operational motherhood, that we are prepared to provide them with the 'Instant Mission Kit', shown in Figure 9.4.

This kit is guaranteed to produce a mission statement of bland, non-operational motherhood, with which no-one will disagree, but which will not change a single thing in the business and the value it provides to the customer – but at least it is quicker than the usual weeks of heart-searching, so you will not waste as much time! Bear in mind it took 300 people to come

Mission Statement Components	Tick as Required
We wannabe:	
... a market leader	
... a total quality supplier	
... a socially responsible producer	
... a green/environmentally friendly firm	
... a caring employer	
... a safeguarder of shareholder interests	
... a global player	
... a provider of excellent service	
... dedicated to improving life on this planet	
... a good corporate citizen	
... a customer-oriented organization	
... a responsible partner with distributors	
... a builder of human dignity	
... with the imagination to think bigger	
... respectful of nature and living things	

Figure 9.4   Piercy's instant mission kit

up with British Energy's somewhat bland statement of mission[12].

This is perhaps a little too cynical and probably reflects battle fatigue from too many fatuous mission analysis sessions with company top managements. Please note, however, I am not alone in such cynicism. Dilbert, the world's greatest business cartoon character, informs us that:

'If your employees are producing low-quality products that no sane person would buy, you can afford to fix that problem by holding meetings to discuss your Mission Statement. A Mission Statement is defined as "a long awkward sentence that demonstrates management's inability to think clearly". All good companies have one.'[13]

Does it ever do any good?

Perhaps surprisingly – yes, it does seem to work for some companies. Anything that forces us to go back to the basics of asking us what we are doing and why has the potential to make a contribution. Probably the best part of the whole thing is challenging our business definition.

In fact, the whole customer mission thing was started off by Theodore Levitt's classic paper 'Marketing Myopia' in 1960[14], which was primarily about business definition in customer terms. This paper laid down the argument that became an article of faith for generations of marketing executives. Levitt tells us that customer needs are fundamental and, by contrast, our specific products and technologies are no more than one way of satisfying that fundamental customer need (so far, so good). The examples given of companies incorrectly defining their businesses have also become classics. The basic questions we are urged to ask are: what business *are* we in; what business *should* we be in; and what business *can* we be in?

But, importantly, our answers are required to be given in terms of customer needs, not products. Levitt's examples included:

Traditional, but inappropriate product or technology-based definitions of the business	Appropriate customer need-based definitions of the business
Railways	Transportation
Oil	Energy
Computers	Information Processing
Photocopiers	Office Productivity

'Things that give us greater insight into the real sources of competition and what really matters to the customer – i.e. meeting the need or solving the problem, not buying our product – cannot be all bad'

Things that give us greater insight into the real sources of competition and what really matters to the customer – i.e. meeting the need or solving the problem, not buying our product – cannot be all bad.

For example, Levitt's view of railways as being in the transportation business in the 1960s could be updated to say that the railway company is actually in the 'communications' business. If this seems far-fetched, consider the following advertising message at the centre of a major advertising campaign run in the UK:

Picture the scene: a tired, scruffy, dishevelled executive arrives home from yet another trip away on business. He finds his wife in the arms of a Spanish dancing instructor, and less than enthusiastic at his arrival. His small child appears and screams at the stranger before him. His dog arrives and bites the ankle of this forgotten intruder. *The message* – do not *travel* on business, use the phone, the fax, the telex, the confraphone, the electronic mail system, and regain your quality of life. *The significance* – all of a sudden British Telecom and the railway companies are direct competitors in the business communications market. And before we discuss that preposterous thought, let us not forget that the much-maligned British railway companies have a major expertise in electronic communications, and substantial potential synergies with the computing and telecoms industries.

This style of analysis is often difficult, but it can produce some very real insights into ways to grow a business, to reposition it, to understand its core strengths and to fend off emerging competition, really by making us think about the things that matter to customers – i.e. their needs.

For instance, mission analysis was useful in identifying different ways to define the business of a British gardening centre firm, at different levels of abstraction from its core business of simply growing plants and selling them. The levels of mission analysis identified were:

- *horticulture* – we grow plants and sell them, and can develop the business by doing more of the same;
- *gardening services* – we add value by providing advisory and information services to support the sale of plants and equipment. We may grow into new markets like garden design services, landscaping and estate maintenance;
- *leisure/entertainment* – we see our role as filling people's leisure time. We add leisure facilities – catering, children's entertainments to create a 'day out'. We develop (probably by leased areas) into new outdoor leisure product areas – camping, caravanning, Do-It-Yourself;
- *dream fulfilment* – we specialize in meeting the needs of the person to whom the perfect home and garden is the ideal and central to their lifestyle[15].

In fact this company chose to pursue the leisure/entertainment mission, and rationalized their operation around this. For these managers mission analysis was central to the practical issue of sorting out how they identified the market, the target customer and the appropriate direction in which to take the business.

The danger is that we get carried away with the excitement and creativity in mission analysis and with the insights it can provide. Mission analysis which forgets the realities of our core business is dangerous, and unhelpful to the people who actually have to run the business.

For example, John Kay[16] links Levitt's analysis of the petroleum industry (meeting energy needs not supplying petrol) to the diversification of oil companies into other energy markets after the 1974 oil strike. The results of this diversification ranged from the disappointing to the disastrous. Few of these activities survive. Oil companies showed little capability for these new areas – they make money by selling oil products, which is what they are good at. Confusing industries and markets is dangerous.

'Defining core business is about identifying our distinctive skills, resources and capabilities, and using these in markets where they give a competitive advantage'

Defining core business is about identifying our distinctive skills, resources and capabilities, and using these in markets where they give a competitive advantage. This is why Marks & Spencer did well in financial services (capitalizing on its reputation with customers), while BT did badly in buying equipment manufacturers (BT is a phone company). The critical issue is whether an activity matches our core capabilities.

This said, certainly many companies will tell you that mission analysis was the single most valuable thing they have *ever* done. Indeed, in some organizations, mission analysis has provided the broad logic for divisionalizing and developing strategies for complex businesses in very simple terms.

One well-known example was a UK brewery which undertook mission analysis at the corporate level, with the results described below:

The brewery's missions	Organizational and market characteristics	Strategies developed
Drink	A static market leading to a traditional bureaucratic organization driven by the pressure of production efficiency and economies of scale.	Compete for market share against competitors by large advertising spends and new brands. Acquire new outlets where possible.
Catering	At the time, a by-product of being in the business of running public houses.	Compete for customer spend by greater variety of food in pubs. Acquire restaurants. Acquire hotels.
Entertainment	Pubs are leisure centres. The expertise is filling people's leisure needs.	Acquisition of gaming clubs, gambling machines, holiday camps, tour operators, private sports clubs.
Chemicals	The unavoidable by-product of brewing.	Strategy of R&D-based collaborations with third parties to exploit the chemical materials in markets as diverse as blood replacement, fish food and genetic engineering.

In this instance mission analysis provided an enduring structure (now more than 20 years old) for developing organizational planning and identifying strategies, on the basis of capabilities in the different customer or user markets, to be competed. However, things change – sometimes dramatically. Eventually, the company withdrew altogether from the drinks and catering business and no longer brews beer, focusing wholly on the entertainment mission.

The sorts of benefits that this kind of market-based mission analysis can give us are:

- defining the market from the customer's perspective, i.e. the need or problem to be solved, so we get better insight into what matters to the customer;
- mapping out the different types of customer market in which we need to develop different types of market strategies and programmes if we are to be a serious player;
- helping us to see where the real competition is coming from, and where it is going to emerge;
- finding us new areas into which we can develop where the link to our current business is our customer base and our capabilities.

On this basis, mission analysis can be used productively, but needs to be used with care to avoid some of the stranger conclusions to which I have alluded.

Table 9.1 IBM's New Principles in 1994*

IBM's New Principles
1 The marketplace is the driving force behind everything we do.
2 At our core, we are a technology company with an overriding commitment to quality.
3 Our primary measures of success are customer satisfaction and shareholder value.
4 We operate as an entrepreneurial organization with a minimum of bureaucracy and a never-ending focus on productivity.
5 We never lose sight of our strategic vision.
6 We think and act with a sense of urgency.
7 Outstanding, dedicated people make it all happen, particularly when they work together as a team.
8 We are sensitive to the needs of all employees and to the communities in which we operate.

* Source: *The Wall Street Journal*, 13 May 1994

There is another type of mission analysis of which we should be aware – the *key value mission*. This is mission analysis which identifies the key values, goals and constraints that we want people to share in running the business.

This is more about motivation and team-building than defining markets, but it too may have something to offer us. Fundamental to Lou Gerstner's programme of cultural change at IBM was the written statement of 'IBM's New Principles' shown in Table 9.1. The goal was to provide a benchmark in the company's attempt to break free from the past and from traditional IBM bureaucracy to build customer focus driven by empowered managers.

So, how do we sort out our market mission?

'mission analysis is potentially confusing and open to abuse'   It is clear from the above that mission analysis is potentially confusing and open to abuse – personally I *hate* being asked about mission. Nonetheless, executives show great enthusiasm for building statements of their vision and mission. If we are going to get involved in this analysis as part of building market strategy and clarifying our value proposition, then at least let's do it systematically.

The problems with mission statements (aside from pretentiousness) seem to be lack of clarity, lack of focus in markets (which is certainly not what Ted Levitt intended) and ambiguity. In fact, what managers say about mission analysis in workshops is things like this:

- the Mission Statements that are produced are qualitative, non-specific, unclear and ambiguous, and so serve little useful purpose in the organization;
- the Mission Statements constructed inevitably seem to represent a trade-off or compromise between the interests of different groups inside and outside the organization – in trying to be 'all things to all people' they end up as largely valueless to anybody;
- to avoid conflict, Mission Statements contain nothing but 'motherhood' – no-one can disagree with what they say, but they have no influence on what people in the organization *do* or *how* they do it;
- Mission Statements are inconsistent – they are self-contradictory in the demands they place upon managers, for example, often in social responsibility imperatives compared to required market position and financial performance;
- Mission Statements are poorly integrated – the different components all make sense on their own, but they look as

though they have been produced in isolation, and they are not compatible and lack realism – for example, injunctions from corporate levels to behave in ways that ignore market and competitive realities;

- Mission Statements try unsuccessfully to encompass everything, rather than recognizing market and SBU differences;
- Mission Statements are so 'visionary' they lose touch with reality in the organization and the marketplace, and have no credibility with line managers – the 'Field of Dreams' approach to mission; and
- Mission Statements are produced that are inward-looking and historically-based, when we desperately need to be market-focused and future-oriented.

These statements are simply compiled from managers' reactions to the mission issue in planning workshops and similar venues. Such comments suggest a pathology of mission in practice, or simply that the reality of the implementation of mission analysis may not be all that is promised by the conventional literature. We should be able to do better than this.

'Such comments suggest a pathology of mission in practice, or simply that the reality of the implementation of mission analysis may not be all that is promised'

Structuring mission content

Views about the desirable content of Mission Statements are many and varied. However, we can distinguish four major areas:

- statements relating to *organizational philosophy*;
- the specification of the *product market domain* or scope for the organization;
- definition of *organizational key values* for participants; and
- the identification of *critical success factors* in the marketplace or industry faced.

These issues vary in *focus* (internal or external) and *scope* (broad and narrow), as shown in Figure 9.5.

Organizational philosophy

Many views suggest that the centre of mission is the definition of the central purpose, or philosophy of the organization, or even creating a form of 'corporate constitution'. Some see this area as encompassing the broad issues: the grand design, quality orientation and atmosphere of the enterprise, and the firm's role

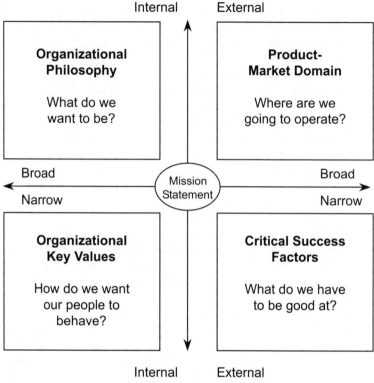

Figure 9.5 A model of mission

in society, or the combination of managerial culture and ethos with social responsibility and public image. More focused perspectives emphasize specific service to internal and external stakeholders, and the identification of values, beliefs, guidelines, aspirations and thus the creation of a unifying force in the organization. In the simplest terms, the underlying question here is 'what do we want this organization to *be* and to *stand for?*'

Product market domain

Others look to mission to define where the organization is to operate, which shifts from a focus on internal to external issues: the definition of the customer base, the product/service offering, location or geographic coverage, and the core technologies or capability to be exploited. In the simplest terms, the central question to be addressed here is '*where* are we going to compete, or what is our *field of operation* and what are our *core capabilities?*'

Organizational key values

This relates to ideas about defining the core values or principles which provide guides to action for members of the organization, or the 'policies and behaviour that underpin the distinctive competence and value system'. Some see this area as building corporate culture and 'selling' corporate beliefs to employees, or motivating employees to achieve the organization's objectives, and even providing the basis for appraisal and reward. In the simplest terms, the central question here is 'what do we want people in this organization to be *good at*, and how do we want them to *behave?*'

Critical success factors

Less easily identified in the traditional approach are suggestions about the external impact of mission. These are taken here as the identification of critical success factors in the market or industry faced. In the simplest terms the central issue here is 'what do we have to be *good at* to *succeed* in this market or industry?'

Analysing mission statements

We can use the structures in Figure 9.5 as a diagnostic tool to confront the mission issue in organizations, either in building a Mission Statement for the first time, or in evaluating an existing statement. The procedure is:

- Summarize the key points of our existing or proposed new Mission Statement.
- From those key points identify the following dimensions of mission: *Organizational philosophy* – what do we see as the enduring purpose of our organization, its unique characteristics, and what it wants to achieve? *Product market domain* – where do we intend to operate and compete, what are our products, what needs do they meet, who are our customers, what technologies will we apply, what are the boundaries of our markets, what are our core capabilities? *Organizational key values* – what values, norms and guidelines do we think are important in our organization, what things do we want people to have in their minds when they make decisions, and carry things out for us? *Critical success factors* – what things do we have to be good at to survive and prosper in our market place?
- Using the structure in Figure 9.5, look at the consistency between the different parts of our mission: do the critical

success factors derived from the mission actually make any sense in terms of the product markets the organization has chosen – or are we trying to be good at things that don't matter? Does the organization's 'philosophy' relate to the key values we try to transmit to people who make decisions in the organization, or are there inherent conflicts because we have not thought things through enough? Do these key values (services, quality, social responsibilities, or whatever) relate directly to the critical success factors in these product markets – or do our internal values have nothing to do with what matters in the marketplace? Has the organization chosen sensible product markets where its philosophy or sense of purpose makes sense? If we work through this process, what conclusions can we reach about: the adequacy of our mission statement; the consistency between internal issues of philosophy and key values, and external issues of product market domain and critical success factors?

- Our conclusions may lead us to revise what we want to reflect in our Mission Statement, or to revise the draft Mission Statement; the critical requirement is to move backwards and forwards between these stages – discussing, revising, testing, rethinking – until we can move from the draft Mission Statement to the final version.

- Finally, we can test our Mission Statement with: our managers, our employees, our shareholders, our customers, and our suppliers.

'a systematic structural analysis of the mission issue takes us forward from the vague, open-ended, waffle that some executives produce'

If nothing else, a systematic structural analysis of the mission issue takes us forward from the vague, open-ended, waffle that some executives produce. Experience in testing this approach in-company suggests it can be a good way to find if there is anything useful here to build market strategy, and to highlight the process of matching our core capabilities with our internal values and with the critical success factors we need outside. In fact, if we regard our company's reputation as an important marketing asset – customer judgements about our philosophy and values may be important in the marketplace as well (see pp. 100–5) – put crudely being seen as ethical and socially responsible may have a marketplace value because it makes our customers more comfortable buying from us.

However, we keep using the terms 'core capabilities', 'competitive advantage' and 'competitive differentiation'. These need much more clarification in progressing the development of market strategy.

Competitive differentiation and positioning

Another difficult issue on which to work with companies is that of competitive differentiation, and the result that it achieves in positioning one company's offering as providing distinctive value in the customer's judgment – and hopefully in the target customer's eyes better and preferable to the alternatives. These words seem to be ones which create problems for executives, perhaps because they sound like vague theoretical notions. Competitive differentiation and positioning are neither vague nor academic, they are about delivering what the customer values, to get the results we want, and to do this we have to find and exploit our core capabilities.

'Competitive differentiation and positioning are neither vague nor academic, they are about delivering what the customer values, to get the results we want'

Competitive differentiation

The best-known approach to simplifying this issue is that provided by Michael Porter of Harvard Business School[17]. Porter told us that in spite of the apparent complexity of competitive strategy, there are two, and only two, sources of competitive advantage: low cost and differentiation. This leads to the identification of three generic strategies, as in Figure 9.6.

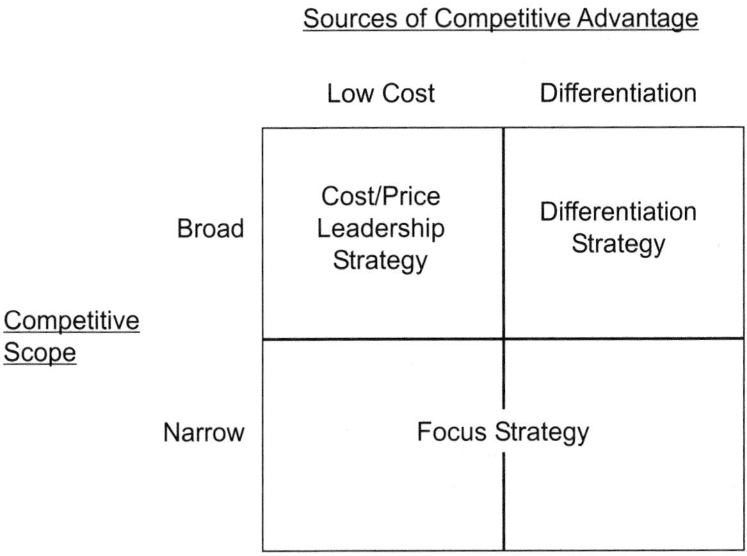

Sources of Competitive Advantage

Figure 9.6   Porter's generic strategies

Porter's view of our competitive choice is that we can compete on a broad or narrow scope (in the same way we have already discussed segmentation), but that we are then either a price leader or a differentiator.

The two most relevant points from Porter's work for our present purposes are: first, we should think in terms of our *own* competitive strategy type (to avoid the danger of becoming a 'stuck in the middle' firm which is weak and vulnerable, because it is neither one thing nor the other – neither a differentiator nor a price leader); second, we can use the structure to see how groups of our competitors are positioned in terms of their strategies – i.e. what are the 'strategic groups' and how well do these groups perform.

For instance, we might be able to break the complex market for personal writing instruments into:

- Broad scope/price leadership – throw-away ball-point pens, generic products.
- Broad scope/differentiators – mass market brands, Parker, Schaeffer, etc., differentiated by branding, design, packaging, and so on.
- Narrow scope/price leadership – own-label pens, badged hotel pens, etc.
- Narrow scope/differentiators – exclusive brands like Cross, Mont Blanc, etc.

It is often very revealing of the reality of what works competitively and what doesn't (i.e. what value means to different customers), to try this simple way of reducing a complex competitive market to a few basic groups. However, this leaves untouched the question of *how* differentiation can be achieved.

Porter is adamant that differentiation must be added to operational efficiency if we are to perform well:

> 'A company can outperform rivals only if it can establish a difference that it can preserve. It must deliver greater value to customers or create comparable value at a lower cost, or do both. The arithmetic of superior profitability then follows: delivering greater value allows a company to change higher unit prices; greater efficiency results in lower average unit costs.'[18]

This comment is important, and raises three significant questions for us in building a market strategy:

- What differences can we establish or exploit between ourselves and the others in this market?

- In what ways do these represent superior value to all or some of our customers in this market?
- Can we sustain this form of differentiation and defend it against 'me-too' imitation by existing or new competitors?

One of the problems we face is that in many markets the spread of approaches, like benchmarking, 'best practice', shared technology and distribution, drives out real differentiation between competing firms and products. Superficial differentiation of products and services that are essentially identical does not fool customers indefinitely (if at all):

'Superficial differentiation of products and services that are essentially identical does not fool customers indefinitely (if at all)'

- As the manufacturers of vacuum cleaners found when confronted by Dyson (see pp. 331–40 for the story).
- As the Andrex brand of toilet paper discovered in the UK – the emotion-tugging Labrador puppy in the TV advertising could only hold prices high for so long, he had a cuddly and soft underbelly wide open to attack from rivals offering better value.
- Indeed, consider the spectacular market success achieved by Direct Line. This operation pioneered telephone-based selling of insurance products with the effect of transforming standards in how insurance is sold in Britain, drastically reducing the prices of policies, and stunning the traditional competitors, but virtually every competitor can imitate telephone selling, and after recovering from the initial shell-shock, this is exactly what they have done.

The issue is real differences that matter to customers – which we can sustain.

Porter's argument is that if competitive strategy is about being different, then the essence is positioning ourselves by choosing to perform activities differently, or choosing to perform different activities than our rivals. For example, all banks and insurance companies offer the same products (as far as customers are concerned), but First Direct and Direct Line introduced direct marketing compared to conventional branch networks and face-to-face selling. On the other hand, IKEA is differentiated from conventional furniture stores by substituting self-service for personal selling, and having customers do their own pick-up and delivery.

The logic is that competition can be seen as 'the process of perceiving new positions that woo customers from established positions or draw new customers into the market'[19], and in this sense it is highly entrepreneurial. Strategic positions are suggested to come from three distinct sources:

- *Variety-based purchasing* – producing a specialized subset of an industry's products or services, i.e. become a specialist.
- *Need-based positioning* – targeting a particular group of customers, for example in exclusive private banking, or in home furnishings by specialized firms like IKEA and Habitat.
- *Access-based positioning* – where customers differ on the best way of reaching them, for example the rural cinema company Carmike provides small cinema services tailored to the needs of rural communities, or First Direct's 24-hour telephone banking service in the UK reaches those who work through conventional banking hours.

In broad terms this asks us to choose: are we a product specialist or a customer specialist? To test that out in real terms for your own business, go back to the Product–Customer Matrix (Figure 8.2), look at each cell in the matrix and ask: will we achieve better results by taking our existing product/service to new customer types, or by adding new products/services to what we sell to existing customers? Or, do we aim to sell more existing products to existing customers (grow within the cell). This quickly highlights what we believe to be our greatest competitive strength.

Porter also points out that approaching competitive differentiation and positioning in this way only produces a sustainable competitive advantage if two further conditions exist:

- competitors cannot imitate or equal our position with their current operations; and
- the activities needed to support the position we want to take in the market fit to each other and to our capabilities.

'We need to combine what we are good at doing with the model of competitive differentiation and positioning – how can we differentiate effectively if we do not understand our capabilities?'

In short, this says for our strategy to be effective, it needs to reflect what we are best at doing – our core capabilities – not what our competitors can do just as well.

Core capabilities

We need to combine what we are good at doing with the model of competitive differentiation and positioning – how can we differentiate effectively if we do not understand our capabilities? Then we can focus on the issue of value to the customer, and the marketing assets we have at our disposal to create the value which underpins competitive positioning.

In a widely-admired *Harvard Business Review* article in 1990, C. K. Prahalad and Gary Hamel[20] examined the characteristics of companies that have succeeded in inventing new markets, quickly entering new markets, and dramatically shifting patterns of customer choices in established markets. They concluded that the common characteristic is that these companies understand, exploit, invest to create, and sustain core competencies. Examples include:

- *Sony* – the capacity to miniaturize;
- *Philips* – optical media expertise;
- *Citicorp* – competence in systems;
- *3M* – competence with sticky tape;
- *Black & Decker* – expertise with small electrical motors;
- *Canon* – skills in optics, imaging and microprocessors;
- *Casio* – competence in display systems.

They see these as the most basic corporate resources, which lead to success in apparently diverse markets and products, and suggest even the largest company is unlikely to have more than five or six core competencies.

This view of core capabilities can be combined with our earlier view of competitive differentiation by thinking about our differentiating capabilities – at the level of the market, segment and customer, which of our capabilities or competencies create value for a customer, differentiate us from competitors, and around which we can build a sustainable market strategy?

It is worth bearing in mind that a company's core competencies may *not* produce differentiating capabilities at the market or customer level. For instance, IBM built an amazingly strong position in the world computer market – in the mid-1980s IBM had 40 per cent of the industry's entire worldwide sales and 70 per cent of all profits. The core competence at IBM was 'big iron' – dealing with big customers and big computers. But, as the market moved towards the personal computer, IBM was poorly positioned to compete – basically smaller suppliers dealing with smaller customers ran rings around IBM. The strategy under John Akers of attacking Microsoft and Intel was a failure. The most critical IBM core competence gave little differentiating capability in the PC market. In fact, the company has been turned round by Lou Gerstner by his vision for an IBM Global Network – global networking requires IBM's expertise in 'big iron'. This area exploits IBM's most basic core competence[21].

Differentiating capabilities

'when we have to build a market position – what competitive differentiation can we use to create value for a customer in this market or segment?'

Differentiating capabilities put together the theories of differentiation and core competencies in a specific market. At this level our concern is when we have to build a market position – what competitive differentiation can we use to create value for a customer in this market or segment?

> 'If you don't have a competitive advantage, don't compete.'
>
> Jack Welch, CEO, General Electric

We need to think very hard about which of our company's core capabilities are valuable to us in a particular market:

- does this capability create value for the customer in this market – if not, it is no use to us in developing a strategy for this market;
- will competitors find it hard to copy this capability – if every company can do this as well as we can, there is no competitive advantage, because we all offer the same value proposition;
- what is the probable duration of the uniqueness – how long have we got before the competition can catch us up;
- who is the primary beneficiary of the capability – does it relate to particular segments of the market, where we should focus;

'perhaps the greatest single barrier to getting market strategy to work effectively is the fact that many executives will tell you that in their business the market is a commodity market, and consequently the only thing that matters is price and product specification'

- does another capability satisfy the same market need – we face competition from substitution;
- is the capability we believe we have really superior to the competition, or are we kidding ourselves?

In the real world, competing on capabilities is a moving target.

However, perhaps the greatest single barrier to getting market strategy to work effectively is the fact that many executives will tell you that in their business the market is a *commodity* market, and consequently the only thing that matters is price and product specification. The reality is, of course, that price and product specifications *do* matter in most markets, but anything and everything can be differentiated. This may sound preposterous, but let us consider it for a moment.

Tom Peters[22] uses the example of the laundrette, turned by one company into a fast-growing success story by twinning it with the wine bar under the slogan – 'Enjoy Our Suds While You Wash Your Duds'. Theodore Levitt[23] has taken examples of basic chemicals like isopropanol, an undifferentiated chemical, and shown large variations in the prices paid by customers in the same market at the same time.

On the other hand, the retail bookselling business in Britain has been traumatized by the abandonment of price protection (the end of the Net Books Agreement) and the entry of multiple supermarkets and Internet retailers as discount book retailers. Much of the traditional industry was prepared to simply curl up and die. In 1997, Waterstones opened a massive new flagship store in Glasgow, which fights off price competition with a highly differentiated offering to customers that exploits the company's strength and delights its customers. The differentiation was not based on outside research but the 'market sensing' of a team of six advocates – senior managers who brainstormed ideas about what sells books and toured the world for new ideas. They defined six key qualities that a bookshop needs to offer its customers: friendliness, service, excitement, generosity, community commit-ment, and an appealing combination of space comfort and atmosphere, termed 'browsability' – they say 'Everybody wants to sit down and read the book they have purchased right away', so this is the kind of bookstore they provide. This provides a highly differentiated market position, which discount retailers cannot emulate[24].

People in the oil business believe they are in a commodity market. An interesting game to play with oil company executives is to challenge them to conceive of a situation where it would be possible to get a 50p a gallon price premium for petrol from the buyer. (I admit to being motivated by the desire to irritate certain such executives, who appear to have been cloned by the 'Smug Corporation'.) This game normally fails because the oil industry's deeply-ingrained belief is that only price and outlet location matter in selling petrol. Interestingly, it is executives from other industries who observe this dialogue and often admit they actually do not *know* the price of a gallon of petrol, and since they do not pay for their own petrol on business trips, probably *would* pay a premium price for such things as: preference in queues, delivery of petrol by an attendant, a quick car wash, a 'free' cup of coffee, clean toilets and bathrooms for 'club members' with keys, preferential access to a phone and fax machine, and a few other services that matter to people travelling on business. This may sound outlandish, but consider the proven efficiency of offering truck drivers in the USA a 'free' breakfast in return for their diesel fuel business (which admittedly may amount to several hundred pounds worth of fuel each time, given the size of the trucks), as opposed to conventional price competition. (It is also highly predictable that if anyone does something like this in the UK, it will probably be a company like Virgin, not the established oil companies!)

Then consider what Tom Farmer did to the car exhaust and tyre business in the UK. Replacement exhausts and tyres are a 'distress' purchase, which none of us want to make, but we *have* to. Farmer's Kwik Fit operation dominates the UK market and has turned a commodity market into a brand loyal one – where the loyalty is to Kwik Fit. Achieved through a variety of means: an obsession with customer satisfaction; a highly idiosyncratic management structure and approach; a large advertising spend; *and* good price deals.

In another, very different, commodity market, the giant South African diamond supplier, De Beers, has effectively put its brand name on diamonds – their vision is that when a young man has fallen in love and spends two months' salary on a diamond engagement ring, the object of his affection will hold out her hand to display the rock, and say 'It's from De Beers'. They are also looking to physically brand each stone with the De Beer's name – invisible to the naked eye, but burnt into a corner of the stone by laser[25]. In similar vein, 2001 saw gold producers investing in re-branding gold to regain consumer favour for the inclusion of gold in jewellery[26] – their slogan is 'glow with gold' and that the warm sensuous richness of gold means that 'warm' is the new cool[27]. Nothing has to be a commodity.

No-one is saying it is *easy,* or necessarily cheap, but with creativity and a simple focus on innovation and novelty in what matters to the customer, there are differentiation opportunities *everywhere.*

At the simplest level, competitive differentiation comes from the three sources identified in Figure 9.7 – the product itself (even if it is a service product); the surround of added-value services which are available (or can be); and a whole set of marketing intangibles (or assets to which we turn our attention in the next section).

'what sources of competitive differentiation open to us will create value for the customer, and build competitive advantage for us in this market, i.e. what are our differentiating capabilities?'

But this leaves open the question – what sources of competitive differentiation open to us will create *value* for the customer, and build competitive advantage for us in this market, i.e. what are our differentiating capabilities?

Useful insights into this question came from Treacy and Wiersema's study *The Discipline of Market Leaders*[28]. Their view is that market leaders dominate

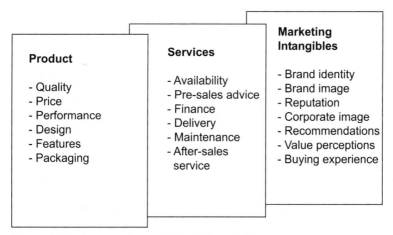

Figure 9.7 Sources of competitive differentiation

their chosen areas by achieving the highest value in the customer's eyes where:

- different customers buy different types of value – few companies excel at everything, so the issue is one of choosing customers and narrowing the value focus, because market leaders excel in offering a specific dimension of venue;
- as value standards rise, so do customer expectations, so you have to improve every year or be outpaced by competitors;
- producing an unmatched level of a particular value requires a superior operating model dedicated to that kind of value.

This leads Treacy and Wiersema to identify the 'value disciplines' followed by market leaders as operational excellence, product leadership and customer intimacy.

- *Operational excellence* – these are companies that deliver a combination of quality, price and ease of purchase that no-one in their market can match. They are not innovators or relationship builders, their value proposition is guaranteed low price and/or hassle-free service. Prime examples are discount retailers.
- *Product leadership* – these are the competitors that continually push products and services into the realm of the unknown, the untried or the highly desirable. Examples of such firms include Intel, Canon and Nike.
- *Customer intimacy* – the customer-intimate company delivers the message 'we take care of you and all your needs' or 'we

give you the best total solution', in the way that IBM did in the 1960s and 1970s in the computer market, and Dell does now.

In the same way that Porter tells us not to be a 'stuck in the middle' company, that is neither low-cost nor differentiated, neither fully broad nor focused in scope, Treacy and Wiersema argue that at the market level, the leaders choose a value discipline and ruthlessly specialize in it. The choice of value discipline commits the company to a particular strategic pathway. These issues force us back to reconsidering how well we understand our customers and how we define and segment the market, and we may not be able to make decisions here until we have worked through issues of marketing assets and the key relationships involved in the strategy.

'These issues force us back to reconsidering how well we understand our customers and how we define and segment the market'

Nonetheless, the important point at this stage is to force us to confront issues of competencies and capabilities, the scope and form of differential advantage and whether any of this creates value for the customer – because no advantage in customer value equals no strategy. Looking at competitive differentiation and positioning should involve us in some painful soul-searching about our core competencies and capabilities, our strategic positioning options, and the route to achieving higher value for a target customer through our differentiating capabilities.

However, we cannot finalize our views on competitive differentiation and positioning without also examining our available marketing assets, and brands in particular.

Marketing assets and brands

As we move from corporate issues like core competencies and strategic position to asking what we have got that can create value for a customer in our market, it is useful to be brutally honest about what marketing assets we really have compared to our competitors (and in some cases, as we will see, what 'marketing liabilities'). Marketing assets refers to all those intangibles, which may impact on the customer's perception of us and our products and services. This includes our history, our reputation, our expertise, and perhaps most importantly our brands. We will review marketing assets generally, but then focus on branding.

What do we mean by marketing assets? In fact, these are revenue- and income-generating resources of the business, which normally cost us a small fortune to create and maintain, and which probably distinguish between the winners and the losers in most markets. However, marketing assets are a bit of a problem for three reasons: they are *intangible*; most businesses do not place any *accounting value* on them (or if they do it is written off as quickly as possible as 'goodwill'); accordingly, they are almost impossible to *monitor* or even to measure in most conventional management accounting systems.

What are marketing assets?

There is no universal framework for listing marketing assets that work for all companies, but we can make a start by thinking about:

- our differentiating capabilities;
- our customer relationships;
- our channel power;
- our company reputation; and
- our brands.

Differentiating capabilities were discussed earlier (see pp. 460–4) as our cutting edge in the market place that grows out of our core corporate competencies and our strategic positioning choices. The test for whether something is a differentiating capability is simple – does it use our resources to give us an advantage over the competitor in the customer's eyes. Examples of what this can mean in practice include:

- Singapore Airlines – while performing a great many commercial air transportation functions well, it is widely acknowledged as the industry leader in *customer service delivery.*
- Nycomed Amersham – a specialized producer of radioactive and related products for medical diagnosis and treatment, it is renowned for its R&D and new product development, but has a *logistics system* that can process orders for radioactive products instantly and deliver them safely and quickly to locations anywhere in the world – with products that are decaying from the moment of production, where the documentation needed to take such materials across national boundaries is fiendish, and where the doctor needs the product tomorrow at the latest, then this company's expensive expertise in logistics gives a unique competitive advantage from the customer's point of view.

- Intuit's 'Quicken' personal finance software dominates the market because this company's culture and organizational processes are totally connected to making the product so *customer friendly* that anyone can use it (see p. 348 for more information about how they do it, and put to shame so many other software producers).

Customer relationships provide a marketing asset in the sense that loyalty and trust give us the ability to defend market scene and open up new markets. We will look at some examples of the advantage of superior customer relationship management in the next chapter (pp. 494–9).

Channel power concerns our dominance or weakness in the distribution channel – our market share in key outlets and share of shelf space in supermarkets for consumer packaged products. If this does not sound important, consider the following case.

Mars launched the Mars Ice-Cream bar (in fact, an obscenely wonderful product) as a major new market entry. The product created a new quality threshold – it turned a child's treat into an adult indulgence. The strategy of turning chocolate bars into ice-creams has been imitated by countless competitors. However, Mars lost money on this product. The reason – Unilever-owned Walls, the market leader, *owned* the distribution channel that mattered: it had a stranglehold on impulse buying outlets like local newsagents. Walls literally owns the freezers in these outlets and does not allow other manufacturers shelf space. With the best branding and marketing communications in the world, Mars could not compete effectively in this market because it did not have the critical marketing asset in distribution needed to succeed[29].

Market information can be a critical marketing asset in the sense that being able to understand the market or customer better and to respond faster and more effectively to customer demands creates competitive advantage. We discussed learning and the importance of superior 'market sensing' in Chapter 7, but to underline the point about information as a marketing asset – consider the customer databases now being built by companies like Tesco and Sainsbury through their loyalty card schemes or through the direct marketing by Virgin Direct in financial services (and it is better quality information too – you may describe yourself as named Santa Claus, aged 102 and of an hermaphrodite inclination, in a yet another nosy and intrusive questionnaire, but not to the people you buy your pension from!). Or, consider the scenario below and ask where the competitive advantage comes from:

'Check into any Ritz-Carlton hotel anywhere in the world and you will be greeted not only by the doorman, but also by a number of small, pleasant surprises. The hotel does not need to ask the name of your employer, your home address, whether you want a non-smoking room, or if your preference is for a non-allergenic pillow. All this information was obtained during your previous visit to the Ritz-Carlton ... you sense that the hotel staff is somehow able to anticipate and respond to your every need, providing you with a feeling of satisfaction that comes from being among people who care about you as an individual. "Why would I ever stay anywhere else?" you wonder.'[30]

Company reputation has always been recognized as a marketing asset (or liability). As buyers become more sophisticated and judgemental, this is becoming an even more significant factor – the company's reputation may impact very directly on brand value for customers. For example, British Gas' entry into the financial services market, with its Goldfish card, represented the use of corporate reputation and identity to open a new market opportunity.

The impact of company reputation on brand value is far more important than the endless (and boring) debate about corporate logo's and headed notepaper. (This said, it is true that companies like BP, Shell, Coca-Cola, Apple, Orange and Nike *do* have clear, concise, constantly recognizable identities that reflect core brand values, while the same cannot be said for companies like British Aerospace, Grand Metropolitan, the City institutions and most pharmaceutical companies[31]).

'The impact of company reputation on brand value is far more important than the endless (and boring) debate about corporate logo's and headed notepaper'

However, what started off with concern about a company's reputation for service, value and quality has now become involved with what customers think about our ethics and environmental responsibility (see back to Chapter 3 for a view on just how far this has gone, pp. 100–112).

For example, an Ogilvy & Mather survey[32] contrasts the view of consumers of some companies as 'efficient bastards' compared to the 'Mr Cleans' at the other end of the scale. The bottom end of the ethical chain in consumers' eyes was represented by companies like Camelot (the National Lottery company), The Sun, Yorkshire Water, William Hill, Ladbrokes and Sky TV.

Add to this suggestions that customers may be reluctant to deal with companies they perceive as unethical and we may have a problem – one recent survey suggested 55 per cent of

'Being seen as a "good corporate citizen" may be a substantial asset that impacts on competitiveness and opens up new opportunities'

consumers would not deal with a company if they disliked its ethics. Being seen as a 'good corporate citizen' may be a substantial asset that impacts on competitiveness and opens up new opportunities[33]. The growing evidence is that these issues matter far more to customers than executives think. There is the prospect of nasty surprises here for the unwary[34].

Perhaps the most widely-recognized marketing asset is the *brand*. Let's open this up as a separate issue, for two reasons: branding is critically important in its own right in many markets, but it also provides a model for the other intangible marketing assets in our portfolio.

Brands and branding

In Chapter 3, I went to some lengths to suggest that we are now in an era of value-based strategy, where relying on a brand (or a customer relationship) strategy to survive is looking increasingly dubious. We said that while 'blind branding' will no longer succeed, brands may be important contributors to value – the goal of 'value branding'. So, at this stage, we need to look at brands as resources – resources which may play a significant role in building and sustaining customer value – which may be exploited in a number of different ways.

Marketing people never stop going on about brands – the company as the brand (e.g. Tesco), the product as the brand (e.g. the Mars bar), the person as the brand (e.g. Richard Branson), the customer as the brand (yes, we'll come back to that one). This is an important issue to sort out in building our market strategy. Let us look at the following questions: different types of branding that occur; why branding remains important to market strategy in an era of value-based strategy; the issue of brand extension strategies and whether they work; and the future of the brand as a central part of market strategy.

'if you want to know what branding is, never ask someone from an advertising agency, unless you like lectures on the philosophy of meaning and have plenty of time'

Types of branding and the big brands

Perhaps the first point is – if you want to know what branding is, *never* ask someone from an advertising agency, unless you like lectures on the philosophy of meaning and have plenty of time. The simplest explanation of a brand was Stephen King's view that: 'A product is something that is made in a factory. A brand is something that is bought by a customer.' In other words, the brand is the 'core identity' we are selling – advertising people like to talk about the 'brand personality' and to give brands human identities – Martini and Coke as 'extrovert' brands that want you to join in, but Timotei shampoo as an 'introvert' brand saying shyly 'you can come to me if you want'[35]. Much talk is of the 'soul' of the brand. (Or as Dilbert would say – 'isn't it amazing we actually get paid for doing this!' Now look, I have been very serious and well behaved so far this chapter, but there are limits!)

Brand strategy is frequently associated with 'creativity' and advertising-based positioning, and not surprisingly comes largely out of consultancies and advertising agencies. For example, Anthony Freeling of McKinseys identifies seven models for creative brand strategy:

- *Classic FMCG* – the fast-moving consumer goods route based on large advertising spend, and practised by companies like Procter & Gamble, Mars, Kraft and Unilever.
- *The Enticer* – frequent changes to product, price and promotion are made to generate constant excitement for the consumer, as used by major retailers and consumer electronics companies.
- *The Individualist* – building sales one at a time, through close personal dialogue with individual consumers, as attempted widely in the financial services market.
- *Transparent Marketers* – whose unique selling point is their honesty about how the market works, for example Daewoo in the car market.
- *Monogamists* – who try to build lifetime relationships with special customers, such as British Airways customer loyalty approach.
- *Benefit Unbundlers* – who over-deliver on what matters most to their customers, but strip out the rest, making consumers a 'partner in value delivery', as with IKEA in furniture, where the customer has to pack, transport and assemble the furniture.
- *The Helpful Brand* – which endears itself to customers by delivering quality and minimizing the time and hassle of shopping; for example, Lexus has bundled up manufacturing with service and repair, and claims to be 'an integrated personal transport package' not just a car brand[36].

Yes, well . . . if nothing else this does firmly underline the link between brand and value proposition (and let's be charitable, even McKinsey consultants have to make a living).

More interesting is the concept that the customer *becomes* the brand – if I sit here typing onto a Virgin computer disk, while the computer's CD-ROM plays the Spice Girls on the Virgin CD purchased from a Virgin Megastore, wearing my Virgin jeans, smelling of my Virgin deodorant, occasionally sipping my Virgin vodka mixed with Virgin cola, while fantasizing about my forthcoming Virgin flight to the US, secure in the knowledge that Virgin Direct is safeguarding my insurance needs and pension requirements, then who or what is the brand? Virgin or Richard Branson? Or me? Certainly more of our thinking should be directed to share of *customer* rather than share of market achieved by a brand.

'more of our thinking should be directed to share of customer rather than share of market achieved by a brand'

However, we should not forget that there may be major difficulties in establishing new brands in existing markets. If you look at the top 50 grocery brands in the UK, very few are new:

4   launched when Queen Victoria was on the throne
16   launched between 1900 and 1950
21   launched between 1950 and 1975 (including the impact of the launch of commercial television in the UK)
9   launched since 1975

This means more than 80 per cent of Britain's top grocery brands are more than 20 years old. A somewhat less than dynamic rate of change and innovation.

Why branding is strategy

'So why do we need to think about branding in developing a market strategy? Because brands add value in the consumer's eyes'

So why do we need to think about branding in developing a market strategy? Because *brands add value* in the consumer's eyes. The functions of branding are to: reduce the customer's search costs (make it easier to find things we want); reduce perceived risk (we have an assurance of familiarity and quality), as well as 'reduce the social and psychological risks' (we get psychological rewards from buying brands that symbolize things we like, so we don't risk owning the 'wrong' product)[37]. Consider how else we could explain the following cases:

● *Coke versus Pepsi* – Panels of consumers are asked to taste samples of Coke and Pepsi: half in *blind tests* (they do not know the brand identities) and half in *open tests* (they can see the containers, the packaging, the logo's, so know which brand is which). In one blind test, 51 per cent preferred Pepsi and 44 per cent preferred Coke. In the corresponding open test, 65 per cent preferred Coke and only 23 per cent preferred Pepsi. There are few more literal illustrations of the power of the brand in adding to value in the customer's eyes[38].

- *Toyota versus General Motors* – In Fremont, California, a joint venture factory produces two virtually identical cars, but one is branded as the Toyota Corolla and the other as the GM Geo Prism. Both cars cost $10 300 to manufacture. In the US car marketplace, the Toyota Corolla sells at a 10 per cent higher price than the GM Geo Prism, holds its value better (so after five years the Toyota trades in for 18 per cent more than the GM), and its market share is twice that of the Geo Prism. It is estimated that Toyota made $128 million more profit than GM from the joint venture. The Toyota brand simply adds more customer value to the product[39].
- *The Savoy Hotel* – In 1997, a letter arrived in the UK from the Czech Republic addressed simply: 'The Manager, the Greatest Hotel in London'. The Royal Mail wrote on the front: 'Try Savoy Hotel, WC2'. That envelope is now the basis for Savoy Group advertising in the US!
- *Heinz Baked Beans* – An old brand, something of a cliché, Heinz baked beans survived a grocery price war in 1996, when some of the supermarkets' own-label beans were priced as low as 3p a can. The power of this brand is such that not only did Heinz customers stay loyal while paying prices nine times higher than the own-labels, the company was actually able to *increase* its price in the same period. In this whole price war, Heinz saw sales revenue dip only by 4 per cent.

Quite simply, brands can *transform markets*, and change competitive structures, because they change how customers look at products, services and suppliers. Consider the following illustrations:

> *'brands can transform markets, and change competitive structures, because they change how customers look at products, services and suppliers'*

- *Financial services* – The financial services sector in Britain – banks, insurance companies, etc. – was characterized for years by very weak branding. The words Provident, Perpetual or Scottish may imply thriftiness, but no distinct brand personality or positioning. Virgin Direct and The Sainsbury Bank (and some others) have been able to take market share in this sector quickly and cheaply by exploiting their brand strength, and the existing players are largely powerless to prevent this. Branding can be a major barrier to entry by new competitors – or not, as the case may be.
- *Cola wars* – In 1996, Pepsi changed its package colour and design from red to blue at the cost of some $500 million, to

deliver more impact for the brand and to differentiate more effectively from its stronger rival, Coke. Coke fought back with a $500 million advertising spend. The products are heavily reliant on image-based advertising – Coke standing for 'America and friendship' and Pepsi as 'California and youth'. Competition between the two companies is fierce and unrelenting. They will do anything to gain or defend market share. Anything that is, except one thing – they will *never* get into a price-cutting war with each other. They tried this in the 1930s and the early 1990s and did not like it. This makes both players vulnerable to new entrants who *will* compete on price. In the UK, this attack has been by Virgin Cola and Sainsbury Cola, both supplied by the Cott company in Canada. Commitment to branding may actually restrict the freedom of brand leaders to respond to new competitors[40].

However, it is also true that in building a market strategy brand identity may also be the biggest *liability* you have to overcome in a market:

● *Skoda cars* – the Czech Republic's main contribution to the motor industry is Skoda cars. For several years, Skodas have been the butt of many jokes:

Q: Why do Skodas have heated rear windows?
A: To keep your hands warm when you are pushing them.

Q: How do you double the value of a Skoda?
A: Fill the tank with petrol.

Q: What do you call a Skoda with a sun roof?
A: A skip.

Q: What do you call a Skoda with twin exhausts?
A: A wheelbarrow.

Q: What do you call a Skoda driver with more than one brain cell?
A: Pregnant

These jokes are based on a widespread belief that Skoda cars are low quality. At one time the cars were very low quality. This is no longer true – they are fine cars which are extremely cheap, but robust, basic vehicles, and they now win prizes. In fact, Skoda buyers are extremely loyal to the brand – it is estimated 72 per cent of first-time Skoda buyers return for a second Skoda purchase. In 1996, Skoda was the highest-ranking European car in the J. D. Powers British customer satisfaction survey and the company is actually now part of the Volkswagen group. Nonetheless, in 1995 when Skoda was preparing to launch a new model in the UK, they did a 'blind and seen' test. With the badges removed, and with no way to identify the car as a Skoda, consumers were impressed with the design of the new vehicle, but with the badge and identity revealed perceptions of the design were markedly less favourable, and the estimated value by potential customers (i.e. price they would be willing to pay) was several hundred pounds lower. To break out of their current niche, Skoda has to overcome *negative* brand equity – where the branding reduces the market value of the product. It looks as though they are doing this incidentally – there is a six-week waiting list for new Skodas across most of Europe.

Even so, in recent years, brands have become a major point of *strategic focus* in companies, and the concept of the brand has been widely applied:

'brands have become a major point of strategic focus in companies, and the concept of the brand has been widely applied'

- In many traditional sectors, like financial services, growing emphasis is on the brand concept instead of individual products and companies, as a way of building greater customer focus.
- The 1996 purchase of the remaining shares in 'The Hard Rock Café' was to unify the Hard Rock brand under Rank ownership, as part of corporate development by Rank as a themed catering and leisure company.
- One dynamic business in the UK is the 'Toni & Guy' franchised hairdressing salons. Owned by the Mascalo brothers, the 'Toni & Guy' brand stands for trendy, youthful hairstyles. The brand range is highly fashionable – the image in the 'Toni & Guy' advertising begs the trendy young person to ask the stylist 'Make me look like that'. From franchising the brand name 'Toni & Guy', the Mascalo brothers turnover around £12m a year, with another £8m from Toni haircare products, and they are taking the brand international.
- 'Brand culling' – brands have become recognized as tradable assets with a market value, and removing brands from the portfolio is now a major strategic issue in companies watched closely by the City. In this sense, brands may be the basis for shaping strategy and reinventing companies. For example, Unilever's 'path to growth strategy' is based on focusing on a few strong brands, such as Dove soap and Magnum ice-creams, in what they call the 'health, hygiene and indulgence sectors', and disposing of many others[41]. Similarly, the drinks group, Diageo, has pursued a successful strategy of focusing on beverage brands – such as Johnnie Walker and Smirnoff – and

Table 9.2   Billion dollar brands*

Rank in 2000	Brand	Country	Brand value 2000 ($Billion)	Brand value 1999 ($Billion)	Change (%)
1	Coca-Cola	US	72.5	83.8	−13
2	Microsoft	US	70.2	56.7	24
3	IBM	US	53.2	43.8	21
4	Intel	US	39.0	30.0	30
5	Nokia	Finland	38.5	20.7	86
6	General Electric	US	38.1	33.5	14
7	Ford	US	36.4	33.2	10
8	Disney	US	33.6	32.8	4
9	McDonalds	US	27.9	26.2	6
10	AT&T	US	25.5	24.2	6
11	Marlboro	US	22.1	21.0	5
12	Mercedes	Germany	21.1	17.8	19

* Source: *Financial Times*, 17 July 2000

reducing its commitment to other activities like the Pillsbury food business and Burger King[42].

● Brands have a balance sheet and income value – Table 9.2 shows the Interbrand/Citibank list of the top twelve global brands and brands values: the 'billion dollar brands'.

● 'Brand extension' – using brand names to enter new product markets and new geographical markets had become a critical issue in many companies. This deserves more detailed consideration below.

It does seem, however, that we can make a powerful case for not neglecting the importance of brands (and other intangible marketing assets) in building market strategy, and the value proposition in particular.

Brand extension strategies

'As executives increasingly talk about "leveraging brand equity", we need to talk more about being realistic about brand extension possibilities'

The value of brands, the difficulty and cost of establishing new brands, and the large ongoing investment in maintaining a brand – all push in the direction of extending or 'stretching' brands into new markets. As executives increasingly talk about 'leveraging brand equity', we need to talk more about being realistic about brand extension possibilities.

Brand extension can be effective but it carries *risks*. Global brands like Toyota, Microsoft and the like have little trouble crossing national and cultural barriers. However, the Interbrand agency's 'black museum' of failed brand moves includes:

- products that have failed to transfer to the UK – a Swiss perfume called 'Kevin', 'Cunto' coffee from Spain, 'Craps' chocolate from France, 'Skum' marshmallows and 'Bums' biscuits from Scandinavia, and the 'Homo Sausage' salami stick from Japan;
- a large Japanese travel firm was surprised at the enquiries it got when it started operating in English-speaking markets, and eventually decided to change the name from the Kinki Nippon Tourist Company;
- the launch of the Ford Pinto in Brazil was not helped by the car's name translating into Portuguese as 'tiny male genitals';
- Rolls-Royce's 'Silver Mist' had to be renamed for Germany, where the original branding means horse manure[43].

However, moving a brand identity can be highly effective – Cadbury brands a cream liqueur, Del Monte brands cook-in sauces and Sainsbury runs a bank. On the other hand, Kellogg, the 'king of cereals', tried to become the 'king of breakfast' with orange juice and failed. Cadbury's brand was extended onto salted snacks, tea bags and instant mashed potato with poor results – the Cadbury name now only appears on chocolate-related products[44].

In the fashion world, the exclusive high couture designer brands have been extended into the middle of the market. Exclusive houses like Ralph Lauren, Calvin Klein and even Tommy Hilfiger take 'diffusion ranges' into the middle of the fashion market with great international success[45]. Similarly, French Connection is taking its brand – and its excellent FCUK logo – from fashion clothes into homewares, like towels and bedlinen, as well as onto eye-glasses, underwear and watches[46].

However, the key issue facing companies is 'brand stretchability' – can you extend the brand and where can you extend it?

'the key issue facing companies is "brand stretchability" – can you extend the brand and where can you extend it?'

Jeremy Bullmore, a director of WPP, has developed a game for advertising and marketing executives he calls 'Brandicide' – the challenge to players is simply to choose a well-known brand and think of extending its name into a new area that would kill the brand stone dead. Bullmore's best effort is: After Eight Bubblegum. Cruder and less subtle opponents might suggest: Persil chocolate,

Cadbury washing-up liquid, a Listerine whisky, Harpic baby food, Skoda condoms, and so on[47]. Interestingly, the Oxo brand name really was taken from the meat-cube onto chocolate and coffee in the 1930s, but the innovations did not last long (which casts some doubts on the new brainwave of putting the Oxo name on hardware)[48].

Peter Wallis, founder of the consultancy SRU, suggests we need to consider both the degree of stretch we are proposing for a brand, and whether the brand personality is suited to that stretch. Wallis distinguishes *degree of brand stretch* as:

- *Licensing* – a strong brand like Harley-Davidson allows the name to be used on cosmetics, and Manchester United's branding goes on clothes and publications.
- *Gentle stretch* – the new branding is in the same sector, for example confectionery brands like Mars badging ice-creams, the Persil brand extending to washing-up liquid from the detergent brand.
- *Unknown territory* – we rely on the relationship with the customer to transfer into a radically new product market – Virgin from music to airlines, Sainsbury's from groceries to financial services, retail banks into stationery and office supplies.

Wallis's test for stretchability is the trust and credibility in the brand – the *brand personality*, which we fail to understand at our peril. Brian Boylan of Wolff Olins, the corporate identity consultants, summarizes the brand stretching dilemma: 'Brands are about promise and delivery. Don't stretch if you can't deliver the promise'[49].

'The big risk is that a failed brand extension will undermine the customer's relationship with the whole brand, not just the extension'

This is an important perspective and it should be remembered before we make big assumptions that our brand's value proposition will transfer and extend to a new product or a new market. The big risk is that a failed brand extension will undermine the customer's relationship with the whole brand, not just the extension.

The future of the brand?

Notwithstanding all this – the traditional brand, and traditional brand management, is under attack from several quarters: own-labels – the undermining of manufacturer brands by retailer brands; the vulnerability of brands to copying and counterfeiting; and the impact of category management in retailing.

The impact of *retailer own-labels* is enormous in many consumer markets. In grocery, in the UK around 30 per cent of all grocery sales are own-label – own-labels account for around 80 per cent of milk and wrapped bread, 60 per cent of frozen peas and fruit juices, more than 50 per cent of yoghurts and fizzy drinks. The dilemma facing brand leaders is to decide whether or not to produce the own-label products which will ultimately undermine their main brands. This is complicated by the continuing belief among many customers that retailer own-labels are actually produced by the brand leaders anyway – this consumer perception has plagued Kellogg over the years in the highly competitive breakfast cereals market.

The retailer brands are not just cheaper, they may be more innovative too – in February 2001, the Co-op's Brio Actipods (capsules of liquid detergents) made it to market ahead of the Unilever and Procter & Gamble brands, to lead the way in the hottest new product area in the detergents field, rather than following. Commentators believe this challenge to leadership with new products is likely to happen increasingly[50].

More frightening than own-labels in food, research by brand specialist CLK suggests that many consumers see no problems with retailer branded products in areas as diverse as: white goods like washing machines and refrigerators; mobile phones; houses through a supermarket estate agency; cars and car servicing; medical services; and package holidays[51]. The own-label phenomenon has a long way to go yet.

'The own-label phenomenon has a long way to go yet'

Yet more aggressive competition which has emerged in UK branded goods markets has been *brand copying* – primarily by retailer own-labels again. In polite circles this is discussed as 'parody as marketing strategy'. While Asda vehemently denies the accusation, interesting parallels exist between a number of its own-label launches and manufacturers' brand leaders:

Manufacturer brand	**Asda brand**
'I Can't Believe It's Not Butter' from Van Den Bergh Foods – a spread in a flat yellow tub with blue print	'You'd Better Believe It' from Asda – a spread in a flat yellow tub with blue print
'Rice Krispies' from Kellogg – a breakfast cereal in a blue box and with a picture of milk being poured on cereal	'Rice Snaps' from Asda – a breakfast cereal in a blue box and with a picture of milk being poured on cereal
'Penguin' – chocolate biscuits for United Biscuits in a flat orange and blue pack	'Puffin' – chocolate biscuits from Asda in a flat orange pack with blue printing

Various brand owners are suing Asda (in some cases very reluctantly because Asda is a major customer for them as well as a competitor) – Asda says it has *not* copied anyone's brand and will fight. In the meantime, own-labels continue to eat into the sales of brand leaders because they are substantially cheaper.

In a totally different category is straightforward, criminal *brand counterfeiting* – i.e. the illegal branding of foods as brands which they are not. Counterfeiting has become a substantial problem for brand leaders like Adidas sportswear, Nike and Reebok sports shoes, and fashion clothes labels as diverse as Levi Strauss, Polo from Ralph Lauren, Armani and Paul Smith. However, the same issue exists for BP with motor oils and for computer software producers. It is illegal, but it is difficult to trace. The real problem is not just the lost sales, but that the brand leader gets the blame for the low-quality product, not the counterfeiter. It is a further serious indication of the vulnerability of a market position that relies on branding.

'The real problem is not just the lost sales, but that the brand leader gets the blame for the low-quality product, not the counterfeiter'

The latest variant of this is the use of brand names by 'cybercriminals' to lure the unwary to their own sites, by using a well-known brand name. For example, in 1999, Intel found that one of its brand names was linked to a pornography site – customers looking for the Intel brand through a search engine were routed to the porn instead[52] (and with the record of the porn visit stored on their computers, which is less than amusing if it is a computer at work). Similarly, at Christmas 2000, children searching for toy brand names like 'My Little Pony' or 'Muppets' were also likely to arrive at pornography sites[53]. This is generally seen as unhelpful to maintaining the integrity of a brand.

A major change overtaking retailing is *category management*. The retailer increasingly defines a category of goods as the focus for merchandising, instead of manufacturers' brands – lunch-time snacks, Friday evening take-homes[54], and so on. The retailer's interest is then on what each manufacturer can offer to improve the performance of the category in the store. This question replaces the issue of brand leadership – the issue is position in the category. The implications are enormous – at Elida Gibbs, for example, brand management has disappeared as new category managers work with the salesforce and each retail customer.

Related to this retail focus are the *category killers* – emerging large-scale discount retailers in specialized product areas. They are characterized by limited product ranges but very low prices – examples include IKEA in furniture, Toys 'R' Us, and Costco in grocery. The transfer of customer priorities to low price further undermines the traditional brand-based strategies of companies in these markets[55].

A variation on category killing with similar results is where a retailer chooses to sell a branded product in circumstances that the brand manufacturer does not want. For example, when the supermarket firm Tesco began to sell Levi 501 blue jeans in 1997 – a heavily branded product supported by its famous image-building advertising – at a price discounted by nearly 50 per cent. Tesco went into the national press with full-page advertisements and the copy line:

> 'SAFE SEATS.
>
> £30.
>
> (LEVI 501'S AT ROCK BOTTOM PRICES)'

Levi's were not terribly amused – their view was that the integrity of their brand is compromised if your Mum can buy them for £30 with the groceries. They tried to prevent Tesco from obtaining supplies. Tesco had played this game before – they sourced the product from Mexico to avoid the Levi embargo. By 2001, Levi's case was still in the European Court – Tesco had four years' sales of the product under its belt, and the preliminary court opinion upheld the retailer's right to continue importing branded goods from outside Europe to sell at 'bargain' prices. The manufacturer's risk is clear – you spend a fortune creating and maintaining a brand image, which is then undermined by a retailer, and there is little you can do to prevent it happening, and when you try you end up the bad guy and the retailer is the 'people's champion'[56].

'The manufacturer's risk is clear – you spend a fortune creating and maintaining a brand image, which is then undermined by a retailer, and there is little you can do to prevent it happening, and when you try you end up the bad guy and the retailer is the "people's champion"'

Branding, value proposition and market strategy

Along with other intangible marketing assets, brands remain a central issue in developing what we will offer the customer as our value proposition. Brands and other marketing assets are resources. They are a means to an end. What we are starting to realize is that the 'end' in question is customer value. This is why, for example, Coca-Cola now talks about 'value marketing' not 'brand marketing', and the chief marketing officer is clear: 'You have to really understand how your brand creates value'[57] (or otherwise). Branding issues are also a main input to our evaluation of market attractiveness and market position (see pp. 431–5). However, there are some major questions to be raised about the implications of relying on brands for sustainable competitive advantage, and the vulnerability of a market position based on branding to competitive attack.

Do we have a value proposition?

If we have got a good idea about our target markets and segments, and have linked our vision and mission to our strategic positioning and thought through our differentiating capabilities, particularly in terms of our marketing assets and brands – the question is: do we have a value proposition for our customer?

Do not just say 'yes' and move on! Try writing it down. If we do not know what we have to offer each of our customers that makes us more attractive than the next to that customer, that we know we can deliver to that customer, then we do not have a market strategy.

For example, the written value proposition for a leading financial services company called their Customer Proposition reads as follows, and describes the position they aim to take in the customer's mind:

- I am more than just a customer with . . .
- All my personal financial needs are met by . . .
- I get top value prices from . . .
- My money is safe with . . .
- I can understand . . .
- I would always recommend . . .
- I find it easy to deal with . . .
- I get the best possible service from . . .
- I can trust . . . to look after my interests
- . . . is where I want to work
- I know that . . . supports people with more than money.

Similarly, Daewoo took fast market share at its launch in the UK through an explicit value proposition that formed the core of its consumer advertising:

- Direct – treating customers differently, with no intermediaries.

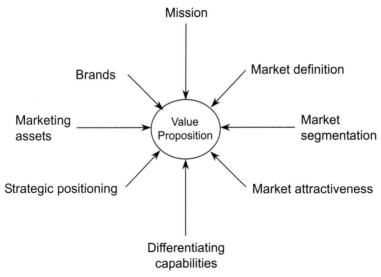

Figure 9.8 Building the value proposition

- Hassle-free – no sales pressure or haggling about prices.
- Peace of mind – features that are traditionally 'extras' are bundled in with every car.
- Courtesy – openly respecting customer needs and preferences throughout the purchase and use process.

There is no fixed format for what a value proposition should look like – but a summary of the factors that should be taken into account is given in Figure 9.8. You can use this framework to check that you have considered all the issues we have raised and how they are linked, and see how each contributes to building a statement of the value for our customers, that will establish a strong position for us in this market.

It must be time for some more awkward questions with which to annoy your colleagues:

REALITY CHECK

THE AWKWARD QUESTIONS ABOUT OUR VALUE PROPOSITION

Have we leveraged our market sensing capabilities so that we truly understand what drives value in the markets we have chosen, and the way in which value is changing for different customer groups? Do we regularly test these ideas with customers to see if we are right, or things are changing?

> Have we made the right market and segment target choices so that we are competing where we have superior value to offer these customers, compared to competitors or substitutes?
>
> Do we have a clear idea about what we want to stand for in the customer's eyes – if we use mission statements, do we do this systematically and thoroughly to make them work for us? If not, why not?
>
> Do we have a clear view of our differentiating capabilities – drawing on corporate competencies to establish what will give us sustainable competitive advantage that clearly differentiates us from the rest as offering superior value?
>
> Have we studied our entire base of marketing assets to see what they contribute to building a strong market position – do we have advantages in company reputation, channel control, market information, and so on?
>
> Have we looked at our branding to see if it provides a sustainable platform for the value proposition that is developing?
>
> Can we write down our value proposition to each major customer group in our market – if we showed this statement to those customer groups would they believe in it, and would it make us stand out from the competition?

These are rich and complex issues, but they are the ones which are essential to building an effective and strong market strategy. However, we have not finished yet; the last strand that links to our market choices and our value proposition is the key relationships that will drive the strategy. We turn attention to this in the next chapter.

Notes and references

1. David W. Cravens, Gordon Greenley, Nigel F. Piercy and Stanley F. Slater (1997), 'Integrating Contemporary Strategic Management Perspectives', *Long Range Planning*, **30** (4), 493–506.
2. Diane Summers (1995), 'Letters Chiefs Aim to Deliver Quality', *Financial Times*, 6 March.
3. Robert Heller (1995), 'The Art of Delighting Customers', *Financial Mail on Sunday*, 6 August.
4. Michael Treacy and Fred Wiersema (1995), *The Discipline of Market Leaders*, New York: Harper Collins.

5. Adrian Slywotsky (1996), *Value Migration*, Boston, MA: Harvard Business School Press.

6. David Hewson (1995), 'Jean Genius: One to One Marketing', *Sunday Times*, 11 June.

7. 'Levi's Woos Youth With Custom-Made Jeans', *Marketing Week*, 17 September 1998.

8. This section draws heavily on Nigel F. Piercy and Neil A. Morgan (1994), 'Mission Analysis: An Operational Approach', *Journal of General Management*, **19** (3), 1–19.

9. Kate Rankine (1998), 'Littlewoods, Age 75, Gets a Lifestyle', *Daily Telegraph*, 18 June.

10. Orit Gadiesh and James L. Gilbert (2001), 'Transforming Corner-Office Strategy Into Frontline Action', *Harvard Business Review*, May, 73–79.

11. Lesley Thomas (1995), 'Millions Spent on Firing Firms With Missionary Zeal', *Sunday Times*, 25 March.

12. Lucy Kellaway (2000), 'Statements That Sum Up Mission Impossible', *Financial Times*, 20 March.

13. Scott Adams (1996), *The Dilbert Principle*, London: Boxtree Press.

14. Theodore Levitt (1960), 'Marketing Myopia', *Harvard Business Review*, July/August, 45–56.

15. I have referred to this case in many speeches and talks over the last couple of years. I used to scoff at the 'dream fulfilment' mission. I stopped after being attacked by a group of very affluent senior managers, who came up to me after my speech and pointed out that the one thing they *loved* in life was their house and garden – and they would willingly drive hundreds of miles to get to a gardening centre which understood their dreams, if only I could tell them where it was! This just goes to show none of us should forget about finding out what really matters to the customer, before jumping to 'obvious' conclusions!

16. John Kay (1995), 'Learning to Define the Core Business', *Financial Times*, 1 December.

17. Michael E. Porter (1985), *Competitive Advantage: Creating and Sustaining Superior Performance*, New York: Free Press.

18. Michael E. Porter (1996), 'What is Strategy?', *Harvard Business Review*, November/December, 61–78.

19. Michael E. Porter (1996), op. cit.

20. C. K. Prahalad and Gary Hamel (1990), 'The Core Competence of the Corporation', *Harvard Business Review*, May/June, 79–91.

21. John Lattice (1996), 'Blue's Legend', *Sunday Business*, 21 April.

22. Tom Peters (1986), *Passion for Excellence*, New York: Harper & Row.

23. Theodore Levitt (1980), 'Marketing Success Through Differentiation – Of Anything', *Harvard Business Review*, January/February, 83–91.

24. Celia Brayfield (1997), 'Bookshops Will Never Be The Same Again', *Daily Telegraph*, 28 March.

25. Richard Tomkins (2001), 'De Beers Looks to Claim Glittering Prize', *Financial Times*, 10 January. 'Troubled De Beers May Brand Diamonds', *Sunday Times*, 28 December 1997.

26. Richard Tomkins (2001), 'Precious Metal With a Badly Tarnished Image', *Financial Times*, 23 March. Richard Tomkins (2001), 'Gold to Play on Warm Image as The "New Cool"', *Financial Times*, 11 May.

27. Notwithstanding any sarcasm I may have unwittingly extended towards this campaign, I really would be happy to receive product samples for evaluation.
28. Michael Treacy and Fred Wiersema (1996), *The Discipline of Market Leaders*, New York: Harper Collins.
29. Alan Mitchell (1995), 'Changing Channels', *Marketing Business*, February, 10–13.
30. Christopher W. Hart (1996), 'Made to Order', *Marketing Management*, Summer, 11–23.
31. Helen Jones (1997), 'Identity Crisis', *Marketing Business*, January, 38–41.
32. Emily Bell (1996), 'Bastards are Losing Out to Mr Clean', *Observer*, 30 June.
33. Ardyn Bernoth (1996), 'Companies Show They Care', *Sunday Times*, 8 December.
34. Meg Carter (1996), 'Consumers Rally to Good Causes', *Independent on Sunday*, 17 November.
35. Oliver Bennett (1996), 'I'm A Tall Blonde Burger', *Independent on Sunday*, 17 November.
36. 'Get Ready for a Brand New Battle', *Marketing Week*, 23 September 1994.
37. Pierre Berthon, James M. Hulbert and Leyland F. Pitt (1997), *Brand Managers, and the Management of Brands*, Boston, MA: Marketing Science Institute, Report No. 97–122.
38. Leslie de Chernatony and Malcolm McDonald (1992), *Creating Brands*, Oxford: Butterworth-Heinemann.
39. *The Economist*, 6 January 1996.
40. Emily Bell (1996), 'Any Colour as Long as it's Blue', *Observer*, 31 March.
41. John Thornhill (2000), 'A Bad Time to be in Consumer Goods', *Financial Times*, 28 September.
42. Rosie Murray-West (2000), 'Brand Focus "Pays Off" for Diageo', *Daily Telegraph*, 8 September.
43. Oliver Bennett (1996), 'I'm a Tall Blonde Burger', *Independent on Sunday*, 17 November.
44. Rufus Olins (1996), 'Elastic Brands', *Sunday Times*, 3 November.
45. Ardyn Bernoth (1996), 'Designers Put London in Fashion', *Sunday Times*, 3 November.
46. Susanna Voyle (2000), 'French Connection Moves Into Bedrooms', *Financial Times*, 20 September.
47. Rufus Olins (1996), 'Elastic Brands', *Sunday Times*, 3 November.
48. Rose Murray-West (2000), 'Unilever Buries the Hatchet After Row Over Oxo Knives', *Daily Telegraph*, 8 August.
49. Quoted in John Willman (1999), 'They'd Like the World to Buy a Shirt', *Financial Times*, 23/24 January.
50. Richard Tomkins (2001), 'Co-op's Capsule Launches Another Soap War', *Financial Times*, 21 February.
51. 'More From the Four', *Marketing Business*, February 1999, 6.
52. Louise Kehoe (2000), 'Leading Brands on the Run', *Financial Times*, 11 October.

53. Fiona Harvey (2000), 'Porn Websites Abuse Brand Names of Toys', *Financial Times*, 16 November.

54. Wal-Mart, the huge US discount retailer, found a strong link between the purchase of nappies and multi-packs of beer on Friday evenings. This reflected young men being told by their partners to pick up some nappies on the way home from work, who then figured that this was a good chance (and maybe a good reason) to stock up on beer as well. It makes sense for the retailer to build displays on Friday afternoon of beer and nappies side by side.

55. 'Killing Off the Competition', *Marketing Business*, April 1997, 11–14.

56. Susanna Voyle and Chris Tighe (2001), 'Win or Lose, Tesco's Fight Will Make It People's Champion', *Financial Times*, 6 April.

57. Quoted in Alan Mitchell (1999), 'Evolution', *Marketing Business*, February, 28.

CHAPTER 10

Market strategy:

Key relationships

The issue we have to confront next is: if we are going to deliver our value proposition to our target markets and segments, on the basis of how we understand these markets, then what are the key relationships that will drive this through, and can we rely on and successfully manage those relationships[1]. The first question is – relationships with who and why?

In formulating their widely-acclaimed approach to relationship marketing, with its particular emphasis on customer retention, Martin Christopher, Adrian Payne and their colleagues at the Cranfield School of Management[2] propose their 'six markets' model. They urge us to address: *internal* markets (individuals and groups within the organization); *referral* markets (sources of word-of-mouth recommendation); *influence* markets (those who shape the marketing environment for us); *employee* markets (because of the critical need to recruit and retain effective members of the organization); *supplier* markets (those who provide us with material, products and services); and *customer* markets (those who buy our goods and services).

This is an excellent framework for developing relationship marketing plans, but falls short of what we need at the strategic level. I propose that the areas where relationship building is most critical in an era of value-based strategy are those shown in Figure 10.1. This underlines that one area of critical relationship importance is with *customers*, and another is with the employees

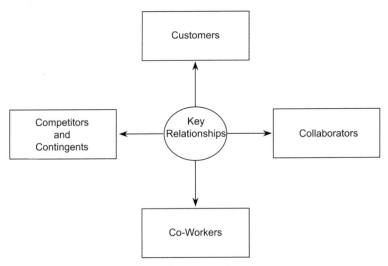

Figure 10.1   The key relationships in marketing strategy

and managers in the company – *co-workers*. However, the difference is that strategically we need to recognize the need to manage relationships with *collaborators* – those with whom we partner in alliances and joint operations, and who are part of our process of going to market; and relationships with *competitors and contingents* – those who, for one reason or another, may try to stop us doing what we want to do in our market strategy.

I am also a bit uncomfortable with Christopher et al. boxing off internal customers as separate from external customers[3]. Clearly, internal customers are important to us because they impact on external customers – unhappy employees and alienated managers are likely to produce unhappy, alienated customers. But in the real world the issue is actually the networks of relationships we start to uncover after five minutes in a real company: employees who are also shareholders and customers; employees who have social and commercial links with our competitors (what else do you expect if we all play the swapping people, headhunting/poaching game); employees who have social and professional links with employees in competitor, supplier and collaborator organizations – e.g. they all go to the same training courses and conferences and exhibitions; employees who have professional links with important influencers and opinion-shapers; competitors' employees who have social and professional connections with our suppliers and collaborators; and so on. If we are serious about analysing the relationships underpinning our strategy,

> '*in the real world the issue is actually the networks of relationships we start to uncover after five minutes in a real company*'

then we need to think about the relationship networks that exist and that can be built. For example, has it occurred to you that, in an e-world, how you talk to your employees can directly impact on your share value:

REALITY CHECK
THE JOY OF E-MAIL

In March 2001, Neal Patterson, CEO and founder of the Cerner Corporation in the health care business based in Kansas City, sent his staff an angry e-mail accusing them of being lazy and unproductive:

> 'We are getting less than 40 hours of work from a large number of our EMPLOYEES. The parking lot is sparsely used at 8 a.m.; likewise at 5 p.m. As managers you either do not know what your EMPLOYEES are doing or you do not CARE. In either case, you have a problem and you will fix it or I will replace you ... NEVER in my career have I allowed a team which worked for me to think they had a 40-hour job. I have allowed YOU to create a culture which is permitting this. NO LONGER.'

He added that 'hell will freeze over' before he increased employee benefits, and that he wanted the car park full by 7.30 a.m. and half full at weekends, before concluding 'You have two weeks. Tick, tock.'

This would have been fine – another CEO working his way to an ulcer – except that a week later his message was copied to a Yahoo financial message board on the Internet. Wall Street analysts and stockbrokers started receiving phone calls from worried share-holders, concerned about what had happened at Cerner to produce such a violent outburst, worried about whether low staff morale would hit performance, and uncomfortable with the CEO's attitude towards his employees.

The share value in the company dropped by 22 per cent. By April it was trading at fully one-third less than before the CEO's e-mail was sent.

Source: Philip Delves Broughton (2001), 'Boss's Angry E-Mail Sends Shares Plunging', *Daily Telegraph*, 6 April.

What we need is an approach that addresses the critical issues, including the following types of relationships:

- with the *customer* – can we keep the promises we have made in the value proposition to our customers?

- with *competitors and contingents* – how vulnerable is our market strategy to competitive attack, how well do we understand our competitors' capabilities and will the strategy survive, and how well do we stand with the market controllers – for example, government regulators, City analysts, shareholders, or key players who exert influence over the customer and the competitor?
- with *collaborators* – does our strategy rely on partnerships with other organizations such as suppliers, distributors, supply chain partners, and so on, and can we manage these relationships effectively?
- with *co-workers*[4] – can and will the employees and managers in this company deliver the quality, the service and the brand values on which the market strategy relies?
- with the *relationship networks* that can support our strategy or provide major barriers.

This is a very neat and tidy model. Do not be surprised if things are somewhat less clear-cut in the real world. It is often difficult to sort out the type of relationships we have with different parties. Ask who is the customer, competitor, collaborator and co-worker in the following cases:

- Company X produces speciality pharmaceutical chemicals for the healthcare industry. They were approached by a customer for a new material to be supplied for clinical diagnostic purposes, which had been designed by the customer's R&D Department. Company X had the production facilities for the new compound, but did not have access to the raw materials needed or the packaging plant required. The customer agreed to supply the raw materials from another source, and arranged for Company X to lease packaging line time at Company Y (Company Y also supplies the customer but is the major competitor of Company X). Company X supplies the new material to the customer in bulk for repackaging and in specialized packaging for laboratory use. The customer packages the bulk material itself. Company X and the customer both sell the bulk material and the packaged material to other healthcare companies, including Company Y. (This is a real situation, but the companies concerned would just as soon not have their names published.) This arrangement has proved profitable for all concerned, it just isn't neat and tidy.
- The Efficient Consumer Response system as originally developed in the US (and adopted in the UK and Europe – see pp. 514–17) involves groups of competing manufacturers and groups of competing retailers sitting down together to

streamline supply chains in terms of logistics, costs and reducing product and promotion proliferation. This process is driven primarily by the retailing organizations providing expertise to their suppliers. Just who are the competitors, who are the customers and who are the collaborators in this scenario?

● There are many cases where companies end up competing with their own distributors. For example, insurance companies sell through Independent Financial Advisors (independent firms and individuals who have direct salesforce operations), and increasingly direct marketing operations. They compete directly (though frequently covertly) with their own distributors.

This does not get us off the hook of evaluating the key relationships that underpin our market strategy. It just means in reality it gets messy. We may have to look at customer, competitor and collaborator relationships when it is the same company we are talking about in each relationship, and this may pose particular problems – if we attack a competitor with a new product which is also a customer for existing products, do we undermine the original business, for example?

'We may have to look at customer, competitor and collaborator relationships when it is the same company we are talking about in each relationship, and this may pose particular problems'

The important point is that if our evaluation here is unfavourable – if our people cannot deliver the values promised to the customer, if our partners will not support our brands, or if our strategy can be wiped out by the competitors or hostile regulators – then we have to think again about our market choices and value proposition, because we have not yet developed a robust market strategy. We will consider each of these areas in turn.

Customer relationships

We looked at the relationship marketing revolution in Chapter 3 (pp. 67–75). Our conclusion was that relationship focus has a great deal to offer – better information about customers, customers who forgive us when we get things wrong, etc. – but that the real test is whether the relationship we have with our customers enhances the value of what we offer them (in their eyes not ours). In fact, a huge amount of what has led up to this point in the strategic pathway is based on the customer relationship. Our starting point was with customer satisfaction and service (Chapter 2), developing superior market sensing capabilities and building customer-focused organizations (Chapter 7), choosing and segmenting markets on the basis of our ability to understand customer relationship requirements (Chapter 8), and building value propositions around different customer groups (Chapter 9).

However, before we go any further, it is time to ask some tough questions:

- Do we know what the relationship with the customer has to be for our market strategy to work?
- Does the customer know and accept this?
- Can we actually deliver that relationship in the customer's terms?

In short, we need to be sure we are not making the mistake of being taken in by 'relationship rhetoric', when we should be focusing hard on relationship reality (see pp. 74–5).

Do not forget that what customers actually see of your 'relationship strategy' is sales promotions and direct communications based on database information – and I personally am delighted to get a personalized letter from the CEO about Heinz Baked Beans, it certainly made my day (not) – and loyalty programmes, or as they have been called 'customer detention' programmes that are intended to tie-in business (or restrict the customer's freedom and choice as some would say). None of this seems particularly related to the philosophy of mutual interdependence that *we* know is what relationship marketing is really about.

Do we know what we want the relationship to be?

If we have got this far and the answer to the question is 'no', then we need to think again! We should be able to write down the relationship with the customer that grows out of our market focus and our value proposition. Try it.

That statement should tell us, if our strategic position and value proposition are going to stand up, then:

'We should be able to write down the relationship with the customer that grows out of our market focus and our value proposition. Try it'

- How close does the relationship have to be – the choices range from essentially a transactional relationship (we are only interested in the one-off sale) through to almost partnership with the customer.

- The *qualities* needed in the relationship – what do we need to have customers believe about us, e.g. our integrity, our service level, our quality, our technology compared to the competition?
- The *life cycle* of the relationship – how long has it got to last for the market strategy to be viable?

Do we have that relationship or can we get it?

This is about getting realistic and challenging any belief that we can take a strong competitive position just by telling customers that we are going to be nice to them (countless millions have been spent over the years on advertising to do just that, and it has not proved very effective). If the relationship positioning we want depends on customer *beliefs* about us – let us find out what they do believe about us by asking them. Many companies are shocked to find that customers have long memories – they remember you and what you did before you got the relationship marketing rhetoric. The critical issue is – are customer beliefs about us supportive to our market strategy or a barrier?

The same applies to *trust*. If our market strategy rests on the assumption that customers trust us, then maybe we should find out if they do. Does our company reputation support our market strategy or create a barrier? Customers do not have to believe you are a wonderful company or trust you with their lives in order for you to do business. People often do business with companies they do not trust. What we have to avoid is building a market strategy that relies on beliefs and trusts which do not exist.

'What we have to avoid is building a market strategy that relies on beliefs and trusts which do not exist'

Can we deliver that relationship?

Getting customers is not the same thing as retaining them, as we saw in Chapter 2. Attracting customers is largely about *making* promises. Retaining customers is much more about *keeping* these promises.

The question at this stage is: when we look at the customer relationship defined by our market strategy, do we have the capabilities to maintain and enhance that relationship? This forces us to look at our internal resources (our people, systems, procedures and structures), but also at the other key relationships we have to manage to maintain the customer relationship.

If we cannot resolve this issue – we need to go back to the value proposition and think again. Making promises to customers that you cannot keep is dangerous. However, there is a lot of technology and structure available to help in keeping the promises – Customer Relationship Management. How seriously major firms are taking the management of customer relationships is well illustrated by the Customer Relationship Management initiative at IBM.

REALITY CHECK

CUSTOMER RELATIONSHIP MANAGEMENT AT IBM

Most of IBM's marketing activities have been embedded in a global Customer Relationship Management (CRM) initiative. The goal is to co-ordinate customer relationships by managing business processes that cut across traditional functional and geographic boundaries to achieve maximum effectiveness. IBM's CRM works through core processes:

- *Market management* – to identify and select core segments.
- *Relationship management* – handles the relationship between IBM and established customers.
- *Opportunity management* – as soon as a sales opportunity is identified, the opportunity manager has the task of finding the right 'opportunity owner', who can offer the right level of expertise and the right level of interaction (e.g. mass customization versus one-of-a-kind), drawing on the next processes.
- *Offering information* – keeping track of every product or solution developed by the company or its business partners, so no-one has to waste tome reinventing the wheel.
- *Skills management* – a worldwide database of IBM people's skills, graded on scales from 1 to 5.
- *Solution, design and delivery* – each offer is tracked to check and result.
- *Customer satisfaction management* – handling customer feedback and complaints.
- *Message management* – co-ordinating all communications with customers.

Fred Schindler, Programme Director of IBM's International Sales Operation, describes the key areas of CRM focus as: improved sales, marketing and services execution worldwide; cross-enterprise integration of global teams and capabilities; better front-office execution and integration; and the disciplined application of customer information to build profitable customer relationships. The most difficult issue proved to be changing culture and behaviour to implement CRM effectively. To back these processes IBM has created several tools; for example, CustomerRoom is a 'virtual meeting place' on the Internet between account teams and customers as a basis for information sharing and collaboration. In January 2000, IBM launched CRM 2000 to accelerate what they describe as their transformation into a leading e-business.

Sources: Alan Mitchell (1997), 'Speeding up the Process', *Marketing Business*, March. Fred Schindler (2000), 'Developing Effective CRM Processes: How IBM Help Their Major Customers To Win', *Proceedings*: 4th International Symposium on Selling and Major Account Management, Southampton, July.

Customer relationship management programmes and systems

Along with e-business, the chances are that Customer Relationship Management (CRM) is going to be one of the hottest things on the agenda in your company in the early 2000s. Whether it stays there will depend on what it delivers after all the excitement about the latest management fad has died down. Certainly, largely fuelled by the fear of being left behind, company expenditure globally on CRM systems is massive – estimated growth path is from $2.8 billion in 1998 to $9 billion in 2002[5]. It is clear the pay-off from CRM also needs to be massive to balance this. The question to ask is whether your market strategy relies on the type of customer relationship that CRM provides. First, however, let's try and clarify a few things about CRM.

'The question to ask is whether your market strategy relies on the type of customer relationship that CRM provides'

What Is CRM?

An excellent question to ask, but somewhat more difficult to answer. One pragmatic view is that the essence of the thing is collecting customer data from all points of contact and storing them in one data pool. In fact, different people use the term to mean different things (a bit like 'marketing', now I think about it). It seems to mean anything from an automated call centre to a company-wide strategy of breaking down barriers between departments and pooling information about customers to enhance customer retention. Malcolm McDonald argues the exact definition depends on who is trying to sell you what, but

CRM is normally taken to be about IT, usually in areas like: data warehouses; customer service systems; call centres; e-commerce; web marketing; operational systems (e.g. order processing, invoicing, etc.); and sales systems (e.g. automated appointment making and contact management) – and then 'the idea is to slam (sorry – integrate, cleanse, unify and present) these systems together, thus enabling the organization to manage its customers flawlessly'. In fact, he says that CRM is about three things: strategy, marketing and IT[6]. Hmmm – so it looks like if you ignore the IT aspects of CRM, we are back to defining the relationship we need with the customer to drive our strategy and finding ways to make that relationship real by integrating what we do around the customer?

So, when does CRM work?

The quickest answer is probably 'when it is used to deliver our value proposition', but that is true without being very helpful. Philip Kotler says that we probably do not need CRM where: customers buy the product only once in a lifetime, the unit value is low, the customer lifetime value is low, customer churn is high throughout the industry, and there is no direct contact between the seller and the ultimate buyer[7]. On the other hand, George Day sees CRM as a 'customer-responsive strategy' that is likely to gain competitive advantage if it:

- delivers superior customer value by personalizing the inter-action between the company and the customer;
- demonstrates trustworthiness;
- tightens connections with customers; and
- achieves the co-ordination of complex capabilities (functions, resources) within the company[8].

So, it seems that if there is a CRM issue it is about whether we can leverage customer retention?

CRM, customer retention and customer selectivity

At the heart of the CRM promise is that we will be able to achieve enhanced customer loyalty (retention) and focus resources on the 'best' customers. The information gained from an integrated CRM strategy has many uses – one is 'firing customers', i.e. reducing service levels or even refusing to do business with 'unprofitable' customers. The argument is that not all

'At the heart of the CRM promise is that we will be able to achieve enhanced customer loyalty (retention) and focus resources on the "best" customers'

customers are valuable; there is an 80:20 relationship for many companies – 80 per cent of the profits come from 20 per cent of the customers. In the banking sector, it is estimated that the top 20 per cent of accounts generate more than 100 per cent of a bank's profits (because the bottom 20 per cent generate losses), and in some segments like credit cards there may be a tenfold difference between the most profitable customers and average accounts[9]. There have already been cases of UK banks closing customer accounts because they were unprofitable[10]. So, part of the attraction of CRM is allowing companies to focus efforts better on the most attractive customers – but only assuming they can define what makes a customer attractive, and how well they can really predict the customer's future behaviour[11].

Dialogue marketing

Another selling point is that CRM systems allow you to get closer to 'one-to-one marketing' by improving the dialogue between the customer and the company. The technology provides a basis for individualized responses to customer queries – the person answering the phone has a full customer record on the screen in front of them – and in developing customized products and services based on information gathered about the customer[12].

The customer information advantage

Underpinning the whole thing is the technology that allows customer information to be collected and retrieved faster and better than previously[13]. That is what allows the better response to customer complaints and requests, the selectivity between customers and the development of customized or individualized offers to customers.

'the technology and the systems alone do not change how a company deals with its customers and more attention is now turning to the changes in structures and processes needed across a company to make CRM happen'

Company-wide change

However, it is also apparent that the technology and the systems alone do not change how a company deals with its customers and more attention is now turning to the changes in structures and processes needed across a company to make CRM happen.

A Chief Relationship Officer?

There are also suggestions around that one of the new roles to be recognized in companies is the Chief

Relationship Officer/Manager, overseeing the integration of company efforts in managing customer relationships.

Is it really that easy?

No, it isn't. There are worrying signs that some companies think CRM is just an extension of customer loyalty programmes, and thus largely tactical[14]. This is likely to lead to a lot of money being spent and little achieved. Others point out that simply building databases and warehouses achieves little unless a company has a strategy and the processes to use the information – the alternative is that CRM becomes no more than the ability to annoy more customers faster than ever before[15]. There is also the worry that if all competitors adopt the same or similar CRM systems and approaches, then they will all look the same to customers – so much for our strategy of competitive differentiation!

There are also a few problems being stored up in policies of 'firing customers' – you better be sure you are not dumping the people who would have been your profitable customers of tomorrow, when your current profitable targets have ceased to be. You need to be sure you are retaining the right customers through your investment in CRM. Figure 10.2 illustrates the dancehall dilemma – why do the ones I fancy never fancy me, and vice versa. Building and reinforcing the loyalty of customers who

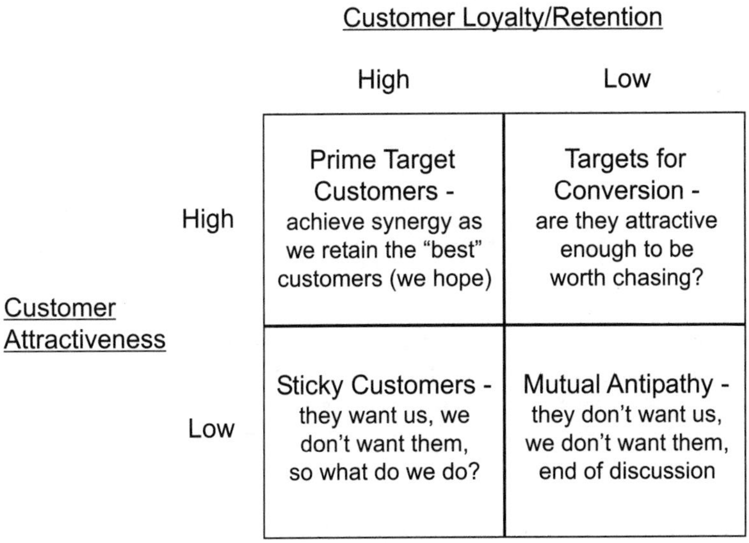

Customer Loyalty/Retention

		High	Low
Customer Attractiveness	High	Prime Target Customers - achieve synergy as we retain the "best" customers (we hope)	Targets for Conversion - are they attractive enough to be worth chasing?
	Low	Sticky Customers - they want us, we don't want them, so what do we do?	Mutual Antipathy - they don't want us, we don't want them, end of discussion

Figure 10.2   The dancehall dilemma – the ones I want never fancy me and vice versa

are attractive (profitable, good future prospects, etc.) may make sense if you are sure you can pick them, but you need to have effective ways of handling other customers too (and ways of recovering the situation if you invest in things like CRM to keep customers who do not pay off).

'we need to think hard about whether CRM approaches can contribute to developing the type of customer relationship that our market strategy needs, and whether our company has the ability to implement more than the superficial trappings of CRM technology'

On balance, the chances are that unless you can achieve the company-wide changes in processes that we discussed earlier (see Chapter 5), then CRM is going to struggle to be anything more than a glorified database.

The bottom line seems to be that we need to think hard about whether CRM approaches can contribute to developing the type of customer relationship that our market strategy needs, and whether our company has the ability to implement more than the superficial trappings of CRM technology. This is potentially a powerful set of tools – the issue is whether they are the right tools for what we are trying to achieve, and whether we can use them to good effect. It may be that we conclude that the issue for us is indeed managing customer relationships, just maybe not CRM systems.

REALITY CHECK
CRM AT BRITISH GAS/CENTRICA

Roy Gardner arrived as CEO at British Gas in 1994, when the company was in a multiple crisis – floods of customer complaints, outrage over 'fat cat' pay rises and punitive supply contracts threatening to bankrupt the business – and the nickname for the business was 'Duff Gas'. By 2001, the same company – now named Centrica – was widely regarded as an outstanding example of a consumer-driven business, and it has quadrupled its value in the space of four years, in which time its shares rose from 58p to 236p. A key element of Gardner's turnaround strategy was an obsession with customer relationship management. His priority was improving customer service – he invested over £100 million in staff training and new equipment, and changed procedures for handling customer problems. He also incorporated customer service targets in managers' bonus schemes. The next stage was to leverage the company's growing customer knowledge. Profit margins on gas would not sustain the business, but the CRM systems uncovered opportunities to sell other things to the same customers – electricity, telecoms, insurance, credit cards. Most surprising, however, was the purchase of the Automobile Association for £1.1 billion. Gardner's reasoning was twofold: that for his customers while the first hassle was getting the home right, the next was the car; and secondly, that he could operate a single back-office and CRM approach for the home business and the car business. The transition was from a gas business to a consumer services company, built around CRM expertise.

Source: Brian O'Connor (2001), 'Centrica Action for Man Who Focuses on the Long Run', *Daily Mail*, 29 March.

Key account management

Closely related to CRM in business-to-business marketing has been the growth in the use of key account management (KAM), sometimes elevated to strategic account management, and now global account management systems to focus efforts on the complex needs of major customers. Driven in part by supplier base reduction and thus the increased importance of each strategic account, KAM is a form of partnering with the company's most important customers, and building an account team around each major partnership. This is still no magic bullet, but it may be a useful way of putting CRM into practice for major clients[16]. It is largely an attempt to put relationships with key customers onto a collaborative footing, so the comments below about collaborative relationships fit here as well.

'Driven in part by supplier base reduction and thus the increased importance of each strategic account, KAM is a form of partnering with the company's most important customers'

Competitor and contingent relationships

Let's talk about relationships with competitors and contingents – they share the characteristic that they may react to what we propose to do and they may stop us.

For a start, we need to be pretty realistic about the type and level of competition in our target markets. This sounds so obvious, but many companies are very poor at putting strategy development into the real competitive environment. This is a route to nasty surprises. We need to give some serious attention to issues like:

- really understanding the competition, particularly in terms of their ability to respond or retaliate to our market strategy;
- continually updating our view of the sources of competition in our market – not just the existing 'me-too' competitors but new entrants, because then we can focus on the level and type of competitiveness in this market.

However, let us get some fundamental issues out in the open before continuing:

- *Every organization has competitors* – whether you accept it or not. Talk to senior people from the police service. These managers say they had no competitors – there is only one police service. What else do you call the amazing growth in private security firms for the home and the business? Then ask yourself why there are more alternative health practitioners in the UK than there are doctors in general practice. Everyone has competitors.
- *We know who our competitors are* – just about every organization says this. An awful lot of them are wrong. Take the examples we looked at earlier: the retail banks who persistently claimed that building societies and insurance companies could not compete in the retail banking market; the airlines who did not believe that 'no frills' operators like easyJet could survive. Competitive myopia is a common condition and can prove fatal.
- *Competitors are in our industry* – many of us tend to identify competitors as firms with the same technology, the same type of products and services as us: this is the industry. Customers are not interested in the 'industry', only in meeting their own needs. The real competition may come from outside our industry: electronic communications reduce the need to travel or freight paper around the world; music competes with clothing for the young consumer's leisure spend; management consultants compete with corporate banks by reducing the need for companies to borrow (e.g. to find stockholding); industrial companies produce their own raw materials instead of outsourcing and turn from customers to competitors.

Sorting out these basics goes before evaluating our relationships with competitors.

Really understanding the competition

Getting to grips with competition is about far more than just listing the companies that sell similar products and services to us.

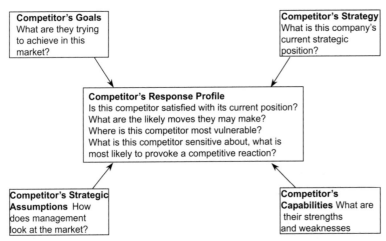

Figure 10.3 Competitor analysis. Source: Adapted from Michael E. Porter (1980), *Competitive Strategy,* New York: Free Press

It is far more about challenging conventional assumptions about what drives our key competitors, understanding their strengths and weaknesses, their limitations and problems, and their likely strategies. A conventional framework for structuring this is shown in Figure 10.3.

This framework suggests we should build a competitor response profile for each key player in the market and constantly revise it. This should help in confronting the likely reactions to our market strategy from each competitor.

The profile should also take into account the psychology of the competition in this market – basically how mean and aggressive are the competitors. For example, try categorizing your competitors in the way shown in Figure 10.4. This involves identifying competitors who will:

'we should build a competitor response profile for each key player in the market and constantly revise it'

- fight to the death in this market, possibly regardless of the short-term commercial consequences;
- show disdain by not reacting to our strategy, because they do not see us as a serious threat worth worrying about;
- counter-attack to protect their own position, but not very aggressively or competently; and
- simply leave us alone, for one reason or another.

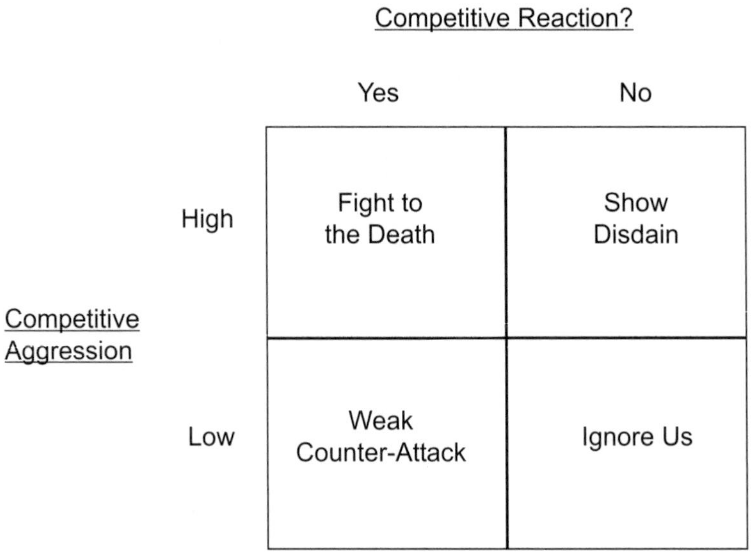

Competitive Reaction?

		Yes	No
Competitive Aggression	High	Fight to the Death	Show Disdain
	Low	Weak Counter-Attack	Ignore Us

Figure 10.4 How ugly are the competitors around here?

Analysis like this can be surprisingly revealing. It is not a wasted effort if you identify the real threats of aggression in the market. The thing to avoid at all costs is the 'fight to the death' competitor, because these conflicts are a fast way of losing a lot of money.

In case this sounds dubious, consider the continuing competitive war between Tesco and Sainsbury. The nature of Tesco's competitive stance can be judged from an often-repeated anecdote from the days of restricted Sunday trading. A Tesco store was reported on Sunday for illegal trading and was fined and ordered to close. The following Sunday, every Sainsbury in a 50-mile radius of that Tesco store was systematically reported for illegal trading and consequently ordered to close. This may have been an unhappy coincidence, but most people suspect not. It does not matter if this story is true – it probably is not (it was more likely a 100-mile radius), and we should never let the facts get in the way of a good story. The point is that when Sainsbury talked about the possibility of a price-cutting campaign and Tesco immediately said it would match every price cut made every inch of the way – everybody believed that Tesco would do exactly that. The market knows, if the major competitor attacks Tesco on price, they will hit back immediately and fully.

REALITY CHECK
THESE GUYS DON'T PLAY NICE

The retail grocery market in Britain is not above playing tricks. Following the takeover of Asda by US retail giant Wal-Mart, Safeway regards Asda as its main competitor. Internal company documents reveal Safeway's 'saboteur shopper' tactics – sending its employees into its rival's stores to cause confusion at busy times, pretending to be customers, clogging up checkouts by demanding price checks at the last minute, causing long queues at counters. The Safeway report gloats of one such campaign: 'The queues on the tills were about 45 feet long and customers were dumping their baskets and leaving …'. Another tactic is large groups of staff arriving outside Asda stores and bombarding customers with Safeway leaflets – at one point in 2000 estimated to be 10 million leaflets a week. Asda simply laughed the tactics off, but may have been more worried by the reaction of Tesco's spokesman on the arrival of Wal-Mart in the UK: 'The Yanks have got a reputation for turning up for wars late and claiming they won them'. A friendly business this is not.

Sources: Richard Price (2000), 'Safeway's Saboteur Shoppers Wage War on Asda', *Daily Mail*, 12 August. 'Talking Heads', *Sunday Times*, 15 August 1999.

Similarly, Coke does not think that McDonalds should serve its competitors' products. Accordingly, it offers McDonalds' franchisees free Coke syrup if they are willing to drop Dr Pepper and serve only Coke brands[17]. On the other hand, look at the behaviour of the big manufacturers of electrical household goods – washing machines, 'fridges, and so on. Far from competing on price these firms stand accused of deliberately restricting supplies of products to discount outlets. They simply do not want to get into that sort of competition[18]. This is not suggestive of cut-throat, fight-to-the-death relationships between these suppliers, but something rather cosier.

Part of the objective in putting strategy into a competitive context is to avoid being trapped in vulnerable positions. If you get into head-on competition with an aggressive market leader, they will fight back, and if they are strong enough they will win. Success comes by avoiding head-on conflict and outmanoeuvring the competition. That success is also about playing to your own strengths and to your competitors' weaknesses.

'If you get into head-on competition with an aggressive market leader, they will fight back, and if they are strong enough they will win. Success comes by avoiding head-on conflict and outmanoeuvring the competition'

If our analysis suggests that we are targeting the same markets with the same value proposition and the same marketing methods as strong, aggressive competitors – why would we expect to be successful?

But where is the competition coming from in this market?

At one level this simply says we should know who the competitors are in this market. Undoubtedly true – but not the full story. We also want to know where the *new competitors* will come from:

- potential new entrants to the market – such as retail firms entering the financial services industry; and
- the threat of substitute products and services that meet the customer's needs, but may come from a different industry or technology – for example, Dyson's entry into the vacuum cleaner market (see p. 332).

Both are vital to know, both are difficult to track. At least so it seems. In fact, if you look at the examples given above – the financial services sector had been told for the best part of two decades that multiple retailers could easily and forcefully attack their sector, and the Dyson product innovation was actually offered to the main competitors (Hoover and Electrolux) before Dyson launched it himself (see pp. 331–40 for the full story). Maybe some nasty surprises shouldn't be? If you need further convincing – go back to the competitive box (pp. 278–82).

Nonetheless, the point to be made is that we need to continually monitor for new competitive threats that may radically change the attractiveness of the chosen market and undermine our value proposition. The test of whether we are getting there is:

- Do we understand the competition well enough to predict their strategic moves, and to maintain our competitive advantage?
- Does this include existing and potential competitors, and potential new technologies coming into the market?
- Does our value proposition give us a specific positioning that plays to our strengths and avoids head-on competition, so that we can build a strong foothold in the market and defend it? If we do not have a competitive differentiation that separates us from the competition in the customer's eyes, then we have no competitive advantage and this market strategy will fail. In this case we need to think again.

This issue has proved so problematic in working with executives, we have developed a specific market sensing technique that focuses on competition (see pp. 390–3).

Now, what about 'contingents', whatever that is supposed to mean[19].

Allowing for critical contingents

As we saw in Chapter 3, one of the defining characteristics of the era of value-based strategy is that there is a whole bunch of people and organizations apparently dedicated to stopping you from putting your strategy into action. To be fair, they could also be one of your major strengths in getting things done faster than your competitors, it just does not seem to work out this way too often. The defining characteristics of our contingents are:

- they are not competitors, but they may react in a similar way to your market strategy;
- they have the potential for restricting your freedom of action, i.e. stopping you from doing what you want to do, either literally or because their actions add to the cost of implementing your strategy;
- the relationship you have with them may be a critical determinant of your ability to put your strategy into effect and deliver your value proposition to your customers.

It is not easy to come up with a definitive list of contingents – it varies too much between companies and markets. However, the list below is illustrative of what we should be thinking about in assessing the strength and direction of the relationships we have and what this means for our ability to implement our intended market strategy.

Shapers

Increasingly, there are forces in the market which shape and change attitudes and beliefs about the industry and our company. For large companies, City analysts and the information they provide to the media are a major determinant of a company's freedom of action. For example, the then-CEO of Marks & Spencer, Sir Richard Greenbury, had a troubled relationship with the City, and when he announced the company's record-breaking profits in May 1998, the City wrote the company's stock down, in reaction

'For large companies, City analysts and the information they provide to the media are a major determinant of a company's freedom of action'

to his statement that trading was getting tougher and he was investing for the long-term future. Subsequently, Greenbury's management succession plans were tracked relentlessly by the media, until Greenbury finally left the company. New CEO, Luc Vandevelde, is attempting a brave turnaround strategy when every move he makes is scrutinized by the analysts and media, every step of the way. This company's pain underlines the importance of managing relationships with powerful shapers of opinion outside the company, or taking the consequences.

One of the most direct impacts of poor relationships with such commentators is that they influence shareholder opinion – possibly more than company management can. For instance, in the midst of the ill-fated attempt at merger with MCI, when BT's chairman, Sir Iain Vallance, was told by an angry shareholder that he was 'an English muffin' because 'American companies eat you for breakfast', he might have anticipated that shareholder pressure was going to force him to reduce the offer for MCI and that the critical deal would fall through, leaving BT's international strategy in tatters. The management of relationships with vocal shareholder groups is becoming increasingly critical for some companies.

Whether stimulated by competitors, the media, government pressure or public opinion, the growing role of regulators in restricting the freedom of actions of companies may be critical. For example, an alliance with American Air was a critical component of British Airways' global strategy in the late 1990s. The then-CEO, Robert Ayling, announced alliance with America, and actually made a press statement stating that the alliance was no business of the European regulators. The regulator's response to this challenge was to crawl all over this deal and impose conditions for approval, until he finally found a way to make the alliance unattractive for both partners. The alliance never happened, and subsequently Mr Ayling left the company. Interestingly, at the same time, Lufthansa's Star alliance did not apparently trouble the regulator, nor KLM's alliance with Northwest. Relationships with regulators may be a critical implementation capability. In fact, winding-up the regulators has become a new competitive weapon in Europe – 'no frills' airlines Virgin Express and easyJet have specialized in running to the regulator every chance they get, much to the discomfort of BA and KLM.

Recommenders

Those who lead opinions for or 'against your products and services may be a critical target for relationship building and sustaining efforts. Indeed, for some this may be the most critical area. For example, in the medical products area, your standing with medical journal writers and medical schools may be a crucial determinant of whether your new products and ways of doing business are accepted by the medical profession. Similarly, in the building products marketplace, architects and designers do not buy the products but they have a decisive role in recommending and specifying them to builders. Relationships with recommenders may be an important advantage or disadvantage for your strategy.

'Those who lead opinions for or against your products and services may be a critical target for relationship building and sustaining efforts. Indeed, for some this may be the most critical area'

Gatekeepers

In some markets, recommenders turn into gatekeepers. For example, in the mainframe computer business it was always the case that the company's IT Department acted as a determinant of whether your products were even considered by management. Right now in the British universities, it is next to impossible to buy a PC other than from Research Machines and Viglen, because of their agreements with university purchasing departments. Never mind that RM and Viglen machines are second-rate and unreliable – that's all the user can buy.

Suppliers

In theory, all competitors have equal access to supplies of materials and resources. In reality, this is rarely so straightforward. For example, Dell is renowned for getting access to new products – the faster chip, the brighter screen – quicker than its competitors, and for obtaining preferential supplies of components which are in short supply. Part of the basis for the anti-trust actions against Microsoft in the US is that it supplies new products selectively to customers, and allegedly tried to make life difficult for Netscape (and its rival Web browser software) by bundling its own Web browser free with the Windows operating system, as well as pressuring some computer manufacturers to sign exclusive deals with Microsoft[20]. Netscape saw its market share collapse, and its stock price fall from $90 to $30, and was subsequently bought by America Online. Your relationships with dominant suppliers may be critical.

Supply chain partnerships

Further, as supply chains are managed as single entities (see the commentary on the ECR programme, pp. 514–17), the relation-

'you do not just have to profile and understand your direct competitors, you need to identify and profile a range of contingent forces as well, to get a view about what type of relationship you have with the important ones, and whether this is a barrier to successfully implementing your strategy'

ship of a company with its supply chain collaborators may define its strategic freedom. For example, in the ECR programme there is a strong push to reduce the number of new product launches, to reduce the number of products that retailers have to stock. This fundamentally restricts the freedom of supply chain members to innovate. For companies involved in these types of supply chain integrations, the ability to implement new market strategies is likely to depend on the ability to successfully negotiate with supply chain partners – suppliers, distributors and even competitors.

What I am saying is that you do not just have to profile and understand your direct competitors, you need to identify and profile a range of contingent forces as well, to get a view about what type of relationship you have with the important ones, and whether this is a barrier to successfully implementing your strategy.

Collaborator relationships

For most firms, going to market has always involved dependence on other firms – suppliers of raw materials and components, advertising agencies, distributors, and so on. The idea that our market strategy relies for success on collaborating effectively with others to get the product or service to the customer is hardly new. We have always been vulnerable to failure in supply or blockages in the distribution channel. However, the issue of collaboration goes a lot further – it includes various forms of *partnership* with other organizations. This increases our dependence on others to drive our market strategy and suggests areas of risk to consider in putting the strategy in place.

Let us consider the following issues: the move from outsourcing (buying-in products and services) to strategic alliances and networks (partnerships of various kinds); the emerging pressure to focus on supply chain management and the Efficient Consumer Response programmes; and the problems of managing partnerships in implementing market strategy. The goal is to identify the critical collaboration links that lie under our market strategy, and to see how vulnerable this makes us.

From outsourcing to alliances and networks

One way of categorizing collaborative relationships is shown in Figure 10.5. This suggests that getting progressively closer to collaboration with others, we can distinguish between:

- *Outsourcing* – an 'arm's length' relationship where we simply contract to buy goods and services on a normal basis, e.g. advertising, market research and direct marketing expertise are typically bought-in expertise. However, we also need to consider the trend to outsourcing critical activities like personal selling and for most firms the unavoidable reality that they will rely on distributors to get their products and services to customers. Some outsourcing may involve enduring relationships and close co-operation.
- *Partnership* – a closer type of relationship where companies recognize each other as partners, and there are varying degrees of inter-company co-ordination and integration.
- *Alliance* – a joint venture where ownership of an activity or operation is shared with a collaborator.
- *Vertical integration* – we fully own the activity or operation[21].

There are many factors driving companies to explore partnerships and strategic alliances as critical components of their market strategies. Quite simply, the use of collaborative

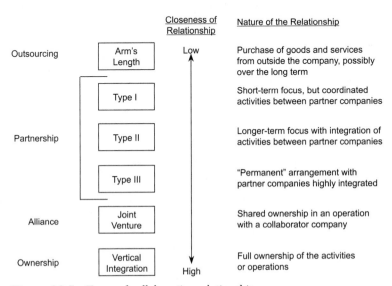

Figure 10.5 Types of collaborative relationship

arrangements has escalated because of conditions of rapid change and high risk in the marketplace, together with demands for skills and resources that exceed a single firm's capabilities. The goals we seek in partnering and alliance include:

- *Cost efficiency* – it may be cheaper to use the expertise of a specialist than to do something in-house: McDonalds has partnerships with regional distributors servicing all outlets in a region to reduce delivery and ordering costs.
- *Customer service* – integration between firms in the supply chain can improve service (and prices) for customers (see the Supply Chain commentary below).
- *Marketing advantage* – integration can acquire greater marketing expertise, gain entry to new markets, and provide better access to technology and innovation. For example, in marketing office equipment in the US, Xerox partners with Ryder, the transportation firm, to deliver and install equipment, reducing costs and retaining price competitiveness. In 1997, British Aerospace announced a deal with Vickers, under which BAe will market Vickers tanks and armoured vehicles in areas like Qatar and Saudi Arabia, where Vickers is weak.
- *Strategic advantage* – an alliance may offer greater market control. For example, in 1997 Dixons, the electrical retailer, sold a 40 per cent stake in its communications offshoot, Link, which retails mobile phones, pagers and faxes, to Cellnet. This has two main effects. First, joint ownership commits both Dixons and Cellnet to the Link venture. Second, it is likely that Vodafone, Cellnet's competitor, will have some trouble finding space for its products in the Link shops.
- *Profit stability and growth* – for many companies, prospects of reduced costs and enhanced profits, and access to more markets and higher market share, are the goals of partnership. More broadly, alliances may provide the opportunity to learn and absorb other companies' skills (although that works both ways).

'competition in the future will no longer be between individual firms, but between alliances of firms'

In some industries now, commentators are suggesting that competition in the future will no longer be between individual firms, but between *alliances* of firms. This is already becoming a significant issue in the airline and computer businesses, and areas like utilities.

For example, early in 1997, Microsoft announced a corporate computing alliance with Hewlett-Packard, to counter the anti-Microsoft alliance created the previous week between IBM, Netscape Communications, Sun Microsystems and Oracle – the Microsoft alliance will further the spread of the

Windows NT operating system, while the IBM alliance aims to weaken Microsoft's control over technology standards. In the British market for electricity and gas supply, rumours in late 1996 were of a prospective alliance between British Telecom and certain of the power companies, for BT to market energy and telecom services together.

These examples are all illustrative of a new type of competition – between alliances and consortia, not individual organizations, which may cause us to rethink some of our assumptions about who can do what.

In fact, there is more – the spread of collaboration, partnership and alliance strategies has led in many industries to the emergence of a wholly new organizational form: *the hollow or network organization*. For example, in the US Calyx & Corolla (C&C) is a good example of a prototype for the network organization. C&C have in effect reinvented the way Americans buy flowers, by selling perishable cut flowers from catalogues (and an Internet site). The C&C network is shown in Figure 10.6 – customers order flowers from C&C's catalogue pictures or website, C&C passes the order electronically to the selected grower (based on stock availability), and Federal Express collects the flowers from the grower (branded with the C&C logo and packaging) and delivers them to the customer. This case is remarkable in two aspects. First, it cuts out three middlemen from the traditional channel for cut flowers (wholesalers, distributors and retailers) and gets flowers to the customer that are up to nine days fresher than flowers bought from a conventional retailer. Second, this is a 'virtual' or 'hollow' organization – C&C adds

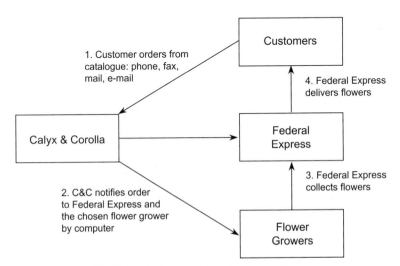

Figure 10.6 The Calyx & Corolla network organization

value through a catalogue and computer links, it does not grow flowers, own warehouses, operate retail outlets, or run a distribution or delivery fleet, and it operates with only a small core staff, so can quickly reposition to follow changing customer requirements[22].

A similar rethinking of a business based on a network of collaborators is shown by the Smart Card announced by Shell, the oil company, in 1997[23]. Shell is at the centre of a consortium of retailers and other companies (Dixons, Currys, Victoria Wine, Vision Express, John Menzies, The Link, Commercial Union, the RAC, Hilton Hotels – with Sainsbury, Next, Allied Domeq and Cellnet potentially joining). The Shell strategy is to take its Smart loyalty card into general shopping, allowing card users to shop, bank and make phone calls, while collecting discount points and air miles in the process. The discount points earned are cashable in any of the consortium members' operations – money spent on Shell petrol could give money off a product in Victoria Wine, and so on. The goal is for the one card to service 70 per cent of the average consumer's expenditure. This strategy too is based on a 'virtual' organization.

Another 'hollow' or 'virtual' organization is The Registry Inc. in the USA. The Registry's core competence is its skill in recruiting software engineers, programmers and technical writers to work on clients' computing and IT projects. Founded in 1987, The Registry's customer account managers identify client needs and then form customized technical teams to service client projects, such as computer system conversions and software development. The Registry has a database of 55 000 technical specialists, with 30 recruiters to locate technical talent and 55 salespeople to put teams together around customer needs. Sales by 1995 were around $100 million[24].

'In some cases collaboration is simply a fast way to get access to a market by using the existing resources of other companies'

In some cases collaboration is simply a fast way to get access to a market by using the existing resources of other companies. For example, a niche of the highly competitive UK grocery market is the time-pressed mobile customer who wants easy one-stop shopping – someone on the way home from work who has no dinner in the house and no catfood. The Budgens supermarket group has outmanoeuvred its larger competitors by a collaboration with Kuwait Petroleum and BP, to open co-branded petrol station forecourt grocery stores, selling ready-meals and fresh and chilled food (and cat food).

One remarkable example of the degree of transformation that may be involved in these new types of organization is shown by ICL – the troubled 'British' computer company, now owned by

Fujitsu. The transformation of this company during the 1990s is so radical that by 1997 ICL no longer had any factories. The company has gone from a traditional manufacturing organization to a computer services company focused on consultancy, outsourcing, electronic commerce, computer training, and the delivery of systems to the retail and finance sectors. ICL's move into new areas, after a period of restructuring and divestment, means they no longer need to own production facilities – ICL is a hollow corporation.

Increasingly, networked ventures are likely to be Internet-based. For example, in the US Cendant, which has Avis, hotel chains and estate agency companies, launched Move.com in 2001, bringing together its diverse brands in a single service to provide house-finding, house financing, removals, car hire and hotel accommodation as a single package.

However, the search for competitive advantage by developing networks based on strategic alliances and partnerships has also seen some major failures:

- When Rover was purchased by BMW, the Rover chief executive actually seemed to believe that the 15-year-old R&D and marketing partnership with Honda would continue – Honda's view about Rover attempting to sell Honda's expertise to BMW was somewhat different and Honda has effectively ended the collaboration.
- IBM and Microsoft were at one stage partners in a strategic alliance, which collapsed because of conflict of interest between the partners.
- British Airways and USAir ended up in court, because BA decided it was better served by an alliance with American Air, and that partnership is dead.
- The alliance between KLM, Royal Dutch Airline and Northwest Airlines was formed in 1990 and took Northwest back into profitability by generating $100 million in new revenue for the partners, but has involved clashes between the partners such as KLM's threat to sue if Northwest carried out a threat to change shareholder rights, and the battle for power continues.
- In 1994, the strategic alliance between Intel, the microprocessor manufacturer, and its biggest customer, Compaq, ran into problems – Compaq objected to Intel's 'Intel Inside' advertising campaign as undermining Compaq by promoting its competitors' computers (which also have Intel chips).
- One recent study of 82 large multinational companies found that less than half the companies operating strategic alliances were satisfied with the effectiveness of those alliances[25].

Indeed, despairing of companies' claims that every alliance and acquisition they make represents 'synergy'[26], one commentator has coined the term 'ygrenys' to describe what they actually get[27]. This word is not actually Welsh – it comes from reversing the word 'synergy'. It describes situations where combining businesses reduces their value instead of increasing it.

'collaboration creates dependence, and we need to think very hard about that vulnerability – how good are we at managing in partnerships, and where will we be left if the partnership fails'

Developing networks of collaborating and allied organizations can provide powerful competitive leverage. However, collaboration creates dependence, and we need to think very hard about that vulnerability – how good are we at managing in partnerships, and where will we be left if the partnership fails.

A particular area of collaboration and partnering that should be noted is in *supply chain relationships*. For consumer goods manufacturers these are of particular note because, as with so many deals with powerful retailers, collaboration largely means doing what you are told. At the extreme, control of supply chains may even take away the manufacturer's right to brand, in favour of the retailer's. Consider the following example.

The focus on the supply chain is seen in the Efficient Consumer Response (ECR) programme in the USA, started in the early 1990s, and launched in the UK in 1996. ECR has been pioneered in the grocery business, but is being extended into the healthcare, airlines and food processing sectors in the US.

The ECR movement is based on 'co-operative partnerships' between retailers and manufacturers, who commit to collaborate in reducing costs in the supply chain. Leading players in the US were Krogers, the leading national supermarket chain, and Procter & Gamble – but by 1995 nearly 90 per cent of firms in the grocery business were applying ECR. In the UK, the participants at the launch were Tesco, Sainsbury, Waitrose, Safeway, Asda and Marks & Spencer from retailing, and Procter & Gamble, Unilever, Mars, Nestlé and Kraft on the supplier side. ECR represents the application of 'lean supply chain' principles to the branded goods business (see pp. 246–9).

The US pioneers of ECR in the grocery business point to the key drivers of what they believe was a survival strategy as factors in traditional channels like:

- *forward buying and diverting* – where retailers do not pass on manufacturer price cuts, but buy in at low prices and take on 'internal' profit, or buy locally where manufacturers have discounted prices and ship the goods elsewhere again to show an internal profit;

- *excessive inventories* – retailers were holding an average more than three months' supplies;
- *damaged and unsaleable foods* – were at unacceptably high levels;
- *complex deals and deductions* – negotiated deals were so complicated that as much as 80 per cent of invoices had to be processed manually;
- *promotion and coupons* – it is estimated that in the US, in 1996, 261 billion promotional coupons were issued, with less than 2 per cent redeemed;
- *new products* – in 1996, 22 400 new products were launched in the US grocery business, dominated by imitative 'me-too' brands, with the expectation that 90 per cent would last less than two years, while the bottom 25 per cent of brands stocked in the supermarket gave retailers less than 1 per cent of their sales.

The ECR programme was a response to this situation, and the goal was to take some $30 billion a year of cost out of the grocery supply chain in the US, by making retail assortments more efficient, by making sales promotion more efficient, by making product replenishment systems more efficient, and by handling product introductions better. The central issue is one of managing flows in the supply chain – flows of product, information and cash. The key elements of ECR are:

- *Category management* – collaborative planning by retailers and manufacturers around groups of products in the store, as they are perceived by customers, not brands as produced by manufacturers, e.g. 'ready meal solutions' grouping together products that replace the home cooked meal, 'laundry' or 'photoprocessing' – typically this has taken 20 per cent of product items off the shelf for good.
- *More efficient promotions* – drastic reductions in the number of coupons and special offers and the substitution of 'value pricing'.
- *Continuous replenishment* – the continual flow of product from manufacturers, with no stock-keeping at retail or wholesale levels, with direct store delivery, with the result that by the end of the first three years of ECR around 20 per cent less stock was held. For example, a package of Procter & Gamble soap powder typically gets to the customer seven days after manufacture instead of four to six weeks (and incidentally contains less preservatives as a result).
- *Electronic data interchange* – the computerization of ordering and payment systems, in a paperless information flow through the supply chain.

- *Performance measures* – new ways of evaluating performance.
- *Organizational change* – for example, Procter & Gamble has replaced its sales organization with its Customer Business Development organization, as part of its commitment to ECR.

Enthusiasm for the power of the ECR strategy in reducing supply chain costs has crossed the Atlantic to Europe. Claims are widespread that across Europe it should be possible to take out £21 billion a year from grocery supply chain costs, or between 5 and 6 per cent of cost. The principles are the same: automated store ordering (point-of-sale scanning data trigger new orders automatically); cross-docking (goods go from suppliers' trucks to retailers' trucks with no time in a warehouse); continual replenishment (to avoid stockholding); and more reliable ordering and payment systems.

This pursuit of operational efficiency in distribution is in many ways superb. However, at the risk of appearing a little cynical it is worth raising a couple of questions about the impact of ECR on market strategy and customer value, rather than just operational efficiency:

- When Don Dufek, ECR Operating Committee Chairman in the US, a champion of ECR and former Senior Vice-President of Krogers, says that ECR is about increasing customer satisfaction and that 'the real power is with the consumer', we all get excited and think ECR is wonderful[28]. But then he tells us how at Krogers they have used ECR to drastically reduce the number of brands on the shelf in collaboration with major suppliers, and how they found with ECR they could increase some product prices to improve profitability. Am I the only one who cannot see how less choice and higher prices will increase my satisfaction as a Krogers' customer? Am I the only one who wonders how small brands from smaller suppliers are ever going to get onto Krogers' shelves, now they are neatly shared out between the big suppliers?
- ECR is an excellent vehicle for reducing operating costs in mature channels of distribution, but its importance is in cost saving (particularly for retailers) not customer satisfaction. I am very pleased for companies that save money, but where is the benefit to me as the customer? The most they could possibly offer is a 5 per cent price cut (and it will probably be much less), and that is not very impressive to me as a customer.
- Why does anyone think that as a customer I care how long the product has been on the shelf – it really makes no difference to me if the can of Coke is three months' old or one week old, because it still *tastes* the same; I am not really interested if the pack of soap powder left the factory eight weeks or eight days

ago, it does nothing to increase the value of the product to the customer. Great increases in operational efficiency – yes. Increase in customer value – no.

- It is also perhaps too cynical to note that Procter & Gamble's disappointing 1996 results brought a large share price fall, and this was attributed mainly to its Efficient Consumer Response programme and particularly its 'value pricing' component[29].

- Why does it seem strange that after years of confrontational and adversarial conflict between retailers and manufacturers, we can accept the 'cease-fire' because of ECR – it looks very fragile in the longer term? Why does it look more like retailers using their market power to demand more cost savings from manufacturers?

- Why do I feel uncomfortable when I hear Paul Polman of Procter & Gamble (UK) talk about 'confusing consumers with meaningless choice', and telling us that even if 40 per cent of existing laundry stock-keeping units (product items) are cut, the category would still meet 95 per cent of consumer needs, and why do I start speculating about the consumers who like choice and the niche market opportunities in the 5 per cent of the market that P&G does not seem to want[30]?

- Why when a branded goods Marketing Manager says: 'if your top five retail outlets say you are joining this club, or face the consequences . . . you join the club and pay your dues' – does this sound a bit more like the real world?

> We have a veto!
>
> We toe ze line.

Whatever view we take – ECR is a reality for those in the grocery business, and it may well spread to other sectors in time. In this situation, the real issue is how the total surplus in the supply chain is divided between manufacturer, supplier and distributor. The question for us then is how it impacts on our value proposition and our process of getting to the market.

More generally, the potential attraction of collaboration and alliance in implementing our market strategy needs to be evaluated carefully against how well partners will carry the value proposition forward, how vulnerable we will be if the collaboration or alliance does not work out, and our capabilities in managing partnerships with other companies.

'the potential attraction of collaboration and alliance in implementing our market strategy needs to be evaluated carefully against how well partners will carry the value proposition forward'

Managing partnerships and collaborations

The signs to look for to judge if a partnership is going to work include the following[31]:

- *Corporate compatibility* – for a partnership to work the cultures and business objectives must mesh. The IBM/Microsoft collaboration probably never stood a chance given the totally different cultures of Bill Gates' irreverent and entrepreneurial software company, and IBM's bureaucracy. The alliance died because the partners were both going after the same market – IBM with OS/2 that Microsoft had produced for it, and Microsoft with Windows that it had produced for itself. Microsoft won.
- *Management style and techniques* – similarities in operating styles help. McDonalds and Coca-Cola share a similar management approach and have an effective and highly integrated partnership. The KLM/Northwest partnership is endangered by Northwest's pursuit of short-term financial gains, and a lack of trust between the two organizations.
- *Mutuality* – the partnership is stronger if both sides get benefits not otherwise obtained, and if there is trust and commitment on both sides.
- *Symmetry* – partnerships between 'equals' stand the best chance.

In fact, some recent research suggests that many of our original ideas about how to manage collaborations are ineffective and we have to think about organizations that form alliances 'co-evolving' though shifting webs of relationships – the issue is learning new ways of managing, not simply plugging in the old ways[32]. We probably also have to get used to the idea that most of the things we measure to plan and control need to be different in an alliance as compared to a single organization[33].

However, if any kind of partnership-based strategy is to be pursued, then it is also necessary to consider the costs and time involved in managing these issues:

- *Establishing the partnership* – identifying, negotiating with and striking a deal with another organization.
- *Monitoring the partnership* – carefully evaluating the effectiveness and strength of the relationship.
- *Strengthening the partnership* – where necessary investing time and effort in the joint activities needed to improve the effectiveness of the partnership.

So, part of our thinking needs to be given to identifying the collaborations and other relationships that underpin going to market with our value proposition. Perhaps the most critical issues are vulnerability and capability – how fragile is our strategy to a failure in key collaborations, and do we have the capability to manage collaborations where they underpin the market strategy? Negative conclusions here may also drive us back to questioning our market choices and the robustness of the value proposition in the real marketplace. We also need to think about the degree to which collaboration may actually undermine our value proposition. For example, many air travellers are beginning to question the honesty of an airline that takes your booking (e.g. KLM) and then puts you on another airline's plane (e.g. Northwest)[34] – presumably if we had wanted to fly Northwest (highly unlikely), then we would have booked Northwest?

Co-worker relationships

We have already emphasized the importance of our people in delivering service and value to put our strategy into effect (Chapter 2), and the importance of pan-company marketing that integrates all the factors that impact on the customer into a single value proposition (Chapter 5). We will not repeat these arguments here. The task at this stage is to look at our value proposition and to question whether our people can and will deliver the promise to the customer. The logic is that we make promises to our customers that will not be kept if the company's internal values do not match[35]. Several points are worth adding.

> *'The task at this stage is to look at our value proposition and to question whether our people can and will deliver the promise to the customer'*

First, do not *assume* that because we have developed a great new market strategy, everyone else in the company is going to agree!

Second, we need to be *realistic* about our capabilities. The question is: can we deliver this strategy to the customer, with these people, these skills, these traditions, this culture, these processes, these structures and boundaries? The question is *not* (usually) if we started again from scratch, could we deliver the strategy?

For example, Frank Cespedes describes the sort of problems faced:

● When IBM planned to release its System 9370 mainframe, the launch was marked by a squabble between product managers and sales managers – the product managers wanted the computer released quickly, but the sales managers wanted to meet quotas of existing products before the launch (when customers would stop buying until the new product was out). The product managers won. The launch was then plagued by lack of co-operation from sales management, and poor product sales.

- At a telecoms firm, a programme of enhanced maintenance and repair services effectively and unwittingly killed the sales of a system upgrade that sales were launching with a major customer.
- At a packaged goods firm, brand and sales units use different measures of retail distribution. Relationships between the units are plagued by misunderstanding and mistrust because they are using different information systems.

Frank's point is that if we want a seamless process of going to market, then we have to work for it. He has developed the idea of 'concurrent marketing' – the goal is better co-ordination of product, sales and service management, but not by vague demands for better 'teamwork', but by carefully developing mechanisms for cross-functional co-operation with clear lines of primary and joint authority, and with new personnel policies that reflect the new priorities in training and career paths[36].

Third, it is easy to underestimate people's capabilities – what they can really do if they are given the chance.

Due to the present economic situation, the light at the end of the tunnel has been turned off until further notice.

The floggings and hangings will continue until morale improves.

For example, as we saw earlier (pp. 350–1), one of the most remarkable stories in the US car business of recent years was the success of Saturn, a subsidiary of General Motors, which has redefined the car buying experience. Saturn's market strategy involved overcoming US buyers' animosity to US cars. They have relied on partnership with many collaborators, but none more important than partnership with the customer and with their employees. The company says the Saturn philosophy is one of partnership, but 'We have nothing of greater value than our people ... We believe that demonstrating respect for the uniqueness of every individual builds a team of confident, creative members possessing a high degree of initiative, self-respect and self-discipline.' Indeed, employees are selected for their compatibility with this culture[37].

However, in most organizations relatively few of our employees and managers are skilled in mind-reading. If we do not discuss, explain, listen, problem-solve and bargain – why would we expect the people in the organization to drive the value proposition for us? More of this when we look at internal marketing (see pp. 666–88).

'If we do not discuss, explain, listen, problem-solve and bargain – why would we expect the people in the organization to drive the value proposition for us?'

However we do it, we need to evaluate our emerging market strategy against the co-worker relationship issue. Our conclusions may even challenge the market choices we have made, and undermine our belief in the value proposition – then we need to do more thinking.

The network of key relationships

We have looked at relationship marketing and alliances and partnerships as components of our market strategy. But, in particular, this chapter has asked us to test our market choices and our value proposition very hard against a number of key relationships:

- the relationship with the *customer*, and with different market segments, in terms of the promises tied up in our value proposition and brands, and whether we can keep those promises;
- the relationship with *competitors* and *contingents* of different kinds, and in particular whether the competitive differentiation and strategic position we have built will stand up against the level and type of competition we will face, and the impact of external actions by others;
- the relationship with *collaborators* of various kinds, and the degree to which outsourcing and partnerships and alliances we may have assumed in developing our market strategy are actually going to work; and
- the relationship with *co-workers* – the people we rely on inside the company to implement and drive the value proposition.

At each stage we have identified new opportunities – to use relationship marketing, to segment the market by relationship type, to position against competitors, to examine new networking possibilities, and so on. But we have also stressed that our conclusions about these relationships and their impact on the market strategy may well drive us back to rethinking market choices and reworking the value proposition.

'these areas of relationship management are not really separate, but part of a hidden network of relationships, which go a long way towards defining our real implementation capabilities and the real implementation barriers our strategy faces'

A last point is that, in reality, these areas of relationship management are not really separate, but part of a hidden network of relationships, which go a long way towards defining our real implementation capabilities and the real implementation barriers our strategy faces. Part of our thinking should be about the network, not just the individual relationships.

For example, Figure 10.7 summarizes the network of relationships that undermined Robert Ayling's strategy at British Airways in the late 1990s. Ayling's strategy of globalization, alliances, cost cutting and premium branding (focused on business-class and first-class passengers) was in ruins by the end of the 1990s. The ability of BA to manage the key relationships needed to support that strategy had failed to materialize: employees were alienated, and there had already been industrial action with the prospect of more; customers were switching brands both to higher service providers and low-cost airlines; the company had antagonized a range of competitors into hostile actions; alliances and distribution channels were a shambles. Over and above these individual problems – failure in each area of the relationship matrix fuels problems in the others – alienated employees do not

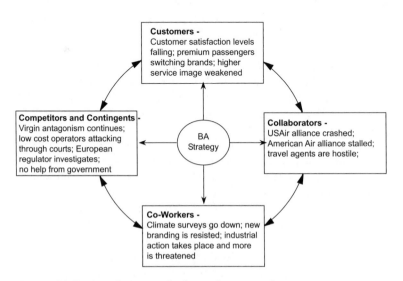

Figure 10.7 British Airways' relationship network

deliver good service to customers; collaborators and competitors stimulate the regulator's interest; hostile competitors impact on employee perceptions of the company; and so it goes on. In many ways what is most worrying is how problems in one area feed off problems in another area of the relationship network, and the situation deteriorates fast. Certainly, BA under Ayling is an excellent example of a company developing a strategy which is wholly dependent on the company's ability to manage a complex network of relationships, ignoring the fact that the company does not have the skills and capabilities required to do this.

It's time to ask some awkward questions about relationships and our market strategy:

REALITY CHECK
THE AWKWARD QUESTIONS ABOUT THE KEY RELATIONSHIPS

Can we identify all the areas of relationships that we need to manage in order to deliver our value proposition effectively to our chosen customer market targets – customers themselves, but also co-workers, competitors and contingents, and collaborators?

Can we write down what we need to have in each of these areas to support the market strategy – how does this compare to reality: what customers really think about us compared to alternatives, the real support for the strategy from managers and employees in the company; the real buy-in from collaborators in alliances and supply chains; and the real threats from major competitors? Do you still have a strategy?

Can we see how a network of relationships underpins our strategy and our ability to deliver value to market targets – and can we identify from this some of the hurdles facing the strategy as the basis for developing a realistic implementation strategy?

So, where have we got to?

The issues raised so far in Part III relating to developing a strategy pathway are fundamental. They are not easy. If you work through them and then work backwards and forwards, you should start to see a robust and distinctive strategy emerging. But there is one last step to consider. In most organizations having a strategy is not enough. We have to have a plan as well! For this reason, the next chapter provides a structure for getting from strategy to a plan.

Notes and references

1. I have to apologize for falling in line with the current usage and adopting the word 'relationship'. It is a well-known fact of human genetics that no male over the age of 16 can use the 'R' word without trembling (and, of course, commitment is even worse).
2. Martin Christopher, Adrian Payne and David Ballantyne (1993), *Relationship Marketing*, Oxford: Butterworth-Heinemann. Adrian Payne, Martin Christopher, Moira Clark and Helen Peck (1998), *Relationship Marketing for Competitive Advantage: Winning and Keeping Customers*, Oxford: Butterworth-Heinemann.
3. But please don't tell them because they can get real mean . . .
4. Further apologies to the reader for using the word 'co-workers' to refer to the employees and managers in our company, but it all alliterates too well with the other relationships and I could not resist!
5. 'CRM Sends Profits Soaring', *Marketing Business*, November 2000, 4. Kim Horner (2001), 'Customer Relationship Management: The Business Challenge', *Marketing Business*, May, xi–xiii.
6. Malcolm McDonald (2000), 'On the Right Track', *Marketing Business*, April, 28–31.
7. Philip Kotler (2000), 'New Marketing for the New Economy', *Proceedings: Society for Marketing Advances Conference*, Orlando, FL, November.
8. George Day (2000), 'Tying in an Asset', in *Understanding CRM*, London: *Financial Times*.
9. Eric Clemons (2000), 'Gathering the Nectar', in *Understanding CRM*, London: *Financial Times*.
10. Richard Tomkins (2000), 'Goodbye to Small Spenders', *Financial Times*, 4 February.
11. Merlin Stone and Bryan Foss (2001), 'Customer Relationship Management: Where Do We Go From Here?', *Marketing Business*, May, iii–viii.
12. Alison Smith (1998), 'Hello Stranger', *Financial Times*, 18 February.
13. Rod Newing (2000), 'Treasures in the Warehouse', in *Understanding CRM*, London: *Financial Times*.
14. Christopher Field (2000), 'Loyalty Cards Are Unlikely to Carry All the Answers', *Financial Times*, 3 May.
15. Malcolm McDonald (2000), 'On the Right Track', *Marketing Business*, April, 28–31.
16. Kevin Walker, Paul Denvir and Cliff Ferguson (2000), *Managing Key Clients*, London: Continuum.
17. 'Coke Offers Incentives to Franchisees to Drop Dr Pepper', *Marketing News*, 7 July 1997.
18. Andrew Alderson and Paul Nuki (1997), 'Stores Accuse Electrical Groups of Discount Cut-Off', *Sunday Times*, 6 April.

19. Well, it may not be elegant English, but it alliterates with the other relationship themes and that is good enough for me.

20. Andrew Cave and Toby Harnden (2000), 'Verdict That Could Spell the End of Bill Gates' Empire', *Daily Telegraph*, 4 April.

21. Douglas M. Lambert, Margaret A. Emmelhainnz and John T. Gardner (1996), 'So You Think You Want A Partner?', *Marketing Management*, Summer, 25–41.

22. David W. Cravens, Nigel F. Piercy and Shannon H. Shipp (1996), 'Network Organizational Forms for Competing in Highly Dynamic Environments: The Network Paradigm', *British Journal of Management*, **7** (3), 203–18.

23. Ray Massey (1997), 'Shell Plays its Ace to Clean Up in Card Market', *Daily Mail*, 13 March.

24. J. Falvey (1993), 'Coming Attractions', *Sales and Marketing Management*, July, 16–21.

25. David W. Cravens, Shannon H. Shipp and Karen S. Cravens (1993), 'Analysis of Co-operative Interorganizational Relationships: Strategic Alliance Formation and Strategic Alliance Effectiveness', *Journal of Strategic Marketing*, March, 55–70.

26. The so-called '2 + 2 = 5 Effect', where the new entity is worth more than the sum of its parts.

27. Richard Northedge (2000), 'Ygrenys: When 2 + 2 No Longer Equals 4', *Financial Times*, 22 February.

28. Don Dufek (1997), 'Essential Elements of ECR', *American Marketing Association Winter Educators' Conference*, St. Petersburg, FL.

29. Richard Tomkins (1996), 'Shares in P&G Slide 4 Per Cent as Sales Slip', *Financial Times*, 25 October.

30. Alan Mitchell (1996), 'P&G Slams Inefficient Marketing', *Marketing Business*, 8 November.

31. Douglas M. Lambert et al. (1996), op. cit.

32. Kathleen M. Eisenhardt and D. Charles Galunic (2000), 'Coevolving: At Last a Way to Make the Synergies Work', *Harvard Business Review*, January/February, 91–101.

33. Karen S. Cravens, Nigel F. Piercy and David W. Cravens (2000), 'Assessing the Performance of Strategic Alliances: Matching Metrics to Strategies', *European Management Journal*, **18** (5), 529–41.

34. Michael Skapinker (1997), 'Codes Can Be Confusing', *Financial Times*, 15 May.

35. William Gordon and Hamish Pringle (2001), *Brand Manners – How to Create a Self-Confident Organization to Live the Brand*, London: Wiley.

36. Frank V. Cespedes (1996), 'Beyond Teamwork: How the Wise Can Synchonize', *Marketing Management*, **5** (1), 25–37.

37. Chad Rubel (1996), 'Partnerships Steer Saturn to a New Marketing Mix', *Marketing News*, 29 January.

CHAPTER 11

Planning marketing:

What do we need to do to get from a strategy to a plan?

HOW DO YOU MAKE GOD LAUGH?

Tell her your plans . . .

Even if we grow an innovative market strategy out of our customer focus and market sensing capabilities, our evaluation of market choices, the development of a value proposition and definition of a strategic position for our business in its market, as well as our evaluation of the underlying relationships on which the strategy is dependent, then we have not finished the strategy job. In almost all organizations we will need to produce a plan.

THE PLAN

In the beginning was The Plan.
And then came the assumptions.
And the assumptions were without form.
And the plan was completely without substance.
And darkness came upon the faces of the workers.
And they did rent their garments and spake unto the
Production Manager, saying 'Yea, it is an unholy crock of s**t
and the stench doth offend us'.

> And the Production Manager went unto the Strategists, saying 'It is a pail of excrement and none may abide its odour.'
> And the Strategists went unto the Business Manager crying unto the heavens, saying 'It is a container of manure, so strong that none here may abide it.'
> And the Business Manager went unto the Director, saying unto him, 'Harken unto me, it is a vessel of fertilizer, and none may abide its strength.'
> And the Director went unto the Vice-President, crying, 'It contains that which aids plant growth, and is very strong.'
> And the Vice-President came before the Senior Vice-President and raising his face before God cried loudly, 'It promoteth growth and it is very powerful – see how we are blessed.'
> And the Senior Vice-President went forward and spake unto the President saying 'Let not your heart be troubled, for this new plan will actively promote the growth and efficiency of the company.'
> And the President looked upon the plan and saw that it was good.
> And lo, the plan became policy . . .

Many people do not like plans, planning or planners. Henry Mintzberg reckons that strategic planning is not strategic thinking, that the goal of those who promote planning is to reduce managers' power over strategy making, and that real strategic change requires inventing new categories not just rearranging old ones[1]. He has a point.

'Strategizing' is the prerequisite, as we saw in Chapter 6, but the trouble is that organizations like written-down plans as well. The companies I work with do not let you do things unless you can put your great strategic ideas into the sort of plan they recognize. This may be stupid, but it is the way things are. It is actually even worse. You are not just going to have to produce a written plan, you are probably going to have to write a plan that looks like everyone else's. This is tedious. However, if you do not produce something that is recognizably a 'plan', as it is understood by your organization, then the chances are that your ideas will be rejected. Regard this as the revenge of the wasters and time-servers in the organization. It is your penance for being a smart ass. Learn to live with it.

'if you do not produce something that is recognizably a "plan", as it is understood by your organization, then the chances are that your ideas will be rejected'

Most companies are terrified of new ideas – in an era of dot.com crashes and failed innovations, this is an even bigger problem than before. Many shout louder about avoiding risk than we can shout about new strategy. You have to make your message palatable.

More positively – if all that creativity, strategizing, innovation and excitement amounts to anything, then it should be turned into a solid business case.

> Never be rude to the alligators,
> until after you have crossed the river.

Mintzberg is right about something else though – planning is a different activity to developing strategy. Gary Hamel goes somewhat further:

'The essential problem in organizations today is a failure to distinguish planning from strategizing. Planning is about programming, not discovering. Planning is for technocrats not dreamers. Giving planners responsibility for creating strategy is like asking a bricklayer to create Michelangelo's Pietà.' [2]

This is stirring stuff for people like me who hate and detest bureaucrats and administrators, but actually Hamel is wrong. Planning can actually be an incredible source of leverage for creating strategic ideas, building momentum for change, and winning people's commitment and enthusiasm for strategic change. (Bricklayers are people too, by the way, and in the building trade probably have some good ideas about strategy, if only we bothered to ask them.) This is about how we manage the process of planning. However, that is the topic for Chapter 13 – concerned with creating plans that build 'ownership' and get driven through to implementation.

'Planning can actually be an incredible source of leverage for creating strategic ideas, building momentum for change, and winning people's commitment and enthusiasm for strategic change'

The goal in this chapter is more modest – we need a structure to articulate our market strategy, to show how we have tested the components of the strategy, and to link the strategy to a marketing programme. This conventional view of marketing planning will provide this final stage in defining our strategic pathway.

A conventional view of marketing planning

Figure 11.1 provides a conventional model of marketing planning. With minor variations, most flow chart models of market-

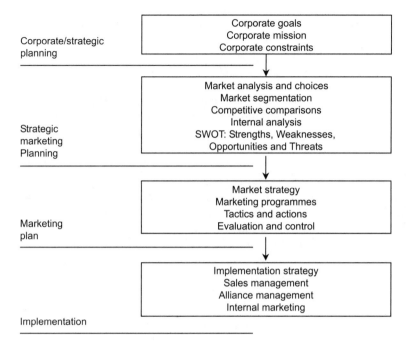

Figure 11.1 Marketing planning

ing planning look something like this. We can put a little flesh on
these bones.

Corporate goals, missions and constraints

Normally, we would expect that the corporate or strategic
planning process (or top management) will define for us what we
are expected to achieve in the specific product market which our
marketing plan is to cover. Ideally, at the start we should have a
clear view of our mission, goals and constraints.

Mission

Corporate mission will either specifically cover our product
market or will show us how to write a market mission for our
specific part of the business (see pp. 442–54). More mundane
parameters should also be defined at the start:

- *Customers* – what type, and which, are to be covered by the
  marketing plan;
- *Products* – which are to be included in the plan and in our view
  of the competitive marketplace;

- *Geographic boundaries* – what are the geographical areas we should include; and
- *Strategic direction* – is this a market where the company wants fast *penetration*, or is prepared to invest for longer-term *development*, or one where we are expected simply to *maintain* the current position, or create a new market position by a *turnaround*, or even one where we are expected to *harvest* what we can get in margins for minimum cost, or to prepare for *divestment?*

'in many practical situations you are likely to find clear guidance here conspicuous by its absence'

In fact, in many practical situations you are likely to find clear guidance here conspicuous by its absence. In the sophisticated multinational branded consumer goods operation and the like – yes, strategic planning will define these things for us. In many situations I suspect, and experience suggests, you will find that Strategic/Corporate Plans either contain nothing other than extended five-year budgets, or they simply do not exist. In that case, these parameters have to be generated within the strategic marketing planning process itself.

Actually, if we see the purpose of marketing planning as getting a match between what we have got and what customers want, and then *doing* it – it makes very little difference if we call it Marketing Planning, or Business Planning, or Strategic Planning, or Business Development, or anything we like really! Lack of formal strategic planning may actually be a great opportunity for us[3]. *Goals* – We would also expect to start marketing planning with some idea of what we are expected to achieve in sales, market share, profitability, cash flow and liquidity, portfolio balance, and so on, in a specified time-frame. It also helps, more than a little, if we know the assumptions that have been made in producing those goals – market growth, new product availability, and so on. As with mission, in the sophisticated, high-technology planning framework, the goals are created for us by the strategic planning process. In many real situations, we have to develop our own goals.

Constraints

'there is some merit in letting our planners know right from the start what they cannot do'

Perhaps less conventional, but equally important, there is some merit in letting our planners know right from the start what they *cannot* do. We need to know what new assumptions are permitted about issues like: personnel, new products and services, changes to the customer base, organizational structure, marketing strategies, new technology, and other critical issues. This is not about being negative, it is about trying to avoid situations where people get excited and produce innovative plans, only to be told about: the 'zero headcount growth' policy; the unacceptability of proposed structural changes; the cancellation of new products; or that certain market strategies are incompatible with 'company policy'.

The foundation for our plan is thus what we are expected to achieve, where and with what, and what we are not able to do. That just leaves the problem of how we are going to achieve the things the company wants.

This sounds incredibly obvious and straightforward – but it isn't. Even if we get management to commit themselves to these issues, there is no guarantee they will not change their minds! The world is full of people who think nothing of moving the goalposts while the game is in progress. But – life is like that. The positive side of this is that if missions and goals are *not* written in tablets of stone, we may be able to go back and renegotiate them when we have seen what we've got, and what the market is doing.

This is the corporate context in which the results of our 'strategizing' have to fit – our market choices, value proposition and key relationship strategies.

Strategic marketing planning

The next, and probably largest, stage in our planning process is review of the marketplace and our resources (normally organized around the marketing mix structure). This suggests that we look at: the market, product policy, pricing policy, distribution policy and communications policy, and pack our proposals about these things together into an integrated plan. The trouble with boxing things off like this is that most of us close each box when we have finished it, and never open it again. One of the points made by William Giles[4], who actually made these things work for real, is that you have to have an iterative approach. In essence, as we go through the stages of the marketing audit, it is vital that we look back at how the new insights change our view of the earlier stages of the analysis. This provides us with the framework into which to fit our market strategy, and to translate it into a marketing programme.

The market audit

The first and probably most time-consuming stage of the strategic audit is the view we take of the marketplace and what makes it work. We have already uncovered the major issues here – market

Table 11.1   The market audit

Focus	Analyse	Objective
Customer needs and buying factors	Customer priorities in the needs to be met through purchase. Customer group differences.	Emphasize customer needs not products, and the differences between potential segments.
Products and customers	Group products by their common need satisfaction characteristics and customers or markets by common characteristics.	Create product and customer definitions reflecting the marketplace, not the technology or the internal operations.
Key products	Identify the key products for each customer group/market, the ones you *have* to have to be a player in this market.	Establish customer group/ market differences in product priorities.
Marketing priorities and critical success factors	Evaluation of most important marketing mix element for each customer group/market and the things the 'winners' get right.	Establish relative effectiveness of marketing mix variables and competitive requirements.
Market segmentation	Product groups and customer types matching.	Define customer-related market segments reflecting differences in *customer* needs.
Company priorities	Compare each match of product and customer to: – potential competitiveness we could achieve; – attractiveness of this business to us.	Isolate areas of high and low priority and niche gaps and opportunities in segments, and the match to our goals and capabilities.
Market sizing and shares	Use emerging segments to value market and its trend, and shares taken by competitors.	Place values on segments to move towards targets.
Life cycle and competitive position	Life cycle stage and competitive position in each segment.	Prioritize market segments and niches.
Competitors	Evaluate: – direct and indirect competition; – enterers and leavers; – major competitors' characteristics.	Identify competitive prospects and our shortfalls.
Marketing environment	Evaluate likely impact of broad changes in markets, law, institutions, technology, etc.	Put planning into the broader content of strategic change in the outside world.

Focus	Analyze	Objective
Market summary	Across the segments, analyse life cycle stage, value, current and required business direction, priority products, marketing mix requirements.	Collate market and competitive positioning.
Market priorities	Across the segments, analyse our market share and sales projections, chances of success, and priorities.	Choose priority market targets.
Critical success factors	What *must* be right to achieve customer priorities.	Specific action list.
Marketing objectives	In priority segments, the key marketing objectives and how they relate to sales and market share.	Isolate major marketing goals, compared to corporate objectives.

segmentation, competitive differentiation, and so on. What we have to do here is systematically evaluate the position on the most critical market issues. A structure for doing this is shown in Table 11.1.

The product audit

We can then focus specifically on product policy issues, and a simplified structure for this is shown in Table 11.2. It is here that

Table 11.2   The product audit

Focus	Analyse	Objective
Competitive performance	In each segment, how well do our products meet customer needs compared to competition?	Identify gaps in matching our products to high priority customer needs.
Product dimensions	For the critical products or customer needs, how well do we perform compared to competitors on the most important dimensions?	Concentrate on strategic differentiating characteristics of products, not just the generic product.
Product lines	For the critical products or customer needs, where do we stand against market standards and where are our specific product gaps and deficiencies.	Develop list of shortfalls and actions to remedy.

we try to get to grips with how well our products meet customer needs, and what the critical product dimensions are from the customer's point of view.

The pricing audit

Closely related to our product positioning is the issue of price compared to competitors, and the critical issue of *value* as it is perceived by the paying customer. Table 11.3 provides a structure for this stage of our analysis.

Table 11.3   The pricing audit

Focus	Analyse	Objective
Product pricing	Within each segment compare our product prices to key competitors, and our price positioning in the segment.	Identify product price positioning.
Market pricing	Within each segment compare our product prices to key competitors, across the segments and for the total market.	Identify market price positioning and relationship with market share.
Price trends	Examine product price index for past and expected future.	Identify risers and fallers.
Value	Compare perceived quality, price position and market share for our company and key competitors.	Break the 'low price = high sales' perception and look for positioning anomalies.
Price levels	For key products, compare our discount structures with key competitors.	Compare our strategy with competitors' and track implications for market share.

The distribution audit

At this stage we look at the distribution and service patterns in the market, and our performance compared to our competitors. A structure for approaching this task is given in Table 11.4.

The marketing communications audit

The goal here is to examine the possibilities and needs for all forms of marketing communications – personal selling, advertising, sales promotion and public relations (see pp. 561–5). We need to

Table 11.4   The distribution audit

Focus	Analyse	Objective
Channels	Map all the channels through which products and services reach the customer, and the amount of market served by each. Look at trends.	Take broad view of channel system and its changes.
Channel services	Identify key service elements of distribution – sales support, technical support, customer service, quality, etc. For each segment evaluate our service performance against key competitors.	Identify gaps in our servicing of the segments.
Channel shares	For key competitors evaluate the proportion of business going through each channel.	Compare our channel strategy to competitors.
Marketing resources	Divide the market geographically or by customer type and compare our coverage in manpower, distributors, sales offices etc. compared to our competitors.	Compare our resourcing to competitors' and relationship to the market shares geographically and by customer type.
Concentration	Within each segment see if the 20:80 rule applies to customer numbers and amount of business done.	Evaluate implications of concentration for our channel strategy.

examine our positioning in the customer's eyes, and to examine the key decision-making units and external influencers who matter, to identify the communications tasks. Messages and media will come out of this. Table 11.5 provides us with a structure for this job.

This is a very sketchy overview of what may be the most revealing and exciting thinking you ever do at the operational level of your company. There is enough here to get started and achieve some major good for your business, but if you want more assistance then go to the marketing planning gurus[5]. There you will find the worksheets, models and analytical techniques.

Remember, the goal here is to test our ideas about market strategy, to put them into the concrete terms that are understood in the company, and to look at the reality of going from the market strategy to the operational marketing plan.

'the goal here is to test our ideas about market strategy, to put them into the concrete terms that are understood in the company, and to look at the reality of going from the market strategy to the operational marketing plan'

Table 11.5   The marketing communications audit

Focus	Analyse	Objective
Brand/corporate positioning	Identify customer perceptions of our company and of our key competitors.	Identify the broad communications tasks.
Decision-making units	Within each market segment, model the DMU, identify the roles played by different people, and the relevant messages and media.	Isolate DMU targets for communication and message.
External influencers	Within each market segment, identify major influence sources and our standing compared to competitors.	Isolate influencer targets for communications and messages required.
Media	Within each segment, identify available media of communication and compare.	Broaden view of communications media.
Media performance	Compare our effectiveness in using each medium and expenditure with key competitors.	Relate effort to market share and areas for development.

Analysis of strengths, weaknesses, opportunities and threats (SWOT)

The conclusions we reach in the marketing audit can be packed into a SWOT analysis. In fact, SWOT analysis can be turned into a very dynamic tool for strategy generation and testing, and we will discuss this in more detail shortly (see pp. 539–47). For the moment, take SWOT as the structure to evaluate the significance of what we have put into the audit.

The marketing plan

There are many ways of formatting a marketing plan: some simple and some complex. Any of the textbooks mentioned above will give you a plan format if you need one. What really matters is that you produce a plan which is comprehensible and credible to your intended audience – company cultures differ wildly on the requirements for written documents of this kind, and you have to adapt to this if you want to be taken seriously. What matters is that you have covered the key issues:

- a summary of the present position in this market;
- if this is an existing market, a forecast of where we are going in this market if we continue with the current strategy (a prognosis);

- our objectives in this market;
- our market strategy – reflecting our key *market choices* – based on our market definition and segmentation, and the market position and attractiveness analysis – our *value proposition* – drawing together our market mission, competitive differentiation and marketing assets – and the *key relationships* to be developed and exploited to drive the strategy;
- the predicted competitive reaction to our strategy;
- our proposed marketing programmes;
- our specific tactics and action plans;
- our financial forecasts.

A framework for addressing these issues is given in Table 11.6. The ultimate in iteration (which really hurts), of course, is that if we get to the last stage – and the financial out-turn is *not* what we want – then we go back to our goals, our marketing audit, and so on . . .

Implementation

Conventionally the production of plans is the end of the process – after all the Action Plan says who should do what. My attitude to this is such that I now urge chief executives to reject out-of-hand, and without right of appeal, *any* plan of *any* kind which does *not* come with a detailed and realistic implementation strategy. It is not enough to produce a great plan and expect other people to go away and make it happen. Implementation is not something we bolt-on at the end of generating strategy – implementation *is* strategy.

'I now urge chief executives to reject out-of-hand, and without right of appeal, any plan of any kind which does not come with a detailed and realistic implementation strategy'

This should be where we are very explicit about issues like the role of sales management in driving the market strategy through to the marketplace, what is needed to manage alliances and partnerships with collaborators and channel members, and the needs for internal marketing to embed the strategy inside the company and make it happen. My views here are now so extreme that we will devote a whole chapter to implementation strategy and internal marketing (Chapter 14).

For the moment it is enough to note that our marketing plan requires an Implementation Strategy that details what *organizational changes* are needed to make the plan happen, what *internal barriers* will have to be crossed, what external relationships have to be managed, and what the real *costs* of these changes are likely to be.

Executives like techniques that give structure to their ideas. About the best technique available for doing that in planning the way we are going to go to market is SWOT analysis.

Table 11.6   The marketing plan

Focus	Analyse	Objective
The present position and prognosis	Current and historical achievements by segment and what will happen to us in this market if we continue as at present.	Provide the context for the plan and quantify the planning gap (what the new plan will achieve over and above what we would get anyway).
Marketing objectives	Specify the volume, market share and market positioning goals to be achieved, to deliver the corporate objectives set.	Translate financial goals into market and customer objectives.
Market strategies	Summarize the key strategies across the market and for each segment. Identifying our market choices, our Value Proposition, and the key relationship aspects of the strategy.	Reduce our ideas to a matrix of market strategies by segment.
Competitive reactions	Evaluate the likely competitive responses to our most visible strategies.	Identify key risks and vulnerabilities, and the need for contingency plans to cope with competitive retaliation.
Marketing programmes	Reduce market strategies to marketing programme requirements in products, prices, distribution and service, and marketing communications.	Identify the programmes needed to make market strategies happen.
Tactics and action plans	Break the segment strategies and programmes into specific lists of tactical actions with responsibilities, timing and cash flows.	Produce detailed action plans.
Evaluation and control	Identify the critical success factors and benchmarks to be monitored to judge progress of the plan, including timing, methods and cost.	Specify the marketing control system.
Financial forecasts	Evaluate the costs and revenue for each segment strategy and its associated tactics over the lifetime of the plan.	Profit and loss accounts by segments, forecasts over the plan period.

Make SWOT analysis work [6]

You should have gathered by now that this is not a 'cook-book' of the latest sophisticated, analytical techniques fresh from the university research laboratory. The *only* analytical technique I will discuss in detail here is SWOT analysis. In fact, in most cases if you use SWOT analysis in the way described below, it may well be the *only* technique you need to start changing the way things are, i.e. getting stuff done, instead of producing beautiful plans which just never get implemented. Now this requires that we do not use SWOT analysis to produce the subjective, meaningful, bland, non-operational, comfortable, biased output it normally gives.

What is SWOT analysis about?

As most people will recognize, SWOT analysis is an incredibly simple, but structured, approach to evaluating a company's strategic position when planning, by identifying the company's strengths and weaknesses and comparing these to opportunities and threats in the market. The major attraction of SWOT analysis is that it is familiar and easily understandable by users, and it provides a good structuring device for sorting out ideas about the future and a company's ability to exploit that future.

However, in practice, the use of this tool has generally become sloppy and unfocused – a classic example perhaps of familiarity breeding contempt! The opportunity comes because the fact that SWOT analysis is frequently done extremely badly does not mean it *has* to be the way the technique is used.

First, however, it should not be forgotten that the reason SWOT analysis has come to be so widely known (and we suggest misused!) is because of its inherent attractions. These are: (a) the technique is simple enough in concept to be immediately and readily accessible to managers – no computer or management scientist is needed; (b) the model can be used without extensive corporate or market information systems – but is flexible enough to incorporate these where appropriate; and (c) SWOT analysis provides us with a device to structure the awkward mixture of quantitative and qualitative information, of familiar and unfamiliar facts, of known and half-known understandings, that characterizes strategic planning.

Experiences with a wide variety of companies and managers suggest that SWOT analysis *can* be made to work, these pay-offs *can* be realized, and real strategic insights *can* be generated and used.

There are a number of very straightforward guidelines to achieve these goals – i.e. we keep the technique because we know how to do it, but we change the rules! The challenge to the reader is to look at how SWOT analysis is used (or neglected) in his/her company's marketing planning and to see whether our guidelines can be made to work.

The 'rules' we propose for using SWOT to produce dynamic results are: (a) focused SWOTs; (b) shared vision; (c) customer orientation; (d) environmental analysis; and (e) structured strategy generation.

Focused SWOTs

'the more carefully we define the area to be evaluated with a SWOT analysis, the more productive the analysis is likely to be'

Experience suggests first that the more carefully we define the area to be evaluated with a SWOT analysis, the more productive the analysis is likely to be. By focusing on a particular issue, and excluding non-relevant material, we can overcome the bland, meaningless generalizations that executives frequently produce if asked to take a global view of their businesses' strengths and weaknesses.

This definition, which should be *rigorously* and *continuously* enforced, has been made effective in analysing issues as diverse as focusing on: a specific *product market* (with parameters defined); a specific *customer segment* in a market; *product policy* in a given market or segment; *pricing policy* in a particular market; *distribution* systems for particular customer groups; *marketing communications* for different customers and members of a defined decision-making unit; and the study of named *competitors* or groups of similar competitors.

The rule we follow is that attention should first be focused on a critical issue to our planning, rather than being global in perspective – because we can always build up the global picture by putting together our focused analyses, and then it will be a better global picture as well. This is a good practical way of getting to grips with some of the issues raised by market definition and market segmentation, that we covered in Chapter 8 (pp. 410–27).

'the very act of focusing starts to highlight major gaps in knowledge and some of the hidden strategic assumptions that managers make'

Apart from anything else, the very act of focusing starts to highlight major gaps in knowledge and some of the hidden strategic assumptions that managers make. For instance, some years ago, in a planning session with a retail bank, to break away from the internal view of a particular market segment, we asked the planners to undertake SWOT analysis for their major competitors. They came back with detailed (and very good) SWOTs of the other retail banks. We asked what about the building societies, the insurance companies, the finance companies. They said that these were not 'serious' players in the 'banking market'! We pointed out that the market was for financial services to solve customer problems, and we started to move slowly towards a totally different conception of where the real competition was coming from – people who do better what matters most to the customer, even if they are not professional, prudent bankers. Their view of the market was swamped by the image of one dominant type of competitor. Flushing out this myth was a major breakthrough. Focus and concentration can have many pay-offs.

Shared visions

Because of its apparent simplicity and ease of communication, we have found SWOT analysis to be an excellent vehicle in working with planning teams or groups of executives. There is little or no barrier created through executives having to learn complex analytical techniques (or succumbing to the temptation to leave it to the 'experts').

We have found that the pay-offs from making SWOT the central focus for group or team planning are numerous: the pooling of ideas and information from a number of sources produces richer results; the SWOT analysis provides a concrete mechanism for expressing team consensus about important issues; and producing a SWOT analysis has the effect of pushing a team towards agreement and flushes out potentially harmful disagreements – indeed, in effect, one can observe managers negotiating the view of the world the company will adopt for its planning. These potential gains arise primarily from participation of diverse interests in planning (see pp. 601–5) – but SWOT analysis provides a mechanism for making participation operational and reaching that potential set of benefits.

'the pay-offs from making SWOT the central focus for group or team planning are numerous'

For example, in the financial services business, another company with which we worked was organized into two semi-autonomous divisions – one serving the retail market and the other the commercial lending market. Undertaking SWOT analysis in joint planning groups proved to be quite literally the first time ever that managers of the two divisions actually found out what their counterparts could do and were doing, and they uncovered many profitable opportunities for collaboration and cross-selling between the divisions – *and* they then did something about them.

Customer orientation

Now we get to the real crunch. The way we can use the SWOT technique in a particularly powerful form is summarized in Figure 11.2. The first requirement is that in evaluating our strengths and weaknesses, we can *only* include those resources or capabilities which would be recognized and valued by the *customer* with whom we are concerned. This helps us to get past the 'motherhood' statements often produced as a list of strengths – service, quality, an established firm, and so on – because we have to define what we believe is *seen* by the customer and is *valued* by him/her.

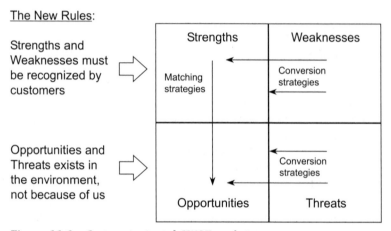

Figure 11.2 Customer-oriented SWOT analysis

For example, our 'great private medical scheme' for employees is *not* a strength for these purposes. It is only relevant if we can say that customers would recognize that we treat our employees well, and this in turn has pay-offs in how they deal with customers and the establishment of long-term relationships. Applying this rule is often a considerable discipline on executives, and in the event of disputes which cannot be resolved about what is a strength and what is not – the joy is that we may actually test our claims with a larger pool of our own people, or even with customers!

'Forcing executives to confront the difference between what they think is important and what customers think is important is a substantial contribution'

Forcing executives to confront the difference between what *they* think is important and what customers think is important is a substantial contribution of this technique. At the end of the day – however unreasonable, irrational, awkward, intolerant, ignorant or plain foolish the 'experts' think customers to be – it is the customers who buy products, not the 'experts'.

In fact, we are, in a very practical way, forcing users of the technique to identify the critical success factors in their business, their customers' needs, and hence factors influencing customer satisfaction. In one company, for example, what executives told us was their strength of 'technical service excellence' turned out to mean to customers that this was a company that sent out Ph.D.-level engineers to *prove* that products had been abused in use, and that warranties did not apply!

Similarly, in working with a secondary retail bank, the key strength identified by banking executives was 'relationship banking', i.e. the availability of skilled, professionally-qualified branch managers to meet and deal personally with customers. This may be true for affluent, high-income customers, but in fact, in the market segments providing critical niches for this company (mainly lower-income consumers and heavy credit users), it was found that the *last* thing such customers normally wanted was frequent meetings with the bank manager. In some ways, the bank's most critical problem was actually to keep the branch managers *away* from the customers!

One problem which regularly emerges is that executives, trying to use the model in this way, claim that the same thing can be listed as a strength *and* a weakness. This is not true, it simply means that we have not gone far enough in our analysis. What we need to do here is to ask the question: which *aspects* of these characteristics are strengths and which are weaknesses? For instance, the commonest 'motherhood' statements might be expanded as shown in Table 11.7.

Table 11.7   Breaking down strengths and weaknesses

'We are an old established firm'

Strengths	*Weaknesses*
Stable suppliers for after-sales	Inflexible
Trustworthy	Old-fashioned
Experienced	No innovation

'We are a large supplier'

Strengths	*Weaknesses*
Comprehensive product range and technical expertise	Bureaucratic
	Offhand with customers
High status/stability reassures customer	No continuity of personal contact

The remaining issue to be addressed is where managers claim that they have a strength (or weakness) which customers do *not* know about and would *not* recognize – but which is too important to leave out of consideration. The easiest way of handling this issue is to include these factors in the list, but to have them boxed-off as 'hidden'. When it comes to the stage of generating strategies, then it is appropriate to consider what would be needed to uncover hidden strengths, if they really are particularly important to the customer and to generating strategies for the future.

Incidentally, for readers who may actually *want* to produce a list of meaningless 'motherhood' statements in their analysis of corporate strengths and weaknesses, we give in Table 11.8 a pro

Table 11.8   A checklist of 'motherhood' strengths statements*

Strengths	Please tick appropriate boxes	Hidden Meanings
High quality	☐	We can't think of any real reason why we do business in this market . . .
Low price	☐	That must explain it . . .
Personal service	☐	We still can't . . .
High value to customers	☐	Our products are a bit expensive, but we still sell some
Old-established firm	☐	We must be OK, we've survived so far
Technologically sophisticated	☐	We know more than the customer
Product strengths	☐	Look at the product, never mind the customer
The 'natural' supplier to this market	☐	We don't know who our competitors are
We are the industry standard	☐	We don't think we have any competition

* This checklist shows some of the most meaningless statements executives have given us to describe their companies' strengths together with our interpretation of their 'hidden meanings'. If the goal of a SWOT analysis is to produce bland, meaningless, non-operational output, the reader can tick off the desired statements (which at least will save some time). Those looking for more useful output from SWOT analysis might prefer to test their own SWOT analysis against this checklist to ensure they are avoiding such traps.

forma of standard 'motherhood' statements of corporate strengths, and the reader has only to tick these off in the boxes provided. Our reasoning is that if the SWOT technique is to be used in this pointless and unproductive way, we can at least save time! If that sounds facetious – it is meant to! The point is that *all* the 'motherhood' statements in this table have been given to us by executives in their planning exercises – which is quite an eye-opener.

Environmental analysis

The same discipline is required to view the opportunities and threats in the environment relevant to our point of focus – the specific market, customer, issue, etc. This turns our attention to the lower half of the model in Figure 11.2.

Here the goal is to list those things in the relevant environment which make it attractive or unattractive to us, and our search for ideas should be as thorough and widely informed as possible. The major difficulty here is that executives tend to jump the gun and put their strategies and tactics down as opportunities – a classic example of self-fulfilling prophesy!

The way out of this trap is the insistence that opportunities and threats exist *only* in the outside world – the things we propose to do about them are our *strategies*. For example, it may be suggested that price-cutting is an opportunity. This is *not* an opportunity in a SWOT analysis – it is a price tactic which we might adopt. We would *only* accept the desirability of price-cutting if, for example, our size gave us greater cost economies than our competitors, and there was an identified, external market opportunity in terms of there being a price-sensitive segment of the market, or the need to meet a competitor's threatened entry to the market with low prices. The rule is that opportunities exist independently of our policies and actions – the actions we plan are our strategies.

> '*The major difficulty here is that executives tend to jump the gun and put their strategies and tactics down as opportunities – a classic example of self-fulfilling prophesy!*'

Structured strategy testing and generation

When we are able to complete all four cells of the SWOT matrix, and we have ranked each item in each category in terms of importance, then the matrix acts automatically as a generator and tester of strategies, as shown in Figure 11.2:

- *Matching strategies* – our central focus is on matching our strengths to opportunities in the outside world. Our logic here is that strengths which do not match any known opportunity are of little immediate value (however proud of them we may be), while highly ranked opportunities for which we have no strengths are food for further thought.
- *Conversion strategies* – more difficult is the design of appropriate responses to highly ranked weaknesses and threats. Here the goal is ideally to convert these factors into strengths and opportunities. In some cases this may be relatively straightforward – a weakness in sales coverage may mean adding to the salesforce, a threat from a competitor may be bought-off by collaboration or merger or neutralized by an advertising campaign, but in other cases we may be unable to think sensibly about converting or neutralizing these factors. In the latter case these factors remain the limiting problems in this business and determine how attractive it is to us.
- *Creative strategies* – finally, we have to recognize that going through this analytical process often simply generates new, creative ideas for how to develop the business. Good ideas should never be discarded simply because they are unusual. Whatever recording we are doing, we should have a box especially for creative ideas that may not fit elsewhere in the model.

Iteration

In this way, the SWOT model gives us a mechanism for structuring and categorizing strategies generated. The final discipline, however, is one of *iteration*. As we identify strategies – to match strengths to opportunities, to uncover hidden strengths, to convert weaknesses, and so on, we should always go back and see how the new situation we are building changes the SWOT model and the broad picture we are painting.

Our output is then ready to be entered into the planning process – for programme building, evaluation, financial appraisal, and ultimately for implementation or action planning.

The challenge

'The guidelines outlined above are incredibly simple to apply, but the disciplines imposed are very severe'

The guidelines outlined above are incredibly simple to apply, but the disciplines imposed are very severe. We know that this approach is effective, and that it turns the SWOT technique into a dynamic and productive tool for strategic audits and strategy generation. Our challenge to the reader is to use the model and the guidelines on his/her own planning and see what happens! Used in this way, SWOT analysis gives us a mechanism for putting ideas about our value proposition and key relationships into tangible form and testing them. It is also a good source of new ideas which can enrich the market strategy.

Incidentally, not for the first time, or the last, I lied to you. The planning stage is not just the receptor for our brilliantly conceived market strategy. It is more likely to be where we share the results of our thinking about market strategy with others, and find that in the cold light of day, some of our ideas are not that great. The planning process provides a ready-made structure for homing in on our strategic assumptions and challenging the most critical. For most of us, this on its own is a tangible step forward.

REALITY CHECK
THE AWKWARD QUESTIONS ABOUT THE PLAN

Do we have a conventional planning framework that we can use to make a sound business case for our market strategy – does it communicate in terms that people understand what it is we want to do, where and how, and does it make financial sense?

Can we show our strategic logic through a systematic marketing audit and SWOT analysis and make it convincing to our colleagues – can we hold our hands on our hearts and say that we have been customer- and environmentally-oriented in how we have evaluated the strategy?

Do we despise ourselves for becoming drones and bureaucrats, or have we learned to live with bureaucracy as a way of getting things accepted in a company?

So, where have we got to?

The goal is that by this stage we have developed a market strategy – we have defined the Strategic Pathway – and we have put those strategic ideas through the sifting process of a strategic marketing audit. The result (we hope) is a customer-focused marketing plan that turns our value proposition into a coherent marketing programme. We should know what we want our company to be about in the market.

However, this is not the end. We turn next to the issues that we have to think about managing in the process of going to market, i.e. to get our market strategy to happen.

Notes and references

1. Henry Mintzberg (1994), 'The Rise and Fall of Strategic Planning', *Harvard Business Review*, January/February, 107–14.
2. Gary Hamel (1996), 'Strategy as Revolution', *Harvard Business Review*, July/August, 69–82.
3. We should perhaps remember, though, the old marketing adage 'there is no such thing as marketing problems only marketing opportunities – unfortunately some of the opportunities may be insoluble!'
4. William Giles (1989), 'Marketing Planning for Maximum Growth', *Marketing Intelligence and Planning*, 7 (3/4), 1–98.
5. William Giles (1989), op. cit. Donald R. Lehmann and Russell S. Winer (1997), *Analysis for Marketing Planning*, 4th ed., New York: McGraw-Hill. Malcolm McDonald (1999), *Marketing Plans*, 4th ed., Oxford: Butterworth-Heinemann.
6. The content of this section draws heavily on two articles by William Giles and me. Much of the creative input to this came from William and his 'Marlow Method' of Marketing Planning. The articles are: Nigel F. Piercy and William Giles (1990), 'Revitalizing and Operationalizing the SWOT Model in Strategic Planning', *University of Wales Business and Economics Review*, 5, 3–10. Nigel F. Piercy and William Giles (1989), 'Making SWOT Analysis Work', *Marketing Intelligence and Planning*, 7 (5), 5–7.

PART IV

The *Real* Issues to Manage in Transforming the Process of Going to Market

CHAPTER 12

Marketing programmes and actions:

But do we ever think our marketing through?

Part I of the book laid down the challenge of focusing on customer value, and Part II added the new and emerging challenges of e-business, totally integrated marketing and creative strategizing. These are the building blocks for market-led strategic change, and our goals in working for a better way of managing the process of going to market. Part III outlined the basic steps in the Strategic Pathway to actually build an effective market strategy. This was all about the content of our market strategy – the things we want to do to transform our process of going to market.

However, Part IV is a bit different. Part IV is about the *context* in which we manage the process of going to market – the processes of decision making involved in developing plans, budgets, implementation strategy, and actions in the market-place. If we are serious about strategic *change* in how our organizations deal with our customers when they go to market, then by the management of these elements of the organizational context for marketing we may be able to achieve some quite dramatic things, i.e. make the market strategy happen. This chapter starts us on this track by looking at what market strategy means in the practical terms of doing things in the marketplace.

Marketing programmes

An overview of the link between our market strategy and actually putting things into effect is shown in Figure 12.1. The theory is remarkably clear – as we have seen from our analysis of market choices, value propositions and key relationships, we build a market strategy which translates into a marketing programme which leads to a market offering. The market responds – with purchases, payment, recommendations to others, and richer customer information. What could be simpler or more straightforward?

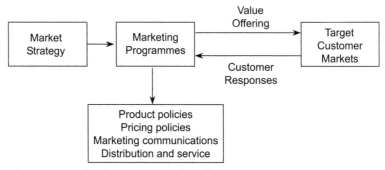

Figure 12.1 Market strategy and marketing programmes

'the translation of our strategy ideas into marketing actions is usually an incredibly weak link in going to market, and we need to test this out'

There is often a major problem here. As we will see shortly, the translation of our strategy ideas into marketing actions is usually an incredibly weak link in going to market, and we need to test this out. It is also worth noting that while the structured marketing programme is a convenient mechanism for *us* in planning and organizing marketing actions, it does not matter one whit to the *customer*. The customer sees only a value offering which he/she evaluates, and probably does not care too much what we go through to produce that value offering. Life is terribly unfair – the reward for neatly and impeccably planning marketing is zero, unless we put together a total package that means superior value to the paying customer.

The structure of the marketing programme shown in Figure 12.1 is the conventional one – the marketing mix, much beloved of every textbook in marketing. I dislike being this conventional. However, we will use the conventional model of the structured marketing programme because it is useful in identifying checklists of the issues to be addressed, and because it is what most companies expect of us – we are almost at the stage where if we cannot recite the elements of the 'marketing mix', no-one will believe we know anything about marketing[1]. In fact, this is the area where it is easiest to acquire expertise and assistance – training, consultants, business graduates, workbooks, computer software, and so on. So, it is enough for us to recognize the main issues here, rather than to cover them all in depth.

Product policies

The principal issues which are usually seen as part of product policy can be summarized as:

- Defining the *product itself*, with its 'bundled-in' services, and its purpose and positioning against the competition.
- Selecting an effective *product mix* to service target markets, including groupings into product lines and ranges that make sense to the customer.
- Creating a *branding policy* that will have meaning and identity for the customer (see pp. 468–80), and to represent our competitive positioning and value proposition, and often also to provide a management focus (e.g. in the form of brand or product management and planning).
- Developing and launching *new products* to meet emerging customer needs, to fill gaps in our product range, or to replace obsolete products.
- Managing *product deletions*, where products are withdrawn from the market.

These are major issues to any organization, and are likely to go way beyond the 'official' remit of many marketing executives (see Chapter 5 if you need convincing). Nonetheless, they are taken as the foundation of the marketing programme – since other marketing policy areas need to be compatible with the reality of the products and services on offer.

A wealth of conceptual and analytical tools exist to support decision making in this area, which we will not open up here, since they are covered in depth in the conventional literature. Examples include: the 'augmented' product model showing the different levels and sources of value which can be offered to the customer (see pp. 460–64); portfolio models to assess the completeness and balance of the product mix; brand management models and planning structures; the product life cycle model, identifying different market conditions and hence effective marketing policies, depending on the stage of life cycle reached; new product development protocols and methods; and product deletion strategies and evaluation techniques.

Pricing policies

The principal issues which make up total pricing policy can be summarized as:

- *Price positioning* in terms of level against competitors and customer expectations (e.g. 'skimming' the market with a high price versus 'penetration' pricing with a low price to gain volume and market share).
- Price *levels and relativities* within the product mix or range, and brand choices we are offering, and the margins created.
- Types and forms of price *discounting* in different customer markets.
- Pricing in different customer *markets*: export versus home; direct sales versus transfers to subsidiaries; bidding versus list prices; key accounts versus general market prices.

'pricing is a "messy" problem, where we have to balance competing internal interests against uncertain and risky external pressures. It is also very high profile – we are exposed to critical scrutiny by customers, competitors, the media, shareholders, and so on'

Generally, it must be said that pricing is a 'messy' problem, where we have to balance competing internal interests against uncertain and risky external pressures. It is also very high profile – we are exposed to critical scrutiny by customers, competitors, the media, shareholders, and so on. Do not be surprised if the CEO is more interested in pricing than any other aspect of the marketing programme.

Perhaps the easiest way of identifying and reconciling the problems in pricing is the model of iteration in Figure 12.2. This is simply a way of recognizing that we have two big sets of shaping factors: the *marketing environment* in the broadest sense, and *organizational factors* – these set the scene and probably set the real limits within which pricing decisions are made. In fact, pricing is worth a little more attention. In many organizations, price is no longer seen as a 'marketing' decision – it is decided higher and elsewhere in the company. This makes price an issue of concern for all managers, not just marketing executives. This was probably one of the first areas where an issue directly impacting on the customer's perception of our value proposition was taken out of the hands of marketing executives in many companies.

PRESSURES FROM THE MARKETING ENVIRONMENT
- Government controls/requests
- City analysis and opinion
- Press and public opinion
- Competitors
- Regulators
- Suppliers and Distributors

PRESSURES FROM WITHIN THE ORGANIZATION
- Corporate goals and controls
- Margin constraints
- Inter-departmental bargaining
- Production capacity
- Costs of administering price changes
- Employee/Trade Union perceptions

Figure 12.2 The messy pricing problem

From a management viewpoint, the process of making the price decision in practice seems to be one of balancing a range of conflicting pressures and trading them off against each other, until we arrive at a price which we can all live with, and which is within the boundaries defined by the marketing environment and the constraints imposed by the organization. This is not a scientific model, but seems to be a good representation of what the pricing problem feels like in practice, and the balancing act that we have to go through.

REALITY CHECK
PRICING FREEDOM?

Consider the price positioning problems faced by a company like British Airways:

- the shareholder pressure is on to maintain margins and rebuild profitability;
- at the same time, operations need you to hit capacity targets by filling seats;

- if you price fares above your competitors, you are accused of 'profiteering' in the media and by your customers, and the regulators ask questions about your market share;
- if you price below your competitors, they run to the European regulator, accusing you of 'predatory pricing' designed to force them out of business;
- if you price high, your employees see this as a signal for higher wages, if you price low, your accountants scream blue murder;
- meantime, travel agents and discounters weaken your control over the price passengers actually pay.

The idea of management's freedom to make strategic pricing choices is increasingly an illusion.

However, the *first* point is that I am constantly astounded and amazed by the predilection of organizations to charge less for their products and services than customers are prepared to pay. In my view, this is called 'giving money away for nothing' – it is what George Cressman has described as 'snatching defeat from the jaws of victory' [2]. Normally it rests on our assumptions that our customers are not just *aware* of competitive prices, but also that they are highly *sensitive* to those prices – hence price determines market share. There is a wealth of evidence that in many markets these assumptions are exactly wrong, and that price is far less significant than we think to how much business we do. Customer value is not determined only by price – see Chapter 3 for the evidence.

This seems to me a fairly neglected issue in many organizations, and one which may offer an excellent start for our market-led strategic change process. Let's talk to the company about what we could do to get *higher* prices, and thus *enhanced margins* for our products through offering superior value to customers in their terms, before we talk about spending more money on marketing! For example, a lot of attention is being given by major companies to 'revenue management' [3], in the sense of looking for opportunities to match high demand with high prices (to enhance margins) and lower demand with lower prices (to gain volume) – such as off-peak travel ticket deals, 'happy hours' in bars, and so on.

This is not as far-fetched as it sounds – it is often amazing what you can find when you put the myths to one side and dig a little deeper into the real price/volume relationship. As they say, people don't look for discounts on Concorde tickets or Porsches.

REALITY CHECK

HIGH PRICES AND MARGINS FROM REINVENTED PRODUCTS

When Gillette launched the Mach3 – the world's first triple-blade razor – they took what many thought was a big gamble. They priced the cartridges 50 per cent above their then-highest price blade, the SensorExcel. In spite of the view of sceptics that they would have to cut prices, they held the price and the Mach3 became the market leader in the US. The secret according to Gillett's CEO is to introduce 'new products that provide benefits people think are worth paying for'. Superior customer value gives the innovator pricing power.

Source: William C. Symonds (1999), '"Build a Better Mousetrap" Is No Claptrap', *Business Week*, 1 February, 47.

A couple of years ago I was working with a well-known computer manufacturer on the problems of developing new marketing strategies for a specific customer market. The executives involved believed that you *had* to price just below IBM, or you would sell nothing. This credo was applied across the board to all their products: the computers (or boxes), software and services. In fact, by the time we finished, their strategy was to *increase* the price of their boxes – because they wanted to be less involved in what was becoming a price-driven commodity market. And to *increase* the price of services, because the service market is growing fast, and service quality is judged by price. The result was, contrary to expectations, they have sold just as many boxes (but at higher margins), *and* consequently have sold more software to be mounted on their machines, *and* have rapidly expanded the services business – indeed, they now earn more revenue from services than selling computers and software.

Shortly afterwards, I did some similar work on strategic marketing planning with a small retail banking company. The target segments they wanted were the conventional banker's 'ideal' market targets – the high net worth individual, the high income individual, the high potential earner, and so on. However, they lacked the image or branch network of the big retail banks, and were thrown back on the conclusion they *had* to compete on price. This is a dangerous conclusion in any business, but perhaps more so in financial services than most. The point is, however, that the amazing thing we found on examining their customer base was that their most profitable type of customer was both highly brand loyal and largely insensitive to price. That most profitable customer was not the high net worth or high income customer – it was secretaries and clerical workers on modest incomes. These consumers apparently prefer a non-glamorous bank, but more significantly: they never use management time, indeed probably never even see a manager; they overdraw every quarter, and so always pay bank charges; they would rather use a cash machine outside than a bank clerk inside the bank; and, if they borrow, they do so on a credit card, at a phenomenally high interest rate.

However, note two things: price is one of the many factors taken into account by the customer; and in neither of these cases was that the message that the company wanted to hear – the computer company loved its computers and the bank wanted to act like NatWest. Nonetheless, these cases simply emphasize that we neglect the realities of pricing at our peril.

'these cases simply emphasize that we neglect the realities of pricing at our peril'

Indeed, one very old game which I still play with some companies, to open up the pricing issue, is that of asking executives to make a snap decision on what they think would improve their bottom line most – a 10 per cent increase in sales, a 10 per cent reduction in costs, or a 10 per cent increase in price? Most executives opt for volume growth or cost-cutting to improve profitability. In fact, however you work the figures the picture will almost inevitably be that price increases give more profit leverage than cost-cutting or selling more. If you try this, you will probably find that the sceptics' response is that this assumes that you can increase price by 10 per cent without losing sales. This brings us back to the real question. *Why not?*

For example, if this intrigues you, consider if any of the following routes to obtaining higher prices may be applicable to your company in one of its markets:

- Is the strength of customer relationship built by the salesforce enough to negotiate higher prices or to build margin protection clauses into contracts?
- Does our value proposition give us enough competitive differentiation that we can get a premium price higher than our competitors?
- Does our segmentation of the market show some types of buyer who are less sensitive to price and where our added value would justify a higher price to the customer?
- Would multiple branding of the product open several price positions in the market instead of just one?
- As we bring new products and new marketing methods to the market, does this give opportunities to skim the market?

Secondly, in most markets the bargain basement is a bad place to be, unless you are really good at doing business that way. Few companies can sustain the very low price position, unless they have a massive cost advantage over their competitors. For example, one of the success stories of the 1980s was the Scottish clothing stores 'What Everyone Wants'. They were the subject of the joke that a shoplifter went on a day-long stealing spree at WEW, and burdened by his haul took a taxi home, only to find the value of his swag was less than the taxi fare. WEW did spectacularly well with rock-bottom clothes prices to meet the needs of the low income customer. By 1997, WEW was in deep trouble and looking to sell off its stores. Plans now centre on transforming WEW into a more upmarket discounter as 'The Store'. However, climbing out of the bargain basement is difficult.

'in most markets the bargain basement is a bad place to be, unless you are really good at doing business that way'

Thirdly, price wars are dangerous and highly contagious. Analysis of the result of price wars in a wide range of industries – computers, mobile phones, air travel, DIY, champagne, electrical goods, cigarettes, newspapers, sports shoes, food retailing, perfume – shows remarkably similar results: margins decline, the weakest companies crash and the product becomes a commodity sold on price only[4]. In 1999, Airbus Industrie, the European civil aircraft consortium, declared losses of £400 million, resulting from contracts won during an intensive price war with Boeing[5]. But the temptations to get into price fights are always there:

- customers may no longer equate low price with low quality as markets become more discerning;
- retailers throughout the world *love* discount sales to shift stock and have some fun;
- over-capacity in an industry is a severe temptation to start price-cutting;
- price may look like a good way for the weaker brands to undermine the brand leader;
- predatory pricing (undercutting competitors to squeeze them out of the business) may be the only response to competition we can think of;
- it makes us look good to everyone if we can say we are reducing prices to increase value to customers.

The harsh reality is that price wars are only likely to be good for you if: customers are highly responsive to prices, your competitors cannot or will not just match your price cuts to restore the status quo in market share, and ultimately you are the lowest-cost

'we should think very carefully before being too aggressive on price, or responding unthinkingly to our competitors' price moves'

producer and can sustain low prices longer than the rest. Otherwise – we should think very carefully before being too aggressive on price, or responding unthinkingly to our competitors' price moves[6].

The *last* point I would make before leaving pricing is that all too often, because they do not have sole control of the pricing decision, marketing executives do not regard price as a marketing variable (they may say they do, because they have read the right books, but they don't really). It may be that price is decided high in the organization, not by the marketing executives. It may be that there are multiple interests to satisfy if we want to change price. On the other hand, it may just be that we are surrounded by *myths* about what prices the market will bear and what they will not, and the real relationship between price and value.

REALITY CHECK
PRICING AN INNOVATION IN VALUE

Strategic pricing for demand creation may be a powerful way to get high volume quickly and establish a market position competitors cannot equal. The Swatch watch transformed the wristwatch from a functional item used to tell the time into a mass-market fashion accessory. The product combined the accurate timepiece with creative designs and emotional appeal. The company's project team had to determine the strategic price for the innovatory product. At the time, cheap, high-precision quartz movement watches from Japan and Hong Kong were dominating the mass market (priced at around $75). The Swatch watch was priced aggressively at $40 – a price at which customers could buy several watches as fashion accessories. The low price left no profit margin available for the Japanese and Hong Kong companies to imitate the Swatch and undercut its price. The Swatch project team worked back from the strategic price to arrive at a target cost, and to design a suitable production system.

Sources: W. Chan Kim and Renee Mauborgne (1999), 'Strategy, Value Innovation and the Knowledge Economy', *Sloan Management Review*, Spring, 41–54. 'The Pioneers of Innovation', *Global Finance*, April 1999, 10.

These factors define the problems of creating and implementing a new pricing policy – they do not change the fact that price is a marketing variable because it is one of the things that matters to customers (but not always in the way that we assume and expect).

The challenge is simple: 'price is how we tell the customer how good we are'. So how good are we telling our customers that we are?

REALITY CHECK

MARRIOTT'S CONCIERGE FLOOR

In the US Marriott hotel chain, in some of the hotels, there is a 'Concierge floor'. The price of a room on the Concierge floor is about $220 compared to about $140 for an ordinary room. For this difference the customer gets: a Concierge lift giving an appearance of security (which is an illusion since all floors are accessible by stairway), but a reality of exclusivity; their 'own' reception desk and staff; 'free' continental breakfasts and coffee; and a room which differs markedly from the standard room in that it contains a bowl of boiled sweets and a TV in the bathroom, but is *identical* in virtually every other respect. You may not be impressed by this, but in my view a 60 per cent price differential buys an awful lot of melon slices, coffee and boiled sweets, and the rest is extra margin. However, to my knowledge, Marriott has never been accused of 'profiteering' or 'ripping off' customers by having a Concierge floor – they are providing an added-value service that one segment of their market is happy to pay for.

We keep coming back to the simple fact that if you offer customers something they value, they will pay you for it, and they do not care what it costs you to provide it. Now let's take pricing policy as a marketing variable and challenge some of the myths!

'if you offer customers something they value, they will pay you for it, and they do not care what it costs you to provide it'

Marketing communications

Probably the most visible and 'glamorous' aspects of the marketing programme are in the area of marketing communications. The key point to make is that however exciting and creative, this is about linking our product and price offer to our customers and nothing else. Creative awards and advertising agency hype notwithstanding, the management problems are: deciding objectives for the communications programme; integrating together the different forms of communication (getting the ad agency and the salesforce doing things

'The key point to make is that however exciting and creative, this is about linking our product and price offer to our customers and nothing else'

even vaguely compatible would be a step in the right direction in many cases); and evaluating in mundane terms like value for money what we are actually getting for our spend on communications (not easy, incidentally, but not impossible).

The communications methods open to us in delivering marketing to the customer can be classified as:

- *Advertising* – using mass media like TV, radio, press, outdoor and transport media to reach large audiences, but also more specialized vehicles like direct mail, exhibitions, trade publications, the Internet, etc., and also including the communications role of product packaging, point-of-sale displays, sales literature, etc., and electronic media (see pp. 165–7).
- *Personal selling* – face-to-face representation by seller to buyer, plus the supporting materials for presentation, display, etc.
- *Sales promotion* – events with short-term objectives, often sharing the same media as advertising, e.g. price cuts, customer competitions and incentives, distributor incentives, 'special offers', collectables, etc.
- *Public relations* – a label greatly abused in practice, but intended to refer to the creation and maintenance of corporate images relevant to different audiences.

Broadly, in each of these areas, the principal issues to be addressed can be summarized as follows:

- Deciding on the *role* of each form of communications in delivering the market strategy to the marketplace, i.e. the target customer. These roles may be quite different, e.g. advertising to the consumer backed by sales efforts aimed at the distributor, but should be compatible.
- Setting *objectives* for each form of communications which represent achieving the role we want it to play. These objectives will have to be set in very different terms. For advertising, objectives may be about altering customer awareness, or changing customer belief about a product. For personal selling, objectives traditionally are more likely to be sales revenue, market coverage and cost-based, although increasingly they are being set in terms of customer relationships. For sales promotion, objectives are likely to be related to specific events, e.g. repeat purchases motivated by collectables, trial rates for new products gained through sampling or special offers, and the like.
- Managing the communications *process*. In advertising and sales promotion this is likely to be about handling relations with external agencies, budgeting, and evaluating the success

of the spend against objectives. In personal selling, this opens up the area of recruitment and selection, training, organization and allocation, remuneration, and evaluation of the field salesforce.

- The *integration* of communications activities. This is not just in deciding what role they should all play but actually arranging it – comparing the messages delivered by sales people to the positioning our advertising is trying to gain, balancing the attractions of short-term gains from a price-cut or special deal with the long-term position we are trying to build for a brand, or simply co-ordinating ad campaigns, sales promotions and sales calls. The goal is what some executives describe simply as getting everyone 'singing from the same song sheet', and it is not easy. For example, consider the equation: 'fantastically effective reduction in stocks held in the channel as a result of continuous replenishment and customer partnering by the salesforce' *plus* 'amazingly effective sales promotion campaign launched by the product manager and the advertising agency' *equals* massive stockouts and unhappy customers.

It may not be very glamorous, but that is about all managers need to know about marketing communications – it is just a means to an end. However, a number of issues behind this are worth bearing in mind.

Most of us are dependent on an advertising agency for creative and media work. This is one of the key relationships we described in Chapter 10. Agency relationships have frequently been problematic[7], but building a relationship of trust and understanding may be an important source of competitive advantage, which should not be underestimated[8]. Nonetheless, agencies still do dumb things – many acclaimed, prize-winning ads fail to deliver value to advertisers, and targeting is often weak, as in the case of small car advertising, still aimed in large part at trendy people in their 20s, in spite of the evidence that three-quarters of all small cars are bought by the over-55s[9]. You need to watch these people.

'many acclaimed, prize-winning ads fail to deliver value to advertisers, and targeting is often weak'

The question of co-ordinating marketing communications has been championed by Don E. Schultz and his 'Integrated Marketing Communications' model[10]. His point is simple – you get the maximum value for money if all your communications come together for the customer in the marketplace to deliver the important message in a consistent and coherent way. However, what he also tells us about in practice is the disintegration of marketing communications, reflecting battles over 'turf' and budget and reward systems that work against integration. He tells us about marketing people working with ad agencies to do one thing, while the sales organization is working with channel members to do something else, and it all sounds terribly familiar. Our value proposition is the vehicle for integrating communications for the elusive 'one sight, one sound' or the 'seamless stream of communication' – so let's just do it that way.

Much attention is also being given to the fragmentation of traditional advertising media (e.g. many more TV channels on cable and satellite), and the creation of new advertising media (from supermarket trolleys to mobile phone messages to the Internet). Some new media are more surprising than others: San Francisco Mexican restaurant owner, Martha Sanchez, could not afford newspaper or TV advertising, so offered free lunches for life to those who would have the restaurant's logo tattooed on their bodies to spread the message; a 1999 Russian rocket took off for the International Space Station with a Pizza Hut logo on its fuselage[11]; Unilever's Comfort Refresh (a clothing and fabric deodorant spray) is advertised in the women's lavatories of pubs and clubs, because that is where you find young females who want to get the smell of cigarette smoke off their clothes[12]. And incredibly, Procter & Gamble is considering moving 80 per cent of its advertising onto the Internet by the mid-2000s[13].

REALITY CHECK
TESTING ALTERNATIVE COMMUNICATION PLANS

An AT&T test of alternative marketing communications plans had the following results:

Plan 1 — spend 70 per cent of budget on advertising and 30 per cent on direct mail.

Result — cost per lead = $200; marketing cost per sale = $6250.

Plan 2 — spend 10 per cent on advertising, 25 per cent on direct mail and 65 per cent on telemarketing.

Result — cost per lead = $67; marketing cost per sale = $444.

Conclusion — trying out new approaches can be critical to profitability.

Source: Adapted from Philip Kotler (2000), 'New Marketing for the New Economy', presented at the *Society for Marketing Advances Conference*, Orlando, FL, November.

However, while there is room for creativity, the fact remains that these advertising media are only a means to an end.

We also have to be realistic enough to recognize that the traditional media of advertising – TV, newspapers, and so on – are rapidly becoming channels of distribution in their own right, in the form of off-page selling and direct response TV advertising. This just helps confuse things further, but then who said life was going to be straightforward? And these are highly important developments for some companies.

Distribution and service policies

Perhaps the 'Cinderella' of marketing for too long was the channels and logistics systems that actually get our products and services into the hands of the paying customer. The problem is that in many instances the control of distribution is located with the operations area, supply chain or distribution management, not with marketing. The trouble with this is that the customer probably does not care too much how we organize it, the customer is typically unreasonable and selfish enough to think that the following is really what distribution is about:

'the "Cinderella" of marketing for too long was the channels and logistics systems that actually get our products and services into the hands of the paying customer'

- Is the product/service available in the outlet *I* want to use, when *I* want to buy it?
- How long do I have to *wait* to get delivery of the product and how *sure* am I it will get here on time?
- Can I get spare parts, maintenance and after-sales service *quickly* and *reliably* and do I *believe* the promises made about spares and maintenance?

In other words, the distribution system, however sophisticated, is about simple service to the customer – and that is why it matters to marketing. The principal *marketing* issues to be addressed in distribution are thus about channels on the one hand and logistics on the other:

- Selecting, motivating and controlling distributors and outlets, although this may sound a trifle optimistic when we look at the realities of retailer and distributor concentration and power in some markets.
- Providing the promise and reality of the delivery and services that the customer wants, through our transportation arrangements, our stockholding, and the location of our warehousing in the marketplace.

'our great products and the excellent value they represent, together with our smart advertising and high-quality selling to the trade, can fall very flat simply because the customer cannot lay hands on the product in the store'

A couple of points should be made before we move on. In many situations, it can be said that our great products and the excellent value they represent, together with our smart advertising and high-quality selling to the trade, can fall very flat simply because the customer cannot lay hands on the product in the store, or get delivery in any sensible time, or we let him/her down because our delivery and service promises are broken.

However, markets change and keeping delivery and services promises may mean we have to change too. In 2000, Avon Cosmetics in the US, after 115 years of 'Avon ladies' selling on the doorstep, took its products into department stores and shopping malls for the first time. Too many of its three million sales representatives worldwide were finding no-one at home, because so many women work away from the home during the day, and many others do not like buying at the door[14].

Strategically the problem is to get our delivery and service lined up with the other elements of marketing, in the market offering made *to* the customer, as it is perceived *by* the customer. This sounds obvious and straightforward but experience suggests that in practice it is not. One of the problems in separating transportation, warehousing, stocking, maintenance and other service issues from marketing is that these people want to do things *their* way, not the *customer's* way.

Tom Peters[15] tells the story of a senior technical manager in a multinational who, to this day, forbids his staff to buy technical equipment from a particular supplier (though it is a superb company that supplies superb products). The reason is that some 10 years earlier when the manager was a departmental executive he bought an instrument from the company and had a small sub-component problem. The supplier sent highly-trained engineers to 'prove' that the sub-component had been abused, so warranties did not apply, and later did not return phone calls, was offensive in correspondence, and so on. The result is the manager's standing order not to buy from that company again. He says: 'I know it's emotional, I know it's irrational, but it's *my money*'. The point I make is not that treating customers shabbily will lose you business – we should know that because it is obvious. The real point is that, 10 years ago, *somewhere* in that instrument supplier, *someone* thought that cracking down on warranty claims was a fine way to save some money, and to build a better bottom line – and s/he was probably rewarded by the organization for doing it.

Again and again you find companies doing things which 'make sense' to them (and they can 'prove' it), but which destroy the long-term value of their brands and the market offering as it is perceived by the customer. The underlying moral is that providing customers with the service levels and types we need in making up the market offering to that customer is likely to cause our transport, warehousing, maintenance and service people to do their jobs worse in *their* terms. This is what the real fight is about. This is why working closer and more effectively with supply chain managers is increasingly a marketing must-do (see pp. 246–50).

It would also be silly to proceed past distribution and communication in marketing without remembering that the Internet gives us a new form of interactive selling, advertising, and distribution and service (see Chapter 4.com) that may change all the rules. It may also substantially increase conflict in the channel as manufacturers and other suppliers bypass traditional distributors – by mid-2001, Dell was not the only large direct seller around; Lego and Mattel offer their entire range online, you can buy a Vauxhall car from the manufacturer's website, and business customers can buy electric motors online direct from ABB[16]. Channel decisions need regular review as a source of competitive advantage through building new and better value for customers.

Direct marketing

In other words, not least of the innovations associated with e-business is the fact that direct marketing channels have become accessible to many more companies – whether as the sole way of doing business (e.g. direct sale of airline tickets by firms like easyJet and Ryanair, or Dell's 'direct business model' for selling computers), or as additional channels for those with established 'bricks and mortar' channels (e.g. Web-based book sales by Waterstones, or home-delivery grocery services by Tesco and Sainsburys). However, direct marketing is broader – for example, it includes direct response TV and print advertising by firms like Daewoo selling cars and Heinz selling food products.

'not least of the innovations associated with e-business is the fact that direct marketing channels have become accessible to many more companies'

Direct marketing has a number of important differences to conventional channels of distribution. For a start, issues of managing distributors, by definition, do not exist, but issues of fulfilment become far more serious (see Chapter 4.com). However, the single most important difference is that direct marketing channels provide a closer customer relationship, with a massive pay-off in information about the customer. Enthusiasts see this as the route to Don Peppers' 'one-to-one marketing', i.e. individualized deals for every customer. This may be somewhat exaggerated if you look at how far this has really got (not very). For example, Sergio Zyman, former advertising VP at Coke, argues that with the fragmentation of the media and increased customer sophistication, mass advertising has lost its ability to move the masses. He believes:

> 'Technology has given people many more options than they had in the past and created a consumer democracy. Everybody has a thousand choices for any product they might want to buy, and there are a million different products competing for their wallets. So marketers increasingly need to find ways to speak to customers individually, or in smaller groups.'[17]

Certainly, recent years have seen the growth of direct marketing approaches: loyalty programmes used to build databases to target consumers; telephone call centres using databases to segment markets as the base for telemarketing campaigns; customer information collected from Internet users being used to target them with new product messages sent by e-mail.

Indeed, some of the impacts of direct marketing strategies and channels are impressive:

- Dell has reinvented the marketplace for selling personal computers, using a direct channel, which provides superior speed of responsiveness to change and greater understanding of customer needs, and which is very difficult for competitors to copy (see pp. 202–5).
- In 2000, DaimlerChrysler announced it was cutting out the middlemen to sell its tiny two-seater Smart city car direct to the consumer through retail outlets in city centres, out-of-town workshops, and Internet sales[18].
- Procter & Gamble have used databases to reach out directly to families with small children in marketing Pampers nappies – individualized birthday cards to babies, reminder letters to parents to move up to the next product size, and so on.
- Nestlé, the Swiss food firm, achieved more than 80 000 membership for its Casa Buitoni Club, increasing purchases of pasta products through a promotional newsletter and recipes in direct communication with the consumer.
- Procter & Gamble have even experimented with the direct marketing of its household products – detergents, toothpaste,

toilet paper, and so on. The direct supply of these products to the home gives the consumer the convenience of home delivery and a good price for bulk purchases, but also takes that consumer out of the marketplace for competitors' products, at least for a while.

Direct marketing is not the answer to every marketing problem; however, it needs to be factored in when we are considering distribution and service choices, and finding new ways to enhance customer value.

Marketing intentions versus market realities

We have covered a lot of ground in attempting to clarify what the substance of going to market is about. Now we reach the stage of testing out which bits matter most to the individual or organization, as part of clarifying what needs to go on our personal agendas for creating market-led strategic change.

The pursuit of market-led strategic change suggests that we are seeking something new. But the issue is whether we have got our marketing 'act' together or not, and what it takes to keep it together. While the marketing programme stuff above gives you the language to 'talk marketing', the next section is the real point of this chapter.

'But the issue is whether we have got our marketing "act" together or not, and what it takes to keep it together'

Getting the marketing act together

One of the major practical problems we face in dealing with this lengthy, overlapping, conflicting, uncertain, messy and complicated set of issues which make up market strategies, marketing programmes and plans, is packing the whole thing together, i.e. creating the 'value offering' that matters to the customer (Figure 12.1). It seems inherent in the nature of the issues we are managing that all too often it goes wrong because we do not succeed in doing this effectively – where effectiveness is judged by the customer not by ourselves.

We may start with grandiose ideas about our missions and our competitive positioning, and how we can achieve these through differentiation and advertising strategy, and the like. However, what matters is the reality of what this turns into in the

'This is about what some have taken as the difference between "intended" and "realized" strategies' marketplace (i.e. what the customer receives, perceives and consequently evaluates).

This is about what some have taken as the difference between 'intended' and 'realized' strategies. Now there is a theoretical argument surrounding this distinction[19], but for present purposes we are dealing with something really very simple:

- *Intended Strategy or Strategic Intent* – what *we* think or want the business to be about in the marketplace.
- *Perceived Strategy or Strategic Reality* – what the business is *actually* about in the marketplace, as it is perceived by the people who run the business, and ultimately as it is perceived by the target customers (the ones we have *lost*, as well as the ones we have gained, incidentally).

Before we set about changing the way we do things, one of the things we should really sort out is where we are now. This is the point of the straightforward strategic gap analysis shown in Figure 12.3 – where we compare our strategic intent (our plans and strategies) to the strategic reality (where we really are in the customer marketplace). In other words, the goal is to evaluate our performance in translating our market strategies into marketing realities in the marketplace. We can do strategic gap analysis to evaluate our present position, before building new strategies and plans, or later as a way of evaluating our success in changing things as well.

For these purposes, strategic intent is what *we* think the business is seen to be doing in the marketplace – the underlying question here is 'for our strategy to be real, what would each part of the marketing programme have to achieve?' – and strategic reality what the people who run the business and the customers tell us the business is *really* about in the marketplace. What we

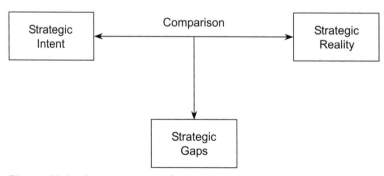

Figure 12.3 Strategic gap analysis

ask is: what is our intention (in the plan or strategy) and what do we actually have, in areas like:

- Our *products and services*, in terms of such issues as quality compared to competitors, fullness of range, image and brand identity compared to alternatives, design attributes, functional features and 'extras', reliability of services, and so on.
- Our *pricing and value proposition*, in terms of the real position in price level against competitors and alternatives (prices customers are quoted and pay rather than published list prices), and how we are seen in 'value for money' terms compared to competitors.
- Our *communications* in terms of the quality and role of our selling efforts and our coverage of the market, the image and awareness created by advertising, the effectiveness of our promotions, and so on, all as compared to our competitors.
- Our *distribution*, in terms of the availability of the product in the marketplace (at the time, in the form, in the place that the customer wants it), the quality of the service provided in terms of waiting time, service provision, maintenance, and so on.
- Our *customer relationships*, in terms of how customers feel about us and how we stand against our competitors.
- Our *strategic positioning*, in terms of the stage of the life cycle our product has reached, the strength of our market position, our success in achieving a differentiation in the customer's eyes, and what we have achieved in customer satisfaction.

The areas you choose will depend on what is most important to your strategy. But bear in mind that on most of these issues we are not looking for sophisticated, research-based quantification to start with – qualitative input in the form of two or three bullet points in each box of the diagnostic is often enough to achieve what we need. More sophisticated inputs can be developed later, if the exercise is paying off for us.

Incidentally, while there is no doubt we are likely to get some useful insights into how well our strategies are translated into reality by completing the analysis *ourselves*, as objectively as possible, and focusing on the strategic gaps which we identify, the real insights come when we ask our *staff* in the field, our *sales and service* people, and our *technical* departments in the company what they believe to be the strategic reality, i.e. let us see what the people who are in touch with the market day-to-day tell us about the reality. There is, of course, only one logical conclusion, which is that ideally we ask our *customers*, and our *distributors*, what is the strategic reality that they perceive in our marketing programme and our strategic positioning. This can be turned into an expensive and sophisticated market research exercise, or it can be much simpler. The point is that the real answer to whether we have got our marketing act together or not can only come from one source – the paying customer. We may have to make do with second best – distributors, sales people, outside experts – but all they are really doing is giving us their views about what matters to the end-paying customer.

There may well be practical difficulties in doing this, but the further you progress down this list of participants in the analysis, the better the results are going to be. With each new set of inputs to understanding the strategic reality as it is perceived by others, we are going to collect new strategic gaps and further ideas for what conclusions we should reach.

> **'With each new set of inputs to understanding the strategic reality as it is perceived by others, we are going to collect new strategic gaps and further ideas'**

There is also a variation which may be useful in applying this diagnostic. We assumed above that our view of strategic intent was both correct and, by implication, fully understood. If we are not completely comfortable with this, we can also test the strategic intent column by asking the same people what the strategic intent was as they understand it, in delivering the strategy to the market. This may well lead us to incorporate in our conclusions quite simply that strategic gaps exist because the key players – like sales people, service staff, distributors, and so on – did not *know* what was required of them in making the strategy happen. In fact, American researchers have suggested that if you really talk to service and distribution employees about their work priorities, it is clear that their *real* mission in most cases is simply to stay out of trouble, i.e. which customers can we ignore and give poor service to, without getting pain from the company? Now compare that to the marketing plan!

The types of issue and question which this process of diagnosis is likely to throw up are:

- Are there serious gaps between what we think the strategy is and what the perceived reality is?
- Why do these strategic gaps exist, what could be done to move the reality closer to the intent; would this be possible and would it pay?
- Are some of the strategic gaps realistically impossible to close, is our strategy hopelessly out of line with our resources and capabilities?
- Where in formulating strategies and planning marketing programmes do we confront the strategic reality as it is

described to us by the salesforce, the distributors, the customer?

- Is the problem one of reformulating the strategy (i.e. moving the intent closer to the reality) or managerial action (i.e. moving the reality closer to the intent)?

I have yet to do this with a company where we concluded there were no important strategic gaps. If done thoroughly this piece of analysis can achieve two major things for us: first, it uncovers how well we translate our market strategies into integrated operational programmes; and second, it forces us to look not just at our goals and creative ideas, but what the operational personnel and the paying customers tell us it really looks like from their point of view. The results can be both revealing and insightful in their own right, but can also push us towards asking how we can actually go about changing and adapting to the realities of the match between our company's capabilities and what matters most in the marketplace.

'The results can be both revealing and insightful in their own right, but can also push us towards asking how we can actually go about changing and adapting to the realities of the match between our company's capabilities and what matters most in the marketplace'

More specifically, the output from this analysis is likely to fall into the following categories which can be handled differently:

- Strategic gaps because the marketing and other departments or functions are poorly integrated – refer to Chapter 5 for some views on this and some tools to close the gap.
- Strategic gaps because line management does not accept the validity of the strategic intent – consider the issue of market sensing and understanding in Chapter 7.
- Strategic gaps because the strategic intent is out of line with corporate capabilities, or they represent aspirations not shared by the people who actually run the business – consider the planning process in Chapter 13.
- Strategic gaps because the marketing programme is not resourced in line with the strategic intent – consider the budgeting problems described in Chapter 13.
- Strategic gaps because there are too many internal barriers to make the strategic intent real – consider the internal market issues in Chapter 14.
- Strategic gaps because when plans and strategic intents were conceived, we did not take the implementation issue seriously – see Chapter 14 on implementation strategy and strategic internal marketing.

REALITY CHECK

AWKWARD QUESTIONS ABOUT MARKETING PROGRAMMES AND ACTIONS

Have we carefully tracked how our market strategy and plan translate into marketing programmes – products, prices, communications, and distribution and service? Have we exploited the full potential of our capabilities in each of these areas to make the strategy real, and also profitable? Are we clear that the strategy comes first and it leads to a programme of action, not the other way round (in spite of what the advertising and salespeople think)?

Have we checked that the progammes and actions linked to our strategy fit together – i.e. are they integrated into a single coherent offer to the customer? Just for once it might be nice if the sales and advertising people were doing something vaguely compatible, wouldn't it?

Have we looked for the strategic gaps – the distance between our strategic intent (what the strategy says we have to be in the customer's eyes) and the strategic reality (where we really stand in the customer's eyes)? Where they exist, do we understand what causes them and what we have to do to reduce them? Does the strategy still make sense when we factor in the costs of filling the strategic gaps, or should we think again?

Our progress so far towards market-led strategic change

Part IV of the book is concerned with confronting the issues that have to be managed to turn our market strategy into reality by delivering superior value to customers. In Part III we saw that market strategy – our strategic pathway – was about a set of complicated and messy issues: customer focus and market sensing, market choices, the value proposition, and the key relationships underpinning the strategy. Inevitably what we found was that the most difficult and uncertain issues are the ones that matter most, because they define what we really have to offer to the customer.

Marketing programmes were defined as the packing together of elements of: product policies, pricing policies, marketing communications, and distribution and service policies. Each of these areas breaks down into a number of sub-components, each with its own technical literature and specialist expertise. For our purposes, however, what matters here is defining a value offering to the customer, which emphasizes the things that matter most to that customer, as described in our market strategy.

However, having unpacked a diverse set of issues, we focused on how well *we* actually put these together to create something of value for the customer – strategic intent versus strategic reality in our marketing and our positioning in the market. Hopefully, this diagnosis will have brought us back to the ground with a bump, after the heady stuff of creativity, new business models, strategizing and strategic pathways!

If we have got anything by now, it is probably a set of issues about changing the way in which our company manages its process of going to market – possibly quite a worrying list in some cases. The next stage is to deal with what we can *do* about that set of issues, and that is the task of the remainder of Part IV of the book, where we examine the key elements of managing the process of going to market, and planning implementation strategy and internal marketing. In short, we have defined the Strategic Pathway in the context of the external market environment (how we understand the market), but for it to become a reality we also need to put it into the context of the internal corporate environment (the operation of critical processes inside the company).

> *'If we have got anything by now, it is probably a set of issues about changing the way in which our company manages its process of going to market – possibly quite a worrying list in some cases'*

Notes and references

1. This is very silly, but reflects the fact that everyone and his uncle has read the books or been on the training courses that preach the importance of the marketing mix.
2. George E. Cressman (1997), 'Snatching Defeat From the Jaws of Victory: Why Do Good Managers Make Bad Pricing Decisions?', *Marketing Management*, Summer, 9–19.
3. Robert Cross (1997), *Hard-Core Tactics for Market Domination*, London: Orion Business Books.
4. David Smith and Matthew Lynn (1993), 'Price Wars', *Sunday Times*, 26 September.
5. Roland Gribben (1999), 'Airbus in £400m Price War Write-Off', *Daily Telegraph*, 17 March.
6. Akshay R. Rao, Mark E. Bergen and Scott David (2000), 'How to Fight a Price War', *Harvard Business Review*, March/April, 107–20.
7. Stephanie Bentley (1996), 'Ad Effectiveness: Measures of Strength', *Marketing Week*, 1 November.

8. Jane Simms (1996), 'Managing the Primal Scream', *Marketing Business*, September, 38–40.
9. Jon Rees (1999), 'Award-Winning Ads Fail to Sell', *Sunday Business*, 22 August.
10. Don E. Schultz and Philip J. Kitchen (2000), *Communicating Globally: An Integrated Marketing Approach*, Chicago: NTC Books.
11. Richard Tomkins (2000), 'Advertising Takes Off', *Financial Times*, 21 July.
12. Richard Tomkins (2000), 'The End of Spin and Grin', *Financial Times*, 2 June.
13. Richard Tomkins (1998), 'Net Ads Fail the Soap Test', *Financial Times*, 28 August. Bruce Horowitz (1998), 'P&G Goal: Conquer Net Advertising Within a Year', *USA Today*, 21 August.
14. Andrew Cave (2000), 'Avon Calls on Big Stores in Makeover Plan', *Daily Telegraph*, 19 September.
15. Tom Peters (1989), *Thriving on Chaos – Handbook for a Management Revolution*, London: Pan Books.
16. David Bowen (2001), 'How to Use the Web as a Recession-Busting Tool', *Financial Times*, 18 January.
17. Sergio Zyman (2000), *The End of Marketing As We Know It*, New York: Harper Collins.
18. Ray Hutton (2000), 'Smart Car Cuts Out the Dealer', *Sunday Times*, 20 August.
19. Henry Mintzberg (1997), 'Opening Up the Definition of Strategy', in Henry Mintzberg and J. Brian Quinn (eds), *The Strategy Process*, 2nd ed., London: Pearson.

CHAPTER 13

Marketing planning and budgeting processes:

How do we create plans with 'ownership' and get the resources we need to make things happen?

The focus of this chapter is managing processes to plan, resource and improve our chances of successfully implementing new strategies in the way we go to market.

Managing the process – marketing planning

Earlier we looked at marketing planning as the framework into which we fit our market strategy, to test it and to communicate it (Chapter 11). However, the aim of this chapter is to look at the planning *process* as a powerful source of leverage for working on achieving market-led strategic change, and actually making market strategy and marketing programmes *happen*. This suggests that we need to look at planning in a rather different light to that shone in traditional marketing approaches.

Many authorities, in textbooks and in training courses, discuss the process of planning as an orderly sequence of steps, in applying rational-analytical techniques to developing market strategies and marketing programmes (see pp. 528–31 for just such a model). Their attention is focused on techniques of analysis, of ever-increasing sophistication, and outputs of carefully-constructed strategic and operational marketing plans, produced to standardized formats with carefully balanced figurework.

Issues like corporate culture, management style, information flows, organizational structures, participation and the like are treated either as facilitating mechanisms or as mere 'context', set aside as trivial, compared to the real business of complex analysis and plan-writing. This approach completely misses the main point. The underlying truth is that these issues are not mere context, they *are* the process.

'The process of planning is significant because the way we design and manage the process will have a direct impact on what goes into the plan, and even more to the point, whether anything useful ever happens as the result of planning'

The *process* of planning is significant because the way we design and manage the process will have a direct impact on what goes into the plan, and even more to the point, whether anything useful ever *happens* as the result of planning. Apart from anything else, it is one of the few chances we have to do something constructive to move the company's culture closer to our market strategy, rather than vice versa. Indeed, it is becoming clear that what a managed planning process offers us is a mechanism to put a handle on organizational development, because the planning process is another form of organizational 'learning' and adaptation (see pp. 347–60). Our goal here is to guide that organizational development and learning towards our market-led goals.

This is a vital point to grasp, because it leads us to a management agenda which *really* matters – *managing* the planning process to get the *results* we want in the customer market. The trouble is that it is precisely this agenda which is normally totally *ignored*.

'There are no real rewards for beautifully designed planning systems incorporating the latest computerized models. The rewards come from getting our marketing act together and getting people excited and motivated enough to drive the market strategy and do the things that matter to customers'

My firm belief is that the most important and productive thing to focus on in planning is not the techniques and formal methods, it is quite simply commitment and 'ownership'. It is a hard life. There are no real rewards for beautifully designed planning systems incorporating the latest computerized models. The rewards come from getting our marketing act together and getting people *excited* and *motivated* enough to drive the market strategy and *do* the things that matter to customers in the marketplace. That is, after all, the only source of real rewards.

Professional planners often object to this view of things. This is understandable – these people love their computer spreadsheets, their planning manuals, their analytical techniques, their 'expert systems', and all the other trappings of formal planning systems. In truth there is nothing wrong with these things – as long as we remember at all times that the goal is to deliver effective market strategies to the paying customer, not just to produce clever plans which never happen. The credo of market-led strategic change should be that we will *not* tolerate the SPOTS syndrome here (Strategic Plan On The Shelf)!

Managing the process – budgeting and resource allocation

Managing planning as a process to create and reinforce market-led strategic change is important. But there is a second area of process that we have to consider, which is directly linked to planning. This is the process of *budgeting*, or *resource allocation* for marketing.

Now if you look at the conventional textbook on marketing, then you will find that budgeting is treated as a very minor issue – a technical exercise of computation to calculate the optimum marketing spend. This is fairly tedious stuff, and accordingly we delegate it to people we don't like and computerize it at the first opportunity. This is not a strategic question. This is stupid. There are few things of more strategic importance than getting the resources you need to do things.

'There are few things of more strategic importance than getting the resources you need to do things'

Indeed, if you talk to marketing executives about budgeting and resource allocation, they normally have a somewhat different view. They talk about issues like these:

- the *'hassle factor'* – the sheer difficulty and inordinate amount of time it takes to get resources, in terms of the papers to be written, the committees to be attended, the bargaining to be done, to get even minor amounts of resources;
- the absolute *refusal* of some organizations to provide resources for anything called 'marketing' let alone something like 'the process of going to market' (yes, I do mean it, even in this day and age);
- the *conflict* over marketing expenditure with accountants and general management;
- the *lack of control* by marketing executives over resource allocation and actually spending the money;
- the *struggle for jurisdiction* over marketing expenditures;

- the dead-weight of *historical views* over how much should be spent on marketing;
- the imposition of *rigid control measures*, that link marketing spend to sales, with the interesting effect that when times get hard and we lose sales and market share, we automatically spend *less* on marketing at precisely that moment when we need to spend *more*;
- the pressure to prove the value of marketing to meet the criteria of *accountability,* which grew up in the recession of the early 1990s;
- the growth of a corporate ethos of being lean, downsizing and '*do more for less*';
- as the process of going to market becomes a *pan-company responsibility* (see Chapter 5), the strength of the marketing budget centre diminishes and responsibility for expenditure becomes unclear;
- *outside interests* drive the company's expenditure in marketing, instead of the market strategy – distributors dictate margins and demand co-marketing deals; suppliers demand partnership and influence over marketing resource use; collaboration strategies eat into marketing resources for internal co-ordination needs.

This is just a little different to the neat set of budgeting techniques that we are given by the textbook, but this is the reality that our marketing executives experience. Now, let's talk about marketing budgeting for real! There can surely be few things more futile and damaging than to get people excited about new plans and innovative market strategies, and then to refuse to resource these plans and strategies.

No – that does *not* mean we expect everything that the marketing department wants to be resourced without question. However, it would be nice if the ground rules were clear from the start, and they were applied consistently.

I will admit that budgeting is one of the things that I am prepared to get nasty about. My advice to those who produce market strategy proposals and plans now is to include 'contingencies'. What this means is that when you go to top management and show them all the great things they can have (sales, market share, customer satisfaction, profit), which is what they said they wanted, and then you show them what it will cost – the two things are *directly* and *explicitly* linked. We have to deliver the message – you cannot have the bag of sweeties, without paying the penny (sorry, but life is like that). If you only want to pay a halfpenny, then you get half the sweeties (or perhaps less).

It sounds silly but expecting market strategy to happen, without resourcing, is not very smart. However, if you stand back and look at what happens in companies, all too often this seems to be exactly what management expects. Sometimes it seems to work too – real champions for the customer cause may well make it happen regardless. This said, if a company does not have a 'marketing budget', will not resource the market strategies it has asked for, and generally makes life difficult on resources – this is a pretty clear signal about real attitudes towards the process of going to market and ultimately towards customers. The second part of this chapter will look at some of the harsher aspects of the *process* of budgeting for marketing.

So what goes wrong with planning?

On the face of things planning seems to offer us just what we have always said we wanted – a way to pursue market-led strategic change, to get our marketing act together, and to give the customer what s/he most values. This is, indeed, the potential. What is equally apparent is that there seem to be a few organizational barriers in the way of realizing that potential.

For a start, research studies throughout the world[1] have long suggested that all is not well with the practice of marketing planning. These studies reveal: that managers see planning as a failure; that planning has been fully adopted by very few British and European companies anyway; that many so-called plans have little or no strategic content and are little more than financial budgets; that there are many managerial objections to doing planning, and that it is widely in 'disrepute' with managers. Since these studies span almost two decades, there may be an issue here! On a far less systematic basis than these studies, over the last couple of years, we have been testing some of these problems out with the companies and managers with which we work. What we have found makes interesting reading.

The benefits of planning

If you look at the sorts of problems that managers describe in their lives – coping with too many different products and markets, missed opportunities, wasted selling efforts, lack of co-ordination in marketing and sales or integration with production and other departments, plans which are budgets not strategic, lack of focus and mission, no sensitivity to customer requirements, and so on – then planning should be a gift from heaven because it helps us sort out just these problems.

So, we trot happily in to see the managers and tell them about what plans can do for them and the hidden benefits of a systematic planning process. However, when we do this, rather than going down on their knees in eternal gratitude as they should, the reaction of managers to the idea of planning seems more associated with comments like:

- We never needed it *before*, so why do we need it *now?*
- Planning takes too much *time* and it *kills* initiative!
- Plans are *inflexible, inaccurate,* and nobody *uses* them anyway!
- Planning is a meaningless, pointless *ritual!*

In fact, much of our current understanding of the real problems of effectively implementing and operating strategic planning in organizations comes from the responses made by groups of executives in planning workshops, and the like, to two wholly naive questions that we have asked: 'What do you want your planning process to achieve for your company?' and 'What goes wrong with marketing planning in your company?'[2].

So, what do you want from planning?

Broadly, the answers from managers to this simple question are as follows:

- *A good plan* – perhaps a largely predictable response, but one which generally refers to plans which are achievable, action-able and capable of being implemented, rather than to technical, analytical sophistication.
- *The creation of teams and the 'ownership' of output* – there is a recurring comment that plans which are not 'owned' by teams of executives are unlikely to gain implementation, even if they are formally approved and accepted by the company. There is widespread concern that planning should achieve commit-ment among executives to 'making it happen', even if this is at the expense of rigour, sophistication and innovation in the planning process itself. Various executives suggested to us in different ways that 'second-rate plans which *happen* are better than first-rate plans which sit on-the-shelf'.

- *Developing a continuous process* – while executives typically do not want to spend more time planning, they *do* want planning to operate continuously, and not to be a 'once-a-year ritual'. We found some disillusionment with planning, paradoxically not just because it consumes managerial time and resources which could otherwise be devoted to 'running the business', but because planning does not become *part* of 'running the business'.

- *Identifying real information needs* – in situations varying from executives experiencing what amounts to technology-led information overload, to those where little real market information existed, executives saw an advantage of planning as a way of isolating and identifying their *real* information needs.

- *Understanding strategy and shaking dogma* – executives often find the concept of market strategy unfamiliar and uncomfortable, but more appositely, quite frequently do not understand what their own company's market strategies *are*, let alone their rationale, and suggested that they had what amounts to culturally based 'dogma' rather than genuine market strategies for the future. Contrary to any expectation that executives want planning to reinforce the existing culture, we were often told that this was a problem, and executives wanted to find ways of shaking and testing the beliefs and values of their culture. This was expressed by one manager as being able to 'think the unthinkable' and even allowed to 'say the unsayable', without the ceiling falling in, when developing and planning new market strategies.

So on the face of things anyway, managers seem to want quite surprisingly reasonable things from planning. This leads directly to our second naive question.

So, why don't you just do it? [3]

Perhaps the most outstanding characteristic of the responses to our second question, about what goes wrong with planning in practice, was that on no occasion that we have recorded did executives complain to us of the lack of either formal planning techniques, computerized models, or statistical information systems. The perceived gap is not scientific planning methodology. Rather, the planning pitfalls executives perceive appear to be in the following areas:

- *Analysis instead of planning* – executives have told us frequently that they see planning as bogged down

'on no occasion that we have recorded did executives complain to us of the lack of either formal planning techniques, computerized models, or statistical information systems'

with analytical techniques and models which are far removed from the realities they perceive, and which do not lead to actionable plans. We spend our time building models, not making plans that someone can take away and do.

- *Information instead of decision* – in similar vein executives have described planning disintegrating into constant demands for more and better information. Some are cynical enough to suggest that the reason for this is that it is easier than making decisions. This too is associated with considerable difficulty in producing an actionable plan from the planning process.

- *Incrementalism* – at its simplest executives have described to us many situations where the primary determinant of a plan is quite simply the previous plan, or at least the previous budget. The planning task then denigrates into negotiating and arguing about minor departures from the previous year, rather than creating new strategies.

- *Vested interests rule* – executives suggest that the powerful in the company exert undue influence over plans, to protect budgets and headcounts, to build empires, and so on. Many manifestations of this were cited: refusal by key players to participate in planning, followed by a rejection of plans by those same players on the grounds of lack of consultation; blockages in the availability of important internal information to planners; sidetracking disputes about jurisdiction and minor company rules and policies; outright, dogged argument against anything which changes the status quo; 'politicking', bargaining and 'horse-trading' outside planning meetings to divert plans from going in unwelcome directions; and so on.

- *Organizational 'mind-set'* – many executives have suggested that conventional planning processes are by definition inward-looking and bounded by 'the way we do things here'. So, they never produce anything new.

- *Resistance to change* – some executives have suggested that strategic change emanating from the Marketing Department is seen as threatening – or even 'unreasonable' – and is often successfully resisted by other departments and organizational interest groups.

- *No 'ownership' or commitment* – it seems in many cases plans are produced (often by staff planners) and accepted by management, but in the absence of 'champions' determined to make them work, nothing ever happens as a result of the planning effort. Plans produced by central planners like 'rabbits out of a hat' seem to do little other than irritate line managers.

- *No resourcing* – executives have pointed out many resource-related pitfalls: the simple refusal by management to provide resources; the rejection of plans with the comment that they are unrealistic because it should have been known all along that resources would not be released; and perhaps the most threatening outcome being approval and acceptance by management of the plan, but rejection of the accompanying resource request (see pp. 614–18).

- *No implementation* – we have received bitter complaints about situations where planning absorbed resources and management time, and even created excitement and support for change, but led to nothing more than a report on a shelf, which was never effectively actioned.
- *Diminishing effort and interest* – largely as a result of lack of resourcing and implementation, executives point out that if planning is to be no more than an annual ritual and managers perceive this, then it is hardly surprising that efforts and interest diminish over time. It becomes a self-fulfilling prophesy that planning is a waste of time[4].

The point is that if you look at what managers say they *want* from planning, and the reasons why it goes *wrong* – there is almost no mention of wanting more sophisticated planning techniques and systems.

Now, the trouble with this is that what we really know a lot about is the techniques and the systems. If you look at the conventional marketing planning textbooks, planning manuals, briefcase planning systems, consultancy advice, management training, and all the rest of it – they are obsessed with model building and computer systems, and analytical techniques. In contrast to this, what managers seem to be telling us is that we are all missing the point about what really matters in making planning effective as far as they and their companies are concerned.

'what managers seem to be telling us is that we are all missing the point about what really matters in making planning effective as far as they and their companies are concerned'

So, we have started to rethink how we work on planning with companies, and have developed an approach which is about *managing* the planning *process*, not just the techniques of planning.

Managing all the dimensions of planning

A multidimensional model of planning

The way we present the planning process to companies now is summarized in Figure 13.1. We suggest that there are at least

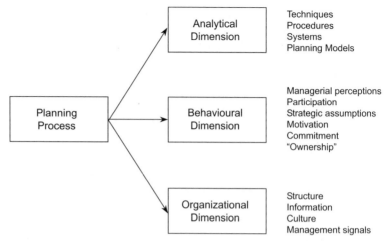

Figure 13.1 A multi-dimensional model of marketing planning

three dimensions of the planning process, and if we are in any way serious about *managing* planning then we have to address all three of these process dimensions, and the consistency between them.

Analytical planning dimension

There is no doubt that to produce effective plans we need the tools for the job – the *techniques* to analyse our problems and opportunities and identify the solutions and strategies; the formal *procedures* and systems to organize our planning and make it part of running the business; a *structure* for our planning to make it comprehensive and manageable; *iteration* to make our planning dynamic and thorough; and a *written plan* as the output capturing our ideas and strategies as a basis for communicating them. I have no quarrel with this element of the planning process, with but two provisos:

- *First proviso*: let us not delude ourselves that this is *all* that planning is about, because then we end up believing that if we can just formalize planning enough and train people in more sophisticated techniques of planning (or perhaps hire 'professional planners' who have this expertise already), then we will improve our performance. There is abundant evidence that it is not enough.
- *Second proviso*: let us be wary of the trap of creating a planning bureaucracy that actually gets in the way of *doing* things. At

the risk of being repetitive, it must be said again, there are no brownie points in the real world for smart, clever, formal plans, until and unless they lead us to effective action in the customer market – which we have already said amounts to no more than being best at what matters most to that customer. Indeed, some of the most exciting and effective planning exercises I have run with managers have been conducted wholly outside their companies' formal, sophisticated, inflexible, inward-looking but legitimate planning systems (see pp. 606–8). At the end of the day, a bunch of dedicated people who care about a problem enough to generate a strategy, and then to go away and do it, cuts more ice in the real world.

However, we do have a couple of problems here. To begin with it is the analytical dimension of planning that we know a lot about – we can train people in financial investment appraisal, the Boston matrix, Porter's structural analysis, PIMS analysis, Business Position Assessment, and other similar models, marketing research techniques, spreadsheets and databases, and all the other paraphernalia; we can design planning schedules and systems; we can write company planning manuals, and so on. We know a lot about these things. The only trouble is that it can all be pointless (and sometimes positively harmful) unless we also sort out the problems that people have in doing planning, and the real attitude of the organization towards the planning.

Behavioural planning dimension

Process means *how* we do things as well as *what* we do. How we do things leads us straight to the problems that our *people* have in building and using marketing plans. The type of issues we have to sort out here have very little to do with formal planning techniques – *managerial perceptions* of planning and the uncertainties they are expected to confront in planning; *participation* levels and types in the planning groups and teams, and managers' attitudes towards this; the hidden *strategic assumptions* that managers make (and believe) about what the company can and should do, and what drives the market; the *motivation* (or otherwise) to make planning effective; the *commitment* to strategic change, or the preference for the status quo; and the '*ownership*' by individuals of the problem of making things happen, without which it is unlikely that too much will ever happen as a result of planning.

'Process means how we do things as well as what we do. How we do things leads us straight to the problems that our people have in building and using marketing plans'

The sad truth is that we know that these things matter, but most of us ignore them when we set up and try to manage our marketing planning.

Organizational planning dimension

Ultimately all of this has to be seen in the context of the organization itself – the *organizational structure*, with all that this means in terms of formal responsibilities, vested interests and power to get things done or stop things happening; the *information* issue, and the problems of access and control of information, the inadequacies, the politics; the *culture* of the organization – 'the way we do things here' – and all the sub-cultures in different parts of the organization; the *management signals* that tell us about the real attitudes and beliefs of management, rather than the lip-service (and if we persist in telling line managers that planning is the number one top priority, but could they do it on Sundays, please, because we are not going to give them any other time or resources, then the signal about real priorities is patently obvious, and we should not be surprised if managers understand it, even if we don't); the existence and direction of *mission and vision* in how the organization is run; and the *hidden norms and values* that really determine what people do in the organization.

'We may not know too much about managing people in planning, but we know even less about matching formal planning to organizational attributes of this kind'

We may not know too much about managing people in planning, but we know even less about matching formal planning to organizational attributes of this kind.

'we know most about what matters least in planning (the analytical techniques and formal systems), and we know least about what matters most (the behavioural and organizational dimensions)'

The conclusion to which I am drawn by examining the literature of planning, by analysing how we train executives in planning, and most of all by studying the practices that I have observed in companies, is that we know *most* about what matters *least* in planning (the analytical techniques and formal systems), and we know *least* about what matters *most* (the behavioural and organizational dimensions), and that we have not even recognized yet the underlying problem of managing these dimensions of planning to give a *consistent*, managed planning process.

Some research evidence

We have done some research to try and substantiate the existence and significance of these hidden dimensions of the planning process. The research was among approximately 200 medium and large UK companies – companies where there is some form of planning (so you would expect them to be above averagely effective in getting the planning act together).

A technical write-up is available elsewhere[5], but the basic question we sought to answer was: 'what predicts the credibility and utilization of marketing plans?' So, the issue is whether we produce plans that people believe in, and use, to run the business. The predictors of plan credibility and utilization that we found in the study were as follows.

Formalization and planning techniques

It was not what we were trying to prove, but nonetheless the degree to which planning was formally organized and documented, and the more that analytical techniques were brought to bear, the higher the credibility and use of the plan (particularly the credibility, incidentally). Actually, this does make sense if you look at what people mean by keeping planning 'informal' – we don't really do *any* planning; we do things the way we always have done them; planning is for chief executives behind closed doors, not the riff-raff out in the field; we pretend to plan, but never let it get in the way of ad hoc, short-term reaction to events as they happen day-to-day; and so on.

'Planning thoroughness'

This factor was to do with three things: whether planning drew on experience and knowledge from all parts of the organization (or the degree to which it did); whether the planning activity was seen to be adequately resourced in time and money; and whether people believed that good planning performance was rewarded in the same way that good operational performance was. So this is really about consultation/participation, and the signals sent by the company to say whether planning is important (or not).

Avoidance of behavioural planning problems

We used a large number of attitude and belief measurements to identify a number of behavioural planning problems at the individual level:

- *Planning recalcitrance* – characterized by people believing that planning was a bore and a ritual, and that it was disorganized, with executives mainly picking on the weaknesses in plans and being easily side-tracked into short-term operational issues.

- *Fear of uncertainty in planning* – executives are seen to resist long-term commitments and to be uncomfortable with long-range forecasting, and so emphasize the present not the future. People resist learning and change, and desperately seek a 'rational' decision-making technique, that will make the decisions for them and take the discomfort away.
- *Political interests* – people see planning as dominated by the vested interests in the company, leading to planning becoming bidding and bargaining for resources, with information sharing precluded and much 'padding' in forecasts and estimates.
- *Planning avoidance* – people are seen to 'go through the motions' in planning, to give compliance not commitment, so nothing gets challenged because planning is about avoiding responsibility for doing anything.

It must be said, when we have presented this material to managers in company workshops, it is normally the behavioural planning problems which start the heads nodding in agreement, and the accusing fingers pointing!

Organizational signals

This was a measure of a number of factors to do with the company's attitude towards strategic planning, towards marketing, and the customer philosophy of management (or lack of it), as perceived by the people who do the planning.

These would seem to be the things that are associated with marketing plans that are credible and actually used. Where this had led us is towards a somewhat different agenda to be addressed in managing planning.

The real management agenda

If we are at all serious about putting a handle on the planning process, so we can use it to unleash our company's potential for market-led strategic change, then the real agenda to be addressed has at least four parts:

- *Techniques and formalization* – It is clear that if we want plans to be credible (the first stage in getting them implemented), then we need to provide a formal system and the appropriate techniques. This seems to be for two reasons – it shows people we are serious about planning how we go to market, and it gives executives the tools to do the job. This is necessary but not sufficient, however.

- *Behavioural issues* – The critical issues here are the *managerial perceptions* of the planning process, with all that this means in terms of their *motivation* to make planning work effectively, and their *commitment* to planning. The variables to be managed here are *training* for the planning job, designing *participation* from a motivational and political viewpoint, and what *signals* managers send about planning.
- *Organizational issues* – The critical question is the degree to which the organization is seen to be, and believed to be, *supportive* of the planning effort. Part of the way into this is the *example* set by senior management, the *resourcing* of planning and the *rewards* of all kinds for good performance in planning. Ultimately, these things are important as they impact on *planning credibility* in the organization, and reflect the surrounding issues of culture, organizational structure and information systems, and so on.
- *Consistency* – While just recognizing the questions above is a great step forward, we also have to think about how we manage the planning process dimensions consistently with each other.

To get to grips with what this may mean, consider some of the conclusions reached by William Giles[6]. William suggested that if we look at what companies achieve in their planning in terms of the sophistication of strategies and plans on the one hand and the ownership and implementation of strategies on the other, we get the picture shown in Figure 13.2 with four scenarios:

'look at what companies achieve in their planning in terms of the sophistication of strategies and plans on the one hand and the ownership and implementation of strategies on the other'

- *Cavaliers – low ownership and weak strategy.* Planning is an annual ritual for the satisfaction of senior management. The documentation is often thick and glossy, full of internal budgets and lengthy 'to do' lists that demonstrate frenetic activity. The whole process may even be delegated to a junior member of staff and rubber stamped by senior management later.
- *Pundits – good planning but low ownership.* Many organizations inadvertently end up here. Planning is done by experts and not shared by those who will eventually implement them. Specialist planning departments are recruited to do the job that really belongs to line management. Strategic decisions become the prerogative of the planners. The plan appears to bear little resemblance to the cut and thrust of real life. It is hard to judge its strategic quality since it is never really put to the test of implementation.

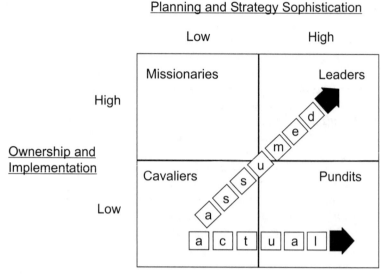

Figure 13.2 Planning sophistication versus ownership

- *Missionaries – ownership high and strategy improving.* The organization is really beginning to move in the right direction. Irrespective of the strength of the strategy, implementation is in full swing. The entire organization knows where it is heading. However, few organizations reach this stage because their preoccupation with improving strategy leads them inevitably towards the ivory tower of the 'Pundits'. 'Missionaries' are in a transient stage. Once ownership has taken root, it is far easier to improve strategy sophistication subsequently without impairing implementation. 'Missionaries' are only a short step from the 'Leaders' position.
- *Leaders – strategy sophisticated and ownership high.* This is where all companies would like to believe they are positioned. In reality, few are. These companies are typified by sustainable market strategies that are well understood by the implementers who have played their part in fashioning them. Departmental and functional boundaries have broken down. People work together in interdepartmental teams that focus firmly on the customer for the good of the entire organization. These organizations are exerting significant influence on their customers and competitors.

If the position of your company on this model is undesirable, then we are back to the question – how do we change? William Giles argued that all organizations start as 'Cavaliers', and in the quest for improvement, the natural progression for most com-

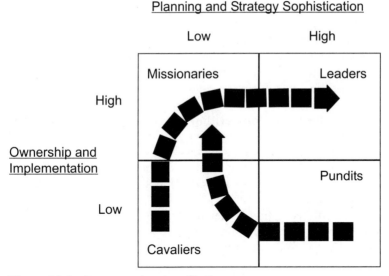

Figure 13.3 Routes to planning effectiveness

panies has been to invest more in the quality and sophistication of planning. This has been accompanied by the assumption that the organization will automatically become a 'Leader'. In reality, organizations move further down the 'Pundits' cul-de-sac, since nothing like the same energy is devoted to ownership issues. The result is the difference between assumed and actual progress shown in Figure 13.3.

William Giles made four observations, which are worth noting:

- *Better planning does not automatically lead to better implementation.* Increasing investment in sophistication without an equal investment in ownership makes planning an ivory tower activity. The planners become 'Pundits' and implementation fails.
- *Over-sophistication hinders ownership.* Once a 'Pundit', additional investment in technical expertise is unlikely to turn an organization into a 'Leader'. The behavioural investment that increases ownership is different to the technical expertise that increases sophistication.
- *Ownership makes implementation work irrespective of strategy.* An organization can only reach the 'Missionary' stage after a significant human investment in behaviour and attitudes of its people. This will be effective if a level of strategy sophistication has not previously been achieved. If it has, it may be necessary to reinvent strategy in order to nurture ownership.

● *Sophistication follows ownership and implementation.* Virtually the only route to becoming a 'Leader' is by being a 'Missionary' first and concentrating on sophistication in the later stages of development. This sometimes means that senior management has to conceal its pride while the transition takes place.

The conclusion is that getting out of the Pundits box may actually mean giving up some planning sophistication and concentrating on winning ownership first – then sophistication can be regained with the support of the people involved – see Figure 13.3. We will see shortly that this can be achieved in several ways.

Now, this is a highly demanding and complex managerial agenda, and we may quite simply not be able to do it all at once. That is fine – let's pick off the problems one at a time.

So what can we actually do?

'there are a number of ways into the problem of managing the planning process, that we can take singly or as a group according to our priorities'

Certainly, when we work on these issues with companies, one of the reactions of managers to the agenda of issues to be addressed in managing planning is that even if they agree with our conclusions – they don't know where to start. This is perfectly reasonable – as we have said, it is a very demanding and lengthy agenda. However, there are a number of ways into the problem of managing the planning process, that we can take singly or as a group according to our priorities. These development approaches are:

● Manage the process.
● The tools for the job.
● Chunking by champions.
● Manage participation.
● Build effective planning teams.
● Facilitate the process.
● Be illogical, turn planning upside-down and inside-out.
● Make implementation strategic.
● Make ownership the top priority.

These practical approaches give us a chance to do things on all three dimensions of our planning process, to see if we can make it work better for us. They all come from experience in working with companies on these issues.

Manage the process

If planning is the way your company gets from strategy to programmes of action – and it is for most of us – then the planning process deserves serious management attention to design it and run it to achieve the things we want. There are many criticisms of planning, which are undoubtedly true for many company planning systems. They are not, however, the unavoidable characteristics of planning. They are the characteristics of *bad* planning. In particular, they are the characteristics of *badly managed* planning.

REALITY CHECK

AN ABRASIVE APPROACH TO MANAGING THE PLANNING PROCESS

3M is a global enterprise manufacturing more than 60 000 products from a base of 112 technology platforms, and consists of 28 autonomous business units, of which the Abrasive Systems Division (ASD) is one. ASD is 3M's original business and operates in a mature market supplying abrasives mainly to manufacturing companies.

At 3M (UK), the early 1990s saw ASD showing falling market share, accompanied by declining staff morale (compared to other company units and benchmark companies outside 3M). The appointment of Stuart Lane as ASD business unit manager in 1992 had three key goals: to restore sales growth to a minimum of 5 per cent p.a., to return gross margin to the levels of the 1980s, and to bring the employee satisfaction level to at least the company average. Lane's first observations shocked him. They showed that people felt: they were not treated with respect or thanked for jobs well done; they lacked freedom to use initiative and make decisions; there was little information sharing and too much bureaucracy.

Lane's first decision was, somewhat perversely, to double the ASD sales growth target from the 25 per cent required by senior management (for 1992–1996) to 50 per cent. In collaboration with 3M's Corporate Marketing business planners he designed what he describes as 'a semi-formal, structured, iterative process' of planning for ASD.

The new planning process started with a two-day planning workshop in Spring 1992, followed by five further workshops over the following three months. Lane sees the workshops as critical to developing a robust plan for ASD, but also the team-building, ownership, enthusiasm and commitment to make the plan happen, as well as confidence among the team members that they were actually going to achieve the ambitious, 'stretch' goals for ASD. Lane was clear from the outset that it was worth sacrificing some sophistication in favour of simplicity and involvement to win people's support.

The planning was linked directly to an implementation process with three key elements: first, a written plan, presented to management, but also reduced to an A5 card containing the essence of the plan in simple and memorable terms; second, the launch of the new plan to the ASD organization at the annual sales conference, and distribution of the A5 cards to be kept at the front of people's diaries; and third, the introduction of Segment Action Teams (with a member of the management team as leader, but including people from sales, marketing, customer service and technical services from different levels in the organization), to take responsibility for segment-specific tactics and programmes. The Segment Action Teams have evolved into a key and permanent part of the ASD structure.

The results achieved by 1996 were: a 53 per cent growth in sales, a 100 per cent growth in gross margin contribution, a 30 per cent increase in market share, and employees satisfaction 12 per cent above the company average. This was achieved, recall, in a mature market showing little growth.

Sources: Stuart Lane and Debbie Clewes (2000), 'The Implementation of Marketing Planning: A Case Study in Gaining Commitment at 3M (UK) Abrasives', *Journal of Strategic Marketing*, **8** (3), 225–40.

'There is another ownership issue here as well – ownership of the job of managing the planning process'

We have talked much about 'ownership' – winning the hearts and minds of the people in the company to get their commitment to implementation of market strategies. There is another ownership issue here as well – ownership of the job of managing the planning process. This is becoming both more difficult and more important, as the responsibility for generating and planning market strategy becomes a pan-company issue not just something that is done by a marketing department.

The observation is simple – if you look at companies where planning really is turning strategizing into operational programmes of action, it is because someone is driving the planning process to achieve this effect (and often without any resources or formal authority to do it).

The tools for the job

If planning is to do what we want, we need to make sure you give the people involved appropriate tools and techniques for planning. Re-read the comments above about planning sophistication (pp. 591–2) and consider again the meaning of the word 'appropriate'. You do not need state-of-the-art technology to do a basic job of turning market strategy into practical action. We have already given you more tools than you probably need:

'You do not need state-of-the-art technology to do a basic job of turning market strategy into practical action'

- a methodology for managing the market sensing process (pp. 390–402);
- structures for analysing customer markets and segments and making choices (pp. 431–5);
- tools for working on market mission and competitive positioning (pp. 442–64);
- methods for analysing relationship issues (pp. 521–3);
- checklists of key issues and plan format (pp. 531–8);
- a customer-oriented SWOT analysis to sift and test strategy ideas (pp. 539–47).

If you make those tools work for you and share them with participants in planning, you will probably be way ahead of most of your competitors in actually getting the important stuff done.

Chunking by champions

One thing we have found in some companies is the tendency to prefer administrative neatness in the company to getting things done in the market. There is a strong danger that by trying to make our planning process all-encompassing, closely integrated with financial and strategic planning, and a 'perfect' system with all the feedback loops covered, and so on, we simply create for ourselves a hopeless bureaucracy.

So, there are two things we can try, almost irrespective of the rest of our formalized planning.

First, let's not start out by trying to solve the problems of the whole universe in a single plan. Let's postpone ruling the world for the moment and focus on one self-contained area of the business. It may be: a vertical market in which we want to develop a stronger position; a market segment which has been ignored; a type of customer with whom we are losing

'Let's postpone ruling the world for the moment and focus on one self-contained area of the business'

out; a new product market; a weak product area; a perennial problem area; or whatever. Let's talk about developing a free-standing plan and market strategy for this area of focus, and see how we get on. This is what has been called 'chunking'.

Second, let's find some people who *really* care about this part of the business. It does not matter whether we talk about 'champions'[7], 'monomaniacs with a mission'[8], 'change-masters'[9], 'mavericks' or 'rebels'[10], 'fixers' or 'marketing subversives'[11]. We know who they are (or if we don't, we should). They are the people in our organizations who will make things happen – possibly, in spite of company policy, lack of resourcing, absence of authority and formal responsibility, and 'insurmountable' barriers to implementation.

It may be 'riding the back of a tiger' (the words of a Managing Director in a company where we did this, not mine), it may be uncomfortable for top managers and staff planners, it may be disruptive, but if things are stuck – let's point the champions at the problem, give them the tools, and let them make it happen for us.

REALITY CHECK

CHAMPIONS WITH A MISSION VERSUS BUREAUCRACY

In one sophisticated, high-technology company with which we worked over several years, the formal planning system was a professional planner's dream. The company is multinational and so has planning at: head office (the big global strategies); geographic zones (e.g. Europe and UK); national level (e.g. UK); business level (product-based divisions); and business units and functions (a matrix structure within each product division). By use of great computer power and the employment of several hundred full-time planners, they integrate and co-ordinate the business through formal planning of impressive complexity and sophistication. There is only one minor problem with this – the real business is just ticking over, and is wide open to attack, as and when the competition feel like it. It is only a start, but they have made some positive steps forward just by forming teams of people who *care* about a particular market (people from all over the company, irrespective of function or seniority), and pointing them at a vertical user market, with the instruction 'create a new strategy for this market, and then do it'. Now, this does not fit in well with the formal planning system. What it has done is to regain lost market share in some customer markets that matter a lot to this company.

It may be messy, but does that really matter if we get new things done? But a couple of points of caution: if you do it, you had better *mean* it; and it involves your *best* people, it is not a dumping ground for the lemons that no-one else wants. Management control comes from how we define the strategic issues and the priorities we place on them, after that it is over to the people who get things done. It is a powerful tool to be used carefully, but it is one we can pick up as we need it.

'Management control comes from how we define the strategic issues and the priorities we place on them, after that it is over to the people who get things done'

Manage participation

Let's talk more generally about *who* should do the planning. Let's talk about *participation* in planning. Now, participation is one of those things that has had a very bad press over the years. The general impression seems to be that participation is some sort of managerial cop-out: we cannot control people so we have to 'share' decisions (with gritted teeth, and when no other choice is apparent); we stick people with the problems we cannot solve (because that will teach them life at the top is not as easy as they thought); or we do it to pay lip-service to 'industrial democracy' and justice and fairness, and so on.

This all misses the main point. That point is that participation is one of the few issues on which we can exert a *direct* influence to shape-up the planning process and the plans that it produces. It is also a route to unleashing the vast reservoir of human ingenuity and resourcefulness that we normally prefer to ignore, or worse we 'police' out of the organization. If we agree that 'ownership' is what really matters in planning, then we have to open up the planning process to those who we want to implement the plan, and who have something at stake.

'participation is one of the few issues on which we can exert a direct influence to shape-up the planning process and the plans that it produces'

In particular, I have no patience whatever with the objection that all participation does is 'waste' time by letting people 'rediscover the wheel'. The easy answer to that is 'no problem, because if *they* discover it, it is *their* wheel not ours, and *they* will make it roll!'

In fact, you may have no choice anyway. We have seen that in many companies multifunctional teams and partnership-based collaborations are operating across traditional functional, and even organizational, boundaries (see Chapter 5). The process of going to market with a customer-focused market strategy and an effective implementation programme is bigger than any department, and many companies now manage that process not departmental plans. Maybe the real skills in planning how we go to market are about how we involve people and help to make teams productive?

So, let's talk about managing participation purposefully to achieve things. Some of the issues to consider are outlined below.

- *Build effective teams for planning* – If we want participation to work we should *design* teams for a purpose. In fact, we know quite a lot about the roles people can play in teams, and broadly what adds to and what detracts from the effectiveness of a team (see the next section for more details).
- *Functional interests* – If our goal is to have people in production, operations, sales, finance or other functions 'buy-in' to plans, then just maybe they would respond positively to being involved in the planning? There is also the point that our plan may actually be better if we include in our thinking the way all the specialist functions see the problem.
- *Discipline interests* – As well as market planners and market researchers, should we involve line managers, and should we have financial analysts or R&D experts, and so on?
- *Political mix* – Should we represent the political, influential and powerful – because they have power and influence we need on our side if the plan is going to happen?
- *Fixers and champions* – What emphasis in team composition do we place on people who care about the problem, and people who get things done in our company?
- *Culture carriers* – How do we include, and to what extent do we include, those who know 'the way we do things here', because that is the constraint on whether the plan gets accepted and implemented?
- *Genuine participation* – How do we achieve genuine participation in making important choices and getting things done. This is not: a token gesture towards consultation which nobody really believes in; manipulating groups of people to do what we want by rigging the agenda; getting people together in a room so you can tell them what to do; 'management meddling' in the detail to make some participants make the 'right' decision. In some companies, this is a serious struggle, which should not be underestimated.

If participation is a problematic issue in your company, then some of the points below about teams and changing the shape of the planning process may be useful.

Building effective planning teams

There is little doubt that effective teams offer enormous power to get things done. There is also evidence that if badly designed and badly managed, teams can create disasters – sometimes quite literally[12]. Used appropriately and sensibly, teams are an incredible mechanism to gain advantages like:

'There is little doubt that effective teams offer enormous power to get things done. There is also evidence that if badly designed and badly managed, teams can create disasters'

- getting across traditional *departmental boundaries* to focus on the processes that matter – such as the process of going to market rather than marketing and operations departmental plans;
- bridging traditional *organizational boundaries* – between members of a group, between seller and buyer, between seller and distributor;
- building real *communication* links between the people who can get things done;
- developing *commitment and ownership* among the people who have to do things if our market strategy is going to become a reality;
- becoming *self-directed* and self-managed groups who drive the process.

The potential gains from the power of teams are phenomenal. Anyone who has worked in a team-based environment will also tell you about the incredible *pain* of working through and with teams!

> Teamwork means never having to take all the blame yourself.

For example, some organizations have a culture of top-down management control and people simply are not prepared for the idea of self-directed teams making decisions for themselves. Ian Ferguson[13], one of the managers involved in the remarkable turnaround of health insurance firm CIGNA, describes the early stages of their team-based operations as characterized by:

- *Chaos* – nothing is defined, roles are unclear, nobody knows quite what to do, people are uncomfortable, arguments and rows start.
- *Conflict* – disagreements abound, there is no consensus about how to operate.

- *False teams* – things are quicker, and it looks like you have a real team, but you don't because there is no real commitment to getting the job done, and conflict and chaos are just under the surface.

In fact, Ferguson says you probably have to go through these stages before you can get to a real team.

'you really do have to recognize that simply writing names down on a sheet of paper does not create a team, just a list'

In some cases you really do have to recognize that simply writing names down on a sheet of paper does not create a team, just a list. It is almost a career-damaging insult these days, but some people do not have natural aptitudes for team working – not 'good team players' – which is not helped by the usual lack of provision of skills training in group-based decision making. Some people are dedicated non-participants – look at the participation games listed in Table 13.1, and see if you can honestly deny that these happen!

Carelessly constructed teams can be a nightmare for all concerned – a clash of personalities and value-systems can be wholly counter-productive. Sal Divita[14] advises watching for the following characteristics of team members as a guide to whether the team will work:

Table 13.1   Games played in teams

The devices used by team members to avoid making any contribution:

The Grand Silence – the ideal game to avoid doing anything, but difficult to sustain indefinitely.

The Hobby Horse – confused by the inexperienced with the *Monologue*, and once under way they are very similar. However, this game requires finding out what the target feels passionately about, which may involve making an effort, which is a breach of the whole spirit of game-playing.

The Monologue – this involves a lengthy statement of opinion by the team leader or the facilitator. This may be brought about by the Grand Silence, or failing this by the 'What do you think?' ploy. Some team leaders thoroughly enjoy this.

I Know, But I'm Not Going To Say – a game only for the skilful, who communicate only through raised eyebrows and facial expressions. A beginner attempting this game is likely to encounter the unpleasantness of:

Uproar – noisy banter and argument, sometimes accompanied by personal accusations and threats, providing the chance to pay off old scores while still not contributing to the team's work.

Martyrdom – when all else fails, then a martyr is elected for the meeting, who is expected to do all the work. Successful players sometimes institutionalize this into a permanent martyr, called the team secretary.

- *Bullies* – whose main satisfaction comes from putting the others down.
- *Challengers* – only interested in what's in it for them.
- *In-Betweeners* – unable to take a position on anything.
- *Traditionalists* – committed to maintaining the status quo.
- *Synthesizers* – driven by the need to make continuous and constant improvements in things.

The dominant values and personalities then predict what will happen: Traditionalists will produce a plan not much different to the present situation; Challengers will produce a positive plan as long as there is something in it for them; In-Betweeners will produce a plan reflecting what they believe management prefers; and Synthesizers will come up with a giant leap forward that no-one else in the company is likely to accept. None of these are likely to be the outcomes we want.

The way through this seems to be how well we design teams and how well we support them.

If we want participation to work we should design teams for a purpose. In fact, we know quite a lot about the roles people can play in teams, and broadly what adds to and what detracts from the effectiveness of a team.

'If we want participation to work we should design teams for a purpose'

What we can try to do is get to the creativity in any group of people, by focusing on the different contributions we want from different team members, and what we want a team leader to do. We need to recognize not just *task roles* (expertise to get the job done, to provide the purpose), but also *maintenance roles* (keeping the group cohesive, to provide the basis of co-operation). The task roles we need may include: *the Initiator* – starts things off, possibly the team leader; *the Clarifier* – interprets and gets things specific; *the Information Provider* – gives expertise, research or knowledge; *the Questioner* – confronts the basic issues for the group; and *the Summarizer* – pulls things together for the group. On the other hand, *maintenance roles* may include: *the Supporter* – gives emotional support to contributors; *the Joker* – provides humour, light relief, release of tension; *the Experience Sharer* – uses personal feelings, experiences to open things up; and *the Process Observer* – stands back and helps free-up blockages in progress. We need to recognize the importance of both types of role and we can look at our planning teams in this light.

Identifying these roles suggests the analytical framework in Figure 13.4. This identifies the scenarios of:

- *Effective Team* – a good balance of task roles to get the work done, and maintenance roles to keep the group together.

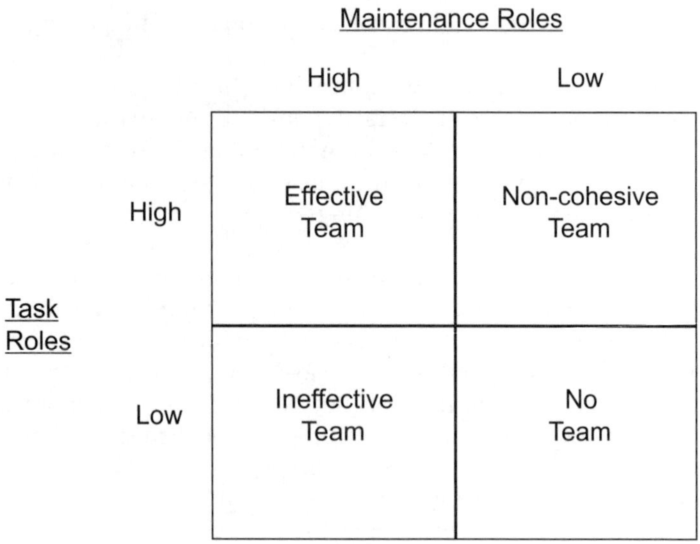

Maintenance Roles

		High	Low
Task Roles	High	Effective Team	Non-cohesive Team
	Low	Ineffective Team	No Team

Figure 13.4 Balancing roles in team design

- *Ineffective Team* – dominated by maintenance roles – everyone has a wonderful time but they do not get the job done.
- *Non-Cohesive Team* – dominated by task expertise, but with no social fabric to hold the group together as a working unit.
- *No Team At All* – a group with no relevant task roles and little cohesion, which is likely to produce no results and turn people off.

The classic research of R. Meredith Belbin[15] tells us more about the characteristics of unsuccessful teams. It is not that they have poor morale or lack of conflict, but unsuccessful teams: lack 'clever' people; parallel the shortcomings of the corporate culture from which they are drawn; have ineffective combinations of roles; have team-role clashes, overlaps or voids; and allocate manpower to roles badly. The Belbin work suggests that successful teams have the following characteristics: (a) team members can make two types of contribution, technical or professional expertise, *and* by taking a team role; (b) each team needs a balance of functional roles and team roles, the ideal mix depending on the team's goals and tasks; (c) team effectiveness is greater when members recognize and adjust to the relative strengths in the group both in technical expertise and ability to engage in specific team roles; (d) personal qualities fit members for some team roles more than others; and (e) a team can use its technical abilities to the best only when it has the needed range of team roles to enhance efficient team work.

However, this leaves the question of how we can support and manage teams to achieve results.

Facilitate the process

If planning involves participation and cross-functional teams and line managers from different disciplines, we can probably do better than just telling them to get on with it, and when can we see that plan, please? (A fair approximation of some company practice, it must be said.)

If the outcome of planning matters to us, we will need to invest time and effort in *facilitating* the process. Indeed, this is one of the things we have learnt from Business Process Re-engineering programmes – teams of managers need help to get things done.

REALITY CHECK

TEAMWORK AT CIGNA EMPLOYEE BENEFITS

CIGNA Employee Benefits is an example of a remarkable company turnaround based on a team-based approach to management of customer service. Ian Ferguson of CIGNA talks about what they had to learn in that company about the skills and processes of facilitating teams. He discusses facilitation skills as:

- *Directing the team* – helping a team to accomplish specific tasks to reach goals, but knowing the amount of direction has to be varied, and not challenging the team's ownership of the process and its outcomes.
- *Supporting the team* – building an environment where people can speak their minds and take appropriate risks, because they are confident they will be listened to.
- *Managing differences* – building the ability for the team to deal effectively with disputes and disagreements.
- *Role modelling* – providing an example of how to behave in teamwork: being open, listening and being listened to. Ferguson calls good facilitation 'the art of nudging'.

CIGNA invested heavily in building process facilitation skills in: consensus decision making and handling difficult team members, and in coaching facilitators as well as the cross-functional teams, in managing its highly effective turnaround.

Source: Ian Ferguson (1994), 'Re-engineering from Top to Bottom', *Banking and Financial Training*, March, 7–12.

Whether facilitation involves re-skilling people inside the company or using outside support, the experience of those companies which built participative team-based processes that work is that you just have to invest in providing facilitation.

Be illogical, turn planning upside-down and inside-out[16]

We can improve the management of the planning process – we can challenge assumptions, we can 'chunk', and we can manage participation and team-based working – but what can we do about the process itself?

The 'logical' sequence of planning

We looked at a conventional sequence of the activities adopted in planning in Figure 11.1. The underlying logic is one of sound, quantified mission and goal definition, followed by appraisal of capabilities and environments, leading to the setting of marketing objectives and the choice of market strategies and tactics. Our problem is that it seems that many conventional writers and consultants on planning actually believe that real planning follows such an orderly and rational sequence of goal setting, analysis and decision making.

'many conventional writers and consultants on planning actually believe that real planning follows such an orderly and rational sequence of goal setting, analysis and decision making'

Indeed, the apparent rationality of such structures cannot be denied. What could be more seductively reasonable than to decide what we want to achieve *before* deciding what we are going to do? In spite of this logic, we suggest that this is a model of a strategic or marketing *plan* not a planning *process* – quite simply, it focuses on what we want to produce and not *how* we produce it. It does not adequately or validly represent the human and organizational realities that we and others have experienced in the practice of planning.

An alternative model of the strategic planning process

An 'illogical' view of the planning process, which differs from the rational, sequential model in a number of important respects, is shown in Figure 13.5.

This model has been created and reinforced by working with many groups of managers facing the prospect of producing strategic plans for their businesses.

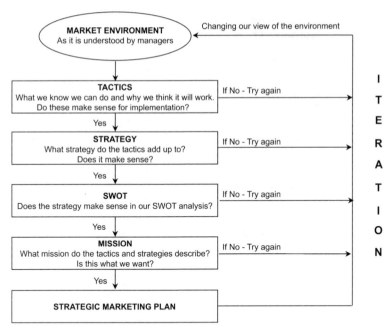

Figure 13.5 'Illogical' strategic marketing planning

For example, at the start of a planning exercise with a financial services company, the view expressed by one senior manager was: 'We know right *now* what needs to be done . . . So, why don't we write the plan now, in five minutes, and we can have some great lunches instead of planning meetings for the next six months!' This offer was extremely tempting but was rejected (honestly, it was). However, reflection suggested that the manager actually had a good point – that groups of line managers *did* have an extensive agenda of tactical issues to be resolved to make their business more effective, and, what is more, those tactical issues had very real implications for what strategies could sensibly be laid down for the business. The seeds of the approach described in our 'illogical' model lie in a variety of such experiences with managers. It must be said that, apart from anything else, with a truculent group of senior managers like these, there was really no other way to proceed anyway!

This process of building a 'pencil sketch' of the marketing plan based on 'known' realities and constraints, which can then be tested and refined and rewritten, has since been encapsulated in the 'Marlow Method' of structured iterative planning by William Giles, which is described by him elsewhere[17]. But let's unpack this model a bit more and see just how 'illogical' it really is.

'First, we take the current understanding of the environment held by a company as a fundamental shaping force on managers' perceptions of what actions are possible and potentially effective'

The market environment (as it is understood by managers)

First, we take the current understanding of the environment held by a company as a fundamental shaping force on managers' perceptions of what actions are possible and potentially effective. The suggestion here is that information and intelligence from the market environment is 'understood' through a filter constructed from past experiences, attitudes and predispositions, and the culture which tells managers what to give attention and what to ignore. This perception of the world is highly imperfect, subjective and biased, but represents *reality* to the people concerned. It is impossible to ignore or avoid this influence on executives' perceptions and we take it as implicitly the initial base-point in planning.

The conventional planning model carries the inherent risk that it will force managers unwittingly to freeze their most critical, and probably their weakest, assumptions as 'tablets of stone' in order to proceed 'logically' through the process. Our view is that this is something to be avoided at all costs, since it removes any possibility of new strategic insights being generated – see back to our discussion of market sensing (pp. 369–79).

The understood environment almost inevitably is associated by managers with a host of tactical proposals based both on current policies and known inadequacies of current implementation of marketing and business strategies. This set of practical ideas about what needs doing in the marketplace tends then to be structured into a set of strategies through a process of rationalization. These tactics-driven strategies can then be tested against the traditional SWOT analysis (see pp. 539–47) and fixed to some concept of a market mission, which can then be tested in turn against managerial aspirations.

Iteration and planning

Clearly the success of the 'illogical' model depends almost wholly on the existence of a process of *iteration* in planning, as shown in Figure 13.5. It is vital that planners move backwards and forwards in the planning system, to test the implications of each new analysis or piece of information on analyses already completed, and to consider their importance for what has yet to be done. Without the painful 'crawling over' the data and the interpretation, the approach we discuss will founder. We suspect this is actually true of *all* approaches to planning anyway, but it is particularly the case with what we describe here.

Planning and information

We should recognize yet again the interdependence of planning and information, or market sensing as we have called it. By starting with the 'known environment' and issues of tactics and implementation familiar and urgent for managers, it is possible to *manage* a process of incremental discovery of new insights and new views of the world. We suggest this to be a more effective route to incrementally challenging the 'dominant reality' or organizational 'mind-set' than swamping executives with new information that they cannot process and which is likely to be avoided (since acceptance would be too great a challenge to the individual's understanding of how the business works).

'By starting with the "known environment" and issues of tactics and implementation familiar and urgent for managers, it is possible to manage *a process of incremental discovery of new insights and new views of the world'*

Behavioural planning constraints

We discussed earlier the emergence of behavioural planning problems (see pp. 589–90). The effect of such factors may be at least partially reduced by allowing planners to focus on what is familiar and relatively certain, and allowing *them* to 'drive' the planning process rather than having it imposed on them. Given the reality of how managers actually do their jobs, there are advantages in starting with the detail of implementation and tactics to gain commitment and involvement, and to work back from this to the development of strategic directions.

Planning horizons and continuity

One of the risks of 'rational' strategic planning is that it separates strategy from running the business. Strategic planning is seen as an unavoidable burden imposed on managers, which is merely an irrelevant distraction from the real job of running the business. We suggest that starting with the problem and opportunities which are closer to the day-to-day managerial reality offers a greater chance of integrating tactics with strategy, and ultimately strategy with tactics.

'One of the risks of "rational" strategic planning is that it separates strategy from running the business'

Planning and change

Strategic planning means change in organizations in order to implement the strategies adopted. It is broadly recognized that change of this kind is likely to meet with resistance – some quite

'a planning process which achieves internal consistency, support from internal coalitions, resourcing from management, and commitment at the delivery level is frequently as effective as we can expect any planning process to be'

above-board, and some hidden in the culture and the power structure of the organization. Getting a reasonable 'fit' between strategies and cultures is widely recognized as essential to gaining successful implementation.

Our view has become that a planning process which achieves internal consistency, support from internal coalitions, resourcing from management, and commitment at the delivery level is frequently as effective as we can expect any planning process to be. In particular, we see this as having advantages over conventional, outward-looking, mission-oriented planning, which formulates strategies the company is not capable of putting into effect.

This is, incidentally, quite different from what some call 'bottom-up' planning. There we just give the whole problem to line managers and ask them to solve it for us. What we have described above is quite different.

Another step forward?

One step we can make towards our goal of market-led strategic change is just to challenge the pervasive conventional, sequential model of strategic planning. A structured, but iterative, planning process of the type described in Figure 13.5 may offer substantial advantages.

The issues for the manager to consider include the following:

- Understand what is really happening in the construction of your marketing plans. In particular, is the process conventional or environment- or tactics-driven?
- Consider the 'understood environment' that planners adopt and its implications for strategies produced.
- Examine the information demanded and used by planners and how this impacts on the strategies and plans produced.
- Evaluate the behavioural planning problems in your planning process, and the degree to which the process you use makes these worse.
- Study the link between your strategic plans and how the business operation is managed day-to-day. Can the process be changed to improve this integration?
- Look at how strategic planning is impacting on the culture of your organization. Can the planning process be managed so as to avoid conflict but to achieve incremental changes in culture?

The real issue to be confronted here is not one of increasingly sophisticated planning models and techniques, nor is it about the more rigorous 'policing' of formal planning systems. The issue is one of facing up to the realities of how executives work and think about their business and taking this as the entry point to strategic planning.

Make implementation strategic

We will not go into detail here, because implementation strategy is the topic of Chapter 14. However, for the moment, note that implementation rates a chapter of its own for two significant reasons.

Firstly, implementation is not something different, it is not what we send the troops away to do when we have done the clever strategic bit for them. Implementation *is* strategy. Any plan which does not spell out in realistic detail precisely how the strategy is going to be implemented should be returned to sender. It is as simple as that. One step we can take, therefore, is to make it clear to all concerned that we expect market strategies to be directly connected to an implementation strategy, or we will not even look at them.

'implementation is not something different, it is not what we send the troops away to do when we have done the clever strategic bit for them. Implementation is strategy'

Secondly, it is no use looking at implementation as some kind of bolt-on accessory that we consider after the main part of the plan has been written. Implementation is *reality*. Implementation problems, costs and opportunities should be part of our earliest thinking, because they tell us what market strategies are worth working-up for the plan, and which are no-hopers (however much market research and clever analysis we do) because they cannot be *done*.

Another step forward we can take is to insist that implementation issues are considered in the planning, not after the plan is written, when people are committed to the plan. If we are serious about making plans happen, we need to think about how we get the support and commitment we need from the people who actually run the business, from top management down to the point-of-sale. Another step towards our goal may be to incorporate an internal marketing plan into our conventional external planning.

Make 'ownership' the top priority

We have argued throughout that what matters at the end of the day is whether our planning produces the 'ownership' and wins people's commitment to make the plan happen. These are fragile and intangible issues.

At least one step forward would be to make it clear to all planning teams that while we will obviously look at their figures and projections, their strategies and tactics, we will also demand, as a prerequisite for accepting any plan, evidence that there is a champion who is determined to make it happen.

'we will also demand, as a prerequisite for accepting any plan, evidence that there is a champion who is determined to make it happen'

People have funny ideas about 'ownership' and commitment. Some time ago I was in a meeting with senior management from an engineering company concerning a project they wanted us to do with one of the company's subsidiaries. My view, which I stated openly, was that unless a key player in the subsidiary was keen enough on the project, and had enough commitment to it, and would take 'ownership' of the problem of making it work, then we were all wasting our time. Their response was 'well, we'll *tell* them to do it!'. I said, 'you will *tell* them to be committed?' and they said 'Yes!'. As they say, I made my excuses and left.

The point of the story is that you cannot demand and legislate for commitment, you cannot police it. You *can* work for it, and hope to unleash its potential.

The silly thing is that we all 'know' a lot about commitment, because we have all read the books and gone on the training courses about it. We all agree that the chances of gaining commitment improve as we move up the spectrum of management action in the following way:

- *Education.*
- Two-way *communication.*
- *Participative* decision making.
- *Support* in the face of barriers.
- *Negotiating* and bargaining.
- *Manipulation.*
- *Coercion.*

We all agree that education, communication and participation achieve long-term commitment to our goals, while manipulation and coercion do not. We all feel good about this. Then we go back to the office, and we *tell* the people what to do, and if they don't do it, then we fix the bastards. We 'get' them through evaluation or reward systems. Alternatively, we create company 'policies'. I have long since come to define company 'policies' as the rules and regulations we create to police the 3 per cent of our employees who work badly (and who don't change what they do because of 'policies'), at the cost of upsetting the 97 per cent of the people who were working properly in the first place (and may not be any more). Coercion and manipulation are easier, faster and are what we know best. The trouble is they don't work.

So, when we look at a plan, let's ask some questions about: enthusiasm, fun, pride, irrational emotional faith, belief, idiosyncratic determination, stubborn support, bloody-mindedness, commitment and 'ownership', as a prerequisite. What is more, let's behave and act as though these things matter too, and that we value 'ownership' as equal to or even above sophistication in planning.

Perhaps the neatest way of putting this issue in a nutshell comes from ever-succinct William Giles:

> *'when we look at a plan, let's ask some questions about: enthusiasm, fun, pride, irrational emotional faith, belief, idiosyncratic determination, stubborn support, bloody-mindedness, commitment and "ownership", as a prerequisite'*

'If it was possible for an entire organization to sing the same song from the same song sheet and face in the same direction at the same time it would be a powerful force. If that song was good, the direction true, and the timing right, it would be a very serious threat to competitors.'[18]

So, where have we got to?

This is probably one of the most important chapters in the book, because it offers a route to getting some real leverage for our goal of market-led strategic change. We started off with a reasonably conventional view of the market planning process in Chapter 11. But for reasons which should now be obvious we restricted ourselves to the basic issues that matter, rather than getting involved in complex models and techniques. The thinking is that getting the basics right is a step forward for most of us. The approach to planning offered here is operational and accessible for *any* organization.

However, the evidence is that all is not well in the practice of planning. Time and time again it goes wrong or never gets past producing simple sales budgets. If we want to unleash the potential for creating and implementing market-led strategic change in planning, then we have to manage the *process* not just the techniques. This opens up a new management agenda recognizing the need to formalize planning and to give people the tools to do the job, but also the behavioural problems and organizational issues in managing a planning process – and trying to manage those dimensions of process compatibly and consistently with each other.

This is a rough and tough agenda. We may not be able to address the whole agenda straight away. So, we have offered a list of things you can try, based on our experiences with a variety of companies: actively *manage* the process; provide people with accessible and appropriate *tools*; don't go for holistic and integrated systems that look good – pick the problems that matter most and aim the *champions* at them; manage the *participation* issue purposefully to achieve momentum for change; *turn planning inside-out* and see if we can get some *real* involvement from the people who actually run the business; build *effective teams* and *facilitate* the team-based process; make the *implementation* a strategic issue, not something we worry about after we have got the marketing plan in place; and look for *'ownership'* and commitment in plans, not just rational logic, and make people believe this is the top priority.

'let's talk about whether we can get the resources to do the things that matter to our customers, and the importance of taking a process-based perspective here too'

That is not a nice neat package – but they are all things that have proved their worth in the real world – i.e. they *can* work in the right hands. Now, let's talk about whether we can get the resources to do the things that matter to our customers, and the importance of taking a process-based perspective here too.

Getting the resources to make marketing happen (or not)

Budgeting is not boring

Far from being the province of accountants, counting the beans, and producing, with the precision and exactness for which their profession is well known, statements of variance against budgets and sales targets, budgeting is about something of critical importance – how do we get the resources we need to get our act together and then to go away and do the things that matter to customers? Put like this, budgeting is an issue of strategic importance, of considerable relevance to whether we make market-led strategic change happen, and one where we also need to get our act together. It is not about mechanical bean-counting. It is not boring.

'budgeting is an issue of strategic importance, of considerable relevance to whether we make market-led strategic change happen'

It is also true that the expenditure on activities like advertising and sales promotion can be headline news for larger companies – attracting both City attention and the trade press to alert competitors to what we are doing.

For example, in the USA, transparency and disclosure means that newspapers like *USA Today* publish 'Pitch and Profit' figures detailing marketing costs and profits across the whole range of consumer packaged grocery products. Even the consumer knows what companies are making on a box of cereal or a can of soft drink. (And with the profit and marketing cost accounting for 69.6 per cent of a soft drink and 69.3 per cent of a pack of breakfast cereal, there is consequently much public pressure for price reductions[19].) The UK has not quite reached that stage yet, but the days when marketing expenditures were 'confidential' are rapidly disappearing.

What is the marketing budget?

This is a very easy question to answer in some companies, because there is *no* marketing budget. This in itself is also a very clear signal about a company's real priorities and attitudes towards customers.

Strictly speaking, the term 'marketing budget' should refer to all the direct and overhead costs associated with the marketing function in a company – or in the 're-engineered' company the costs of the process of going to market. The marketing budget in companies seldom means this.

The problem is that accountants face considerable technical difficulties in allocating 'marketing' costs to products anyway, and frequently do not bother – in effect they treat marketing as a type of overhead expense. This is related to the philosophy of cutting marketing expenditure when sales go down – along with the other 'overheads', like the canteen, secretarial support, maintenance and a few other non-essentials like training. This leads to the next problem below as well.

In any case, we have seen that 'marketing' itself means very different things in different companies – normally we would not expect to be held responsible for things we do not control, so if we have no control over order processing, or transport, or even things like selling costs and distributor commission, then we would not normally expect to have budgetary control for these items exerted over us. Even accountants agree with this principle.

In fact, there is some evidence of exactly the reverse happening in some companies – the marketing budget is made up of costs over which the marketing department has little or no jurisdiction.

'in some companies – the marketing budget is made up of costs over which the marketing department has little or no jurisdiction'

REALITY CHECK
WHO REALLY CONTROLS THE MARKETING BUDGET?

In one industrial chemicals company, the newly-appointed Marketing Director faced a major barrier in obtaining even modest sums for the new promotional campaigns which were central to his plans. On the face of things, the company's view seemed hardly surprising – the marketing budget already accounted for some 5 per cent of sales, which is high for an industrial company. However, the reality was that more than 95 per cent of that budget consisted of two items: commission paid to distributors, and the costs of the order processing office. In fact, distributor commission rates were set and controlled by the Finance Director, and Order Processing is a fixed administrative cost of being in the business. The accounts showed a massive marketing budget, which was unlikely to be increased, while the discretionary spending open to the Marketing Director was close to zero. He did, however, get the 'blame' in the company for high marketing costs.

Incidentally, this type of situation is not restricted to the unsophisticated company. One of the interesting observations of the blue-chip fast-moving consumer goods companies is that where marketing and advertising expenditure is truly massive, marketing executives may have the least *real* control over the size of the spend or its allocation between products and markets. In these companies, it seems that because marketing expenditure is *so* large, and *so* visible, marketing budgeting is an issue for the Board, not the Marketing Department.

However, in the present setting, we are most interested in the control of the level of marketing expenditure, rather than the accounting system and its peculiarities. For our present purposes, the 'marketing budget' refers to those items of expenditure and other resources we need the company to commit in order to implement our plans and strategies. Issues of technical accounting principles in deciding what goes in what budget can be left to one side for the moment.

It should also be noted that our interest is the *resources* we need, not just financial budgets. Obviously, in many cases we need money. But the real resource backing we need may mean other things as well – people, space, computer time, management time, training and development of skills, and so on. This is the real resource issue – what we need to make market strategies and plans *happen*.

You cannot really prove anything

Probably the source of most of the problems in getting resources for marketing is the fact that at the end of the day there is one critical uncertainty – we can never *prove* that particular marketing expenditures have achieved particular results, and we can never *prove* that the budget we are requesting will achieve exactly what we are predicting. We are back to the 'Black Box' called the market shown in Figure 13.6. We can easily measure expensive *inputs* to the Black Box (advertising, salesman time, promotion, discounts, and so on) and we can measure *outputs* (sales, market share, cash flow, profits, and the like). What we can never do in any practical way is say what inputs create what outputs or when.

'we can never prove that particular marketing expenditures have achieved particular results, and we can never prove that the budget we are requesting will achieve exactly what we are predicting'

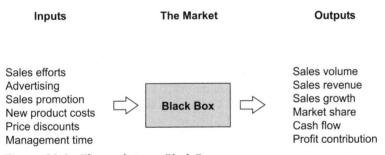

Figure 13.6   The market as a Black Box

My academic colleagues will object to this, and produce complex mathematical computerized models that analyse hundreds of years of past results and make allowances for cumulative and lagged effects, and all the rest of it. Similarly, technofreaks tell us that we can read sales and profit results in real time, so we must be able to prove things. I repeat that, at the practical level, when you are standing in the Boardroom pitching for a marketing budget, you cannot *prove* anything. I know of no practical way around this central and critical uncertainty.

This remains with us whether we are trying to defend existing budgets against cost-cutting, or trying to obtain new resources to implement a new marketing strategy. You can run, but you can't hide – you cannot prove what you need:

We say . . .	They say . . .
we spent 2 per cent of sales last year and hit the target	but it was a great product and the market was growing, so you would have hit the target anyway
we need a £100K advertising spend for the new product	how do you know it won't sell anyway, and anyway that gives us a ridiculously high percentage of sales?
to make the plan work we require a budget for promotion	well we never needed one before, and we've done OK so far
if we double the marketing spend we can increase profitability	you're not serious, are you?

and so it goes on . . .

That is why marketing budgeting is never really just the application of textbook budget-setting techniques. It is probably also why some companies are doing their best to manage without budgets – since 1977 the bank Svenska Handelsbanken has been managed without budgeting, with outstanding performance results. The drinks company Diageo has redesigned its strategic planning to focus on 'value drivers' instead of budgets[20]. This is probably the way forward, but for the moment most of us work in organizations that have total belief in budgeting, so we are stuck with it for the time being.

So how do you get a handle on marketing budgeting?

Budgeting is a process issue just like planning, and the same general points apply. First, we will look briefly at the conventional view of marketing budgeting. Second, we will turn to the reality of how marketing budgeting processes actually operate in organizations. Third, we will use these realities to see where we need to focus our attention.

The conventional view of marketing budgeting

Just like planning, the *process* of marketing budgeting has three dimensions (analytical, behavioural and organizational, see pp. 585–8). Just like planning, virtually all the attention has focused on the analytical techniques, rather than the bits of the process that matter most to results. However, let's start with a quick look at these analytical techniques.

Most experts approach this in one of two ways: either prescribing what budget-setting techniques we *should* use in marketing, or describing what techniques managers *actually* use.

Prescriptive approaches to marketing budgeting

The prescriptive wisdom of the experts offers us the following tools for setting marketing budgets.

Economic analysis

Economic theorists give us the principle of marginality – we should go on spending on marketing until the marginal income from the marginal unit of expenditure is equal to its cost, because until that point income exceeds expenditure, and because this is how to maximize profits. Now that is really good practical stuff that we can all take away and use!

Management science models

Econometrics offers us a wide variety of mathematical models to determine the optimum marketing and advertising spend. Some of the models available are very elegant with complex calculations to balance many influences on effectiveness. However, as is often said, there is only one problem with management science models – managers never use them. In fact, when they do, they probably use them for the 'wrong' reasons, but we will get on to that issue shortly.

Corporate budgeting approaches

Faced with the critical uncertainty about the sales response to marketing efforts, the managerial literature offers a number of ways of trying to sort things out so we can get things done. These approaches include: programme budgeting, output budgeting, and the 'objective and task' model. Of these, the most commonly prescribed (and claimed by managers to be in use) is the 'objective and task' model.

The 'objective and task' approach seems to solve the problem for us by taking the uncertainties away and organizing things logically:

- Translate corporate goals into marketing *objectives* (e.g. our corporate goal of 10 per cent growth in product sales revenue requires a 50 per cent growth in customer awareness, 20 per cent growth in trial of the product, and 2 per cent growth in distribution coverage).
- Define the *tasks* required to achieve these marketing objectives (e.g. media advertising to achieve awareness, sampling to achieve product trial, and trade promotions to gain distribution coverage).
- *Cost out* these tasks (how much advertising, sampling and promotion will be needed, and the expenditure required).
- The sum of these costs is the *marketing budget* for the product.
- Repeat this for each product and market in the marketing plan to get the total marketing budget.

Now that is nice and straightforward. Of course, all we have really done is build a gloss of logic and methodology to hide the real guessing about how we turn corporate goals into marketing objectives in the first place, how much we need of each marketing activity to achieve the objectives, and so on.

Strategic budgeting guidelines

In 1982, the Cahners Publishing Company published a set of marketing budgeting guidelines. These were produced by The Strategic Planning Institute using the PIMS database. Fifteen years on, those guidelines still look good, and are still way ahead of conventional corporate budgeting rules. The Cahners guidelines can be summarized as:

- *Market share is important.* The higher your market share, the more you should spend to protect it. (High market share is not an excuse to reduce investment because you have 'won'.)
- *New products.* New products require higher advertising and marketing expenditure than established products. If your plan involves introducing several new products, you cannot do it with the same 'percentage to sales' figure that keeps existing products going.
- *Growth markets.* Markets or segments growing more than 10 per cent a year will require a higher-than-average advertising and marketing spend. You cannot keep up with fast growing

markets by spending the same 'percentage to sales' that you spend in slower growth markets.

- *Plant capacity utilization.* If you are operating at less than 65 per cent of capacity, you should consider increasing advertising and marketing expenditure.
- *Prices.* Products with low unit prices require higher advertising and marketing support than products with high unit prices. Premium priced products and heavily discounted products should get more advertising and marketing support than products with average prices.
- *Customer spending percentage.* Products that account for less than 5 per cent of a customer's annual purchases need more advertising support than those accounting for a high percentage of the customer's purchases.
- *Quality.* Higher quality products generally require higher advertising and marketing expenditure. Quality does *not* sell itself.
- *Product lines.* Companies with broad product lines should budget more than companies with narrow product lines (there is less economy of scale).
- *Product standardization.* Standard, off-the-shelf products need higher advertising and marketing expenditure than custom, made-to-order products[21].

These principles are based on analysis of the PIMS data covering the performance of many companies. They are intuitively reasonable. Which of us could say that we follow them? Which of us does not have a Finance Director who would rubbish every one?

Judgemental budgeting models

Perhaps the last resort of those who despair of ever sorting out the budgeting issue in marketing is to lay down guidelines or go for 'me-too' budgeting. Guidelines are normally 'percentage of sales' ratios or 'unit rates'. 'Me-too' budgeting looks at what our competitors do – the 'pooled wisdom' approach. This is tantamount to saying that we don't know what we are doing, but we will assume our competitors do, and copy them. What is even better is that you can spend literally thousands of pounds getting the information to copy them. Logically, these guidelines are a nonsense. They do, however, simplify the problem so we can deal with it and get on.

'Perhaps the last resort of those who despair of ever sorting out the budgeting issue in marketing is to lay down guidelines or go for "me-too" budgeting'

Sequential models

Those who like to play safe pack all these approaches together so we do each calculation in turn and keep going until we get to a figure that we like.

There are really two objections to the prevailing wisdom about how we *should* budget for marketing. One objection is *technical* – these models do nothing to overcome the central Black Box uncertainty about the marketplace, they obscure it and hide it away. In any case, they often demand information and resources we do not have. The other objection is *organizational* – anyone who believes you set budgets and get them by plugging-in models of this kind (sophisticated and mathematical, or crude and judgemental) can surely never have participated in a real budgeting decision in a real organization and seen what really goes on?

Descriptive approaches to understanding marketing budgeting

'the best possible predictor of this year's marketing budget is last year's marketing budget (plus or minus a bit depending on inflation and company profitability)'

We get a bit closer to the reality if we look at the somewhat sparse evidence about how budgeting actually happens and what managers tell us it is like.

Precedent

Again and again it has been shown that the best possible predictor of this year's marketing budget is last year's marketing budget (plus or minus a bit depending on inflation and company profitability). We may not like it, but it happens to be true. (It is also not as bad as it sounds, because the alternative of 'zero-base budgeting' usually sets the scene for a massive, time-consuming, political bun-fight.)

Incrementalism

It follows that most of the management attention focuses not on total budgets, but on the changes we want to make to what is set by precedent. This means we take the £1 million as read, and fight about the extra £10 000.

Calculation models

When managers are asked directly what methods they use to set marketing budgeting, they tell us about: *rules-of-thumb*, like percentages to sales (last year's sales in the unsophisticated company, and next year's forecast sales in the 'state-of-the-art' sophisticated marketing company); *affordability* – we spend what we can 'afford'; maintaining a share of *industry spend*; maintaining *parity* with the competition; and the *'objective and task'* approach. What this really tells us is that people recognize that the problem of getting the 'right' budget is so complex that we cannot solve it, so we use a simplification device. We know it gives the 'wrong' answer, but we *have* to make decisions and get on with things.

Experiential

As a result of the crude budgeting techniques we use, we take a 'suck it and see' approach, i.e. try it and see what happens, then try something else.

Negotiation

Perhaps the most significant point here is that budgets are not really calculated, they are bargained and negotiated. And bargaining and negotiation are about influence and control (or the lack of those things).

The reality of the budgeting process

The conventional view of marketing budgeting is concerned with analytical techniques varying from complex simulation models to simple 'percentage of sales' approaches. To be fair, these methods all have their place. But let's talk about some of the cruder realities of what it takes to get our marketing strategies resourced, and why we sometimes don't. To get started on the search for reality, consider the case of the Worldwide Computer Corporation.

REALITY CHECK
WORLDWIDE COMPUTER CORPORATION

The Situation. WCC was a long-established computer manufacturer based in the UK, but operating worldwide. In view of its size and the diversity of its customers, WCC was organized into a number of 'business centres', each concerned with a single area of business — either a customer type, a geographic area, or a specialized product application. One of these business centres was concerned with meeting the specialized needs of a single customer — International Telecommunications Ltd (ITL). Existing sales turnover of this WCC business centre was £30M, representing approximately 14 per cent of the UK market (i.e. ITL's expenditure in the UK on computer products and services).

The business centre did not have any formal budget for advertising or sales promotion, but the 'operating expenses' of the business centre amounted to approximately £1M. This figure includes the costs of sales personnel in contact with various parts of the customer organization, in-house service personnel providing a pre- and post-sales service and advisory function, and a small amount of expenditure on sales literature and public relations events (e.g. Wimbledon tickets, golf matches, theatre outings, and the like) to facilitate contacts with the customer.

The goal of the unit's market planning exercise was to develop strategies to turn the business centre into a £100M turnover business within five years. Although this involved more than tripling the size of the WCC business centre, this represented only 25 per cent of the estimated market at ITL (i.e. the UK spend). Although the planning gap facing the WCC managers seemed considerable, a laborious process of defining user segments in the market was carried out. This changed the picture dramatically from one of a single customer whose need was for computers, to six user-oriented segments with different needs, which could be met with different combinations of products and services. As a consequence, it was possible to define various marketing targets for information and persuasion at a variety of locations in ITL, and to plan very distinct mixes of activities to attach each segment.

The starting point was the current position, where sales to ITL were £30M, divided between hardware (40 per cent), software (40 per cent) and services (20 per cent). The company's estimates of the gross margins, i.e. cost of goods sold before the operating expenses of the business centre (marketing costs), were: hardware 20 per cent, software 50 per cent, services 60 per cent. The new market plan involved a large increase in the personal selling effort, and sales promotion and advertising targeted in the chosen market segments. The five-year out-turn was estimated sales (at current prices) of £100M, divided between hardware (10 per cent), software (40 per cent) and services (50 per cent), and gross margins were assumed constant. However, to achieve this result required that the marketing spend should increase from £1M to £6M.

The dilemma facing the business centre managers was how this budget requirement could be justified to senior management, i.e. can a sixfold increase on the marketing budget be justified to grow the business from £30M to £100M sales turnover, even though it increases profitability of the business centre as well?

The Problem? Now at this point some companies would be jumping up and down with excitement and building action plans. This was not the position in WCC. The business unit managers pointed to sales growth and enhanced profitability resulting from an increased marketing budget. Company management took the stand that to increase 'operating expenses' from 3 per cent of sales to 6 per cent of sales was against company 'policy', particularly since this involved increasing the expenditure sixfold. The culture of this company was adamantly opposed to such levels of marketing expenditure, regardless of the effect on growth and profitability. There is *no* rational analytical technique that resolves the issue.

The Result? Bargaining and negotiation started but led to complete deadlock. The chief executive started the search for a buyer of the business unit, prime among the potential purchasers being ITL. When 'rational' approaches are deadlocked, the man with the power makes the decision, and it may not be the decision you wanted.

The Moral? Now let's talk about what budgeting is really about.

Real marketing budgeting processes

If you ask managers about the marketing budgeting process you get a very different view to that in the textbook. They do not tell us about methods of calculation, they tell us bluntly about who actually *runs* budgeting in their companies. They tell us about bottom-up[22] budgeting and top-down budgeting.

In fact, ground-breaking research by the Marketing Communications Research Centre at Cranfield[23] identified a number of variations:

- *Bottom-up budgeting* is where initiative lies at the product management level, and resource demands are pushed up through the organization – this is rarely found now.
- *Bottom-up/top-down budgeting* involves more negotiation and involvement of other departments, but initiative remains at the product level.

'If you ask managers about the marketing budgeting process you get a very different view to that in the textbook. They do not tell us about methods of calculation, they tell us bluntly about who actually runs budgeting in their companies'

- *Top-down/bottom-up budgeting* involves far greater control by top management over marketing budgets, and changes the basis for negotiation.

To these variations, I would add one of my own from my work in this area:

- *Top-down budgeting* – the man at the top says how much you get and there is no room for negotiation[24].

These pragmatic views of what the marketing budgeting process is like in practice differ according to: where the *initiative* lies for marketing resource demands; who *runs, controls* and *influences* the resource-claiming process for marketing; the amount and type of *negotiation* involved; and who is involved and *participates* in marketing budgeting – what level of management, what other departments, what interdepartmental committees, and so on. This leads to quite an interesting question.

What really determines marketing budgets?

'the resources we actually see companies putting behind marketing are determined by the nature of the budgeting process and the context in which it operates'

If we forget, for the moment, about budgeting techniques, then the evidence suggests that the resources we actually see companies putting behind marketing are determined by the nature of the budgeting process and the context in which it operates.

Marketing budgets are influenced and determined by factors like these:

- *Power* – the power of the marketing function (if there is one) relative to other players in the organization, in terms of organizational structures, participation in important decisions, and status.
- *Strategic contingencies* – just how important and critical a company believes its market problems and its customers are.
- *Process control* – who sets the rules and the agenda for the budgeting process, which interests participate in the budgeting decisions, who chooses the 'rational' techniques to be used in calculating marketing budgets?
- *Political influence* – who controls the information, and exerts control over what people think?
- *Bargaining and advocacy* – how good people are at building cases and doing deals to get resources.
- *Corporate culture* – the acceptability or otherwise of resource claims for marketing in the historical frame of reference of 'the way we do things here'.

This is not the place to unpack academic research about these different issues. It *is* the place to say that these are the issues to be addressed in managing the marketing budgeting process.

The real management agenda

The conclusion I put forward is very similar to that we reached when examining the planning process – putting a handle on a process like marketing budgeting does not involve learning cleverer analytical techniques, it involves getting to grips with the messy realities of the behavioural and organizational dimensions of the process. Getting the resources needed to transform the process of going to market may be the biggest implementation challenge you face. This is the real management agenda for marketing budgeting.

'Getting the resources needed to transform the process of going to market may be the biggest implementation challenge you face. This is the real management agenda for marketing budgeting'

If you see marketing budgeting as a major blockage to making marketing happen in your company and achieving market-led strategic change, then consider the following points.

- Making sense of the budget and resource issues is easiest in the context of the specific problems we have uncovered in analysing our marketing performance and context in the earlier parts of the book, and strategic planning is a vehicle for capturing and articulating these problems. So weld marketing planning and marketing budgeting together.
- Figuring out why we have resourcing problems and what we may be able to do about them involves getting a handle on the *process* and its context – who runs the marketing budgeting in our company and who influences what happens? This may be painful, but is more productive than building analytical models and getting hurt when they are ignored.
- Bear in mind that there are few things more politically explosive in organizations than resource allocation. Careers and corporate empires hang on these issues. Some marketing resource problems we will never solve. Others we may be able to do something about. In both cases we can carry these issues forward to our implementation strategy.

Budgeting for marketing is frequently a highly problematic area for executives, and the new realities for companies mean it is likely to stay that way or get worse. We have tried here to put a handle on the organizational realities of getting marketing

'The important point is that we should see marketing budgeting as a process, and as a process which is inseparable from the planning process'

resourced, as well as looking at budget-setting techniques. The important point is that we should see marketing budgeting as a *process*, and as a process which is inseparable from the planning process. The underlying truth is that all too often marketing seems to happen *in spite* of the attitude of companies towards budgets and headcounts. If we are serious about market-led strategic change, then we cannot escape the conclusion that it comes with a price tag.

REALITY CHECK

THE AWKWARD QUESTIONS ABOUT PROCESSES

Do we know what people think about planning and budgeting in our company? Are our processes just bureaucratic rituals that change nothing, or are the processes designed to support strategy and organizational change? If not the latter, why not, and what are we going to do about it?

Are we clear that planning and budgeting processes need to fit together – the budget is the bill for the strategy and programme in the plan, and managing them as separate processes makes no sense. If we are stuck with company systems that do not fit together (e.g. budgets decided in January, plans made in June), how do we find a way around this?

Can we get support for designing planning and budgeting as managed processes – with analytical, behavioural and organizational dimensions that need to be chosen with consistency in mind? Are there ways in to this problem, with top management support, to transform planning (and budgeting) from bureaucracy to change management and builders of commitment and enthusiasm? Is it time to shake up the way these things are done in our company to achieve better results – how do we start?

This is probably a good moment to turn attention to the biggest process issue of all – strategy implementation.

Notes and references

1. Gordon Greenley (1983), 'Where Marketing Planning Fails', *Long Range Planning*, **16** (1), 106–15. Gordon Greenley (1988), 'Managerial

Perceptions of Marketing Planning, *Journal of Management Studies*, **25** (6), 575–601. Lloyd C. Harris (1999), 'The Problems of Initiating Planning', *Long Range Planning*, **32** (1), 85–102. Malcolm McDonald (1999), *Marketing Plans*, 4th ed., Oxford: Butterworth-Heinemann. Branislaw Verhage and Eric Waarts (1988), 'Marketing Planning for Improved Performance: A Comparative Analysis', *International Marketing Review*, Summer, 20–30.

2. Nigel F. Piercy and Neil A. Morgan (1994), 'The Marketing Planning Process: Behavioral Problems Compared to Analytical Techniques in Explaining Marketing Planning Credibility', *Journal of Business Research*, **29**, 167–78. Nigel F. Piercy and Neil A. Morgan (1990), 'Organizational Context and Behavioural Problems as Determinants of the Effectiveness of the Strategic Marketing Planning Process', *Journal of Marketing Management*, **6** (2), 127–44.

3. One manager showed me a rubber stamp he keeps on his desk, which prints the message 'JFDI'. This politely translates into 'Just "Flipping" Do It', which he stamps onto bureaucratic memos and executives' excuses for inaction. I too now have one of these stamps. It doesn't make people do things, but it is very satisfying.

4. Getting people excited about planning and then letting them down because nothing happens is not smart. It is like pushing into the queue in a Glasgow pub – you can do it, but only once.

5. Nigel F. Piercy and Neil A. Morgan (1994), 'The Marketing Planning Process: Behavioral Problems Compared to Analytical Techniques in Explaining Marketing Planning Credibility', *Journal of Business Research*, **29**, 167–78.

6. William Giles and Nigel F. Piercy (1994), 'Managing the Market Planning Process', in Sidney J. Levy (ed.), *Marketing Manager's Handbook*, Chicago: Dartnell Company.

7. Tom Peters and Nancy Austin (1988), *Passion for Excellence*, New York: Harper & Row.

8. Peter F. Drucker (1979), *Adventures of a Bystander*, New York: Harper & Row.

9. Rosabeth Moss Kanter (1983), *The Change Masters: Corporate Entrepreneurs at Work*, London: Unwin.

10. Vijay Sathe (1988), *Culture and Related Corporate Realities*, Homewood, IL: Irwin.

11. Thomas V. Bonoma (1986), 'Marketing Subversives', *Harvard Business Review*, November/December, 113–18.

12. Paul F. Levy (2001), 'The Nut Island Effect: When Good Teams Go Wrong', *Harvard Business Review*, March, 51–61.

13. Ian Ferguson (1994), 'Re-engineering from Top to Bottom', *Banking and Financial Training*, March, 7–12.

14. Sal Divita (1996), 'Being a Team Player is Essential to Your Career', *Marketing News*, 9 September.

15. R. Meredith Belbin (1996), *Management Teams: Why They Succeed or Fail*, Oxford: Butterworth-Heinemann. R. Meredith Belbin (2000), *Belbin: Beyond the Team*, Oxford: Butterworth-Heinemann.

16. This section draws heavily on an article by William Giles and me, and William takes credit for most of the originality: Nigel F. Piercy and

William Giles (1989), 'The Logic of Being Illogical in Strategic Marketing Planning', *Journal of Marketing Management*, **5** (1), 19–31.

17. William Giles (1995), 'Marketing Planning for Maximum Growth', in Michael J. Thomas (ed.), *The Gower Marketing Handbook*, 4th ed., Aldershot: Gower.

18. William Giles (1990), *Marketing Kinetics*, Marlow: Strategic Marketing Development Unit (STRATMAR).

19. 'Cereal Makers Not the Only Ones Milking Profits', *USA Today,* 13 June 1996.

20. Tom Lester (2000), 'Cutting the Planning Ties That Bind', *Financial Times*, 9 May.

21. Bob Lamons (1995), 'How to Set Politically Correct Budgets', *Marketing News*, 4 December.

22. Personally I dislike this term. This is because many years ago I worked for a man who claimed to have been Sales Director for the launch of the first roll-on deodorant in the UK. The story is that the product was imported from the USA and marketed with the American packaging and user instructions. The product had to be withdrawn from the market after only a few months. The American package included the instruction on the glass tube of deodorant 'Push Up Bottom'. Unfortunately, some UK consumers had done precisely this, and not only did it do nothing for their personal freshness but it was quite painful! The story is probably apocryphal, but I doubt that you will use the term 'bottom-up budgeting' in the same way ever again!

23. Marketing Communications Research Centre (1981), *Setting and Allocating the Communications Budget*, Cranfield, Beds.: Cranfield School of Management.

24. Nigel F. Piercy (1986), *Marketing Budgeting – A Political and Organizational Model*, Beckenham: Croom Helm.

CHAPTER 14

Implementing market strategies:

The role of strategic internal marketing

ANOTHER MONTH ENDS . . .

All targets met.
All systems working.
All customers satisfied.
All staff eager and enthusiastic.
All pigs fed and ready to fly . . .

Our progress towards market-led strategic change

By this stage we should have accumulated a fairly lengthy list of new things to try, and things to put right, in how our organization goes to market. The issue now is quite simple – implementation, or making it happen, for our companies and for our customers, in the real world. In an ideal world, of course, there would be no need for a chapter on implementation. It would be redundant because we would already have an innovative and sustainable market strategy bringing our differentiating capabilities to bear to deliver superior value to our customers. Oh, if only . . .

If that is what it is like in your company, then you may not need what follows here. However, if that is what you believe, you are probably wrong. Most of us are not working in companies like that, and for us implementation is worth a lot more attention. Maybe we should start off by asking ourselves a few basic questions: why do we need to make an issue out of implementation; why do we need internal marketing; why do we need employees on our side; and why do we need managers on our side?

Why do we need to make an issue out of strategy implementation?

Because evidence suggests that up to 80 per cent of company change initiatives fail[1]. In fact, the implementation issue cannot be avoided. Indeed, some would go as far as to say that implementation *is* strategy – on the grounds that without a systematic management approach to the execution of plans and strategies, they simply will not happen, and so remain ideas which never become strategy in any really sense. Others suggest that implementation is *different* to strategy – it is the difficult part. They argue that finding out what a company needs to do in its markets is easy, it is putting new things into effect that is difficult[2]. Whichever view is taken, to ignore implementation when we look at market strategy is to ignore an important part of the reality which executives face.

'without a systematic management approach to the execution of plans and strategies, they simply will not happen'

There is no need, however, to make implementation issues complex or abstract – this defeats the object. Our focus is quite simply described as 'making strategy work', and identifying the things that are needed to get from the plans to the action. There is a problem, however. While executives and organizations have become increasingly aware of theories of market strategy and the technical tools of market analysis and strategic market planning, there has been much less attention given to the processes involved in executing plans and strategies. The result has been described as executives being 'strategy-sophisticated' but 'implementation-bound'[3], and this still seems to be the familiar situation in many companies. In short, we need to do far better in responding to the executive's question: 'we know what marketing *is*, but how do we *do* it?'

The urgency of this topic is underlined by the frequent failure of plans, and the strategies they represent, to reach the marketplace and achieve the results promised. The underlying problem is that in most situations market strategies have to survive in a corporate and organizational environment, which may provide fundamental barriers to successful change.

The approach we have developed to work on this has two elements: building implementation strategies for our market strategies, and turning these into internal marketing programmes to match our external marketing programmes.

Actually it is a big leap forward for many companies just to recognize implementation as a serious issue anyway. But even when we do, it becomes clear that all too often we lack the practical tools and techniques for getting the act together and creating an implementation strategy. Well, things are changing. This is a gap which we can now try to fill. Implementation is the new focus, and we are learning fast.

'Implementation is the new focus, and we are learning fast'

However, do not be misled. This is no pushover and we have no easy 'quick fix' answers. Marketing implementation is *different* to what we have looked at so far, and in many situations it is infinitely more *difficult* than creating clever market strategies and impeccable marketing plans. It is also potentially *dangerous* to the champions of change, personally and to their companies' performance, if we get it wrong. However, it also *matters* more as well.

The goal of this chapter is to open up the implementation issue. We can build up to this in the following way. To start, we can look at why we have implementation problems at all and the problems we face in getting people to put the implementation question on the management agenda in the first place. Then we can look at the sources of the barriers to getting market strategies to work, as they are perceived by executives.

The end-product, to which we are progressing, is the early identification and evaluation of the implementation problems facing our plans and strategies, and the identification of the strategies needed to overcome those barriers. This feeds into the operational techniques of internal marketing. That is why we need to make an issue out of strategy implementation.

'The reaction of some executives when we talk about internal marketing is that they have enough problems already in dealing with the external market, without getting involved in all this stuff'

Why do we need internal marketing?

The reaction of some executives when we talk about internal marketing is that they have enough problems already in dealing with the external market, without getting involved in all this stuff. Some people have a different view:

REALITY CHECK

THE INTERNAL CUSTOMER INSIDE THE COMPANY

Sir Tom Farmer is founder and chief executive of the successful UK car exhaust and tyre company, Kwik Fit plc – now owned by Ford. He describes the development of his business in the following terms. He refers inevitably to his corporate advertising message 'You can't get better than a Kwik Fit fitter' and suggests 'Now people leave school wanting to become Kwik Fit fitters, and women dream of falling in love with one!' This leads Farmer to perhaps his most revealing statement: 'In any business there are two types of customer – *internal* customers and *external* customers'. One is the person with the sick motor car, but the other is the person who has to crawl underneath the wet, dirty, rusty, unpleasant vehicle and fix it. The business depends on both types of customer. This is not sentimentality – Farmer started with one shop in Edinburgh in 1971 and ended up with a £480 million public company with almost 1000 outlets, expanding into Europe and with a successful insurance arm. When Ford purchased Kwik Fit in 1999, they paid £1 billion, earning Farmer £78 million for his shareholding. Of course, Farmer had the advantage that he left school at 14, so had never been on courses that teach how 'proper' managers manage.

This stands up well against our experiences in working with executives from a wide range of manufacturing and services businesses, as well as public sector bodies in health care, museums and the like. We have been struck forcibly and repeatedly by one major barrier to putting strategies and plans into effect. That barrier is provided by the people, the systems and procedures, the departments, and the managers whose commitment and participation are needed to implement strategies effectively, i.e. the *internal customers* for our plans and strategies.

For instance, Thomas Masiello[4] concludes from his research, in the USA, that in a range of different industries typically:

- most functional areas do not understand the concept of being driven by customer needs, and if market plans exist they are not told about what is in them or what they mean;
- consequently, most employees do not see how their jobs have anything to do with customers or customer needs;
- most functional areas do not really understand the roles of the other functions in the company, so they have no basis for co-operation; and

- most functional areas have little or no meaningful input to the market direction of the company (this includes people like customer service engineers, R&D executives, and so on).

Some people go as far as to suggest we should think of our company as an 'employer brand', as well as a customer brand, and fit the two sides of the brand together better[5]. The basic point is maybe we need to do something about internal customers of all kinds to get our act together with the external customer.

'Some people go as far as to suggest we should think of our company as an "employer brand", as well as a customer brand, and fit the two sides of the brand together better'

The trouble is that the conventional training and development of executives, quite reasonably, has focused on the *external* environment of customers, competitors and markets, and the matching of corporate resources to marketplace targets. The argument we now present to executives is that, while analysing markets and developing strategies to earn a living in the external marketplace remains quite appropriately our central focus, it is frequently not enough on its own to achieve the implementation of market strategies.

In addition to developing marketing programmes aimed at the external marketplace, to achieve the organizational change that is essential to make those strategies work, there is a need to carry out substantially the same process for the *internal marketplace* within our companies.

The silly thing is that it seems that the reality in many organizations is there is an explicit assumption that plans and strategies will 'sell' themselves to those in the company whose support and commitment are vital. When made explicit in this way, this is just as naive as making similar assumptions that, if they are good enough, our products will 'sell themselves' to external customers.

We have frequently been surprised that those same executives who have been trained and developed to cope with behavioural problems – like 'irrational' behaviour by consumers and buyers, or the problems of managing power and conflict in the distribution channel, the need to communicate to buyers through a mix of communications vehicles and media, and trying to outguess competitors – have taken so long to arrive at the conclusion that these same issues have to be coped with *inside* the company. The paradox is that we dismiss the 'better mousetrap' syndrome for our external markets, but adopt exactly this approach in expecting managers and operatives, whose support we need, to make a 'beaten path' to the planner's office.

Why do we need employees on our side?

Because it works. Some managers have the insight to build their whole approach around the issue of employee commitment and buy-in to strategy:

REALITY CHECK
NICE PEOPLE TO DO BUSINESS WITH

Hal Rosenbluth is CEO of Rosenbluth International, one of the world's largest travel management companies – 2001 turnover of £3.8 billion and operating in 24 countries. Rosenbluth has a very distinctive view about how to treat his employees and why. His view is that employees come first, and customers come second. His initiatives with his 5000 'associates' include: his 'Crayola survey', where staff are invited to send him crayon drawings showing their feelings about the company; and his 'Ambassadors' Council' in which randomly selected employees are flown to the Philadelphia head-quarters to discuss with senior management how to improve the business. Some strategies are highly counter-intuitive, such as the investment in video-conferencing to enable customers to reduce their travel commitments. Rosenbluth says he has always dreamed of creating a company based on friendship. He has actually asked some customers to stop doing business with his company – because he will not subject his employees to rudeness on the telephone. He looks for one main thing in employees (and potential acquisitions) – they need to be nice people. It is perhaps unsurprising that this company has a reputation for being nice people to do business with.

Source: Alison Maitland (2001), 'Always Nice People To Do Business With', *Financial Times*, 20 March.

In fact, there are many reasons why a management approach like this is increasingly relevant:

> 'Many jobs still require big, expensive machines. But in an age of intellectual capital, the most valuable parts of those jobs are the human tasks: sensing, judging, creating and building relationships.' [6]

Conversely, if you do not win the commitment and support of your employees for what you are trying to do, your customers may pay a high price:

REALITY CHECK

THE WAITERS' GAME

Waiters in restaurants often have to tolerate abuse from their supervisors (the irascible chef and *maître d'* who feels s/he has to live up to this image), and unreasonable customers (that's you and me, remember). While they cannot get back at the supervisors, the customers are another matter ...

- one waiter describes how when a customer complained about the sauce on his steak, the waiter simply took it outside and licked the sauce off, before re-presenting the glistening steak to the customer;
- a waitress describes her revenge on a customer who clicks his fingers and tugs her apron to get attention – she wipes his morning croissant around the lavatory rim before serving it, and says she finds this extremely cathartic so on these occasions her smile is quite genuine;
- many servers describe spitting in the food and drink of irritating customers;
- those who complain about cold coffee may find that the rim of the cup is steam-heated for a moment or two to produce an amusing yelp of pain when it touches the customer's lip;
- another waiter returns tips he regards as inadequate with the loud and embarrassing comment 'I couldn't possibly, you clearly need this more than me';
- an industry expert opines 'If you don't tip at least 10 per cent, I bet you have ingested your waiter's saliva at least once'.

Now, try me again, what was that you were saying about 'customer service' and 'service quality'? Let's go back to the idea of the employee as terrorist and that is more like the truth in this industry.

Source: Chris Brooke (1998), 'Take a Tip and Be Nice to the Waiter', *Daily Mail*, 9 February.

In many cases, we can go yet further. The revitalization or transformation of a company may be in large part dependent on: incorporating employees fully in the challenge to change the ways they deal with conflict and learning; leading differently to maintain employee involvement; and instilling the disciplines that will help people learn new ways of behaving and sustain that new behaviour[7]. Managers who fail to get their employees to

'Managers who fail to get their employees to understand what they are doing and why, and to build their enthusiasm, should not be surprised when change programmes turn into disasters or an expensive joke'

understand what they are doing and why, and to build their enthusiasm, should not be surprised when change programmes turn into disasters or an expensive joke[8].

Why do we need managers on our side?

Because managers are people too (mostly). The implementation and internal marketing issue is not just about front-line employees. This was the whole point about talking about total integration in Chapter 5 – you need the buy-in of managers throughout the organization to drive strategy through. It is also the case that managers who do not like the change you are working for may prove adept at stopping it from happening:

REALITY CHECK
HOW MANAGERS CAN BLOCK CHANGE

Bob Garrett describes from his research how 'ready, aim, fire' approaches by companies to implementing change produce confusion, demoralization and resistance to change. Emotional reactions to planned change run through: *denial* – managers refuse to believe the change is real, and continue working as before, hoping everything will be alright; *fear* – when the change does not go away, managers' denial gives way to fear (what will it do to me) and energies are diverted into playing politics; *grieving* – people lose enthusiasm and energy as they grieve for the way things used to be; *resistance* – a mixture of denial, fear and grieving lead to resistance to change, whether active or passive.

Work at a leading financial services company identifies how groups and managers can resist change in the following ways:

The '*Dangerous Enthusiasts*' are high in energy but low in understanding, and run around the organization demanding rapid change without authority, and little understanding of the goals of the change. The '*Yes ... But*'s are those who understand very well what the changes were about, but have little inclination to do anything about them ('yes ... but' is a polite way of saying 'no' without actually saying it). Capable of producing devastingly logical reasons why they cannot implement the change now or in the foreseeable future, if pushed they turn nasty and use the '*Malicious Obedience*' defence – 'I did exactly what you asked, no more and no less. If things went wrong,

Energy

	Low	High
High	The "Yes ... But"s or Malicious Obedience	The Ideal
Low	The Dinosaurs	The Dangerous Enthusiasts

Understanding

it is not my responsibility because you gave the orders.' The 'Dinosaurs', on the other hand, are not malevolent – they just do not understand what is going on, and they do not want to play anyway. The implementation goal is to move the other groups towards 'The Ideal' – those with understanding of the change needed and the energy to implement it.

Sources: Bob Garrett (1999), 'Never-Ending Challenge of Change', *Financial Times*, 10 December. Bob Garrett (2000), *Twelve Organisational Capabilities: Valuing People at Work*, London: Harper Collins.

The bottom line is that we should insist that it is not acceptable or reasonable for managers to adopt a 'don't blame me' attitude as a response to organizational barriers to strategic change or to the 'irrational' behaviour of those who hold different views about the desirability of that change. Real commitment to improving the process of going to market *must* involve a managerial duty of creating the culture and conditions necessary to permit strategic change to happen.

'Ah, but you can't change culture ... ' (whine, whine, sniff, sniff)

We all repeatedly use the word 'culture' in the context of implementation and internal marketing. Indeed, people increasingly recognize that the culture of a company can be one of its most important sources of successful innovation and competitive advantage[9]. Some even say that the culture is the brand[10]. It is certainly one of the most distinctive attributes of a company – for better or worse:

REALITY CHECK

THE SIGNS OF A CULTURE OF COMPLACENCY

Royal Dutch/Shell is the world's second largest company, and it was renowned throughout the oil industry for its hierarchical and bureaucratic management structure that valued predictability, order and stability above all else, favouring technical competence above commercial achievement.

Most oil industry people have their favourite stories about the workings of Shell's culture:

- executives at Shell were always encouraged to come up with three scenarios when considering any course of action, with the result they always chose the middle one because it was the 'safest' compromise (the number of options requested from executives has now been reduced to two);
- in Gabon, oilmen say that Shell employees have buried expensive oil exploration equipment that was surplus to requirements, because they could not face the bureaucratic obstacles of reassigning it elsewhere;
- the MD of Shell's Global Exploration notes 'In the past many Shell people believed that 14 signatures on a piece of paper somehow made it a better piece of paper';
- an oilman recalls arriving on a delayed flight to an African capital, being collected by a Shell driver, and being driven to an important meeting at the stately pace of 30 mph. The oilman begged the driver to go faster, but the driver pointed out that, because it was a Shell car, there was a speed governor on the car. Exasperated oil executive: 'What do you do when you want to get somewhere in a hurry?' Driver: 'I take a taxi, of course!'

The challenge facing Shell is to break free of the old culture of bureaucracy and predictability, to cope with the massive demands now facing the energy industry.

Sources: Robert Corzine (1998), 'Shell Discovers Time and Tide Wait For No Man', *Financial Times*, 10 March. Robert Corzine (1998), 'Bureaucracy and Waste the Stuff of Legend', *Financial Times*, 10 March.

The trouble is that many of us do no more than pay lip-service to culture, because someone told us we could not change it.

In fact, one of the most irritating reactions I have encountered in working with executives on implementation and internal marketing projects comes from a certain type of snivelling 'it won't work here' person, usually located in human resource management[11]. These people seem to have some hang-up about the word 'culture'. They whine that 'culture *is* the company', and that you 'can't change culture' and that 'social engineering is bad'. I am sorry if this offends people who theorize about this type of thing. Basically, this view is garbage. You can change the culture of any organization. You may not like what it takes or what it costs, but you can do it. In some cases, it is the only thing you can do.

'one of the most irritating reactions I have encountered in working with executives on implementation and internal marketing projects comes from a certain type of snivelling "it won't work here" person, usually located in human resource management'

REALITY CHECK
CHANGING CULTURE TO IMPLEMENT STRATEGY

Early in 2001, IBM was the only large US technology company that was not issuing revenue or profit warnings to investors – and that includes Dell. It was not always so. IBM fell from grace as an admired company in the late 1980s and early 1990s, with sluggish sales and net losses for three years at the beginning of the 1990s. John Akker's strategy of attacking Intel and Microsoft was a failure. The IBM of the 1990s had a monolithic sales-led culture, based on powerful geographic sales territories, no longer providing the right mix of skills and responsiveness appropriate for the changing IT marketplace.

Incoming CEO, Lou Gerstner, arrived in the company in 1993, but spent most of his first few months with customers, sending a clear message to the Big Blue culture about the mind-set required to turn the company around. His turnaround strategy was not a complex new corporate plan but a simple move to a strong customer-needs focus, leading to the development of integrated technology solutions drawing on all of IBM's R&D, product, service and software skills.

Gerstner announced that failure to willingly and actively support the changes required to turn the company around could kill the strategy and the company. 'Pushback', he said, would not be tolerated. Senior executives who attempted to block Gerstner's initiatives were removed from the company. IBM broke free from the 'robber barons' controlling the all-powerful geographic sales regions in a massive restructuring programme linking product groups to customer markets (instead of regions) – Industry Solution Units. The issue was not structural efficiency, but culture change. The new structure has account executives bypassing the geographical region managers who previously controlled their careers to report to the industry group heads. Many of the new industry group heads were appointed from outside the company, and had not come up through the traditional IBM salesforce route, so did not owe their allegiance to the geographical region sales managers. The company moved from its traditional focus on short-term sales revenue to customer-based measures of market performance, and marketing activities were embedded in a global Customer Relationship Management initiative.

IBM of 2001 is a different company to IBM of 1993 when Gerstner arrived. The culture has changed. The driving forces have been strong leadership, restructuring and changing performance measures, but most of all changing the people.

The fight at retailer Marks & Spencer to turn that troubled business around is not being conducted by managers who are afraid to change the culture. M&S in the 1990s took its traditional culture of smugness and complacency just a little too far, and paid the price as customers walked away and sales and share value collapsed. The new Chairman, Luc Vandevelde, is from outside the M&S culture, and shows no hesitation in making decisions that will change the culture – new managers like George Davies of Next and Asda fame are being brought in to implement critical changes; the CEO Peter Salsbury – a long-term M&S man – has departed the company; and large layers of middle management 'culture carriers' around head office are being removed from the company. That company's recovery strategy relies on changing its culture.

Repeat after me: 'You can change culture . . .'

Implementation versus strategy [12]

Traditionally, implementation has been regarded as what follows after new market strategies have been created, plans have been written, approval has been obtained, and what remains is simply a matter of telling people what to do and waiting for the results to happen. If we think about implementation at all, then we see it as the logistics of getting things organized:

- we focus on developing the organizational arrangements needed for the new strategy – allocating responsibilities across departments and units, and maybe creating new organizational structures where necessary;
- we allocate resources in the form of budgets and headcount to support the activities underpinning the strategy to the appropriate parts of the organization;
- we produce 'action lists' and 'action plans' and do presentations to tell people the way things were going to be done; and
- we develop control systems to monitor outcome performance in sales, market share, profit, and so on, to evaluate the success of the strategy, and to take remedial action if things are not turning out how we want them.

'it is illogical to plan strategies that are not firmly rooted in the organization's capabilities, and yet we seem to set up planning systems to do precisely this'

There are some very substantial problems in approaching implementation in this way. Firstly, it is illogical to plan strategies that are not firmly rooted in the organization's capabilities, and yet we seem to set up planning systems to do precisely this. Secondly, organizational structure and resource allocation are important, but on their own they are very weak, and usually very slow, approaches to the organizational change inherent in many new market strategies. Thirdly, outcomes like sales, market share and profit are what we want to achieve, but the driver of these outcomes is likely to be the behaviour of people in the organization who impact on what the customer receives in service and quality, which suggests we should focus on the behaviour not just the outcomes.

'The "dichotomy" between strategy formulation and implementation that exists in many organizations is fraught with dangers'

Organizational processes which treat implementation as an afterthought when the real work of generating innovative strategies and writing strategic plans has been done are counter-productive for a number of reasons. The 'dichotomy' between strategy formulation and implementation that exists in many organizations is fraught with dangers:

- It ignores or underestimates the potential link between market strategy and a company's unique implementation capabilities and weaknesses – strategies should logically exploit the things we are good at doing, and avoid dependence on the things that our competitors do better.

- More generally, it risks ignoring the competitive advantage which may be achieved by identifying and exploiting the organization's core capabilities and competencies in each market, by reflecting the views of the 'professional planner' in the corporate ivory tower, not the understanding of those who are working in the marketplace concerned.

- It encourages a weak linkage between strategy plans and operating plans – strategies which cut across operating plans and budgets and do not fit departmental plans are likely to be ignored and undervalued inside the organization.

- It ignores the hidden but often highly significant 'inner workings' of the organization – the culture and how it shapes people's behaviour; boundaries between functions, regions and organizational interest groups which may provide barriers to communication and co-operation; and the role of the powerful and influential in the organization.

- It may prevent a company from ever exploiting 'time-based' market strategies, or from realizing first-mover or pioneer advantages in a market – traditional approaches to implementation are too slow and cumbersome to support fast change in market strategy. For example, in markets where the most important competitive advantage comes from the company's ability to execute effectively a succession of appropriate, but increasingly short-lived, strategic initiatives (for example, as Canon has done in bringing new computer equipment to market), then traditional approaches to planning and strategy and implementation provide an insurmountable barrier to market success.

- It ignores the practical problems of understanding the real capabilities and practical problems faced, as a company moves into operating through a network of collaborations and strategic alliances with other companies.

'If we separate strategy from implementation in how we run things then we create problems for ourselves'

If we separate strategy from implementation in how we run things then we create problems for ourselves. Traditional approaches do little to overcome these self-induced barriers to change. Quite simply, we need better ways of integrating strategy and implementation.

In fact, we need to dig even deeper. There are many examples of market strategies that fail not because they are weak strategies, but because they fail other tests. David Jobber suggests the underlying reasons are:

- they do not fit with an organization's culture, and the people do not support them and make them effective;
- they are not supported by key management players, perhaps because they involve unwelcome change or because they compete with other projects for resources;
- they do not fit existing planning and budgeting systems, and so 'fall in the cracks' and fail to become formally recognized in the company or to get the resources they need;
- they do not sit well on the existing organization structure of departments and units, so are neglected or given only lip-service, and fail through lack of ownership[13].

These types of problem are unlikely to be solved through management advocacy, presentations, internal communications to *tell* people the way things should be done, or management sabre-rattling and threats. They are unlikely to be overcome by tighter control systems and budgeting, or reorganization. These are the types of barriers that drive us to look more closely at the implementation issue in transforming the process of going to market.

So, what is the beef about implementation?

How *can* implementation be seen as an afterthought by so many companies? Many of us have concluded that the market strategy which looks good, makes managers feel good, but has no effect whatever on the realities of running the business and changing its direction is a harmful and expensive waste of time. In fact, as shown above, in many cases the real problem is not strategizing and planning, it is *implementation*.

The underlying danger is that we constantly underestimate the degree and type of change that will have to happen if our plans and strategies are to succeed. It is not enough to talk about organizing things and producing action lists on their own – we have to put a handle on the deep-seated, strategic change in our organization that we need for the market strategy to *happen*. This is the real implementation beef.

'Many of us have concluded that the market strategy which looks good, makes managers feel good, but has no effect whatever on the realities of running the business and changing its direction is a harmful and expensive waste of time'

In fact, marketing implementation failures often occur for a number of very simple reasons, even if actually *solving* implementation problems is seldom easy. At least if we can see where implementation goes wrong we can make a start. It comes down to issues like the following.

Separation of planning from management

If we organize, staff, operate and organizationally separate planning and the strategy process from line management of the business, we create a fundamental divide, which may be difficult to bridge. Planning which is perceived as something different from running the business is unlikely to succeed. Imposing grandiose market strategies on line management is unproductive, ineffective and even destructive. The routes around this problem may be: job rotation – we do not have professional staff planners, we take executives out of line management for a period to work on marketing planning; or more simply managed participation, as discussed in Chapter 13 – we involve line management directly in strategizing and planning (see pp. 599–600). Admittedly, participation of line executives is expensive in cost, time, the conflicts to be confronted and, not least, in terms of top management stress – but if we are serious about making market strategy work, that may be the price we have to pay.

Hopeless optimism

Perhaps because of the isolation and separation of staff planners, from running the business, all too many of the plans we see are so far removed from practical reality that it is probably just as well that they never get to the implementation stage. We certainly need vision, but not fiction. This is why we proposed in Chapter 13 the radical approach of turning the whole planning process upside-down and inside-out (see pp. 606–11). Whilst this may not be the solution in all situations, it can do two things: it can provide an antidote to the more extreme lunacies of the ivory tower strategic planner and analyst; and it can tell line managers that what they are doing is important and has long-term implications.

Implementation is recognized too late

'Examining implementation issues after we have already committed ourselves and everyone else to what we are going to do is ineffective'

Possibly also as a result of planners' isolation from the operation, and the sheer excitement of identifying and researching new strategies, we often never face up to the implementation issue until it is too late. Examining implementation issues *after* we have already committed ourselves and everyone else to what we are going to do is ineffective for two reasons: first, we end up with the strategic plans which *cannot* realistically be implemented with the resources, people, capabilities and systems that we actually have; and we persist stubbornly with strategies which make sense economically only because we have totally ignored the real organizational change and implementation costs. Implementation realities really do need to be an integral part of our planning, not something we think about afterwards.

Denial of implementation problems

Perhaps partly as a result of the last point, some planners (and, in particular, some top managers) deny the existence of barriers, obstacles and hurdles in implementing strategic plans – 'if this is the way we *say* it is going to be, then this is the way it is *going* to be!' Sabre-rattling statements by top management make them feel good, and make the planner's life a lot easier, because s/he has been *told* there is no such thing as an implementation problem, so clearly there isn't one! Unfortunately, life is rarely quite this simple. All our evidence suggests that many of the most significant implementation barriers are covert, and become more covert but not less problematic when they are driven underground by macho top management posturing. We ignore such issues at our peril.

'many of the most significant implementation barriers are covert, and become more covert but not less problematic when they are driven underground by macho top management posturing'

Implementation bolted-on at the end

It seems likely that many of the problems we have observed, as outlined above, are created or at least worsened because we still see implementation in many planning systems as something bolted-on at the end of the planning, when the 'real' work has been done, just to tidy up the loose ends. This is *exactly* the wrong way to see implementation! In some ways this reflects the attitude that producing plans is clever, while going away and putting them into effect is an inferior activity to be left to others. If that sounds exaggerated, just look at who gets the 'brownie points' in *your* organization's career paths – the planners or the doers? Implementation is effective only when it is clearly *integrated* with the rest of the strategy process and *before* the plan is finalized.

Fixation

When managers rush into a decision because they cannot tolerate the uncertainty surrounding an issue, premature decisions may lead them to become fixated on the features of an apparent solution, even after repeated failures to make it work. Implementation researcher, Paul Nutt, highlights the importance of developing a range of options, but particularly the early involvement of the people involved[14].

Implementation is a black box

Lastly, we find cases where senior managers over-react, and when the signal is sent by the organization that a market strategy will be 'difficult' to implement, we dump it immediately before we get burnt fingers. We have found that often when implementation barriers are carefully and explicitly broken down into sources and types of obstacles, into key players for and against, alongside each of our key strategy items, two things can be achieved. Firstly, some of the barriers actually disappear – they were just the myths and stereotypes of the corporate culture. Secondly, once we flush out the real implementation issues explicitly and in detail, we may be able to construct implementation strategies to cope with the problems and to get the strategy to happen. At the very least we end up with an explicit and detailed case for changing a strategy that will be too expensive to implement. At best, we create an implementation strategy that matches each major element of the plan. We will look at this issue in detail in this chapter.

These are just some of the underlying problems we have found when companies have trouble with making their plans happen. Perhaps the most basic point is that we have to learn to cope with the fact that a lot of the time our formal structures, processes, and ways of doing things will be out-of-line with the needs of the marketplace, and accept that messy and unorthodox things that work are better than neat systems that don't.

'market strategies and marketing plans which do not confront implementation realities contain the seeds of their own failure – so let's not be surprised when they fail'

Let's get to grips with the fact that market strategies and marketing plans which do not confront implementation realities contain the seeds of their own failure – so let's not be surprised when they fail. Let's do something about it instead!

But we don't have a problem (so kindly take your smart ideas and get lost!)

Perhaps the most basic reason of all why market-led strategic change and hence the implementation issue are completely

Table 14.1   The four-stage approach to avoiding change just because something has happened

Stage	What we say is . . .
1	There may be something happening . . . but we don't need to do anything.
2	There really is something happening . . . but we should do nothing.
3	There really is something major happening . . . but there is nothing we can do.
4	Something major has definitely happened . . . we probably could have done something, but it's too late now!

* Source: 'The Foreign Office Standard Approach', adapted from Jonathan Lynn and Anthony Jay (1987), *Yes, Prime Minister*, London: BBC Books

ignored by companies is quite simply that they do not believe that they *have* a problem, or that they need to *change* anything, or even if they do think things are going wrong they will not change – until it is too late. Table 14.1 illustrates just such an approach to avoiding change, revealed by *Yes Prime Minister*. Does it sound familiar?

Let us assume that we have agreed that some things need changing in the way your organization goes to market – because if you have used the MLSC approach, it is unlikely you will have concluded that all is 100 per cent perfect in your company's process of going to market. What we are suggesting is that organizations (and, indeed, different parts of the same organization) differ dramatically in two important respects:

- the perception that there is a problem which should be taken seriously (or conversely that there really isn't a problem at all); and
- the willingness to try something new to solve the problem (or, on the other hand, the lack of willingness so to do).

We can put this together to produce the picture shown in Figure 14.1. So, a first step in getting to grips with the marketing implementation issue is to ask where we are currently on this model. Which of the following best describes the situation in your company, department or unit:

- *Closed Minds* – We do not accept that we have any kind of problem in the market that could not be solved by a new brochure, the salespeople working harder, or sending our junior staff on training courses. Therefore, why *should* we change? And, anyway, we're not *going* to change! The Closed Minds can be mightily frustrating. It is no accident that our

Table 14.2   The snake

If you see a snake . . .

1   Do not write me a memo about it.

2   Do not commission a consultant's report to identify the snake's characteristics.

3   Do not form a committee to review the 'snake situation' and to adjudicate on departmental snake responsibilities.

4   Do not apply to Human Resources to appoint a Manager of Snake Affairs.

5   Do not go home pretending that you have not noticed the snake and hope it has gone away by the morning.

KILL THE SNAKE!

(then say sorry to whoever owned the snake, and explain that it has gone a bit limp)

---

graphic shows a gentleman studying the ground in front of him, with his rear stuck in the air. One Chief Executive has assured me that he was so frustrated in his attempts to build customer responsiveness in a bureaucratic and slow moving company, he sneaked in at the weekend and put on every office wall a copy of the 'Kill the Snake' sign shown in Table 14.2. He says it did not change much, but it irritated the bureaucrats and that made him feel better!

- *Worried Stayers* – Yes, we *know* we've got problems; yes, we *know* we are under threat, but if we just stick to doing things our way it's bound to come right in the end, isn't it? Besides, it cheaper. (This is similar to waiting for a bus that never turns up, and refusing to budge from the bus stop, because we are convinced it is at that precise moment that the bus will arrive.)

- *Frightened Rabbits* – OK, we've got some problems, but please keep extremely quiet about it, because the trick is to keep still in the middle of the road and concentrate very hard on staring at those headlights coming towards us . . . Our graphic shows just such a warm, cuddly bunny-wunny waiting to be flattened by a truck.

- *Blissful Ignorance* – We are always open to new ideas and thoroughly enjoy talking about them, but we don't think *we* need them, because *we've* got it right already, so 'if it ain't broke, don't fix it!' Delightful people – as the graphic shows they are always reading the *Financial Times* and *Harvard Business Review* – they just never *do* anything, because they don't think they need to.

- *Ready to Go* – Yes, we've got a problem in the market, and yes we want to solve it. The graphic shows a friendly face. Give us

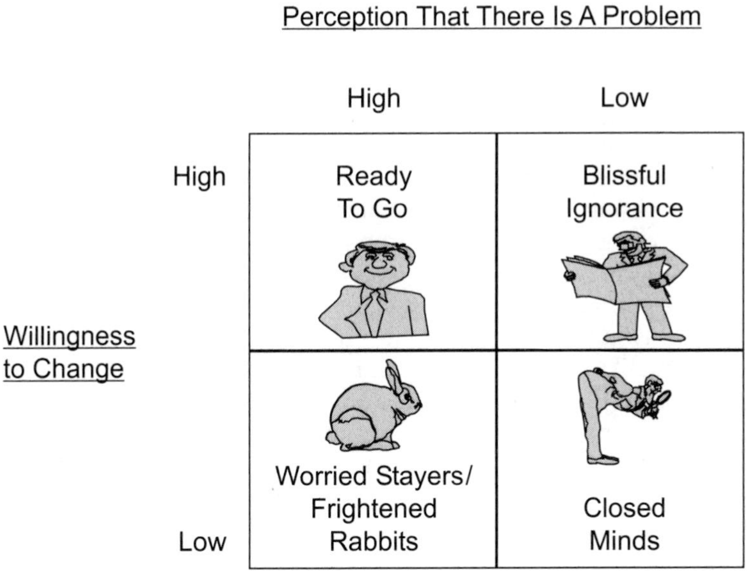

Perception That There Is A Problem

Figure 14.1 Recognizing the implementation problem and preparing for change

the tools and we will find the resources, commitment and money to use them and make it happen. It is important, though, that this should be measured and planned change not panic leading to the 'headless chicken' scenario. We have to avoid what has been called by cynical commentators on government policy the 'Politicians' Syllogism', i.e. *Step One*: We must do something. *Step Two*: This is something. *Step Three*: Therefore we must do this[15].

Now, that sounds harsh. How could it be that we have problems in the market and we do not ever see them? Quite easily, if you look at our analysis of the market sensing issue! But there is more to it than this.

Tom Bonoma and Bruce Clark[16] make some interesting observations on this issue with their 'Marketing Performance Assessment' framework. To start with, they point out the following basics:

- Satisfaction with marketing performance depends on what management *expected* in the first place. Jubilation or despair depends not just on the actual results achieved, but on the psychological distance between what was thought achievable and what was achieved. If we expect poor results and get mediocre ones we may be highly delighted. This has, of course, nothing to do with the potential we might have achieved.

- How much marketing effort we have to make to get a given result depends on our skills and our structures. As a consequence, we may get good results with minimal effort, or bad results with massive efforts, depending on the match between what we have got and what the market needs. This complicates further seeing whether we have got a marketing problem, or if one is on the way.
- Our results depend on the environment – market trends, competitive action, and so on. Our results may look good because of external factors totally outside our control – we may even do well *in spite* of our marketing competence (or strictly our lack of it), if we are in the right place at the right time. Of course, relying on such good fortune continuing carries a bit of a risk.

The point is that seeing how good or bad our marketing performance is may be far from straightforward.

Now, consider the different strategies for achieving market-led strategic change that are implied from Figure 14.1:

- *Illuminate the problem* – if the goal is to move from 'Blissful Ignorance' to 'Ready To Go', then the problem is changing the perception that 'we don't have a problem'.
- *Unfreeze the inertia* – if the goal is to move from 'Worried Stayer'/'Frightened Rabbit' to 'Ready to Go', then the problem is increasing the willingness of the organization to do something about the problem.
- *Illuminate the problem and/or unfreeze the inertia* – if the goal is to open the 'Closed Minds', then this is the most problematic situation of all. Perhaps the most difficult choice here is where do you start – can you do both things at the same time and move straight to 'Ready to Go', or do you work on one thing at a time and go through the 'Blissful Ignorance' or 'Frightened Rabbit' stage on the way? That choice will depend on prevailing conditions.
- *Create a new reality* – when the people are 'Ready to Go', then the goal is to build a programme of market-led strategic change and drive it through to implementation.

However, the underlying question we have yet to tackle is: why are there implementation problems anyway?

So, why doesn't it work?

Before we jump to conclusions about where things need changing (or in anticipating future difficulties), let's just consider how planning and strategy building goes wrong. Figure 14.2, adapted from Tom Bonoma[17], is a good starting point.

The strategy versus the implementation skills

This suggests that the trouble with diagnosing implementation problems is that you have to think about the strategy (which may be appropriate or inappropriate) as well as execution skills (which may be good or bad) to try to decide what is going wrong. The possible situations to consider are:

- *Success* – if we have a sound strategy, matched by good implementation skills, then we would reasonably expect success in meeting our targets for growth, share, profits, and so on, as long as our expectations in setting these targets were realistic.
- *Trouble* – we may conclude the strategy is good (it is the right thing to do), but our skills and capabilities for implementing it are poor. The strength of the strategy may never become

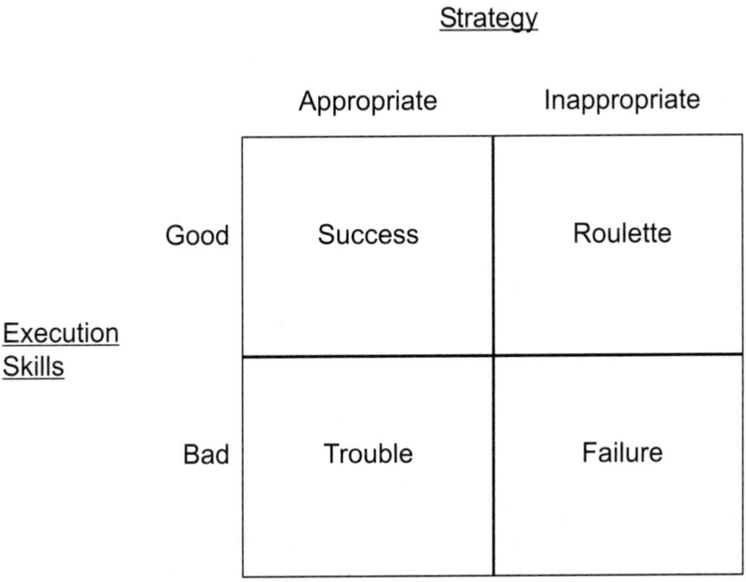

Strategy

		Appropriate	Inappropriate
Execution Skills	Good	Success	Roulette
	Bad	Trouble	Failure

Figure 14.2 Diagnosing the marketing implementation problem

apparent, because we are bad at putting it into effect. This is, of course, what we normally assume to be the explanation when things go wrong – after all it is obvious that our *great* plans and strategies go wrong only because of the incompetence of line management in the field!

- *Roulette* – this is a gamble because we rely on excellence in our implementation skills and capabilities to drive a weak strategy. This gives us time to improve the strategy. Otherwise we end up in the failure box.
- *Failure* – a weak strategy and poor implementation skills. This is hard to diagnose because the weakness of the strategy is hidden by the implementation failure. The danger is we invest more and more effort to improve the execution of an inappropriate strategy.

This may sound an obvious analysis to do before we act on implementation failures – if so, why do so few of us actually think it through like this?

However, it does get more complicated if we allow for the fact that life is inherently unfair – things change. Notwithstanding our wise words about matching strategy to our differentiating capabilities (see pp. 460–4), the unavoidable consequence of market-led strategic change is that you may have to reposition to survive in a market, in ways which require new capabilities, and the inevitable consequence of real markets is that strategies do not stay appropriate for ever. The implementation issue may change because of the degree of *stretch* we are asking from people in the company.

'the unavoidable consequence of market-led strategic change is that you may have to reposition to survive in a market, in ways which require new capabilities, and the inevitable consequence of real markets is that strategies do not stay appropriate for ever'

For example, consider the model in Figure 14.3, which raises the question of whether we need 'strategies for stretch or more of the same?' The judgement we make here is likely to be highly indicative of the type of implementation barriers we face and the approaches needed to develop an effective implementation strategy.

Where our market strategy is essentially a continuation of the type of approach we usually take – i.e. *'Conventional Strategies'* – it follows there is probably going to be a good fit with the company's capabilities, and relatively few new implementation problems. An example of this type of strategy from the retail sector is the growth from increased market share achieved by sales promotions, new product launches, competitive price positioning, and so on. The implementation tasks here are probably mainly concerned with action planning, resource

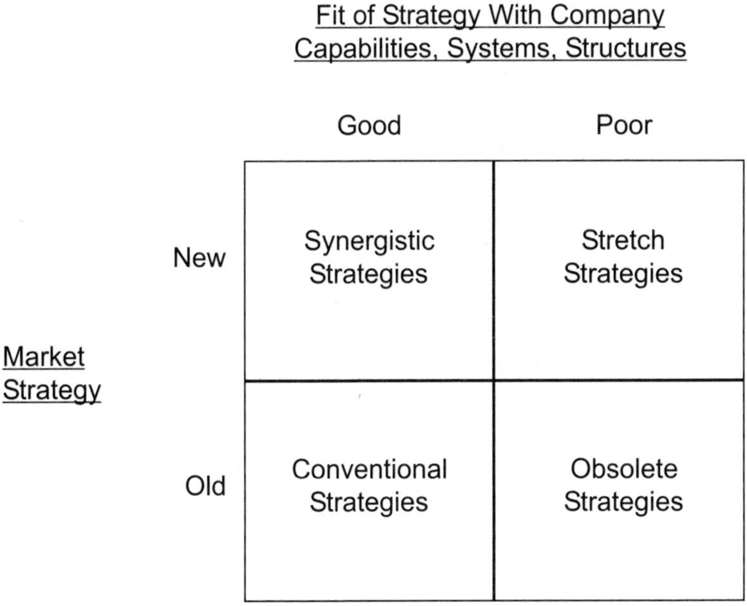

Fit of Strategy With Company
Capabilities, Systems, Structures

		Good	Poor
Market Strategy	New	Synergistic Strategies	Stretch Strategies
	Old	Conventional Strategies	Obsolete Strategies

Figure 14.3 Organizational strategies

allocation, internal communications and the day-to-day leadership skills of line management.

On the other hand, look at the case of '*Synergistic Strategies*'. This is where we have developed new market strategies to achieve the things we need in the external market, but they are designed around existing company capabilities and systems. We may be doing new things – but they are the things we know how to do and have the resources to do. An example from the retail sector is the move of major players like Sainsbury and Tesco into petrol retailing and financial services – entry into totally different product markets but based on customer franchise and sound retailing skills. Implementation strategy may be about no more than resource acquisition, action planning and internal communications, so that managers know what the new strategies are.

What is more worrying is where our plans and strategies are relatively conventional for the company, but have a poor fit with company capabilities, systems and structures – critical people have left, we have been left behind by the competition, or perhaps the market has changed in its requirements. Then we are left attempting to drive '*Obsolete Strategies*', which are familiar but no longer appropriate to the company. A classic example was the determination of *Encyclopaedia Britannica* to continue selling books through direct selling, when the market was moving to CD-ROM (see pp. 370–1). The problems then are surviving the short-term with what we have got, but as quickly as possible developing new strategies to cope with new realities.

This leads to the case of *'Stretch Strategies'* – the new things we need to do to perform in the changing external marketplace, but which are unfamiliar and currently do not fit well with the company's capabilities and systems. An example of this type of strategy is provided by the move of computer companies from selling technology to relationship-based marketing of solutions to customer problems, involving huge changes in culture and priorities. These strategies may be the only route to marketplace success – but only if we can execute them effectively. In this situation, we may need to think not just about what we have to do to develop organizational learning and changing internal systems and structures to implement the strategy, but also about what we have to do to develop a programme of organizational change, and ultimately how we manage the processes of strategy building to win commitment and support for new strategies.

'The greatest risk is that we confuse Synergistic Strategy with Stretch Strategy – that way we assume there is no implementation issue to address'

The greatest risk is that we confuse Synergistic Strategy with Stretch Strategy – that way we assume there is no implementation issue to address.

ASSUME

This is the word that makes an

ASS

out of

U

and even worse, out of

ME

However, before jumping to easy conclusions about why things go wrong – let's test our great strategies and how we handled them first.

Testing out the strategy versus blaming the salesperson

Before we can expect our market strategies to achieve any-thing, we need people to know about, to understand, to believe in, to accept, and then to do them. This applies both to top management whose support we need, right down to field people, whose actions and commitment we depend on.

MANAGEMENT MESSAGE TO THE SALESFORCE

We didn't say it was your fault . . .

We just said we were going to blame you.

Some of the basic questions we should ask are set out in Figure 14.4. *First*, if we have not produced a *coherent* and *complete* strategy that is linked to tactics and actions, we can hardly be surprised if nothing happens as a result of it. How many of the plans and strategies that never 'happen', are really no more than vague, grandiose management aspirations and ego trips, or at the other extreme are no more than projected financial budgets?

'How many of the plans and strategies that never "happen", are really no more than vague, grandiose management aspirations and ego trips'

Secondly, if we produce brilliant ivory tower plans that, realistically, are impossible for this company, with this management, at this time, can we really expect any more than lip-service (and that only if we are lucky)? Here again, Tom Bonoma[18] has outlined some of the common scenarios we create for ourselves:

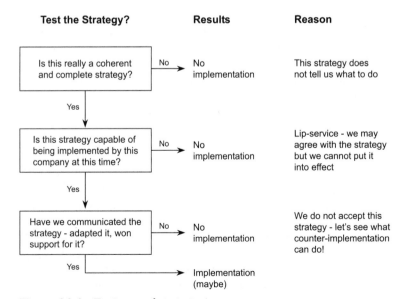

Figure 14.4 Testing market strategies

- *Management by assumption* – we assume 'someone' will get the nitty-gritty work done, so in reality 'no-one' does.
- *Structural contradictions* – we create strategies that our systems and structures simply *cannot* deliver.
- *Empty promises marketing* – we build programmes which rely on abilities and resources we have not got and cannot get.
- *Bunny marketing* – we have no clear strategy, so we create a profusion of plans instead. (The analogy is the man with lots of rabbits who needed an ox, but no matter how much he bred more rabbits, he never seemed to end up with an ox.)

Thirdly, if we are not prepared to make the effort to communicate and to win support (adapting our plans if need be), non-acceptance and counter-implementation must surely follow, rather than 'ownership' and commitment.

Indeed, some would say that one of the outstanding skills of middle management throughout the world is *counter-implementation* – dogged, pervasive, determined and effective efforts to ensure that something will *not* happen. If that sounds exaggerated, consider the 'D's of counter-implementation, and see how many you recognize in your company:

- *Deflecting goals* – we say to the planner 'what you want (A) is just a little bit too "ambitious", so let's go after something a little bit more modest instead (B)' (where, of course, B is not even vaguely related to A).
- *Diverting resources* – the money, the people and the time are suddenly absorbed in 'urgent' work elsewhere (with profuse apologies), but never to return.
- *Dissipating energies* – if enough hassle and aggravation are created, you can wear most people down eventually.
- *Delaying decision* – if you can put things off long enough, the troublemakers may leave or just lose interest and forget about it, or it may just be too late.
- *Destroying credibility* – rumour, innuendo, and even the right sort of praise can make anyone suspicious about a new plan and its sponsors. Consider for a moment the instructions in the excellent *Yes Prime Minister*[19] for rubbishing someone or something threatening, by offering support: *Stage One*: express absolute support. *Stage Two*: list all the praiseworthy features, especially those which make the person unsuitable for the job, or the project impossible to accept. *Stage Three*: continue to praise these qualities to the point where they become positive vices. *Stage Four*: mention the bad points by defending and trying to excuse them.

- *Deflating excitement* – if the problem is that people are getting excited about a new strategy and are in danger of making it happen, then make them feel bad about it, and take the fun out of it – that should slow them down.
- *Depth charge* – if all else fails, outright conflict and attack may work, particularly if they don't see it coming until it is too late, maybe because you 'forgot' to ask them to the meeting that matters.

However, the real point is that if you ignore people by not listening to them and not actively working for their support – do not be surprised if they turn on you. Let's just think that one through before we blame the salesperson for our failed plans and strategies.

What about execution?

With all this said, however well-developed and resear- **'one critical**
ched are our market strategies, and however carefully **resource we should**
we evaluate implementation issues and build imple- **absolutely not**
mentation strategies, one critical resource we should **ignore is the**
absolutely not ignore is the ability of our line **ability of our line**
managers to put plans into effect – their execution **managers to put**
skills. Quite simply, however much strategy we talk **plans into effect –**
and however many plans we write, in reality, the way **their execution**
the strategy implementation process is managed at the **skills'**
interpersonal level is likely to be one critical determinant of implementation success. In fact, in many cases it is true
that managers' personal skills of leadership and action may have
to *substitute* for having the right structures and administrative
policies – because external markets change faster than companies
can respond with their formal systems. One way of looking at
managerial execution skills is as follows:

- *Interacting skills* – this refers to how a manager behaves and influences the behaviour of those around him/her, and includes leadership by example and setting the standards by providing a role model, as well as bargaining and negotiating and using power to get the right things to happen. In most organizations, the managers who have superior interacting skills are well known for their bias for action and getting things done.
- *Allocating skills* – this is about how a manager sets the agenda for others by budgeting time, money and people around the highest priorities to achieve implementation, even if this is at

the expense of 'fair play' and administrative 'neatness'. In some cases this may even involve 'cheating' the system to get things done, and reward those who perform – even if this is not formally approved behaviour.

- *Monitoring skills* – refers to how the manager develops and uses feedback mechanisms that focus on the critical issues for success, rather than just the information provided by the company's information systems. This may involve face-to-face discussions, participation in key tasks, and coaching, more than score-keeping and awarding penalties.
- *Organizing skills* – in the sense not of designing formal organizational arrangements, but of networking and arranging and fixing things to achieve the right kind of action[20].

The importance of these issues is that managers' execution skills represent a hidden but vital resource for strategy implementation. This is a resource we need to consider when we look at the internal market and ask questions like: what are we really good at doing here, and who do we need on our side to make the strategy happen?

However, with all this said, our strategies *may* fail because they are put into effect badly. At one level, this may be relatively straightforward – the skills needed are not available, things are done badly, and so on. This can happen to any company – you think you are close to the customer, you train people, you set up systems and processes, and it is all rendered obsolete because the market changes. One level of the execution problem is that a great gap opens up between what we do and what the market wants, while we are looking the other way. The remedy here is simple – close the gap.

'at a deeper and more worrying level, a company may have learned routines for implementing strategies which are flawed and ineffective – but, in spite of the flaws, we continue with the routine'

However, at a deeper and more worrying level, a company may have learned routines for implementing strategies which are flawed and ineffective – but, in spite of the flaws, we continue with the routine. This is what Chris Argyris calls 'designed error'[21]. The problem is that we not only have to find out what is wrong with the implementation process, but also why we continued unaware that it was wrong, or why when we knew it was wrong we still did nothing about it, i.e. the defensive routines that people have to protect themselves from the discomfort and disruption of having to change.

The real execution or implementation barrier is not gaps in skills, or even recalcitrant attitudes and change-resisting behaviour from line managers and operatives. The real barrier is those defensive routines and the 'designed error' that they protect from challenge. If we are to get to grips with an implementation *strategy*, then we have to confront these issues.

Building implementation strategies

The approach here is described in more detail in articles by myself and Ken Peattie[22], looking at how successful implementors really do it, in a variety of different companies. The sorts of issues with which we need to grapple hinge around questions like these:

- *Basic objectives* – what do we need to make the market strategy work, what resources are necessary, who controls those resources?
- *Problems* – what are the most critical elements, who controls them, will they co-operate with us, will they respond with delays, resistance, and so on; how will we cope with these tactics?
- *Games* – what counter-implementation games are people likely to play?
- *Delays* – how much delay should we build into the plan, how much negotiation is going to be needed?
- *Fixing the game* – what senior management help can we expect, who can we use as a political 'fixer', can we build coalitions that will help us, what do we have to do to establish a 'contract for change' with key players in the organization?

The underlying goal is to anticipate implementation barriers as early as possible, to allow us to steer a path between ignoring such problems, or seeing them as totally intractable. The logic is of four stages in developing implementation strategies, and of iteration backwards and forwards between those four stages to build a complete picture in the way shown in Figure 14.5. The output is either movement forward in terms of generating an Implementation Strategy, or feedback to the planning process indicating that some barriers cannot be overcome and the relevant strategies are likely to fail if not adapted in some significant way. (It should be borne in mind though that 'significant'

'The underlying goal is to anticipate implementation barriers as early as possible, to allow us to steer a path between ignoring such problems, or seeing them as totally intractable'

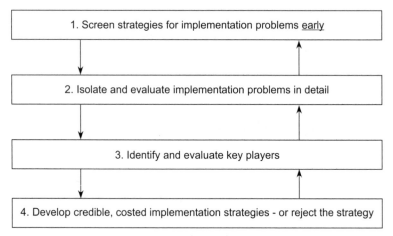

Figure 14.5   Screening strategies for implementation problems

adaptation of strategies to make them more easily implemented may come down to no more than 'relabelling' the strategies.) The four stages are as follows.

Screening strategies for implementation problems

At the earliest stage possible, we screen the strategy possibilities we have identified for implementation barriers, in terms of the acceptability of each key strategy to the company. In particular, note that the *earlier* this issue is faced, the less wasteful the planning process will be for two reasons: first, if there is an absolute barrier, and a strategy is not capable of being implemented, it can be abandoned or 'shelved' before it has used up too much time and effort; however, secondly, if we identify problem areas early enough we can devote more time to solving them. Implementation barriers may be fundamental cultural mismatches, but often down-to-earth factors like obtaining a budget or headcount – where company policies forbid increased expenditure, or recruitment, or simply expenditure on something like advertising – may be seen as 'wasteful' by the corporate culture.

As shown in Figure 14.6 we can sift our strategies through a matrix to identify the following categories. The *'Losers'* should probably be discarded. More discussion is usually generated about *'Low Risk/Low Pay-off'* and *'Pushover'* strategies, on the grounds that if they are acceptable to the company, then possibly they should be more central to the strategic plan. However, it is the *'Conflicts'* we are likely to want to focus on, because these are high in priority but low in acceptability.

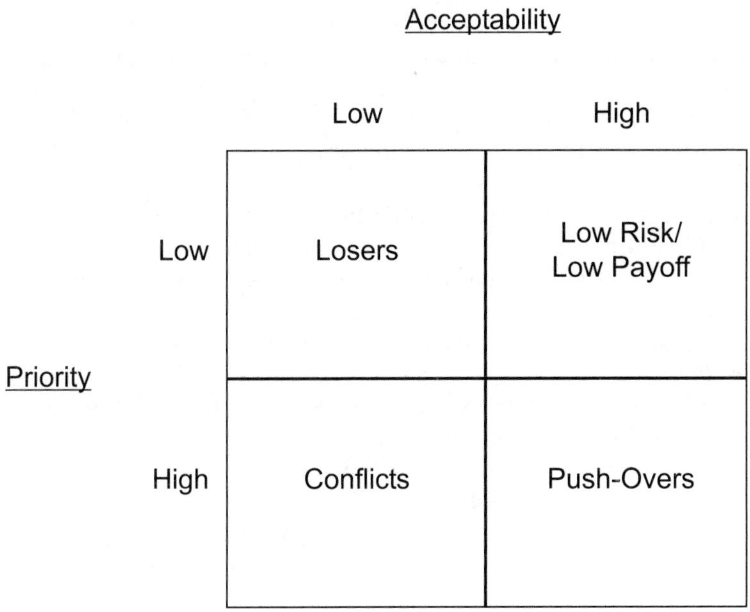

Acceptability

		Low	High
	Low	Losers	Low Risk/ Low Payoff
Priority	High	Conflicts	Push-Overs

Figure 14.6 Priority and acceptability of a strategy

Isolating and evaluating implementation problems

Once we have isolated the strategies which, at first sight, are high priority *and* low acceptability, then these can be further analysed. We can examine the forces surrounding the implementation of these key strategies facing implementation barriers, and try to see the balance between opposing and favourable forces and the likely impact of the various factors identified. It is not unusual, for instance, to find that some of the reasons 'why not' for a strategy, which are apparently 'insoluble', when tested are not as overpowering as we first thought.

While generally the picture which emerges from isolating problems should give us an overview of all those significant factors of different kinds in the company which relate to getting our strategy implemented, and which are most important, we will probably need to refine and reconsider this overview in two ways. First, we can evaluate the key players in our implementation problems. And, second, we can ask what else would have to happen to move the issues, to see if this changes the picture.

Evaluating key players in implementation

First, if our thinking has produced little insight into what is likely to prevent things happening, or what we have to do to make them happen, we may not have got to the heart of the problem – so we may have to be a lot more specific about the people, the departments, the committees, and so on, that we have to cope with.

Broadly, the categories into which our key players will fall are (as shown in Figure 14.7) as follows:

- *Influential Supporters* – With these key players the goal is to utilize and reinforce this source of support for what we are trying to achieve. We will be concerned to ensure that these key players stay on our side, and remain involved in the decision with which we are concerned.
- *Influential Opposition* – These are the key players who are influential and involved, but almost inevitably will oppose our plans. First, we have to consider whether their influence is great enough to outweigh our supporters (or vice versa). If it is, we may want to consider whether there are strategies we can employ to win their support – perhaps by doing 'deals' on things important to them, or by negotiating, or by 'selling' our ideas to them. Alternatively, we may want to consider what may be done to reduce the influence of intractable opponents. We may consider how these key players might be eased out of the decision-making unit – by the action of a senior player who is on our side, or perhaps more surreptitiously by removing them from the circulation list, or influencing the agenda for the decision-making unit!

Attitude of the Key Player To This Issue	Influence of the Key Player Over This Issue: High	Influence of the Key Player Over This Issue: Low
Supportive	Influential Supporters	Non-Involved Supporters
Opposed	Influential Opposition	Non-Involved Opposition

Figure 14.7 Key player matrix

- *Non-Involved Supporters* – With these key actors, who are not influential in the decision but who support our goals and plans, the main possibility to consider is what may be done by us or them to increase their influence – the reverse of the tactics above for Influential Opposition!
- *Non-Involved Opposition* – These are the parties providing unhelpful 'noise' in the system, but since they are not directly influential we may not see these as a major threat. However, if it seems likely that their influence will increase or they provide support for Involved Antagonists, then we may need to allow for this extra problem and consider the appropriate stance to take.

The final stage involves packing all the problems and their possible solutions together, to see if we can succeed in generating an implementation strategy.

Developing implementation strategies

By going through the implementation issues in this detailed way, we hope to turn apparently intractable, unbeatable barriers into things which may be moved, at least a little. Naturally, in taking this approach we have to accept that some things cannot be overcome – however creative our implementation tactics and strategies may be.

'we have to accept that some things cannot be overcome – however creative our implementation tactics and strategies may be'

The underlying goal is 'de-mystifying' the barriers to making plans work in different situations. Experience suggests that it is very easy to see some elements of a strategic plan as impossible to implement, not because they fail to make financial sense, but simply because they are innovative, different to how 'we do things here', are against 'company policy', fly in the face of 'organizational myths', and so on. Working with planners on such issues suggests that breaking barriers down into their constituent parts and addressing them at this level frequently leads to the conclusion that strategies may be feasible after all, if we can integrate an appropriate implementation strategy with our strategic plans, and if we are prepared to look into the organizational realities of how things happen in our companies.

So far, we have an approach to open the closed minds by illuminating the problems and unfreezing the inertia. First, we test our strategies for their adequacy and then we break down implementation barriers into their smallest components and see what we can do about them. We do this early, systematically, and iterate between the strategy and the barrier. Then, we can either say that a strategy should be abandoned, or that we know what to do to make it work. We can then use an internal marketing framework to put implementation strategy into effect.

Strategic internal marketing

What we are now calling 'strategic internal marketing' has the goal of developing a type of marketing programme aimed at the internal marketplace in the company that *parallels* and *matches* the marketing programme aimed at the external marketplace of customers and competitors.

'the implementation of external market strategies implies changes of various kinds within organizations – in the allocation of resources, in the culture of "how we do things here", and even in the organizational structures needed'

This model comes from the simple observation that the implementation of external market strategies implies changes of various kinds within organizations – in the allocation of resources, in the culture of 'how we do things here', and even in the organizational structures needed to deliver our market strategies effectively to our customer segments. Such changes may not be welcomed by those most directly affected.

Internal marketing seems to be coming of age as a way of coping with this type of strategic change – in 1997, research by Marketing Forum found that nearly 80 per cent of their delegates came from organizations committed to communication with employees, and for companies with a total marketing budget of more than £20 million, three-quarters have a dedicated internal marketing budget.

In practical terms, the attraction of internal marketing is that exactly those same techniques of analysis and communication, which are used for the external marketplace, can be adapted and used to market our plans and strategies to important targets within the company. Indeed, one of the major attractions of talking about 'internal marketing' instead of culture change, implementation and so on is that we know how to *do* it. The goals of the internal marketing plan are taken directly from the implementation requirements for the external marketing plan and the objectives to be pursued. Depending on the particular circumstances this process might include:

- gaining the support of key decision makers for our plans – and all that those plans imply in terms of the need to acquire personnel and financial resources, possibly in conflict with established company 'policies', and to get what we need from other functions like operations and finance departments;

- changing the attitudes and behaviour of employees and managers, who are working at the key interfaces with customers and distributors, to those required to make plans work effectively;
- winning commitment to making the plan work and 'ownership' of the key problem-solving tasks from those units and individuals in the firm, whose working support is needed; and
- ultimately managing incremental changes in the culture from 'the way we always do things' to the 'the way we need to do things to be successful' and to make the market strategy work.

In short, *that* is why we need an internal marketing strategy. Now let's go into more detail about what it is.

But, what is 'internal marketing' anyway?

Internal marketing is not my invention, and the term is somewhat ambiguous, reflecting the views of different people who have used the technique in different settings. This is clearer if you look at the sources of internal marketing.

Service marketing and quality

The original and most extensive use of internal marketing was in improving the quality of service at the point of sale in service businesses like banking, leisure, retailing, and so on – the so-called 'moment of truth' for the services marketer. Some call this 'selling the staff', because the 'product' promoted is the person's job as a creator of customer service and value. Now, I have nothing against efforts to introduce a bit of customer care in the retail store or the bank – a tad less offensiveness and arrogance in dealing with paying customers is all to the good. However, all too often these internal marketing programmes are, in practice, essentially tactical and restricted to the operational level of the organization.

In fact, there is a substantial theoretical underpinning for this form of internal marketing, which comes mainly from the 'Nordic School of Services', and the pioneering work of people like Evert Gummesson[23] and Christian Gronroos[24].

'all too often these internal marketing programmes are, in practice, essentially tactical and restricted to the operational level of the organization'

Indeed, in all fairness to advocates of this form of internal marketing, there is a lesson here for us all, if we believe that our carefully prepared market strategies are let down by the quality of implementation at the point of sale. It is apparent and obvious that marketplace success is frequently largely dependent on employees who are far removed from the excitement of creating market strategies – service engineers, customer services departments, production and finance personnel dealing with customers, field sales personnel, and so on. These are all people called 'part-time marketers' by Evert Gummesson[25] – they impact directly and significantly on customer relationships, but are not part of any formal marketing organization, nor are they typically within our direct control. Indeed, one of the advantages of thinking about the process of going to market instead of conventional marketing is that it should help us identify who are the important 'part-time marketers' who participate in the process just as much as marketing people do.

REALITY CHECK
FREEING PEOPLE TO BE THEMSELVES

It is worth bearing in mind that quality and service improvement does not mean programming people to do what they are told. It may be more about freeing people's abilities by letting them be themselves. As British Airways has struggled to regain its advantage in customer service, its Operation Breakthrough told staff to tear up the service manuals and relax and be themselves. The results were interesting:

Announcement to Euro-commuters on the Paris–London evening flight: 'For your in-flight entertainment today, you can watch the cabin crew attempt to feed you all and clear it all up before we touch down at Heathrow.'

Result: amused customers (previously an infrequent occurrence at BA).

Indeed, for example, recent US research suggests we should all think more carefully about the impact of such things as organizational communications on employees – as 'advertising's second audience'[26]. The chances are that employees are more aware and more influenced by our advertising than are our customers, so we should use that productively to deliver messages to employees.

REALITY CHECK
ADVERTISING TO THE INTERNAL CUSTOMER

National press advertising by the Automobile Association in 1998:

**'AA
retail staff are
among the best in
the business.
We would recommend them to anyone.'**

This is heart-warming stuff, spoiled only by the subsequent decision of the de-mutualized AA to close its retail operations in 1999!

Some companies take this very seriously to good effect. Think of the Day's Inn TV advertising in the USA which says 'Thank you for staying with us' – to the *staff* not just the guests. Then ask yourself when you last said that to the people in your company who handle customers! (Really this is about recognizing that we don't get people's commitment just because they work for us – we have to work hard to win their 'hearts and minds' if we want commitment instead of just compliance.) An interesting example of where this can lead is Kinko's Copiers.

REALITY CHECK
CAN WE COPY KINKO'S?

Kinko's is a US company that positions itself as 'the world's branch office' – it offers 24-hour facilities for photocopying, computer services, audio-visual production, video-conferencing and Internet access, and post office services. In fact, the company started as a single rented Xerox machine in an old hamburger stand in California and has expanded to locations throughout the US, and is growing in Europe and the Far East. The founder, Paul Orfalea, has understood throughout how important office services are to his customers – high-quality production and reliable despatch of documents may mean survival or death to a small business; a curriculum vitae is not just a photocopying job, it is the prospect of employment for the customer who comes in off the street. However, Orfalea is adamant about something else, for he says and means: 'If you never take care of your co-workers, you won't be able to take care of your customers ... The attitude of our workers is our *biggest* competitive advantage.' This belief is central to how he has successfully differentiated and owned this simple service business. Anyone can open a copy shop – but it won't be a Kinko's.

Source: Chad Rubel (1999), 'Treating Co-Workers Right is the Key to Kinko's Success', *Marketing News*, 29 January, 14.

'The critical issue is consistency between strategies, tactics and implementation actions. This suggests that real culture change is a central part of the process of going to market effectively'

At the same time, we are learning that, while there is no one 'right' strategy in a given product market situation, there are good and bad ways of *delivering* market strategies which determine whether they succeed or fail. The critical issue is consistency between strategies, tactics and implementation actions. This suggests that real culture change is a central part of the process of going to market effectively. At its simplest, the disgruntled employee produces the disgruntled customer, and then we all have problems. Tom Bonoma has hit this nail right on the head: 'treat your employees like customers, for your customers will get treated like employees'[27]. Given how appallingly badly so many of us treat our employees, the real enormity of the task becomes apparent! Internal marketing focusing on customer service and quality strategies can help here.

Internal communications

The largest growth in this area has been investment in internal communications programmes of various kinds – where 'communication' is understood as telling our employees what is going on, and delivering messages which support the business strategy. Conventionally, where it happens at all, it tends to be a responsibility of the Human Resources Department[28]. This is a start, but there is a danger we miss an important point: communication is a two-way process – we are supposed to listen as well as tell people things.

Perhaps the most visible sign of commitment to internal communications to win employee commitment to strategies of customer service is the huge investments made by some successful companies, to build programmes that justify management changes to employees and explain the background to things like media stories about the company[29]. Indeed, BT has actually formally merged internal communications with public relations.

Obviously, it is good if employees know when the 'special offers' are and deliver against our value proposition promises at the point of sale. It is even better if they actually feel they are being treated as 'trusted insiders' by the company.

The manifestations are mundane: company newsletters, conferences, training, video-conferencing, satellite TV transmissions, interactive video, e-mail, and so on. The trouble is most of this is about instructing and informing people rather than winning their real involvement and participation.

REALITY CHECK

INTERNAL COMMUNICATIONS?

A word to the wise who believe that internal communications are about giving employees a videotape of the CEO's latest 'morale-boosting' speech – at least have the decency to make sure the tapes are long enough to record an episode of *Eastenders* (because that's what most of them are going to be used for).

This may be why internal communications go wrong. Peter Bell of the Added Value Internal Communications Consultancy has described from his work with companies the emergence of in-company barriers to internal communications 'that halt or distort the flow of information, whether they take the form of misunderstandings and misconceptions, hidden agendas and internal politicking, or even myths'[30].

Is this why, whatever company you visit, the presentations come with the same stock artwork, the same canned music, and the same zooming and flashing words (thank you very much for your contribution, Microsoft)? Even as you read this, how many middle managers are there in the world doing TV-style fades between 'virtuous circles' and three-pronged strategies? What is this obsession with 1950s style drawings of men at desks and women with briefcases to deliver the message that 'People Are Our Greatest Asset'? Why is it that regardless of all this, the message in the presentations always seems to be the same: sell more and work harder?

However, even more telling about how we may miss the point is the view of Chris Argyris of Harvard Business School. Argyris also says that many internal communications strategies are misconceived to the point of being completely counter-productive. He cites the case of a chief executive who was determined to

'many internal communications strategies are misconceived to the point of being completely counter-productive'

improve his company's performance in innovation and time to market, and formed special task forces to work on this issue. The task forces found that every new idea in the company was subjected to 275 separate checks. By redesigning channels of internal communication, 200 of these checks were eliminated, which dramatically reduced the time to get a new idea to market. A success story? Not according to Argyris. He says the chief executive *failed*, because at no stage did he ask the really unsettling questions like 'how long have you known that we have had an excessive number of barriers to innovation?' or 'what is it that prevented you from questioning these practices?'[31].

This highlights the fundamental problem in many internal communications programmes – they become about telling and persuading, not listening. This is internal *selling* not internal *marketing*.

What is really encouraging, though, is that we can see many of our current success stories *are* actually going to enormous efforts to *listen* to their employees' feedback, and to react positively to it, to improve the value they deliver to their customers.

REALITY CHECK

IT ASDA BE ASDA

The supermarket firm Asda, now owned by Wal-Mart, managed its remarkable turnaround, in part, simply by tapping into the wisdom of its 85 000 staff, to involve them in the day-to-day running of the company. In 1995, the company launched its 'Colleague Circles' (Asda calls its employees 'Colleagues' as a point of principle). The Colleague Circles produce suggestions for improving customer services, and the best are presented at an annual meeting – the National Circle. The idea is to make it easy for staff to present ideas and thoughts based on their experiences in doing different jobs. It is also important that management listens and takes action. For example, one suggestion was simply that landscaping supermarket car parks with roses means that litter and trolley collectors regularly get spiked, which they do not enjoy – so the landscaping was changed to pot plants and trees. The other source of staff feedback is the 'Tell Archie' scheme (the then chairman was Archie Norman) – allowing staff to pass comments direct to the chairman, and *always* to receive a reply direct from him. Norman's goal was to create a culture where everyone takes some responsibility for improving the business.

Source: David White (1999), 'Good Ideas Come From Little Boxes', *Financial Times*, 15 September.

Listening to employees can be done, and it seems more effective in changing attitudes and building commitment than sending out yet more insanely boring company newsletters.

'Listening to employees can be done, and it seems more effective in changing attitudes and building commitment than sending out yet more insanely boring company newsletters'

Innovation management

Closer to what we have in mind here as internal marketing strategy is the use of the internal marketing framework to place, and gain use of, innovations like computers and electronic communications in the IT field. These applications use tools of market analysis and planning to cope with and avoid resistance to change. The argument here is that people in an organization are customers for our ideas and innovations. This encourages us to:

- look at customer needs – even in hierarchical companies people are not robots waiting to be told what to do, so making the effort to understand their needs increases the likely effectiveness of innovation;
- delivering the goods – the needs of customers tell us what matters most to them;
- raising unrealistic expectations – is as dangerous with internal customers as it is with external customers[32].

Corporate positioning

Others talk of internal marketing in terms of creating awareness, understanding of and co-operation with functions, departments or processes inside the company. This is about creating an image, and just letting people know we are there and what we do. This may be of particular significance, for example, to gaining influence for the non-integrated marketing department (see pp. 230–1), in the absence of formal power or 'clout' in the company, or of sharing the idea that we are all involved in managing the process of going to market, rather than it being what marketing executives do. This form of internal marketing is also becoming more significant as formal marketing organizations disappear in some companies, and are replaced by new organizational arrangements like process-based teams, network collaborations, and so on (see Chapter 5). The need to explain who does what and how things operate becomes more important not less.

'This form of internal marketing is also becoming more significant as formal marketing organizations disappear in some companies, and are replaced by new organizational arrangements like process-based teams, network collaborations, and so on'

Internal markets instead of external markets

The terms internal market and internal marketing have also been applied to internal relationships between different parts of the same organization – making them suppliers and customers as a way of improving the focus on efficiency and value. This is common in total quality management programmes, and in wider applications like the reform of the UK National Health Service.

This can lead to some interesting issues. For example, work with the R&D division of a major brewery suggested that the internal customer issues were really about the type and degree of dependence between the internal supplier (in this case the provider of R&D solutions to process problems in the brewery) and the internal customer (here the production and sales units of the brewery) – which in turn reflects the freedom of either internal supplier or customer to deal with third parties outside the company. (And where third party collaborations *had* to be handled via the R&D Division, we counted this as the same as them supplying their own expertise.) It was interesting in the brewery that managers in R&D had never previously taken the idea of customers seriously, and this approach gave that a start in segmenting their internal customer market, and developing better ways to handle relationships with different types of customer.

The other interesting lessons learned in the brewery case were: not only do some technologists not understand marketing, they do not *want* to understand it; there is a real need for professional specialists inside organizations to acquire the awareness and skills needed for customer relationship building. It can all go horribly wrong though:

REALITY CHECK

INTERNAL MARKETING MAY BE BAD FOR YOUR HEALTH

A prestigious health insurance company moved to a huge new office block, with an expensive, state-of-the-art catering facility built next to the office block in the company's new 'park'. Concerned with issues of efficiency in the internal market, management pressured the manager of catering to 'sell' the new restaurant and catering facilities to employees, and proposed to evaluate his success by restaurant usage rates by employees. As an entrepreneurial sort of fellow, he toured the new offices (his marketplace), and quickly arranged for the removal of all kettles, coffee machines, soft drink machines, snack facilities and microwaves and toasters, with which employees had equipped themselves, and then pressured departmental managers to enforce company rules about employees not eating or drinking at their work stations. The result is a high usage figure for the catering facility – employees have nowhere else to get food or drinks. Management is delighted. However, they now have to deal with a bunch of very unhappy employees who are getting meaner by the day and are liable to lynch the catering manager some day soon (a serious risk, in fact, since the company is in Texas).

There are some interesting issues here, which may be relevant to our companies, but there is another dimension to internal marketing as well.

Strategic internal marketing (SIM)

Finally, there is the use of SIM as the direct parallel to our external market strategy and marketing programme, which aims at winning the support, co-operation and commitment we need inside the company, if our external market strategies are to work. This is the view of internal marketing we are mainly taking here, although it is informed by the other types of internal marketing which have a longer history. The key issue here is the organizational and cultural change needed to make marketing happen.

'The key issue here is the organizational and cultural change needed to make marketing happen'

What does strategic internal marketing look like?

We know why we need it and where it comes from – but what does it involve? The logic here is really quite straightforward.

The structure of SIM

A structure for an internal marketing programme, as we have used it with companies, is summarized in Figure 14.8. The easiest way to make practical progress with *internal* marketing, and to establish what it may achieve, is to use exactly the same structures that we use for planning *external* marketing. This suggests that we should think in terms of integrating the elements needed for an internal marketing mix or programme, based on our analysis of the opportunities and threats in the

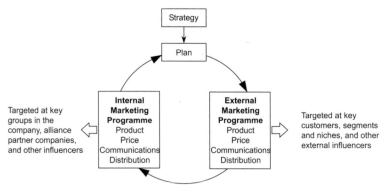

Figure 14.8 Internal and external marketing

internal marketplace represented by the company with which we are working. This is shown in Figure 14.8 as a formal and legitimate extension of the planning process.

In fact, in this model, we take the internal marketing programme not only as an *output* of the planning process and the external marketing programme, but also as an *input*, i.e. constraints and barriers in the internal marketplace should be considered and analysed as a part of the planning process at both strategic and tactical levels. For our proposals to make sense in practice, we rely on this iterative relationship.

The starting point is that the market strategy and the planning process may define an external marketing programme in the conventional way, and less conventionally the internal marketing programme needed to make it happen. However, it may well be that internal barriers suggest to executives that some external strategies are not capable of being implemented in the time-scale concerned, and we have to feed back into the planning process the message that some adjustments are needed.

'What we are trying to make explicit for executives is the need to balance the impact of both internal and external market attributes'

More positively, however, it is equally true that our analysis of the internal market may suggest new opportunities and neglected company resources which should be exploited, which in turn impact on our external marketing plan and thus on the planning process. What we are trying to make explicit for executives is the need to balance the impact of both internal and external market attributes on the strategic assumptions that they make in planning.

The structure of such an internal marketing programme can be presented in the following terms:

- *The product* – At the simplest level the 'product' consists of the market strategies and the marketing plan in which they are written up. What is implied, however, is that the product to be 'sold' is those values, attitudes and behaviours which are needed to make the marketing plan work effectively. These hidden dimensions of the product may range from increased budgets and different resource allocations, to changed control systems and criteria used to evaluate performance, to changed ways of handling customers at the point of sale. At the extreme the product is the person's job – as it is redefined and reshaped by the market strategy. We may be able to identify positive 'product benefits' – ways in which the market strategy will make people's working lives more enjoyable. There may also be negatives – changes people will not like, which brings us to price.

- *The price* – The price element of the internal marketing mix is not *our* costs, it is concerned with what we are asking our internal customers to 'pay', when they buy-in to the product and the marketing plan. This may include the sacrifice of other projects which compete for resources with our plan, but more fundamentally the psychological cost of adopting different key values, and changing the way jobs are done, and asking managers to step outside their 'comfort zones' with new methods of operation. The price to be paid by different parts of the internal marketplace, if the marketing plan is to be implemented successfully, should not be ignored as a major source of barriers and obstacles of varying degrees of difficulty.

- *Communications* – The most tangible aspect of the internal marketing programme is the communications media and the messages used to inform and to persuade, and to work on the attitudes of the key personnel in the internal marketplace. This includes not only written communications – such as plan summaries and reports – but also face-to-face presentations to individuals and groups who are important to the success of the plan. Broadly, we should remember that to assume that simply 'telling' people will get them on our side is likely to be as naive inside the company as it is outside. It is important to consider the full range of communications possibilities and associated goals, as we would with external customers, and we should not forget to budget the time and financial costs which may be associated with these activities. In reality, just letting people know what we are trying to do would be a step forwards for most of us! At the simplest level the purpose of our internal marketing communication may be served by a video presentation explaining things, or a roadshow taking the message out to the regions and the distributors. But real communication is two-way – we listen, we adapt, we focus on our audience's problems and needs (see pp. 611–13).

- *Distribution* – The distribution channels' element of the mix is concerned with the physical and socio-technical venues at which we have to deliver our product and its communications: meetings, committees, training sessions for managers and staff, seminars, workshops, written reports, informal communications, social occasions, and so on. Ultimately, however, the real distribution channel is lining up of recruitment training, evaluation and reward systems behind marketing strategies, so that the culture of the company becomes the real distribution channel for internal marketing strategies. In fact, Dave Ulrich[33] makes some radical points about this, which are worth confronting. He says that if we really want complete customer commitment from our external customers, through interdependent, shared values and shared strategies, then we should give our customers a major role in our: staff recruitment and selection decisions; staff promotion and development decisions; staff appraisal, from setting the standards to measuring the performance; staff reward systems, both financial and non-financial; organizational design strategies; and internal communications programmes.

Now that is *really* using our human resource management systems as the internal marketing channel. That is *really* taking the internal and external customer issue to its logical conclusion. The companies taking this seriously and trying it in the USA are minor players like General Electric, Marriott, Borg-Warner, Ford Motor Company, Hewlett-Packard, Honeywell, and some even less significant organizations! Just try thinking about that for a minute or two. Then, let's talk to our HRM people about our joint interests (see back to pp. 250–1).

However, in an era of downsizing and dumbsizing, one of the questions managers ask is often – but how can you use internal marketing when you are telling people that their departments are closing and their jobs are going? I had trouble with this until I looked around and saw that this is exactly what the best companies are capable of doing.

REALITY CHECK

ULTIMATE INTERNAL MARKETING

Kate Owen, a senior manager at the British Petroleum Group, describes how in the period from the late 1980s to the mid-1990s that major company slimmed from 120 000 employees to around 60 000. In the 1980s, BP had eleven businesses ranging from a computer company to a minerals business to a cooked meats and animal foods business. By 1995, they had three businesses: BP Exploration to find the oil and gas, BP Oil which refines and markets the fuel, and BP Chemicals. She does not say these changes were easy or free from pain – far from it. She does describe moving from a complex, bureaucratic organization, with 89 standing committees and a huge head office, to a vastly leaner business. She describes the struggle to change the values of the people in the organization, to give them power, and to have them accept radical change in structure and process. She also describes how executives actively participated in the planning and execution of strategies that led to the removal of their own jobs from the company. There were many financial safeguards for managers in this position, which is one of the costs of change, but nonetheless people worked with management to remove their own jobs, and that is simply amazing.

Internal market research

It also follows that we can use our market research techniques inside the company to get to grips with who has to change, in what way, how much, and what the patterns are, in our internal marketplace.

Finally, as with the external marketing programme, we should not neglect the importance of measuring results wherever possible. This may be in terms of such criteria as people's attitudes towards the market strategy and their commitment to putting it into practice, or customer perceptions of our success in delivering our promises to them – or, perhaps more appositely, our lack of success as presented by complaints and so on.

Internal marketing targets

Again, in exact parallel with the conventional external marketing plan, our internal marketing programmes should be directed at chosen targets or segments within the market. The choice of key targets for the internal marketing programme should be derived directly from the goals of the external marketing programme, and the types of organizational and human change needed to implement market strategies. The internal marketplace may be segmented at the simplest level by the job roles and functions played by groups of people, e.g. top management, other departments, and marketing and sales staff.

'The choice of key targets for the internal marketing programme should be derived directly from the goals of the external marketing programme, and the types of organizational and human change needed to implement market strategies'

Alternatively, we might look beyond job characteristics to the key sources of support and resistance to the external marketing plan which are anticipated, to identify targets for reinforcement, or for persuasion and negotiation. Perhaps at the deepest level we might choose our targets on the basis of the individual's attitudes towards the external market and customers, and the key values that we need communicated to external customers, together with people's career goals.

For instance, one approach used successfully in internal marketing of IT has been to apply the diffusion of innovation models, widely recognized in conventional consumer research. The idea here is to identify and specifically target the 'opinion leaders' in the company (regardless of rank or functional specialization), because if they can be persuaded to change, the rest will gradually follow.

Increasingly, internal marketing may also be concerned with partners in alliances and networks, where the issue is positioning our market strategies with employees and managers in alliance organizations. Indeed, as organizations become more complex and reliant on the effectiveness of networks of collaborators, this may become a major role for internal marketing.

The hidden face of strategic internal marketing

In fact, as well as giving us a model for analysing internal marketing needs, we can go further because this structure also provides a practical route to get to grips with the 'corporate environment' for market strategy.

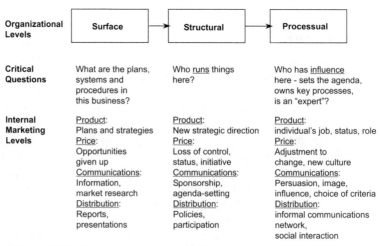

Organizational Levels	Surface	Structural	Processual
Critical Questions	What are the plans, systems and procedures in this business?	Who runs things here?	Who has influence here - sets the agenda, owns key processes, is an "expert"?
Internal Marketing Levels	Product: Plans and strategies Price: Opportunities given up Communications: Information, market research Distribution: Reports, presentations	Product: New strategic direction Price: Loss of control, status, initiative Communications: Sponsorship, agenda-setting Distribution: Policies, participation	Product: individual's job, status, role Price: Adjustment to change, new culture Communications: Persuasion, image, influence, choice of criteria Distribution: informal communications network, social interaction

Figure 14.9 Levels of internal marketing

The model in Figure 14.9 suggests that when we get to a company we may start by asking about the techniques, the systems and so on, but behind this the really important questions are 'who *runs* the organization?' and 'who has *influence* in this organization?'

On this basis, we have developed a crude analytical device used to encourage managers to go beyond the superficial aspects of how their organizations work in planning internal marketing, to distinguish between a level of *surface* analysis, which is primarily about plans, techniques and systems, and the level of *structure* and *process* analysis. This can have the effect of widening the debate from simply the presentation of the plan to the company to the more difficult and covert issues of power and culture in companies in the way shown.

At the rational level, for example, the 'product' is the marketing plan or strategy, but the additional dimensions suggested are the implied changes in culture and environmental perceptions, and the status of others in the company, while at the most covert level the 'product' implies the existence or threat of changes in the individual's role or job design which are needed to implement the marketing strategy. Similarly, the 'price' people are asked to 'pay' starts simply as the alternative opportunities given up, but at deeper levels involves the status and loss of control they may feel, and the psychological adjustment to strategic change required of others in the company.

We have found that managers are far more comfortable using the term 'internal marketing' to focus attention on the elements of the corporate environment inside the company that need to be changed in order to implement marketing plans, and that this terminology provides an acceptable and legitimate framework for unpacking the issues in the company. It may sound tacky, but it works! The issue is getting to grips with the processes inside the organization, not just sending out glossy brochures.

'managers are far more comfortable using the term "internal marketing" to focus attention on the elements of the corporate environment inside the company that need to be changed in order to implement marketing plans'

REALITY CHECK
GE's 'WORKOUT' MODEL

The US multinational, General Electric, has developed an integrated approach to managing change implementation, in the form of its WorkOut programme – since used by many other organizations, such as the British insurance company Eagle Star.

Eagle Star was part of BAT, the tobacco and financial services group, but has since joined Zurich Financial Services. In the 1990s, Eagle Star lost hundreds of millions of pounds in the mortgage indemnity market, and was renowned in the motor insurance business for pursuing market share regardless of losses.

Patrick O'Sullivan joined Eagle Star as CEO in 1997, with the goal of changing the company's culture and turning around its performance. He described what he found as 'Happy Valley' – staff getting more and more rewards: flextime, benefits, bonuses, unrelated to the company's performance – and almost no-one aware of how bad the company's situation had become. He spent his early days with the company telling staff how bad things were and that change was coming. He encountered quiet resistance from a layer of senior and middle managers – he labelled them the 'permafrost' – and much cynicism from staff, who had seen seven CEOs come and go in the space of eight years.

O'Sullivan turned to the WorkOut programme as a way of implementing change, and started with his most innovative department – telesales. The goal of WorkOut, as developed by GE, is to shorten and improve decision making and enhance responsiveness to customers by using the collective intelligence of the entire company, not just a management elite. It works by employees generating proposals, which are costed and presented to three-day 'town meetings', where senior management is held to account. They have to give an on-the-spot 'yes' to fast implementation, or 'no' with credible reasons why the proposal cannot go ahead. Some degree of 'showmanship' is involved. One Eagle Star meeting featured a lady dressed in black bin-liners, carrying 75 balloons to represent the £75 it costs every time a customer is lost, which the audience was asked to burst, prior to hearing a set of proposals from telesales to improve customer retention.

O'Sullivan reports significant improvements in response time and productivity in telesales. His 'permafrost' has also thawed – only one of the eleven-strong management committee remains with the company.

Following the merger with Zurich, the WorkOut programme has been adopted by around 25 per cent of Zurich's businesses – the Zurich insurance services businesses report a verified saving of £15.4 million in the first two years.

Source: Andrew Bolger (2000), 'How Eagle Star Was Saved by a High-Flier', *Financial Times*, 30 June.

But, does internal marketing really work?

An easy question to ask, but a difficult one to answer. Certainly, the case evidence suggests that internal marketing has something to offer in achieving the sorts of strategic change we want. Consider the following examples drawn from our work with different types of organizations.

'the case evidence suggests that internal marketing has something to offer in achieving the sorts of strategic change we want'

A museum

Perhaps some of the simplest examples of the real barriers to implementing customer-focused market strategies come from the public sector, where the marketing concept is still regarded as innovative. In one case, for instance, the new marketing director of a public sector museum was trying to implement a strategy of converting an open-air museum site into a historical 'theme park'.

While apparently broadly supported by the organization (i.e. lip-service is paid), there were substantial barriers slowing down and reducing effective implementation. One such barrier was the operating personnel and the traditional culture of the museum. Quite simply, personnel were being asked to abandon their training as custodians and protectors of exhibits, and to become entertainers in costume who encouraged the 'customer' to handle and use exhibits. There was a major difficulty in achieving the transition for employees from 'policeman' to 'entertainer'.

More covertly, at a deeper cultural level, the senior managers of the organization have some considerable distaste for commercialization of their traditional 'business' by their political masters. Accordingly, they must give open support for obvious reasons, but real commitment is less easily obtained.

'the senior managers of the organization have some considerable distaste for commercialization of their traditional "business" by their political masters'

This pervasive attitude impacts on allocations of budget, manpower and the priorities imposed by the organization. It is these issues which provide the real agenda for this senior marketing executive – not the problems of generating a creative and innovative market strategy and plan for the museum.

We have found similar problems in other public service organizations faced with imperatives to become 'market oriented' and 'commercial'. The internal attitudes and potential resistance to income-generating activities from managers and operatives from the 'public service' tradition – hidden behind approving lip-service to marketing concepts – pose the most serious (but the most covert and difficult) barrier to actually implementing the new market strategies being devised by executives in such organizations.

A corporate bank

Another case example involves one of the secondary banks in the UK. The bank consists of a large retail branch network, backed by a number of small specialist units at the London centre. One of these units is Corporate Banking, servicing mainly multinational company headquarters in the City of London. The plan developed by this unit created a new market strategy of servicing medium- and large-sized corporate customers in all areas covered by the retail branch network (currently in the Retail Branch managers' remit), with the goal of a substantial increase in market share in the corporate market for the group.

On the face of things, the internal marketing needs were to inform branch managers of the new strategy, and to use this to reduce the pressure from the network for more staff to cover the corporate market. Branch managers were required to provide sales leads and market intelligence to the centre. Admittedly, branches would lose potential income, but they had never succeeded in realizing much of that potential anyway.

However, at the political level, an apparently rational strategy was deeply tied up with the power struggle within the organiza-tion – in terms of the centralization of control of the branches, the clash of cultures between technical City-based bankers and banking 'salesmen' in the field, and indeed ultimately the actual survival of the corporate banking unit. The real 'price' to be paid by branch managers was far more than potential loss of income – it was far more to do with a loss of autonomy for the branch manager in the local area, and a downgrading in status to an operator of 'commodity' consumer and small business banking.

The internal marketing strategy evolved has proved far more problematic than the external strategy. The key elements were written and spoken sponsorship from the chief executive – epitomized by a short memo to all branch managers, reading 'The train is now leaving the station. You are either on it or . . . ' – as well as joint planning between branch managers and corporate banking executives to gain some participation and communication between the branch managers and the corporate banking executives. This has been reinforced by operating on the evaluation/reward system to offer the branch manager some financial gain from assisting the corporate executive to exploit 'his' area, and greater rotation of staff between the branches and the centre.

Progress continues, but the company has paid a substantial price for the new corporate banking strategy, in time spent on winning branch managers round, and in increased managerial staff turnover at the branch level. It would be wrong to suggest that internal marketing offers easy answers to the problems of implementing market-led change. What is shown is the additional insight which can be generated, leading to an agenda of implementation issues at various levels. It should be said also that the case demonstrates vividly that the external strategy and its direct costs may be only the tip of the iceberg compared with the efforts and costs required to create change through an internal marketing strategy.

'the external strategy and its direct costs may be only the tip of the iceberg compared with the efforts and costs required to create change through an internal marketing strategy'

A retail financial services organization

In a medium-sized financial services organization, the central strategy, designed by the central Marketing Department and championed by the new General Manager, was 'cross-selling' between two divisions: the retail banks and the finance company. The concept was that since the banks and the finance company shared the same geographical areas, it would make sense for the bank to refer commercial loan business to the finance company, and for the finance company to push its commercial customers into banking with the group. Indeed, it was such an obvious strategy the new General Manager could not understand why it had not already happened.

At a wholly rational level, this strategy was the product and the price was the commission sacrificed by managers in referring business across divisions rather than selling more of their own products. Distribution and communication was by written plan, presentation at sales conferences, and so on. The effect in Year 1 of the new strategy was zero results in cross-selling.

Of course, if you dig deeper, as we had to, the product is really not just cross-selling, it is a changing role for the branch manager and increased control at the centre.

The most intractable issues were the hidden political and cultural barriers represented by the costs to managers of collaborating closely with divisional counterparts historically perceived, at best, as competitors – cultural barriers made worse by differences in ethnic and educational background and professional training between the divisions. The approach taken here hinged on the formation of joint planning and problem-solving teams, and the redesign of the management information system to allow clear measurement of the implementation and success of the new strategy.

Progress with implementing the cross-selling strategy continues in this company – with some remaining conflicts and breakdowns. Success is difficult to evaluate but recent discussions with branch managers suggest awareness of what they themselves describe as a change in the 'culture' of their company, and quite tangible operational changes in how the two operating divisions work together. Cross-selling is now happening in a significant way.

In one sense this is a success story – they now *do* cross-selling. But, if you look at the real cost to the business of getting cross-selling to happen – the strategy is an unmitigated disaster. At current levels, it will take about 20 years for the margins earned through cross-selling to pay back the cost of the joint-planning team exercise, let alone the staff turnover they created on the way. In these terms the strategy is an abject failure.

'if you plan your internal marketing strategy at the same time as your external market strategy, your financial evaluation may actually mean something, because it will include the real costs of implementation'

One of the lessons we have learned is that if you plan your internal marketing strategy at the *same time* as your external market strategy, your financial evaluation may actually mean something, because it will include the *real* costs of implementation. You may well reject a market strategy when you see the 'hidden' costs of implementation.

So, does it work?

It is impossible to say conclusively. The case evidence suggests that it helps, but it is difficult to generalize. But, where companies do make the internal marketing effort, it seems to have a good effect, and many more companies are now formalizing it in the search for effective implementation of market strategies that 'stretch' their companies. There are some cases that suggest that internal marketing may be the ideal vehicle to build the collaboration between market management and human resource management that we discussed earlier (see pp. 250–1). So, there may be value in adding an internal marketing structure to our market-led strategic change – because the evidence is that currently most of us simply don't bother.

How do we plan internal marketing?

The real joy of internal marketing strategies and programmes is that we can *directly* translate our external marketing policies, using *precisely* the same tools and techniques, and even present the plan in the same format:

'The real joy of internal marketing strategies and programmes is that we can directly translate our external marketing policies, using precisely the same tools and techniques'

- *Internal market strategy* – asks us to work out, in broad terms, an internal market strategy that is needed to gain the successful implementation of an external market strategy. It is here that we need to confront the real implications of our external market strategy for the internal customer – the decision makers, managers, operatives and others, without whose support, co-operation and commitment the external strategy will fail. This is the most critical question in the whole internal marketing exercise. It should not be skimped. It may be worth consulting the people directly concerned – doing internal market research. It is certainly worth incorporating some diversity of opinion. As we learn more, we can come back and redraft and rethink our conclusions here. It is here that we should take a view of what it is likely to cost us to achieve these things and the deadline for achieving them to implement the external marketing strategy on time.
- *Internal market segmentation* – is about identifying the targets in the internal marketplace around which we can build internal marketing programmes, which are different in what we have to achieve and how we are going to do it. This may not be straightforward, but is the route to real insights into the internal market problem, and effectiveness in how we cope with that problem. The most obvious way of identifying internal segments may be by role or function, or location, and this may be sufficient. It might be more productive to think of who are the innovators and opinion leaders who will influence others. We might approach this more directly in terms of the role that different people will play in implementing the external strategy and the problems they may face in this, or simply how much different people will have to change to get the external strategy to work.
- *Internal marketing programmes* – specify what internal marketing programmes will be needed in each internal market segment to achieve the objectives we have set. In each area we need to collect our thoughts about the rational issues but also

the human and cultural issues. To us the product may be a great new marketing plan that we need to inform people about (internal marketing communications), through formal presentations (internal marketing distribution), adjusting commission and evaluation systems as need be (internal marketing price). To the internal customer, the same plan may be about disruption and threat (product), loss of initiative and status (price), imposed without consultation by management (communication), and rigorously 'policed' through coercion (distribution). If internal marketing is about anything it is about confronting and coping with this conflict. It is this confrontation which will drive us away from thinking about internal marketing as writing customer care brochures and doing great plan presentations, towards coping with the human and organizational realities of what strategic change takes and costs. This is also the stage to take a look at the cost implications of what we now see to be necessary in our internal marketing: Does the internal marketing cost mean that the external market strategy is no longer attractive? Do we have to account for internal marketing cost which is more than we expected, but bearable? Do we have to change the external strategy to reduce the internal marketing cost? Are there cheaper ways of achieving the critical internal marketing goals?

- *Internal marketing evaluation* – what we can measure to see if we are getting there, ideally quantified and objective-reduced customer complaint rates, or higher customer satisfaction scores. This may be ambitious and we should not abandon important objectives because they are difficult to evaluate – we may have to settle for a subjective or qualitative evaluation, which is better than nothing. There is some logic not just in introducing new measurements relevant to what we are trying to change, but keeping those measurements broad – the danger is that we are fixated with the 'old' measures we have always used (e.g. short-term financial targets), when we would do better reviewing broader issues (such as employee behaviour or skills developed)[34].

'**Strategic internal marketing directly parallels our external market strategy and is a route to achieving implementation of those external strategies**'

The logic is simple – we can use our familiar and established marketing techniques to package and work on our problems *inside* the company. Strategic internal marketing directly parallels our external market strategy and is a route to achieving implementation of those external strategies. It is no more than a means to an end, but one which gives us important tools in the right circumstances.

So, what now?

The critical point to which we have been building throughout this discourse on market-led strategic change – building a customer-focused organization that delivers solid value to customers in their terms, defining our Strategic Pathway, and managing the organizational context for the process of going to market and sales – is implementation. The approach to implementation described here has tried to pull our thoughts together around the simple notion that the only thing that matters in all this is what we actually deliver to a paying customer.

However, when we focus on implementation, we can separate out a long-term and a short-term issue. The short-term issue is what has mainly occupied us so far – getting things to happen *now*. The longer-term issue is about how we manage things to *avoid* the implementation problems we have considered here.

What this means is that there is a need to consider both process management and execution skills in implementation. The difference is that managing the strategy process has the goal of integrating implementation and change issues with the market strategy, with the goal of avoiding the emergence of implementation barriers. On the other hand, execution skills are concerned with how to manage a way through the change problems and barriers, which stand in the way of market strategy. While these are different approaches, they are not mutually exclusive, and in most practical situations we will need to give attention to both.

The reasons for this are suggested in Figure 14.10. The implementation scenarios suggested are:

- *Weak Implementation*, where the management of process and execution skills is inappropriate to drive a market strategy.
- *Management-Driven Implementation*, where the emphasis is on leadership and control by management to put a strategy into effect and to overcome problems or barriers which may exist.
- *Implementation-Driven Strategy*, where the emphasis is on exploiting the capabilities of the existing organization and adapting strategies to 'fit' with this reality.
- *Integrated Strategy and Implementation*, which achieves implementation by both managing key processes and applying management execution skills.

The 'Weak Implementation' scenario is largely based on managers assuming that once plans and strategies are written, then people will go away and make them happen. Some

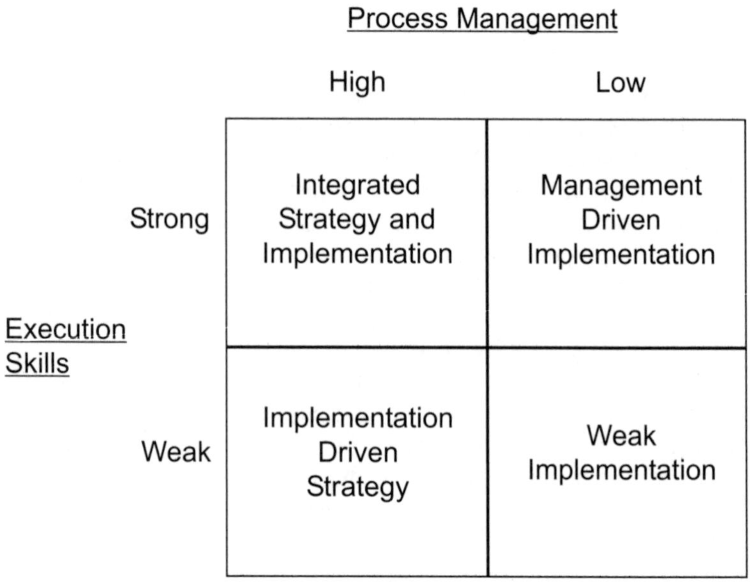

Process Management

	High	Low
Strong	Integrated Strategy and Implementation	Management Driven Implementation
Weak	Implementation Driven Strategy	Weak Implementation

Execution
Skills

Figure 14.10   Execution skills versus process management in marketing implementation

managers make these assumptions implicitly in how they approach things, and then get upset when their edicts and commands are not put into effect or are implemented half-heartedly or haphazardly. Any market strategy that matters to an organization deserves to have implementation taken more seriously than this.

The 'Management-Driven Implementation' scenario is probably closest to the traditional view of how things should be managed. The emphasis is on line management to take charge, to overcome obstacles, to lead, to coerce, and to make things happen – it relies on high-quality management execution skills to overcome implementation barriers. It is quick to put into practice and in the short-term may achieve change, but the problem is it lacks longer-term effectiveness in sustaining change.

The 'Implementation-Driven Strategy' scenario is where the focus of market strategies is dominated by exploiting existing capabilities and skills in the organization, mainly by adapting market strategies to 'fit' with the organization's existing competencies. This is also quick to be put into effect, and will keep implementation costs low. It is weaker in achieving strategic change because the emphasis is on exploiting what we already have, not developing new capabilities – this is fine until the point when our capabilities do not provide what the market wants, i.e. our strategy becomes outdated by market change.

Table 14.3 Implementation scenarios

	Weak Implementation	Management-Driven Implementation	Implementation Driven Strategy	Integrated Strategy and Implementation
Characteristics	Ignores implementation	Focuses on the management of execution and behaviour	Focuses on exploiting capabilities of existing organization and matching to strategy	Emphasizes building strategy and implementation together
Timing	N/A	Fast	Fast	Slow
Cost of implementation strategy	None	Medium	Low	High
Ability to manage strategic change	None	Short-term: high Long-term: low	Short-term: low Long-term: low	Short-term: low Long-term: high
Implementation effectiveness	None	Medium	High	High

The 'Integrated Strategy and Implementation' scenario is the ideal to which we aspire. Implementation is not an issue because it is fully integrated with the market strategy, and we are not forced to cling to existing skills and processes, because part of developing strategy is developing the appropriate processes, structures, skills and capabilities to drive the strategy. It is slower to achieve and expensive, and in the short-term not outstandingly effective. It is probably the only route to long-term sustained strategic change. It is also the scenario we understand least well, and find rarely in practice. We will assume, however, that this is the situation to which we aspire.

The characteristics of these different implementation scenarios are summarized in Table 14.3. A good question for the executive to raise at this point is: which of these scenarios sounds most like how we do things in our company, and how can we improve the way we do things? Integrating strategy and implementation is likely to be the only real way to cope with the challenges we have detailed throughout the earlier chapters.

'A good question for the executive to raise at this point is: which of these scenarios sounds most like how we do things in our company, and how can we improve the way we do things?'

REALITY CHECK

**THE AWKWARD QUESTIONS ABOUT
IMPLEMENTATION AND INTERNAL MARKETING**

How much of an issue is implementation in our company? Do people dismiss the issue? Do things get done the way we want – or are there barriers and hurdles to strategy implementation? What did our analysis of strategic gaps suggest the big implementation challenges would be?

How good are we at building implementation realities into our thinking about strategy right from the start – do we, for example, make full use of the hidden capabilities and distinctiveness in our company in building strategy? Do we allow for the costs of change when we evaluate strategic options?

Do we make our implementation priorities explicit and clear in a formal implementation strategy that goes along with our market strategy?

Is there scope for improving our implementation performance through a formal internal marketing strategy? What could we achieve with this mechanism – who would we involve inside the company and from outside (e.g. customers)?

How well are we doing in working towards the situation where strategy and implementation are an integrated issue in our company's thinking and behaviour, so we may really be able to say that there is no implementation problem here?

With that broader challenge laid down, it only remains to overview the managerial agenda for market-led strategic change.

An agenda for market-led strategic change

This book is about transforming the company's process of going to market. That transformation is achieved by being *market-led*, and by managing the difficult, messy and uncomfortable process of *strategic change* which this implies for organizations.

I said at the outset that this was a book for the person who wants to change the way the company goes to market, and who will champion that change and drive it through the company. This is not a simple task. Much of what we have considered here is about building an effective agenda for change – an agenda which probably has both open and hidden levels! But this agenda is our central focus, if we are to take the challenge of market-led strategic change seriously.

'Much of what we have considered here is about building an effective agenda for change – an agenda which probably has both open and hidden levels!'

So, what are the real problems?

At its simplest, the entire logic of this book is based on the observation that the *real* problems for virtually all organizations are incredibly obvious and straightforward. The real problems are generally not about the lack of sophisticated skills and techniques. The challenge is to look at the whole process which creates a market offering of value to customers. This is much broader than looking at 'marketing' in the conventional sense – it involves everyone in the company and it crosses traditional departmental boundaries and even organizational boundaries to focus our attention firmly on what the customer gets that creates value for that customer and differentiates us from the competition.

Like all processes, the process of going to market has several dimensions (see pp. 585–8) – it is about more than analysis, strategizing and plan-writing, it also has behavioural and organizational dimensions. While the analytical dimension is concerned with building customer focus and a market strategy that is linked directly to marketing programmes, the behavioural dimension is concerned with the people issues in the process, and the organizational dimension is concerned with the real context in which the process operates.

The behavioural dimension is concerned with things like: the real attitudes that people show towards customers and customer service and their underlying beliefs about what matters in the market, their commitment to customers and their ownership of the problem of making market strategies effective, as well as their ability and willingness to cross traditional boundaries to get things to happen. The organizational dimension is concerned with the culture of the organization and the leadership and role model provided by managers, as well as organizational structures that reinforce traditional arrangements as opposed to cross-functional team building, and underpinning all this the way the organization understands the market.

The consistency between these dimensions is concerned with managing the process of going to market so as to deliver the value offering to the customer, and is concerned with implementation effectiveness. This is the real test – have we fallen into the trap of a value proposition offering customer value and service in which our people do not believe, and which our organization cannot deliver?

This brings us back to the point of Market-Led Strategic Change. Let's just remind ourselves of what that means.

Market-led . . .

The logic we have pursued is that if you cut through the corporate trappings to the real substance – there is only one thing that links and integrates everything and gives a purpose to everything, and that is the customer. Being market-led means put the customer and customer value at the top of the management agenda, and using that as the focus for how we manage the organization and achieve our corporate objectives. It is about interpreting customer demands and needs to the key players inside the organization and changing their priorities. It is about the integration of all company activities and investments around what matters most to our survival – the customer – for what we do. For a start, strategy needs to be creative, accessible and exciting, not bureaucratic and mysterious – the strategic pathway is one way to handle this issue.

'Being market-led means put the customer and customer value at the top of the management agenda, and using that as the focus for how we manage the organization and achieve our corporate objectives'

This is not about being reactive and drifting helplessly with the vagaries of the randomly changing marketplace. Far from it. It is about purposefully focusing on the customer and aiming our resources at being best at what matters most to our customer – the things that create superior customer value.

We have the tools to achieve this – market sensing, the customer-focused organization, market strategies and marketing programmes. We all too often do not *use* them very effectively, but they are there.

. . . Strategic change

The sad truth is that, for most of us, tackling these underlying, basic problems is not about fine-tuning and marginally improving tactical and technical marketing performance. It is about deep-seated, fundamental strategic change in our organizations. It is about changing cultures, challenging the status quo, breaking the inertia, coping with obstacles and resistance to change, changing the distribution of power and how management controls the operation – just a few trivial issues like that!

The point is that just because strategic change is difficult, it does not mean we ignore it – we have to create it and manage it. When all is said and done *nothing* is impossible.

Anyway, it has frequently amazed me in working on strategic planning with diverse organizations to see unconventional, way-out strategic ideas initially dismissed out-of-hand by the prevailing wisdom – only to see those same strategic ideas successfully implemented later, because someone cared enough to make it happen. *Nothing* is impossible. It may be difficult. It may be costly. It is *not* impossible. Perhaps the greatest boon of the Internet is that it shows the 'impossible' becoming possible, on a daily basis.

> **'Nothing *is* impossible. It may be difficult. It may be costly. It is not impossible'**

Market-led strategic change

So, MLSC has two components. The first – being market-led – is about the up-front content, focus and integration of our value offering to become better at doing the things that matter to the paying customer. The second – strategic change – is about coping with the revolution created by being market-led. Now, let's consider the real management agenda.

Creating the momentum for strategic change starts with isolating and defining the strategic issues, i.e. establishing the agenda to be addressed. That is the real control that managers exert over an organization. In Chapter 1, I described this as the ten steps to transforming the process of going to market. Those ten steps can be seen in the following outline or checklist for focusing management attention on MLSC, and packing together the material we have covered in the book looks like this:

What do we have to change?

> The process of going to market, not 'marketing' in the conventional sense (Chapter 1)

> Company-wide ownership of the process of going to market – total integration of the activities that create value for customers – not marketing 'specialization' (Chapters 1 and 5)

> Our attitudes towards our customers and the relationships we have with them (Chapter 2)

Our understanding of the customer value imperative – not just brands and 'relationships' and the era of the sophisticated customer (Chapter 3)

The ways in which e-business will be integrated into the process of going to market (Chapter 4.com)

Making market strategy a creative and innovative activity, not just repetitive bureaucracy – strategizing (Chapter 6)

Routes to change

Superior market sensing capabilities and achieving enhanced customer focus, as a foundation for the strategic pathway (Chapter 7)

Rethinking critical market choices, segments and niches that shape the strategic pathway (Chapter 8)

Developing and testing the value proposition to our customers that is the centre of the strategic pathway (Chapter 9)

Managing the key relationships that underpin the strategic pathway (Chapter 10)

Developing a coherent plan out of the strategizing, not vice versa (Chapter 11)

How to change

Turning strategy into programmes of action (Chapter 12)

Managing the key processes of planning and budgeting to build ownership and action (Chapter 13)

Developing implementation and internal marketing strategies to manage change (Chapter 14)

How you choose to approach this agenda will depend on your circumstances and the most urgent issues for your company. In the right situation, the MLSC structure can be turned into a company-wide programme. The agenda can be integrated into an existing management training and development programme, leading to training and development work for our key executives. It can be addressed as part of organizational development, leading to changes in our structure, systems and procedures. It may simply be the agenda for the next Board meeting or a Director's workshop. In other situations we may have to pick the issues off, one at a time, using whatever resources and support we can get. The important thing is to get started.

This MLSC agenda follows the structure of the book, leaving the action planning stage to be covered in the final chapter. However, there is the last question of getting started to consider first.

But where do we start?

In times of turbulence and change we need to think very seriously about what we need to do to help managers cope. When we look at our programmes of change, then one test is to ask 'what are we doing to help and support our managers to do the following things':

- to understand the 'big picture', not just day-to-day running-the-business decisions;
- to identify the alternatives open to us;
- to learn from best practice in leading companies everywhere, including competitor and partner organizations;
- to make sense of the future and the role managers have to play in shaping that future;
- to build networks of information that cut across traditional boundaries and reinforce our learning; and
- to answer the manager's top three questions[35].

REALITY CHECK

THE AWKWARD QUESTIONS

Well, of course, one thing you could do to decide where to start is to go back to the 'Awkward Questions' at the end of each chapter. These were the Reality Checks that you skipped over, assuming that they were just those irritating 'ending-off bits' that people put in at the conclusion of chapters. However, since you chose to skip over them as beneath your contempt, now you need them, I'm not going to tell you what pages they are on. So there!

Actually, one very nice summary of the options is provided by William Band[36], a Canadian consultant. In the same way that we have done here, Band argues that the greatest barriers to success in the struggle for a customer focus came from traditional organizational structures and processes, and employee attitudes and beliefs – so, he says, the way we manage organizations and people will have to change. In the same way that Tom Bonoma talks about the critical 'marketing subversives'[37], who take advantage of 'loose' money, people and time, to make marketing work, in spite of the company's policies and procedures, Band talks about marketing's 'organizational revolutionaries' attacking the status quo with planned change strategies (and allies in human resource management, see pp. 250–1). Band argues that where you start depends on how *fast* change is needed and where the *leadership* comes from, and he identifies the following options:

- *Annexation* – start with the part of the organization that is most willing to change and has the greatest chance of success, and add extra 'chunks' later.
- *Perestroika* – where top management leads the change process, dragging the organization behind, screaming and kicking.
- *Guerilla campaign* – a bottom-up, hidden, selective exploitation of opportunities for change as they occur.
- *Palace coup* – those who want change take control.

There are many excuses available for ignoring the imperative for change and improvement:

'I guess one person can make a difference . . .
but most of the time they probably shouldn't'

(attributed to Marge Simpson of the Simpson Family)

Making change happen is a personal commitment and a personal risk. Sometimes you got to take risks! As John F. Kennedy once said 'If not us, who? If not now, when?'. It may be somewhat unoriginal and trite (and why break the habit of a lifetime now), but the following seems to be a wholly appropriate thought with which to end this book:

'Somewhere in the African jungle this morning a gazelle will wake up. The gazelle knows it must run faster than the slowest lion, otherwise it will die. Somewhere else in the jungle a lion wakes up. The lion knows it must run faster than the slowest gazelle, otherwise it will starve. The moral is whoever you are, wherever you are, you better wake up and start running . . . '

Notes and references

1. Lyn Bicker (1999), 'Twenty Things You Didn't Know About Change', *Financial Times*, 5 January. Emiko Terazono (1999), 'Re-Engineering Faces the Highest Risk of Failure', *Financial Times*, 1 October. Vanessa Houlder (1998), 'Justify the Need for Change', *Financial Times*, 1 January.

2. The late Tom Bonoma was fond of remarking that: 'The average table-top could tell you what you should be doing. A piece of fauna in the field outside could tell you what your strategy should be. The issue is whether you can do it.'

3. Thomas V. Bonoma (1985), *The Marketing Edge: Making Strategies Work*, New York: Free Press.

4. Thomas Masiello (1988), 'Developing Market Responsiveness Through-out Your Company, *Industrial Marketing Management*, **17**, 85–93.

5. Kevin Thomson (1999), 'Folk Lore', *Marketing Business*, May, 40–41.

6. Thomas Stewart (1998), *Intellectual Capital*, New York: Bantam Books.

7. Richard Pascale, Mark Millman and Linda Gioja (1997), 'Changing The Way We Change', *Harvard Business Review*, November/December, 127–39.

8. Jeanie Daniel Duck (2001), *The Change Monster: The Human Forces That Fuel or Foil Corporate Transformation and Change*, New York: Crown Business.

9. Peter Mitchell (1998), 'Innovation in the Right Place', *Financial Times*, 17 April.

10. Alan Mitchell (1997), 'Evolution', *Marketing Business*, May, 48.

11. . . . and when was it we allowed Personnel Departments to start calling themselves Human Resource Management?

12. This section relies heavily on the material in: Nigel F. Piercy and Frank V. Cespedes (1996), 'Implementing Marketing Strategy', *Journal of Marketing Management*, **12**, 135–60. Frank V. Cespedes and Nigel F. Piercy (1995), 'Implementation of Strategy', in Malcolm Warner (ed.), *International Encyclopaedia of Business and Management*, London: Rout-ledge. Nigel F. Piercy (1998), 'Implementing Marketing Strategies', in Colin Egan and Michael J. Thomas (eds), *Strategic Marketing*, Oxford: Butterworth-Heinemann.

13. David Jobber (1996), 'Theory Without Practice', *Marketing Business*, February, 51.

14. Quoted in Vanessa Houlder (1998), 'Justify the Need for Change', *Financial Times*, 1 January.

15. Jonathan Lynn and Anthony Jay (1987), *Yes Prime Minister, Volume II*, London: BBC Books.

16. Thomas V. Clark and Bruce Clark (1990), 'Assessing Marketing Perform-ance', in Thomas V. Bonoma and T. K. Kosnik (eds), *Marketing Management: Text and Cases*, Homewood, IL: Irwin.

17. Thomas V. Bonoma (1985), *The Marketing Edge: Making Strategies Work*, New York: Free Press.

18. Thomas V. Bonoma (1985), op. cit.

19. Jonathan Lynn and Anthony Jay (1987), op. cit.

20. Thomas V. Bonoma (1985), op. cit.

21. Chris Argyris (1985), *Strategy, Change and Defensive Routines*, New York: Harper & Row.

22. Nigel F. Piercy and Kenneth J. Peattie (1988), 'Matching Marketing Strategies to Corporate Culture: The Parcel and the Wall', *Journal of General Management*, **13** (4), 33–44. Nigel F. Piercy (1989), 'Diagnosing and Solving Implementation Problems in Strategic Planning', *Journal of General Management*, **15** (1), 19–38.

23. Evert Gummesson (1988), *Marketing: A Long Term Interactive Relationship*, Gottenburg: Anderson Sandberg Dheen Ltd.

24. Christian Gronroos (1983), *Strategic Marketing and Management in the Service Sector*, Cambridge, MA: Marketing Science Institute.

25. Evert Gummesson (1990), *The Part-Time Marketer*, University of Karlsstad, Research Report 90:3.

26. Mary C. Gilly and Mary Wolfinberger (1996), *Advertising's Second Audience: Employee Reactions to Organizational Communications*, Cambridge, MA: Marketing Science Institute.

27. Thomas V. Bonoma (1990), 'Employees Can Free the "Hostages"', *Marketing News*, 19 March, 14–15.

28. Alan Mitchell (1994), 'The People Factor', *Marketing Business*, October, 24–28.

29. Alan Mitchell (1994), 'The Message not the Media', *Marketing Business*, November, 21–24.

30. Quoted in Alan Mitchell (1994), 'The Message not the Media', *Marketing Business*, November, 21–24.

31. Quoted in Alan Mitchell (1994), 'The Revolution Within', *Marketing Business*, January, 22–25.

32. Sal Divita (1996), 'Colleagues are Customers: Market to Them', *Marketing News*, 21 October.

33. Dave Ulrich (1989), 'Tie the Corporate Knot: Gaining Complete Customer Commitment', *Sloan Management Review*, Summer, 19–27.

34. Keith Ruddle and David Feeny (1997), *Transforming the Organization: New Approaches to Measurement, Management and Leadership*, Oxford: Templeton College. Vanessa Houlder (1997), 'Wider Picture Provides the Best Score', *Financial Times*, 18 July.

35. The manager's top three questions are always the same. They are: (1) What about me? (2) What about me? (3) What about me?

36. William A. Band (1991), *Creating Value for Customers: Designing and Implementing a Total Corporate Strategy*, New York: John Wiley.

37. Thomas V. Bonoma (1986), 'Marketing Subversives', *Harvard Business Review*, November/December, 113–18.

Case 6   Trolleywars*
The next generation

The British grocery business illustrates the continuing struggle for market leadership and competitive positioning and repositioning in a large, intensely competitive and highly dynamic sector. Recent years have seen: major changes in managerial leadership at the top of most of the established companies in the grocery business; widespread public attacks on price levels and the frequent declaration of 'price wars' by the leading competitors; the entry of the US retailer Wal-Mart into the British market through the purchase of Asda; and the polarizing of competitive activity into large out-of-town superstores on the one hand, and local convenience stores on the other. We pick up the story of the grocery sector in the late 1990s and look at the strategic pattern emerging in the early 2000s.

'We pick up the story of the grocery sector in the late 1990s and look at the strategic pattern emerging in the early 2000s'

The major competitors in the British grocery market are: Tesco, Sainsburys, Asda (Wal-Mart), Safeway, and a group of smaller players including companies like Somerfield, the Co-op and Budgens. By 2001, *Retail Intelligence* estimated that Tesco was holding 25.1 per cent of all supermarket trade, compared to Sainsbury (17.6 per cent), Asda (14.5 per cent) and Safeway (11 per cent). The large lead opened up by Tesco partly reflects its greater emphasis on non-food products than Sainsbury, but also the fact it is outselling its rival. In fact, the shares of the grocery business through the 1990s, estimated by the Institute of Grocery Distribution, are shown in Table 1 and other statistics in Table 2.

The positioning of the main competing brands is broadly that: Tesco leads in customer service – 'every little helps'; Asda is the consumer's champion – 'everyday low prices'; Sainsburys 'makes life taste better'; and Safeway makes shopping easier – 'fresh to go'.

'Tesco leads in customer service – "every little helps"; Asda is the consumer's champion – "everyday low prices"; Sainsburys "makes life taste better"; and Safeway makes shopping easier – "fresh to go"'

Historically, the competitive structure of the British supermarket sector through the 1980s and early 1990s was dominated by J. Sainsbury, more than 120 years old and in the sixth generation of founding family management. Sainsbury was positioned on its strength in product and store quality and customer service, and had achieved the status of a British 'institution'. Sainsbury had led the way for the increasingly sophisticated British grocery consumer to exotic new foods and an innovative range of high-quality wines and household

---

* This case material has been prepared on the basis of discussions with industry executives and published secondary sources.

Table 1   Market shares in the UK grocery sector*

	1990 (%)	1991 (%)	1992 (%)	1993 (%)	1994 (%)	1995 (%)	1996 (%)	1997 (%)	1998 (%)	1999 (%)
Tesco	9.7	9.9	10.1	10.4	11.4	13.4	14.2	14.8	15.2	15.6
Sainsbury	11.0	11.3	11.9	12.1	12.3	12.2	12.2	12.4	12.2	11.8
Asda	6.8	6.5	6.3	6.5	6.7	7.2	7.8	8.3	8.5	8.9
Safeway	7.1	7.2	7.3	7.5	7.6	7.3	7.6	7.6	7.6	7.4
Morrisons	1.4	1.7	1.7	1.9	2.2	2.4	2.5	2.5	2.6	3.0
All others	64.0	63.4	62.7	61.6	59.8	57.5	55.7	54.4	53.6	53.3

* Source: Institute of Grocery Distribution (2001)

Table 2   The main supermarket groups in Britain*

	Number of employees	Number of stores	Total sales area (sq ft)	Weekly sales (£ per sq ft)	Profit on sales (%)
Tesco	185 600	568	14.6 m	21.12	5.9
Sainsbury	175 600	391	10.9 m	18.59	7.6
Asda	76 600	218	8.8 m	13.77	5.3
Safeway	75 200	500	9.3 m	14.10	6.9

* Source: Key Note Publications (1999)

products, and pioneered superstores and high-quality own-label products. Sainsbury was market leader in every sense.

The second competitor was Tesco. Tesco had grown as a downmarket discount retailer, with origins in the market stalls of the East End of London and growth through early self-service stores in London and Essex. By the 1960s, Tesco was one of Britain's fastest growing companies, and the company started to drop its cheap and dowdy downmarket image and attacked the middle of the market. However, in the early 1990s, Tesco was badly wrong-footed by the economic recession – the company was behind Sainsbury in quality, service and market reputation, and its market share was under attack in a value-oriented market by price discounters like Aldi.

Behind the main players were smaller competitors like Safeway, Asda and Kwik Save – each potentially threatening, but each with its own problems in the 1980s and early 1990s. However, the structure of the old grocery market and the strategic positioning of the main players changed – some say changed forever – in 1995.

The day in 1995 that Sainsbury finally lost market leadership in the British supermarket sector was headline news in many national newspapers. Comments were made about the 'end of an era' in Britain, particularly since Sainsbury lost its market share leadership to Tesco, its traditional rival with its 'pile it high, sell it cheap' background. The trauma was not so much the loss of a few market share points, but genuine loss of market *leadership* – in quality, innovation, customer service and the ability to change in line with customers' requirements. (Indeed, in the 1970s and early 1980s, Tesco led on market share, but was never recognized as 'market leader'.) Nonetheless, this was the time when reality caught up with reputation.

> **'Sainsbury lost its market share leadership to Tesco, its traditional rival with its "pile it high, sell it cheap" background. The trauma was not so much the loss of a few market share points, but genuine loss of market leadership'**

The loss of leadership in market share for Sainsbury resulted from a steady erosion of the lead over Tesco. Sainsbury had lost share primarily to Tesco, but also to Asda and Safeway. The financial performance of Sainsbury also deteriorated dramatically in this period. In 1993–96, Sainsbury shares slumped more than 30 per cent from 579p to 404p, underperforming against the FTSE index by 48 per cent and the supermarket sector by 28 per cent. The Sainsbury family owns some 40 per cent of the company, and in the 1992–1996 period some £1.2 billion was wiped off the value of its holdings. This decline has not been stopped by further profit warnings by the company to the City.

By 1996, Tesco's rate of sales growth was three times faster than Sainsbury's, and by 1997 forecasts suggested Tesco had become a significantly bigger profit earner than Sainsbury. In 1997, Tesco continued to increase profit levels, while Sainsbury and Safeway both issued profit warnings to the City, and Tesco sales were almost a third higher than Sainbury's. At that time, analysts did not believe that Sainsbury could ever regain market leadership. This was reflected in the relative performance of their shares – compared to the rest of the retail sector, Tesco clearly outperforms Sainsbury by a wide margin, and in 1996 Tesco share value equalled Sainbury's for the first time. The signs in 1997 were that Sainsbury had no effective strategy to recover the position and the gap achieved by Tesco was increasing.

By the start of 2001, the sector was characterized by Asda and Tesco fighting the battle to see which could claim to be the lowest price or 'best value' food retailer, while Sainsbury's had conceded defeat in the price war and is trying to differentiate itself on the basis of quality, Safeway is also cutting prices, and Wm Morrison is trying to keep up with its larger rivals in prices to retain its value-conscious customers in the north of England. Each of the major competitors faces different but equally demanding challenges in the early part of the 2000s.

> **'Each of the major competitors faces different but equally demanding challenges in the early part of the 2000s'**

Not least of those challenges come from a government that: vilified supermarkets in its 'rip-off' Britain campaign, subjected the sector to a two-year Competition Commission investigation, threatened to make them scrap free car parking, and suggested tougher planning restrictions on new developments. Chats between Prime Minister Tony Blair and Wal-Mart are said to have eased the American company's entry to Britain through its purchase of Asda, with promises of lower prices. The government also had a fair attempt at blaming the supermarket companies for the 2001 'foot and mouth' epidemic. The Labour Party early signalled its intention to look at supermarkets again, when re-elected in June 2001.

Tesco Stores

'Tesco is the market leader in the British grocery and supermarket sectors, but more than this it is a world-class retailer on an international stage'

Tesco is the market leader in the British grocery and supermarket sectors, but more than this it is a world-class retailer on an international stage. Tesco is admired throughout the world for its skills in market responsiveness, customer service, cost management and supply chain excellence. Its e-commerce venture – Tesco Direct – is globally recognized as the best Internet grocery operation in the world. The status of the company is seen in its solid growth in share value into 2001 (see Figure 1). Tesco is Britain's largest private sector employer – with 20 000 additional jobs announced in April 2000 – and is the standard against which other retailers in Britain are judged.

It should be noted that CEO Terry Leahy blames his flat share value in the 1998–2000 period as the market undervaluing Tesco due to media attacks on 'rip-off Britain' and the government's Competition Commission investigation into supermarkets. With those problems behind him, he has shown rapid growth in share value and market capitalization (see Table 3). Indeed, Leahy was extremely angry at the time that the low share price left him vulnerable to potential overseas predators while he was taking the

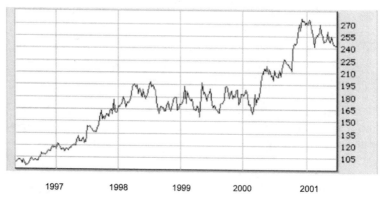

Figure 1 Tesco plc share performance, 1997–2001

Table 3   Tesco financials, 1997–2001

	1997	**1998**	**1999**	**2000**	**2001**
Turnover (£m)	13 887	16 452	17 158	18 796	20 988
Pre-tax profit (£m)	750	760	842	933	1 054
Earnings per share (p)	7.83	8.86	9.37	10.2	11.3
Dividend per share (p)	3.45	3.87	4.12	4.48	4.98
Market capitalization (£m)	7 580	11 364	11 983	11 497	18 197

business forward during 2000. He does not take kindly to people who mess with his business. He may have felt slightly better when he announced profits in 2001 that had gone through the £1 billion barrier for the first time, having become Britain's most profitable retailer already in 1999.

'Leahy was extremely angry at the time that the low share price left him vulnerable to potential overseas predators while he was taking the business forward during 2000. He does not take kindly to people who mess with his business'

The history of Tesco

Tesco was founded by Jack Cohen (later Sir John) from his food trading activities in the post-War East End of London, and the business was associated from its earliest growth with high-volume, low-price retailing with limited service and quality in merchandising – encapsulated in Cohen's 'pile it high, sell it cheap' slogan.

The strategic development of this business is largely associated with the leadership of Ian (now Lord) MacLaurin. An engineering apprentice, MacLaurin was hired in 1958 by Cohen personally, apparently because of his cricket prowess. MacLaurin became the protégé of Arthur Thrush, Retail Director, and became Chairman in 1973 – fighting an early and highly significant boardroom battle to start a new image for Tesco by abandoning the downmarket Green Shield trading stamps collectables, which had been the major Tesco marketing ploy of the 1960s. MacLaurin's aspirations for making Tesco the best player in the supermarket sector were met with derision inside and outside the company.

MacLaurin as Chairman was partnered with David Malpas as Managing Director – credited by many as the 'brains' underpinning MacLaurin's strong leadership. MacLaurin's strategy in the 1980s was founded on opening new stores in out-of-town locations, with much higher levels of quality and value than Tesco had previously attempted. The substantial change in the Tesco organization needed to implement this strategy is associated with MacLaurin's autocratic management style. He was always addressed by directors as 'Chairman' to his face, but also referred to in this way in his absence.

Although the company's aggressive price-cutting had caused some liquidity problems in the 1980s, the major challenge was in the early

'Having moved the operation progressively into the middle of the market, Tesco was wrong-footed by the economic recession of the early 1990s'

1990s. Having moved the operation progressively into the middle of the market, Tesco was wrong-footed by the economic recession of the early 1990s. Tesco's market share was under attack from price discounters like Aldi, while it still had not caught up with Sainsbury in non-price competitiveness.

The bad times of 1992 led to a series of internal changes and marketing initiatives. MacLaurin abandoned his role as 'retail dictator' and gave much freedom to Terry Leahy, a marketing man in the succession line for Chief Executive, who drove a number of critical marketing programmes: the introduction of 'value lines' that matched or undercut discounters on commodity items, while maintaining margins on most of the range; establishing smaller inner-city Tesco Metro stores, to supplement out-of-town superstores; the launch of the Clubcard loyalty programme, which doubled the company's sales growth; mounting an effective challenge to high street chains, like W. H. Smith, in the sale of newspapers, magazines and books; adopting new technological innovations at the point of sale, such as consumer operated scanning; a 1996 customer care programme creating 4500 new jobs in Tesco stores, including customer assistants in blue waistcoats to pack bags, unload trolleys, fetch forgotten items and replace damaged goods, and experiments with all-night opening in key locations.

In 1997, Tesco was in the headlines again for its conflict with the manufacturers of branded designer goods, which Tesco had started to stock and sell at discounted prices. Brands sold without the manufacturer's 'permission' (and sourced from third parties), included Levi 501 blue jeans, as well as Chanel, Christian Dior and Clarins perfumes and cosmetics. These disputes continued into the 2000s.

Marketing Director, Terry Leahy, became CEO when MacLaurin and Malpas retired in 1997, inheriting control of the market leader in the UK grocery business. Leahy had been a working class Liverpool boy, who won a scholarship to grammar school and then studied business at the University of Manchester Institute of Science and Technology, working as a Tesco shelf-stacker in the holidays. He went from university to the Co-op and then on to a variety of marketing and commercial roles at Tesco. He is a quiet man, unlike the forceful MacLaurin, but it was MacLaurin who picked him out as his successor some years before the hand-over. His industry peers regard him as the best retailer of his generation. It is perhaps more regrettable that he is a fanatical Everton supporter.

'Leahy's explanation for how Tesco continues to outperform its rivals is simple – he says the key is "listening to our customers", but also coming up with good ideas first'

The Leahy strategy

Leahy's explanation for how Tesco continues to outperform its rivals is simple – he says the key is 'listening to our customers', but also coming up with good ideas first – such as the 'virtual assistant' in stores, allowing customers to scan in bar-codes on products to check ingredients and other information, without finding a human assistant. He is also prepared to be infuriating to the powers that be, in pursuit of popularity with shoppers – in July 2000, he reintroduced pounds and ounces to product packaging (alongside the metric weights required by European law), because the evidence was that his shoppers preferred the old measures. At the time, Marketing Director Tim Mason said: 'We're not anti-European, but we are pro-shopper'.

Competition

Tesco remains aggressive on pricing and refuses to concede price leadership to Asda's 'every day low prices' claims. The 'value for money' principle is central to how Tesco operates. Early 2001 saw a further £70 million price-cut package, codenamed Project Gordon, to open a gap with Asda – the Tesco/Asda price positioning had been neck and neck throughout 2000, with each company claiming the lead and that the others' comparisons were wrong. Asda retaliation is regarded as inevitable. Industry figures show Tesco as 9 per cent cheaper than Sainsbury and 14 per cent cheaper than Safeway. Estimates suggest that Tesco has put £1 billion into price cuts since 1996. Interestingly, however, an internal company memo reveals that Tesco has not fully communicated its pricing position to consumers – research suggests 81 per cent of Sainsbury shoppers and 79 per cent of Safeway customers do not believe that Tesco is cheaper.

Certainly, the initial fears that Tesco would not be able to stand up to the might of Wal-Mart after its purchase of Asda were groundless. Tesco has continued to grow sales (after a brief stall in growth rates in 1999) and margins, in spite of fierce price competition, much at the expense of Sainsburys. In the non-food sector, Tesco is able to go to market with prices up to 20 per cent lower than rivals like Boots and Dixons.

Supply chain dominance

Tesco led the British supermarket sector into superior supply chain management, and was an early advocate of the Efficient Consumer Response programme. Stockholding and distribution costs have been minimized through constant replenishment systems, and new Tesco stores are built with very limited warehousing space – with walls designed to be removed and warehousing turned into selling space at the earliest opportunity. Tesco's supply chain management receives little publicity, but is recognized by peers as one of the most advanced in the world.

'Tesco's supply chain management receives little publicity, but is recognized by peers as one of the most advanced in the world'

Product ranges

Tesco is committed to a strategy of further extending its higher-margin non-food product sales – Leahy wants to double the proportion of his business coming from non-food from its 3 per cent level in 2000. Indeed, at Christmas 2000 alone, it sold 14 000 DVD players and 8000 widescreen TVs. In fact, the company's impressive sales growth at this time was largely driven by strong demand for electrical goods and mobile phones, and plans are to increase the number of stores that can stock the full non-food product range. In fact, at the beginning of 2000, Tesco was rumoured to be planning a bid for Marks & Spencer to extend its non-food positioning (though after weeks of talks the bid was not finally made). Leahy has not ruled out the possibility of a joint venture with a clothing company to fight Asda's popular George brand.

In addition, the financial services operation has been successful – by 2001 Tesco owned the fastest growing credit card in the UK. With the banks closing rural branches, Leahy was quick to extend the range of banking services available to customers at Tesco checkouts. In 2000, the company started to offer car insurance including breakdown cover through its petrol stations.

In 1999, Tesco started selling motor scooters from selected stores – the Far East-built 'Tescooters' – imported through the grey market, which many saw as a signal that the company's long-awaited entry to the car distribution market would not be far off. Another experimental 'toe in the water' was the 1999 plan for a leisure and travel division.

E-Commerce

'Rumours were that the Internet business would be floated, but Leahy's stated view is that this is "core business" and he is keeping it'

Tesco Direct's online operation has grown quickly and has created a business unit valued in 2000 at around £3 billion. Rumours were that the Internet business would be floated, but Leahy's stated view is that this is 'core business' and he is keeping it. He plans to extend the online operation to his international stores, as well as aiming at 100 per cent coverage of the UK. Leahy makes no secret of the fact that he plans to become the UK's top e-commerce business, as he extends the product range on offer from grocery into CDs, books, videos and clothing, with future plans for electrical products. The plan revealed in 2000 was to make at least 50 per cent of online revenue from non-food sales. Some of this growth is being driven by joint ventures – for example, with Otto Versand, the German catalogue company, to sell baby accessories and home furnishings through the website.

In 2000, Tesco announced a new £45 million deal with iVillage.com in the US, to launch a new Internet service aimed at women in the UK and Ireland. At the start of 2001, Internet sales had reached the £250 million level, making Tesco Direct a larger e-tailer than Amazon.co.uk, with predictions of £300 million in the next year.

International expansion

Tesco's international ventures have not always been successful – in 1993 they bought the French food retailer Catteau, only to admit defeat and sell the business four years later. However, Leahy has always been committed to an international strategy for Tesco. The goal is to have 45 per cent of sales from overseas by 2002. Indeed, even by the end of 2000, nearly half of Tesco's floorspace was already overseas, and plans included new stores in the key emerging markets of Eastern Europe and Asia. The plan is for international operations to contribute £150 million profit by 2002. Following expansion into Thailand, South Korea and Taiwan, December 2000 saw plans to move into Malaysia with 15 hypermarkets, at a cost of £215 million, in partnership with a local trading group. Stores in Japan and China have also been planned.

In July 2000, Leahy was reported to be in advanced stages of talks to buy Germany's largest hypermarket group, Real, for £3 billion.

Partnership

When the share price was depressed during 1999 and early 2000, Tesco looked like a potential victim for an overseas predator, following in the footsteps of Wal-Mart's acquisition of Asda. The recovery of the share value makes this less likely. However, some investors believe that Tesco needs to partner in order to get bigger and build the business on a global basis. For example, if Wal-Mart were able to acquire all or some of Safeway's stores to bolster the Asda operation, then the domestic marketplace would be very less attractive for Tesco. Analysts have suggested a Tesco/Carrefour merger would dwarf Wal-Mart's European operations, while other candidates suggested have been Casino, one of France's largest super-market chains, or Ahold of the Netherlands. Leahy remains non-committal on this topic, and emphasizes the strength of organic growth.

'When the share price was depressed during 1999 and early 2000, Tesco looked like a potential victim for an overseas predator, following in the footsteps of Wal-Mart's acquisition of Asda'

Performance

In April 2001, Leahy posted Tesco's first £1 billion profit, along with plans to create 20 000 new jobs (half in Britain). This was a 13 per cent rise in pre-tax profits, and a 12 per cent growth in turnover, with non-food sales reaching 15 per cent of the total.

J. Sainsbury plc

The loss of market leadership

Even today, Sainsbury remains approximately 40 per cent in family ownership. However, retaining that ownership has cost the Sainsbury

Table 4 J. Sainsbury financials, 1996–2000*

	1996	1997	1998	1999*	2000
Turnover (£m)	12 267	13 395	14 500	16 433	16 271
Pre-tax profit (£m)	712	609	691	888	509
Earnings per share (p)	29.3	24.0	28.7	30.9	24.0
Dividend per share (p)	12.1	12.3	13.9	15.3	14.3
Market capitalization (£m)	6 823	5.824	8 942	7 380	5 446

* 13 months

family dear. The family stake was worth £3 billion in 1995, but only £2.2 billion at the start of 2000. On the other hand, if they had invested the money in Tesco, their stake would have been worth £6 billion by 2000! However, that situation does provide the company with protection from predators for the time being, as long as family patience lasts. The company's financial performance in the period 1996–2000 is summarized in Table 4.

David Sainsbury, who became Chairman and Chief Executive in 1992, represented the sixth generation of family leadership. However, dramatic erosion of the company's market position coincided with David Sainsbury's tenure – indeed, although in 1996 some City analysts said he had only kept his job by virtue of his family name, the underlying sources of the problems go back further.

'Sainsbury's market success was based on bringing new food and wine assortments to the market, including its strong own-label products – at times reaching 60 per cent of the product assortment on sale'

Sainsbury's market success was based on bringing new food and wine assortments to the market, including its strong own-label products – at times reaching 60 per cent of the product assortment on sale in Sainsbury stores – merchandised as high-quality products in well-designed stores, surrounded with a higher level of customer service than competitors. This strategy was associated mainly with the leadership and vision of John Sainsbury.

Lord (John) Sainsbury was an autocrat, feared throughout the organization, but widely respected as 'a man with a gut instinct for the grocery business'. Lord Sainsbury's management style rested on rigid lines of command, with power concentrated in the hands of a small family-dominated group at the centre of the company. The Sainsbury culture was seen from outside as smug and arrogant, cautious and conservative, secretive, and with considerable animosity between Sainsbury and its suppliers. These structures and this culture drove an effective strategy through the 1970s and 1980s, but they were not well suited to managing change and being responsive to market developments. It should be recalled, however, that when John Sainsbury became Chairman in 1969, the business was weak and underperforming against both Tesco and Marks & Spencer, and it was his management team that turned Sainsbury into the most profitable British retailer in 1992. Times have not always been good. He may have had a foul temper, but he also had an unshakeable belief in Sainsbury's core values – quality food at low prices – and was recognized as a brilliant retailer.

David Sainsbury was a shyer and more cerebral man, with many interests outside business. His focus of attention, on assuming the chairmanship, was on expansion into the USA with successful purchases of Shaws and Food Giant (since proving problematic and time-consuming), and in diversification, rather than the core UK grocery business. His preference was a more consensual management style, consulting with people about decisions, in a company which has no experience of working this way. A senior executive with a rival chain was quoted in 1997: 'Lord Sainsbury ran an incredible tight ship. The staff were used to being barked at, and then the extremely nice David Sainsbury took over with this loose management style, and everything ground to a halt.'

Executives reported that staff morale had hit rock-bottom. The Chairman wanted the culture to change in a very traditional company, but managers saw two previous chairmen – John and Robert – still at head office, looking over David's shoulder. Reports indicated that low morale was leading to an unusually large number of specialist buyers leaving to join competitors.

Meanwhile, outsiders criticized Sainsburys for 'resting on their laurels' and sticking to old strategies at a time of fierce and innovative competition from Tesco, Asda and Safeway, who were more responsive and flexible in keeping up with market changes. The largest example of the Sainsbury company's inability to respond to market change and competitive pressure was the loyalty card strategy. In 1994, as part of its renewed marketing efforts, Tesco launched its loyalty card programme – the Tesco Clubcard. The Sainsbury Chairman's response was to rubbish this ploy as 'electronic Green Shield stamps', and effectively declare business as usual. (This was in spite of the major success of the Spend and Save loyalty card in Sainsbury's DIY company Homebase.) The Tesco Clubcard was a major success from launch – by the end of 1996 there were 9 million Clubcard members who shared £58 million worth of vouchers and coupons.

> **'The largest example of the Sainsbury company's inability to respond to market change and competitive pressure was the loyalty card strategy'**

As the Tesco success unfolded, Sainsbury's response was confused and unclear. By the end of 1995, Sainsbury announced, after conflicting statements, its own loyalty card launch. However, much competitive ground had been lost, and the signs were that Sainsbury's lack of initiative, and the final 'me-too' response, did not recover the ground lost. Indeed, analysts suggest that much of the profit fall in Sainsbury's 1996 performance could be blamed on the costs of coming too late to market with its Reward loyalty card – in January 1997 the City saw a £60 million

'Sainsbury in the 1990s paid the price for ignoring Tesco's policy of acquiring sites for what they had disparaged as "silly prices"'

profit reduction as largely the result of the costs of the Reward card scheme.

In addition, Sainsbury in the 1990s paid the price for ignoring Tesco's policy of acquiring sites for what they had disparaged as 'silly prices'. When planning permission became more difficult to get, Tesco had a bank of land for new larger stores and Sainsbury was left trading out of smaller, older sites in many towns. Sainsbury was not just late in the loyalty card, it was also left to follow Tesco's leadership in opening 'metro' stores in town centres, and it was slow to invest in reducing prices and launching 'value lines'. Management was slow to see how things were changing in the marketplace. One insider is quoted as saying:

> 'We were beginning to lose market share and our customers were going to Tesco. But the business went into denial. We blamed the customers. We almost thought it was their fault they were not buying more. We refused to see that life had changed. We saw our customers as Volvo-driving, Windsmoor-wearing Penelope Keith types, but Tesco was much more in tune with the way the country had changed: people wearing baseball caps backwards and in their trainers all the time. Those that had a stake in the past kept talking about the glory days. Huge divisions began to open up and infighting became inevitable.'

The loss of top position in the UK grocery business, however, was not just down to being outsold by the ever more aggressive Tesco. It was also because Sainsbury was outbid by Tesco for the Scottish supermarket chain Wm Low in 1995, when Tesco paid £247 million for Low's stores.

The Sainsbury response to loss of market leadership and continued fierce competition was sluggish and piecemeal, and analysts suggested that existing company management was unable to develop a strategy of recovery. The Chairman's explanation that decline was because 'we haven't communicated well', confused many in the City, but was regarded by industry specialists as symptomatic of the lack of strategic direction in the company. One industry insider commented of David Sainsbury's performance that 'once he got the top job, he was a bit like a rabbit in the headlights'.

The most immediate response to loss of market leadership at Sainsbury was internal restructuring. The Chairman/Chief Executive role was split to create two joint Chief Executives, with one of these posts filled by moving

'The most immediate response to loss of market leadership at Sainsbury was internal restructuring'

Dino Adriano from heading the successful Homebase DIY chain to run the British supermarket business. A new Marketing Director was hired – Kevin McCarten, with a track record at P&G, Woolworth and Superdrug – although it has been suggested that he was blocked from the outset in his change strategies by the Sainsbury 'old guard'. The company announced a number of customer service initiatives – e.g. home delivery, a free breakdown rescue service for consumers shopping at its stores, checkout bag-packers, but did little to promote them, or to target its large advertising spend at winning customers back from Tesco.

The major strategic platform promised by the company was a series of price-cutting campaigns. While some smaller rivals may have been vulnerable to price-cutting, Tesco stated publicly it would match any Sainsbury price cuts. Critics also pointed out the need to slaughter several 'sacred cows' at Sainsbury. The dogged determination to maintain the private label business – around 50 per cent of its product lines in-store – conflicts with the strength of leading food brands, and reduces customer brand choice compared to Tesco. The unwillingness to try new store formats – like Tesco's successful smaller in-city Metro stores – had to change.

Sainsbury attempted to regain this initiative by announcing the Sainsbury Bank, to lead the way in supermarket-based financial services. Critics suggested this strategy failed to address the problems in the core grocery business, and would bring problems of its own – not least because banks are highly unpopular with customers when they say 'no' to loans, account applications and other services, and when they increase charges. Some critics also draw attention to Sainsbury's history of strained supplier relationships as a suspect basis for an alliance with a financial services company.

'Some critics also draw attention to Sainsbury's history of strained supplier relationships as a suspect basis for an alliance with a financial services company'

Nonetheless, early in 1997 the Sainsbury Bank opened in 244 stores, underwritten by a £30 million investment by the company, as a start to going national during 1997. The Sainsbury Bank represents an alliance with the Bank of Scotland, and offers Visa credit cards (where use earns Reward loyalty points) and an instant access savings account – personal loan, mortgage and insurance products are planned. City reactions are highly favourable, judging the Sainsbury banking products to be flexible, convenient and highly competitive compared to conventional banks.

Changes at the top

In May 1998, the company announced that David Sainsbury would retire as Chairman in November that year, to pursue a full-time career as a Labour peer. He is said never to have looked as happy as the day he made this announcement, although suffering the ignominy of seeing Sainsbury share price rising on account of the news. Sir George Bull, former Chairman of Grand Metropolitan, became Non-Executive Chairman, with Dino Adriano as Chief Executive – a 35-year Sainsbury veteran.

A month after David Sainsbury left, Adriano had to announce that things had got worse – the extremely irritating 'Value to Shout About'

'the extremely irritating "Value to Shout About" advertising campaign with John Cleese had not merely insulted Sainsbury staff, it had failed to attract customers either'

advertising campaign with John Cleese had not merely insulted Sainsbury staff, it had failed to attract customers either and had to be abandoned. Cleese was paid £400 000 to make adverts bawling at staff through a megaphone, and far from convincing people the store had bargains, managed to alienate many better-off customers. Critics pointed out they made Sainsbury look like the 'pile it high, sell it cheap' Tesco of the 1970s. While the high cost of the campaign ate into margins, the most it achieved was to have shoppers visit stores to 'cherry-pick' the keenly priced items and then leave – average spending was lower.

Adriano's position was saved for the time being by City attention turning to the Asda/Kingfisher merger talks.

With disappointing profit levels, Adriano focused on cost-cutting, leading to 2000 job losses, and trying to impact on the hierarchical culture by naming employees 'colleagues' and introducing new team kit – baseball caps and sweatshirts in 'living' orange. He was publicly committed to sticking with existing plans to reposition the brand and continue its 'value for money' brand proposition. He was also planning 200 new convenience stores to counter the impact of Tesco Metros. One City analyst commented on Adriano's strategy:

> 'This is an example of a moronic statement of strategy. Sainsbury's problem is that it has mediocre or average product quality and presentation and it charges too much. Either it gets the product quality up to the level that justifies the prices or it cuts the prices.'

'Insiders reported that the company was still dominated by its buying process and its products, not by customers or marketing'

Others investors were openly sceptical about whether Sainsbury's management really understood the depth and seriousness of its problems. Fears were expressed that Adriano's approach was going to fall between two stools: in a price contest with Tesco and Asda he would be bound to lose, while at the same time further weakening Sainsbury's reputation for quality. Insiders reported that the company was still dominated by its buying process and its products, not by customers or marketing.

The next advertising campaign was themed as 'Making Life Taste Better'. This was the third change of brand advertising strategy in three years.

Causing a major trauma to the company and its investors, in the autumn of 1999 the *Wall Street Journal* published one of its journalists' shocked impression of shopping at Sainsbury in Camden Town. The article stressed filthy displays contaminated with leaks of chicken blood, displays encrusted with dirt, and truculent staff:

> 'On a busy Saturday afternoon in one of the busiest outlets, many shelves are empty, there's sour milk dripping from the dairy case, and long lines have formed at checkout counters — half of which were unstaffed. When asked questions, one employee shrugs and another just walks away.'
>
> *Wall Street Journal*, October 1999

In October 1999, Adriano's publicity stunt to show his human side backfired badly on the 'Back to the Floor' television programme. Adriano was seen turning up at a store in a chauffeur-driven car, made a fool of himself trying to control a line of trolleys, did not know what products were sold at the store, and shocked staff with his £500 000 pay package. The programme further underlined the remoteness of Sainsbury management from the shopfloor. Spookily, it was the same month that, on Sir George Bull's instructions, he handed over day-to-day control of the supermarket chain to his ambitious deputy, David Bremner, while remaining as Chief Executive. Outsiders saw this arrangement as farcical. In January 2000, Bremner became Managing Director and two weeks later Adriano was forced to resign. City rumours were that the search was on for a merger partner or buyers for the company, probably from Europe.

The man from the Pru

In January 2000, Sainsburys announced the appointment of Sir Peter Davis, Chairman of the Prudential insurance organization, as Chief Executive from March that year. In fact, Davis had left Sainsbury in 1986 after ten years with the company, because his route to the top job was blocked by family members. Indeed, Davis was one of the team that in 1978 helped Sainsbury recapture market leadership from Tesco.

Davis now says that deciding on the direction for change was easy: 'One of the interesting things is that the customer research all says the same thing as our staff were saying. We had fallen behind in a number of areas — product quality and availability, and store formats. We had lost the oomph that used to be there.'

'One of the interesting things is that the customer research all says the same thing as our staff were saying'

Shortly after assuming office, Davis' view in June 2000, was that: costs were too high compared to competitors; margins of 4 per cent compared poorly with the 6 per cent of rivals; the infrastructure was seriously out of date; and the stores were run-down. His underlying aims were to expand e-commerce, refurbish the stores and improve efficiency. June 2000 saw a 23 per cent decline in Sainsbury profits, triggering an 11 per cent fall in share price, and the gap between Sainsbury and Asda looked to have closed. Asda had been reported as the number two supermarket company by Verdict in January, on the basis of regular shoppers. However, Davis firmly ruled out joining the price war being run by Tesco and Asda, relying on a quality strategy, with new superstores to be opened and e-commerce development accelerated.

Davis said it would take three years to turn the company round, though admitting privately that he would need signs of recovery within 18 months. His vision for Sainsbury is that he wants it to be the retail chain, which is automatically seen as the first choice for quality and freshness, but remains affordable. Davis shares the traditional Sainsbury passion for quality food and it underpins his strategy for recovery. His goal is to make shopping at Sainsbury 'more special for more customers'.

Early on, Davis made personnel changes – the first departures being within eight days of his arrival, when Managing Director David Bremner and Kevin McCarten were asked to leave. Davis wanted to take direct charge of the supermarkets, which make up 85 per cent of the business, not leave them in Bremner's hands. McCarten was the Marketing Director responsible for the disastrous 'Value to Shout About' advertising and the newly-created Stores Director. Kevin Whitbread, who had worked for Davis when he was previously at Sainsbury, became Retail Director of the supermarkets. Davis also plans to sell Sainsbury's London head offices building – an important symbolic action, but also moving to new offices that accommodate a smaller number of head office personnel.

'Davis also plans to sell Sainsbury's London head offices building – an important symbolic action, but also moving to new offices that accommodate a smaller number of head office personnel'

Davis promised £100 million investment in improving out-of-date stores, systems and distribution. In fact, the situation had become so bad that in some stores that lack of refrigeration units meant it was impossible to display full product ranges. He set about overhauling IT strategy and outsourced the process management to Accenture. In March 2001, Sainsbury revealed a strategic partnership with Excel to manage the upgrading of its supply chain. The existing supply chain was poorly integrated and inefficient – getting products to stores costs Sainsbury 12 per cent of sales, around £2 billion a year – and the weakness of the supply chain is a major constraint on growth. The company had been running with 1980s IT, and 20-year-old distribution depots, while competing with world-class supply chains at Tesco and Asda. Davis promised £600 million a year cost cuts by 2004.

On the brand-building front, Davis used Jamie Oliver, the *Naked Chef*, in advertising because of his perceived classlessness – the word 'taste' became the theme running throughout the company's advertising and publicity. Fashion guru, Jeff Banks, was hired to produce a range of fashion clothing for Sainsbury stores.

Davis kept his promise to dispose of the Homebase DIY chain in a complex deal completed just before Christmas 1999 – the Homebase chain was sold to Schroder Ventures for £416 million in cash and a deferred payment of £71 million, but Sainsbury retains freehold properties which have been leased back to Homebase, with a further £259 million for eventual disposal. A further £219 million comes from the sale of 28 development sites to Kingfisher. Sainsbury reinvested £31 million for a 17 per cent stake in the business.

In addition, Davis had to get Sainsbury out of a disastrous foray into Egypt, which had been initiated by Bremner as a personal project – taking a £100 million hit by selling out to the local partner.

In April 2001, Sainsburys was looking to buy a number of stores from Boots, to allow expansion of the local store format, but rumours were of a deeper partnership being developed between the two retailers which may lead to new-format joint ventures to strengthen both in the fight against Tesco and Asda Wal-Mart.

Davis also made big moves into e-commerce with a variety of joint ventures (he had been responsible for the launch of the Egg Internet banking service while at the Pru). Mid-2001, Sainsbury was spending heavily on upgrading online shopping services to try and close the gap with Tesco Direct, as part of a seven-year technology outsourcing contract with Accenture.

Davis has, importantly, conceded price leadership to Tesco and Asda – he does not intend to be the cheapest grocer, but plans to compete on quality. Sainsbury's stated October 2000 plan was to match Tesco prices on 1000 key lines, but to be up to 1.5 per cent more expensive elsewhere.

'Davis has, importantly, conceded price leadership to Tesco and Asda – he does not intend to be the cheapest grocer, but plans to compete on quality'

Although Davis says it is not the real issue, regaining market leadership may be a possibility. Late in 2000, rumours of a break-up of Safeway suggested that Sainsbury would pick up the largest pieces. Davis said he would not initiate a move on Safeway, but would like the stores (particularly in Scotland, where Sainsbury coverage is weakest). The deal did not happen in 2000, but Davis is suspected of casting his eyes over Somerfield and Morrisons for similar reasons.

Rebuilding the Sainsbury position

By April 2001, the effects of the Davis strategy were being seen. First quarter sales growth was 6.9 per cent and shares reached 400p. He reiterated though that the goal was not market share versus Tesco, but rebuilding profits. July quarterly results were also encouraging. Davis said the improvement had come simply from 'listening to our customers', reducing the 'clutter' in the stores, and the new 'Naked Chef' advertising showing Sainsbury's 'passion for food'. The impact of the events through this period of Sainsbury's history is shown in Figure 2.

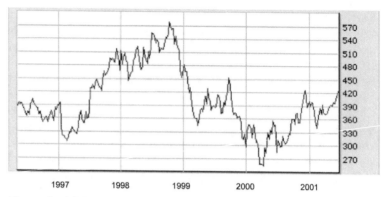

Figure 2 J. Sainsbury plc share performance, 1997–2001

Asda Wal-Mart

As third player in the market in the 1990s, Asda showed no aspiration to market share leadership, but under the leadership of Archie Norman, the company established a strong and highly differentiated position in the market. Norman joined Yorkshire-based Asda in 1991 on the basis of experience as a McKinsey consultant and five years as a finance director at Kingfisher, the owner of Woolworth and Comet. The prospects at Asda did not look good – many of the stores were in poor condition and the company had debts of £1 billion and needed a further injection of £700 million to survive.

During the 1980s, Asda had lost touch with its roots as a northern-based discounter. In trying to imitate the success strategies of Sainsbury and Tesco, the company had allowed its good-value image to erode and had alienated its traditional customer base, without appealing to a new base. Asda had also acquired 60 stores from Gateway in 1989, in an attempt to expand from its northern base, and gained massive debts. In fact, by 1995, Norman had brought in a profit of £246, tripling profits in three years, with a net cash flow of £4.2 million, leading share price up from 27p to 102p, and established Asda as Britain's third largest grocer.

Part of Norman's strategy had been to change the Asda culture to reinforce the 'good-value ethos'. Although a man who criticizes the 'cult of the personality' in business, Norman has been described in the trade as 'the Gazza of food retailing, he is constantly playing to the crowd'. His management style was characterized by an ethos of austerity – expensive company cars disappeared; head office executives were sent to stores to pack bags at checkouts on the busiest days at Christmas; the executive box at York races went. The reason for

'Part of Norman's strategy had been to change the Asda culture to reinforce the "good-value ethos"'

abandoning perks was said in the company annual report to be because they 'carry a sense of status and hierarchy antipathetic to the corporate culture'. The new management style also involved: 'red hats' – headquarters staff who need time to think could put on a red baseball cap, which means no-one will speak to them for two hours; 'listening groups' held weekly in 200 stores as a forum for ideas and complaints; and asking staff to select a product and creatively promote it, to win the keys to a red Jaguar for a month.

When Norman arrived at Asda, he started his 'Day Zero' turnaround strategy. The centre of the strategy was to present Asda to the customer as the most competitive discounter among the top four supermarket chains. In large part, Norman's strategy was modelled on that of Wal-Mart in the US. The implementation of this strategy by Norman was described variously as 'outspoken', 'slightly wacky' and 'playful', and the process of embedding ground-breaking standards of customer service has included such tactics as: 'pet stops' in-store for families to leave animals while they shop; 'brolley patrols' where shop assistants escort customers to their cars with umbrellas to protect them from the rain; in-store events like 'singles nights' and 'fancy dress days' – with the first couple to marry as a result of an Asda 'singles night' offered the opportunity to have the wedding ceremony in the store and the reception in the store cafeteria; and checkouts with red carpets for big spending customers. This is all part of what Marketing Director, Michael Fleming, described as a strategy of bringing 'theatre and life' into supermarket retailing.

Norman pursued his position as the leading discounter by a series of attacks on price-fixing arrangements. Going after discounting opportunities in pharmaceuticals, toiletries and books that break free of price-fixing, Norman reinforced his own strategic position and also focused price-cutting onto far higher margin products than staple commodity groceries. Asda gained enormous publicity for these moves, and Norman was portrayed as a 'pioneering shopper's champion'. These moves continued into 1999, and encompassed Calvin Klein toiletries and Ray-Ban sunglasses among others. While Asda held back from a loyalty card, Norman aggressively counter-attacked Tesco's Clubcard by telling customers that Asda would honour the Tesco money-off coupons sent to Clubcard holders, and advertised that Asda's prices are lower 'every day'.

> **'Going after discounting opportunities in pharmaceuticals, toiletries and books that break free of price-fixing, Norman reinforced his own strategic position and also focused price-cutting onto far higher margin products than staple commodity groceries'**

With the recovery phase completed, Asda fought to maintain the momentum of success – 'Operation Breakout'. The strategic options for British retailers are basically the same for all players: expand overseas; increase non-food product lines; and acquire other retail businesses in Britain. Norman joined the other major players in pursuing higher margin non-food areas like clothes and electrical goods. At Asda, the basis for expansion in clothing was the 'George' range – designed by, and named for, George Davies, the creator of Next. Norman set an ambitious target of making the George brand the second-largest clothing brand in Britain, after Marks & Spencer. He continued to pursue the high margin over-the-counter medicine market and the possibility of discounting if price-fixing agreements could be abolished (the price-fixing rules ended mid-2001). Asda planned to become the first supermarket to open book stores to compete directly with traditional book retailers, and along with Boots investigated the possibility of locating doctors and other health care services on store premises. Norman had acquisition ambitions within the UK, but his first priority was upgrading existing stores to increase the range of fresh foods, and trying to recreate a market-stall atmosphere in restyled butchery, bakery and delicatessen departments.

In 1995, Asda became heavily involved in a head-to-head price war with Tesco on fresh produce, with both sides selling products below cost to gain advantage. The war petered out as the potential for mutual damage became clearer. Early in 1997, Asda launched 'Value Cannonball', a price campaign led by the message that, unlike rival loyalty schemes, savings for customers at Asda were immediate, and to fight off the effect of Kwik Save's new own-label range. City reactions were cautious based on fears that Asda's margins were levelling off and cost pressures mounting. However, in early 1999 Asda launched a further price war, adopting the Wal-Mart term 'Rollback', saying it was going back to 'permanently low prices'.

'City reactions were cautious based on fears that Asda's margins were levelling off and cost pressures mounting'

By this stage, Norman was looking to his personal political ambitions by standing for Parliament, retaining the Chairman's role but with Allan Leighton, formerly Marketing Director at Mars, in position as his successor. The impact of the Asda turnaround in the mid-1990s on share price is shown in Figure 3.

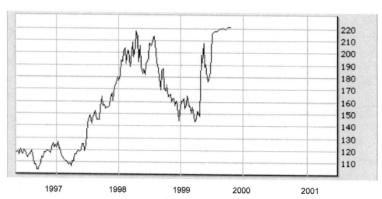

Figure 3 Asda plc share performance, 1997–1999

The next phase

In 1998–1999, Archie Norman engaged in talks with Sir Geoffrey Mulcahy of Kingfisher to set up a £17 billion all-share merger, which appeared to be going ahead in June 1999 – Mulcahy had just spent five weeks on the road with Allan Leighton convincing sceptical shareholders of the attractions of the deal. On 14 June at 7.00 in the morning, Norman phoned Mulcahy with the words 'Geoffrey, we've got a little problem...', to give him two items of news: first, that the merger of Asda with Kingfisher was off; and, second, that Asda was being taken over by Wal-Mart in a £6.7 billion cash deal which was to be announced to the stockmarket as soon as their phone call was ended. It is thought that Mulcahy did not wish Norman to 'have a nice day'.

The Wal-Martians

With 2000–2001 sales of $191 billion and more than 1.2 million employees in 5200 stores throughout the world, Wal-Mart is the largest retailer, and indeed the largest private sector employer in the world. Sam Walton was a small-time merchant who operated variety stores in Arkansas and Missouri, who established Wal-Mart in 1962. Walton's heirs are now the richest people in America. The underlying Wal-Mart principles were from the start high value, low prices and a warm welcome. Wal-Mart is well known for a distinct culture established by its founder: People Greeters to welcome shoppers at the entrance to the store; the 'ten foot attitude' – if a customer comes within ten feet of a Wal-Mart associate, s/he must be looked in the eye, greeted and offered help; the 'sundown rule' – try to answer all requests by sundown on the day they are received; 'aggressive hospitality' to exceed customer expectations; the 'Wal-Mart cheer'; and low prices, every day. Wal-Mart's strategy rests on customer service and awesome cost-cutting technology – the slogan is 'we sell for less, always' – and the computer system is said to be on a par with that of the Pentagon in Washington. Wal-Mart has massive buying power – for example, it buys more from Procter & Gamble than the whole of Japan. They are robust with suppliers. Says one: 'They're great folks, but just don't mess with them.' Wal-Mart has a reputation for an aggressive competitive policy, which few rivals have survived for long. The staff – the 'Wal-Martians' – are motivated by a culture of praise, backed by financial incentives for showing initiative and friendliness towards customers. Commentators suggest that the genius of Wal-Mart is its ability to combine low prices with superior customer service.

'Initial reactions to the merger were panic. People talked about the "worst nightmare of Western European retailers"'

Initial reactions to the merger were panic. People talked about the 'worst nightmare of Western European retailers', Tesco executives saw their share value dip and debated whether to recall Terry Leahy from a trip to the Far East, newspapers and politicians revelled in the prospect of lower prices for consumers as Asda started to 'piggy-back' on Wal-Mart's buying power and supply chain strengths. A Tesco spokesman growled the somewhat bad-tempered comment that 'the Yanks have got a reputation for turning up for wars late and then claiming they won them'. Nonetheless, companies as diverse as Boots and Dixons were seen as likely victims of Wal-Mart's non-food merchandising strengths.

Since Asda had been closely modelled on Wal-Mart by Norman and Leighton, there appeared to be little culture clash – one commentator suggested that it was like 'coming home to mommy'. Nonetheless, employees and managers are being sent to the US to learn Wal-Mart skills and methods. However, management turnover at Asda Wal-Mart has been high. Three members of Asda's eight-strong board have left. As anticipated, in November 1999 Archie Norman left the new group. Late in 1999, Allan Leighton was promoted to head up Wal-Mart's European operations, but left the company seven months later to pursue a range of other part-time commitments, shortly before the poor results in Wal-Mart's German operation became clear. Tony Campbell, Deputy Chief Executive, has retired. In November 2000, George Davies, founder of the George clothing range at Asda, left the company to join Marks & Spencer, followed three months later by five members of his Asda team. Justin King, in charge of the hypermarket division, has also left.

'In July 1999, Asda announced plans to open ten Asda Wal-Mart superstores over the following five years, the first opening in Bristol in July, accompanied by price cuts up to 60 per cent on branded goods'

In July 1999, Asda announced plans to open ten Asda Wal-Mart superstores over the following five years, the first opening in Bristol in July, accompanied by price cuts up to 60 per cent on branded goods.

Within two weeks of the take-over, Asda announced 15 per cent price cuts on top branded products, with the cuts to be extended to 4000 products by the end of the year. By September 1999, Wal-Mart revealed plans to cut Asda's prices by up to a fifth, across the board, with the intention of bringing prices down to US levels within 18 months, the biggest impact to be in non-food products. In the autumn of 1999, Asda contrasted its 9.5 per cent year-on-year sales growth with 5.4 per cent growth at Tesco and declines of 0.4 per cent at Sainsbury, 5.0 per cent at Safeway and 8.3 per cent at Somerfield. By the start of 2000, Asda claimed to already be 9 per cent cheaper than its main competitors. Mid-2000 saw price cuts targeted on non-food products competing with Boots, Mothercare, Dixons, W. H. Smith and Currys, and planned entry into BT's phone business, the jewellery business and financial services, as well as the possibility of cut-price car sales.

Wal-Mart is rumoured to be looking at other UK acquisition possibilities – Somerfield, Safeway and Sainsbury have all been mentioned in the food sector, though non-food targets could include Kingfisher, Boots, or even Marks & Spencer.

However, at the start of 2001, some doubts began to be made about the Wal-Mart impact in Britain, and its ambition to displace Tesco as market leader, with fears that Asda's growth is slowing. Not least of the reasons is that Tesco and Safeway appear to have gone into overdrive. It may also be the case that Wal-Mart has never before competed head-on with a retailer as strong as Tesco.

Safeway

Although one of the largest retail chains in the US, the British Safeway chain, acquired by Argyll in 1987, is in fourth place, with a market share only half that of the market leader, and very much second division to Tesco and Sainsbury. The Argyll group's (now known as the Safeway Group) purchase of the Safeway business (for £681 million from its US parent), and Presto stores, led to the conversion of the larger Presto stores to the Safeway brand and the sale of the Low Cost discount stores to the Co-operative Retail Services, while the smaller Presto stores were sold to the Spar voluntary group. The Presto brand is maintained in Scotland and the north-east of England. The company's recent financial performance is summarized in Table 5.

Table 5   Safeway plc financials, 1996–2000

	1996	1997	1998	1999	2000
Turnover (£m)	6 069	6 590	6 979	7 511	7 659
Pre-tax profit (£m)	429	421	340	341	236
Earnings per share (p)	24.8	27.5	25.0	25.0	16.4
Dividend per share (p)	12.8	14.1	14.1	14.4	8.64
Market capitalization (£m)	3 506	3 877	4 120	2 739	2 044

Safeway's market position in the 1990s rested on a very large advertising campaign with the prize-winning 'Look Who's Talking Now' television advertisements dubbing adult voices and conversations into the mouths of small children in-store. These ads achieved extremely high consumer awareness scores. This campaign was associated with Safeway's determination to become more customer oriented. In 1995, Safeway's advertising spend was £39 million (compared to £26 million by the market leader Tesco, £40 million by second-placed Sainsbury, and £16 million by Asda in third place in the market). Underpinning this, were major investments to upgrade stores and improve service quality, and also major restructuring as part of the 1993 'Safeway 2000' review. This review led to the formation of task forces reporting to board level and supported by external consultants.

'A critical process was the development of the "Safeway customer proposition" and the central customer promise that Safeway were concerned with "Lightening the Load"'

A critical process was the development of the 'Safeway customer proposition' and the central customer promise that Safeway were concerned with 'Lightening the Load'. The Safeway repositioning after 1994 was based on brand and service – executives freely admitted that while they followed market prices, they did not claim to be a price leader, although they rejected Sainsbury's claim that there was as much as 4% price difference.

The brand message in the advertising campaign was that Safeway would do everything to make the shopping trip easier – for example, by the roving teams of 'Queue Busters' used to home in on queues at checkouts and counters, and simply by having more staff on the shopfloor to handle customer queries and customer service.

The implementation of the brand strategy also rested on a campaign concerned with 'Getting the Basics Right Every Time' at store level. The strategy involved developing the product range to have broader appeal – research in the Safeway 2000 project found that the company was perceived as strong with single people and pre-family couples but not in the family shopping market. While the 'Safeway Savers' was a value-oriented positioning, major efforts were also made to improve the range of customer services offered in-store and upgrade store layout and design. An 'ABC' loyalty card followed in response to Tesco's Clubcard launch. Much of the development was based on customer feedback - for example, the company's 'family connections' panel of 1500 consumers to discuss perceptions of Safeway and developing service needs.

Safeway also favoured a process of internal 're-energizing' in the form of the MAD (Make a Difference) campaign – focusing on the customers' propositions and having all employees and managers think about the working styles and practices needed to support the company's strategy. Behind the repositioning of Safeway was the closure of unprofitable stores, and some 3000 job cuts. However, by 1996 the company was planning the opening of large stores, and the creation of 5000 new jobs; in line with improving profitability and market share. In 1997, talks were held with Asda about a possible merger, but were abandoned for fear of intervention by the competition authorities. Shortly afterwards, Somerfield showed willingness to receive a friendly bid, but this also fell through.

The late 1990s

Under the leadership of Colin Smith as CEO, Safeway made solid progress in its repositioning strategy through the mid-1990s. However, the period 1997–99 saw dramatic falls in sales growth, a string of profits warnings and the collapse of the share price – see Figure 4.

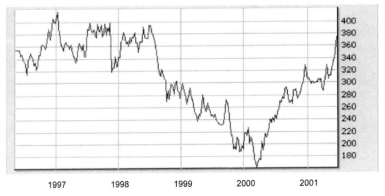

Figure 4 Safeway plc share performance, 1997–2001

City opinion at this time was that Safeway could no longer survive as an independent in a market dominated by Tesco and Sainsbury, and was in play for a predator. May 1999 saw Safeway buying back 10% of its own shares rather than investing in its store-opening programme.

> **'City opinion at this time was that Safeway could no longer survive as an independent in a market dominated by Tesco and Sainsbury'**

Don't cry for me Argentina

July 1999 saw the appointment of Carlos Criado-Perez as Safeway's Chief Operating Officer, with a brief to turn around underperforming stores. Amid widespread calls for Colin Smith's resignation as CEO, and for more retail expertise to be brought onto a board dominated by finance people, Criado-Perez was to be groomed as the eventual successor to Smith. Criado-Perez brought more than 20 years' retail experience to the company, most recently with Wal-Mart's international division. However, his appointment triggered the departure of Roger Partington, director responsible for marketing and business development, because his route to the CEO post was now blocked.

Responsible for stores, marketing, training and logistics, Criado-Perez first concentrated efforts on improving the stores' presentation and cutting prices. He also caused controversy when he asked for a donation of £20 000 from manufacturers to help promote each line they supplied (most had little option other than to pay up), his letter read: 'We look forward to you joining us in the campaign, and anticipating a favourable response, we will take the liberty of sending you an invoice on Friday of this week.'

'Criado-Perez was predictably dubbed "The Jackal" at this time'

As the fall in share price continued, in November 1999, at the end of his first ten weeks with the company, Criado-Perez abruptly replaced Colin Smith as CEO. Criado-Perez was predictably dubbed 'The Jackal' at this time. Asked if Safeway could survive in the face of fierce competition from Tesco, Sainsbury and Asda Wal-Mart, he said 'Are you serious? We're going to win. We're not going to just survive.'

However, with Safeway profits and shares still declining, both Asda and Morrisons were viewed as potential predators. In fact, the Competition Commission enquiry into supermarkets prompted by the accusation of 'rip off' Britain, and the Trade Secretary's slow response to its report, bought Safeway some breathing space. Merger and takeover activity was on hold until the Commission's findings were public. While the uncertainty continued into 2000, Sainsbury was rumoured to be part of a group putting together a bid, which would give Sainsbury the pick of Safeway's stores on the break-up of the company. The attraction to Sainsbury was heightened by the prospect of overtaking Tesco as market leader through this route.

A recovery strategy

The first part of Criado-Perez's strategy was selective, targeted price-cutting to boost sales and win customers back, but also making major investments in upgrading the larger stores and extending product ranges, particularly into non-food items. Store managers were given greater autonomy to vary prices and merchandising, and a bonus scheme which could double their wages. He also dropped the national 'Look who's talking' advertising campaign, in favour of local advertising. Some 300 head office jobs were axed, and directors were sent back to the shop floor. His strategy also placed more emphasis on fresh foods, shelf availability, and customer service improvements.

'he dismissed the ABC loyalty card as "a useless piece of plastic", and dumped it'

Though once seen as integral to Safeway's survival, he dismissed the ABC loyalty card as 'a useless piece of plastic', and dumped it, at a saving of £50 million. His thinking was that with sales per square foot some 25% less than rivals, he should concentrate on absorbing that slack through sales growth – growth without the costs of further capital investment. In the view of one analyst at the time: 'With Tesco following Asda into everyday low pricing, and Sainsburys swimming around like a headless turtle, there is room for a mid-market position.' It looked like the target competitor for Safeway was Sainsbury. Certainly, the battered morale among Safeway management was improving only a few weeks into the new CEO's reign.

At the centre of Criado-Perez's strategy was using local promotions to drive up sales and to convert occasional Safeway shoppers into loyal customers. While these goals are shared by all retailers, the difference in Safeway's approach was to run promotions on a localized store-by-store basis, largely driven by store managers. This approach is common in the US, but anathema to rigidly centralized British and European retail chains. The strategy is based on the philosophy that retailing is essentially local, and the intention is to compete in specific local neighbourhoods. The effect is also to improve morale at the local store level. One impediment was that the Competition Commission expressed concern to Safeway about prices varying between stores, but Safeway felt comfortable this would not be a barrier because they were not a dominant player.

The new-style store approach involves large areas devoted to fresh food and ready meals, offering higher than average margins, with counters staffed by young, brightly-dressed employees trained in the arts of 'retail-tainment' – many have been sent on acting courses. Criado-Perez is determined to make shopping at Safeways an enjoyable and different experience. His weight is behind the 'Fresh to go' concept, and fresh-food experts have been recruited from Marks & Spencer, featuring made-to-order coffee, pizza, pasta and noodles. Café Fresco is a high quality in-store Mediterranean-style restaurant.

Somewhat colourful in his expressions, Criado-Perez argues Safeway is the 'guerrilla against the gorillas'. The 'gorillas' are his giant rivals Tesco, Sainsbury, and Asda Wal-Mart, against whom he promises to hit first and where least expected. His guerrilla tactics include massive local price cuts on selected lines (60% or more off the existing price), and dawn raids on rivals' car parks littering them with leaflets to spread the news.

> **'Criado-Perez argues Safeway is the "guerrilla against the gorillas"'**

Safeway is now split into 40 regions, and has around 20 offers moving around the country, with the aim of disorienting competitors. Rivals have immediately pledged to match Safeway prices, and Criado-Perez says: 'So, of course, we help them. We fill their car parks with Safeway adverts so all their clients can benefit from our offers in their stores. They last about 15 minutes – those offers do about six months of sales in one week so they don't have the supplies and have to take the banners down.' One competitor, facing the supply chain disruption that ensues from Safeway's guerrilla tactics, concludes 'The man is a nightmare.' His 'hit and move' strategy continued through 2000, and led to an ugly row with Asda, the latter infuriated with Safeway blocking its checkout queues and advertising its special offers in Asda car parks. There has been some retaliation – in August 2000, Safeway customers were sent a spoof e-mail falsely purporting to come from 'the Safeway team', reading 'We are pleased to announce that from Monday Safeway will be increasing prices on all our goods by 25%. If this doesn't sound good to you then you can p*** off to another supermarket chain such as Tesco or Sainsbury.'

Mid-2000 saw a fall in profits, reflecting the costs of repositioning the business – redundancies, a £9 million hit on property disposals, and millennium wages. However, by November, with sales growth back in the 7% region and a 11.5% increase in half-year profits, as well as a million additional customers shopping with Safeway, after his first year as CEO, Criado-Perez announced plans to convert 25 Safeways into huge hypermarkets. He promised a 'futuristic' view of what a hypermarket could do – certainly a switch in emphasis to household goods, DIY, and health and beauty products, but not clothing or electricals. He also announced his intention to be the UK's first choice for food shopping.

In May 2001, Criado-Perez reported a one-third growth in pre-tax profits and 6% sales growth for the year. The first phase of his recovery strategy – the 'four pillars' of 'great offers, outstanding fresh foods, consistent availability, and top-class service' – was in place, and was being followed by the second phase: new store formats and product ranges. The impact on share prices can be seen in Figure 4.

Somerfield

The origins of the Somerfield brand illustrate the problems that confronted David Simons on joining the company (then Isosceles) as Chief Executive in 1993 – at the company's all-time low when its debt had reached £1.3 billion. The company started in 1964 as a chain of the early self-service stores founded by Frank Dee, who opened 70 stores under his own name. By 1970 those stores had become part of Linford Holdings. In 1977 Linford Holdings bought Gateway – a 14-unit chain named for 'Bristol – Gateway to the West'. By the end of 1977, there were more than 100 stores around the country operating as Gateway. In 1983 the Frank Dee stores were brought under the Gateway brand, and Linford Holdings was renamed the Dee Corporation. For the next few years the Dee Corporation expanded through a series of mergers and acquisitions, gaining ownership of Keymarkets, Lennons, International Stores, Fine Fare and Carrefour Hypermarkets. In 1988 the Dee Corporation was renamed the Gateway Corporation.

A major turning point came in 1989, when Isosceles bought Gateway for £2.1 billion, and sold 60 of the larger stores to Asda. In 1990, the first Somerfield store was opened, trading alongside the Gateway stores, but with a greater emphasis on fresh food. However, by 1992 it was necessary for Isosceles to ask its banks for a halt to the repayment of its £1.3 billion debt, to avoid bankruptcy and to refinance. In 1993 David Simons joined the company as Chief Executive, when an operating company - Somerfield Holdings – was formed to separate the store business from the debt held by the parent company Isosceles. It was at the time of the Somerfield flotation that Simons declared that his next task would be to acquire Safeway – and he made regular approaches for some time afterwards.

Simons quickly launched the Price Check campaign – a deep price cut strategy taking up to 15% off major brand prices – which triggered a price war driving prices down across the whole grocery sector, and turned a 15% sales decline for Gateway into 11% growth. By 1994 the decision had been made to phase out the now somewhat tarnished Gateway brand name and replace it with Somerfield stores, and a cheaper chain called Food Giant. Sales and profit recovery continued, with sales of £3.05 billion in 1994 and £3.14 billion in 1995. In 1994, Gateway undertook a radical re-branding, moving its stores progressively from the 'shabby' Gateway image to the more upmarket Somerfield brand. By 1996 operating margins had increased from 1.75% to 2.65% and a market flotation was announced. After a painful 7 years, the City judged that the company had turned the corner. Simons boasted that he had saved Britain's fifth largest food retailer from collapse.

'Simons boasted that he had saved Britain's fifth largest food retailer from collapse'

Nonetheless, analysts saw the high street image of the stores as shabby and downmarket. The company had come through a period when the competition had invested heavily in customer loyalty, while Somerfield had to rely on existing customers – leading to lost market share. The company had demonstrated strength in low price marketing – its 1990s price-cutting campaign took market share back to 7% from the low of 3%, but its capabilities for customer service improvement and quality-based strategies seemed limited, not least because the company's trading margins were around 3% compared to the sector average of 7%.

However, the Somerfield image change seemed to have worked – the supermarkets had a strong emphasis on fresh food. By 1996 the rate of change of stores from the Gateway brand to Somerfield was running at 100 per year. The total chain consisted of 610: 275 Somerfields, 28 Food Giants, and 307 Gateways. The Somerfield operation was also differentiated by its high street-based locations, compared to the increasingly criticized out-of-town developments of its major competitors.

The urge to merge

Simons' continued approaches to Safeway were rebuffed – particularly after Safeway saw its opportunity to merge with Asda disappear and did not want to be second prize. Simons also held merger talks with Booker, the cash-and-carry grocery business, Budgens, and the Iceland chain. Indeed, to some analysts the company's continued attempts to do deals raised questions about its own strategy, and whether it was looking for opportunistic short-term gains rather than focusing on its core business. In February 1998, Somerfield announced takeover talks with Kwik Save, going ahead as a £1.4 billion all-share deal in March that year – promising huge cost savings for the combined group.

'In February 1998, Somerfield announced takeover talks with Kwik Save'

Kwik Save

In the late 1990s, from its north Wales base, Kwik Save held around 4% of the market with around 870 stores – slightly ahead of Somerfield. Kwik Save's strategy was to occupy a distinct niche position in the market – it concentrated on supplying quality brands at heavily discounted prices. The strategy was wholly focused on price. Store quality and services were low, the stores were dark, and had old-fashioned turnstile entrances and unfriendly staff – but the major brands were cheap. Analysts suggested Kwik Save was operating in the 'dark ages' in many areas – its supply chain management was rudimentary with store deliveries 2 or 3 times a week, instead of daily like its competitors. For this reason, stockouts were frequent, shown by gaps on the shelves and there was no prospect of a loyalty card because the company's systems and IT were not sophisticated enough to handle it. For the same reason customers could not use Switch debit cards on the Kwik Save checkouts.

The company hit the financial headlines in November 1996. Kwik Save's profits up to August 1996 had fallen from £125 million to £80 million, as a result of competitive pressures from the larger supermarket chains on the one hand, and sharply targeted, focused overseas discounters like Aldi and Netto on the other. The superstores had stolen Kwik Save's price advantage, while the aggressive continental discounters were trying to steal their custom-ers too. Shares slumped from a year's high of 612p to 300p.

Kwik Save retained its prominent position in the financial press by announcing the results of a £4 million strategic review conducted by Anderson Consulting. The highlight of the review was the proposal to close 107 loss-making stores, shedding some 2000 jobs, although the seriousness of the redundancies was reduced by the existing high staff turnover. The 1996 accounts had an exceptional change of £87 million to cover store closures, and redundancy costs, removing most of the year's profit earning. Some analysts suggested that up to 300 stores would eventually have to close. The Anderson consultants recommended a strategy of 'New Generation Kwik Save', involving a new range of own-label products, more fresh and convenience foods, and longer opening hours. Industry experts commented that all those things were already available in the superstores, and queried the potential competitive advantage for Kwik Save. The opportunity to imitate Asda's strategy did not exist either, because Asda had large stores and a residual value-for-money image, and Kwik Save has neither of these.

In the face of vocal opposition from Kwik Save concessionaries, Simons' strategy was to attempt to move Kwik Save upmarket, by converting the stores into the Somerfield format. In January 1999, Somerfield announced outstanding results of combined sales for the new group of around £5.8 billion and profits of £223 million, pushing shares up to 430p. This was a 31% increase in profits, showing no dilution in operating margins because of the lower-quality Kwik Save stores. Simons claimed that the 10 pilot conversions of Kwik Save stores – doubling the product range, adding fresh produce, deli, and bakery – had increased store income by 5% on average as they attracted better-off customers. Simons also announced that he had decided to restrict future information about Kwik Save sales performance, though revealing that Somerfield like-for-like sales had risen 3.4% while those at Kwik Save had fallen 3.1%. The Kwik Save challenge remained. Kwik Save's 872 stores made less sales than Somerfield's 472, and the £1 billion conversion programme was in its early days. Simons emphasized the benefits of the combined purchasing power of the group, and announced experiments with home delivery and more branches on Elf petrol station forecourts.

However, by July 1999, Simons admitted that he was having problems converting the Kwik Save stores to the more up-market Somerfield format – only 30 of the 70 conversions at £420 000 a time were judged to be successful. Grudgingly, Simons decided not to convert the 350 Kwik Save stores used for 'big trolley' purchases, but to spend £160 000 each on refurbishing them. Even so, with 70 stores earmarked for closure, he insisted on continuing to convert a further 460 Kwik Save stores to the Somerfield format. Staff morale at Kwik Save hit rock bottom.

By the end of 1999, Andrew Thomas had resigned as Chairman, criticized for not standing up to Simons, to be replaced by Louise Patten (widely-respected and formerly a Bain & Co consultant, bringing strategic advice to the board), and Simons' recovery plan consisted of selling 140 large Somerfield stores and 300 Kwik Save shops. If sold these would have left Somerfield with 850 neighbourhood outlets generating £3 billion of sales. The goal was to refocus on high street convenience stores. At the time, analysts doubted that Somerfield had the strong brand, management skills, or good locations to achieve this in the face of competition from Tesco and Sainsbury local stores. One commentator suggested the problem was that Somerfield had been created with the stores that no-one else wanted and lacked a strong relationship with the consumer. Simons' underlying strategy seems to have been to make Somerfield a more attractive purchase for one of the big food retailers.

'The goal was to refocus on high street convenience stores'

The real Kwik Save aftermath

By September 1999, Simons was facing angry shareholders whose stock had fallen from a 1998 peak of 481p to a low of 162p, mainly as a result of the Kwik Save takeover. The costs of integrating Kwik Save had been totally underestimated, and there were doubts that the integration could be made to work. Simons was accused of running the company for short-term gains instead of long-term profitability. Meantime, research showed huge defections of Kwik Save customers to Asda – switches worth around £100 million in sales were estimated, with some of the converted stores losing as much as 50% of sales. The reality faced was that up-market rivals were now out-discounting Somerfield or Kwik Save and customers were defecting from the Somerfield mid-market format. In addition, Simons had gone for fast cost-savings by putting huge Kwik Save volumes through the Somerfield distribution network – but before the system had been sufficiently strengthened to cope.

After three profits warnings in four months, investors questioned the continued viability of the Somerfield retail model, as well as the futures of CEO David Simons and chairman Andrew Thomas. The strengthening of Asda following the takeover by Wal-Mart looked like intensifying a price war that Somerfield could not win.

Trying to recover the situation

'This was a strategic U-turn that undermined the rationale for the Kwik Save merger in the first place'

Simons' response was to attempt to sell 500 stores to attempt to repair the damage done by the merger. This was a strategic U-turn that undermined the rationale for the Kwik Save merger in the first place, the new emphasis being to avoid head-to-head competition with the larger super-markets. These plans did not succeed. By February 2000, after setting out to sell 140 larger Somerfield stores and 350 Kwik Save outlets, Simons had buyers for only 45 stores.

Simons' whole strategy was to try to reposition the group as a neighbourhood food retailer – admitting that he could no longer compete with Tesco and Asda for the 'big trolley' shop. But he failed to sell off enough outlets or to stem the falling sales and profits. It was at this time that Simons fell out with the Somerfield board over his plans to take the group private with funding from private equity firms.

A change in leadership and strategy

When Somerfield and Kwik Save merged, they had a combined market value of £1.2 billion. By February 2000, Somerfield was worth £242 million. The collapse in Somerfield's share price is shown in Figure 5.

In March 2000, David Simons was removed from his job at Somerfield. One insider was quoted as saying: 'he lost control of the business. He was focusing on image rather than trading'. Another said about the failed Kwik Save integration: 'He was just too heavy-handed with Kwik Save. He went for the quick easy wins' – such as rapid closure of the Kwik Save head office in North Wales – 'When you leave a business without an infrastructure, you leave it vulnerable'.

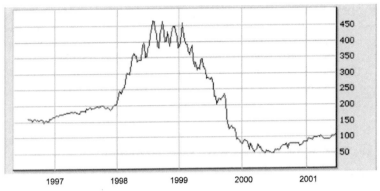

Figure 5 Somerfield plc share performance, 1997–2001

Acting Chairman Louise Patten announced that the group was no longer in discussions with potential bidders – tentative offers were rumoured to be at a share price well below 100p, which was unacceptable to directors – as these were a 'distraction' from managing the business. At this point shares were valued at around 57p. There was some speculation that Simons would retaliate by raising a bid for the company backed by private equity.

Simons was replaced as CEO by Alan Smith, from Punch Taverns, and previously Managing Director of Kingfisher's B&Q and Superdrug chains. Shortly after, in May 2000, John von Spreckelson was recruited as Chairman from his position at Budgens, with a history of turning around underperforming retailers in the UK and Europe.

The signs of an immediate strategy change by the new management team were the halting of the programme of store disposals, and closing the 24–7 home shopping firm. The bids from venture capitalists for the 350 Kwik Save stores were simply not high enough to be worthwhile. The new team had decided on rebuilding the Kwik Save heritage, as well as retaining the larger Somerfield stores that had been up for sale. The 406 stores due to be converted into Somerfields were now to stay as Kwik Save, with a high priority to tackle low staff morale and associated stock shortages and poor customer service.

'The new team had decided on rebuilding the Kwik Save heritage'

Table 6 Somerfield plc financials, 1996–2000

	1996	**1997**	**1998**	**1999**	**2000**
Turnover (£m)	3 161	3 201	3 484	5 898	5 466
Pre-tax profit (£m)	92.0	105	(11.1)	209	(14.5)
Earnings per share (p)	29.3	29.4	(3.60)	31.8	(3.00)
Dividend per share (p)	–	10.2	11.4	13.2	1.50
Market capitalization (£m)	–	543	1618	1684	281

In January 2001, von Spreckelson claimed that the business had stabilized, but that a full turnaround would take five years. The second half of 2000 had seen falling turnover, with Somerfield like-for-like sales down 5.3% and Kwik Save's down 11.1% (although he claimed to have had a better Christmas 2000 than Sainsbury). He reported a pre-tax loss of £21.7 million, after an exceptional gain of £22.2 million from selling stores. The company's financial performance over this period is shown in Table 6.

Other key players in the market

Wm Morrisons

Morrisons, with 105 stores and £3 billion sales, is a medium-sized, value-for-money chain that competes strongly in Asda's traditional heartland of the north of England and Scotland (though with a small number of stores in the south of England as well). The company's growth and financial performance is shown in Table 7. In fact, the company has delivered sales and profit growth every year since it went public in 1967. Morrisons' performance has earned it a place in the FTSE index of Britain's most valuable 100 companies.

Table 7 Wm Morrison financials, 1997–2001

	1997	1998	1999	2000	2001
Turnover (£m)	2 176	2 297	2 534	2 970	3 500
Pre-tax profit (£m)	136	151	170	189	219
Earnings per share (p)	5.28	6.06	6.84	7.57	9.05
Dividend per share (p)	0.85	1.05	1.23	1.50	1.80
Market capitalization (£m)	1 122	1 935	2 337	1 981	2 781

The company is run by 68-year-old Sir Ken Morrison as Executive Chairman, who took over his father's market stalls in Bradford when he was 20. He is regarded as one of the best retailers in Britain. The Morrison family holds stock worth around £900 million, and the business has succeeded where conventional advice suggested it would fail. Morrisons has an extremely low cost base – underlined by the 1970s décor in its head office, which has not been redecorated for around 30 years – and low prices. Loyalty schemes have been rejected out of hand, in favour of consistently low prices – 'pounds not points is our motto', says Morrison. Morrison regards himself as a 'hands-on manager', and specializes in looking in the dustbins at his stores to find out what has been going on (which is why he tends not to

'Morrisons has an extremely low cost base – underlined by the 1970s décor in its head office, which has not been redecorated for around 30 years – and low prices'

wear an expensive suit). Margins are also protected because much of what Morrisons sells is produced in-house – the company operates its own abattoir, produces its chilled and frozen foods, and manufactures its own packaging.

Sir Ken and the family continue to ignore institutional investors' politically correct suggestions that there should be non-executive directors on the board, to conform with modern thoughts about corporate governance. Sir Ken's view from his Bradford office seems to be that he would rather spend the money on an extra checkout operator.

Question: What's the difference between a supermarket trolley and
a non-executive director?

Answer: A supermarket trolley has a mind of its own.

The company's very straightforward strategy has been to increase sales at the expense of weaker competitors through selective price cuts, and to convert new customers through good value and full stock availability – 'we are happy to carry stocks rather than miss a sale' says Morrison in dismissing competitors' constant replenishment systems. It has made particular gains at the expense of Somerfield – mainly former Kwik Save customers transferring their business to Morrisons rather than Somerfield.

Morrisons has been widely discussed as a take-over target. The Morrison family hold 38 per cent of the company, but it is unlikely that any of the family members will run the business after Sir Ken Morrison's retirement. However, in 2000 the company declared itself in the market to make acquisitions if

'The company's very straightforward strategy has been to increase sales at the expense of weaker competitors through selective price cuts, and to convert new customers through good value and full stock availability'

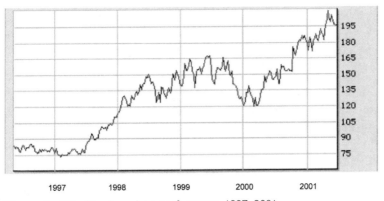

Figure 6 Wm Morrison share performance, 1997–2001

any of the larger supermarkets are obliged to dispose of sites by the Competition Commission, and had been looking at acquiring some former Kwik Save stores from Somerfield.

In fact, Morrisons continues to outperform most of its larger rivals – growing 2001 profits 16 per cent to £219 million on sales growth of 18 per cent to £3.5 billion. Store openings and refurbishments take the total to 114. As sites become available (a major constraint for a smaller firm) Morrisons plans to extend its coverage of the south of England. The performance of Morrison's shares is shown in Figure 6.

Budgens

Budgens is run by Martin Hyson, who took over as CEO when John von Spreckelson left to go to Somerfields. At the start of 2001, Budgens achieved growth rates on a par with its much larger rivals. Sales were rising at the rate of 2.5 per cent, compared to a 0.7 per cent rise at Sainsbury and a 1.1 per cent dip at Somerfield. Half-year profits were up to £8.6 million (held back by the £1.2 million cost of closing its home delivery business), with operating margins constant at 4.1 per cent. The company's financial performance is summarized in Table 8.

Table 8   Budgens plc financials, 1996–2000

	1996	1997	1998	1999	2000
Turnover (£m)	303	321	363	411	421
Pre-tax profit (£m)	7.58	9.08	10.5	12.6	14.6
Earnings per share (p)	3.50	3.60	4.56	4.80	4.81
Dividend per share (p)	1.25	1.40	1.60	1.85	2.20
Market capitalization (£m)	71.7	66.1	122	110	111

'Budgens is continuing its roll-out of neighbourhood convenience stores. Larger stores have been closed in pursuit of a strategy of recreating the village convenience store'

With annual sales of around £420 million, Budgens is continuing its roll-out of neighbourhood convenience stores. Larger stores have been closed in pursuit of a strategy of recreating the village convenience store. With a current total of 219 outlets, Budgens plans a further 50 of its franchise stores – Budgens Local. Musgrove, the Irish food distributor now holding 28 per cent of Budgens shares, is expected to assist in the development of Budgens Local format. Hyson has scrapped his predecessor's B2 Division – 50 stores formerly trading as 7–11s, and intends to operate the refurbished stores as Budgens Locals. The company is also in the market for acquisition opportunities, in retail as well as bakery operations.

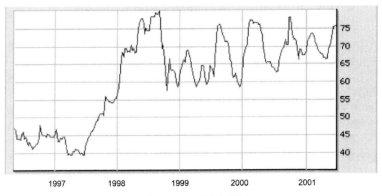

Figure 7 Budgens share performance, 1997–2001

The £15 billion convenience grocery market is attracting more competitors, although currently they have failed to equal Budgens' performance. The convenience format has several attractions – consumer lifestyle changes have driven up demand for fresh convenience foods like ready meals and salads, and reduced the time consumers are prepared to spend preparing a meal. Growth rates in convenience products are substantially higher than the general food and drinks market, and there is a clear role in providing top-up shopping for those who make their main weekly purchase at a large supermarket. However, this market is highly fragmented – independent retailers take about 57 per cent and 'symbol' retailers like Spar another 12 per cent. The Co-op takes just under 10 per cent, but companies like Budgens, Alldays and Forbuoys take only about 2 per cent each. In 2000, Kingfisher started trials of convenience food stores modelled on the US 7–11 format.

In fact, Tesco is rethinking its Metro store strategy, and Sainsbury has not fulfilled the promises of its Locals. It has been suggested that this places Budgens as a take-over target – the impediment being the major shareholder, Rewe Handelsgruppe of Germany. The performance of Budgens' shares is summarized in Figure 7.

The Co-op

The British co-operative movement in retailing was born 157 years ago to combat consumer exploitation in the north of England. Long referred to as 'the sleeping giant of the high street', by the end of the 1990s the Co-operative Wholesale Society (CWS) was made up of 50 mutual retail societies, though the 15 largest account for 90 per cent of its trade. Its sister organization, and one of its owners, is Co-operative Retail Services (CRS). As a mutual, the Co-op movement is owned by its members and returns its profits to them as dividends on purchases. As recently as 1985, the Co-op could have claimed to be the UK's leading grocery retailer (as well as banker, insurance provider, funeral director and agricultural operator). Indeed, in the 1950s, CRS alone had 26 per cent of the retail food market.

However, in food retailing the Co-op's position has been displaced by the large supermarket groups. Critics blamed the Co-op's bureaucracy, lack of innovation, and too many personal fiefdoms battling with each other, instead of improving the business. One senior insider said in 1999: 'Its rivals have good stores with well-motivated staff and clear brand propositions backed up by consistent advertising, while the Co-op has rotten stores, with poorly trained staff, an ageing customer base and no-one knows what it represents any more'.

'in food retailing the Co-op's position has been displaced by the large supermarket groups'

A fundamental problem for CWS is the independence of the individual societies, which has held back the development of a truly national approach to product ranges and retail strategy. In 1997, CWS fought off a £1.2 billion take-over bid organized by Andrew Regan – he planned to realize assets and return the proceeds to members.

Co-operative Retail Services chose to focus on the superstore format, in direct competition with the large supermarket firms. However, with only around 20 superstores out of a total of nearly 500 stores, critical mass was small.

However, the closeness of local co-op societies to their local communities provides a strength in convenience retailing – small neighbourhood stores, responsive to local needs, and exploiting the co-op image as a concerned and ethical retailer, supporting the local community. Together, CRS and CWS have around 1000 stores in high street locations – many exactly the type of sites that Tesco and Sainsbury are desperately trying to acquire for their Tesco Metro and Sainsbury Central and Local formats. Since 1999, CWS has been renaming its convenience stores Welcome. The Co-op has also resurrected its traditional 'divi' – the precursor to loyalty schemes – in electronic form. The scheme pays a 5 per cent cash rebate (a substantially larger pay-out than the Tesco or Sainsbury loyalty card schemes).

'The Co-op has also resurrected its traditional "divi" – the precursor to loyalty schemes – in electronic form'

The late 1990s saw escalating losses at CRS, with sales static at around £1.5 billion, in spite of investments in store refurbishment, new information systems, improved distribution and product development. The refurbishments revealed wholly inadequate financial systems in the company, as well as major supply chain weaknesses. Declining profits at CWS have led to growing pressures for CRS and CWS to merge, and to unite their buying groups. In 1999, CRS sold its non-grocery businesses – Living and Homeworld stores – to focus on food, with 3000 jobs lost in the process.

In 1999, CRS and CWS looked at beginning their first combined marketing campaign ever, and combined their purchasing into a single £4.5 billion buying group. Finally, in 2001, after decades of talks and at what was at least the fourth attempt, CRS and CWS agreed to merge into the

Co-operative Group, with Graham Melmoth as Chief Executive, creating a £4.7 billion a year business, with 1100 stores and 50 000 employees. The combined buying power put the Co-op around fifth in the UK supermarket league – behind Tesco, Sainsbury, Asda and Safeway, but ahead of Somerfield and Morrisons. In May 2001, the new Group reported a profit of £131 million, wiping out CRS losses of £80 million and a one-off merger cost of £20 million. Underlying retail trading profit (stripping out contribution from the Co-op Bank) was £50 million, compared to a combined CWS/CRS loss of £29 million the previous year. The focus on convenience stores is continuing – 146 new stores opened in 2000. The Group is also emphasizing 'market town stores' – mini-markets in rural locations where the major store groups do not trade, with 31 new stores opening in this format in 2000. The Group also operates Co-op2U for online shopping.

Points to ponder

1 Thinking about the supermarket business is a good way of making sense of what market-led strategic change is about, and what transformations in the process of going to market actually look like. Almost all of the themes we have discussed are illustrated here, and it is a sector in which we almost all participate – as customers if nothing else. Just consider:

- how customer demands have evolved and escalated;
- how all the companies converged on low prices as the way to enhance customer value, but are now diverging and trying to find new ways of building value strategies;
- how e-commerce is developing and breaking down traditional boundaries;
- how the organizations are evolving better ways of delivering value – for example, in the relationship between branding and supply chain strength;
- the ways in which the competitors are coping with a sector where traditional market boundaries have disappeared, and they are trying to achieve differentiated positions in new market spaces;
- the pressure for greater customer focus and the dangers of poor market sensing;
- the ways in which markets are being redefined and new targets emerging and companies are trying to develop different value propositions;
- the range of internal and external relationships the competitors have to manage in surviving and performing better;
- the critical issue of being able to implement new strategies through company processes and people.

2 There are probably two good ways to think about these issues. The first is to consider the sector as a whole and look at the trends and changes. The other is to adopt the perspective of one of the companies and to consider what that company can do to improve its position and performance.

3 However you look at it though, this is an area of business that underlines beautifully the power of market-led strategic change, and the unavoidable necessity for transforming the process of going to market.

Index